Please ask for accompanying CD at library counter.

Internet Core Protocols

The Definitive Guide

Internet Core Protocols
The Definitive Guide

Eric A. Hall

O'REILLY®

Beijing · Cambridge · Farnham · Köln · Paris · Sebastopol · Taipei · Tokyo

Internet Core Protocols: The Definitive Guide
by Eric A. Hall

Published by O'Reilly & Associates, Inc., 101 Morris Street, Sebastopol, CA 95472.

Editor: Mike Loukides

Production Editor: Nicole Arigo

Cover Designer: Edie Freedman

Printing History:

February 2000: First Edition.

Library of Congress Cataloging-in-Publication Data:

Hall, Eric A.
Internet core protocols : the definitive guide / Eric A. Hall.
p. cm.
Includes bibliographical references.
ISBN 1-56592-572-6 (alk. paper)
1. Internet (Computer network) 2. Computer network protocols. I. Title.

TK5105.875.I57 H355 2000
004.6'2--dc21

99-089559

ISBN: 1-56592-572-6 [5/00]
[M]

Table of Contents

Foreword

The Internet began as a research effort to link different kinds of packet-switched networks in such a way that the computers that were attached to each of the packet networks did not need to know anything about the nature of or the existence of any networks other than the ones to which the host was directly connected. What emerged was a layered design that used encapsulation to carry end-to-end "Internet" packets from the source host, through intermediate networks and gateways to the destination host. The first Internet incorporated three wide/medium area networks including the ARPAnet, the Atlantic Packet Satellite net (SATNET), and a ground mobile Packet Radio network (PRNET). Eventually it also included the first 3 MB/s Ethernet developed at Xerox PARC in 1973.

Now, some twenty-five years after the first designs, there are hundreds of thousands of networks comprising the Internet, serving an estimated 45 million computers and 150 million users. Moreover, the original speeds of the trunking circuits in the constituent networks have increased from thousands of bits per second to billions of bits per second, with trillions of bits per second lurking in laboratory demonstrations. As the Internet has grown, its complexity and the number of people dependent on it have both increased substantially. But the number of people with detailed understanding of the protocols and systems that allow the Internet to work represent a declining fraction of the total population of users or even operators of such networks.

Worse still is the fact that the number of protocols and services in use on those networks has also increased from a handful to hundreds. While it used to be that a single super-administrator could manage the routers, domain name servers, mail servers, and other resources on the network, we are now faced with so much specialization that it seems impossible for any one person to follow everything. At many of the larger firms, there are entire departments that do nothing but manage the network routers, while other groups manage the dial-up servers and still others manage the web and mail systems, domain name systems, and newsgroups.

This is a serious problem. Large corporations can afford to hire specialists who understand their respective parts of the overall picture, but most companies can't afford an army of specialists, and have to make do with a handful of network engineers who have to know "whatever's necessary." Furthermore, debugging and analyzing Internet problems defies specialization. Problems often arise because of the interactions between different parts of the network. If email isn't being delivered, is the problem with the mail server itself? Or has something gone wrong with routing, the domain name system, or with the low-level protocols that map Ethernet addresses to Internet addresses? It may be unrealistic to expect one person to diagnose problems in all of these areas (plus a dozen more), but many network operators face this challenge daily.

When problems do occur, administrators have a variety of tools available for debugging purposes. This includes packet analyzers that can show you the inner core of the network traffic, although they won't tell you what that traffic means. Another set of tools is the vendor's own documentation, although more often than not the vendor's documentation is based on the same misreading of the specs as the problematic software. One of the last alternatives is for the administrator to prowl through the protocol's technical specifications in order to determine where the problem really lies. But when it's 4 a.m. and the web server in Chicago keeps dropping its connection to the database server in Atlanta, these specifications are of limited use. These documents were written largely as strict definitions of behavior that should occur, and generally do not describe ways in which the protocols might be made to fail.

That's why these books were written. Throughout this series, Eric Hall takes you behind the scenes to discover the function and rationale behind the protocols used on IP networks, offering thorough examinations of the theory behind how things are supposed to work. Furthermore, Hall backs up the tutorial-oriented discussion with packet captures from real-world monitoring tools, providing an indispensable reference for when you need to know what a particular field in a specific packet is supposed to look like. In addition, Hall also discusses the common symptoms of what things look like when they break, providing detailed clues and discussions on the most common interoperability problems.

This three-way combination of tutorial/reference/debugging-guide essentially makes these books all-inclusive "owner's manuals" for IP-based networks. They are attractive volumes for any network manager who works with Internet technologies, particularly as the Internet continues to go through the growing pains resulting from near-exponential growth. Even though there are already more than 44 million devices connected now, all indications point to there being nearly a billion devices online by 2006, including IP-enabled sensors, garage door openers, video recorders, IP-telephones, and all other manner of office and home appliances. And of course, may of those devices will need new protocols. The Net is going to get a lot more complicated.

The research networks we linked long ago have given way to networks being adapted for interplanetary distances (in which a different form of "the speed problem" emerges). Already planned is an Internet-enabled Mars base station, together with a set of interplanetary gateways that will link these networks back to Terra Firma. The NASA Mars missions begun in 1998 will continue well into the second decade of the next millennium. A part of the plan for these explorations includes the formation of a network of Internets: an interplanetary Internet. Perhaps someday it will be the lifeline of communication for explorers and colonists to our neighboring planets, the moon, and the satellites of the larger planets in the outer solar system.

Back here on Earth, however, there will be plenty to occupy our attention as the Internet continues its relentless growth. We will need the help of books like the ones in this series to analyze problems arising on the Internet we already have, as well as the ones planned for the future.

—Vint Cerf

Preface

It's 4:45 p.m. on a Friday afternoon, and you're looking forward to going home early for a change. All of a sudden the telephone rings. It's one of your users, unable to connect to the email server, yet again. Worse, he has to send a report to his boss before he can go home, which means that you've got to get the problem sorted out before *you* can go home.

But before you can fix anything, you've got to know what the problem is exactly. Is the user providing the wrong username or password? Is the user running an old email client that's incompatible with some new features on your brand-new server? Maybe the user's mailbox is locked by another process? Or are there basic network-connectivity problems keeping the computers from even being able to communicate?

Unfortunately, the unprecedented success and wide-scale adoption of Internet protocols and application services has resulted in an equally unprecedented number of complexities. And although there is a wealth of literature and documentation on how to implement a specific vendor's product, rarely can you find detailed information on how the underlying protocols used by those products are implemented. There's likely to be reams of documentation on the nifty email filters, but not a word will be printed on which POP3 or SMTP commands are supported. This makes troubleshooting difficult, to say the least. Worse, when vendors start pointing fingers at each other, you're stuck trying to figure out the problem on your own.

The point is, in order for you to be able to effectively design, implement, manage, and support different implementations of Internet-based, standards-centric protocols and services, you must educate yourself on how they actually work. Everything eventually boils down to the protocols (including the failed commands and the errors they generate). The fastest road to solution-ville is by understanding what's going on at the protocol level.

It's at times like this that you need to be able to capture the traffic on your network—and more importantly—be able to understand the packets that you're looking at. The purpose of this book is to show you the ins-and-outs of the most common protocols found on today's Internet-centric networks. Throughout this book, you'll find background information on the design of each of the core protocols used on TCP/IP networks, as well as detailed reference information that discusses the options and parameters available with each of them. Additional volumes in this series will explore the application-layer protocols in the same manner. When used in conjunction with a protocol analyzer, this book will prove to be a lifesaver when you need to find out why something isn't working exactly right.

Audience

This book is primarily intended for people who design, build, manage, or support computer networks using Internet-based protocols and services. While this book may be useful to power users and programmers, it is intended mostly to be used as a reference for people who live and breathe TCP/IP.

This book is optimized for people who already have a basic understanding of computer networks and how they work, and who may already know a little bit about how TCP/IP works, but who also want to know a lot more on the subject. If you don't know how to assign IP addresses to your computer, then you shouldn't be looking for help here. Instead, see *TCP/IP Network Administration* by Craig Hunt or *Windows NT TCP/IP Network Administration* by Craig Hunt and Robert Bruce Thompson (both books are published by O'Reilly & Associates, Inc.). However, if you want to know more about IP's Time-To-Live or Type-of-Service parameters and how they can affect your network, then this is the book for you.

Also, it is important to note that this book is not meant as a reference for any specific implementations or applications. While I may mention a specific implementation, it is for illustration purposes only, and should not be used instead of the official product documentation.

Organization

This book deals with the basic building block protocols that provide the networking and transport services that all TCP/IP applications and services use. There are chapters on IP, UDP, TCP, and the common support protocols like ICMP, IGMP and ARP. The end of this book also contains appendixes on material that is indirectly related to how these protocols function.

Here's a more detailed, chapter-by-chapter breakdown:

- Chapter 1, *An Introduction to TCP/IP*, provides a history of TCP/IP, its design objectives, and an overview of the inter-relationships between the different protocols.
- Chapter 2, *The Internet Protocol*, discusses the Internet Protocol in detail, including fundamentals of IP addresses, packet forwarding, the limited reliability services offered, fragmentation, and prioritization.
- Chapter 3, *The Address Resolution Protocol*, illustrates how IP devices are able to locate each other on a network, and the variations of ARP that are commonly used for different types of tasks.
- Chapter 4, *Multicasting and the Internet Group Management Protocol*, describes how multicasting works on a network, and how devices register with multicast routers in order to participate in distributed multicast feeds.
- Chapter 5, *The Internet Control Message Protocol*, discusses the error-reporting services used by IP, how the different ICMP messages are implemented, and also shows how the interactive services offered over ICMP can be used to diagnose your network.
- Chapter 6, *The User Datagram Protocol*, explores the lightweight, error-prone transport protocol used by applications that don't need TCP's reliability service.
- Chapter 7, *The Transmission Control Protocol*, covers all the major aspects of this excruciatingly complex transport protocol, including the flow-control, reliability, network- and application-management services that are used by almost every Internet-based application today.
- Appendix A, *The Internet Standardization Process*, discusses the process by which Internet developers write proposals that eventually become standards, and also describes the authoritative bodies that oversee the process.
- Appendix B, *IP Addressing Fundamentals*, provides a detailed discussion on IP addresses and their formatting rules.
- Appendix C, *Using the CD-ROM*, contains installation instructions for Shomiti Surveyor Lite, the network analysis tool that is on the accompanying CD. The CD also contains all of the published RFCs available, as well as the captures used in the book.

Each chapter is divided roughly into three sections: an introduction to the protocol, the details of the protocol's syntax, and some real-time usage and troubleshooting notes. How you read this book will depend on who you are and what you're trying to do.

Beginners

If you're new to TCP/IP networks and want to learn more about the general concepts and architectural issues of the protocol suite (or of the Internet in general), you should read Chapter 1, *An Introduction to TCP/IP*, followed by the introductory material in Chapter 2, *The Internet Protocol*, and Chapter 7, *The Transmission Control Protocol*. By reading this material, you'll get a sound understanding of how TCP/IP really works.

Working managers

If you're responsible for managing a network and are looking for a thorough understanding of the core protocols, then you may want to read the introductory material provided at the beginning of Chapter 2, *The Internet Protocol*, Chapter 7, *The Transmission Control Protocol* and Chapter 5, *The Internet Control Message Protocol*. In fact, you probably should do this as soon as possible, *before* you start having problems. You can then come back and read the reference material and troubleshooting tips whenever problems do crop up.

If you're already having some kind of problem with a particular protocol or service, then you should probably start capturing packets, and study the detailed reference sections for the specific protocols that are giving you grief. Study the packet captures, and try to see where things start breaking down. Then look at the packets that are having problems, locate the appropriate parts in the reference section of the appropriate chapter, and see if you can figure out what the problem might be.

Finally, the CD contains Shomiti Surveyor Lite, a full-featured tool for analyzing network traffic. (For more information about this product, contact Shomiti at *www.shomiti.com*.) It also contains the full text of all the RFCs—another tool that no network manager should be without. Ultimately, the RFCs (and not this book) define how your network should work. Granted, the RFCs are all available online, but if your network isn't working, you might not be able to access them. With this book, a network analyzer, and the RFCs, you'll have everything you need for a late-night troubleshooting session—except coffee.

How to Read This Book

This book does not use any code samples, and only rarely uses program output in examples or illustrations. When the latter is used, a screenshot of the application is always supplied, and the program output is not displayed "in-line" with the book's text.

Terminology

Most network managers refer to data that is sent across a network using generic terms such as "packet" or "datagram." However, as TCP/IP has evolved, a variety of terms have been used to describe the units of data that are transmitted by specific protocols. RFC 1122 brought all of these terms together and defined the usage for each term according to specific protocols. These terms are used throughout this book in the same manner.

Frame
: A *frame* is the unit of data that is sent across a network using the link-layer protocol appropriate for that network. This includes link-layer encapsulation technologies such as Ethernet II frames, 802.3 Ethernet frames, or Token Ring frames.

IP datagram
: An *IP datagram* is the unit of data that is managed by the Internet Protocol, including whatever data is being transmitted, as well as the IP headers associated with that data. In essence, an IP datagram is the unit of data that IP works with explicitly.

IP packet
: An *IP packet* is another term for IP datagrams, although this term is most often used to refer to the datagram portion of a frame, rather than referring to the datagram itself. For example, a sending and receiving system will look at an IP datagram as a single entity, while that datagram may have been split into multiple IP packets for transmission across a set of intermediary networks. Typically speaking, hosts deal with IP datagrams, while routers deal with IP packets.

Message
: A *message* is the unit of data sent from one of the upper-layer protocols (such as UDP or TCP), including the data being transferred and the related transport-specific headers associated with that data. Although most of the time the message data will be generated by an application-specific protocol, ICMP and IGMP also communicate with IP directly and will therefore also generate message data. Messages eventually become the data portion of an IP datagram.

TCP segment
: Although the headers and data that are generated by TCP are considered to be *messages*, TCP messages can be spread across multiple messages. In this scenario, the messages are typically referred to as *segments*.

Images

Throughout this book, a variety of images are used to represent different types of network devices, including hosts, routers, modems, and other infrastructure equipment. In order to minimize any possible confusion, these symbols are shown in the three figures in this Preface to provide a common interpretation throughout the various chapters.

For example, Figure P-1 shows the common symbols that are used for Token Ring and Ethernet networks, the symbols used for application clients and servers, and a network router.

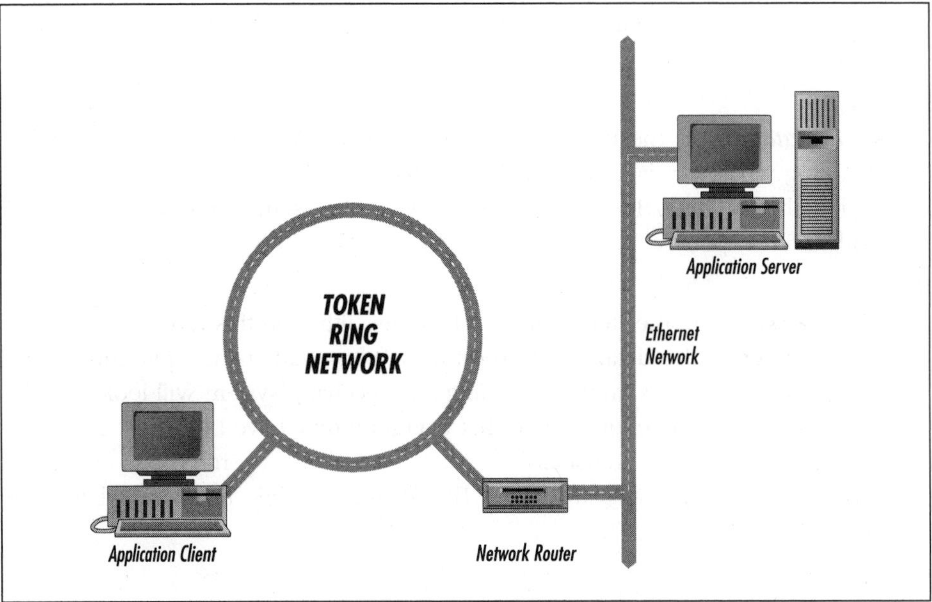

Figure P-1. Common symbols used with local area networks

Figure P-2 shows the symbols that are commonly used to represent wide area networks (WANs), including those that incorporate modems, satellites, microwave radio, and generic WANs (such as Frame Relay or leased-line networks). Notice that the figures used for network routers, application clients, and servers are the same as those used for LAN-based topologies.

Note that sometimes a generic host will be identified using the "Application Client" symbol, indicating that the device is either sending data to or receiving data from another network device, which may be another client or server, indicating that the role played by the devices is irrelevant to the discussion at hand.

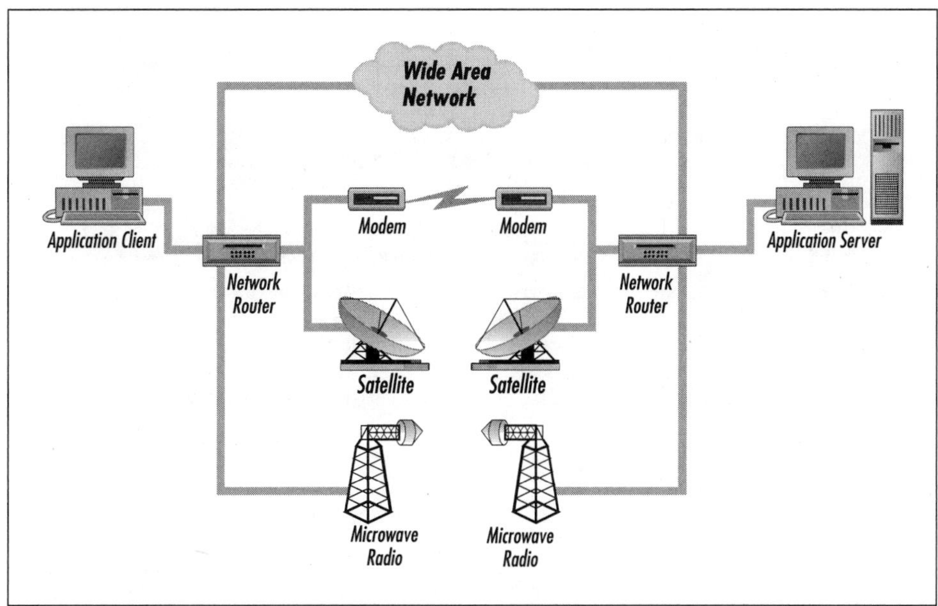

Figure P-2. Common symbols used with wide area networks

The Author's Test Network

Almost all of the packet captures and examples used throughout this book are based on my own test network, as is shown in Figure P-3. The operating systems used on that equipment are listed in Table P-1.

Table P-1. Operating Systems Used on the Author's Test Network

Component	Operating System
Ferret	Microsoft Windows NT Workstation 4.0, Service Pack 4
Arachnid	Microsoft Windows NT Server 4.0, Service Pack 4
Krill	Digital Unix 4.0d
Froggy	Apple MacOS 8.5
Weasel	Novell NetWare 5.0
Greywolf	RedHat Linux 5.2
Dial-Client	Microsoft Windows NT Workstation 4.0, Service Pack 4
Bacteria	Microsoft Windows 98
Fungi	Sun Solaris 7 (Intel)
Sasquatch	Cisco IOS 11.3
Canary	Sonic SonicWall Firewall v3.1

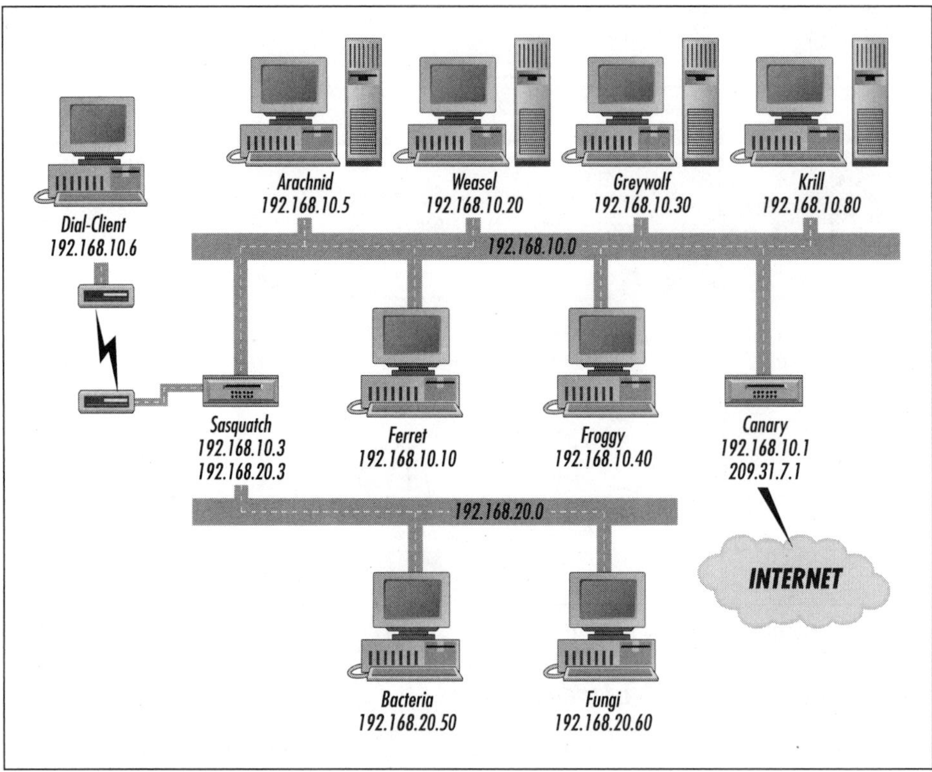

Figure P-3. Network devices on the author's test network

Font Conventions

The following conventions are used in this book:

Italics
: is used for filenames, directory paths, URLs, hostnames, and emphasis.

The owl icon designates a note, which is an important aside to the nearby text.

The turkey icon designates a warning relating to the nearby text.

How to Contact Us

We have tested and verified the information in this book to the best of our ability, but you may find that features have changed (or even that we have made mistakes!). Please let us know about any errors you find, as well as your suggestions for future editions, by writing to:

O'Reilly & Associates, Inc.
101 Morris Street
Sebastopol, CA 95472
1-800-998-9938 (in the U.S. or Canada)
1-707-829-0515 (international/local)
1-707-829-0104 (fax)

You can also send us messages electronically. To be put on the mailing list or request a catalog, send email to:

info@oreilly.com

To ask technical questions or comment on the book, send email to:

bookquestions@oreilly.com

We have a web site for the book, where we'll list information, errata, and any plans for future editions. You can access this page at:

http://www.oreilly.com/catalog/coreprot/

For more information about this book and others, see the O'Reilly web site:

http://www.oreilly.com

Acknowledgments

I would like to thank several people who have helped make this book happen. In particular, I'm indebted to Bob Quinn from Stardust Forums for his work on Chapter 4, *Multicasting and the Internet Group Management Protocol,* Greg Shipley for his feedback on Chapter 5, *The Internet Control Message Protocol* (which resulted in a major rewrite), Barry Margolin, who pointed out holes in each of the chapters and Appendix B, *IP Addressing Fundamentals* in particular, and Bob Packer, the CTO of Packeteer, Inc., who contributed heavily to both the conceptual and practical aspects of Chapter 7, *The Transmission Control Protocol.* Many questions were also answered by a variety of participants from the TCP-IMPL mailing list. I'm extremely grateful for the unselfish assistance that those folks provided.

I'm especially indebted to Mike Sullenberger, who provided detailed comments, criticisms, and compliments on each and every chapter in this book. Without Mike's feedback, this book would be riddled with errors.

On another note, I never really understood why so many people thanked their editors in the acknowledgments, but now I do. Michael Loukides makes things happen. This book would never have been possible without his many efforts, would never have been written without his determination, and would never have been shipped without his flexibility.

In addition, I would like to thank Tim Bean at Shomiti Systems, who worked hard to give us access to Surveyor Lite for distribution with this book, allowing you to use the same decoding tools that we did. Thanks also goes to Fritz Nelson and Kevin Cooke at *Network Computing Magazine*, who gave me writing assignments (and thus kept me funded) during this book's development.

1

An Introduction to TCP/IP

If you've been using TCP/IP-based networking products for any length of time at all, you're probably already aware of how IP addressing, routing, and other fundamental aspects of the Internet family of protocols work, at least from a user's perspective.

What you probably don't know—unless you've been formally trained in these subjects—is what makes TCP/IP work from the wire's perspective, or from the perspective of the applications in use on your network. This chapter provides you with an introduction to these viewpoints, providing you with a better understanding of the nature of the traffic on your network.

A Brief History of the Internet

Before you can understand how TCP/IP works—or why it works the way it does—you first have to understand the origins of the networking protocols and the history of the Internet. These subjects provide a foundation for understanding the basic design principles behind TCP/IP, which in turn dictate how it is used today.

TCP/IP presented a radical departure from the traditional computer networking services in use during its development. In the early days of commercial computing (the late 1960s), most companies bought a single large system for all of their data processing needs. These systems used proprietary networking architectures and protocols, which primarily consisted of plugging dumb terminals or line printers into an intelligent communications controller, each of which used proprietary networking protocols to communicate with the central hosts.

Most of the early computer networks used this hierarchical design for their proprietary network protocols and services. As users' computing requirements expanded, they rarely bought a different system from a different vendor, but instead added new components to their existing platforms or replaced the existing system with a newer, larger model. Cross-platform connectivity was essentially unheard of, and was not expected. To this day, you still can't plug an IBM terminal into a DEC system and expect it to work. The protocols in use by those devices are completely different from each other.

As the use of computers became more critical to national defense, it became clear to the U.S. military in particular that major research centers and institutions needed to be able to share their computing resources cooperatively, allowing research projects and supercomputers to be shared across organizational boundaries. Yet, since each site had different systems (and therefore different networking technologies) that were incompatible with the others, it was not possible for users at one site to use another organization's computing services easily. Nor could programs easily be ported to run on these different systems, as each of them had different languages, hardware, and network devices.

In an effort to increase the sharing of resources, the Advanced Research Projects Agency (ARPA) of the Department of Defense (DOD) began coordinating the development of a vendor-independent network to tie the major research sites together. The need for a vendor-independent network was the first priority, since each facility used different computers with proprietary networking technology. In 1968, work began on a private packet-switched network, which eventually became known as ARPAnet.

ARPAnet was the world's first wide-area packet-switching network, designed to allow individual units of data to be routed across the country as independent entities. Previous networks had been circuit-switched, involving dedicated end-to-end connections between two specific sites. In contrast, the ARPAnet allowed organizations to interconnect into a mesh-like topology, allowing data to be sent from one site to another using a variety of different routes. This design was chosen for its resilience and built-in fault-tolerance: if any one organization were bombed or otherwise removed from the network, it wouldn't affect the rest of the organizations on the network.

During this same time period, other network providers also began interconnecting with the ARPAnet sites, and when these various networks began connecting to each other, the term "Internet" came into use. Over the next few years, more organizations were added to the ARPAnet, while other networks were also being developed, and new network technologies such as Ethernet were beginning to gain popularity as well.

All of this led to the conclusion that networking should be handled at a higher layer than was allowed by the ARPAnet's packet-switching topology. It became increasingly important to allow for the exchange of data across different physical networks, and this meant moving to a set of networking protocols that could be implemented in software on top of any physical topology, whether that be a packet-switched WAN such as ARPAnet or a local area network (LAN) topology such as Ethernet.

TCP/IP to the Rescue

In 1973, work began on the TCP/IP protocol suite, a software-based set of networking protocols that allowed any system to connect to any other system, using any network topology. By 1978, IP version 4 (the same version that we use today) had been completed, although it would be another four years before the transition away from ARPAnet to IP would begin. Shortly thereafter, the University of California at Berkeley also began bundling TCP/IP with their freely distributed version of Unix, which was a widely used operating system in the research community.

The introduction and wide-scale deployment of TCP/IP represented a major ground-shift in computer networking. Until the introduction of TCP/IP, almost every other network topology required that hardware-based network nodes send traffic to a central host for processing, with the central host delivering the data to the destination node on behalf of the sender. For example, Figure 1-1 shows a host-centric networking architecture. In this model, devices are attached to a centralized system that coordinates all network traffic. A user at a terminal could not even send a screen of text to a printer without first sending the data to the central host, which would parse the data and eventually send it to the printer for printing.

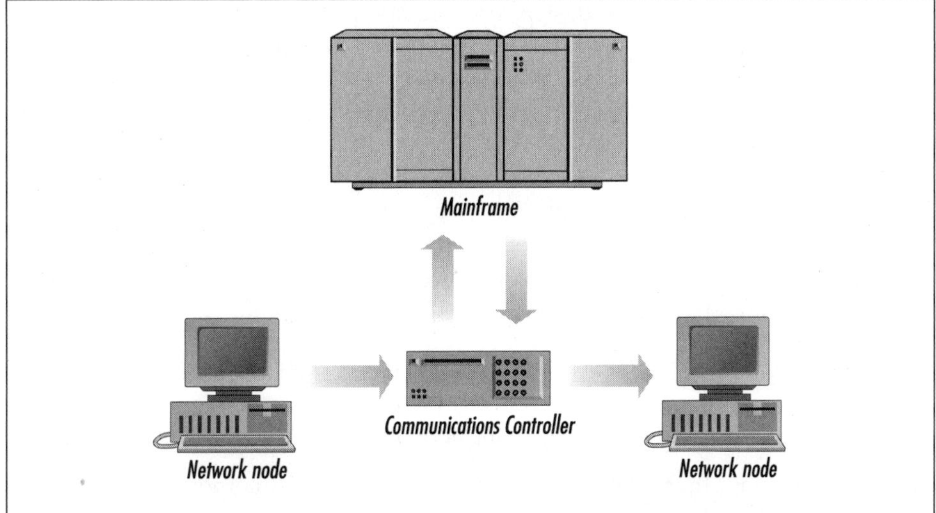

Figure 1-1. Host-centric networking

But with TCP/IP, each network device was treated as a fully functional, self-aware network end-point, capable of communicating with any other device directly, without having to talk to a central host first. IP networks are almost anarchic, with every device acting as a self-aware, autonomous unit, responsible for its own network services, as illustrated in Figure 1-2.

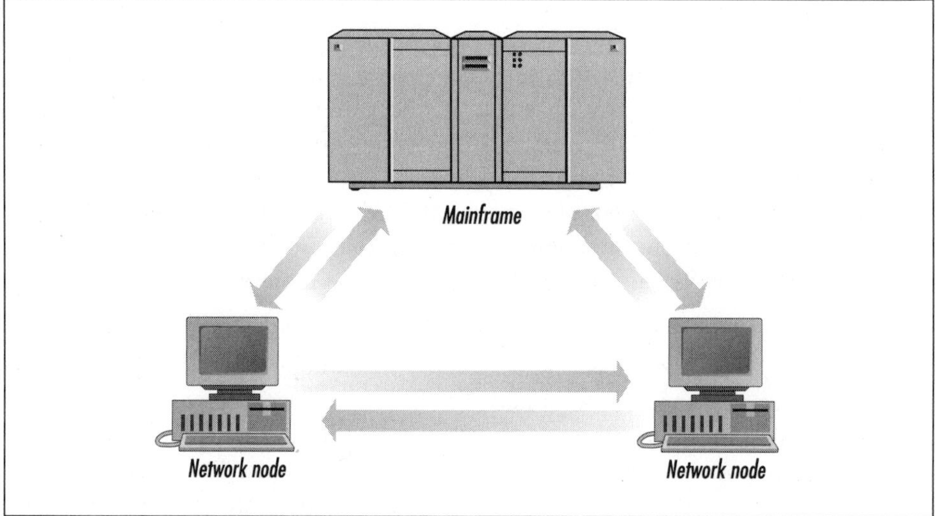

Figure 1-2. Node-centric networking

This design allowed for application- and resource-sharing on a national scale, since a top-down model simply would not work with millions of widely distributed devices. In addition, this design also provided reliability in case any part of the network was damaged, since a host-based model would simply stop functioning if the central host was destroyed or disabled.

The Internet Today

Over time, the ARPAnet evolved into an open "network-of-networks" using TCP/IP, with educational, commercial, and other organizations connected to each other through an interwoven mesh of networks. Today this type of mesh architecture is far less common, replaced by a much more structured hierarchy.

Rather than organizations connecting to each other directly, most organizations now connect to a local network access provider who routes network traffic upwards and outwards to other end-point networks.

Generally speaking, there are only a handful of top-level Internet Service Providers (ISPs), each of which provide major interconnection services around the country or globe. Most of these firms are telecommunications companies that specialize in large-scale networking (such as long-distance providers like MCI WorldCom and Sprint).

Below these top-level carriers are local or regional access providers who offer regional access and lower-speed connection services to end users directly (these mid-level carriers are sometimes referred to as Internet Access Providers, or "IAPs"). This design is represented in Figure 1-3.

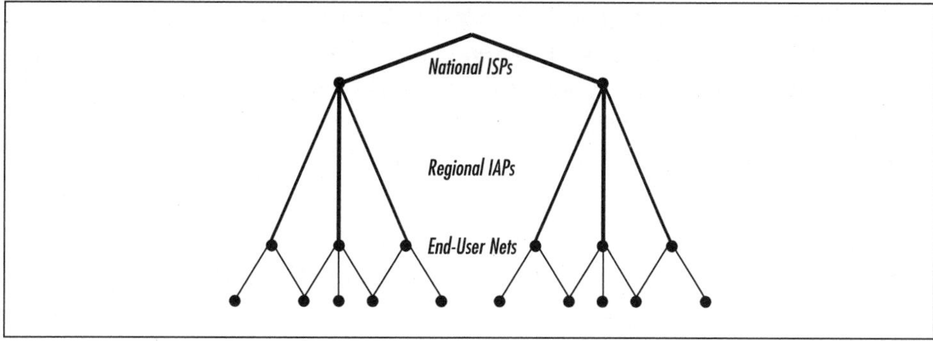

Figure 1-3. The hierarchical architecture of the Internet

Visually, the Internet can be thought of as a few major networking companies who provide large-scale "backbone" services around the world, followed by a large number of secondary providers that resell bandwidth on those networks. At the end of the line are the end-leaf organizations that actually generate the traffic that crosses these networks.

The Internet, Defined

Simply having a lot of interconnected networks does not by itself mean that you have the "Internet." To "internet" (with a lowercase "i") means to interconnect networks. You can create an internet of Macintosh networks using AppleTalk and some routers, for example. The term "Internet" (with a capital "I") refers to the specific global network of TCP/IP-based systems, originally consisting of ARPAnet and the other research networks.

There have been lots of private and public networks that have offered a multilayer network design (private SNA* networks from the 1980s are a good example of this). Therefore, the Internet in particular is a collection of networks that support host-to-host communications using TCP/IP protocols.

* SNA stands for Systems Network Architecture, a proprietary IBM networking protocol.

Under this definition, the network is made up of intelligent end-point systems that are self-deterministic, allowing each end-point system to communicate with any host it chooses. Rather than being a network where communications are controlled by a central authority (as found in many private networks), the Internet is specifically meant to be a collection of autonomous hosts that can communicate with each other freely.

This is an important distinction, and one that is often overlooked. For example, many of the private networks have offered mail-delivery services for their customers, allowing a user on one network to send email to another user on another network, but only by going through a predefined mail gateway service. Conversely, the Internet allows users to exchange mail directly, without going through a central politburo first. In this regard, the Internet is a collection of self-deterministic, autonomous hosts.

Having hosts communicate with each other directly is not enough to make the Internet, however. Many networks have offered users the ability to communicate directly with other hosts on those networks, and those networks have not been considered as parts of the Internet per se. For example, there have been many private DECnet networks that have offered this capability, and Novell offers a similar service using IPX today.

The last key criteria is that the Internet is a collection of networks that allows host-to-host communications through voluntary adherence to open protocols and procedures defined by Internet standards. Therefore, in order for these networks to be parts of the Internet, they must also use Internet protocols and standards, allowing for vendor-neutral networking.

This is perhaps the most important part of the entire definition, since the use of consistent protocols and services is what allows the Internet to function at all. For example, it is not enough for a private network to allow users to send email messages to each other directly. Rather, those users must use the same protocols and services to exchange email messages, and those protocols must be defined as Internet standards.

TCP/IP's Architecture

A key part of understanding the distributed nature of TCP/IP is the realization that TCP/IP is a modular *family* of protocols, providing a wide range of highly segmented functions. TCP/IP is not a single monolithic protocol, but instead is a collection of protocols that range from application-specific functions like web browsing down to the low-level networking protocols like IP and TCP.

One common tool used for comparing different kinds of protocols is the OSI* Reference Model, which is a simplistic breakdown of networking functions from the physical wiring up to the applications that run on the network. By comparing TCP/IP to the OSI Reference Model, it is easier to understand how each of the major protocols interact with each other.

An Introduction to the OSI Reference Model

The OSI Reference Model is a conceptual model that uses seven "layers" to identify the various functions provided by a network, and these seven layers can be used to compare different protocols using a common framework. Each layer within the OSI Reference Model has a very specific function, and each layer depends on the other layers in order for the entire model to function properly. Each layer only communicates with the layers immediately above or below it. If there is a problem at one layer, it is the responsibility of that specific layer to provide feedback to the layers surrounding it.

The OSI Reference Model is extremely useful as a tool for discussing various network services. For example, if we were to look at a simple network service such as printing a document to a locally attached printer, we could use the OSI Reference Model to determine how this simple task was being achieved. We could also use the model to determine how printing over a Novell network was done, or how printing over a TCP/IP network was accomplished. Because all three of these examples use the same model, they can all be compared to each other even though they all use extremely different technologies to achieve the same objective.

Not all networking technologies have seven layers, nor do they all match up to the seven layers in the OSI Reference Model exactly. Most of them do not match it except in small, specific ways, although all of them can be compared to the model with a little bit of thought. This flexibility is what makes it such a popular tool.

The following list briefly describes each of the seven layers and the purpose each serve. Remember that this is a conceptual model, with very little direct meaning to the real world.

The physical layer

The physical layer is concerned with the physical wiring used to connect different systems together on the network. Examples include serial and parallel cables, Ethernet and Token Ring cabling, telephone wiring, and even the specific connectors and jacks used by these cabling systems. Without strictly standardized definitions for the cabling and connectors, vendors might not implement them in such a way that they would function with other implementations, which in turn would make it impossible for any communication

* OSI stands for Open Systems Interconnect, an alternate suite of network protocols.

whatsoever to occur. Each of these wiring systems therefore follows very strict standards, ensuring that network devices will at least be able to communicate without having to worry about issues such as voltage and impedance.

The data-link layer

The data-link layer defines how information is transmitted across the physical layer, and is responsible for making sure that the physical layer is functioning properly. Some networks—such as the public telephone network, radio, and television—use analog sine-waves to transmit information, while most computer networks use square-wave pulses to achieve this objective. If there are any problems with transmitting the information on the physical cabling (perhaps due to a damaged wire or circuit), then this layer must deal with those errors, either attempting to retransmit the information or reporting the failure to the network layer.

The network layer

The network layer is used to identify the addresses of systems on the network, and for the actual transmission of data between the systems. The network layer must be aware of the physical nature of the network, and package the information in such a way that the data-link layer can deliver it to the physical layer. For example, if a telephone line is the physical layer, then the network layer must package the information in such a way that the data-link layer can transmit it over an analog circuit. Likewise, if the physical layer is a digital Ethernet LAN, then the network layer must encapsulate the information into digital signals appropriate for Ethernet, and then pass it to the data-link layer for transmission.

On many networks, the network layer does not provide any integrity checking. It simply provides the packaging and delivery services, assuming that if the data-link layer is not reporting any errors then the network is operational. Broadcast television and radio work in this manner, assuming that if they can transmit a signal, then it can also be received. Many digital networking technologies also take this approach, leaving it up the higher-level protocols to provide delivery tracking and reliability guarantees.

The transport layer

The transport layer provides the reliability services lacking from the network layer, although only for basic transmission services, and not for any application- or service-specific functions. The transport layer is responsible for verifying that the network layer is operating efficiently, and if not, then the transport layer either requests a retransmission or returns an error to the layer above it. Since higher-level services have to go through the transport layer, all transport services are guaranteed when this layer is designed into the network software and used. Not all systems mandate that the transport layer provide reliability, and many networks provide unreliable transport layers for nonessential services such as broadcast messages.

The session layer
The session layer is responsible for establishing connections between systems, applications, or users. The session layer may receive this request from any higher layer, and then will negotiate a connection using the lower layers. Once a connection is established, the session layer simply provides an interface to the network for the higher layers to communicate with. Once the higher layers are finished, the session layer is responsible for destroying the connection.

The presentation layer
The presentation layer provides a consistent set of interfaces for applications and services to utilize when establishing connections through the session layer. Although these interfaces could also exist at the session layer, that would burden it unnecessarily. It is better to have the session layer only manage sessions and not worry about verifying data or providing other extended services. An example of a service provided by the presentation layer is data-compression, allowing applications to take advantage of the performance gains that compression provides without forcing the applications to develop these services themselves, and without forcing the transport layer to provide this service when it may not always be needed.

The application layer
Finally, the application layer provides the network's interface to end-user application protocols such as HTTP and POP3. This layer should not be confused with the part of the end-user application that displays data to the end user. That function is an entirely separate service, and is outside the scope of the OSI Reference Model.

Although every network must use all seven layers of the OSI Reference Model in some form or another, not every network design provides distinct protocols or services that match all seven layers precisely. TCP/IP is one such networking design, with many layers that do not match up to each of the layers used by the OSI Reference Model.

Comparing TCP/IP to the OSI Reference Model

TCP/IP does not strictly conform to the OSI Reference Model. Some portions of the OSI Reference Model map directly to some of the protocols and services provided by TCP/IP, while many of the layers do not map to each other directly at all. For example, the actual delivery of data over the network is handled at the physical layer, and in this case, the wire is the physical layer. There are no services in TCP/IP that correspond with the physical or data-link layers. Rather, IP passes data to a network adapter's device driver, which provides an interface to the data-link layer in use with the physical layer.

Figure 1-4 shows how TCP/IP matches up with the OSI Reference Model. Notice that TCP/IP does not provide any physical or data-link layer services directly, but instead relies on the local operating system for those services.

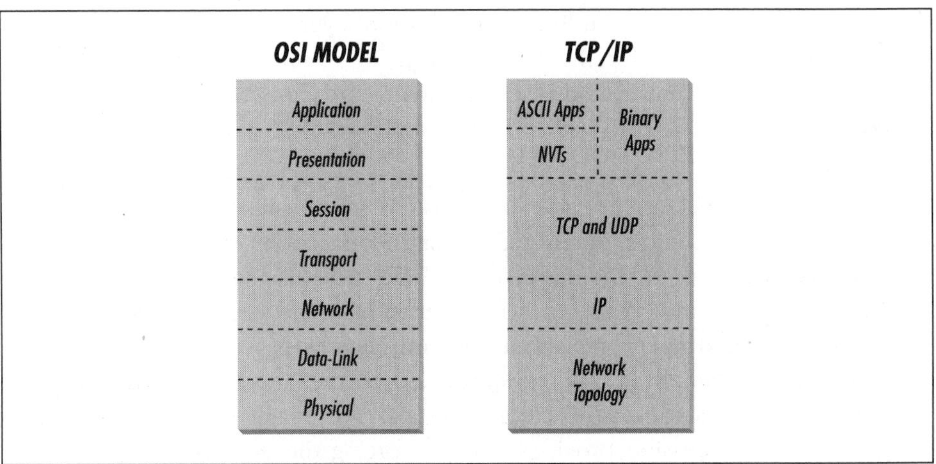

Figure 1-4. TCP/IP in comparison to the OSI Reference Model

The specific layers offered by TCP/IP include:

The Internet Protocol

IP itself works at the network layer of the OSI reference model. It is responsible for tracking the addresses of devices on the network, determining how IP datagrams are to be delivered, and sending IP packets from one host to another across a specific segment. In essence, IP provides a virtual representation of the network that is independent of any of the individual network segments, acting more like a national delivery service than a local courier service.

The Transport Protocols (TCP and UDP)

TCP/IP provides two protocols that work at the transport layer: TCP and UDP. TCP provides a highly monitored and reliable transport service, while UDP provides a simple transport with no error-correcting or flow-control services. It is also interesting to note that TCP and UDP also provide session layer services, managing all of the connections between the different hosts. When an application protocol such as HTTP is used to exchange data between a web client and a web server, the actual session-management for this exchange is handled by TCP.

Presentation Services

TCP/IP does not provide a presentation layer service directly. However, some applications use a character-based presentation service called the Network Virtual Terminal (NVTs are a subset of the Telnet specification), while others might use IBM's NetBIOS or Sun's External Data Representation (XDR) programming libraries for this service. In this regard, TCP/IP has many presentation layer services that it *can* use, but it does not have a formal service that every application protocol *must* use.

Application Protocols (HTTP, SMTP, etc.)

TCP/IP provides an assortment of application protocols, providing the end-user applications with access to the data being passed across the transport protocols. These protocols include the Simple Message Transfer Protocol (SMTP), which is used by electronic mail systems to move mail messages around the Internet, and the Hyper-Text Transfer Protocol (HTTP), which is used by web browsers to access data stored on web servers, among many others.

All of these services get called upon whenever an application wants to exchange data with another application across the Internet. For example, a mail client will use the SMTP application protocol whenever a user wants to send a mail message to a remote mail server, and the SMTP protocol uses rules defined by the NVT specification whenever it exchanges data with TCP. In turn, TCP provides error-correction and flow-control services back to SMTP. IP is used to move the TCP segments between the source and destination networks, while hardware-specific protocols (like Ethernet-specific framing) will be used to move the IP packets between the various systems on the network itself.

TCP/IP Protocols and Services In-Depth

Whenever data is exchanged between two applications across a TCP/IP network, each of the major layers provided by TCP/IP come into play.

This can be seen with email clients that use the Simple Message Transfer Protocol (SMTP) to send mail to a local server, as is shown in Figure 1-5. The email software on the client contains local application-specific code for parsing and displaying email messages, but everything else is done with network protocols such as SMTP, TCP, and IP.

As data is passed through each of the different layers, packets are generated that contain two distinct elements: headers and data. As information is passed down through the protocol stack, each layer encapsulates the previous layer's information (including both the header and the data) into a new packet, containing a new layer-specific header and the newly minted data segment. This process is shown in Figure 1-6.

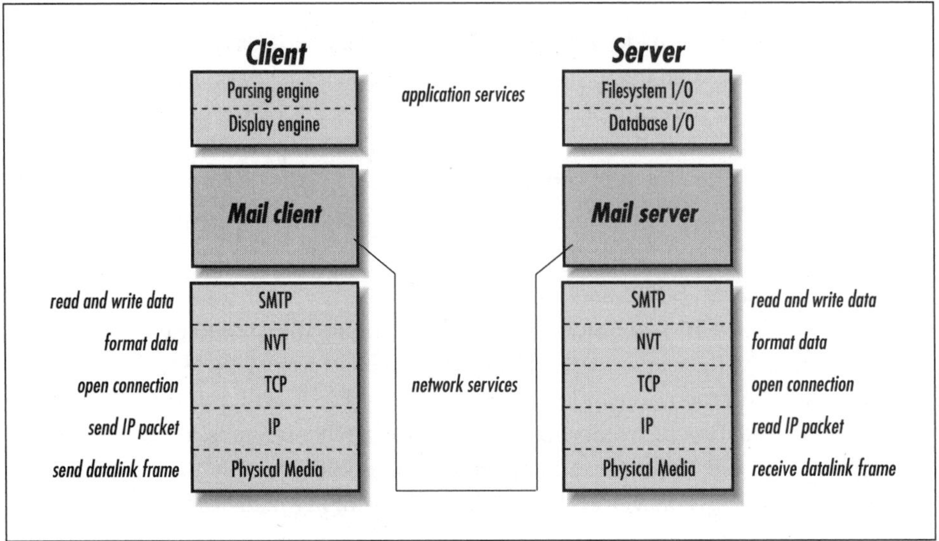

Figure 1-5. Some of the layers used by TCP/IP applications

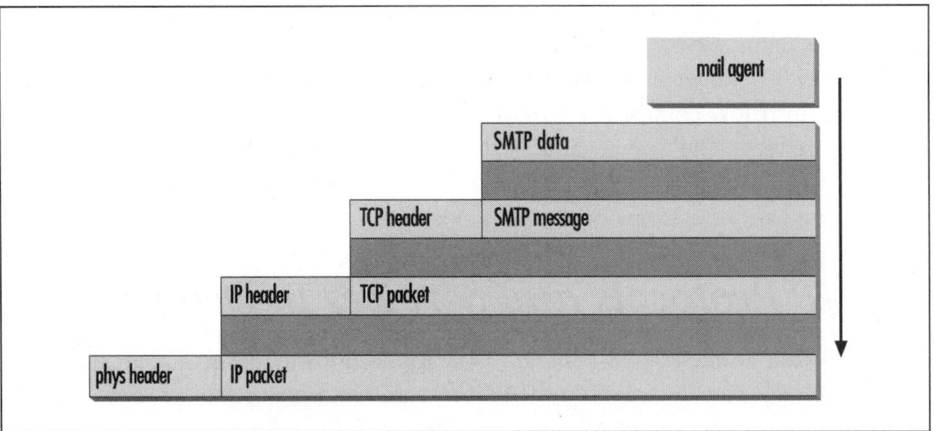

Figure 1-6. The sub-parts of layers

At the bottom-most layer, the physical network is used to transfer bits of data (called "frames") between two devices on the network. IP packets are contained within these network-specific frames. The only reason IP is used for this process is because the data can go over a variety of different network topologies, and as such the TCP/IP applications must have a way of addressing and routing traffic consistently, regardless of the specific networks in use.

Embedded within the IP datagrams are TCP segments, which provide a reliable virtual circuit for the SMTP application protocol to use. TCP does things like open a connection between two application protocol end-points, resend lost data, remove duplicates, and exert flow control, each of which is beyond the simple delivery function of IP itself, yet is common enough to be useful as a separate, distinct service.

The SMTP application protocol contains application-specific semantics. In this case, this might consist of an SMTP command such as "RCPT TO ehall" and an application-specific response code such as 250 ("okay"). Note that the commands and data used by SMTP conform to the NVT specification, which prescribes how the data should be formatted, the types of data allowed, and so forth, although SMTP is doing all of the real work.

As can be seen, each of the layers in the TCP/IP suite provide specific functionality to the layers above and below it, making the overall design extremely modular. It is this modularity that makes TCP/IP so powerful, and also what makes it so complex.

Data-Link Services

When two devices on a network communicate with each other, they don't use IP to do so. Rather, they use protocols that are specific to the wire itself. For example, devices on an Ethernet segment use a predefined series of electrical impulses to communicate with each other. Whenever an Ethernet device wants to send data to another device on the same network, it raises and lowers the voltage of the shared medium so that a series of "on" and "off" voltage patterns are generated. These changes in voltage are interpreted as bits by the other devices on the network.

The changes in voltage are dictated by protocols that are specific to the different types of physical networks. Ethernet networks have data-link protocols that will not work with technologies like Token Ring. Similarly, modems use protocols specific to different types of modem technology.

Much of IP's functionality is determined by the physical media that the IP device is connected to. When an IP device has information that it needs to send to another device on the same wire, it has to understand the characteristics of the wire in order to prepare the information so that is usable for that particular medium.

One of the issues that IP has to deal with is the mechanisms used for the network-specific addressing. Just as physical networks have to provide mechanisms for encapsulating and disseminating data on the wire, they also have to provide a way for devices to locate each other, using addressing methods defined by the low-level protocols.

On shared networks, each device must have a unique hardware address in order for devices to indicate which node the traffic is for. Ethernet networks use a 48-bit

Media Access Control (MAC) address for this purpose, while Frame Relay networks use Data-Link Connection Identifier (DLCI) addresses, and so on. This concept is illustrated in Figure 1-7, where IP traffic for 192.168.10.40 is sent to the Ethernet address of 00:00:c0:c8:b2:27, using Ethernet-specific signalling.

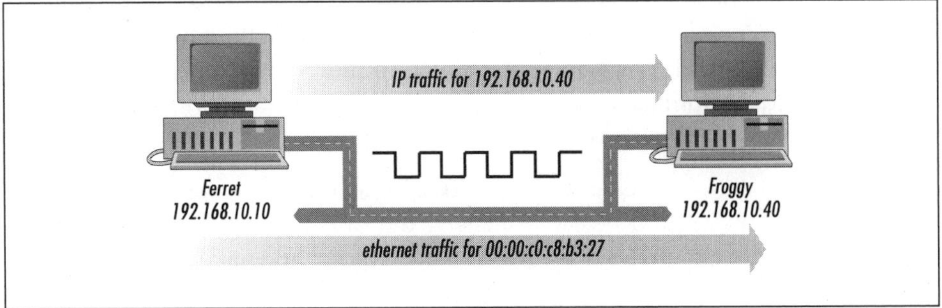

Figure 1-7. Topology-specific protocols and addressing

In contrast, modems are point-to-point; only two devices can communicate over any given circuit. As such, modem circuits don't use addresses per se, but instead just send and receive data over dedicated "transmit" and "receive" wires as needed. The same is true of T-1 lines and most other point-to-point circuit-based networks.

In all of these cases, the IP stack running on the local device must understand the addressing mechanisms used by the hardware, and implement it accordingly, just as it must understand the framing characteristics and signalling mechanisms in use on the physical network.

The Internet Protocol

When an IP-enabled device wants to send data to another IP node, the data-link services on that device convert the IP datagrams into a format usable by the local network medium, and then send the data to the destination system using the addressing and framing mechanisms dictated by the network.

These steps occur on each of the networks that an IP datagram traverses on its way to the final destination system. If an IP datagram were sent from a dial-up user working at her home in Los Angeles to a server in Rome, Italy, the number of networks that would be crossed could be quite high. But at each step of the way, the data would be transmitted using the low-level protocols appropriate for each of the particular networks being crossed.

In this regard, IP provides a virtual representation of the global Internet to the hosts that are on it. IP provides a datagram formatting and addressing mechanism that is not dependent upon any of the specific characteristics of the individual networks that make up the global Internet. Data can be sent to an IP address, and the data will be encapsulated and transmitted according to the rules of each of the intermediary networks, with the IP datagram being used to provide delivery clues to the sending, receiving, and intermediary devices. Essentially, routing occurs at the network layer (IP), while delivery occurs at the data-link layer (Ethernet, modems, whatever).

This concept is illustrated in Figure 1-8. In that example, data sent over a modem would be encapsulated into a form usable by the dial-up connection. Once received, the data would be determined to be an IP datagram, and would then get converted into a form that was usable by the LAN connection and sent out again. The receiving system (Ferret) would eventually get the packets.

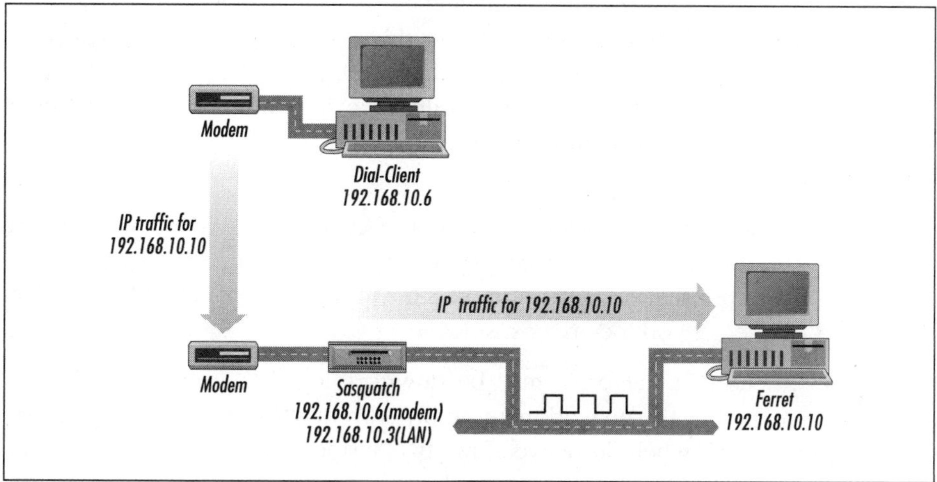

Figure 1-8. IP datagrams versus the topology-specific protocols

One thing to keep in mind is that this was the primary design goal of IP, allowing it to scale beyond the packet-switched networks that made up the original Internet (which could not be grown easily or cheaply). Without moving to a virtual networking protocol like IP, the Internet would still be using packet-switching networks, and we'd all have WAN connections on our desktops instead of Ethernet or Token Ring (or, more likely, we wouldn't be using IP). But by leveraging the virtual nature of IP, we can use any network we want anywhere we want, and the IP data will still be deliverable across any of them.

One side effect of this design is that the IP datagram is a separate entity from the IP packets that are being used to transfer the datagram from the source to the destination. Whenever a device needs to send data, it will form an IP datagram containing both the data that needs to be sent and whatever headers are required to deliver the data over IP to the destination system. However, as this datagram is sent across the network, it will be shipped as a series of packets that get created and destroyed by each network device that processes or forwards the datagram on to its final destination. In essence, the datagram becomes a series of packets, each of which can go anywhere they need to in order for the datagram to be delivered.

Another interesting aspect of IP is that it does not guarantee that any of these packets will ever get delivered at all. A system may be able to send the data, but the data may not be received intact, or the data may be ignored by the destination system due to high processing loads or some other reason. Although some networking topologies provide an intelligent retransmission mechanism in case data is lost, many of them do not. As such, IP's designers had to assume that data would get lost sometimes.

In this regard, IP offers absolutely no guarantees, leaving it up to higher-layer protocols to perform this function if required. For this reason, IP can be thought of as being unreliable, particularly in the sense that application designers (and users) should not assume that every IP datagram will arrive at its destination intact. Some people refer to this as "best-effort" delivery, while others refer to it jokingly as "best-of-luck" delivery.

Another key design goal of IP was the concept of datagram independence. The IP protocol does not dictate that all datagrams must travel the same route. In fact, IP dictates just the opposite: any datagram can travel across any network path that the devices on the network deem most suitable.

For example, a user in California may be downloading data from a host in Ireland, and some part of the network may simply stop functioning. The sending system (or a router somewhere in between the two systems) would eventually detect this failure and would begin forwarding datagrams through a different network path. This feature gives IP a robust and flexible foundation, allowing networks to become self-healing, in a sense.

Since each datagram is independent, it is likely that some datagrams will take different paths to the same destination. As such, one datagram may end up crossing a satellite link, while another datagram crosses a fiber-optic line. When this happens, the second datagram will likely arrive at the destination system before the first datagram does. In another situation, the satellite link may experience some sort of problem that results in the first datagram getting sent twice.

In both of these cases, the network has caused the IP datagrams to get out of synch. But since IP is simply a virtual representation of the network, it does not care when this happens. If sequencing is important to an application, then it has to implement that service directly or by using TCP (appropriately the Transmission Control Protocol) for transport-layer services.

Another related concept is fragmentation. Assume for a moment that the sending system were on a high-capacity network such as Token Ring, while the destination system were on a low-capacity dial-up connection. Since the sending system generates datagrams according to the characteristics of the local network, it generates large datagrams appropriate for the Token Ring frames.

But when the next system tries to relay the IP datagram to the dial-up recipient, the IP datagrams are too large for the dial-up network to handle in one frame. When this happens, the datagram must be split into multiple fragments, with each of the fragments being sent across the network as independent entities. Each fragment follows all of the other rules outlined earlier, thus being capable of getting lost in transit, routed separately, or arriving out of sequence.

When the fragments arrive at the destination system (*if* they arrive), then they need to be reassembled into their original datagram form. However, this only occurs at the final destination system, and not at any intermediary routers, since any of the fragments could have gone off in another direction.

Taken together, these services make IP a highly unreliable and unpredictable network protocol. Datagrams can get lost or may be broken into multiple packets, all without warning. The only thing IP does is move data from one host to another, one network at a time. Of course, users have little interest in applications that must be provided by a higher-level protocol than either IP itself (for example, TCP) or the application.

Remember this rule: The Internet Protocol is *only* responsible for getting IP datagrams from one host to another, one network at a time.

For more information on IP, refer to Chapter 2, *The Internet Protocol.*

The Address Resolution Protocol

Since two IP devices on the same physical medium communicate with each other using the low-level protocols specific to that physical medium, the two devices must locate each other's hardware addresses before they can exchange any data. However, each networking topology has its own addressing mechanisms that are different from all of the others, and IP has to be able to locate hardware addresses for each of them.

Since there are so many different types of networking topologies, it is not possible for IP to be imbued with the specific knowledge of how to build the address mappings for each of them explicitly. Attempting to do so would be an extraordinarily inefficient use of the IP software's basic functionality, preventing the rapid adoption of new networking topologies and introducing other fundamental problems into the network.

Instead, the Address Resolution Protocol (ARP) is used as a helper to IP, and is called upon to perform the specific task of building each address mapping whenever address conversion is required. ARP works by issuing a broadcast on the selected medium, requesting that the device using a specific IP address respond with its hardware address. Once the destination device has responded, the sending system can establish communication with the receiving system and start sending data to the discovered hardware address. This process is shown in Figure 1-9, with 192.168.10.10 issuing a lookup for 192.168.10.40, who responds with its local Ethernet hardware address.

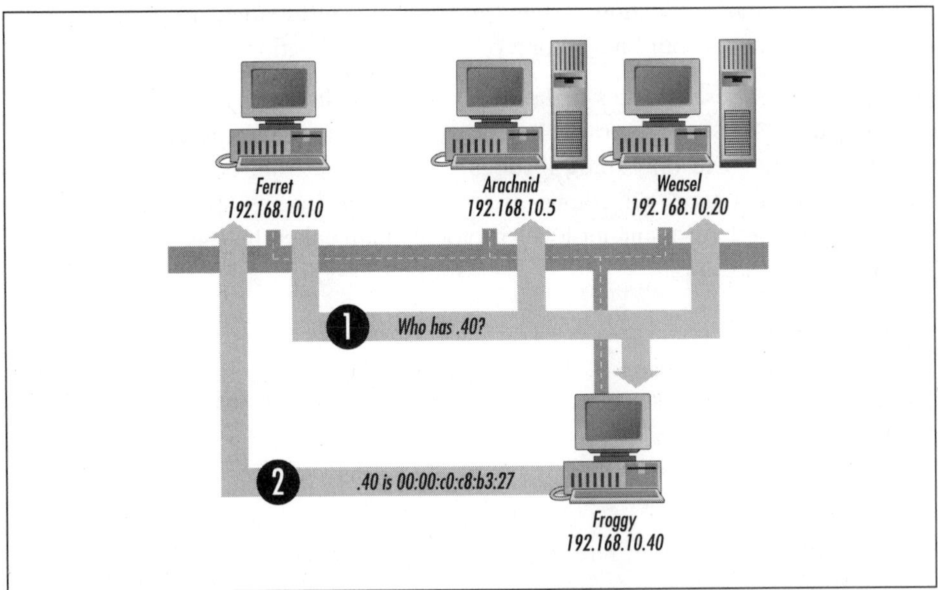

Figure 1-9. Using ARP to locate the hardware address associated with a known IP address

The ARP requests and responses work at the physical layer and are embedded directly into the frames provided by the low-level protocols in use on the physical medium. ARP messages do not use IP, but instead are entirely separate protocols.

For more information on ARP, refer ahead to Chapter 3, *The Address Resolution Protocol.*

The Internet Control Message Protocol

From time to time, IP datagrams will fail to get delivered. This may be due to errors in the datagram structure, a general network outage, or a delivery timeout. IP doesn't really care about these problems, since it never promised delivery in the first place. However, applications care about these problems very much. They would like to be able to react to a failure, either by taking an alternative course of action, or by at least informing the user that a problem has occurred.

IP uses the Internet Control Message Protocol (ICMP) for error-reporting services. When a system needs to report a problem that is preventing delivery from occurring, it generates an ICMP message that describes the general problem, and then sends it back to the original sender of the original datagram. ICMP messages are not sent when a packet is lost in transit or when some other transient error occurs. Rather, ICMP error messages are only sent when there is a detectable problem that is preventing certain packets or datagrams from being delivered due to a specific reason. This indicates that the sending host should probably stop trying to send those kinds of datagrams to this specific destination system, or that a different path should be used.

Even if two IP-enabled systems are able to communicate effectively, there are no guarantees that everything will work, since the data inside the datagrams may be corrupt, or packets may get lost without any ICMP errors being generated. IP is an unreliable network protocol by its very definition, and as such does not provide any guarantees. ICMP does not change this fact.

ICMP runs on top of IP, allowing it to traverse the global Internet just as easily as TCP or UDP messages. This seems a bit confusing to many people: if an IP datagram could not be delivered, it would not seem that an ICMP error—delivered over IP—would make it back to the original sender. However, remember that most delivery errors occur due to problems on the *next* leg of the network, and that the original IP datagram at least made it as far as the system that's reporting a problem. In this scenario, the network between the original sender and the host that's reporting the problem is likely to be functioning properly.

There are a variety of ICMP message types, and not all of them are limited to reporting on network errors. There are also ICMP "query" messages, useful for diagnosing and testing the network interactively. The most common of these are the ICMP Echo Request and Echo Reply query messages, which are better known as *ping* to most users.

For more information on ICMP, refer to Chapter 5, *The Internet Control Message Protocol*.

The Transport Protocols

Application protocols do not communicate with IP directly, but instead talk to one of two transport protocols: TCP or UDP. In turn, these transport protocols pass data to IP, which encapsulates the data into IP datagrams that get sent over the network. In essence, the transport protocols hide the network from the application protocols so that they do not have to deal with packet-sizing and other issues, while also shielding the network from having to multiplex the application protocol traffic (a task that IP can leave to the transport protocols).

For example, both UDP and TCP provide a multiplexing service to application protocols by way of application-specific port numbers. Essentially, port numbers act as virtual post office boxes for messages to be delivered to within a single host, allowing multiple applications to run on a single host. When datagrams arrive at a destination system, they are handed off to the transport protocol specified in the datagram, which then delivers the transport-specific message data to the port number specified in the header of the message. In this manner, many different application protocols can run on the same host, using different port numbers to identify themselves to the transport protocols.

The transport protocol that an application protocol uses is determined by the kinds of network- and application-management services that are required. TCP is a reliable, connection-oriented transport protocol, providing error-correction and flow-control services that can tolerate IP's knack for losing packets. Conversely, UDP is an unreliable, message-centric transport protocol that offers little functionality over IP alone. There are many applications that need to use one of these models or the other, and there are a handful of applications that use both of them. A good example of an application that could use them both is a network printer.

If many users share a network printer, all of them need to be kept informed of the printer's availability. Using UDP, the printer could send out periodic status messages such as "out of paper" or "cover open." The software on the client PCs would then pick up on these status updates, changing the desktop icon appropriately, or notifying an administrator that something has gone awry. UDP allows the printer to notify everyone of these updates simultaneously, since it's not a big deal if some of these updates get lost.

This concept is illustrated in Figure 1-10, in which the printer at 192.168.10.2 is periodically sending out UDP broadcasts, indicating its current status. Network systems that are interested in that information can monitor for those updates and can change their desktop icons or management station software appropriately. If a system does not receive one of these updates for some reason, then it will probably get the next update message, so it's not a big deal.

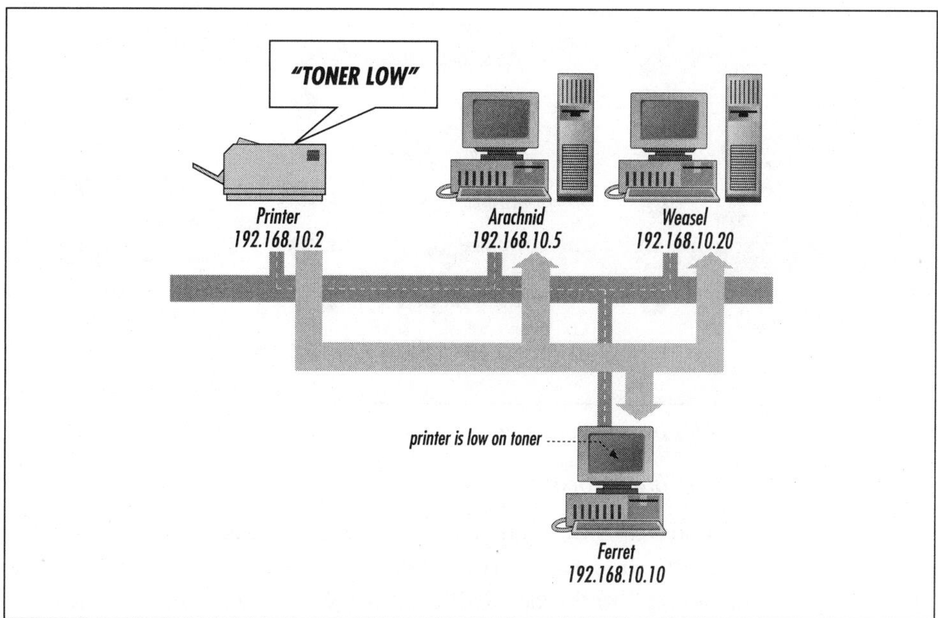

Figure 1-10. Using UDP to broadcast status updates

Conversely, when a user wants to print a file, she would prefer to use TCP, since that would ensure that the printer received all of the data intact. When the user wants to print, the client software on the end user's PC establishes a TCP session with the printer, sends the data to the printer's software, and then closes the connection once the job was submitted.

If the printer is functioning properly, it accepts the data, and uses the error-correction and flow-control services offered by TCP to manage the data transfer. If the printer is not available (perhaps it is out of paper, or low on toner), then it sends an appropriate message using the existing TCP connection. This ensures that the client is notified of whatever problem is preventing the print job from being serviced.

This process is illustrated in Figure 1-11. Here, the desktop PC is trying to print a file to the printer, but since the printer is out of toner, it rejects the connection. Because TCP is a reliable, circuit-centric protocol, the client is sure to get the message, even if it didn't get all of the UDP broadcasts sent earlier.

As you can see, both TCP and UDP provide functionality that is above that offered by IP alone, and both protocols are required to build an effective set of network applications.

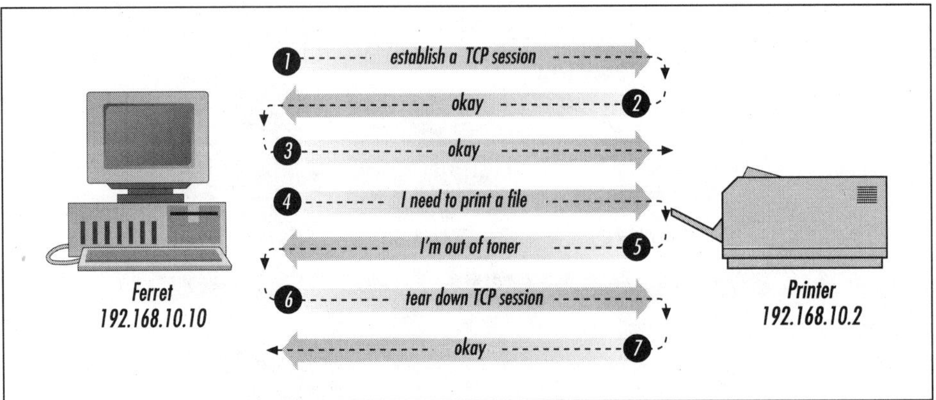

Figure 1-11. Using TCP for transaction-oriented applications

The Transmission Control Protocol

TCP provides error-correction through the use of a connection-oriented transaction. Whenever an application needs to send data to another host, TCP builds a "start" segment and sends it to the destination node. When the other system sends a "start" segment back (along with an acknowledgment that it got the first segment), a monitored conversation between the two systems begins.

TCP works in much the same way as a telephone conversation. When an application wants to trade data with another system, it first tries to establish a workable session. This is similar to you calling another person on the phone. When the other party answers ("Hello?"), they are acknowledging that the call went through. You then acknowledge the other party's acknowledgment ("Hi Joe, this is Eric"), and begin exchanging information.

If at any time during the call parts of the data exchange are lost ("Sorry, what did you say?"), the sender retransmits the questionable data. If the connection degrades to a point where no communication is possible, then sooner or later both parties simply stop talking. Otherwise, once all of the data has been exchanged, the parties agree to disconnect ("See ya"), and close the call gracefully. TCP follows most of these same rules, as is illustrated in Figure 1-12.

TCP segments are encapsulated within IP datagrams. They still rely on IP to get the data where it's going. However, since IP doesn't offer any guarantees regarding delivery, TCP has to keep track of the status of the connection at all times. This is achieved through the use of sequence numbers and acknowledgment flags embedded within the TCP header. Every byte of data sent over TCP must be acknowledged (although these acknowledgments are usually clumped together). If one of the systems does not acknowledge a segment, then TCP will resend the

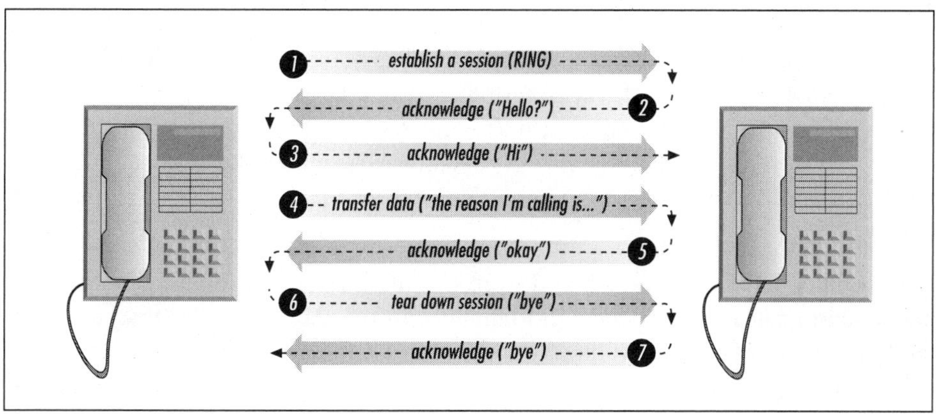

Figure 1-12. TCP virtual circuits versus telephone calls

questionable data. This provides error correction and recovery functions that overcome IP's unreliable nature.

The use of sequence numbers also allows TCP to implement flow control and other services on top of IP. Applications can send as much data as they need to, and TCP will break the data into chunks that will fit within IP segments. If the receiving system is unable to process data quickly enough, it can tell the sending system to slow down, thereby reducing the likelihood that data will get lost.

In addition, it is important to realize that TCP offers a byte-stream service for applications to use whenever they need to read and write data. Whenever an application needs to send data—whether that data is a 20-byte message or a two-megabyte file—the application can send the data in a stream to TCP, where it will be converted into manageable chunks of data that are sent (and tracked) over IP cleanly. Once the IP datagrams are received by the destination system, the data is made available to the destination application immediately, where it can be read and processed.

Applications such as the Internet's Simple Message Transport Protocol (SMTP) and Hypertext Transfer Protocol (HTTP) both require the reliable and controlled connection services that TCP provides. In addition, these types of application protocols also benefit from TCP's streaming model, allowing the applications to send data as a continual stream of bytes that will be read and processed by the recipient upon their arrival. Without these services, mail messages sent over SMTP and GIF images sent over HTTP would not flow smoothly, and would likely get garbled. And since TCP provides these services directly, applications do not have to embed these routines within their internal application code.

For more information on TCP, see Chapter 7, *The Transmission Control Protocol*.

The User Datagram Protocol

Not every application requires guaranteed delivery, and these applications typically use UDP for transport services. Unlike TCP, UDP sends only the data it has received from the application, and makes no pretense towards guaranteed delivery or flow control or anything else. As such, UDP is much like IP, but is the protocol that applications use to communicate with each other, rather than using IP directly.

UDP is much like a postcard. If you were travelling around a foreign country, you might send postcards to friends and family from the different cities that you visit, informing them of recent events. You wouldn't worry about the postcards getting delivered quickly, or even if they got lost entirely, since you'll probably send more postcards from the next town anyway. You wouldn't necessarily *want* the postcards to get lost, but at the same time you wouldn't rely on the postcards for any urgent business (like "send money to the embassy"). For anything important, you'd use the telephone (TCP) to ensure that your message arrived intact and was processed correctly.

You may wonder why a UDP protocol exists, when it would seem that IP could serve the same function. The reason is simple: IP doesn't do anything but get datagrams from one host to another. IP doesn't provide any application interfaces or management services. UDP does provide these services, and it provides a consistent environment for developers to use when writing low-overhead network applications. UDP also provides application multiplexing services through the use of port numbers, allowing many application protocols to be used on a single host. Trying to do this with IP would require either a lot more transport protocols, or an application multiplexing layer within IP directly, neither of which would be very efficient.

Another benefit of UDP is that it offers a message-centric delivery model, allowing chunks of data to be sent as single IP datagrams (instead of being streamed over virtual circuits like they would with TCP). For example, a UDP-based application protocol can write a four-kilobyte block of data to UDP, and that block will be handed to IP directly. IP will then create an IP datagram that contains the entire four kilobytes, and send this data as a series of IP packets to the destination system (according to the rules defined for the network medium in use). Once all of the data arrives, the IP datagram is reassembled and the entire four-kilobyte UDP message will be handed to UDP for processing.

In this model, it is easy for applications to exchange record-oriented data (such as a fixed-length file or a database record), since the entire record can be read by a single operation. Since the IP datagram (and thus the UDP message) will be contained in a single message, if the client has received any of the data, then they will receive *all* of the data in that message. Conversely, TCP would require that the client continually read the queue, waiting for all of the data to arrive, and having no clear indication of when all the data for that record had arrived (without also using application-specific markers in the data stream, anyway).

Also, applications that need fast turnaround or that already have their own internal error-correction routines can make good use of UDP because of its low overhead. Some database software packages can be configured to use UDP, and many file transfer protocols also use UDP because it is a light, fast, and message-centric protocol that is easier and faster than TCP, and that does not require the overhead of TCP's virtual-circuit model.

For more information on UDP, refer to Chapter 6, *The User Datagram Protocol.*

Presentation Services

Whenever application protocols wish to communicate with each other, they must do so using a predefined set of rules that define the types of data that will be exchanged. For example, if an application protocol is to use textual data, then those characters must have the same byte-order and binary values on both systems. For example, one system cannot use US-ASCII while the other system uses EBCDIC characters. Nor can one system pass data in "big-endian" form to a processor that only understands "little-endian" data, since the bits will be interpreted backwards.

For these reasons, the application protocols must agree to use certain types of data, and must also agree on how to present that data so that it is interpreted consistently. Typically, this falls under the heading of "presentation layer services," with some network architectures providing detailed presentation-layer specifications that cover everything from character sets to numeric formatting rules. However, TCP/IP does not have a formally defined presentation layer. Instead, it has many informal mechanisms that act as presentation layers, with each of them providing specific kinds of presentation services to different kinds of applications.

Most of the application protocols used on the Internet today use the Network Virtual Terminal (NVT) specification for presentation services. NVTs are a subset of the Telnet specification, and provide a basic terminal-to-terminal session that applications use to exchange textual data. The NVT specification defines a simple definition for the characters to use (seven-bit, printable characters from the US-ASCII character set) and end-of-line markers.

However, NVTs do not provide for much in the way of complex data types, such as numeric formatting. If an application needs to exchange a complex piece of data—including extended characters, long integers, and record markers—then NVTs can not be used alone. For this reason, a variety of other presentation-layer services are also used with TCP/IP applications, although typically these services are restricted to vendor-specific applications and offerings.

One presentation service that is popular with Microsoft-based applications is IBM's NetBIOS, a set of network APIs that provide functionality suitable for PC-based network applications. Another popular service is Sun's External Data Representation (XDR) service, a set of APIs that are useful for passing complex data types. Yet another popular service is the Distributed Computing Environment's Remote Procedure Call (DCE RPC) mechanism, useful for passing network-specific data between highly dissimilar hosts.

Each of these mechanisms is popular with different groups and for different reasons. But most Internet-based applications use just NVTs since they are usable on a wide variety of systems. Remember that many of the computing systems in use on the Internet are still quite old and are incapable of supporting anything other than seven-bit ASCII text.

Application Protocols

A variety of application protocols exist that provide standardized mechanisms for the exchange of information across vendor bounds. Among these are file transfer protocols such as FTP, Gopher, and HTTP; groupware and electronic mail services such as SMTP, POP3, IMAP4, and NNTP; and protocols for locating network resources such as DNS, Finger, and LDAP, among many others.

It's important to realize that client applications generally consist of two distinct components: the application protocol (such as HTTP or POP3), and an end-user interface that displays information. For example, a web browser uses HTTP (the protocol) to retrieve HTML and GIFs from a web server, but the code for displaying that data is a separate service that is not covered by the protocol specification.

For more on the common application protocols found on the Internet today, refer to the book *Internet Application Protocols*, which covers most of these protocols.

How Application Protocols Communicate Over IP

Almost all IP applications follow the same basic model: a client sends a request of some kind to a server running on another system, and the server examines the request, acts upon it in some form, and then possibly returns some form of data back to the client. This is not always the case (many UDP-based "servers" do not return any data, but simply monitor network activity), but it holds true for most applications.

Server-based applications (like an email server or web server) are generally loaded by the operating system when the computer is started. The servers then go into a "listen" state, watching for incoming connections. Conversely, client applications will only establish a connection when some sort of action is required (like "get new messages").

Applications communicate with the transport protocols through the use of "ports," which are unique I/O identifiers used by the transport protocols and the specific instance of the application protocol. "Ports" are conceptually similar to the mailboxes used at your local post office. When a letter comes in for a recipient, it is placed into a known mailbox reserved for that specific recipient. Whenever the recipient comes by, he will pick up any messages in that mailbox and process the data at his convenience.

Similarly, ports provide TCP and UDP with a way to deliver data to higher-layer application protocols. Every time an application protocol opens a connection to one of the transport protocols, it will allocate a port from the transport protocol, and then use that port for all network I/O. Any traffic that is destined for that particular application will be routed to the appropriate port for the application to deal with.

Just as every device on an IP network has a unique IP address, every instance of every application protocol also has a unique port number that is used to identify it to the transport protocols on the local system. This concept is illustrated in Figure 1-13, which shows how UDP reserves ports for specific applications. Any UDP or TCP messages that come into a system will be identified as destined for a specific port number, and the transport layer will use that information to route the data to the correct application.

Some applications can open many simultaneous network connections, and in this case, each instance would get its own port number. One example of this is the ubiquitous web browser, which can open many simultaneous connections to a remote web server, depending on the number of files that need to be downloaded from a web page. Each of these HTTP connections will get created as independent network connections, with each of the connections having unique port numbers for the client side of the connection. Once the web browser finishes downloading the objects, then each of the individual connections will be closed.

Every connection between a client and a server consists of four pieces of information: a source IP address, a source port number, a destination address, and a destination port number. All together, these four pieces of information make connections unique. For example, if a web browser were to open two connections to a web server, then the IP addresses of both hosts would be the same. In addition, the well-known server port number (80) would also be the same.

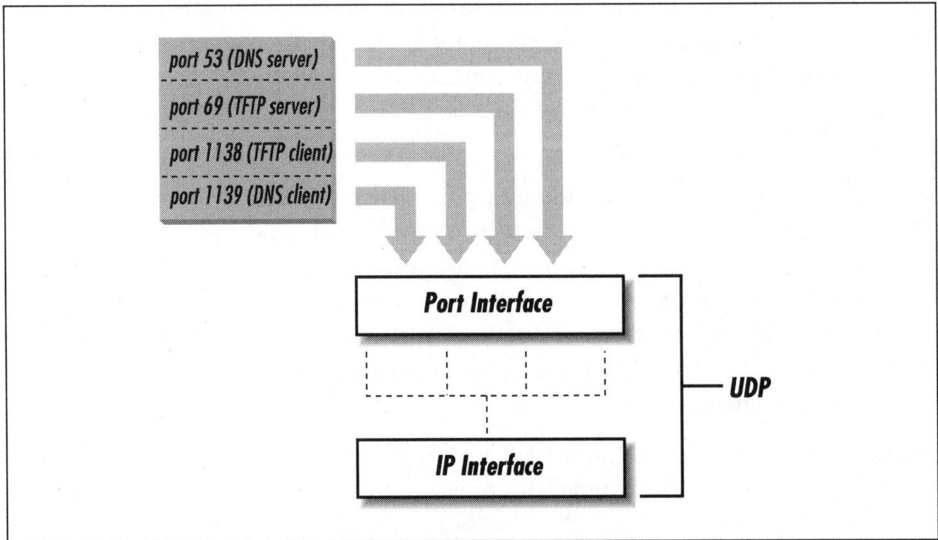

Figure 1-13. Application-level multiplexing with port numbers

Therefore, in order for the individual connections to be unique, the client must use a different port number for each of the unique connections. Servers do not care if a single client asks for multiple connections, as long as each connection comes from a unique port number on the client, since each connection must be uniquely identifiable to the server.

This four-way identifier is called a "socket pair" in IP lingo, and is the basis of all communications for all application protocols. A "port" identifies a connection point in the local stack (i.e., port number 80). A "socket" identifies an IP address and port number together (i.e., port 80 on host 192.168.10.20 could be written as "socket 192.168.10.20:80."). A "socket pair" refers to a distinct connection between two different applications, including the IP addresses and port numbers in use by both. Each individual connection requires that the socket pair contain at least one unique element.

Servers Listen for Incoming Connections

Most server-based IP applications use what are referred to as "well-known" port numbers. For example, an HTTP server will listen on TCP port 80 by default, which is the well-known port number for an HTTP server. This way, any HTTP client that connects to HTTP servers can use the default of TCP port 80. Otherwise, the client would have to specify the port number of the server that it wanted to connect with (you've seen this in some URLs that use *http://www.somehost.com:8080/* or the like, where "*8080*" is the port number of the HTTP server on *www.somehost.com*).

Most application servers allow you to use any port number you want. However, if you were to run your web server on TCP port 8080 for example, then you would have to tell every Internet user that your web server was *not* accessible on TCP port 80. This would be an impossible task. By sticking with the default, all users can connect to your web server using the default of TCP port 80.

Some network administrators purposefully run application servers on non-standard ports, hoping to add an extra layer of security to their network. However, it is the author's opinion that security through obscurity is no security at all, and this method should not be relied upon by itself.

There are a number of predefined port numbers that are registered with the Internet Assigned Numbers Authority (IANA). All of the port numbers below 1024 are reserved for use with well-known applications, although there are also many applications that use port numbers outside of this range.

In addition to the reserved addresses that are managed by the IANA, there are also "unreserved" port numbers that can be used by any application for any purpose, although conflicts may occur with other users who are also using those port numbers. Any port number that is frequently used is encouraged to register with the IANA.

For a detailed listing of all of the port numbers that are currently registered, refer to the IANA's online registry (accessible at *http://www.isi.edu/in-notes/iana/assignments/port-numbers*). To see the well-known ports used on your system, examine the */etc/services* file on a Unix host, or the *C:\WinNT\System32\Drivers\Etc\SERVICES* file on a Windows NT host.

Clients Open Connections to Servers

In contrast to server-based applications that are always listening for incoming connections on a fixed port number, client applications will use a randomly assigned port number for their end of the connection. Whenever an IP application needs to send data, the transport protocol will allocate a random port number above 1024 and use this port number for all incoming and outgoing data associated with that application.

For example, when a POP3 client is used to establish a connection with a mail server, the client application will pass an application-specific command to TCP, specifying the server's IP address and port number as the destination. TCP will then add its own information—including stuff like the port number of the local

POP3 client—and hand the entire package off to IP for delivery. IP then does its best to get the message to the destination system.

When the mail server's IP stack receives the datagram, it verifies that it contains a TCP segment, and then hands the contents off to TCP for further processing. TCP will see that the destination port number refers to the local POP3 server, and then hand off the original application command. Once the server has processed the command, it will reverse the process, sending whatever data it generates back to the port number and IP address in use by the client. Once the transaction is finished, the client's TCP port will be released. Any subsequent connections would require a new connection be opened, with a different port number being allocated by the client.

2

The Internet Protocol

Summary	The Internet Protocol provides a basic delivery service for transport protocols such as TCP and UDP. IP is responsible for getting data to its destination host and network. IP is not reliable, so the effort may fail.
Relevant STDs	2 (*http://www.iana.org/*); 3 (includes RFCs 1122 and 1123); 4 (RFC 1812, republished); 5 (includes RFCs 791, 792, 919, 922, 950, and 1112)
Relevant RFCs	781 (Timestamp Option); 791 (Internet Protocol); 815 (Fragmentation Reassembly); 919 (IP Broadcasts); 922 (Broadcasting on Sub-Nets); 950 (Sub-Net Recommendations); 1108 (Security Option); 1112 (IP Multicasting and IGMP v1); 1122 (Host Network Requirements); 1349 (Type-of-Service Flags); 1455 (Data-Link Security TOS Flags); 1812 (Router Requirements); 2113 (Router Alert Option)

As we learned in Chapter 1, *An Introduction to TCP/IP*, a variety of protocols are used for moving application data between different systems. We saw that hardware-specific protocols are used by devices when they need to exchange data directly, that the Internet Protocol is used to get IP datagrams across the different network segments to their final destination, and that TCP and UDP provide transport and connection management services to the application protocols used by end-user applications.

Although each of these layers provides unique and valuable services, the Internet Protocol is perhaps the most important to the overall operation of the Internet in general, since it is responsible for getting data from one host to another.

In this regard, IP can be thought of as being like a national delivery service that gets packages from a sender to a recipient, with the sender being oblivious to the routing and delivery mechanisms used by the delivery agent. The sender simply hands the package to the delivery agent, who then moves the package along until it is delivered.

For example, a package that is shipped from New York to Los Angeles is given to the delivery service (let's say UPS), with instructions on where the package has to go, although no instructions are provided on how the package should get to the destination. The package may have to go through Chicago first; the delivery agent at the New York UPS office makes that routing decision. Once the package reaches the Chicago UPS office, another delivery agent at that facility decides the best route for the package to take in order to get to Los Angeles (possibly going through Denver first, for example).

At each juncture, the local delivery agent does its best to get the package delivered using the shortest available route. When the package arrives at the Los Angeles facility, then another agent does its best to get it to the final destination system, using the destination address provided with the package to determine the best local routing.

Similarly, it is the function of IP to provide relaying and delivery decisions whenever an IP datagram has to be sent across a series of networks in order for it to be delivered to the final destination. The sending system does not care how the datagram gets to the destination system, but instead chooses the best route that is available at that specific moment. If this involves sending the datagram through another intermediary system, then that system also makes routing decisions according to the current condition of the network, forwarding the data on until it arrives at the destination system, as specified in the datagram's header.

The IP Standard

IP is defined in RFC 791, which has been republished as STD 5 (IP is an Internet Standard protocol). However, RFC 791 contained some vagaries that were clarified in RFC 1122 (Host Network Requirements). As such, IP implementations need to incorporate both RFC 791 and RFC 1122 in order to work reliably and consistently with other implementations.

RFC 791 begins by stating "The Internet Protocol is designed for use in interconnected systems of packet-switched computer communication networks. The Internet protocol provides for transmitting blocks of data called datagrams from sources to destinations. The Internet protocol also provides for fragmentation and reassembly of long datagrams, if necessary, for transmission through 'small packet' networks."

RFC 791 goes on to say "The Internet Protocol is specifically limited in scope to provide the functions necessary to deliver a package of bits (an Internet datagram) from a source to a destination over an interconnected system of networks. There are no mechanisms to augment end-to-end data reliability, flow control, sequencing, or other services commonly found in host-to-host protocols."

That pretty much sums it up. A source system will send a datagram to a destination system, either directly (if the destination host is on the local network) or by way of another system on the local network. If the physical medium that connects the sending and receiving systems offers enough capacity, IP will send all of the data in one shot. If this isn't possible, the data will be broken into fragments that are small enough for the physical medium to handle.

Once the datagram is sent, IP forgets about it and moves on to the next datagram. IP does not offer any error-correction, flow-control, or management services. It just sends datagrams from one host to another, one network at a time.

Remember this rule: the Internet Protocol is responsible *only* for getting datagrams from one host to another, one network at a time.

IP Datagrams Versus IP Packets

Hosts on an IP network exchange information using IP datagrams, which include both the units of data that contain whatever information is being exchanged and the header fields that describe that information (as well as describing the datagram itself). Whenever a device needs to send data to another system over an IP network, it will do so by creating an IP datagram, although the datagram is not what gets sent by IP, at least not in the literal sense.

Instead, IP datagrams get sent as IP packets, which are used to relay the IP datagrams to the destination system, one hop at a time. Although in many cases an IP datagram and an IP packet will be exactly the same, they are conceptually different entities, which is an important concept for understanding how IP actually works.

This concept is illustrated in Figure 2-1. In that example, Ferret needs to send an IP datagram to Fungi. However, since Fungi is on a remote network, Ferret has to send the packet containing the datagram to Sasquatch, who will then send another packet to Fungi.

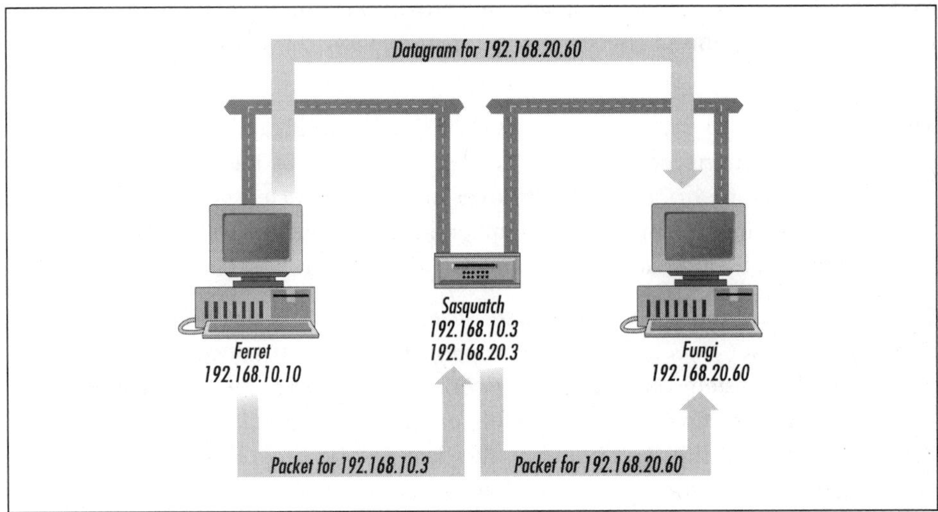

Figure 2-1. IP datagrams versus IP packets

IP datagrams contain whatever data is being sent (and the associated IP headers), while IP packets are used to get the datagram to the destination system (as specified in the IP headers). These IP packets are sent using the framing mechanisms defined for the specific network medium in use on the local network, and are subject to network events such as fragmentation or loss. However, the datagram itself will always remain as the original piece of data that was sent by the original sender, regardless of anything that happens to any of the packets that are used to relay the datagram.

For example, Figure 2-2 shows a four-kilobyte datagram that is being sent from Ferret to Fungi. Since this datagram is too large for the Ethernet network to send in a single frame, the datagram is split into four IP packets, each of which are sent as individual entities in individual Ethernet frames. Once all of the IP packets are received by the destination system, they will be reassembled into the original datagram and processed.

This model is necessary due to the way that IP provides a virtual network on top of the different physical networks that make up the global Internet. Since each of those networks have different characteristics (such as addressing mechanisms, frame sizes, and so forth), IP has to provide a mechanism for forwarding datagrams across those different networks reliably and cleanly. The datagram concept allows a host to send whatever data needs to be sent, while the IP packet allows the datagram to actually get sent across the different networks according to the characteristics of each of the intermediary networks.

This concept is fundamental to the design nature of the Internet Protocol, and is the key to understanding how IP operates on complex networks.

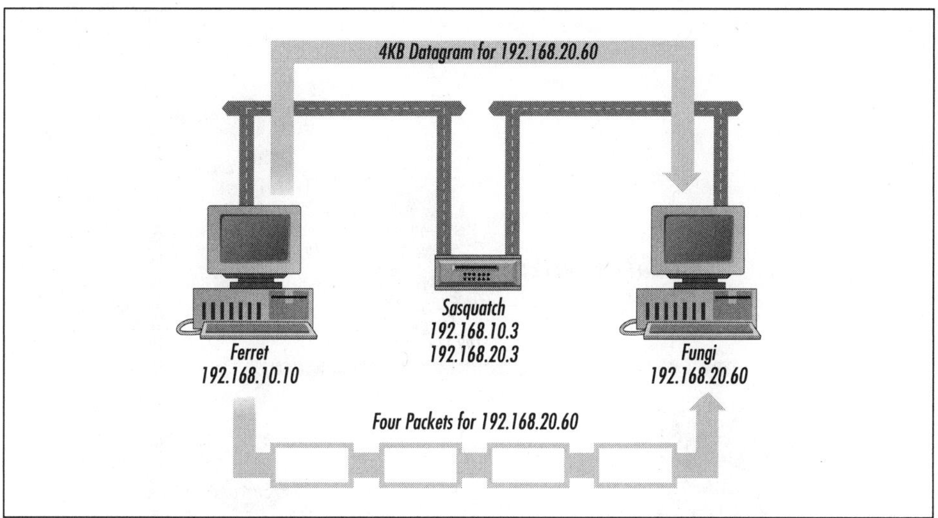

Figure 2-2. Datagram fragmentation overview

Local Versus Remote Delivery

The IP header stores the IP addresses of both the source and destination systems. If the destination system is on the same physical network as the sending system, then the sender will attempt to deliver the datagram directly to the recipient, as shown in Figure 2-3. In this model, the sender knows that the recipient is on the same local network, so it transmits the data directly to the recipient, using the low-level protocols appropriate for that network medium.

However, if the two systems are not connected to the same IP network, then the sender must find another node on the local network that is able to relay the IP datagram on to its final destination. This intermediate system would then have to deliver the datagram if the final recipient was directly accessible, or it would have to send the datagram on to yet another intermediary system for subsequent delivery. Eventually, the datagram would get to the destination system.

A slightly more complex representation of this can be seen in Figure 2-4. In that example, the sending system knows that the destination system is on a remote network, so it locates an intermediate system that can forward the data on to the final destination. It then locates the hardware address of the forwarding system, and passes the data to the intermediate system using the low-level protocols appropriate for the underlying medium. The intermediate system then examines the destination IP address of the datagram, chooses an exit interface, and sends the data to the final destination system using the low-level protocols appropriate to that network.

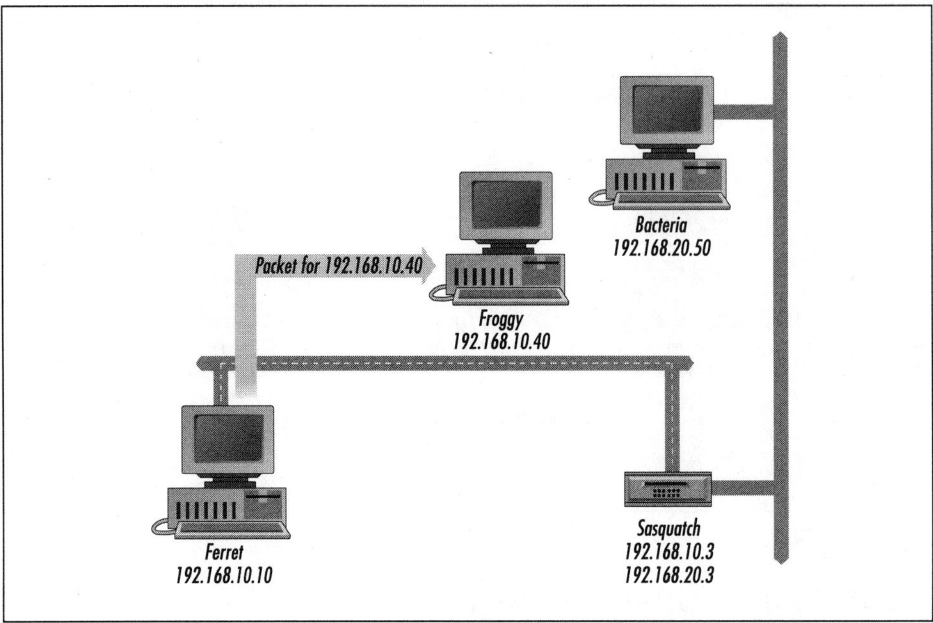

Figure 2-3. An example of local delivery

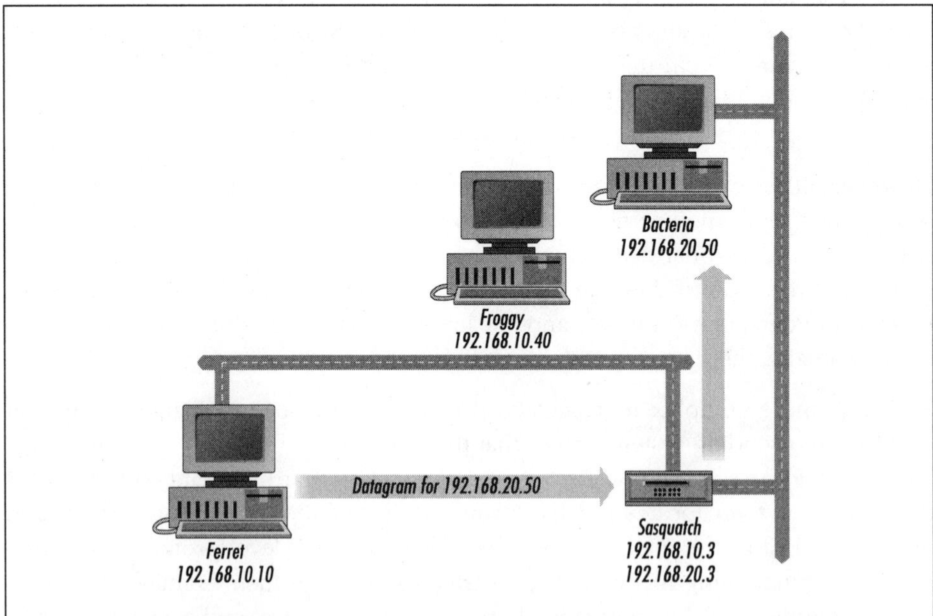

Figure 2-4. An example of routed delivery

The two network models shown in Figure 2-3 and Figure 2-4 are both relatively simple, and each represents the majority of the traffic patterns found on internal corporate networks. Most networks only have a few segments, with the target being no more than a handful of hops away from the originating system.

But once datagrams start travelling over the Internet, things can get very complex very quickly. Rather than having to deal with only one or two routers, all of a sudden you may be looking at a dozen or more hops. However, IP handles complex networks the same way it handles small networks: one hop at a time. Eventually, the datagrams will get through. This concept is illustrated in Figure 2-5, which shows five different network segments in between the sending and destination systems.

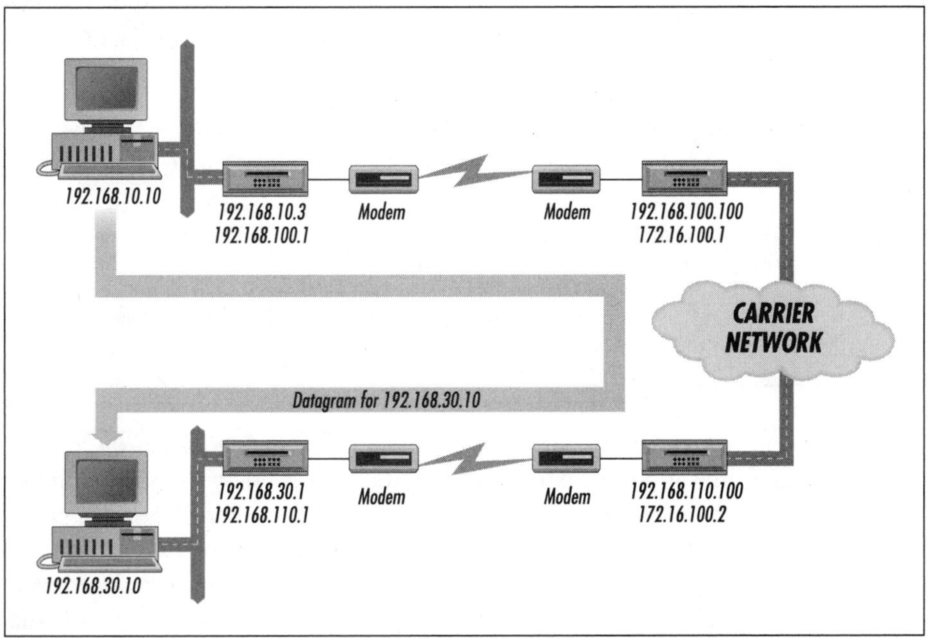

Figure 2-5. A complex, multi-hop network path

In the example shown in Figure 2-5, the sender has to give a packet to the local router, which will send another packet off to a router at the other end of a modem connection. The remote router then has to forward the data to yet another router across the carrier network, which has to send the data to its dial-up peer, which will finally deliver the datagram to the destination system. In order for all of this to work, however, each router must be aware of the path to the destination host, passing the data off to the next-hop router.

How IP finds remote hosts and networks

Every IP device—regardless of the function it serves—must have an IP address for every network that it is connected to. Most systems (such as PCs) only have a single network connection, and therefore only have a single IP address. But devices that have multiple network interfaces (such as routers or high-load devices like file servers) must have a dedicated IP address for every network connection.

When the IP protocols are loaded into memory, an inventory is taken of the available interfaces, and a map is built showing what networks the system is attached to. This map is called a routing table: it stores information such as the networks that the node is connected to and the IP address of the network interface connected to that network.

If a device only has a single interface, then there will be only one entry in the routing table, showing the local network and the IP address of the system's own network interface. But if a device is connected to multiple networks—or if it is connected to the same network several times—then there will be multiple entries in the routing table.

In reality, just about every IP device also has a "loopback" network, used for testing and debugging purposes. The loopback network is always numbered 127.0.0.0, while the loopback interface always has the IP address of 127.0.0.1. This means that routing tables will generally show at least two entries: one for the physical connection and one for the loopback network.

When a system has to send a datagram to another system, it looks at the routing table and finds the appropriate network interface to send the outbound traffic through. For example, the router shown in the top-left corner of Figure 2-5 has two network connections: an Ethernet link with the IP address of 192.168.10.3 and a serial connection with an IP address of 192.168.100.1. If this router needed to send data to 192.168.10.10, then it would use the Ethernet interface for that traffic. If it needed to send datagrams to 192.168.100.100, it would use the serial interface. Table 2-1 shows what the router's routing table would look like based on this information.

Table 2-1. The Default Routing Table for 192.168.10.3

Destination Network	Interface/Router
127.0.0.0 (loopback network)	127.0.0.1 (loopback interface)
192.168.10.0 (local Ethernet network)	192.168.10.3 (local Ethernet interface)
192.168.100.0 (local serial network)	192.168.100.1 (local serial interface)

However, such a routing table would not provide any information about any remote networks or devices. In order for the router to send an IP datagram to 172.16.100.2, it would need to have an entry in the routing table for the 172.16.100.0

network. Systems are informed of these details by adding entries to the routing table. Most TCP/IP packages provide end-user tools that allow you to manually create and delete routing entries for specific networks and hosts. Using such a tool, you could inform the router that the 172.16.100.0 network is accessible via the router at 192.168.100.100. Once done, the routing table for the local router would be similar to the one shown in Table 2-2.

Table 2-2. The Routing Table for 192.168.10.3 with a Remote Route Added

Destination Network	Interface/Router
127.0.0.0 (loopback network)	127.0.0.1 (loopback interface)
192.168.10.0 (local Ethernet network)	192.168.10.3 (local Ethernet interface)
192.168.100.0 (local serial network)	192.168.100.1 (local serial interface)
172.16.0.0 (remote carrier network)	192.168.100.100 (next-hop router)

Since the router already knows how to send datagrams to 192.168.100.100, it now knows to send all datagrams for 172.16.100.2 to 192.168.100.100, under the assumption that the remote router would forward the packets for delivery. By adding entries for each network segment to the local routing table, you would be able to tell every device how to get datagrams to remote segments of the network. Such a routing table might look the one shown in Table 2-3.

Table 2-3. Complete Routing Table for 192.168.10.3, Showing Entire Network

Destination Network	Interface/Router
127.0.0.0 (loopback network)	127.0.0.1 (loopback interface)
192.168.10.0 (local Ethernet network)	192.168.10.3 (local Ethernet interface)
192.168.100.0 (local serial network)	192.168.100.1 (local serial interface)
172.16.100.0 (remote carrier network)	192.168.100.100 (next-hop router)
192.168.110.0 (remote serial network)	192.168.100.100 (next-hop router)
192.168.30.0 (remote Ethernet network)	192.168.100.100 (next-hop router)

Unfortunately, you would have to add entries for every segment of the network to every device on the network in order for everything to function properly. Each router would have to have a map showing every network and the routers that were to be used for that network. This task can be a lot of work, and is also highly prone to human error.

Several application protocols can be used to build maps of the network and distribute them to all of your systems without human intervention. The most popular of these for private networks is the Routing Information Protocol (RIP), which uses UDP broadcasts to distribute routing tables every thirty seconds. Another popular protocol is Open Shortest Path First (OSPF), which provides the same basic functionality as RIP but with more detail and less overhead. For external networks, neither of these protocols works well enough to support a significant number of networks, and other protocols (such as the Border Gateway Protocol) are more common for those environments.

In common practice, most network administrators run these dynamic routing protocols only on their routers (but not on their hosts) since they tend to consume a lot of CPU cycles, memory, and network bandwidth. They then define "default" routes at the hosts, pointing them to the router(s) that serve the local network that the host is attached to. By using this model, clients need to keep only one entry in their routing tables, while the dedicated routers worry about keeping track of the overall network topology.

Table 2-4 shows what this might look like from the perspective of our example router. Notice that it has routing entries only for the locally attached networks, and that it now knows to send any other datagrams to the default router at 192.168.100.100. That router would then forward all of the datagrams that it gets to its default router as well.

Table 2-4. A Simplified Routing Table for 192.168.10.3

Destination Network	Interface/Router
127.0.0.0 (loopback network)	127.0.0.1 (loopback interface)
192.168.10.0 (local Ethernet network)	192.168.10.3 (local Ethernet interface)
192.168.100.0 (local serial network)	192.168.100.1 (local serial interface)
0.0.0.0 (default route)	192.168.100.100 (next-hop router)

Default routes can be built manually (using the tools provided with the IP software in use on the local system), or can be assigned during system boot (using a protocol such as BOOTP or DHCP). In addition, a protocol called Router Discovery can provide network devices with default route information dynamically, updating the devices' routing tables as the network topology changes.

The examples shown earlier illustrate that managing routing tables can be complex, even with relatively small networks. Unfortunately, the Internet consists of several hundred thousand such networks. If all of the routers connecting these networks together had to be tracked by all of the other routers, there would be so much router-management traffic that nothing else could get through. The Internet would collapse under its own weight.

Route aggregation

New address assignment schemes are being deployed that allow routes to be aggregated together. Now, when you request a block of Internet addresses from your Internet Service Provider, the ISP must assign one from a larger block that has already been assigned to them. This allows routing to happen at a much higher level. Rather than ISPs having to track and advertise thousands of network routes, they only have to advertise a few super-routes.

The ISP will still have to track all of the networks that are under it, but it won't have to advertise them to other ISPs. This feature cuts down on the amount of backbone router-update traffic immensely, without losing any functionality.

Geography-based aggregation schemes are also being deployed. For example, any network that begins with 194 is somewhere in Europe. This simple assignment allows major routers on the Internet to simply forward traffic for any network that begins with 194 to the backbone routers in Europe. Those routers will then forward the datagrams to the appropriate regional ISP, who will then relay the datagrams on to their final destination.

This process is conceptually similar to the way that area codes and prefixes help the phone company route a call. Telephone switches can route a long-distance call simply by examining the area code. The main switches in the remote area code will then examine the telephone number's three-digit prefix, and route the call to the appropriate central office. By the time you finish dialing the last four digits of the phone number, the call is practically already established.

By using aggregated routing techniques, IP datagrams can be moved around the Internet in much the same manner. Aggregation allows routers to use much smaller tables (around 50,000 routes instead of two million routes), which keeps CPU and memory requirements as low as possible, which, in turn, allows performance to be higher than it otherwise would be if every router had to keep track of every network's router path.

For more information about hierarchical routing, refer to "Classless Inter-Domain Routing (CIDR)" in Appendix B, *IP Addressing Fundamentals*.

Datagram Independence

In the preceding section, we used an analogy of a telephone number to illustrate how routers are able to route datagrams to their final destination quickly, based on the destination IP address. However, we should also point out that IP packets are not at all like telephone calls.

Telephone networks use the concept of "circuits" to establish a point-to-point connection between two users. When two people establish a telephone call, a dedicated point-to-point connection is established and is preserved for the duration of the call. In contrast, IP networks treat every individual IP datagram as a totally unique entity, each of which is free to travel across whatever route is most suitable at that moment.

For example, if a user were to retrieve a document from a remote web server, the server would probably need to generate several IP datagrams in order to return the requested material. Each of these datagrams is considered to be a unique and separate entity, totally unrelated to the datagrams sent before or after.

Each of these datagrams may take whatever path is deemed most appropriate by the routers that are forwarding them along. Whereas the first datagram sent from the web server to the requesting client may travel across an underground fiber-optic cable, the second datagram may be sent across a satellite link, while a third may travel over a conventional network. This concept is illustrated in Figure 2-6.

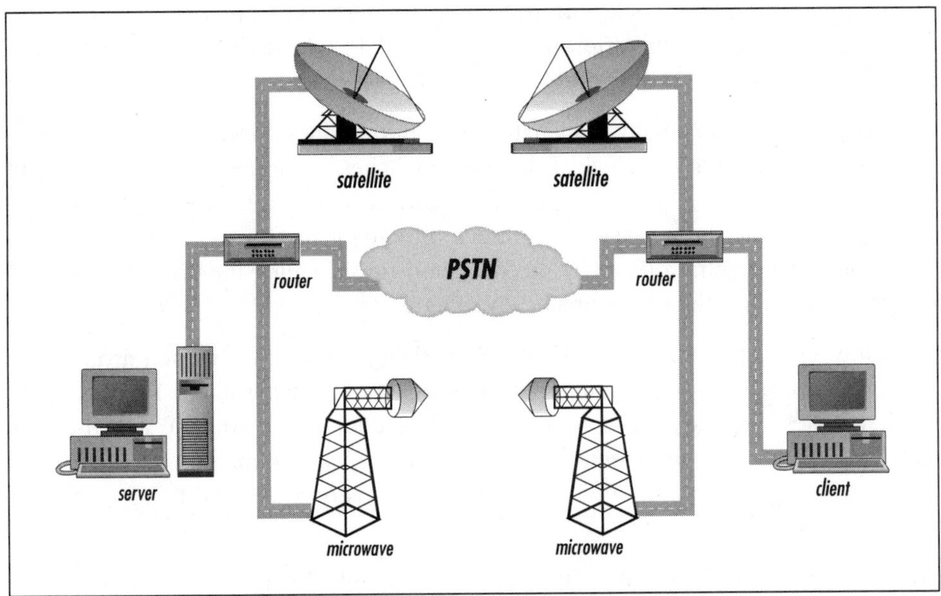

Figure 2-6. Every IP datagram is an individual entity and may take a different route

These routing decisions are made by the routers in between the source and destination systems. As the network changes, the routers that are moving datagrams around will have to adapt to the changing environment. Many things can cause the network to change: network cables can be ripped up, or downstream routers can become too busy to service a request, or any number of other events can happen to cause a route to become unavailable.

A result of this independence is that datagrams may arrive at their destination out of sequence, since one of them may have gone over a fast network, while another may have been sent over a slow network. In addition, sometimes datagrams get duplicated, causing multiple copies of the same packet to arrive at the destination system.

This architecture is purposefully designed into IP: one of the original design goals for the Internet Protocol was for it to be able to survive large-scale network outages in case of severe damage caused during war-time. By allowing each datagram to travel along the most-available path, every datagram's chances of survival increases dramatically. IP does not care if some of them happen to arrive out of sequence, get lost in transit, or even arrive multiple times; its job is to move the datagram, not to keep track of it. Higher-level protocols deal with any problems that result from these events.

Furthermore, by treating every datagram as an individual entity, the network itself is relieved of the responsibility of having to track every connection. This means that the devices on the network can focus on moving datagrams along, and do not have to watch for the beginning and end of every web browser's session. This feature allows overall performance to be as high as the hardware will allow, with as little memory and CPU requirements as possible.

Housekeeping and Maintenance

Every system that receives a packet—whether the system is the final destination or a router along the delivery path—will inspect it. If the packet has become corrupt or has experienced some other form of temporary failure, then the packet will be destroyed right then and there. Whenever one of these transient errors occurs, the datagram is destroyed rather than being forwarded on.

However, if a problem occurs that is semi-permanent—for example, if the current device does not have a routing table entry for the destination network, or if the packet does not meet certain criteria for forwarding across the next-hop network—then IP may call upon the Internet Control Message Protocol (ICMP) to return an error message back to the original sender, informing them of the failure. Although the datagram will still be destroyed by the last-hop device, it will also inform the sender of the problem, thereby allowing it to correct whatever condition was causing the failure to occur.

This distinction between transient and semi-permanent failures is important. Transient errors are caused by no fault of the sender (such as can happen when the Time-to-Live timer expires, or a checksum is miscalculated), while semi-permanent failures are problems with the packet or network that will always prevent delivery from occurring over this path. In the latter case, it is best either to inform the sender of the problem so that it can take whatever corrective actions are required, or to notify the application that tried to send the data of the problem.

Chapter 5, *The Internet Control Message Protocol*, discusses the error messages that are generated by ICMP whenever a semi-permanent problem is encountered. However, the remainder of this section also discusses some of the transient problems that may occur with IP delivery in particular.

Header checksums

Part of this integrity-checking service is handled through the use of a checksum applied against the IP datagram's header (but *not* against the data inside of the IP datagram). Every device that receives an IP datagram must examine the IP header and compare that information with the value stored in the header's checksum field. If the values do not match, then the datagram is assumed to be corrupt and is discarded immediately.

The data portion of the IP datagram is not verified, for three reasons. First of all, a device would have to examine the entire datagram to verify the contents. This process would require additional CPU processing time, which is more often than not going to be a waste of time.

Second, the data portion of an IP datagram always consists of a higher-level datagram, such as those generated by TCP and UDP. Since these protocols provide their own error-checking routines, the recipient system will have to conduct this verification effort anyway. The theory is that datagrams will move faster if routers do not have to verify their contents, a task which will be handled by the destination system anyway.

Finally, some application protocols are capable of working with partially corrupt data. In those cases, IP would actually be performing a disservice if it were to throw away datagrams with invalid checksums, since the application protocol would never get it. Granted, most applications do not work this way, but most applications will also utilize some form of error-correction service to keep this from becoming a problem.

Time-to-Live

Another validation service provided by IP is checking to see if a datagram has outlived its usefulness. This is achieved through a Time-to-Live field provided in the IP datagram's header. When a system generates an IP packet, it stores a value in the Time-to-Live header field. Every system that forwards the packet decreases the value of the Time-to-Live field by one, before sending the datagram on. If the Time-to-Live value reaches zero before the datagram gets to its final destination, then the packet is destroyed.

The purpose of the Time-to-Live field is to keep datagrams that are caught in an undeliverable loop from tying up network resources. Let's assume that a pair of routers both have bad information in their routing table, with each system pointing to the other for final delivery. In this environment, a packet would be sent from one router to the other, which would then return the packet, with this process repeating forever. Meanwhile, more packets may be introduced to this network from external devices, and after a while, the network could become saturated.

But by using a Time-to-Live field, each of these routers would decrement the value by one every time it forwarded a packet. Eventually the Time-to-Live value would reach zero, allowing the datagram to be destroyed. This safeguard prevents routing loops from causing network meltdowns.

The strict definition of the Time-to-Live field states that the value is a measure of time in seconds, or any forwarding act that took less than one second to perform. However, there are very few Internet routers that require a full second to perform forwarding, so this definition is somewhat misrepresentative. In actual practice, the Time-to-Live value is decremented for every hop, regardless of the actual time required to forward a datagram from one network segment to another.

It is also important to note that an ICMP failure-notification message gets sent back to the original sender when the Time-to-Live value reaches zero. For more information on this error message, refer to "Time Exceeded" in Chapter 5.

The default value for the Time-to-Live field should be set to 64 according to the Assigned Numbers registry (*http://www.iana.org/*). In addition, some of the higher-layer protocols also have default Time-to-Live values that they are supposed to use (such as 64 for TCP, and 1 for IGMP). These values are really only suggestions, however, and different implementations use different values, with some systems setting the Time-to-Live on all outgoing IP datagrams as high as 255.

Fragmentation and Reassembly

Every network has certain characteristics that are specific to the medium in use on that network. One of the most important characteristics is the maximum amount of data that a network can carry in a single frame (called the Maximum Transmission Unit, or "MTU"). For example, Ethernet can pass only 1500 bytes in a single frame, while the typical MTU for 16-megabit Token Ring is 17,914 bytes per frame.

RFC 791 specifies that the maximum allowed MTU size is 65,535 bytes, and that the minimum allowed MTU size is 68 bytes. No network should advertise or attempt to use a value that is greater or lesser than either of those values. Several RFCs define the specific default MTU values that are to be used with different networking topologies. Table 2-5 lists the common MTU sizes for the most-common media types, and also lists the RFCs (or other sources) that define the default MTU sizes for those topologies.

Table 2-5. Common MTU Sizes and the Related RFCs

Topology	MTU (in bytes)	Defined By
Hyperchannel	65,535	RFC 1374
16 MB/s Token Ring	17,914	IBM
802.4 Token Bus	8,166	RFC 1042

Table 2-5. Common MTU Sizes and the Related RFCs (continued)

Topology	MTU (in bytes)	Defined By
4 MBs Token Ring	4,464	RFC 1042
FDDI	4,352	RFC 1390
DIX Ethernet	1,500	RFC 894
Point-to-Point Protocol (PPP)	1,500	RFC 1548
802.3 Ethernet	1,492	RFC 1042
Serial-Line IP (SLIP)	1,006	RFC 1055
X.25 & ISDN	576	RFC 1356
ARCnet	508	RFC 1051

Since an IP datagram can be forwarded across any route available, every IP packet that gets generated by a forwarding device has to fit the packet within the available MTU space of the underlying medium used on the transient network. If you're on an Ethernet network, then IP packets have to be 1500 bytes or smaller in order for them to be carried across that network as discrete entities, regardless of the size of the original datagram.

There are really two concepts at work here: the size of the original IP datagram and the size of the packets that are used to relay the datagram from the source to the destination. If the datagram is too large for the sending system's local MTU, then that system has to fragment the datagram into multiple packets for local delivery to occur. In addition, if any of those IP packets are too large to cross another network segment somewhere between the sender and final recipient, then the packets must be fragmented by that router as well, allowing them to be sent across that network.

On an isolated network, size rarely matters since all of the systems on that network will share the same maximum frame size (a server and a client can both use at most 1500-byte datagrams, if both of them are on the same Ethernet segment). However, once you begin to mix different network media together, size becomes very important.

For example, suppose that a web server were on a Token Ring network that used 4,464-byte packets, while the end users were on a separate Ethernet segment that used 1500-byte packets. The TCP/IP software on the server would generate IP datagrams (and packets) that were 4,464 bytes long (according to the MTU characteristics of the local network), but in order for the IP datagrams to get to the client, the router in between these two segments would have to fragment the large packets into smaller packets that were small enough to move over the Ethernet network, as illustrated in Figure 2-7.

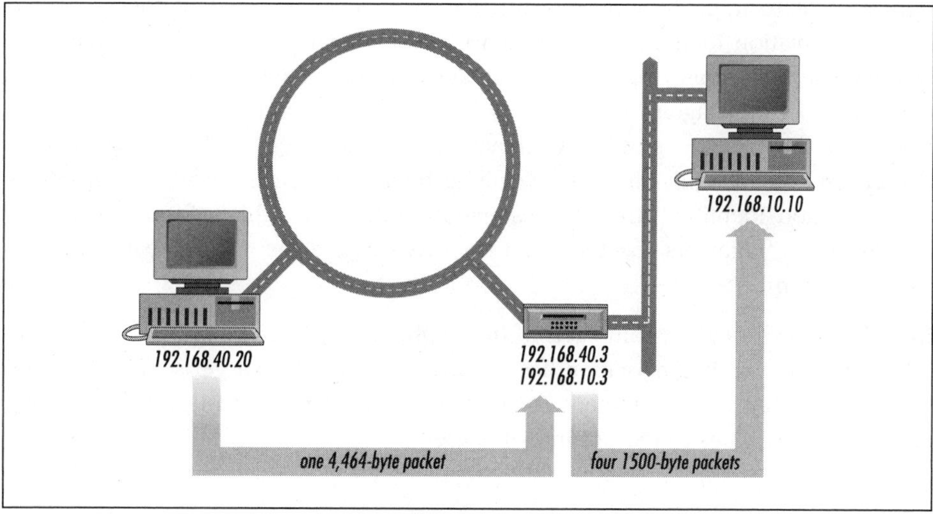

Figure 2-7. One 4,464-byte packet being split into four 1500-byte packets

During the act of fragmentation, the router will do several things. First of all, it will examine the size of the data that is stored in the original packet, and then it will create as many fragments as are needed to move the original packet's data across the smaller segment. In the example shown in Figure 2-7, a single 4,464-byte IP packet would require four IP packets in order to travel across the 1500-byte Ethernet (the mathematics behind this process will be explained in a moment).

In this example, the destination host may not be able to reassemble the original datagram, since the datagram is larger than the MTU of the local Ethernet connection. RFC 1122 states that hosts must be able to reassemble datagrams of at least 576 bytes, and should be able to reassemble datagrams that are "greater than or equal to the MTU of the connected network(s)." In this case, the local MTU is 1500 bytes, although the original datagram was four kilobytes, so it is possible that the destination system would be unable to reassemble the original datagram. Although most systems do not have problems with this, it should not come as a surprise if a wireless hand-held device cannot reassemble 65 KB datagrams sent from high-speed servers.

When the original 4,464-byte packet was fragmented, the headers of each of the new 1500-byte IP packets would be given whatever information was found in the original packet's header, including the source and the destination IP addresses, the Time-to-Live value, the Type-of-Service flags, and so on.

With regards to fragmentation in particular, the most important of these fields is the Fragmentation Identifier field, which is used to mark each of the fragments as belonging to the same original IP datagram. The Fragmentation Identifier field is really more of a Datagram Identifier, and is a 16-bit "serial number" that gets generated by the sending system whenever a datagram gets created. Whenever a packet gets fragmented, all of the resulting fragments use the original datagram's Fragmentation Identifier, and the destination system uses this information to collect all of the fragments together, and then reassemble the original datagram into its original form.

In addition, two fields within each of the fragments' IP headers will also be set, to reflect the fact that fragmentation has occurred. The fields that get set are the Fragmentation Offset and a Fragment Flags field (the latter is used to provide ordering and reassembly clues to the destination system).

Fragmentation Offset
: This field is used to indicate the byte-range of the original datagram that a specific fragment provides. However, only the *starting* position of the byte-range is provided in this field (the remainder of the packet is assumed to contain the rest of that fragment). This starting position is stored in terms of eight-byte (64-bit) blocks of data. The Fragmentation Offset identifier allows the receiving system to re-order the fragments into their proper sequence once all of the fragments have arrived.

Fragment Flags
: This field provides clues as to the current fragmentation status (if any). There are three one-bit flags, although only the last two are currently used. The first bit is reserved for future use and must always be set to 0. The second bit indicates whether or not fragmentation is allowed (0 means fragmentation is allowed and 1 means do not fragment). The third and final bit is used to indicate whether a current fragment is the last (0), or if more fragments will follow this one (1).

In addition to these changes, the Total Packet Length field for each of the newly minted IP packets also gets set according to the size of the fragments (rather than the size of the original datagram).

The resulting IP packets are then sent over the Internet as independent entities, just as if they had originally been created that way. Fragments are not reassembled until they reach the destination system. Once they reach the final destination, however, they are reassembled by the IP software running on the destination system, where they are combined back into their original datagram form. Once the original datagram has been reassembled, the IP datagram's data is forwarded to the appropriate transport protocol for subsequent processing.

There are a few rules that you must remember when trying to understand how IP fragments get created:

- Fragmentation only occurs on the data portion of a packet.
- Packet headers are *not* included in the fragmentation process. If the original datagram is 4,464 bytes long, then at least 20 bytes of that datagram are being used to store header information, meaning that the data portion is 4,444 bytes long. This 4,444 bytes is what will get fragmented.
- Each new fragment results in a new packet that requires its own IP headers, which consume at least 20 bytes in each new packet generated for a fragment. The IP software must take this factor into consideration when it determines the maximum amount of payload data that can be accommodated in each fragment, and thus the number of fragments that will be required for a particular MTU.
- Fragmentation must occur on an eight-byte boundary. If a datagram contains 256 bytes of data, but only 250 bytes can fit into a fragment, then the first fragment contains only 248 bytes of data (248 is the largest number divisible by eight that's less than 250). The remaining 8 bytes (256 – 248 = 8) will be sent in the next fragment.
- The Fragmentation Offset field is used to indicate which parts of the original datagram are in each fragment, by storing the byte count in quantities of eight-byte blocks. Rather than indicating that the starting position for a fragment's data is "248 bytes," the Fragmentation Offset field will show "31 blocks" (248 / 8 = 31). Also, note that the block count starts with 0 and not 1. This means that the 32nd block will be numbered 31 instead of 32.

As shown in Figure 2-7, in order for the original 4,464-byte IP datagram to be sent across the Ethernet network segment, four IP fragments will have to be created. Each of the new packets will contain an IP header (copied from the original datagram's header), plus however much data they could carry (although the quantity has to be divisible by eight). The result is four unique fragments, as shown in Figure 2-8.

The relevant fields from the original IP packet are shown in Table 2-6.

Table 2-6. Headers from the Original 4,464-byte Packet

Fragment	Fragment Identifier	Reserved Flag	May Fragment Flag	More Fragment Flags	Fragment Offset	Packet Length
1	321	0	0	0	0	4,464

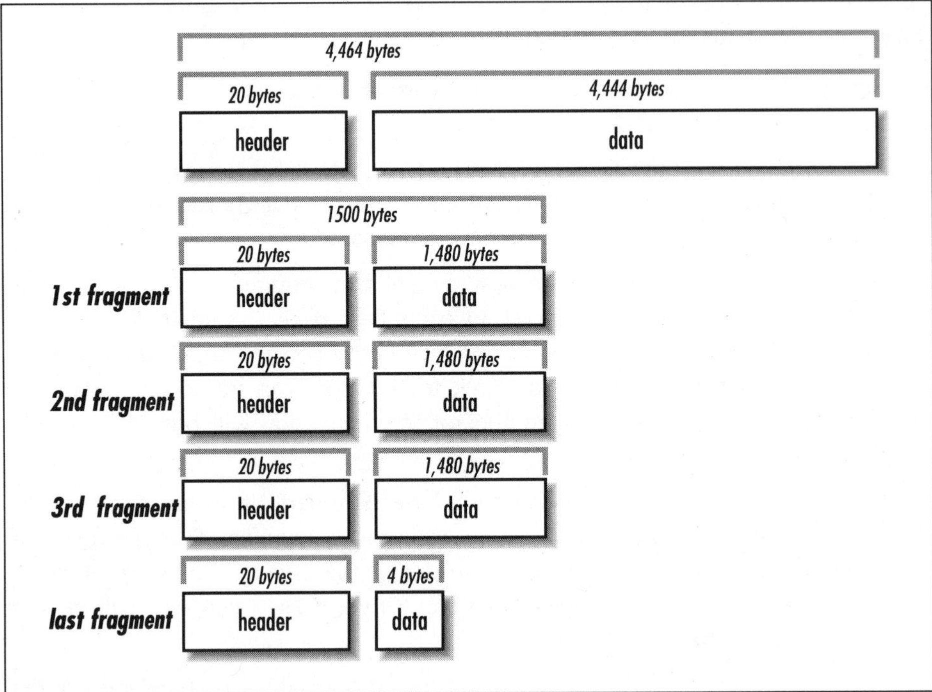

Figure 2-8. The mathematics of datagram fragmentation

After converting the single 4,464-byte IP packet into four 1500-byte IP fragments, the headers of each fragment will appear as shown in Table 2-7.

Table 2-7. Headers from Four 1500-byte Fragments

Fragment	Fragment Identifier	Reserved Flag	May Fragment Flag	More Fragment Flags	Fragment Offset	Packet Length
1	321	0	0	1	0	1,500
2	321	0	0	1	185	1,500
3	321	0	0	1	370	1,500
4	321	0	0	0	555	24

Each of the fragments contains the following header information:

- Each fragment belongs to the same original datagram, so each of them share the same "serial number" in the Fragmentation Identifier field (321 in this case).
- The first bit in the 3-bit Flags field is reserved, and must be marked 0.

- Each packet may be fragmented further, so the "May Fragment" flags are marked 0.
- The "More Fragments" flag is used to indicate if more fragments are following after this fragment. Since the first three fragments all have another fragment coming behind them, they all have the More Fragments flag marked 1, while the last fragment identifies the end of the set by having a 0 in this field.
- Since the first fragment marks the beginning of the original data, the Fragment Offset field starts at 0. Since the first fragment held 1,480 bytes of data, the second fragment would have its Fragmentation Offset field set to 185 (1480 / 8 = 185). The second fragment was also able to store 1,480 bytes, so the Fragment Offset flag for the third packet will be set to 370 ((1480 × 2) / 8 = 370). The third fragment was also able to hold 1,480 bytes, so the fourth fragment's Fragment Offset flag will be set to 555 ((1480 × 3) / 8 = 555).
- In addition, each new IP packet created during the fragmentation process will also have its Total Packet Length field set to the size of the resulting IP packets, rather than set to the size of the original IP datagram.

In order for the destination system to reassemble the datagram, it must read the fragmentation-specific headers in each of the fragments as they arrive and order them into their correct sequence (as indicated by the Fragment Offset field). Since each fragment may arrive out of sequence (due to a slower link, a down segment, or whatever), the destination system has to store each fragment in memory until all of them have arrived before they can be rearranged and the data processed.

Once all of the segments have been received, the system will examine their headers and find the fragment whose Fragment Offset is 0. The IP software will then read the data portion of the IP packet containing that fragment, recording the number of eight-byte blocks that it finds. Then it will locate the fragment that shows the Fragment Offset needed to continue reading the data, and then read that fragment's data into memory. This process will continue until all of the data has been read from all of the packets. Once a packet has been read that has the "More Fragments" flag set to 0—and if each of the Fragment Offset fields matches up without leaving any holes in the final datagram—then the process is complete.

If all of the fragments do not arrive within the predefined time (normally 60 seconds on most Unix-like systems), then all of the fragments will be destroyed, and an error message will be sent to the original sender, using the ICMP "Time Exceeded" error message. For more information on this error message, refer to "Time Exceeded" in Chapter 5.

This process can get fairly tricky, and it may seem like an awful lot of overhead. However, there are many benefits offered by fragmentation. First and foremost, fragmentation allows IP to use whatever packet sizes are required by the underlying medium. Furthermore, any traffic that is local to your own network probably won't require fragmentation, so you can use large packets on your local network. If IP were forced to use a lowest-common-denominator approach of very small packets for all data, then local performance would always be miserable. But by using a flexible MTU size, the local network can run at full speed, with fragmentation only occurring whenever large datagrams must leave the local network.

RFC 791 states that all systems must be able to send an IP datagram of at least 576 bytes. Indeed, many of the early IP routers required that IP datagrams be cut into 576-byte fragments if they were to be forwarded over a different media (regardless of that media's MTU capacity).

In addition, there are some techniques that can be used by a sending system to determine the most efficient segment size when sending data to a remote network, thereby preventing fragmentation from occurring. TCP connections use a "Maximum Segment Size" header option that can be used to determine the MTU of the remote network, and most IP systems implement a technology called "Path MTU Discovery" that allows them to detect the largest available MTU on the end-to-end connection. For more information on the Maximum Segment Size option, refer to "Maximum Segment Size" in Chapter 7, *The Transmission Control Protocol.* For more information on Path MTU Discovery, refer to "Notes on Path MTU Discovery" in Chapter 5.

Prioritization and Service-Based Routing

One of the key differences between IP and other networking protocols is that IP offers direct support for prioritization, allowing network hosts and routers to send important packets before less important packets. This feature is particularly crucial with applications that are sensitive to high levels of delay resulting from network congestion.

For example, assume that an organization has two high-speed networks that are interconnected by a relatively slow wide area network (WAN), and that a lot of data has to cross the WAN frequently. In this example, the routers could forward data across the WAN only at whatever rate was allowed by the WAN itself. If the WAN were fixed at a maximum throughput of 256 KB/s, then the routers on the WAN could only send 262,144 bits across the WAN in a single second. This may be plenty of bandwidth for a few terminal emulation sessions—or even for a couple of simultaneous database updates—but it would not be enough for several simultaneous streaming video feeds in conjunction with those other applications.

The problem is that the routers just wouldn't be able to forward enough data across the WAN for all of the applications to work smoothly. The routers would have to start dropping packets once their buffers began filling up or as the queuing delays exceeded the maximum Time-to-Live values on some of the packets. UDP-based applications may not care much about these dropped packets, but TCP-based applications care very much about lost packets. They would attempt to resend any data that had not yet been acknowledged, and if congestion was sustained for a long period of time, then those applications would eventually just timeout.

This may not matter with some applications, but it would be a very big deal with some others, particularly those that are crucial to the operation of the business itself. For example, if users were unable to enter sales orders into a remote database, the problem would be somewhat greater than if they were unable to access a recreational video.

In order to ensure that congestion doesn't break the mission-critical applications on your network, IP supports two key concepts: prioritization and type-of-service handling. Every IP datagram has an 8-bit field (called the "TOS byte") that consists of a three-bit precedence field used for prioritization and a four-bit field that indicates specific handling characters desired for a datagram (the last bit is currently unused).

By using three bits for precedence, IP has eight levels of prioritization (0 through 7), which provide eight distinct priority levels to all IP traffic. Table 2-8 lists the values of the Precedence field and their meaning as defined in RFC 791, with the highest priority level being 7 and the lowest being 0.

Table 2-8. The Precedence Flags and Their Meaning.

Precedence	Definition
0	Routine (normal)
1	Priority
2	Immediate
3	Flash
4	Flash Override
5	Critical
6	Internetwork Control
7	Network Control

Using these priority values, you could assign database applications a higher priority level than the streaming video traffic. The routers would then sift through data that was waiting in the queue, sending the higher priority traffic before sending the lower priority traffic. In this model, the database traffic would be sent out first, while the streaming video traffic would be forced to wait until bandwidth was available. Your mission-critical applications would continue to function smoothly, while the less-critical applications would take a back seat, possibly suffering dramatic performance losses.

The remaining four bits of the TOS byte provide administrators with the ability to implement per-datagram routing based on the characteristics of the datagram's data. Thus, an IP datagram that contains Usenet news traffic can be marked as desiring a "low-cost" service, while Telnet traffic can be marked as desiring a "low-latency" service.

Originally, there were only three types of service defined in RFC 791. These services were identified with unique bits that were either on or off, depending on whether or not the specific type of service was desired. However, this interpretation was modified by RFC 1349, which added a fourth service class, and which also stated that the bits were to be interpreted as numeric values rather than independent flags. By making them numeric, the four bits provided for a maximum of sixteen possible values (0 through 15), rather than four distinct options (although the values cannot be combined and must be used independently).

There are a number of predefined Type-of-Service values that are registered with the Internet Assigned Numbers Authority (IANA). Some of the more common registered values are shown in Table 2-9.

For a detailed listing of all of the Type-of-Service values that are currently registered, refer to the IANA's online registry (accessible at *http://www.isi.edu/in-notes/iana/assignments/ip-parameters*).

Table 2-9. Type-of-Service Values and Their Meaning

Value	Service	Description
0	Normal	When all of the Type-of-Service flags are off, the IP datagram is to be treated as a normal datagram, and is not to be given any special handling. Almost all IP datagrams are marked with all zeroes in the Type-of-Service field.
1	Minimize Delay	The Delay flag is used to request that IP route this packet over a network that provides lower latency than normal. This may be useful for an application such as Telnet, where the user would want to see their keystrokes echoed back to them quickly. The Delay flag may be set to either 0 (normal) or 1 (low delay).
2	Maximize Throughput	The Throughput flag is used to request that IP route this packet over a network that provides higher throughput than normal. This may be useful for an application such as FTP, where the user would want to download a lot of data very quickly. The Throughput flag may be set to 0 (normal) or 1 (high throughput).

Table 2-9. Type-of-Service Values and Their Meaning (continued)

Value	Service	Description
4	Maximize Reliability	The Reliability flag is used to request that IP route this packet over a network that provides the most reliable service (perhaps as indicated by overall up-time, or by the number of secondary routes). This may be useful for an application such as NFS, where the user would want to be able to open a database on a remote server without worrying about a network failure. The Reliability flag may be set to 0 (normal) or 1 (high reliability).
8	Minimize Cost	The Cost flag was added by RFC 1349 and was not defined in RFC 791. For this reason, many systems do not recognize or use it. The Cost flag is used to request that IP route this packet over the least expensive route available. This may be useful for an application such as NNTP news, where the user would not need data very quickly. The Cost flag may be set to 0 (normal) or 1 (low cost).
15	Maximize Security	RFC 1455—an experimental specification for data-link layer security—states that this flag is used to request that IP route this packet over the most secure path possible. This may be useful with applications that exchange sensitive data over the open Internet. Since RFC 1455 is experimental, most vendors do not support this setting.

In addition, the IANA's online registry also defines a variety of default Type-of-Service values that specific types of applications should use. Some of the more common application protocols and their suggested Type-of-Service values are shown in Table 2-10. For a detailed listing of all of the suggested default Type-of-Service values, refer to the IANA's online registry (accessible at *http://www.isi.edu/in-notes/iana/assignments/ip-parameters).*

Table 2-10. Suggested Type-of-Service Values for Common Application Protocols

Application Protocol	Suggested TOS Value
Telnet	8
FTP Control Channel	8
FTP Data Channel	4
Trivial FTP	8
SMTP Commands	8
SMTP Data	4
DNS UDP Query	8
DNS TCP Query	0
DNS Zone Transfer	4
NNTP	1
ICMP Error Messages	0
SNMP	2

It is important to note that not all of the TCP/IP products on the market today use these values. Indeed, many implementations do not even offer any mechanisms for setting these values, and will not treat packets that are flagged with these values any differently than packets that are marked for "normal" delivery. However, most of the Unix variants on the market today (including Linux, BSD, and Digital Unix) do support these values, and set the appropriate suggested default values for each of the major applications.

Administrators that have complex networks with multiple routing paths can use these type of service flags in conjunction with TOS-aware routers to provide deterministic routing services across their network. For example, an administrator might wish to send low-latency datagrams through a terrestial fiber-optic connection rather than through a satellite link. Conversely, an administrator might wish to send a low-cost datagram through a slower (but fixed-cost) connection, rather than take up bandwidth on a satellite connection.

By combining the type of service flags with the prioritization bits, it is possible to dictate very explicit types of behavior with certain types of data. For example, you could define network filters that mark all Lotus Notes packets as medium priority and tag them with the low-latency TOS flag. This would not only provide your Notes users with preferential service over less-critical traffic, but it would also cause that traffic to be routed over faster network segments. Conversely, you could also define another set of filters that marked all streaming video traffic as lower priority and also enable the high-bandwidth TOS flag, forcing that traffic to use a more appropriate route.

As long as you own the end-to-end connection between the source and destination systems, you can pretty much do whatever you want with these flags, and you should be able to queue and route those datagrams according to the flags that you set. Keep in mind, however, that most ISPs will not treat these datagrams any different than unmarked datagrams (otherwise, you'd mark all of your packets with the high-priority and minimize-latency flags). Indeed, if you need a certain type of service from an ISP, then you will mostly likely end up paying for a dedicated link between your site and the destination network, since you will not be able to have your datagrams prioritized over other customer's packets across the ISP's backbone.

The IP Header

IP datagrams consist of two basic components: an IP header that dictates how the datagram is treated and a body part that contains whatever data is being passed between the source and destination systems.

An IP datagram is made up of at least thirteen fields, with twelve fields being used for the IP header, and one field being used for data. In addition, there are also a variety of supplemental fields that may show up as "options" in the header. The total size of the datagram will vary according to the size of the data and the options in use.

Table 2-11 lists all of the mandatory fields in an IP header, along with their size (in bits) and some usage notes. For more detailed descriptions of these fields, refer to the individual sections throughout this chapter.

Table 2-11. The Fields in an IP Datagram

Field	Bits	Usage Notes
Version	4	Identifies the version of IP used to create the datagram. Every device that touches this datagram must support the version shown in this field. Most TCP/IP products use IP v4. *NOTE: This book only covers IP v4.*
Header Length	4	Specifies the length of the IP header in 32-bit multiples. Since almost all IP headers are 20 bytes long, the value of this field is almost always 5 (5 × 32 = 160 bits, or 20 bytes).
Type-of-Service Flags	8	Provide a prioritization service to applications, hosts, and routers on the Internet. By setting the appropriate flags in this field, an application could request that the datagram be given higher priority than others waiting to be processed.
Total Packet Length	16	Specifies the length of the entire IP packet, including both the header and the body parts, in bytes.
Fragment Identifier	16	Identifies a datagram, useful for combining fragments back together when fragmentation has occurred.
Fragmentation Flags	3	Identifies certain aspects of any fragmentation that may have occurred, and also provides fragmentation control services, such as instructing a router not to fragment a packet.
Fragmentation Offset	13	Indicates the byte-range of the original IP datagram that this fragment provides, as measured in eight-byte offsets.
Time-to-Live	8	Specifies the remaining number of hops a datagram can take before it must be considered undeliverable and be destroyed.
Protocol Identifier	8	Identifies the higher-layer protocol stored within the IP datagram's body.
Header Checksum	16	Used to store a checksum of the IP header.
Source IP Address	32	Used to store the 32-bit IP address of the host that originally sent this datagram.
Destination IP Address	32	Used to store the 32-bit IP address of the final destination for this datagram.

Table 2-11. The Fields in an IP Datagram (continued)

Field	Bits	Usage Notes
Options (optional)	varies	Just as IP provides some prioritization services with the Type-of-Service flags, additional special-handling options can also be defined using the Options field. Special-handling options include Source Routing, Timestamp, and others. These options are rarely used, and are the only thing that can cause an IP header to exceed 20 bytes in length.
Padding (if required)	varies	An IP datagram's header must be a multiple of 32 bits long. If any options have been introduced to the header, the header must be padded so that it is divisible by 32 bits.
Data	varies	The data portion of the IP packet. Normally, this would contain a complete TCP or UDP message, although it could also be a fragment of another IP datagram.

As can be seen, the minimum size of an IP header is 20 bytes. If any options are defined, then the header's size will increase (up to a maximum of 60 bytes). RFC 791 states that a header must be divisible by 32 bits, so if an option has been defined, but it only uses eight bits, then another 24 zero-bits must be added to the header using the Padding field, thereby making the header divisible by 32.

Figure 2-9 shows an IP packet containing an ICMP Echo Request Query Message, sent from Ferret to Bacteria. It does not show any advanced features whatsoever.

The following sections discuss the individual fields in detail.

Version

Identifies the version of IP that was used to create the datagram. Most TCP/IP products currently use IP v4, although IP v6 is gaining acceptance. *NOTE: This book only covers IP v4.*

Size

Four bits.

Notes

Since the datagram may be sent over a variety of different devices on the way to its final destination, all of the intermediary systems (as well as the destination) must support the same version of IP as the one used to create the datagram in the first place. As features are added, removed or modified from IP, the datagram header structures will change. By using the Version field, these changes can be made without having to worry about how the different systems in use will react. Without the Version field, there would be no way to identify changes to the basic protocol structure, which would result in a frozen specification that could never be changed.

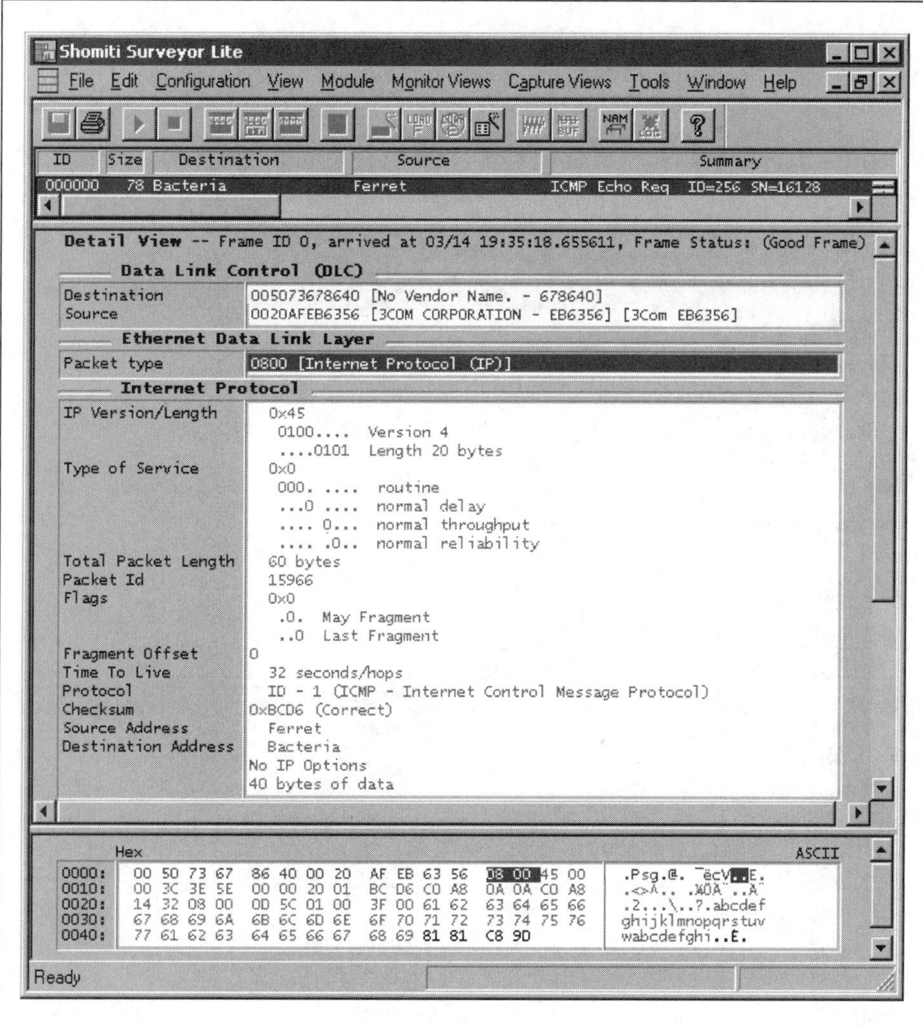

Figure 2-9. A simple IP packet

Almost all TCP/IP products currently use IP v4, which is the latest "standard" version. However, a new version, IP v6, is rapidly gaining supporters and acceptance in the Internet community. It should also be pointed out that IP v4 is the first "real" version of IP, since prior versions were only drafts that were not widely deployed. *NOTE: This book only covers IP v4.*

Capture Sample

In the capture shown in Figure 2-10, the Version field is set to 4, indicating that this packet contains an IP v4 datagram.

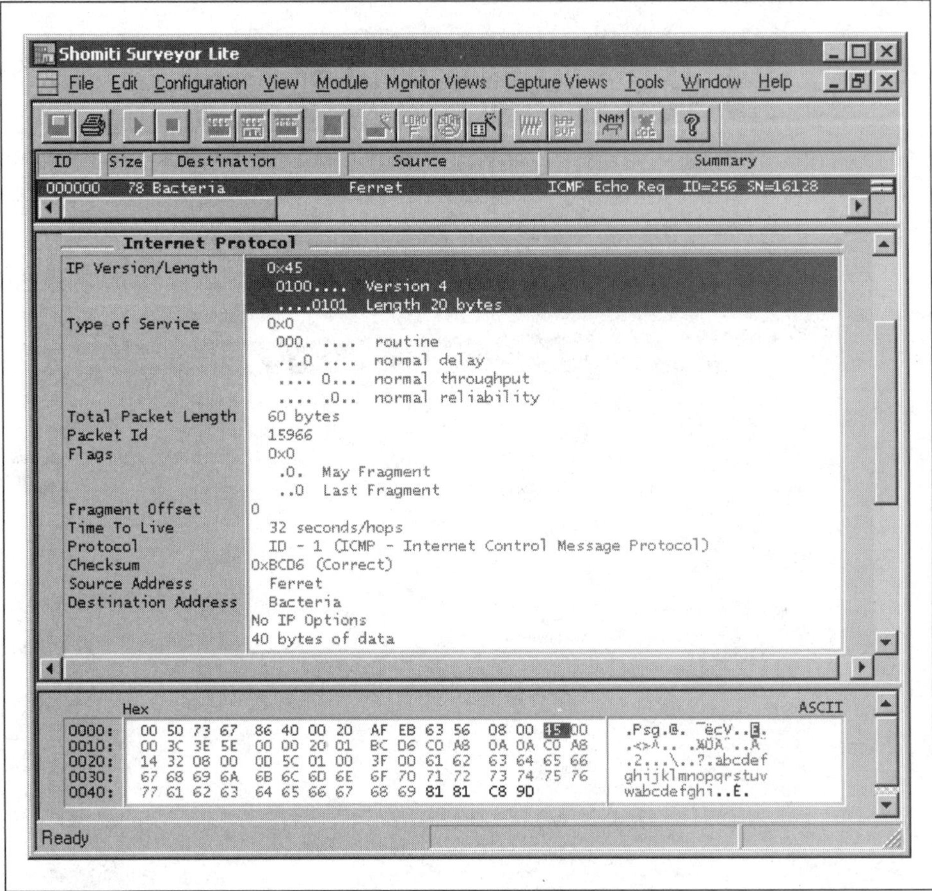

Figure 2-10. The Version field

Header Length

Specifies the size of the IP header, in 32-bit multiples.

Size

Four bits.

Notes

The primary purpose of this field is to inform a system where the data portion of the IP packet starts. Due to space constraints, the value of this field uses 32-bit multiples. Thus, 20 bytes is the same as 160 bits, which would be shown here as 5 (5 × 32 = 160). Since each of the header's mandatory fields are fixed in size, the smallest this value can be is 5.

If all of the bits in this field were "on," the maximum value would be 15. Thus, an IP header can be no larger than 60 bytes (15 × 32 bits = 480 bits = 60 bytes).

Capture Sample

In the capture shown in Figure 2-11, the Header Length field is set to 5, indicating that this packet has 20-byte header (20 bytes / 32 bits = 5), which is the default size when no options are defined.

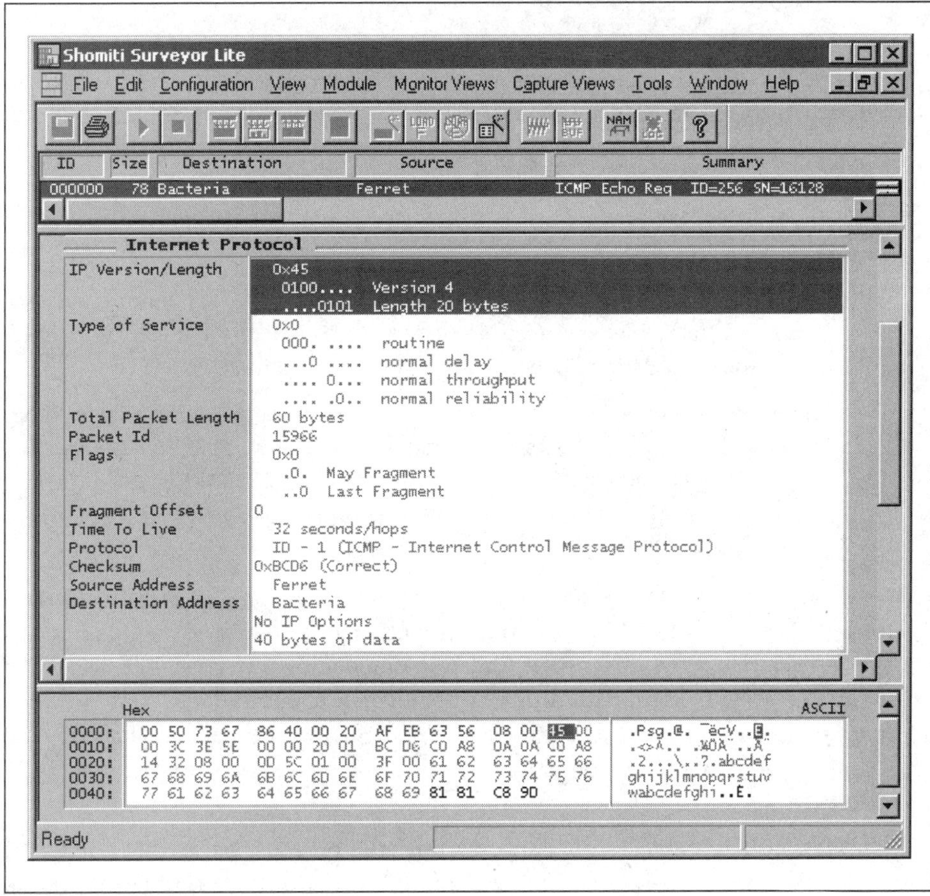

Figure 2-11. The Header Length field

See Also

"IP Options"

"Padding"

"Total Packet Length"

Type-of-Service Flags

Provides prioritization capabilities to the IP datagrams, which are then acted upon by the applications, hosts, and routers that can take advantage of them. By setting these fields appropriately, an application could request that the datagrams it generates get preferential service over other datagrams waiting to get processed.

Size

Eight bits.

Notes

Although the Type-of-Service flags have been available since IP v4 was first published, there are only a handful of applications that actually use them today. Furthermore, only a few IP software packages and routers support them, making their use by applications somewhat moot. However, as more multimedia applications and services are being deployed across the Internet, the use of Type-of-Service flags has increased dramatically, and should continue to do so.

Effectively, the Type-of-Service field is divided into two separate groups of flags. The first three bits are used to define Precedence, while the remaining five bits are used to define specific Type-of-Service options.

The Precedence flags are used to determine a datagram's priority over other datagrams waiting to be processed by a host or router. The Precedence flag uses three bits, allowing it to be set from 0 (normal) to 7 (highest priority). Table 2-8 earlier in this chapter shows the precedence values and their meanings, as defined in RFC 791.

The next four bits are used to indicate various other Type-of-Service options. In RFC 791, only three bits were used to define Type-of-Service handling characteristics. However, the usage and implementation of these bits has been redefined in RFC 1349, with four bits being used to represent a numeric value ranging from 0 (normal datagrams) to 15 (highly secure path requested). The currently-defined values for these flags and their meanings are listed back in Table 2-9.

The last bit from this byte is currently unused and must be zero (0). RFC 791 states that the last two bits are unused, although RFC 1349 added the Minimize Cost Type-of-Service flag, which used up one of them.

Capture Sample

In the capture shown in Figure 2-12, no precedence or special-handling flags have been defined. Also note that Surveyor does not show the Minimize Cost flag, and most products don't understand it.

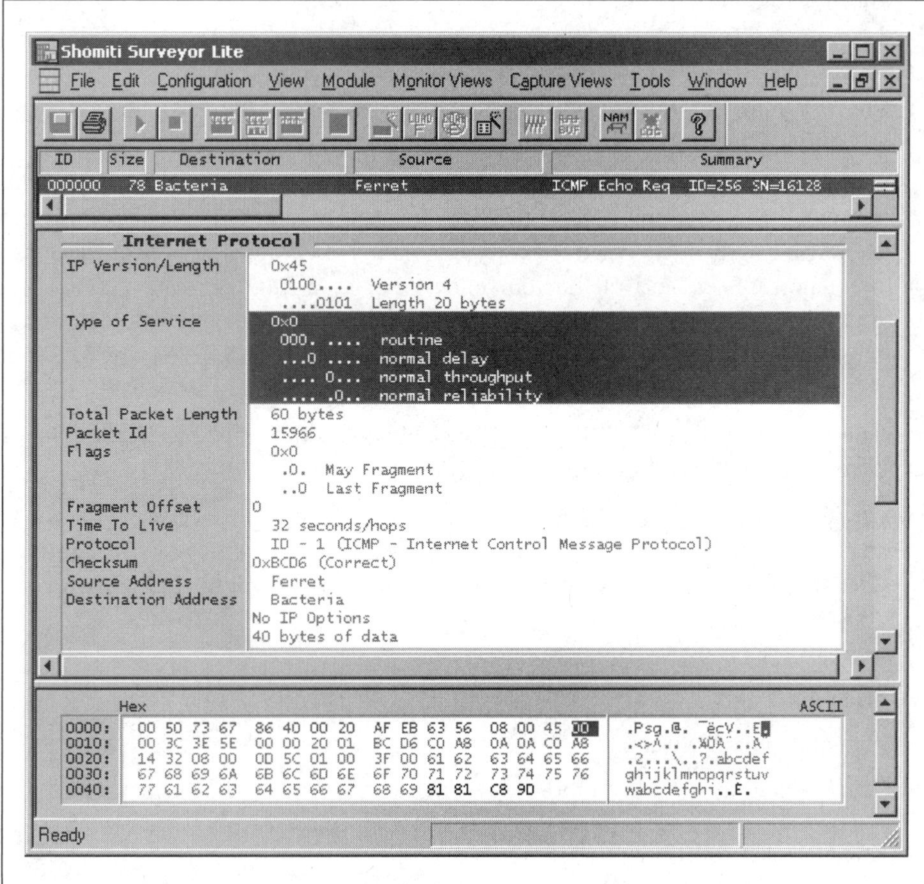

Figure 2-12. The Type-of-Service flags

See Also

"Prioritization and Service-Based Routing"

"IP Options"

"Notes on Precedence and Type-of-Service"

Total Packet Length

Specifies the length of the entire IP packet, including both the header and data segments, in bytes.

Size

Sixteen bits.

Notes

The primary purpose of this field is to inform a system of where the packet ends. A system can also use this field to determine where the data portion of the packet ends, by subtracting the Header Length from the Total Packet Length.

The latter service is especially useful when fragmentation has occurred. Whenever a fragment indicates that another packet is following (set with the "More Fragments" flag), the system will add the value provided in the current fragment's Fragmentation Offset field to the length of the current fragment's data segment. The resulting value will then be used to determine which fragment should be read next (discovered by examining the values stored in the Fragmentation Offset field of the remaining associated fragments). By combining the Fragmentation Offset and Total Packet Length fields from each of the fragments that are received, the recipient can determine if there are any holes in the original datagram that need to be filled before it can be processed.

The minimum size of an IP packet is 21 bytes (20 bytes for the header, and 1 byte of data). The maximum size is 65,535 bytes.

Capture Sample

In the capture shown in Figure 2-13, the Total Packet Length is set to 60 bytes. Twenty of those bytes are used by the IP header, meaning that 40 bytes are used for data.

See Also

"Header Length"

"Fragmentation Offset"

"Fragmentation and Reassembly"

Fragmentation Identifier

A pseudo serial number that identifies the original IP datagram that fragments are associated with.

Size

Sixteen bits.

Notes

Every datagram that gets generated has a 16-bit "serial number" that identifies the datagram to the sending and receiving systems. Although this field is actually a "datagram identifier" of sorts, it is not guaranteed to be unique at all times (16 bits isn't very large), and is really only useful for identifying the datagram that incoming fragments belong to.

When fragmentation occurs, the various fragments are sent as separate IP packets by the fragmenting system, and treated as such until they reach their final destination. The fragments will not be reassembled until they reach their final destination. Once there, however, the destination system must reassemble

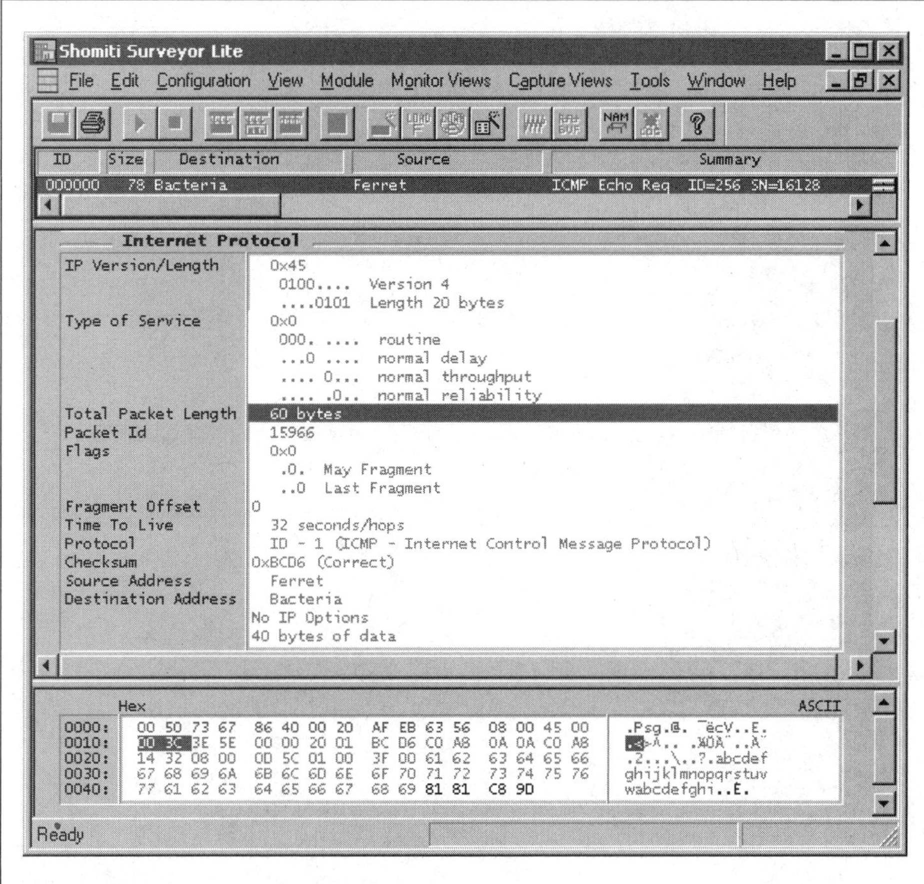

Figure 2-13. The Total Length field

the fragments into the original IP datagram, and the Fragmentation Identifier field is used for this purpose.

Since this field is only 16 bits long, it does not provide a permanently unique serial number, and over time many packets may arrive with the same Fragmentation Identifier, even though those packets have never been fragmented. For this reason, the receiving system must not use this field to determine whether or not fragmentation has occurred (the Fragmentation Flags must be used for this purpose). Instead, the system must use this field only to collect fragments together when the Fragmentation Flags indicate that fragmentation has occurred somewhere upstream.

Capture Sample

In the capture shown in Figure 2-14, the Fragmentation Identifier (or Datagram Identifier, or Packet Identifier) is shown as 15966.

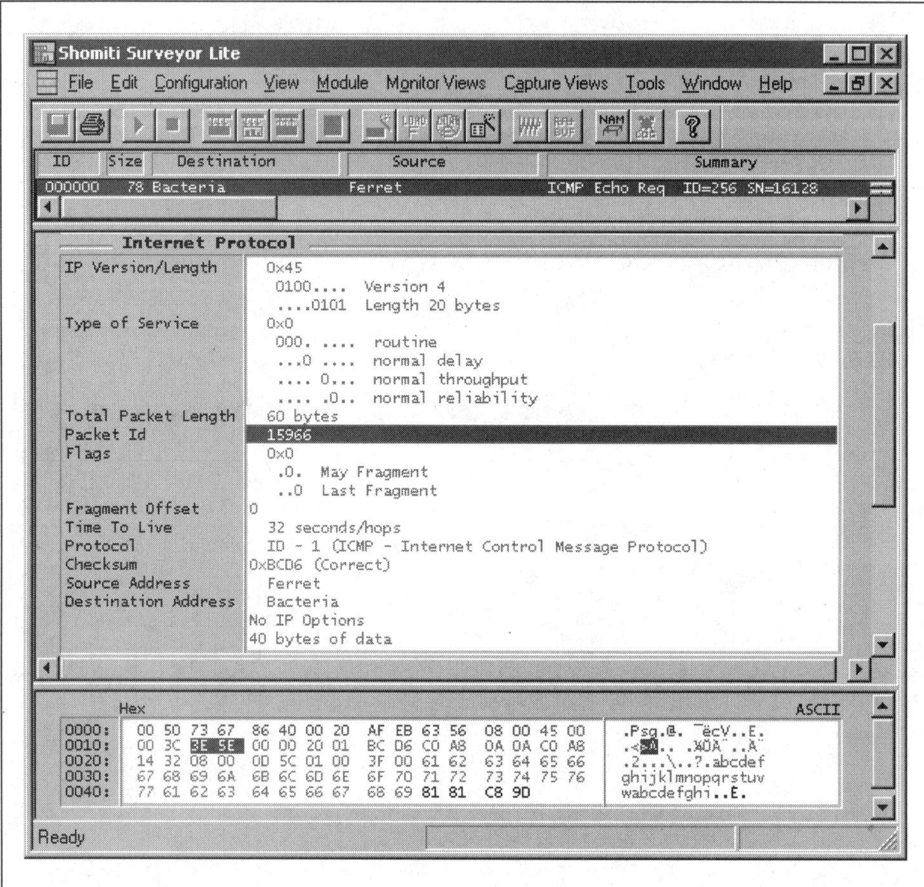

Figure 2-14. The Fragmentation Identifier field

See Also

“Total Packet Length”

“Fragmentation Flags”

“Fragmentation and Reassembly”

Fragmentation Flags

Identifies certain aspects of any fragmentation that may have occurred. The flags also provide fragmentation control services, such as instructing a router not to fragment a packet.

Size

Three bits.

Notes

There are three bits available in the Fragmentation Flags field. The first bit is currently unused, and must be marked 0. The remaining two bits are used as follows:

- *May Fragment.* The May Fragment flag is used to indicate whether or not an IP router may fragment this IP packet. An application may choose to prevent a datagram from becoming fragmented for any number of reasons. It is important to realize, however, that if an IP router cannot fragment a datagram that is too large to travel over a particular network segment, then the router will destroy the IP datagram. The May Fragment flag can be set to 0 ("may fragment," the preferred default) or 1 ("do not fragment").
- *More Fragments.* The More Fragments flag is used to indicate whether or not there are any other fragments associated with the original datagram. The More Fragments flag can be set to 0 ("last fragment," the default) or 1 ("more fragments are coming"). If an IP datagram has not been fragmented, this flag is set to 0.

Capture Sample

In the capture shown in Figure 2-15, the More Fragments flag is set to 0, indicating that this packet has not been fragmented.

See Also

"Total Packet Length"

"Fragmentation Identifier"

"Fragmentation and Reassembly"

Fragmentation Offset

Indicates the *starting* byte position of the original IP datagram's data that this fragment provides, in 8-byte multiples.

Size

Thirteen bits.

Notes

The first fragment's Fragmentation Offset will always be set to 0, indicating that the fragment contains the first byte of the original datagram's data.

The Fragmentation Offset field is used by the final destination system to figure out which fragment goes where in the reassembly process. Since there are no fields that provide a "fragment sequence number," the destination system must use this field in conjunction with the Total Packet Length field and the More Fragments flag.

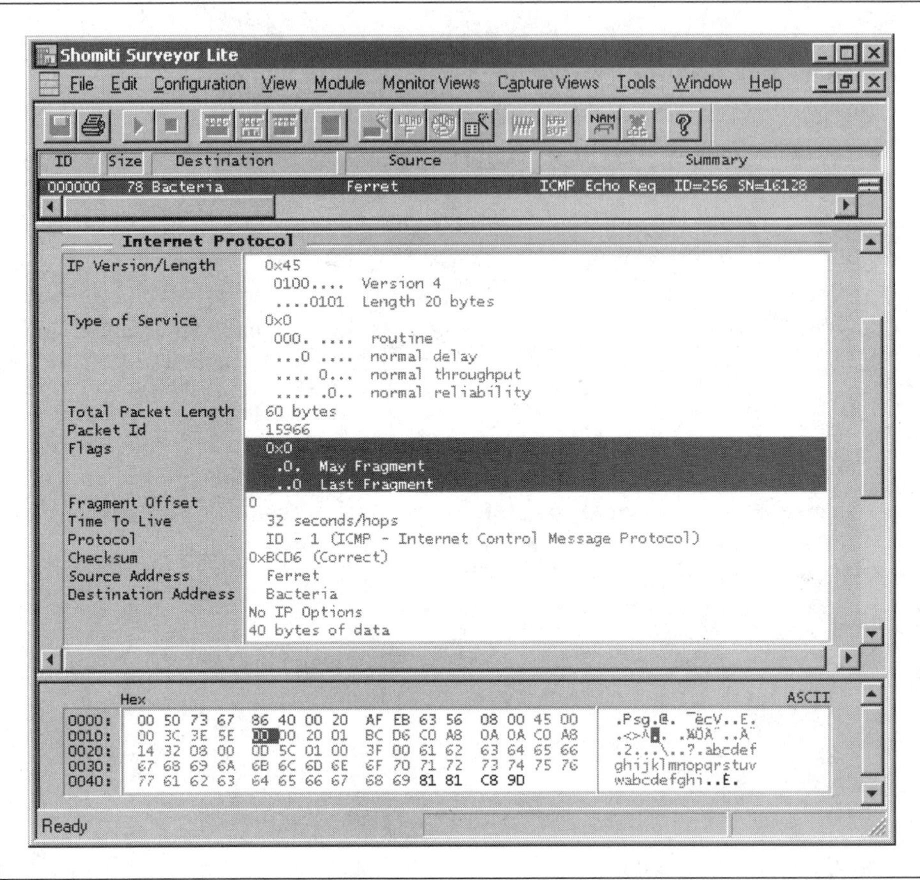

Figure 2-15. The Fragmentation Flags field

For example, let's assume that an IP datagram's data has been split into two 64-byte fragments. The first fragment's IP header will show a Fragmentation Offset of 0, indicating that it contains the first few bytes of the original IP datagram's data. After subtracting the value of the Header Length field from the Total Packet Length, the IP software will be able to determine that the fragment's data is 64 bytes long. In addition, the More Fragments flag will be set to 1, indicating that more fragments are coming.

The next fragment will then show a Fragmentation Offset of 64 bytes, although this will be provided in an 8-byte multiple so the Fragmentation Offset field would actually show the value of 8. After subtracting the Header Size value from the Total Packet Size value, the IP software will determine that the fragment's data is 64 bytes long. Finally, the More Fragments flag will be set to 0, indicating that this fragment is the last.

By using all of these fields and flags together, the IP software is able to reassemble datagrams in their correct order.

Note that if an IP datagram has not been fragmented, the Fragmentation Offset field should be set to 0, and the More Fragments flag should also be set to 0, indicating that this packet is both the first *and* the last fragment.

Capture Sample

In the capture shown in Figure 2-16, the Fragmentation Offset field is set to 0 (the first byte of data).

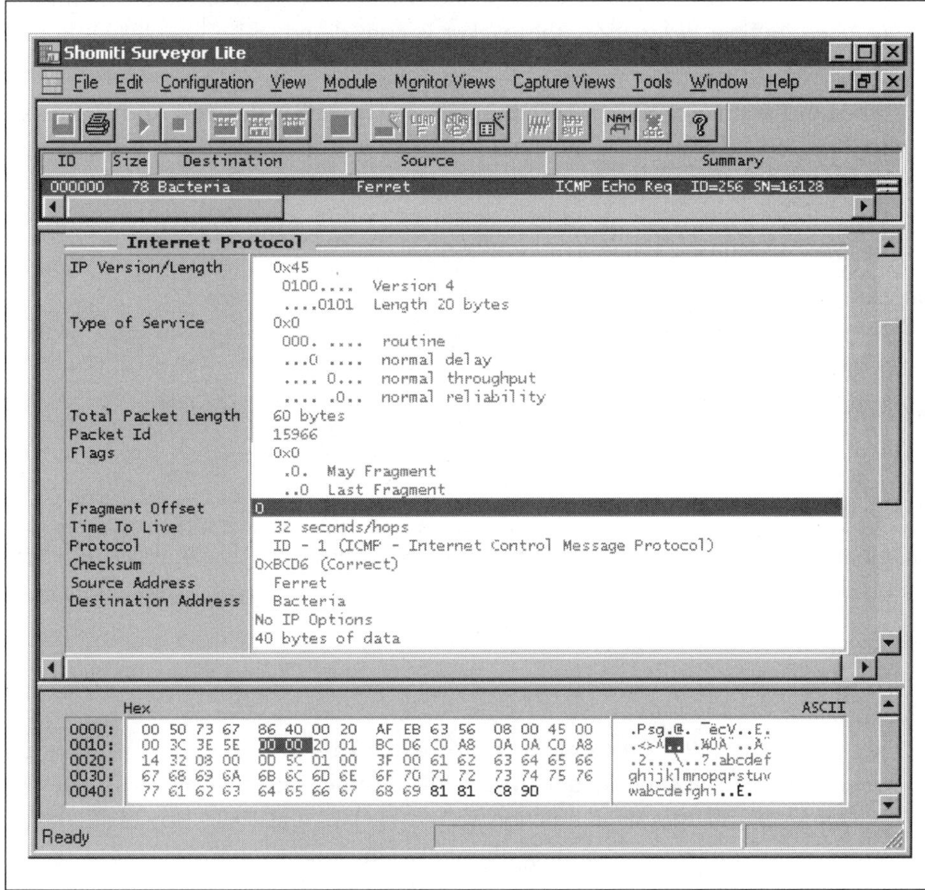

Figure 2-16. The Fragmentation Offset field

See Also

"Total Packet Length"

"Fragmentation Flags"

"Fragmentation and Reassembly"

Time-to-Live

Specifies the maximum number of hops that a datagram can take before it must be considered undeliverable and destroyed.

Size

Eight bits.

Notes

When a source system generates an IP datagram, it places a value between 1 and 255 in the Time-to-Live field. Every time a router forwards the packet, it decreases this value by one. If this value reaches zero before the datagram has reached its final destination, the packet is considered to be undeliverable and is immediately destroyed.

Since this is an 8-bit field, the minimum (functional) value is 1 and the maximum is 255. The value of this field varies by its usage and the specific implementation. For example, RFC 793 (the document that defines TCP) states that the Time-to-Live value should be set at 60, while some applications will set this field to values as high as 128 or 255.

Capture Sample

In the capture shown in Figure 2-17, the Time-to-Live field is set to 32 (which would mean either "32 hops" or "32 seconds").

See Also

"Housekeeping and Maintenance"

Protocol Identifier

Identifies the type of higher-level protocol that is embedded within the IP datagram's data.

Size

Eight bits.

Notes

Remember that IP works only to move datagrams from one host to another, one network at a time. It does not provide much in the way of services to higher-level applications, a function served by TCP and UDP. However, almost every other protocol (including these two transport protocols) uses IP for delivery services.

Normally, the entire higher-level protocol message (including the headers and data) is encapsulated within an IP datagram's data segment. Once the IP datagram reaches its final destination, the receiving system will read the data segment and pass it on to the appropriate higher-level protocol for further processing. This field provides the destination system with a way to identify the higher-layer protocol for which the embedded message is intended.

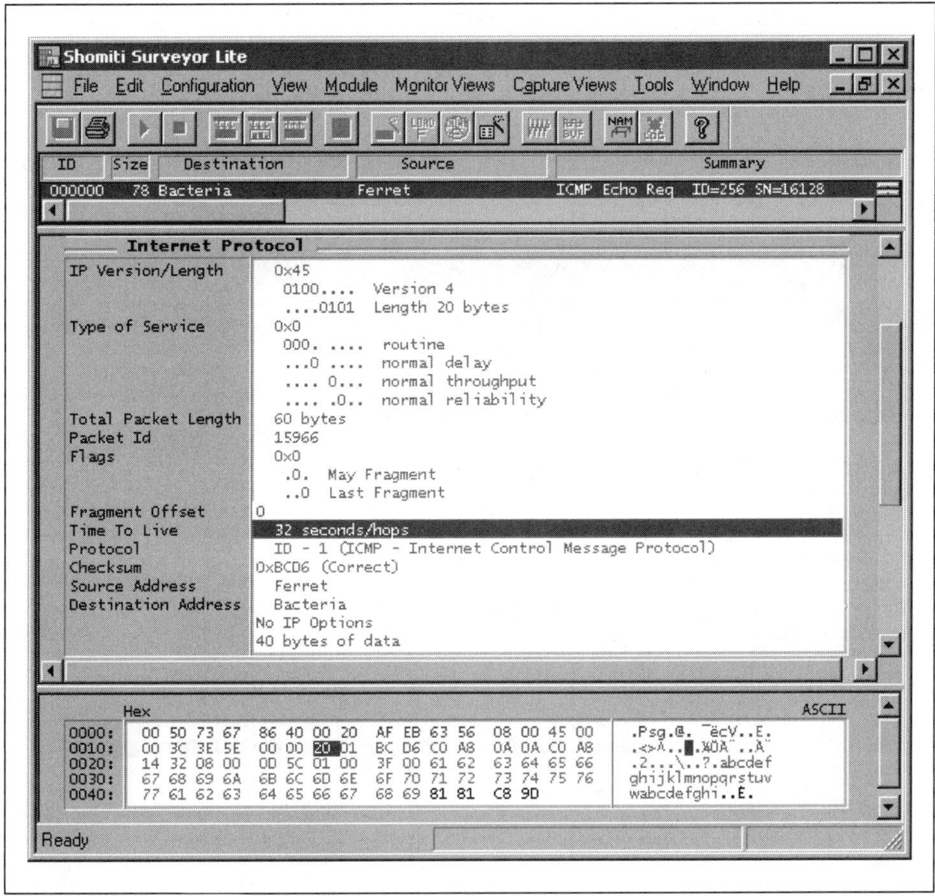

Figure 2-17. The Time-to-Live field

Table 2-12 lists the four most common protocols, and their numeric identifiers.

Table 2-12. The Most Common Higher-Level Protocols and Their Numeric Identifiers

Protocol ID	Protocol Type
1	Internet Control Message Protocol (ICMP)
2	Internet Group Message Protocol (IGMP)
6	Transmission Control Protocol (TCP)
17	User Datagram Protocol (UDP)

There are a number of predefined protocol numbers that are registered with the Internet Assigned Numbers Authority (IANA). For a comprehensive list of all the upper-layer Protocol Identifier numbers used by IP, refer to the IANA's online registry (accessible at *http://www.isi.edu/in-notes/iana/assignments/protocol-numbers*).

Capture Sample

In the capture shown in Figure 2-18, the Protocol Type field is set to 1, indicating that the datagram contains an ICMP message.

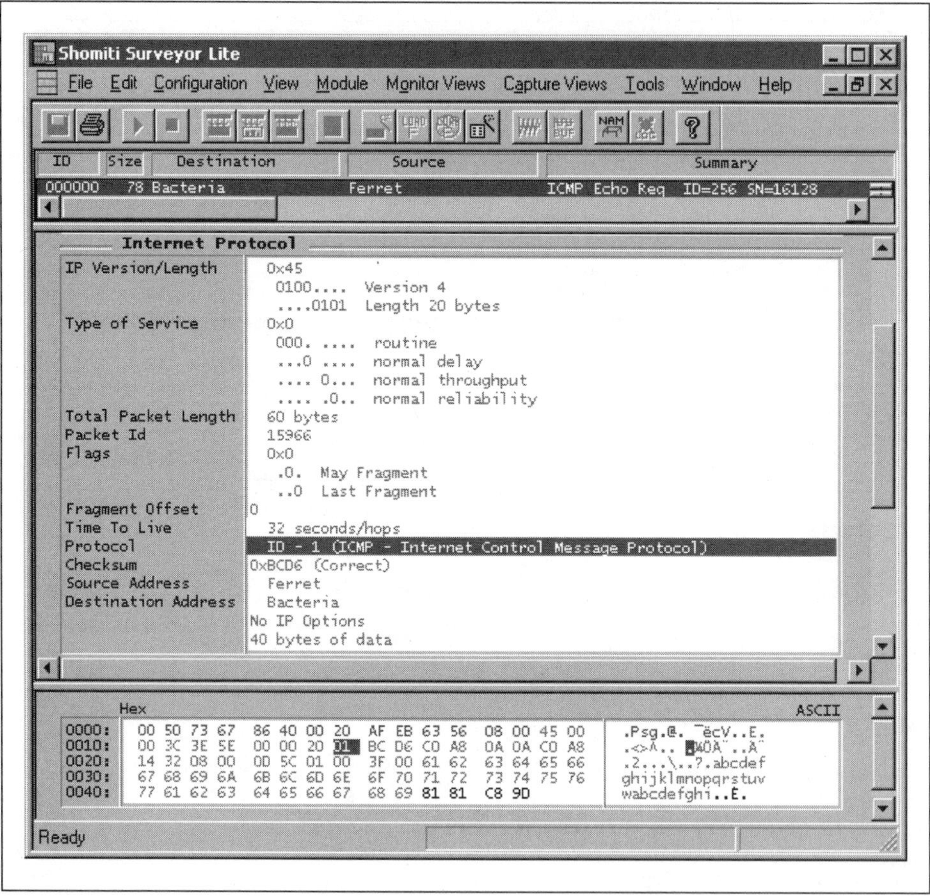

Figure 2-18. The Protocol Type field

Header Checksum

Used to store a checksum of the IP header, allowing intermediary devices both to validate the contents of the header and to test for possible data corruption.

Size

Sixteen bits.

Notes

Since some portions of an IP datagram's header must be modified every time it is forwarded across a router, the sum value of the bits in the header will change as it gets moved across the Internet (at the very least, the Time-to-Live value should change; at most, fragmentation may occur, introducing additional IP headers, flags, and values). Whenever the header changes, the local system must calculate a checksum for the sum value of the header's bits, and store that value in the Header Checksum field. The next device to receive the IP datagram will then verify that the Header Checksum matches the values seen in the rest of the header. If the values do not agree, the datagram is assumed to have become corrupted and must be destroyed.

Note that the checksum only applies to the values of the IP header and not to the entire IP datagram. This is done for three reasons. First of all, a header is only going to be 20 to 60 bytes in length, while an entire datagram may be thousands of bytes long, so it is much faster to calculate only the header's checksum. Also, since the higher-layer protocols provide their own error-correction routines, the data portion of the datagram will be verified by those other protocols anyway, so it makes little sense to validate the entire datagram when validation will occur at a later stage. Finally, some applications can deal with partially corrupt data on their own, and so IP would be performing a disservice if it threw away corrupt data without ever giving the application a chance to do its job.

Capture Sample

In the capture shown in Figure 2-19, the Header Checksum has been calculated as hexadecimal "bc d6", which is correct.

See Also

"Housekeeping and Maintenance"

Source IP Address

Identifies the datagram's original sender, as referenced by the 32-bit IP address in use on that system.

Size

Thirty-two bits.

Notes

This field identifies the original creator of the datagram, but does not necessarily identify the device that sent this particular packet.

Capture Sample

In the capture shown in Figure 2-20, the Source Address field is shown here as Ferret, which is 192.168.10.10 (or hexadecimal "c0 a8 0a 0a").

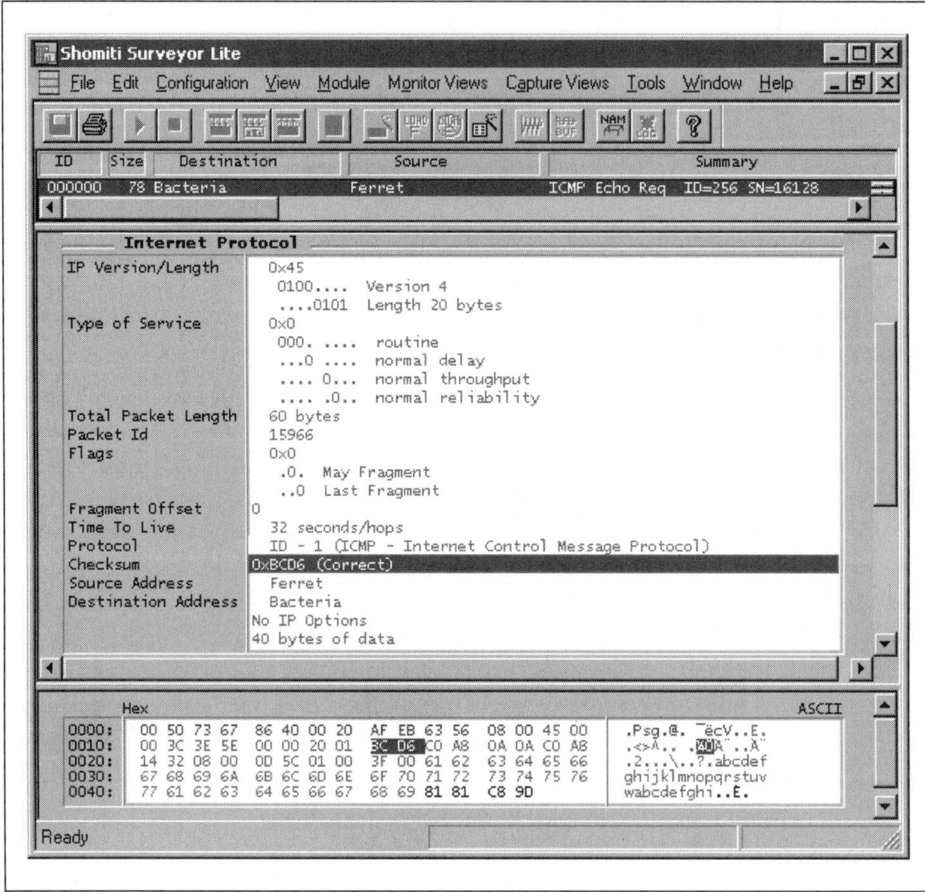

Figure 2-19. The Header Checksum field

See Also

"Destination IP Address"

Destination IP Address

Identifies the 32-bit IP address of the final destination for the IP datagram.

Size

Thirty-two bits.

Notes

This field identifies the final destination for the datagram, but does not necessarily identify the next router that will receive this particular packet. IP's routing algorithms are used to identify the next hop, which is determined by examining the Destination IP Address and comparing this information to the local routing table on the local system. In order for a packet to be delivered to

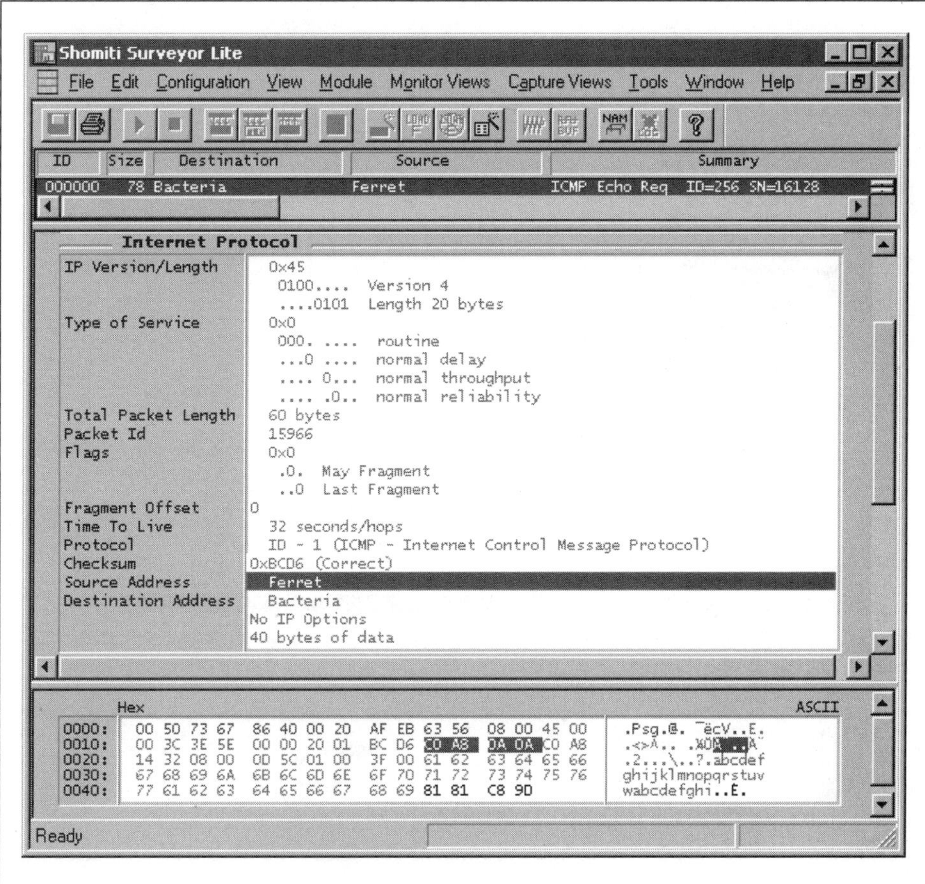

Figure 2-20. The Source Address field

the final destination system, that system's IP address must be provided in the header and must always remain in the header.

Capture Sample

In the capture shown in Figure 2-21, the Destination Address is shown as Bacteria, which is 192.168.20.50 (or hexadecimal "c0 a8 14 32").

See Also

"Source IP Address"

"Local Versus Remote Delivery"

IP Options

Everything an IP system needs to deliver or forward a packet is provided in the default headers. However, sometimes you may need to do something special with a datagram, extending its functionality beyond those services provided by the

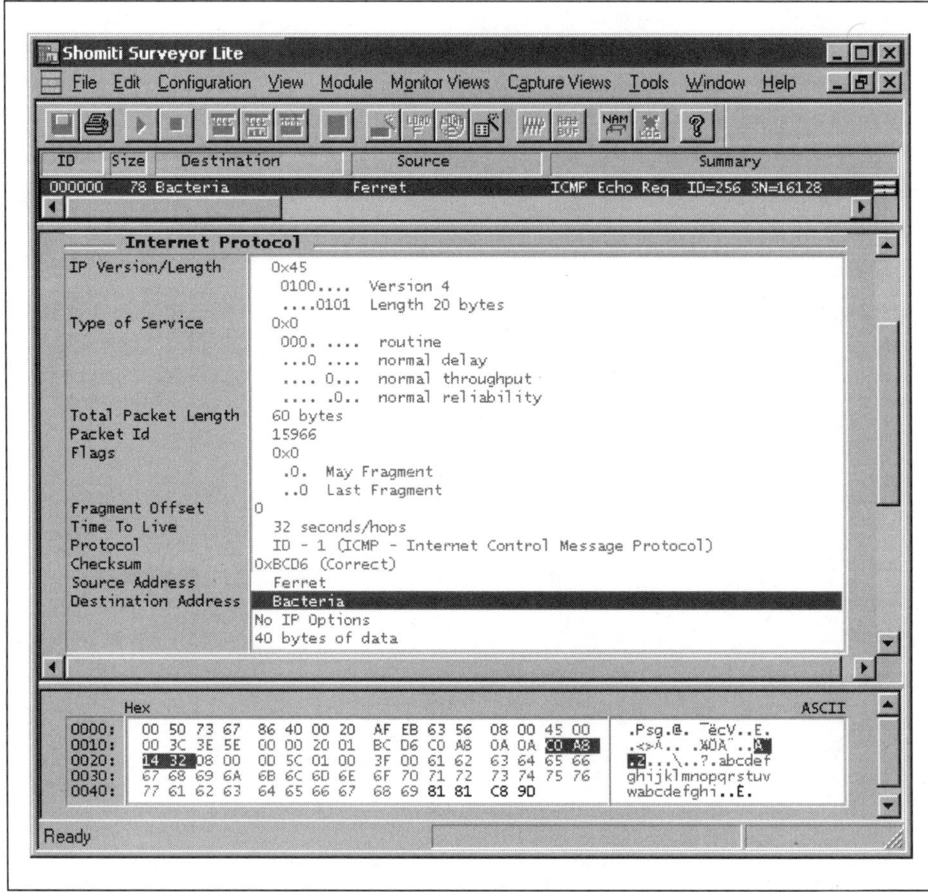

Figure 2-21. The Destination Address field

standard header fields. IP Options provide a way to introduce special-handling services to the datagrams or packets, allowing a system to instruct a router to send the datagram through a predefined network, or to note that the path a datagram took should be recorded, among other things.

Size

Varies as needed. The default is zero bits, while the maximum is 40 bytes (a restriction imposed by the limited space that is available in the Header Length field).

Notes

Options provide special-delivery instructions to devices on the network, and can be used to dictate the route that a datagram must take, or to record the route that was taken, or to provide other network-control services. Options are not mandatory, and most IP datagrams do not have any options defined.

However, all network devices should support the use of options. If a device does not recognize a specific option type, then it should ignore the option and go ahead and process the datagram as normal.

By default, no options are defined within the IP header, meaning that this field does not exist. An IP header can have as many options as will fit within the space available (up to 40 bytes), if any are required.

Each option has unique characteristics. For more information on the various options and their ramifications, refer to "Notes on IP Options" later in this chapter.

Capture Sample

In the capture shown in Figure 2-22, the packet does not have any options defined.

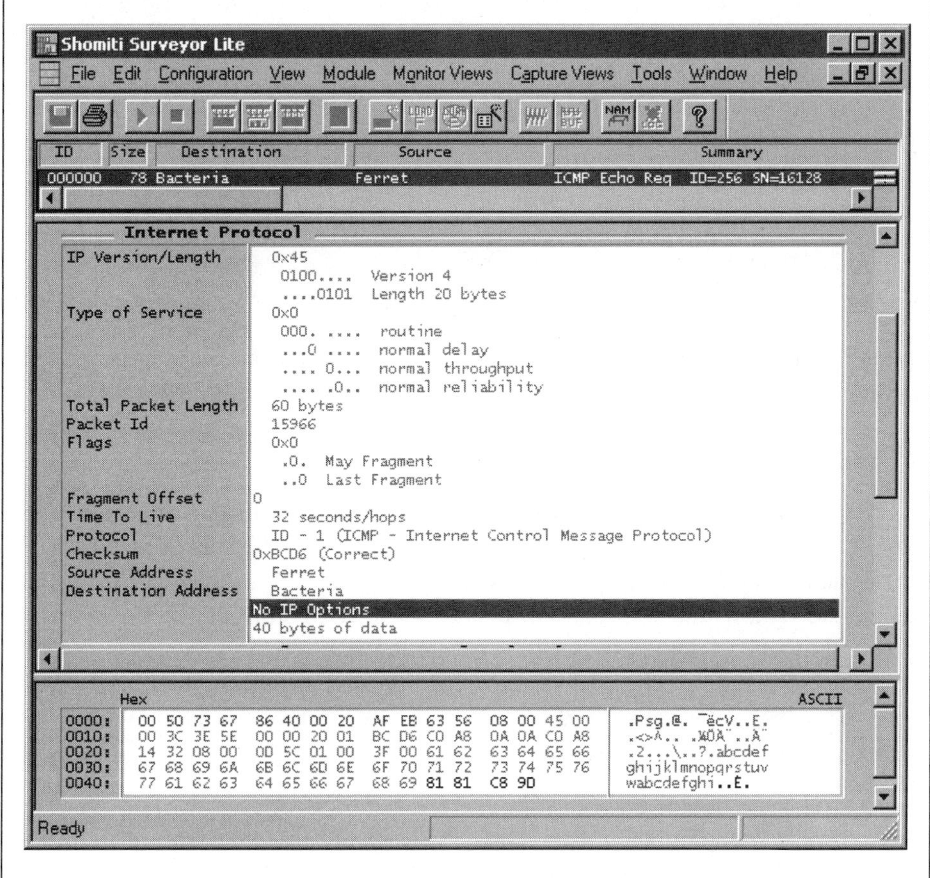

Figure 2-22. The IP Options area

See Also

"Header Length"

"Padding"

"Fragmentation and Reassembly"

"Notes on IP Options"

Padding

Used to make an IP datagram's header divisible by 32 bits.

Size

Varies as needed.

Notes

The length of an IP header must be divisible by 32 bits if it is to fit within the small Header Length field. Most IP headers are 160 bits long, since that's the size of a normal header when all of the mandatory fields are used. However, if any options have been defined, then the IP header may need to be padded in order to make it divisible by 32 again.

See Also

"Header Length"

"IP Options"

Notes on IP Options

There can be many options in a single IP datagram, up to the amount of free space available in the IP header. Since an IP header can only be 60 bytes long at most—and since 20 bytes are already in use by the default fields—only 40 bytes are available for options.

Options are identified using three separate fields as shown in Figure 2-23: Option-Type, Option-Length, and Option-Data. The Option-Type field is used to indicate the specific option in use, while the Option-Length field is used to indicate the size of the option (including all of the fields and Option-Data combined). Since each option has unique characteristics (including the amount of data provided in the option-data field), the Option-Length field is used to inform the IP software of where the Option-Data field ends (and thus where the next Option-Type field begins).

The Option-Type field is eight bits long and contains three separate flags that indicate the specific option being used: copy, class, and type.

- The first bit from the Option-Type field indicates whether or not an option should be copied to the headers of any IP fragments that may be generated. Some options—particularly those that dictate routing paths—need to be

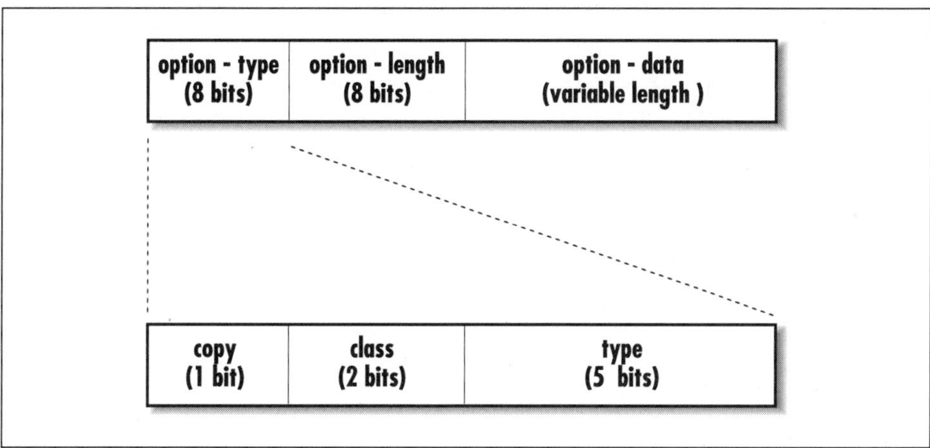

Figure 2-23. The IP Option-Type sub-fields

copied to each of the fragments' headers. Other options do not need to be copied to every fragments' headers, and will only be copied to the *first* fragment's header instead.

- The next two bits define the option "class" (an option class is a grouping of options according to their functionality). Since there are two bits, there are four possible classes, although only two are used. Class 0 is used for network control options, while class 2 is used for debugging services. Classes 1 and 3 are reserved for future use.
- The last five bits of the Option-Type field identify the specific option, according to the option class in use. Table 2-13 lists the most commonly used IP options. Each of these options is described in detail in the next sections of this chapter. For a detailed listing of all of the IP Options that are currently registered, refer to the IANA's online registry (accessible at *http://www.isi.edu/in-notes/iana/assignments/ip-parameters*).

Table 2-13. The Option-Type Definitions, Including Their Classes, Codes, and Lengths

Class	Code	Bytes	Description
0	0	0	End of option list
0	1	0	No operation
0	2	11	Security options (for military uses)
0	7	varies	Record route
0	3	varies	Loose source routing
0	9	varies	Strict source routing
0	20	4	Router alert
2	4	varies	Timestamp

The Option-Length field is used to measure bytes of data, so a value of 1 would mean "one byte." Since the Option-Length field is eight bits long, this allows for a maximum of 255 bytes of storage space to be specified, although the complete set of options cannot total more than 40 bytes (a restriction incurred from the Header Length's size limitation).

The following sections discuss the IP options in detail.

End of Option List

Used to mark the end of all the options in an IP header.

Class and Code
: Class 0, Code 0

Size
: Eight bits.

Copy to all fragments?
: May be copied, added, or deleted as needed.

Defined In
: RFC 791.

Status
: Standard.

Notes
: This option comes after all of the other options, and not at the end of every option.

The End of Option List option does not have an Option-Length or Option-Data field associated with it. It simply marks the end of the options in use with a specific IP header. If this option does not end on a 32-bit boundary, then the IP header must be padded.

No Operation

Used to internally pad options within the Options header field.

Class and Code
: Class 0, Code 1

Size
: Eight bits.

Copy to all fragments?
: May be copied, added, or deleted as needed.

Defined In
: RFC 791.

Status

Standard.

Notes

Sometimes it is desirable to have an option aligned on a certain boundary (such as having an option start at the 8th, 16th or 32nd bit off-set). If this is the case, the No Operation option can be used to internally pad the Options header field.

The No Operation option does not have an Option-Length or Option-Data field associated with it. It is used by itself to pad the IP Option field by a single byte. If more padding is required, the No Operation option can be used again, as many times as needed.

Security Options

Used to specify military security flags. This option is used only on military networks.

Class and Code

Class 0, Code 2

Size

Eighty-eight bits.

Copy to all fragments?

Yes.

Defined In

RFC 791.

Status

Standard.

Notes

Security options allow datagrams to classify their contents as being anywhere from "Unclassified" to "Top Secret," and also provide mechanisms for determining if a device is authorized to send certain types of traffic. Because of the highly vertical nature of this option, I suggest that people who are interested in using it should refer to RFC 1108, which deals with it in detail.

Record Route

Provides a facility for routers to record their IP addresses, allowing a system to see the route that an IP datagram took on its way from the original source to the final destination.

Class and Code

Class 0, Code 7

Size

Varies as needed.

Copy to all fragments?

No (first fragment only).

Defined In

RFC 791.

Status

Standard.

Notes

If a system wishes to have the route recorded, it must allocate enough space in the IP header for each device to place its IP address in the related Option-Data field.

In order to facilitate this process, the Record Route option has a separate 8-bit "pointer" field that is placed at the beginning of the Option-Data field. The pointer indicates the byte position where the IP address of the current router should be recorded. If the pointer is greater than the option length, then no more room is available. If there is sufficient space, then the router will write its four-byte IP address at the location specified by the pointer, and then increment the pointer so that it points to the next offset in the Option-Data field. (Interestingly, RFC 791 states that "if there is some room but not enough room for a full address to be inserted, the original datagram is considered to be in error and is discarded.") The process will continue until there is no more space, or until the datagram is delivered to its final destination.

Due to the limited space available, this option is not very useful on the open Internet.

Loose Source Routing

Identifies a network path that the IP datagram should take, with variations allowed as long as all of the defined routes are taken at some point.

Class and Code

Class 0, Code 3

Size

Varies as needed.

Copy to all fragments?

Yes.

Defined In

RFC 791.

Status

Standard.

Notes

Loose Source Routing allows an originating system to list landmark routers that a datagram must visit on the way to its destination. In between these landmark routers, the datagram may be sent wherever the network tells it to go.

In order to facilitate this process, the Loose Source Route option uses an 8-bit pointer field that is placed at the beginning of the Option-Data field. The pointer indicates the byte position that contains the next landmark to be visited. Once a landmark has been visited, the pointer is moved to an offset that points to the next landmark. If the pointer exceeds the option-length value, then no more landmarks can be used, and normal routing takes over.

Each router that touches the datagram will also record its own IP address in the option-data as well, as specified in "Record Route" in the previous section of this chapter. Due to the limited space available, this option is not very useful on the open Internet.

There are some security concerns with this option. By specifying a route that datagrams must take, it is possible for an intruder to mark external datagrams as being internal to your network. Normally, any datagrams sent in response to these datagrams would never leave your network, although by specifying a source-route, the hacker can tell your systems to send the datagrams to him *by way of his own routers.* For this reason, most firewalls block incoming packets that have this option defined.

Strict Source Routing

Identifies a network path that the IP datagram *must* take, without exception.

Class and Code

Class 0, Code 9

Size

Varies as needed.

Copy to all fragments?

Yes.

Defined In

RFC 791.

Status

Standard.

Notes

Strict Source Routing allows an originating system to list the specific routers that a datagram must visit on the way to its destination. No deviation from this list is allowed.

In order to facilitate this process, the Strict Source Route option uses an 8-bit pointer field that is placed at the beginning of the option-data field. The pointer indicates the byte position that contains the IP address of the next router to be visited. Once a router has been visited, the pointer is moved to an offset that points to the IP address of the next router. If the pointer exceeds the option-length value, then no more routes can be used, and normal routing takes over.

Each router also records its own IP address in the moving list of landmarks, as specified in "Record Route" earlier in this chapter. Due to the limited space available, this option is not very useful on the open Internet.

As with Loose Source Routing, there are some security concerns with this option. By specifying a route that datagrams must take, it is possible for an intruder to mark external datagrams as being internal to your network. Normally, any datagrams sent in response to these datagrams would never leave your network, although by specifying a source-route, the hacker can tell your systems to send the datagrams to him *by way of his own routers*. For this reason, most firewalls block incoming packets that have this option defined.

Router Alert

Used to inform a router that the current IP packet has some peculiarities that should be studied before it is forwarded on.

Class and Code

Class 0, Code 20

Size

Thirty-two bits.

Copy to all fragments?

Yes.

Defined In

RFC 2113.

Status

Proposed Standard, Elective.

Notes

Typically, routers will blindly forward datagrams that are destined for a remote network host or network. They do not normally process datagrams unless those datagrams are explicitly addressed to the router (as indicated by the

Destination Address field), or are broadcasts or multicasts that the router is participating in.

However, sometimes the data in a datagram is of such a nature that the router should examine it closely before simply forwarding it on. For example, an experimental form of Path MTU Discovery currently under development requires that routers return bandwidth information about the last network that the probe crossed before reaching the router. In order for this to work, the router has to process the datagram—which is actually destined for a remote host—see that it is a request for MTU information, and then return the requested data. Without this option, the router would simply pass the datagram on to the next-hop router or final destination system.

The two-byte Option-Data field used with Router Alert allows for 65,535 possible numeric codes. The only currently defined code is 0, which states that routers should examine the datagram before forwarding it on. The other 65,534 codes are currently undefined.

Timestamp

Identifies the time at which a router processed the IP datagram.

Class and Code
: Class 2, Code 4

Size
: Varies as needed.

Copy to all fragments?
: No (first fragment only).

Defined In
: RFC 791.

Status
: Standard.

Notes

The Timestamp option is conceptually similar to the Record Route option, with the critical exception being that the router will also place a timestamp into the Option-Data field (actually, the source device can choose the specific information that it wants to have recorded).

In order to facilitate this process, the Timestamp option uses an 8-bit pointer field similar to the pointer found in the Source Route and Record Route options, as well as a four-bit overflow field, and a four-bit set of flags.

The overflow field provides a counter for the routers that could not register their timestamps. This allows an administrator to see how much of the network they could not record, due to lack of space. The flags are used to define the behavior that an administrator wishes the routers to adhere to. These behaviors are listed in Table 2-14.

Table 2-14. Flags Used with the Timestamp Option

Flag Value	Description
0	Timestamps only (do not record router addresses)
1	Record router addresses, followed by timestamps
2	Match timestamps with preexisting router addresses

Timestamps are recorded as 32-bit integers that represent the number of milliseconds since midnight, Universal Time.

As the datagram is passed around the Internet, the routers use the pointer to indicate the byte position where they should write their data. Once a router has been visited, the pointer is moved to an offset that points to the next 32-bit field where timestamp recording should occur. If the pointer exceeds the option-length value, then no more timestamps can be recorded. At this point, routers should begin to increment the overflow counter as the datagram moves through the network. Interestingly, RFC 791 states that "if there is some room but not enough room for a full timestamp to be inserted, or if the overflow count itself overflows, the original datagram is considered to be in error and is discarded."

Due to the limited space available, this option is not very useful on the open Internet.

IP in Action

Although IP is responsible only for getting datagrams from one host to another, one network at a time, this seemingly simple service can actually get quite complex. An IP device has to route traffic to the appropriate network whenever a datagram needs to be forwarded; it has to break large datagrams into smaller pieces whenever datagrams have to be sent across a small network; and it has to make decisions based on the priority of the data.

Notes on IP Routing

Since IP is designed as a node-centric networking protocol, every device has equal access to the network. In this model, any device can communicate with any other device directly, without requiring the services of a centralized host. Nodes do not send traffic to a central host for processing and relay services, but instead communicate directly with the destination system, if possible.

When this is not possible—such as when the two hosts are on separate networks—then the sending device has to locate another device to relay the traffic to the destination system on its behalf. Even in this situation the sending device is still self-deterministic, since it chooses which local device it will send the datagrams to for forwarding.

The process of choosing an intermediate forwarding device is called routing. Whenever a device needs to choose a forwarder, it looks at a local list of available networks and forwarders (called the "routing table"), and decides which interface and forwarder is the most appropriate for the specific datagram that needs to be sent.

As was discussed in "Local Versus Remote Delivery" earlier in this chapter, the routing table on a system can be built using several different tools. To begin with, most systems build a basic routing table that shows the available network interfaces and the networks they are attached to. This information can then be supplemented with manual entries that identify specific forwarders for specific networks and hosts, or a simple "default route" for all non-local networks.

In addition, routing protocols can be used to automatically update the routing tables on the hosts of a network that changes often. Some of the more-common routing protocols in use today on corporate networks are Routing Information Protocol (RIP), Open Shortest Path First (OSPF), and Router Discovery (RDISC). However, these protocols are not able to scale up to the quantity of routes that are found on the Internet backbone, and protocols such as the Border Gateway Protocol (BGP) are more common in those environments.

Figure 2-24 shows a Windows NT 4.0 system with a fairly typical routing table. By looking at the "Active Routes" list, we can see the routers and networks that this device knows about explicitly.

The routing table shown in Figure 2-24 looks somewhat complicated, but in reality is not that difficult to understand. The first thing we can tell (from the "Interface List") is that the PC is connected to three distinct networks: the "loopback" network (which is common to all IP devices), a local Ethernet network, and a dial-up network (which is currently inactive).

The "Active Routes" list shows all of the networks and forwarders that this device knows about. The first entry shows a destination of "0.0.0.0" (the default route for this device), with a forwarding gateway address of "192.168.10.3". Any datagrams that this host does not know how to deliver will be sent to that router for delivery.

The next two entries show the local networks that are currently active on this host, including the loopback network ("127.0.0.0") and the local Ethernet network ("192.168.10.0"). In addition, the subnet masks for those networks are shown, as are the IP addresses of the local network interface points on this system for those

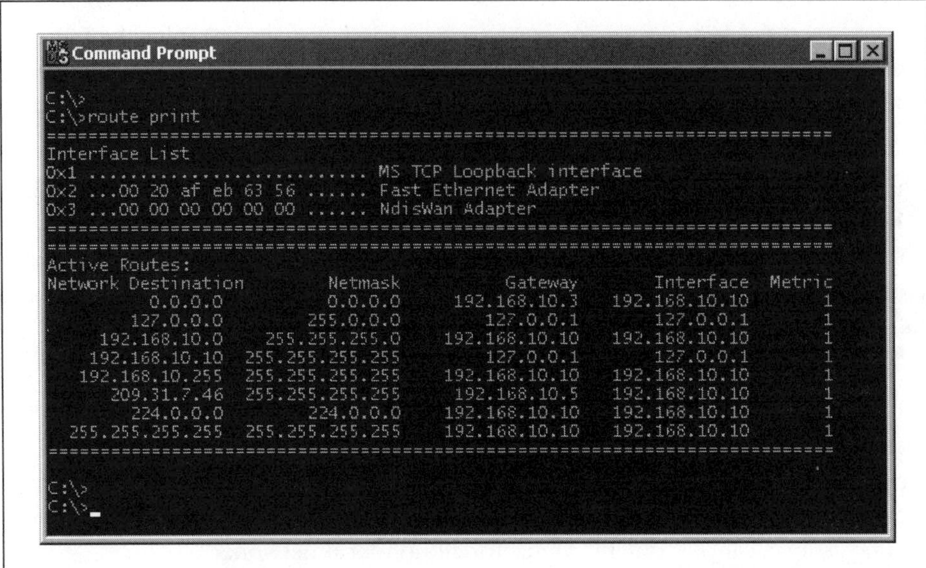

Figure 2-24. The routing table on a Windows NT 4.0 PC

networks. This information provides the local host with the data it needs to route datagrams from the internal TCP/IP software to the appropriate local network.

In addition, there is a routing entry for the local Ethernet device explicitly, which indicates that any traffic bound for that network should be sent to the loopback address for delivery. This would indicate that *all* traffic is sent to the local loopback interface for forwarding and that the loopback adapter is in fact a forwarder.

The remaining entries show less-granular routes for general purpose network traffic. For example, the routing entry for "192.168.10.255" is a broadcast address for the local network, and the routing table shows that any traffic for that address should be sent to the Ethernet card for delivery. The last two entries show the all-points multicast address of "224.0.0.0" and the all-points broadcast address of "255.255.255.255", with both entries listing the local Ethernet card as the forwarder.

Most systems have similar routing tables, although they may not show as much information. For example, Figure 2-25 shows the routing table from a Solaris 7 client, which also has loopback and Ethernet interfaces. However, these entries do not show the detailed level of routing that the Windows NT 4.0 host does.

Notice also that the routing table in Figure 2-25 does not show explicit routing entries for the network interface cards like the Windows NT 4.0 host does. This is because Solaris uses a different networking kernel design than NT (the latter routes local traffic through the loopback interface, while Solaris passes it directly from the kernel to the network interface).

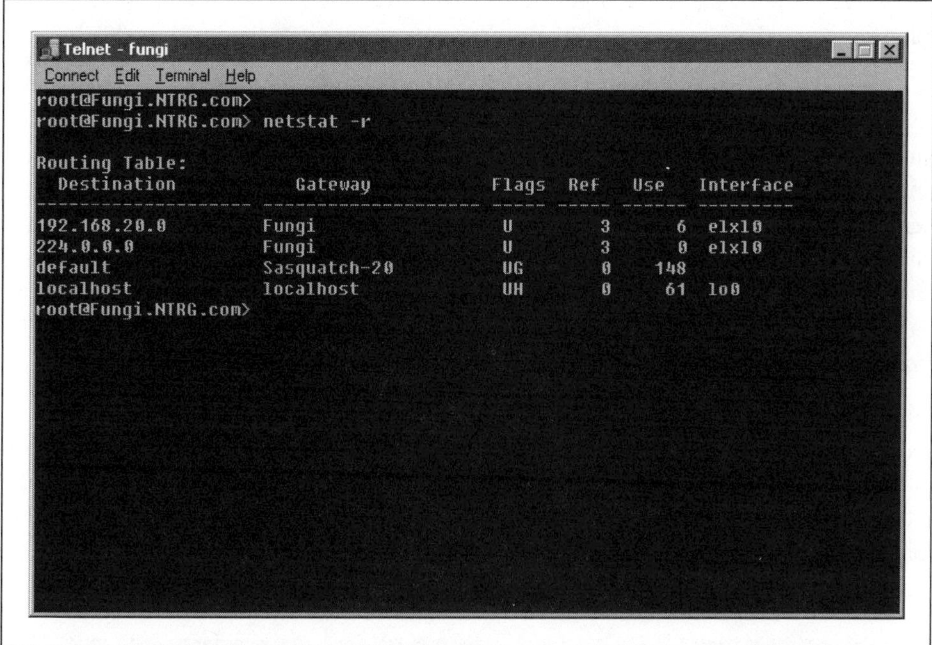

Figure 2-25. The routing table on a Solaris host

Most TCP/IP implementations also provide a *traceroute* program that can be used to see the route that datagrams are taking to get to specific destination systems. These programs typically send an ICMP or UDP message to an explicit destination system, setting the IP Time-to-Live value to a low value so that it will be rejected by routers along the path. This results in the intermediate systems returning ICMP error messages back to the sending system, which can then display the list of routers that rejected the forwarding requests. The *traceroute* program is described in detail in "Notes on traceroute" in Chapter 5.

Notes on Fragmentation

As discussed in "Fragmentation and Reassembly" earlier in this chapter, each of the different network topologies have different Maximum Transfer Unit (MTU) sizes, which represent the maximum amount of data that can be passed in a single frame. On Ethernet networks, the MTU is typically 1500 bytes, while 16 MB/s Token Ring has a default MTU size of 17,914 bytes. Some networks have smaller MTUs, with the minimum allowed value being just 68 bytes.

Whenever an IP datagram needs to be sent across a network to another device, the datagram must be small enough to fit within the MTU size constraints of the local network. For example, if the local network is Ethernet, then the IP datagram must be 1500 bytes or less in order for the datagram to get sent across that network. If the datagram is larger than 1500 bytes, then it must be split into multiple fragments that are each small enough to be sent across the local network.

Most of the time, datagrams do not require fragmentation. On local networks, every device uses the same MTU size, so local packets are never fragmented. And most of the networks in use on the Internet (either as destination networks or intermediate ISP networks) are capable of handling packets that are 1500 bytes in length, which is the largest size that most dial-up clients will generate. The only times that fragmentation typically occurs is on mixed local networks that have Ethernet and Token Ring (or other large-frame networks), or when a host on an Ethernet network tries to send data to a dial-up user that is using a small MTU size. In either of these situations, fragmentation will definitely occur.

In addition, fragmentation occurs if the application that is generating the datagram tries to send more data than will fit within the local network's MTU. This happens quite often with UDP-based applications such as the Network File Service (NFS). This can also be forced to happen through the use of programs such as *ping*, simply by specifying a large datagram size as a program option.

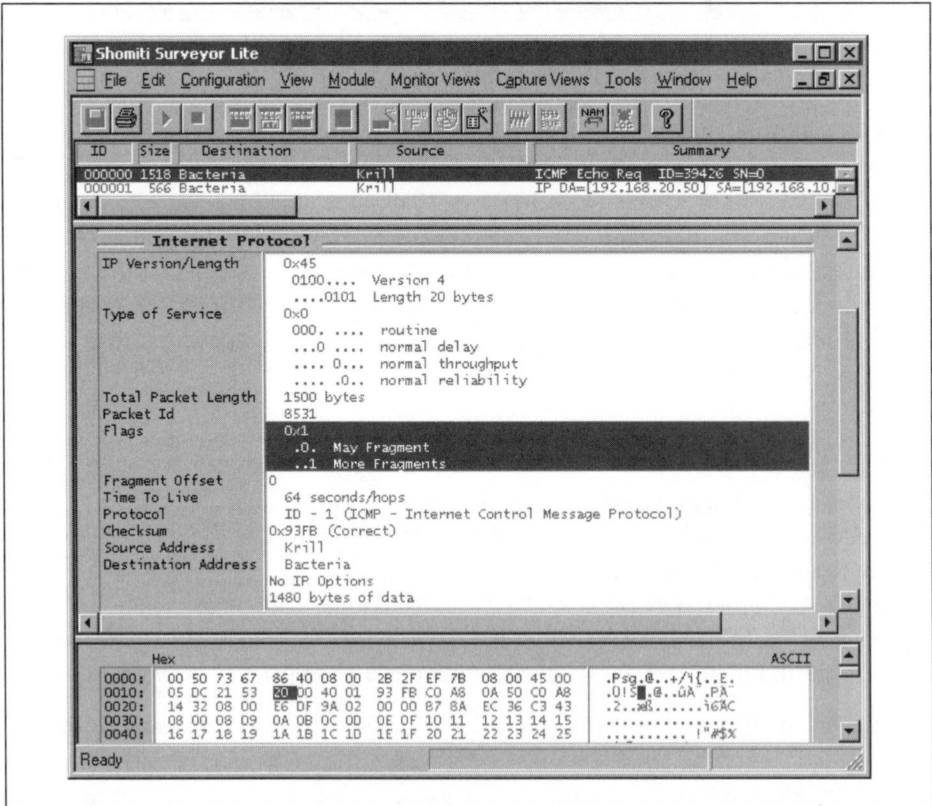

Figure 2-26. The first fragment of a large datagram

For example, Figure 2-26 and Figure 2-27 show a large ICMP message being sent from Krill to Bacteria that was too large for the local network to handle, and so the datagram had to be fragmented into two packets. What's most interesting about this is the fact that Krill fragmented the datagram before it was ever sent, since it could not create a single IP packet that was large enough to handle the full datagram.

Figure 2-26 shows the first fragment of the original (unfragmented) datagram, and Figure 2-27 shows the second (last) fragment. Notice that the Fragmentation Identifier field is the same in both captures, and that the first fragment has the More Fragments flag enabled, while the last fragment does not.

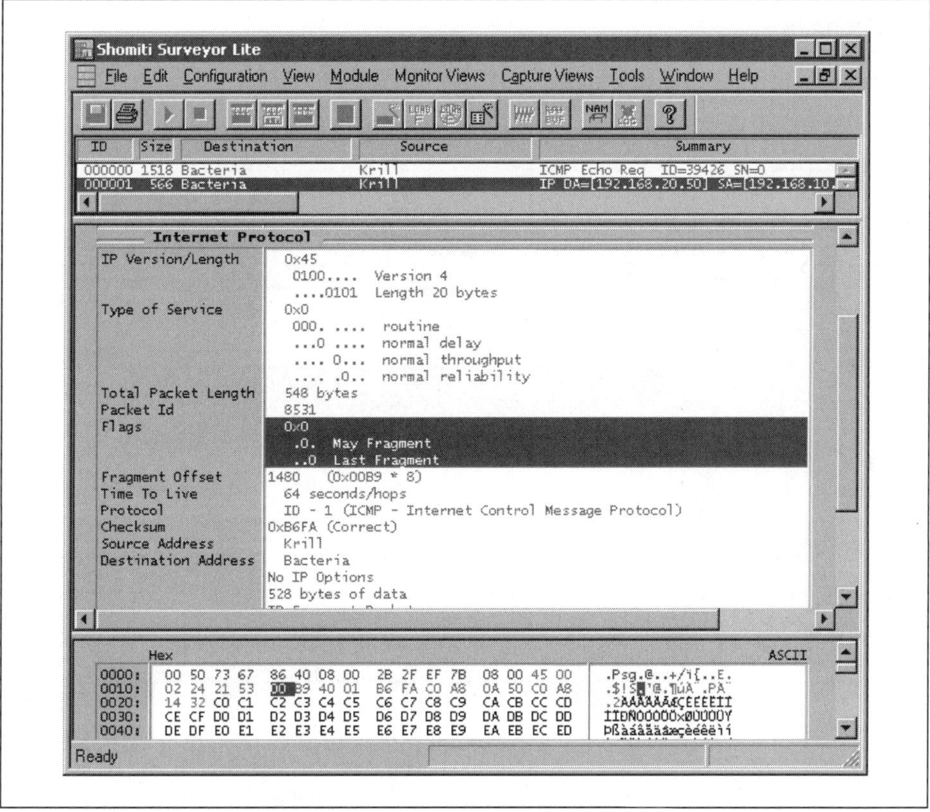

Figure 2-27. The second fragment of a large datagram

Also, notice that Figure 2-26 shows the Fragmentation Offset as 0, which indicates that the first fragment contains the starting block of data from the original datagram, while Figure 2-27 shows the Fragmentation Offset as 1480, which indicates that the last fragment contains data starting at that byte.

For more information on fragmentation-related issues, refer to "Fragmentation and Reassembly" earlier in this chapter.

Notes on Precedence and Type-of-Service

Applications can use the Precedence and Type-of-Service flags to dictate specific per-datagram handling instructions to the hosts and routers that forward the datagrams through a network. For example, the Precedence flags allow applications to set specific prioritization flags on the datagrams they generate, allowing them to define a higher-priority over normal traffic. Using this field, a database client could flag all IP datagrams with a higher priority than normal, which would inform the routers on the network to prioritize the database traffic over normal or lower-priority traffic.

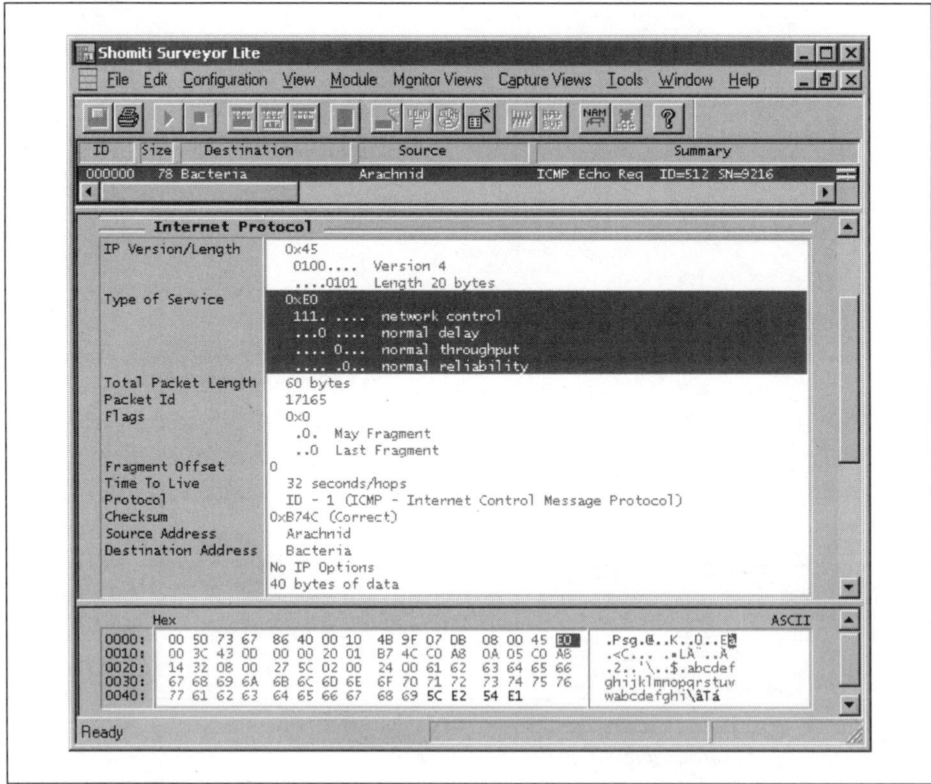

Figure 2-28. An IP packet with a precedence of 7

Figure 2-28 shows an ICMP Echo Request Query Message sent from Arachnid to Bacteria, with a Precedence value of 7 in the IP header's Type-of-Service field. This IP packet would be given a higher priority over any other packets with a lower priority value, assuming the router supported this type of special handling operation (many routers do not offer this type of support).

Besides prioritization, the Type-of-Service byte also offers a variety of different special-handling flags that can also be used to dictate how a particular datagram should be treated. A Telnet client could set the "Minimize Latency" Type-of-Service flag on the datagrams that it generated, requesting that routers forward that traffic across a faster (and possibly more expensive) network than it might normally choose, for example. In addition, an FTP server could set the Maximize Throughput flag on the IP datagrams that it generated, requesting that routers choose the fastest-available link, while a Usenet News (NNTP) client could set the Minimize Cost flag, if it desired.

Figure 2-29 shows a Telnet client on Bacteria setting the "Minimize Latency" Type-of-Service flag on a Telnet connection to Krill. This packet would then get routed over a faster network than any packets that were not marked with these flags, assuming the router supported this type of operation (many routers do not offer this type of support).

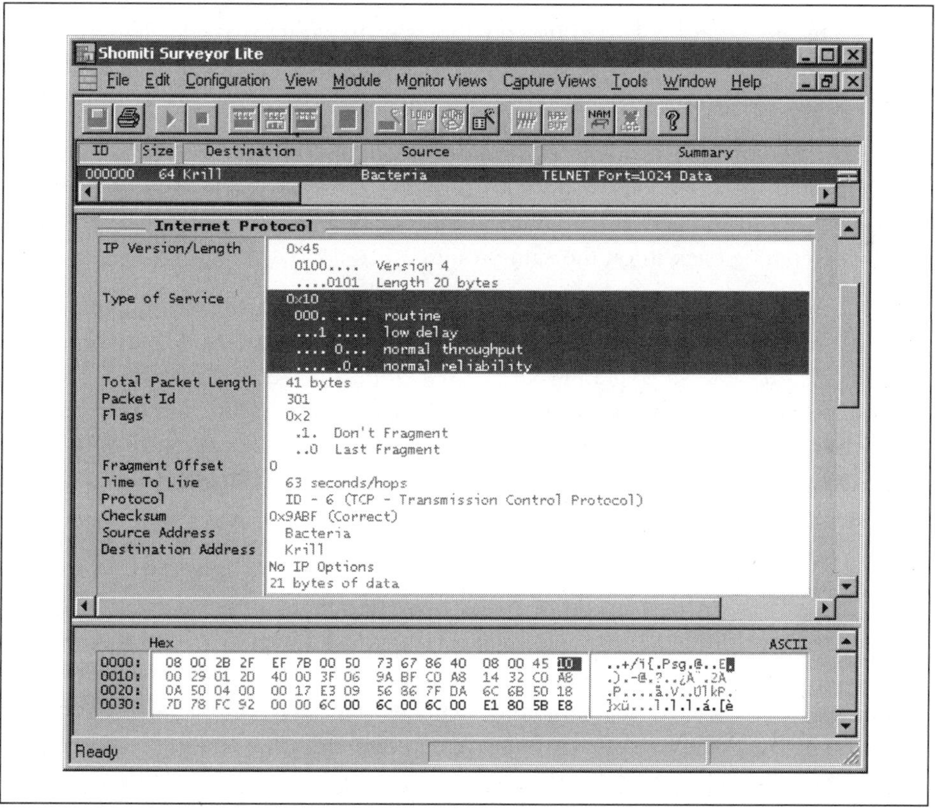

Figure 2-29. A Telnet connection with the "Minimize Latency" Type-of-Service flag enabled

For more information on these flags and their usage, refer to "Prioritization and Service-Based Routing" earlier in this chapter.

Troubleshooting IP

Since IP provides only simple delivery services, almost all of the problems with IP are related to delivery difficulties. Perhaps a network segment is down, or a router has been misconfigured, or a host is no longer accepting packets.

In order to effectively debug problems with IP delivery, you should rely on the ICMP protocol. It is the function of ICMP to report on problems that will keep IP datagrams from getting delivered to their destination effectively. For more information on ICMP, refer to Chapter 5.

Misconfigured Routing Tables

The most common cause of connectivity problems across a network is that the routing tables have not been properly defined. In this scenario, your datagrams are going out to the remote destination, and datagrams are being sent back to your system but are taking a bad route on the way to your network. This problem occurs when the advertised routes for your network point to the wrong router (or do not point to any router).

This is a very common problem with new or recently changed networks. It is not at all unusual for somebody to forget to define the route back to your new network. Just because the datagrams are going out does not mean that return datagrams are coming back in on the same route.

The only way to successfully diagnose this problem is to use the *traceroute* program from both ends of a connection, seeing where in the network path the problem occurs. If you stop getting responses after the second or third hop on outbound tests, then it is highly likely that the router at that juncture has an incorrect routing entry for your network, or doesn't have any entry at all. For more information on *traceroute*, refer to "Notes on traceroute" in Chapter 5.

Media-Related Issues

Since IP packets are sent inside of media-specific frames, there can be problems with some network media that will manifest when used with IP packets. For example, some network managers have reported problems with network infrastructure equipment such as Ethernet hubs and switches that have problems dealing with full-sized (1500-byte) packets. In those situations, you will need to use ICMP to probe the network for delivery problems through equipment that is acting suspicious.

One way to do this is to send incrementally larger ICMP Echo Request messages to other devices on those networks, testing to see where they stop working. If the hub or switch stops forwarding data to all of the attached devices after a certain point, then it is possible that the device itself could be eating the packets. However, it is also entirely possible that the problem lies with your own equipment. In order to verify your suspicions, you should test connectivity using another system with a different network adapter (since your adapter may be the true culprit). However, if only one or two devices fail to respond, then the problem is likely to be with the adapters or drivers in use with those systems.

In addition, some network managers have reported problems with wide-area networking equipment that interprets some bit patterns from the IP packet as test patterns. In those cases, the WAN equipment may eat the packets. The packets that are most problematic are those that contain long sequences of ones or zeros, although packets that contain alternating ones and zeroes have also been problematic for some users. If you have reproducible problems with some of your WAN links, you may want to look at the data inside of the IP packets to see if you have any long strings of specific bit patterns, and then use a program such as *ping* to verify that the test pattern is causing the problems.

Fragmentation Problems

In addition, a variety of fragmentation-related problems can crop up that will prevent datagrams from being successfully delivered. Since IP will process only a complete datagram (and more importantly, will discard an incomplete datagram), fragmentation problems will cause a substantial number of retransmissions if an error-correcting protocol is generating the IP datagrams.

Fragmentation problems can occur in a variety of cases, although the most common cause is due to the sender attempting to detect the end-to-end MTU of a network using Path MTU Discovery, but an intermediary device does not return ICMP Error Messages back to the sending system. The result is that the sender continues trying to send packets that are too large to be fragmented, with the Don't Fragment flag enabled. For a comprehensive discussion on Path MTU Discovery and the problems that can result, refer to "Notes on Path MTU Discovery" in Chapter 5.

Other fragmentation problems can occur when using infrastructure equipment that is under heavy load, or when the network itself becomes somewhat congested. In those situations, a device that is fragmenting packets for delivery of another (smaller) network is losing some of the fragments, or the network itself is losing the packets. These problems can be difficult to diagnose, since *ping* tests using small or normal-sized messages across the network may perform just fine.

The best way to diagnose these problems is to send large ICMP Echo Request messages to the remote system, forcing fragmentation to occur on the network. If some (but not all) of the ICMP query messages are responded to, then it is likely that a device or segment on the network is eating some of the fragmented packets. For a detailed discussion on using *ping* to test the network, refer to "Notes on ping" in Chapter 5.

3

The Address Resolution Protocol

Summary	The Address Resolution Protocol provides a mechanism for IP devices to locate the hardware addresses of other devices on the local network. This service is required in order for IP-enabled systems to communicate with each other.
Relevant STDs	2 (*http://www.iana.org/*); 3 (includes RFCs 1122 and 1123); 37 (RFC 826, republished); 38 (RFC 903, republished)
Relevant RFCs	826 (Address Resolution Protocol); 903 (Reverse ARP); 1122 (Host Network Requirements); 1433 (Directed ARP); 1868 (UnARP Extension); 2131 (DHCP and DHCP ARP); 2390 (Inverse ARP)

When two IP-enabled devices on the same network segment want to communicate, they do so using the low-level protocols and addressing mechanisms defined for the specific medium in use.

For example, Ethernet devices use Ethernet-specific addresses when they communicate with each other, while Frame Relay networks use Frame Relay-specific addresses.

In order for IP systems to communicate with each other, they must first be able to identify the hardware addresses of the other devices on the same network segment that the local device is on. This service is provided by the Address Resolution Protocol.

The ARP Standard

ARP is defined in RFC 826, which has been republished as STD 37 (ARP is an Internet Standard protocol). However, RFC 826 contained some vagaries which were clarified in RFC 1122 (Host Network Requirements). As such, ARP implementations need to incorporate both RFC 826 and RFC 1122 in order to work reliably and consistently with other implementations.

RFC 826 introduced the concept of an Address Resolution Protocol as a useful way for devices to locate the Ethernet hardware address of another IP host on the same local network. As it turns out, ARP is also useful for many network topologies—not just Ethernet—and has since become incorporated into most of the other network topologies. All LAN media—and many WAN media—now use ARP to locate the hardware addresses of other IP devices on the local network.

When a device needs to send an IP packet to another device on the local network, the IP software will first check to see if it knows the hardware address associated with the destination IP address. If so, then the sender just transmits the data to the destination system, using the protocols and addressing appropriate for whatever network medium is in use by the two devices. However, if the destination system's hardware address is not known, then the IP software has to locate it before any data can be sent. At this point, IP will call on ARP to locate the hardware address of the destination system.

ARP achieves this task by issuing a low-level broadcast onto the network, requesting that the system that is using the specified IP address respond with its hardware address. If the destination system is powered up and on the network, it will see this broadcast (as will all of the other devices on the local network), and it will return an ARP response back to the original system. Note that the response is not broadcast back over the network, but is instead sent directly to the requesting system.

This process is illustrated in Figure 3-1. In that example, Ferret issues an ARP request for the hardware address associated with 192.168.10.40 to the network-specific broadcast address in use on that LAN. When Froggy sees the ARP request, it unicasts an ARP reply (containing Froggy's hardware address) to Ferret directly. Having gained the information it needed, Ferret can then send whatever data it has for Froggy to that host's hardware address, using the protocols that are specific to the underlying network medium.

ARP packets work at the data-link layer, the same as IP packets. As such, ARP packets are completely separate from IP packets; they even have a different protocol ID of 0806, instead of 0800 as used with IP.

ARP packets contain several fields, although only five of them are used to provide the bulk of ARP's functionality: the hardware address of the source, the IP address

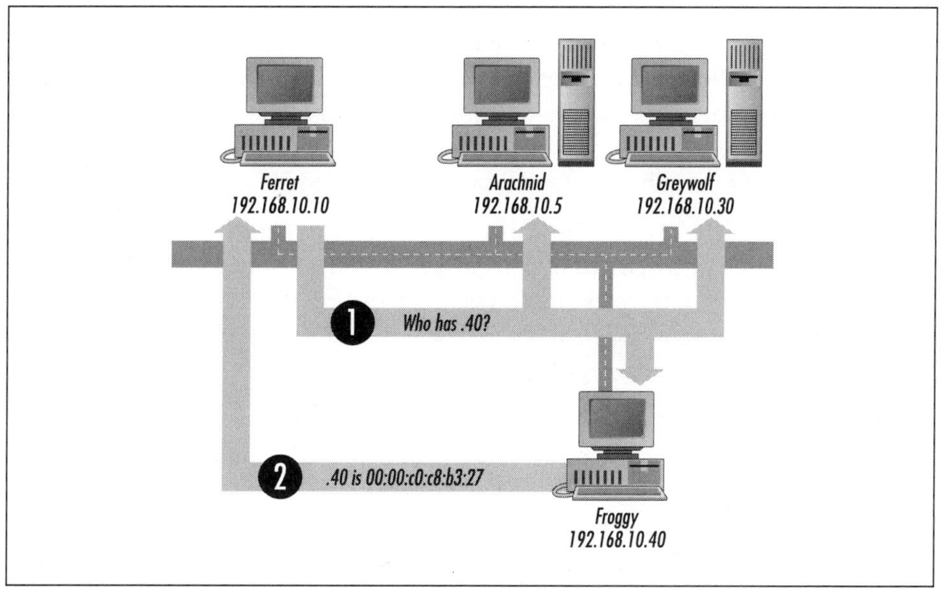

Figure 3-1. An overview of ARP

of the source, the hardware address of the destination, the IP address of the destination, and a "message-type" field that indicates whether the current ARP packet is a request or a response to a request.

When a device issues an ARP request, it fills in three of the four address-related fields, providing its own hardware and IP address, as well as the IP address of the target (the target's hardware address is unknown, so that field is filled with zeroes). In addition, it will set the message-type field to indicate that the current packet is an ARP request, and then broadcast the request onto the local network for all devices to see.

All of the local devices should monitor the network for ARP broadcasts, and whenever they see a request for themselves (as indicated in the destination IP address field of the ARP request), they should generate a response packet and send it back to the requesting system. The response packet will consist of the local device's IP and hardware addresses (placed into the sender fields), and the IP and hardware address of the original sender (placed in the destination fields of the response packet). The response will also be marked as such, with the message-type field indicating that the current packet is an ARP response. The new ARP packet is then unicast directly to the original requester, where it is received and processed.

Note that there is no timeout for an ARP request. The packet is sent and that's all there is to it. If a response comes back, that's great. If not, then ARP itself does not care, although the IP stack itself probably does care, and will continue to issue ARP lookups. However, this is also dependent upon the implementation of ARP, and how it deals with queuing. Many implementations only have room in the ARP lookup queue for a single packet for each of the hosts being queried. If an ARP request is not satisfied and another packet arrives from IP for the host being queried, then the first query will likely be aborted, and a second query will be issued. If the host is not responding to the ARP queries—but IP is trying to send multiple datagrams to that host—then there will be multiple queries for that host.

In this model, a higher-layer protocol such as TCP may notice that a problem has occurred and attempt a retransmission, which would in turn generate another IP packet (and another ARP request). Other protocols (such as UDP and ICMP) will not do this, however, and will simply treat a failed ARP lookup as a general timeout error (if a timer is being kept).

For example, if you try to use the *ping* program to test a host that is powered off, that host will not be able to respond to ARP broadcasts, and as such the local ICMP software will not be able to send an ICMP Echo Request message to the destination system. However, *ping* may continue generating ICMP Echo Request messages, which will result in multiple ARP lookups. *ping* may report timeout errors to the user for each of the failed lookups (since no response was received to the ICMP Echo Request message that was never actually sent over the network), although these errors will be generated by *ping*, and not by ARP.

The ARP Cache

When the requesting system gets an ARP response, it will store the hardware and IP address pair of the requested device into a local cache. The next time that system needs to send data, it will check the local cache, and if an entry is found it will go ahead and use it, eliminating the need to broadcast another request.

Likewise, the system that responded to the ARP broadcast will store the hardware and IP addresses of the system that sent the original broadcast. If it did not do so, it would have to issue an ARP broadcast to find out where to send the ARP response.

Since all of the systems on the network will see the ARP broadcast, they could go ahead and capture the IP and hardware addresses of the sender, storing this information in their own caches. However, doing this might cause existing entries in the cache to be flushed (an especially problematic issue with systems that have small caches), so only those systems who *already* have the sender's IP address in their cache should *update* their entries. Hosts that do not already have the device in their cache should ignore the broadcast.

Cache size issues

Most systems have a very limited ARP cache, with only enough room for a few entries. These entries will be overwritten as needed—a problem for busy networks.

For example, if a client system frequently accesses a variety of different servers (one for mail, one for web, one for routing, one for database, etc.), and its ARP cache was smaller than the number of systems it was connecting to, then it would have to overwrite entries in the cache on a continual basis. It would issue an ARP broadcast, cache the result, and then overwrite that entry with the results from another ARP broadcast for a different system a few moments later. If this problem were multiplied by hundreds of devices, the network could theoretically become saturated with ARP broadcasts.

Likewise, if many clients are accessing a single server, and if the ARP cache on that server is too small to hold entries for all of the clients, then the ARP cache on the server may get flushed continually. This would require the server to issue ARP requests whenever it needed to send data back to the clients. This in turn would flush even more entries, forcing the cycle to be repeated endlessly.

Note that many large, multiuser systems and network routers have very large ARP caches to prevent these types of problems from occurring in the first place. For example, high-end Cisco routers have an ARP cache that is large enough to hold several hundred entries, since the router is likely to exchange data with each PC on the local network quite frequently. Having a large cache on these types of devices is essential to smooth operation, since otherwise the servers and routers could communicate with only a few PCs simultaneously.

Cache timeout issues

Systems should flush entries from the ARP caches after they have been unused for a while. This allows well-known IP addresses to be moved to a different machine—or for a well-known machine to be given a new IP address—without communication problems coming about due to stale (and invalid) address mappings. ARP cache timeout values that are too high will cause problems whenever a host is assigned a different IP address, since the other hosts who have an older entry in their caches will still try to send data to the old (and invalid) hardware address.

Conversely, an ARP timeout that is too short will also result in problems, especially on busy networks with lots of devices. If network clients are constantly flushing their ARP caches due to short timeout values, then many broadcasts will be required. This hurts performance, since the IP software will not be able to send any data until an ARP broadcast has been sent and responded to.

RFC 826 does not give a specific timeout value for ARP cache entries, so each vendor implements this value differently. On desktop PCs, the timeout value can be quite low, with entries expiring after just 120 seconds on Windows 95 systems. Conversely, many server-class systems will set the timeout value to be ten minutes or more, while some routers set the timeout as high as four hours. These types of systems typically benefit from having high timeout values, since the client systems do not change addresses very often, and provide their new hardware address whenever they switch to a new IP address (by issuing ARP queries).

You may need to ask your system vendor for the default ARP timeout value, or for instructions on how to change it. However, RFC 826 does state that if a device sees an ARP packet whose IP address is already in the cache, then any timeout clocks for that entry should be reset. This helps the already-cached data to survive for as long as possible.

Static caching

To get around some of the problems encountered with entries expiring and being over-written, many products provide tools for adding static entries to the cache that never expire. On some systems, static entries are cleared from the cache when the system is restarted, requiring they be added again, while on other systems the static entries are more or less permanent, remaining until they are manually purged or until space is needed in the cache.

There are some benefits that come from using static ARP entries. Some network administrators incorporate static entries into an overall network security strategy. By adding static ARP entries for every device on the network, an administrator can prevent someone from using somebody else's IP address to access a sensitive host. Another benefit of static cache entries comes from the elimination of frequent lookups, since clients will always have ARP cache entries for the servers they use most frequently.

However, this benefit can also cause management headaches if systems are moved or renumbered frequently. If the network adapter is changed on a server—or if a well-known IP address is moved to another computer—then the static cache entry for that device will be invalid on all of the systems that have it. Systems will be unable to communicate until the static entries have been purged.

Proxy ARP

Sometimes it is useful to have a device respond to ARP broadcasts on behalf of another device. This is particularly useful on networks with dial-in servers that connect remote users to the local network. In such a scenario, a remote user might have an IP address that appears to be on the local network, although the user's system would not be physically present (it would be at a remote location, connected through the dial-in server).

Systems trying to communicate with this node believe that the device was local, and would use ARP to try and find the associated hardware address. However, since the system is remote, it would not see (nor respond to) the ARP lookups.

Normally, this type of problem is handled through Proxy ARP, which allows a dial-in server to respond to ARP broadcasts on behalf of any remote devices it services.

Figure 3-2 shows a dial-up client connected to an Ethernet network using an IP address that is associated with the local Ethernet network. Whenever another device on the network needed to locate the hardware address of the remote user, it would issue an ARP Request for that IP address (as shown in step one in the figure), and expect an Ethernet address back in the ARP Response.

However, since the dial-up client is actually on a remote network, it would not see the ARP request (unless bridging were enabled over the connection, which is highly unlikely). Instead, Sasquatch should respond to the ARP Request on behalf of the dial-up system, providing its own Ethernet address in the ARP Response packet (as shown in step two in the figure). Essentially, Sasquatch would trick the other hosts into thinking that it was the remote system.

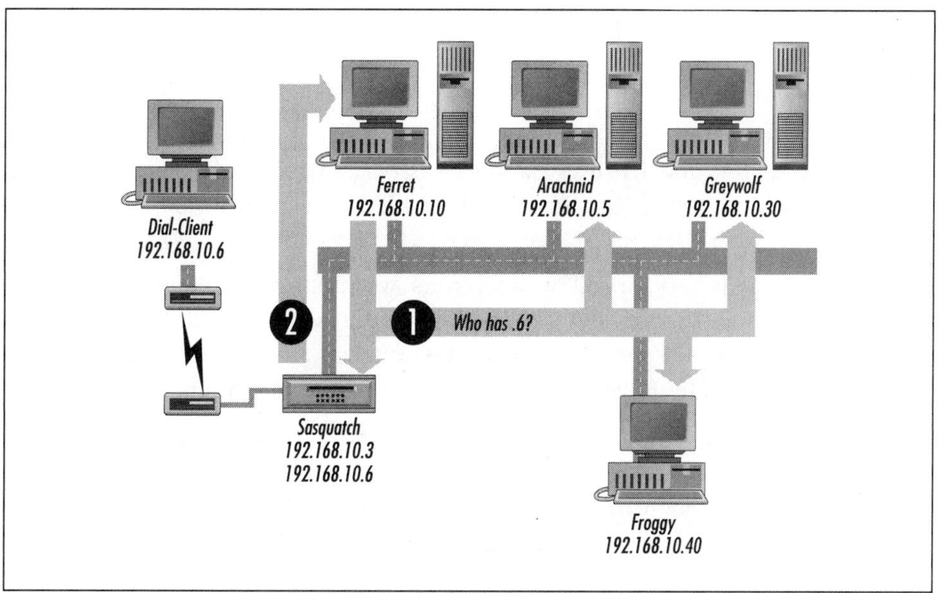

Figure 3-2. An overview of Proxy ARP

Having gained the necessary information, the other devices on the local network could then start communicating directly with the communications server (using the low-level protocols appropriate for the medium). The communications server would accept the packets on behalf of the dial-up user, see that they were intended for the dial-up host (as shown in the destination address field of the IP header), and forward them on.

Some interesting problems can occur with Proxy ARP, especially in regards to mobile users who frequently connect and disconnect with multiple dial-in servers that share a modem pool or ISDN line. Whenever a client connects to an application server on the local LAN, ARP entries are stored in the server's cache, and if the user were to disconnect from the dial-up server and reconnect to another dial-up server on the same LAN (negotiating the same IP address for both connections), the application server's ARP cache entry for the client would still point to the first dial-up server's hardware address. This situation would prevent the application server from being able to communicate with the client, at least until the Proxy ARP entry in the server's cache was flushed. This particular problem can be resolved in a variety of ways, however, with the most common solution being the use of Gratuitous ARP on the dial-up servers in the pool.

Variations on the ARP Theme

Just as an IP device can locate the hardware address for a specific IP address, so can a device locate the IP address associated with a known hardware address. Two variations on ARP take advantage of this capability, although for very different purposes:

Inverse ARP
: Inverse ARP works exactly the opposite of regular ARP. Rather than a device needing to find the hardware address associated with a known IP address, Inverse ARP is used to find the IP address for a known hardware address.

Reverse ARP
: Reverse ARP is used to allow a diskless workstation to request its own IP address, simply by providing its hardware address in an ARP request broadcast. A Reverse ARP server will see this request, assemble an ARP response that contains an IP address for the requester to use, and then send it back to the requesting device. The workstation will then use this IP address for its networking activity.

In addition, three other variations on ARP have been developed that attempt to overcome some of the problems that have proven to be common on IP networks:

DHCP ARP
: DHCP ARP is used by devices that obtain an IP address using an address-allocation protocol such as DHCP. The purpose of DHCP ARP is to allow the device to probe the network for any other device that may be using the assigned IP address already, prior to actually trying to use the address. This process helps prevent problems with duplicate or overlapping address assignments, as the requester can just reject the assignment if another device responds to the DHCP ARP query.

Gratuitous ARP
: Gratuitous ARP is used when a device issues an ARP broadcast for the sole purpose of keeping other devices informed of its presence on the network.

There is no information gained by the requesting device in this scenario. However, other devices that already know about this device will update their cache entries, keeping them from expiring too quickly.

UnARP

Similarly, UnARP provides a mechanism for de-registering ARP entries. When a device wishes to leave the network, it can issue an UnARP broadcast, causing the other devices to clear their ARP caches of entries for this device.

DHCP ARP, Gratuitous ARP, and UnARP can each be extremely useful when managing networks that change frequently.

Inverse ARP (InARP)

The design goal for ARP was to allow an IP system to locate the hardware address associated with the (known) IP address of another system on a local network. Inverse ARP—which is documented in RFC 2390—works in the exact opposite manner, instead allowing a system to locate the IP address associated with a known data-link address. This feature is necessary when the devices are known to each other at the data-link layer, but the IP addresses of those systems are not known, which will prevent the two systems from being able to communicate with each other using IP. This is a common scenario on networks that share data-link addresses across different physical networks, such as Frame Relay and ATM.

Frame Relay networks are somewhat different from traditional networks in that the devices themselves do not have hardware addresses. Instead, the devices have addresses for each of the circuits that they are connected to (known as "data-link connection identifiers," or DLCI addresses). Whenever a device needs to send data to another device, it sends the data to the DLCI address that is associated with the specific circuit that the destination device is available through.

From IP's point of view, if a device wants to send IP packets to another device on the Frame Relay network, then the sender must have an ARP cache of sorts that maps destination IP addresses to specific circuit identifiers, allowing the sender to transmit data for a known IP address through the correct Frame Relay circuit. Typically, Frame Relay access devices must be manually configured with this mapping information, showing that DLCI 153 is associated with the IP address of 192.168.30.122, for example. In this model, the sender is using a static ARP entry for each of the circuits that it is connected to. This scenario does not scale well, to say the least, particularly with Frame Relay networks that have hundreds of circuits (and therefore hundreds of IP-to-DLCI mappings).

This is the problem that Inverse ARP solves: by sending a query to each of the circuits that a device is attached to, a device can automatically build circuit-to-IP address mappings on a somewhat-automated basis. Once the destination systems on the far end of those circuits receive the Inverse ARP requests, they will respond with the IP address they are using on that specific circuit, allowing the sender to build these maps automatically.

Figure 3-3 provides a rough illustration of how this concept works. In that example, one of the devices wants to know the IP address of the other device at the far end of circuit 153, so it sends an Inverse ARP request through that circuit. The remote system sees the incoming request and responds with an Inverse ARP response that shows the IP address that is associated with that virtual circuit. Note that if the remote system were connected to multiple circuits, it would need to have different IP addresses for each of the circuits it were connected to (per-interface IP addresses are required in order for basic IP routing to work across the network).

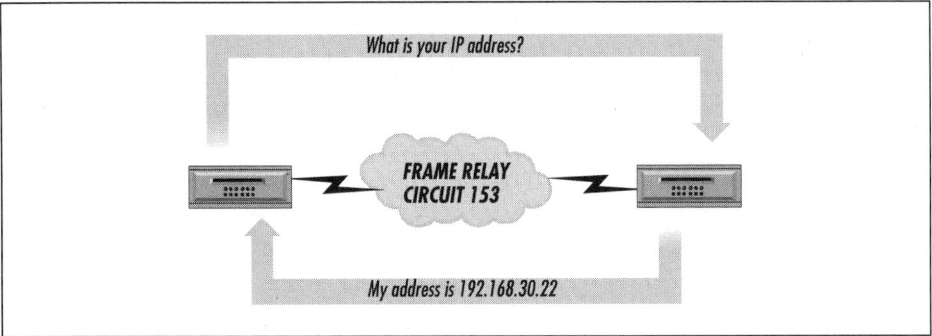

Figure 3-3. An overview of Inverse ARP

Every device on the Frame Relay network can go through this process, sending Inverse ARP requests through every circuit defined on the network, until all of the devices discover the IP addresses in use by all of the other devices. This information can then be used to build workable ARP caches for each of the systems. Note that these ARP entries should be treated the same as any other type of ARP data, with address pairs getting flushed or updated as needed by the system.

An interesting aside here is that Frame Relay circuits can have different circuit identifiers at each end, depending upon the number of switches in between the two end-points. In that scenario, the two end-points will have different circuit identifiers for the IP addresses in their ARP caches. For example, the sending router shown in Figure 3-3 may see the circuit as DLCI 153, while the recipient may see the circuit as DLCI 298. However, since the end-points only communicate with the circuit (and not with the remote system directly), the hardware address associated with the remote IP address is somewhat irrelevant.

Although the model put forth by Inverse ARP could be incorporated into Ethernet and other LAN-based topologies, it has not yet been done so to my knowledge. Generally speaking, there is no need for these services on a local network where every device shares the same physical medium. Frame Relay and ATM networks are unique in that devices can share a data-link connection while not being connected to the same physical network medium.

For more information on Inverse ARP, refer to RFC 2390. For more information on using IP with Frame Relay networks, refer to RFC 2427. For more information on using IP with ATM networks, refer to RFC 2225.

Reverse ARP (RARP)

Reverse ARP (RARP) is most often used with diskless workstations that do not have a permanent IP address, or that do not have sufficient resources for storing a permanent IP address. Whenever such a device needs to obtain an IP address for its own use (generally at boot time), it issues an ARP broadcast that contains its own hardware address in both the Sender and Recipient Hardware Address fields. Note that the Sender and Recipient Protocol Address fields would be zeroed out.

A special host (called a RARP server) watches for RARP broadcasts (RARP packets have their own unique ethertype of 8035). When one is seen, the server attempts to find an entry for the requesting device's hardware address in a local table of IP-to-hardware address mappings. If a match is found, it returns a RARP response to the requesting device, providing it with the IP address needed to continue the boot process. This process is illustrated in Figure 3-4.

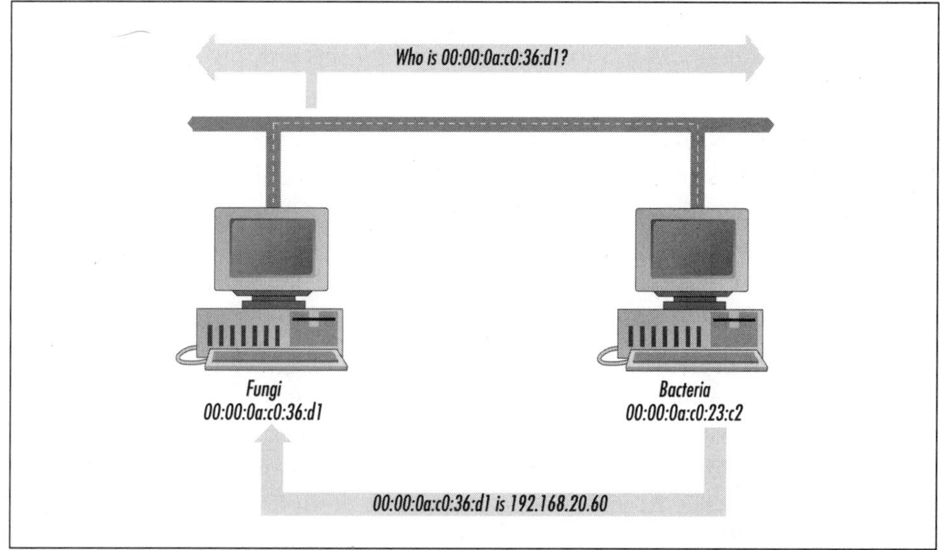

Figure 3-4. An overview of Reverse ARP

Although RARP was functional enough to be useful, it did not offer much in the way of comprehensive resource configuration. RARP did not provide for automatically determining the subnet mask in use on the network, the routers available, or much of anything else. For this reason, RARP is used much less frequently today than it has been in the past, with most devices having long ago moved to the BOOTP or DHCP configuration protocols for address-assignment and configuration services. You probably won't see it in use except on networks that have lots of older equipment.

For more information on RARP, refer to RFC 903.

DHCP ARP

One of the key differences between DHCP and RARP is that DHCP uses a shared pool of addresses when assignments are made, rather than using fixed entries like RARP does. This allows a network manager to share a limited number of IP addresses among a large number of hosts, instead of having to assign fixed addresses to each host. Although this makes life a little easier for the administrator in one sense, it can also make life more difficult, particularly when it comes to making sure that more than one device is not trying to use the same address at the same time. This is particularly problematic when users do not release the address they have been assigned and another device starts trying to use it, or when a user has manually configured his system to use a specific address that is also being assigned out of the DHCP pool.

In order to minimize the opportunity for this problem to occur, RFC 2131 (the DHCP RFC) stated that devices should verify the integrity of the address they are getting from the DHCP server before they accept the assignment. RFC 2131 also defined a specific ARP request format to be used for this purpose, in order to keep other systems from getting confused by the ARP request.

With DHCP ARP, the requesting device issues a normal ARP request, except that instead of putting its own IP address in the Source Protocol Address field, it puts in "0.0.0.0". The rest of the packet looks like a normal ARP request, with the local hardware address in the Source Hardware Address field, the questionable IP address in the Destination Protocol Address field, and the Destination Hardware Address field containing zeroes.

This combination of fields serves two purposes. First of all, by providing the local hardware address in the Source Hardware Address field, a device that is already using the questionable address will see the ARP request and will be able to respond to it (ARP does not use IP for delivery, so it does not need an IP address for responses to work). At the same time, the lack of an IP address in the Source Protocol Address field prevents the other systems on the network from updating their ARP caches. Otherwise, the IP address provided in the Source Protocol

Address field would cause the other network devices to update any existing entry in their caches, even though another system may be using that IP address.

This process is demonstrated in Figure 3-5. In that example, Greywolf has been assigned an IP address from the DHCP server, but it tests the assignment using a DHCP ARP request before attempting to use it. In that case, it would create an ARP request packet, and set the Destination Protocol Address field to the address that it had been assigned by the DHCP server. Then it would fill the Destination Hardware Address and Source Protocol Address fields with zeroes.

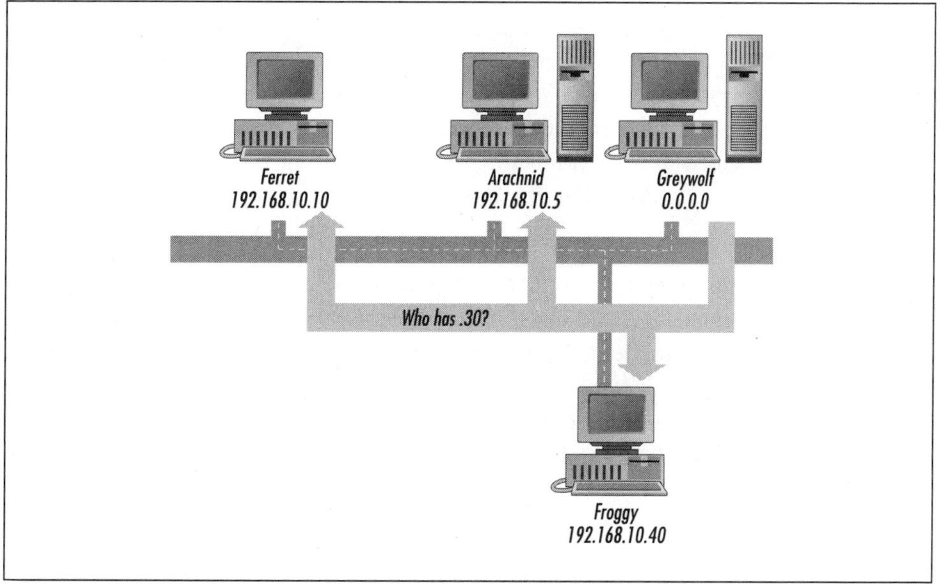

Figure 3-5. An overview of DHCP ARP

If Greywolf does not receive a response to the query, then it can assume that no other device on the local network is using that IP address, and start using it. If Greywolf did receive a response, however, then it should reject the IP address offered by the DHCP server, and restart the assignment process.

It is important to note that just because a client does not receive a response from a DHCP ARP request does not mean that the IP address is safe to use. For example, another device may have that address permanently configured, but may also be powered off at the moment the DHCP ARP was issued. When that device was powered back on, it would try to use the permanently assigned address, resulting in addressing conflict problems (such as reset TCP connections, unexpected ICMP messages, and other such problems). Furthermore, not every device understands the DHCP ARP format, and many older systems will just ignore an ARP request that has zeroes in the Source Protocol Address field. In fact, the UnARP protocol explicitly uses ARP responses instead of requests for just that reason.

RFC 2131 also suggests that clients "should broadcast an ARP reply to announce the client's new IP address and clear any outdated ARP cache entries in hosts on the client's subnet." However, there is some confusion in regards to this clause. Most systems implement this type of functionality using the Gratuitous ARP mechanism, which uses a broadcast ARP request message (rather than an ARP reply). Although RFC 2131 clearly states that devices should issue ARP replies, many implementations will use an ARP request for this service.

For more information on DHCP ARP, refer to RFC 2131.

Gratuitous ARP

Simply put, Gratuitous ARP is where a device broadcasts its own hardware and IP address pair, solely for the purpose of causing other devices to update their ARP caches. Remember that systems will not *add* new devices that they see in a broadcast (as this may cause the cache to flush more important entries). However, they will gladly *update* any entries that are already in the cache.

When a Gratuitous ARP request is broadcast, the sender puts its hardware and IP address information into the appropriate sender fields, and also places its IP address in the destination IP address field. It does not put its hardware address in the destination hardware field, however. Other devices on the network see this broadcast, and if they have the sender's information in their cache already, they either restart the cache entry's countdown timers or modify the entry to use the new hardware address (in case the network adapter on the sending host has been changed).

This process can be particularly useful with servers that communicate with many different clients frequently; the frequent use of Gratuitous ARP messages causes those clients to update their cache entries frequently, thereby keeping the clients from having to constantly reissue queries whenever they want to connect to this server. Furthermore, Gratuitous ARP messages can also be useful when a system frequently dials into a modem pool that is served by multiple communications servers, and the user has pre-selected an IP address to use for her connection. In that environment, the address being used may be associated with a different hardware address from one of the other communications servers (from one of the previous connections). By using Gratuitous ARP, the active dial-up server will ensure that all of the hosts on the LAN have the right hardware address in their ARP caches.

This process is illustrated in Figure 3-6, which shows Ferret issuing an ARP Request for its own IP address (192.168.10.10).

Nobody should reply to the ARP request, since nobody else should have the IP address listed in the destination field. If anybody does reply to the Gratuitous ARP

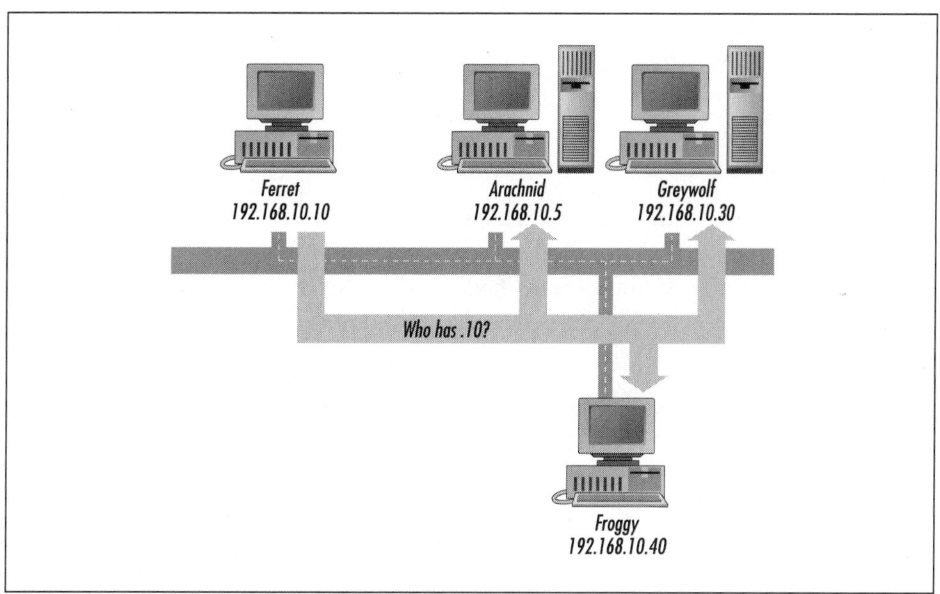

Figure 3-6. An overview of Gratuitous ARP

broadcast, it would be because the responding host was also using the same IP address of the sending system. In this case, both systems should notice that there is an addressing conflict, and may choose to display a warning message on the system console stating that another host is using the local host's IP address.

In fact, many hosts use Gratuitous ARP whenever they come online just for this purpose, since it offers a cheap way to test for address conflicts on startup. Unfortunately, the use of Gratuitous ARP in this way can actually cause some problems to occur, and is not always a good idea. For example, if a misconfigured host issues a Gratuitous ARP for an IP address that is already in use by another device, then any clients who see that broadcast will update their ARP caches to use the new hardware address being published, even though the new mapping may point to the wrong host. From that moment on—or at least until the cache entries are updated—those clients will try to send data to the misconfigured host, rather than to the original (proper) host.

DHCP ARP is probably a better mechanism to use when testing for addressing conflicts on startup, since it allows the sender to detect whether or not another device is using the IP address before it actually tries to use it. Furthermore, the use of zeroes in the Source Protocol Address field prevents the other systems from updating their ARP caches with this host's information, which may be the more prudent choice.

UnARP

As discussed in "The ARP Cache" earlier in this chapter, there are no Time-to-Live mechanisms defined in the ARP standard. Each vendor implements its own ARP timers, ranging anywhere from two minutes to twenty minutes and more. This wide diversity can cause several problems.

For example, a DHCP client may be assigned an IP address, use it for a while, and then release it. Moments later, another client may be assigned the same IP address from the DHCP server. If any systems had the first DHCP client's hardware address stored in their cache, they would not be able to communicate with the new DHCP client.

One possible solution to this problem that has been proposed is UnARP, another variation on the ARP theme as defined in RFC 1868. UnARP dictates that a special ARP packet should be broadcast whenever a node disconnects from the network, explicitly telling other devices that the node is going away, and that the cache entry for that host should be flushed. This warning would allow another device (such as another DHCP client) to reuse the IP address immediately, without having to worry about stale caches causing any problems.

Essentially, UnARP is an unsolicited ARP response with zeroes in the Source and Destination Hardware Address fields that get broadcast across the network, as illustrated in Figure 3-7.

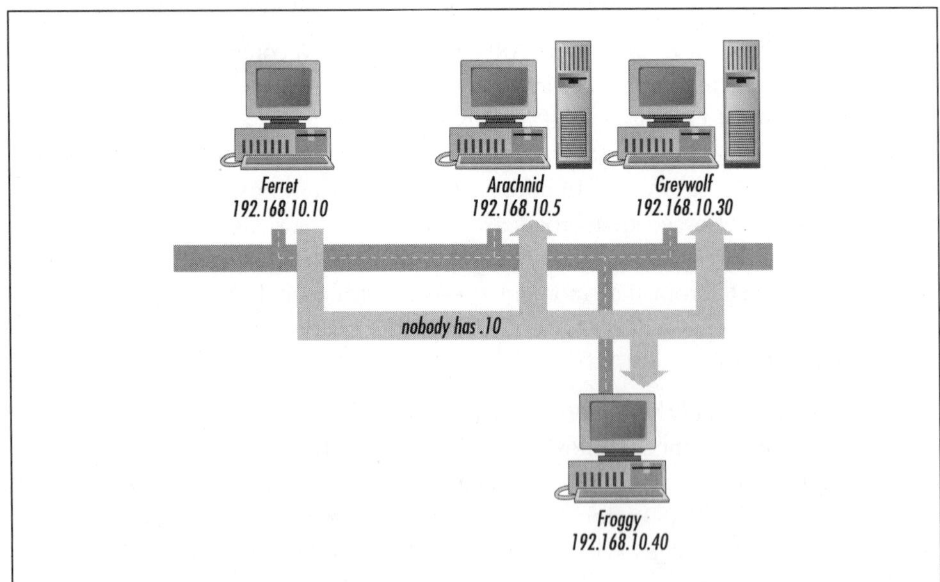

Figure 3-7. An overview of UnARP

There are some key concepts to UnARP that are subtle enough to be easily missed:

- Zeroes are used in the Source and Destination Hardware Address fields to indicate that no hardware address is associated with the IP address provided in the Source Protocol Address field. In addition, the Hardware Address Length field is also set to zero.
- UnARP uses an ARP *response* packet rather than an ARP request packet. This is because UnARP uses zeroes in the hardware address fields, which could break lesser-bred ARP implementations that were expecting data in those fields. Since devices do not typically monitor for unsolicited ARP responses, support for UnARP would therefore require special code within the device, helping to minimize problems that might result from using zeroes in the hardware address fields.

Note that RFC 1868 is defined as an experimental RFC, and therefore many vendors do not support it. You should check with your vendor to see if it is among those that do.

For more information on UnARP, refer to RFC 1868.

The ARP Packet

An ARP packet works at approximately the same layer as IP. It communicates with the data-link services provided by the physical medium, and as such, ARP is a separate protocol than IP (and is identified separately by any network that both categorizes the protocols being carried in the low-level frames and supports ARP directly). The ethertype for ARP is 0806 as opposed to the ethertype for IP, which is 0800.

According to RFC 826, an ARP packet is made up of nine fields. The total size of the packet will vary according to the size of the physical addresses in use on the local network medium.

The fields in an ARP packet are listed in Table 3-1.

Table 3-1. The Fields in an ARP Packet

Header Field	Bytes	Usage Notes
Hardware Type	2	Identifies the medium-specific address type being requested.
Protocol Type	2	Identifies the higher-layer protocol information being discussed (which is always IP as far as we're concerned).

Table 3-1. The Fields in an ARP Packet (continued)

Header Field	Bytes	Usage Notes
Hardware Address Length	1	Specifies the size of the physical medium's hardware address, in bytes. Since each network uses different physical addressing mechanisms, this field is required for other fields further in the ARP packet.
Protocol Address Length	1	Specifies the size of the higher-layer protocol's address, in bytes. This is always 4 (32 bits) for IP.
Message Type	2	Identifies the purpose for this ARP packet ("request" or "response").
Source Hardware Address	varies	Identifies the hardware address of the system issuing the ARP broadcast.
Source IP Address	varies	Identifies the higher-layer protocol address of the system issuing the ARP broadcast. This field's value will be 4 when IP is in use.
Destination Hardware Address	varies	Identifies the hardware address of the system responding to the ARP broadcast.
Destination IP Address	varies	Identifies the higher-layer protocol address of the system responding to the ARP broadcast. This field's value will be 4 when IP is used.

Notice that the ARP packet's format does not provide Time-to-Live or Version fields. This deficiency has caused a considerable amount of difficulty. Since there is no Time-to-Live field, every implementation uses its own cache timeout mechanisms, which results in inconsistent views of the network. Also, since there is no Version field, it is not possible to change the protocol's structure (such as adding a Time-to-Live field) without causing incompatibilities between the different implementations.

Figure 3-8 shows a capture of two ARP packets: an ARP Request from Ferret to the local broadcast address, and an ARP Response from Krill back to Ferret. These two packets will be used to illustrate the ARP packet throughout the rest of this section.

The following sections discuss the fields of the ARP packet.

Hardware Type

Identifies the hardware address type being requested, in decimal format. This would be 1 for DIX–Ethernet, 6 for IEEE 802.x Ethernet, 7 for ARCnet, etc.

Size

Sixteen bits.

Notes

Since ARP is used for getting the hardware address associated with an IP address—and some systems allow an IP address to be associated with multiple types of hardware—there must be a way to request the specific type of

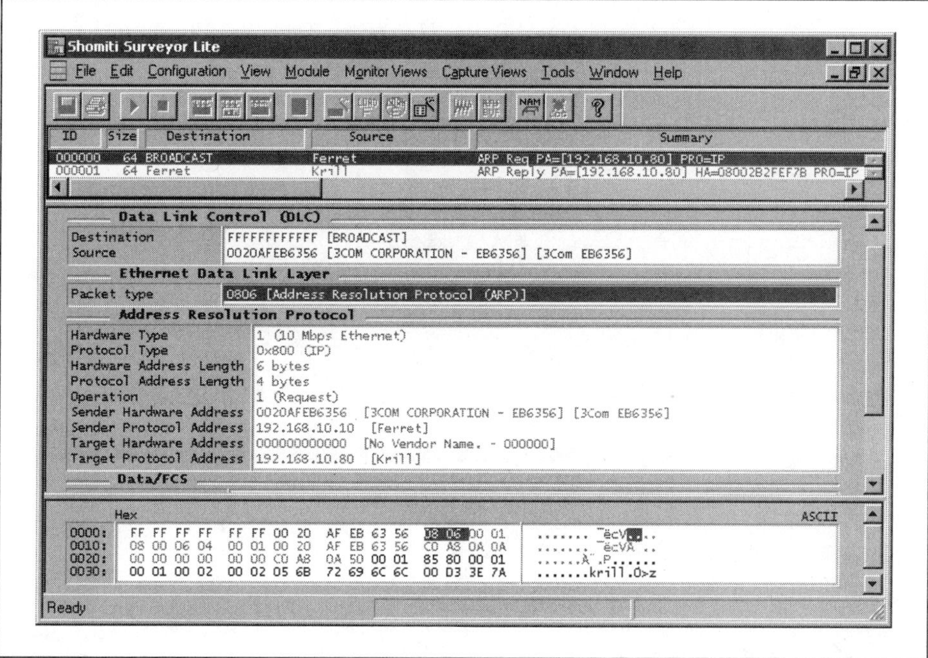

Figure 3-8. Two ARP packets

hardware address desired. Two devices on the same Ethernet LAN would want to communicate using the Ethernet-specific addresses, and the ARP request needs to be able to ask for that kind of address specifically.

The Hardware Type field uses decimal codes to indicate the address type being requested. Some of the more common hardware types are listed in Table 3-2. For a detailed listing of all of the known hardware types that are currently registered for ARP, refer to the IANA's online registry (accessible at *http://www.isi.edu/in-notes/iana/assignments/arp-parameters*).

Table 3-2. The Hardware Types Listed in RFC 1700 (Internet Assigned Numbers)

Hardware Type	Decimal Code
DIX-Ethernet and FDDI	1
IEEE 802 (includes 802.3 Ethernet and 802.5 Token Ring)	6
ARCnet	7
LocalTalk	11
SMDS (Switched Multimegabit Data Service)	14
Frame Relay	15
ATM (Asynchronous Transfer Mode)	19
Serial Line	20

Capture Sample

In the capture shown in Figure 3-9, the Hardware Type field is set to hexadecimal 0001, the code for DIX-Ethernet.

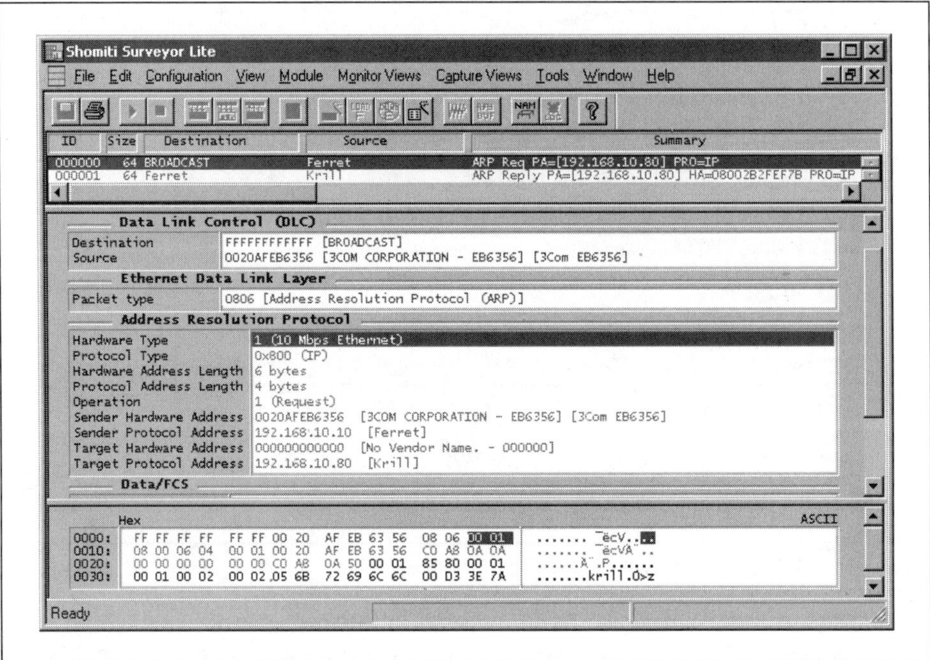

Figure 3-9. The Hardware Type field

See Also

"Hardware Address Length"

"Source Hardware Address"

"Destination Hardware Address"

Protocol Type (IP)

Identifies the higher-level protocol in use. For the purpose of this book, this field always contains the topology-specific identifier for the IPv4 protocol.

Size

Sixteen bits.

Notes

Since ARP talks to the physical medium's data-link interface directly, it is not tied specifically to IP and can be used by any higher-level protocol seeking the hardware address associated with a higher-level protocol address (such as IPX, or DECnet, or whatever). For this reason, the Protocol Type field must define the higher-level protocol the request is referring to (which is always IP, as far as this book is concerned).

For Ethernet networks, the value for IP would be hexadecimal 0800 (which equates to the decimal value of 2048, the Protocol Type for IP).

Capture Sample

In the capture shown in Figure 3-10, the Protocol Type is set to hexadecimal 0800, the code for IP.

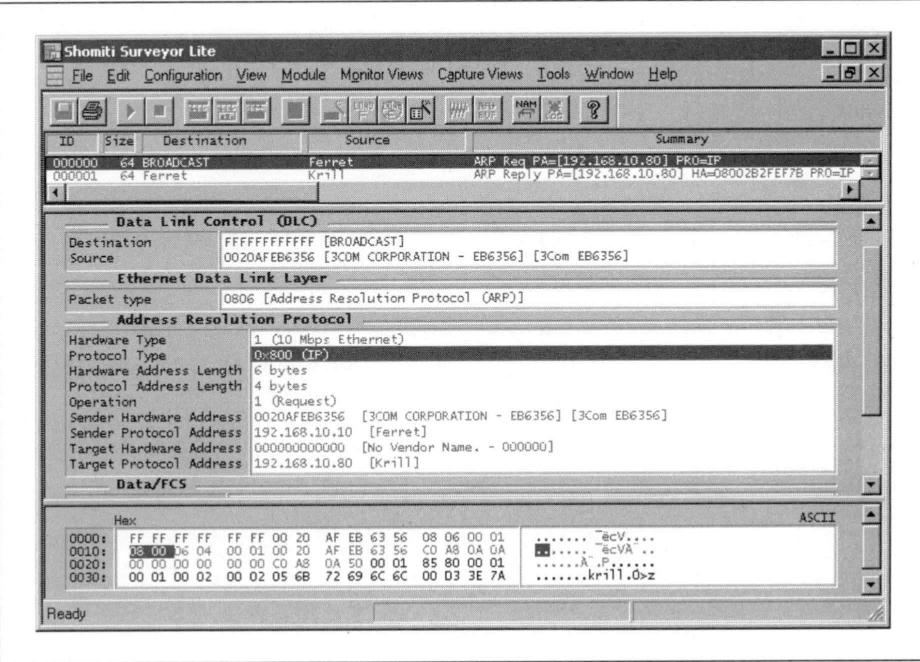

Figure 3-10. The Protocol Type field

See Also

"Protocol Address Length"

"Source Protocol (IP) Address"

"Destination Protocol (IP) Address"

Hardware Address Length

Specifies the length (in bytes) of the hardware addresses provided in the Source and Destination Hardware Address fields.

Size

Eight bits.

Notes

Since each network uses different physical addressing mechanisms, this field is required in order to make sense of the Source and Destination Hardware Address fields further in the ARP packet. Table 3-3 shows some of the most common hardware types and the sizes of their hardware addresses (in bytes).

Table 3-3. The Address Sizes of Some Hardware Types

Hardware Type	Size (Bytes)
Digital-Intel-Xerox (DIX) Ethernet	6
IEEE 802.3 Ethernet	6
IEEE 802.5 Token Ring	6
ARCnet	1
FDDI	6
Frame Relay	2, 3, or 4
SMDS	8

Capture Sample

In the capture shown in Figure 3-11, the Hardware Address Length field is set as hexadecimal 06, which indicates that the Source and Destination Hardware Address fields are six bytes (or 48 bits) long, the norm for DIX-Ethernet.

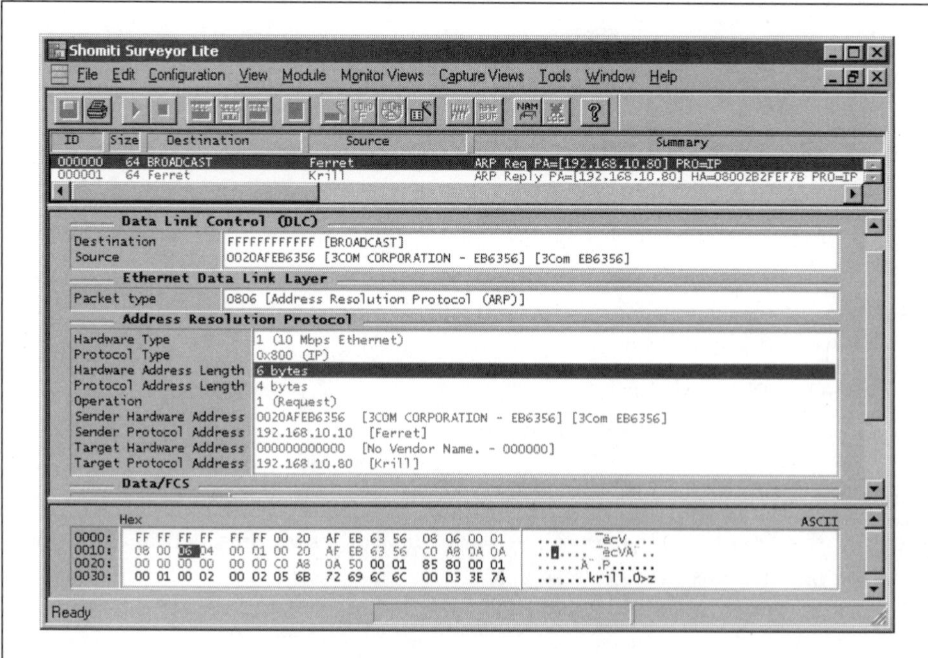

Figure 3-11. The Hardware Address Length field

See Also

"Hardware Type"

"Source Hardware Address"

"Destination Hardware Address"

Protocol Address Length

Specifies the length (in bytes) of the higher-level protocol address found in the Source and Destination Protocol Address fields. For IP, this value is always 4 (32 bits / 8 = 4 bytes).

Size

Eight bits.

Notes

ARP can be used with many different higher-level protocols (ARP isn't restricted to IP), and since each higher-level protocol uses different addressing mechanisms (IP addresses are considerably different from IPX and DECnet addresses), this field is required in order to make sense of the Source and Destination Protocol Address fields further in the ARP packet.

When IPv4 is specified in the Protocol Type field, the value of the Protocol Address Length field is always 4, since IP addresses are 32 bits (four bytes) long.

Capture Sample

In the capture shown in Figure 3-12, the Protocol Address Length field is set to hexadecimal 04, indicating that the Source and Destination Protocol Address fields are four bytes (or 32 bits) long, the norm for IP.

See Also

"Protocol Type (IP)"

"Source Protocol (IP) Address"

"Destination Protocol (IP) Address"

Message Type

Identifies the purpose for this ARP packet.

Size

Sixteen bits.

Notes

ARP by itself supports two basic operations: a request for the hardware address associated with a protocol address, and a response to an earlier request. Similarly, RARP also supports the notion of request and response operations, as does Inverse ARP.

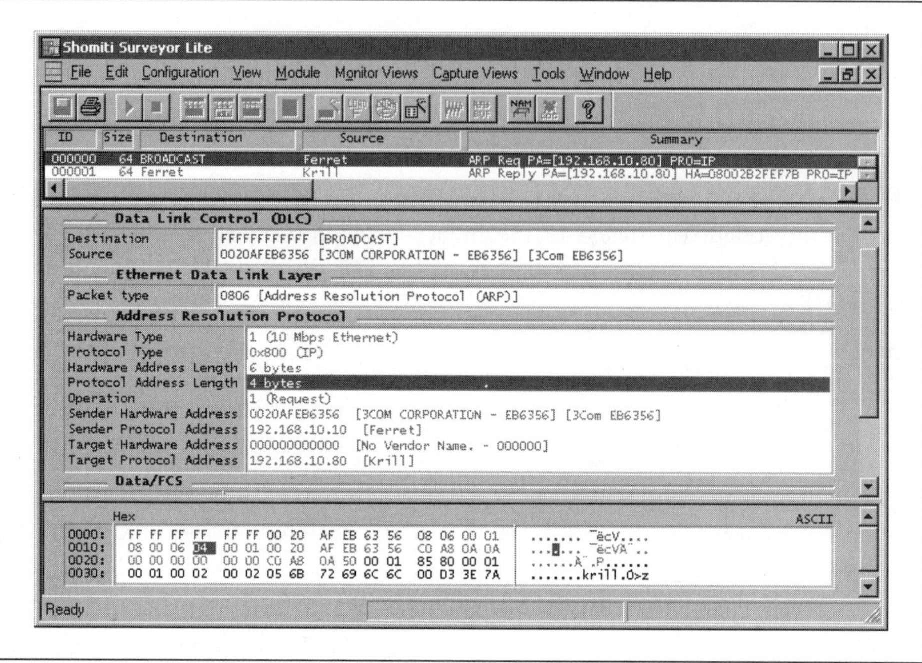

Figure 3-12. The Protocol Address Length field

The Message Type field is used to inform other systems on the local network which of these operations are being called upon. Table 3-4 lists the Message Type codes and their uses.

Table 3-4. ARP Message Type Codes and Their Meanings and Uses

Message Type	Usage Notes
1	ARP Request
2	ARP Response
3	Reverse ARP Request
4	Reverse ARP Response
8	Inverse ARP Request
9	Inverse ARP Response

If an ARP packet contains an ARP request (or if the packet is for a Gratuitous ARP), then the Message Type field will be set to 1. If the ARP packet contains an ARP response (or if the packet is for an UnARP operation), then the Message Type field will be set to 2. RARP uses 3 for requests and 4 for responses, while Inverse ARP uses 8 and 9, respectively.

Capture Sample

In the capture shown in Figure 3-13, the Message Type field is set to hexadecimal 0001, which indicates that this packet is an ARP Request.

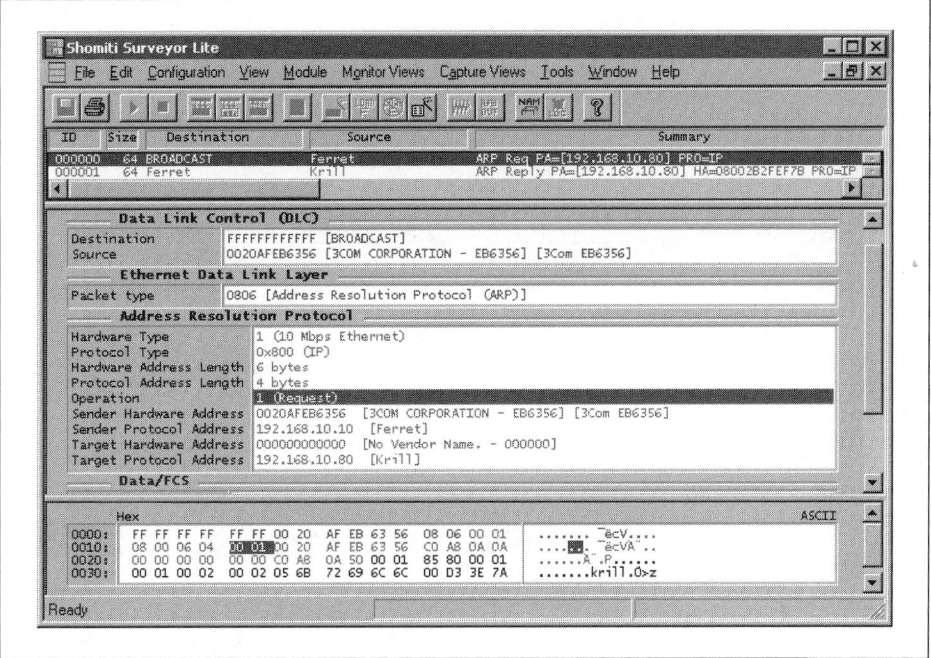

Figure 3-13. The Message Type field

Source Hardware Address

Identifies the hardware address of the system issuing the ARP packet. The packet may be either a request or a response.

Size

Varies according to the physical medium in use. Refer back to Table 3-3 for a listing of the most common hardware addresses and their lengths.

Notes

Every ARP exchange consists of two distinct packets: the original request and a response to the request. The Source Hardware Address field indicates the sender of this specific ARP packet. If the ARP packet is a request, then this field contains the hardware address of the device that is sending the request. If the ARP packet is a response, then this field contains the hardware address of the device that is sending the response.

Capture Sample

In the capture shown in Figure 3-14, the Source Hardware Address field is set to 00:20:af:eb:63:56, which is the 48-bit Ethernet address of the sender, in hexadecimal.

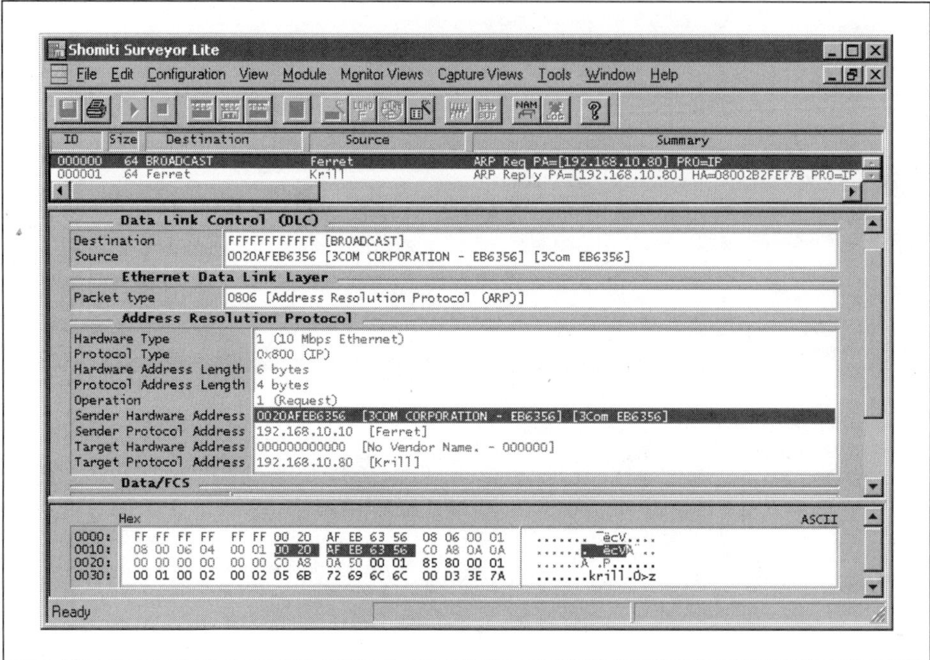

Figure 3-14. The Source Hardware Address field

See Also

"Hardware Type"

"Hardware Address Length"

"Destination Hardware Address"

Source Protocol (IP) Address

Identifies the higher-level address of the system issuing the ARP packet. The packet may be either a request or a response.

Size

Varies according to higher-level protocol in use. With IP, this field is four bytes (32 bits) long.

Notes

Every ARP exchange consists of two distinct packets: the original request and a response to the request. The Source Protocol Address field indicates the sender of this specific ARP packet. If the ARP packet is a request, then this field contains the IP address of the device that is sending the request. If the ARP packet is a response, then this field contains the IP address of the device that is sending the response.

Capture Sample

In the capture shown in Figure 3-15, the Source Protocol Address shows the 32-bit IP address of 192.168.10.10.

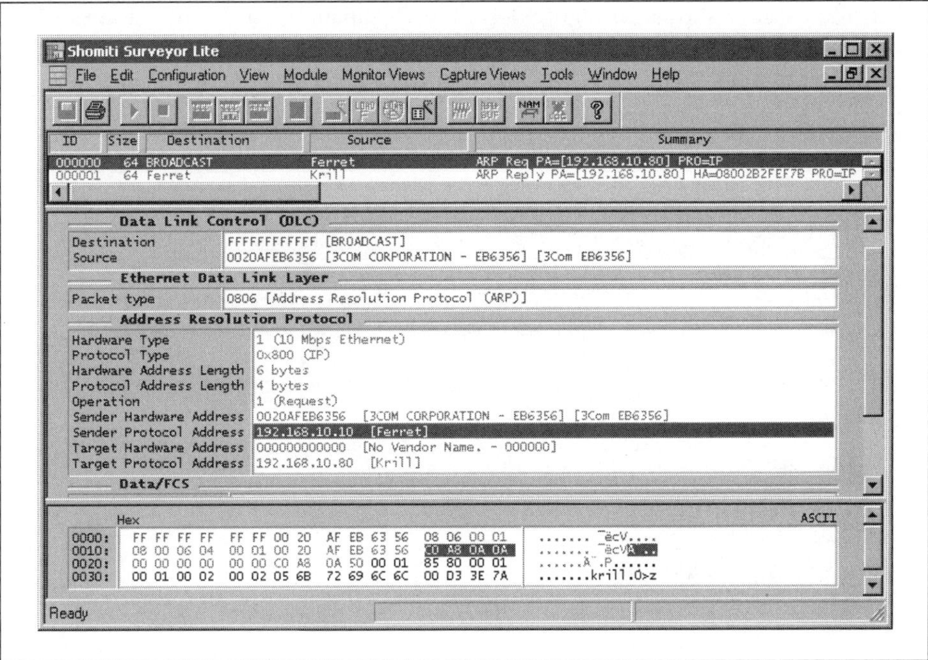

Figure 3-15. The Source Protocol Address field

See Also

"Protocol Type (IP)"

"Protocol Address Length"

"Destination Protocol (IP) Address"

Destination Hardware Address

Identifies the hardware address of the ARP packet's destination, which could be either a broadcast (as used in requests) or a specific system (as used in responses).

Size

Varies according to the physical medium in use. Refer back to Table 3-3 for a listing of the most common hardware addresses and their lengths.

Notes

Every ARP exchange consists of two distinct packets: the original request and a response to the request. The Destination Hardware Address field indicates the recipient of this specific ARP packet. If the ARP packet is a request, then this field will probably be empty, since the hardware address is unknown. If the ARP packet is a response, then this field contains the hardware address of the device that sent the original request.

Capture Sample

In the capture shown in Figure 3-16, the Destination Hardware Address is set to hexadecimal 00:00:00:00:00:00, indicating that the sender does not know the destination system's hardware address (as is normal with ARP request packets).

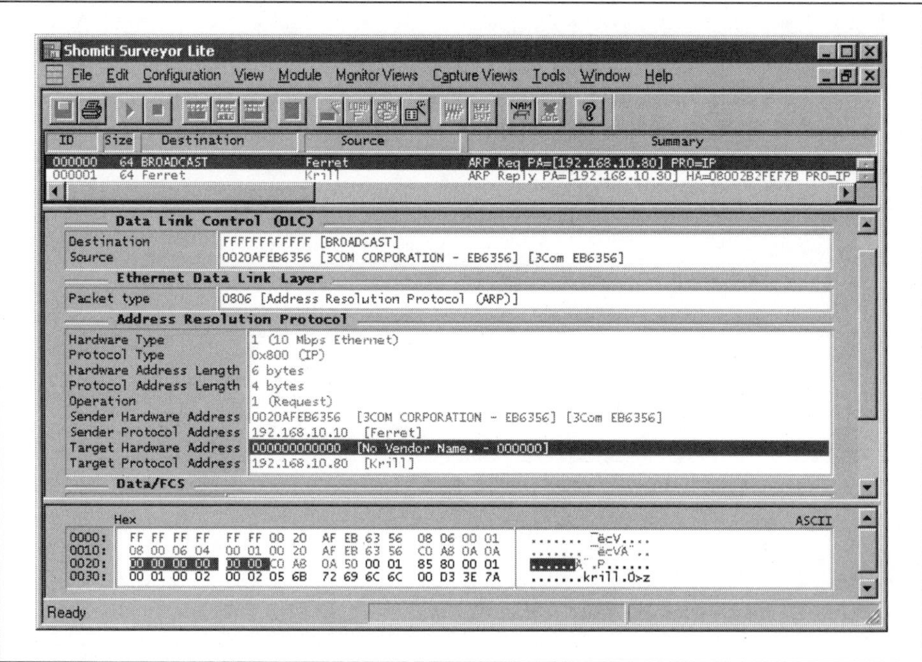

Figure 3-16. The Destination Hardware Address field

See Also

"Hardware Type"

"Hardware Address Length"

"Source Hardware Address"

Destination Protocol (IP) Address

Identifies the higher-level protocol address of the ARP packet's destination. The packet may be either a request or a response.

Size

Varies according to higher-level protocol in use. With IP, this field is four bytes (32 bits) long.

Notes

Every ARP exchange consists of two distinct packets: the original request and a response to the request. The Destination IP Address field indicates the recipient of this specific ARP packet. If the ARP packet is a request, then this field will contain the IP address of the device being looked up. If the ARP packet is a response, then this field will contain the IP address of the device that sent the original request.

Capture Sample

In the capture shown in Figure 3-17, the Destination Protocol Address field is set to the IP address of 192.168.10.80.

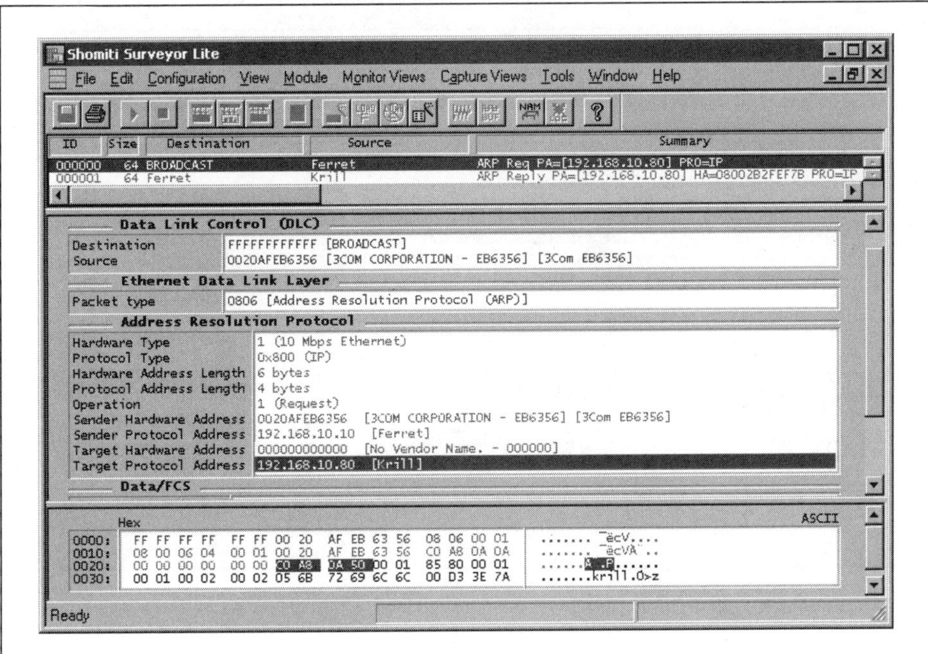

Figure 3-17. The Destination Protocol Address field

See Also

"Protocol Type (IP)"

"Protocol Address Length"

"Source Protocol (IP) Address"

ARP in Action

ARP is an extremely simple protocol. There are no headers or timers or anything else. Nor is there any negotiation or identification management: ARP packets get sent but they aren't tracked or managed in any shape or form.

A Typical Exchange

The ARP captures shown in Figure 3-18 and Figure 3-19 represent a typical ARP exchange.

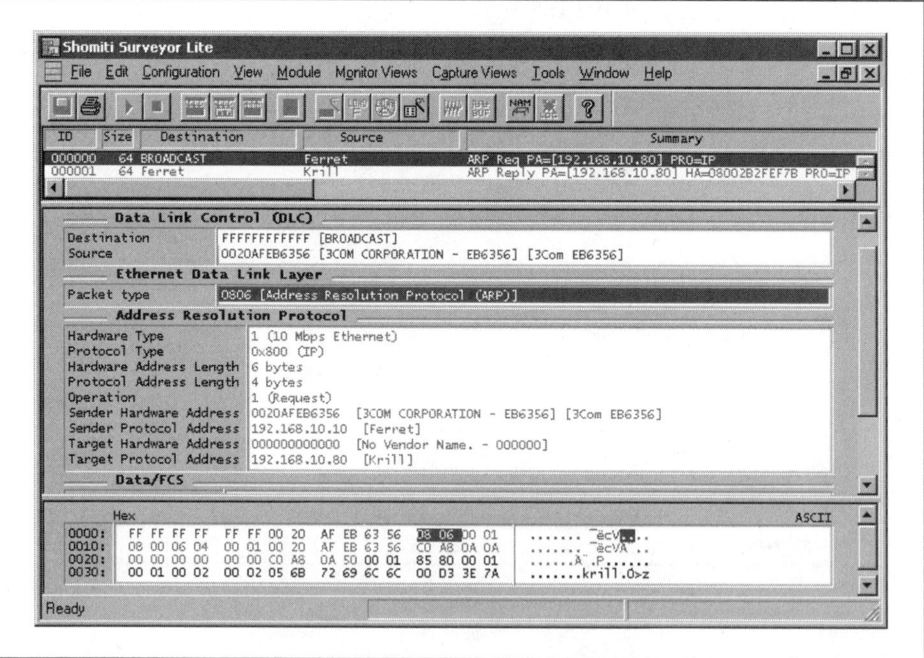

Figure 3-18. An ARP request from Ferret, seeking Krill's hardware address

The packet shown in Figure 3-18 is an ARP request from Ferret, seeking the hardware address associated with 192.168.10.80. The devices are on a DIX-Ethernet segment, and are so identified by the Hardware Type field being set to 1. Furthermore, the Hardware Address Length field is set to 6, which equals the 48-bit hardware addresses used by DIX-Ethernet. In addition, the devices are using IP for their higher-level protocol, so the Protocol Type field is set to hexadecimal 0800 while the Protocol Address Length field is set to 4, which represents the 32-bit addresses used by the IP protocol.

Since the packet shown in Figure 3-18 is an ARP request, the sender puts its IP address (192.168.10.10) and Ethernet address (00:20:af:eb:63:56) into the Sender-related fields, puts the destination system's IP address (192.168.10.80) into the Destination IP Address field, and puts zeroes into the Destination Ethernet Address.

The packet shown in Figure 3-19 is the ARP response that was returned for the ARP Request shown in Figure 3-18. This packet is coming from Krill (Ethernet address of 08:00:2b:2f:ef:78) and is being sent directly to Ferret.

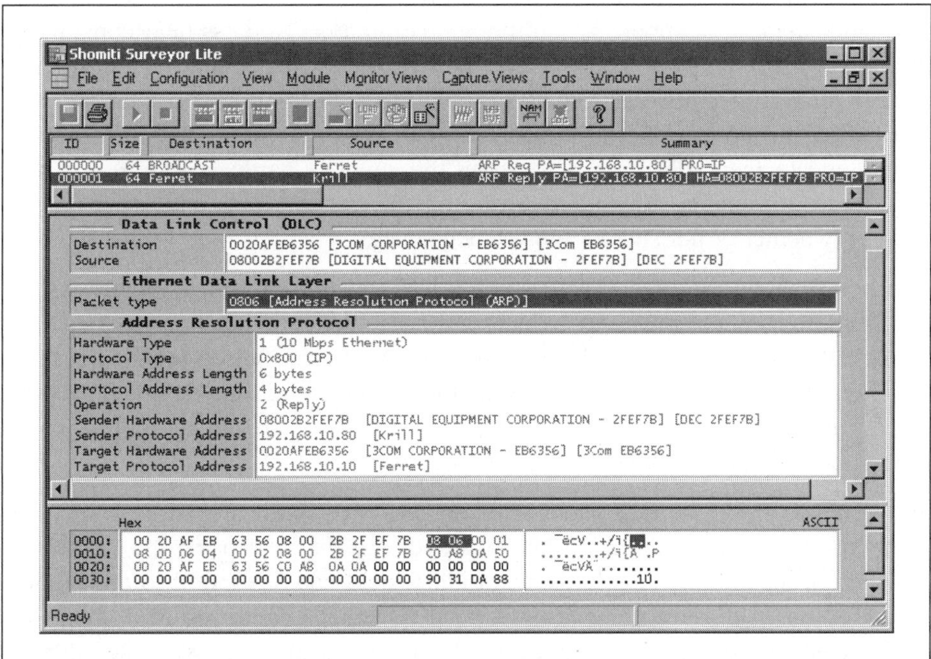

Figure 3-19. An ARP response from Krill back to Ferret

Notice that the response message has taken the source-related data from the original packet and has placed it into the destination-specific fields of the response packet. In addition, the ARP response also has the 48-bit DIX-Ethernet address associated with the requested IP address, as well as the IP address itself. Once this packet arrived back to Ferret, it would update its local ARP cache with this mapping, and keep it there until it was updated by another ARP packet, had expired, or the cache space was needed by another mapping.

Notes on DHCP ARP

RFC 2131 (the DHCP specification) defined a special type of ARP request that could be used to probe the network whenever an IP address had been assigned from DHCP, in case another device on the network was already using that IP address. This is an important service, since DHCP allows multiple devices to share an IP address, although those devices are not supposed to use the same IP address at the same time. In order to keep problems to a minimum, the use of the DHCP ARP probe allows a device to verify that no other devices are using the IP address before this device starts to do so.

The DHCP ARP packet looks like a regular ARP request packet, except that the Source Protocol Address field of the request is set to 0.0.0.0. This is done to prevent the ARP caches on other devices from being updated with any new information, since that only happens when the Source Protocol Address field contains an IP address that is already in the cache. If the DHCP client issued a regular ARP request (or a Gratuitous ARP request) for the assigned IP address using that same address in the Source Protocol Address field, then the other network devices would update their ARP caches to show the sender's hardware address, which would cause problems if another device on the network was still using that IP address (whether or not such usage was legitimate).

Figure 3-20 shows the host Fungi issuing a DHCP ARP request to the network for the IP address of 192.168.20.60 (which is the IP address it has been assigned by the DHCP server). Notice that the Source Protocol Address field is set to 0.0.0.0 (as specified by RFC 2131), while the Destination Hardware Address field is filled with zeroes, and the Destination Protocol Address field is set to the IP address being probed (as specified by the ARP specification).

Since the DHCP ARP request packet contains a Source Hardware Address field that points to Fungi's own Ethernet address, any device that was using the IP address specified in the Destination Hardware Address field could respond to the request with a unicast ARP response packet. If such a response were received, then RFC 2131 states that Fungi should reject the DHCP lease, and then restart the address-assignment procedure.

If no response was received, then Fungi could assume that no other hosts were using this IP address, and could begin using it for its networking services. However, this can be a fatal assumption, since responses may have failed to be sent (or received) for a variety of different reasons, ranging from physical-layer bridges that do not forward broadcasts, to the conflicting device being powered off at the moment the ARP request was issued.

In addition, RFC 2131 states that upon successfully completing the DHCP ARP process, Fungi should broadcast an ARP response to its own DHCP ARP message. By

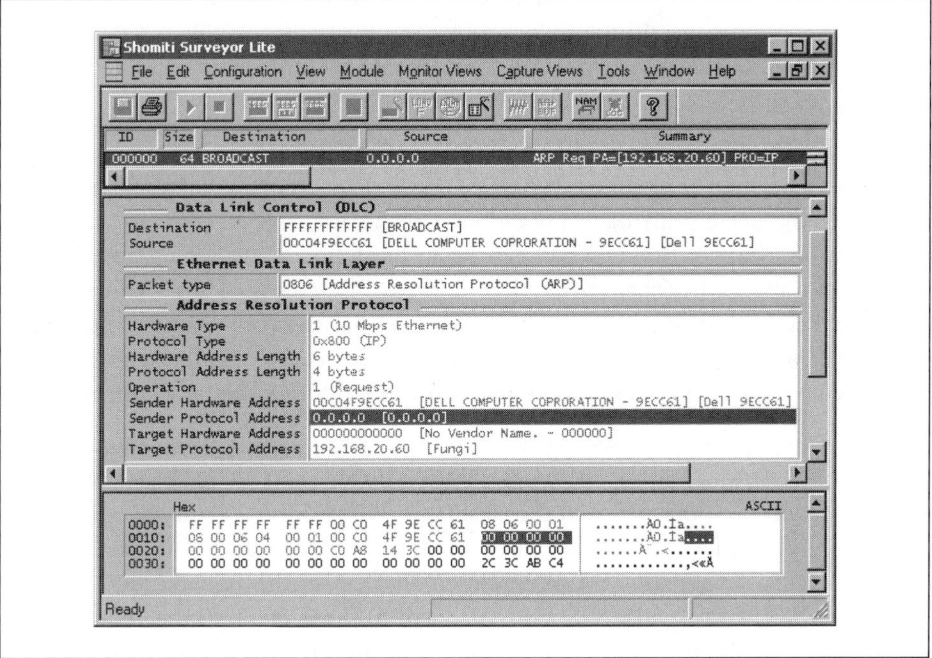

Figure 3-20. A DHCP ARP request packet

broadcasting the ARP response, other devices on the network would see the new Source Hardware Address and Source Protocol Address mapping, and update any entries in their ARP caches for that IP address, thereby preventing any other problems from occurring as a result of stale ARP entries.

However, most implementations do not broadcast an ARP response, but instead broadcast a new Gratuitous ARP. This is because many older systems do not process an ARP response that is not intended for the local machine directly. Therefore, the use of the broadcast request form that is typical of Gratuitous ARP packets is more widely accepted and offers a better chance of the intended operation succeeding.

For more information on DHCP ARP, refer to "DHCP ARP" earlier in this chapter. For more information on Gratuitous ARP, refer back to "Gratuitous ARP" also in this chapter, and refer ahead to the next section, "Notes on Gratuitous ARP" (the latter of which shows a Gratuitous ARP being issued by Fungi after the DHCP ARP shown in Figure 3-20 was sent).

Notes on Gratuitous ARP

As we discussed in "The ARP Cache" earlier in this chapter, one of the biggest problems that comes from devices that maintain hardware-to-IP address mappings in their local ARP caches for long periods of time is the fact that devices can and do change hardware or IP addresses. But the other devices will not be able to communicate with those systems until the ARP cache entries have expired or been replaced.

This process is particularly problematic for systems that act as servers for a network (perhaps sharing email or database services), since many clients may be trying to communicate with that system but will not be able to, due to stale ARP cache entries. Another problem that can occur quite frequently comes from dial-up clients who always negotiate a fixed IP address, regardless of the dial-up server they connect to. In that situation, the servers on the network may still have ARP cache entries for the last dial-up server that the user connected through, and will therefore be unable to communicate with the client through the new connection.

In both of these examples, stale ARP cache entries are causing fundamental communication problems, as the network devices try to send IP packets to the old hardware address associated with the destination IP address. Gratuitous ARP offers a solution to this problem by allowing devices to broadcast an ARP query for their own IP address. When this happens, other devices on the network will see the Source Hardware Address and Source Protocol Address fields in the request, and will update any entries for that IP address that are already in their ARP caches. Devices who do not already have a mapping in their cache will simply ignore the packet.

This concept is illustrated in Figure 3-21. In that example, Fungi is issuing a Gratuitous ARP to the local network, providing its own IP address in both the Source and Destination Protocol Address fields, as well as providing its own hardware address in the Source Hardware Address field.

Notice also that the Destination Hardware Address field contains the topology-specific broadcast address (FF:FF:FF:FF:FF:FF for DIX-Ethernet in this example), rather than the all-zeroes address that is normally used with ARP requests. This is a common feature found with implementations that use Gratuitous ARP whenever they are initialized.

Any device that sees this broadcast—and that also has a cache entry for the IP address of 192.168.20.60—updates its ARP cache to reflect the hardware address being provided in the Source Hardware Address field. Devices that do not have an entry for that IP address in their caches will simply ignore the packet.

A point worth making here is devices that have this Source Hardware Address in their ARP caches—but that do not have the Source Protocol Address in their cache—will still ignore the message. The ARP specification does not make any provisions for devices to update their ARP caches based on an existing hardware

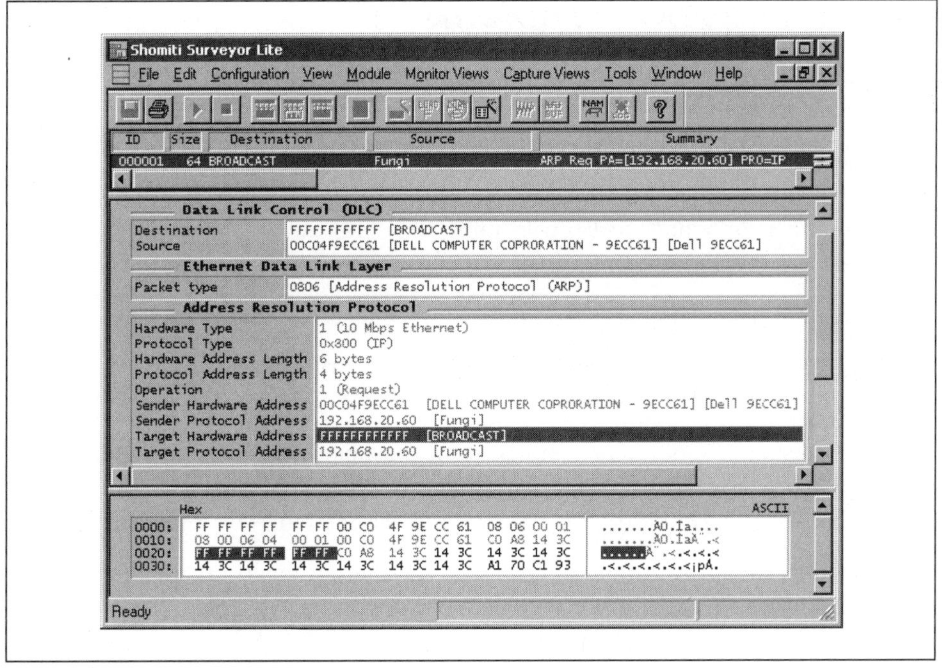

Figure 3-21. A Gratuitous ARP advertisement

address. Instead, if this device has been given a new IP address, then it is to be treated as a new entry in the ARP cache.

Although some implementations also use Gratuitous ARP broadcasts to detect addressing conflicts, this is not a particularly good idea, since it causes any existing entries in the ARP caches to be overwritten with the new data. Since the new device may be the one that is misconfigured, this updating action causes any other devices on the network that have rightfully updated their caches to have entries for the wrong device.

For this reason, devices should use the DHCP ARP mechanism for the purpose of detecting IP address conflicts, rather than using Gratuitous ARP broadcasts. Since DHCP ARP broadcasts only use 0.0.0.0 in the Source Protocol Address field, they do not cause other devices to update their ARP caches.

For more information on Gratuitous ARP, refer to "Gratuitous ARP" earlier in this chapter. For more information on DHCP ARP, refer to "DHCP ARP" and "Notes on DHCP ARP", both found earlier in this chapter (the latter of which shows Fungi issuing a DHCP ARP request in an effort to detect any other devices that are already using the IP address of 192.168.20.60).

Debugging ARP Problems

Since ARP is such a simple protocol, there aren't many problems that can crop up with it. Most of the problems that do arise are exhibited elsewhere. You probably wouldn't know that a problem was directly related to ARP unless you knew what some of the common symptoms were.

In addition, it is important to keep in mind that ARP can fail on its own, yet not appear to be an ARP-related problem. If the destination host specified in the original ARP request were down or otherwise unreachable, then it obviously would not receive (nor respond to) the original request. In such a case, the original sender would be unable to get a hardware address and would therefore be unable to send any IP packets to the destination device.

This is a substantially different concept from the host being able to send data to the recipient, even if that data is being ignored. While it may seem irrelevant (we can't send data in either case), it is an important distinction.

If a host wanted to send data to another system, then it would first have to get the hardware address. If it could not get the hardware address, then no IP data would get sent at all. Under normal circumstances, it would be able to get the hardware address although IP delivery might still fail. An application should be able to tell the difference between these two types of failures, as they may have different ramifications for the end user.

For example, if you try to use the *ping* program to test a host that is powered off, that host will not be able to respond to ARP broadcasts, and as such the local ICMP software will not be able to send an ICMP Echo Request message to the destination system. So, the ICMP software may return timeout errors to the user through the *ping* application. This is a different failure from the host taking too much time to respond, from routing errors preventing the ICMP packets from being sent or returned successfully, or from any other form of errors that may be keeping *ping* from working properly. Instead of ICMP failing (as the results might indicate), the truth would be that the sending system was the one having problems. This is a subtle but important difference, and one that should be kept in mind when diagnosing connectivity problems.

Lots of ARP Requests from Network Clients

If you have a lot of ARP requests from network clients, then you probably have too small of a cache on the client systems. Most client systems have a very small ARP cache, and will gladly flush through it on a continuous basis if you force them to connect to a multitude of servers. Either refer to your system documentation for instructions on how to increase the ARP cache, or else replace the IP software you have with something better.

Increasing the size of the ARP cache may cause other problems for the client, due to an increased demand for memory, CPU time, and other resources. Another option for you to consider is to consolidate a multitude of servers into a single large system.

Frequent flushing of cache data at the client can also result when ARP timeout values are set too low. If your clients only check email every thirty minutes, but the ARP timers expire after twenty minutes, then the clients will have to issue ARP requests every time they check their mail. On a large network with hundreds of devices per segment, this activity can generate a substantial amount of traffic. You may want to either lengthen the cache timeout values or implement a periodic Gratuitous ARP process on the servers.

Bursted Duplicate ARP Requests

Whenever a system tries to send data to a local destination system that does not have an entry in the sender's ARP table, the ARP module on the sender will try to locate the device's hardware address using an ARP query. If the sender tries to send a lot of packets to that destination system in a burst, then the ARP module may end up issuing several queries in a burst as well.

Although RFC 1122 recommends that ARP not issue duplicate lookups at a rate faster than once per second, some systems ignore this recommendation and cause each of the generated IP packets to also trigger an immediate ARP request. Some systems will wait for at least one second before issuing a subsequent ARP lookup, although those systems still may lose data as the higher-layer protocol continues to submit data faster than this.

Most ARP agents can only keep track of one lookup to any given host at a time. As such, if they receive an IP packet for a device while an ARP lookup for that device is already in progress, then the first packet in the ARP queue will get destroyed, and another lookup may get generated for the second packet. If the end-point applications are not using TCP or some other reliable protocol, then the packet will be lost forever. This situation is particularly problematic with ICMP- and UDP-based applications that generate many IP packets in a single operation. For more information on those scenarios, refer to "First Packet from ping Always Fails" in Chapter 5, *The Internet Control Message Protocol*, and "Datagrams Are Corrupted or Never Sent" in Chapter 6, *The User Datagram Protocol*.

Clients Can't Connect to Network Resources

If your DHCP clients are coming and going frequently (due to short DHCP lease timers or due to clients releasing their leases when they aren't needed), then it is likely that you will encounter connectivity problems due to old entries in other systems' ARP caches.

You may also encounter this problem with users who frequently connect and disconnect from multiple dial-in servers on the same Ethernet LAN, and who always use the same IP address regardless of the dial-in server that they connect to. Since these servers will provide Proxy ARP services to the remote users, it is highly likely that the ARP caches on the various network devices will get out-of-synch at some point.

One solution to this problem would be to cut back on your DHCP or dial-in lease activity. Essentially, this solution suggests that you try to minimize the hardware and IP address changes, and do your best to keep them synchronized for as long as possible.

Another option would be to seek out DHCP and dial-in servers that support UnARP or Gratuitous ARP. UnARP would cause the cache entries on the local devices to get flushed when the DHCP or dial-in addresses were released, while Gratuitous ARP would update any devices on the local network with the new hardware address associated with the dial-up system's IP address.

ARP Tables Are Fine, but Still No Connections

It is entirely possible that a device has responded to an ARP request packet, but that the device is not on the network. How can this be? Proxy ARP. Check to see if a device is responding to ARP requests on behalf of a non-local system.

4

Multicasting and the Internet Group Management Protocol

Summary	IP multicasting allows IP datagrams to be sent to explicit hosts on multiple networks simultaneously. This is different from traditional broadcasting in that not all hosts have to process the data, and hosts on remote networks can also receive the datagrams. The Internet Group Management Protocol provides a mechanism for IP devices to register with multicast routers, indicating the multicast groups they are interested in participating in.
Protocol ID	2
Relevant STDs	2 (*http://www.iana.org/*); 3 (includes RFCs 1122 and 1123); 5 (includes RFCs 791, 792, 919, 922, 950 and 1112)
Relevant RFCs	1112 (IP Multicasting and IGMPv1); 1122 (Host Network Requirements); 1469 (Token Ring Multicasting); 2236 (IMGP v2)
Related RFCs	1075 (Distance Vector Multicast Routing Protocol); 1256 (Router Discovery); 1584 (Multicast Extensions to OSPF); 2365 (Administratively Scoped IP Multicast); **2588** (IP Multicast and Firewalls)

When a system needs to communicate with other hosts on the local network, it typically does so either by broadcasting a packet to every host on the local network or by sending unicast datagrams to a specific destination.

Another alternative that can be used is "multicasting," a technique that lets a system send data to a group address. Any hosts that are monitoring that group address will receive the data, while every other device on the network will simply ignore it.

This model is particularly useful for applications that require a host to send data to multiple destinations simultaneously, but would be hindered by the limitations found with broadcasts.

For example, applications such as streaming audio require that a host be able to send data to multiple hosts simultaneously. While it may seem that general-purpose broadcasting can be used for these types of applications, it is not necessarily the most efficient model to use. For one thing, broadcasts are meant for *every* host on the *local* network. As such, they will not reach hosts that are on remote networks (most routers filter out broadcast traffic). But if a host on a remote network needed to receive that data, then the broadcast traffic would have to be re-broadcast to the remote network, getting sent to every host on that remote network, regardless of whether or not they wanted the traffic.

Furthermore, with broadcast traffic, every device on the local network has to monitor all of the packets and then decide if the data is needed by any local applications. If the data wasn't useful, then it still had to be processed before this fact was discovered. With bandwidth-intensive applications like network multimedia, this traffic results in every system on the network spending a large amount of computing resources examining and then discarding unwanted messages. But by using multicasts instead of broadcasts, hosts can choose which network streams they want to monitor, and higher-layer protocols will only have to process the packets they are specifically interested in. Hosts that do not want any data from a particular multicast group will not have to process anything extra.

In short, multicasts allow for broadcast-like activity, while providing explicit support for remote hosts and networks on a selective basis. This is a particularly important service with bandwidth-intensive applications like network multimedia, but also is useful for any application that requires a host be able to communicate with multiple systems simultaneously.

For example, the Router Discovery protocol (defined in RFC 1256) makes extensive use of multicasting to allow devices to automatically locate the routers on a network, and there is a draft proposal that proposes to imbue DNS clients with the ability to locate DNS servers automatically using this same model. There are even proposals for using multicast transfers with TFTP to send data to multiple hosts simultaneously, and for replicating Usenet newsfeeds to multiple servers with a single stream (instead of many large unicast transfers).

Multicasts are useful for all of these applications, allowing data to be sent to multiple systems simultaneously, rather than sending it on a point-to-point basis to each of them discreetly. In fact, anything that can benefit from a single feed to multiple, distributed destinations can benefit from IP multicasts.

The IP Multicasting and IGMP Specifications

IP multicasting is documented in RFC 1112, which is included in STD 5 (the IP standard). As such, IP multicasting is a part of STD 5, and is therefore considered to be an Internet Standard protocol. All hosts are required to implement multicasting into their IP stacks if they are to be compliant with Internet standards.

In addition to the IP multicasting services, RFC 1112 also defined IGMPv1, a follow-up to IGMPv0 (originally published in RFC 998). IGMPv2 was introduced in RFC 2236 as an update to IGMPv1, and has gained a substantial number of implementations. Some IGMP implementations only support IGMPv1 while others support IGMPv2 and v1.*

Of the differences between IGMPv1 and v2, the most notable addition in IGMPv2 was the addition of the "Leave Report" message, which allows a host to inform the network that it is no longer interested in receiving IP datagrams for a specific multicast group. This feature is required for networks that use data-link services that do not support multicasting directly (such as PPP). This chapter focuses on IGMPv2 primarily, and only mentions IGMPv1 when there is a significant difference.

RFC 2236 states that the Protocol ID for IGMP is 2. When a system receives an IP datagram that is marked as containing Protocol 2, it should pass the contents of the datagram to IGMP for further processing. However, note that IGMP is not a transport protocol and is not used for the delivery of multicast *data*. Rather, IGMP is a control protocol like ICMP, useful for informing devices of network events and changes.

It is also important to note that although all hosts are required to implement IP multicasting, they are not required to implement IGMP. If they do not implement IGMP, however, then they cannot tell local multicast routers that they wish to receive multicast packets. Although a host can send any data it wants to a multicast group IP address, hosts can only receive multicast data reliably if they implement IGMP. Most of the multicast-aware systems in use today implement IGMP, as well as the basic support for multicast services.

The default Time-to-Live value for IP datagrams sent to a multicast address is "1 hop", unless the sending application explicitly specifies a larger value. Also, it should be noted that IGMP messages are only meant to be received and processed by devices on the local network, and as such the Time-to-Live value for IP datagrams that contain IGMP messages should always be "1 hop". Although multicast data can be sent across router lines, IGMP messages should never be forwarded.

---

* IGMP stands for Internet Group Management Protocol.

An Introduction to IP Multicasting

In essence, IP multicasting is a function of the IP address in use by a particular "multicast group." If a user wants to send an audio presentation to a variety of distributed hosts simultaneously, then that user would send the data to an IP address that was associated with a particular multicast group. Any hosts that were listening for traffic destined for that IP address would then receive the data and process it accordingly, while other hosts would simply ignore it.

The application protocol used for such a feed could be a RealAudio stream sent as a bunch of UDP messages over IP. These messages would not look any different from the same data being sent to a single destination system or to the local broadcast address. The only difference between the multicast datagrams and their unicast or broadcast equivalents would be the destination IP address in use with those datagrams: the unicasts would point to a specific destination system, the broadcasts would point to all hosts on the local network, and the multicasts would point to a group address.

In the IP world, multicast group addresses are known as Class D addresses and include all of the IP addresses in the range of 224.0.0.0 through 239.255.255.255. Each of the individual addresses in this range refer to specific multicast groups, many of which are associated with a specific application or service.

There are a number of predefined, reserved addresses that are registered with the Internet Assigned Numbers Authority (IANA). For example, all of the addresses in the range of 224.0.0.0 through 224.0.0.255 are reserved for use with routing protocols and other low-level, infrastructure-related services. Some of the more common registered addresses are shown in Table 4-1. For a detailed listing of all of the multicast groups that are currently registered, refer to the IANA's online registry (accessible on the Web at *http://www.isi.edu/in-notes/iana/assignments/multicast-addresses*).

Table 4-1. Some Common Multicast Group Addresses

Multicast Address	Description
224.0.0.1	All local multicast hosts (including routers). Never forwarded.
224.0.0.2	All local multicast routers. Never forwarded.
224.0.0.4	DVMRP routers. Never forwarded.
224.0.1.1	Network Time Protocol.
224.0.1.24	Microsoft's Windows Internet Name Service locator service.

Besides the reserved addresses that are managed by the IANA, there are also "unreserved" addresses that can be used by any application for any purpose, although conflicts may occur with other users who are also using those multicast addresses. Any group address that is frequently used is encouraged to register with the IANA.

Any host can send data to a multicast group address simply by providing the multicast group address in the destination field of the IP datagram. Any hosts that are listening for traffic sent to that group address will pick up the data.

If an application wishes to participate in a local multicast group as a listener, all it has to do is inform the local system's IP stack and network adapter of the group address to be monitored. If this step is not performed, then the system will likely ignore traffic going to the multicast group addresses of the applications in use. By registering with the local interface, any data sent to the multicast address in use by the application will get picked up and monitored by the local system and then get delivered to the local application for processing. The following section, "Local Multicasting", describes this process in detail.

If an application wishes to participate in a distributed multicast group across a router, then the application must still perform the local registration tasks described above, but it must also register its desire to receive traffic for that group address with any local multicast routers. This step is required before multicast routers will forward any remote multicast datagrams for that group address onto the local network. "Distributed Multicasting" later in this chapter describes multicasting over multiple networks in detail, while "Managing Group Memberships", also later, describes the registration process.

Local Multicasting

Remember that IP datagrams (and IP addresses) are used only to represent a consistent view between IP-enabled devices, and that when two devices on the same local network want to communicate with each other they will use the topology-specific protocols and addresses defined for the local network medium to actually exchange data. For example, two hosts on the same local Ethernet segment will use Ethernet framing and addressing mechanisms when they want to exchange IP data, with the IP packets being passed in the Ethernet frames. Meanwhile, hosts on Token Ring networks will use the protocols and addressing mechanisms specified in the Token Ring standards when they want to exchange data.

These same rules apply with multicast traffic, which must also use the low-level protocols and addressing rules defined for whatever medium is in use with the local network. When multicast IP packets are being passed around the network, they are really being sent in a form that uses the multicasting services that are provided by the underlying network topology.

Most shared-medium networks provide three distinct types of addressing:

Unicast

Unicast data is sent from one device to another, using an explicit destination address. Devices on the network must monitor the network traffic, looking for any frames that are marked for their local hardware address. With Ethernet, this is a 48-bit address typically written in hexadecimal notation as something like c0:14:3d:22:1e:04.

Broadcast

Broadcast data is sent from one device to every other device on the local network, using a broadcast address specific to the network topology. Devices on the network must monitor the network traffic and read any frame that is marked for the broadcast address. With Ethernet, the 48-bit broadcast address is "all on," typically being written in hexadecimal notation as ff:ff:ff:ff:ff:ff.

Multicast

Multicast data is sent from one device to a specific multicast group address. Devices on the network choose which multicast groups they want to participate in, and then monitor the network traffic, looking for any frames that are destined for one of those multicast groups (ignoring any other frames that are going to any other multicast group addresses). Ethernet offers a variety of multicast group addresses, ranging from 01:00:5e:00:00:00 to 01:00:5e:7f:ff:ff.

In order for IP multicast traffic to be sent to multiple hosts simultaneously, the IP multicast addresses must be mapped to the multicast addresses in use by the local network, and the local IP stack must inform the local network adapter of the multicast groups that the adapter should be listening for. Unless the hardware is listening for traffic sent to the hardware-specific multicast addresses, the IP software (and thus UDP and the application-layer protocols) will never get the IP packets.

Some conversion is usually required in the process of mapping multicast IP addresses to multicast hardware addresses. For example, the range of available Ethernet multicast addresses only provides 23 of the 48 available bits for defining specific multicast group addresses, although IP uses 26 bits from the 32-bit Class D address block to identify specific multicast groups. Therefore, to map IP multicast addresses onto Ethernet multicast addresses, the last 23 bits from the IP multicast address are mapped onto the 23 bits available for the Ethernet multicast address.

For example, Figure 4-1 shows a multicast packet bound for 224.0.0.1 being sent to the Ethernet group address of 01:00:5e:00:00:01. The last 23 bits of the IP address (0000000 00000000 00000001) have simply been copied to the Ethernet group address block of 01:00:5e:00:00:00.

This mapping results in some overlap, with some multicast groups sharing a single Ethernet multicast address. In this case, the IP software on the destination

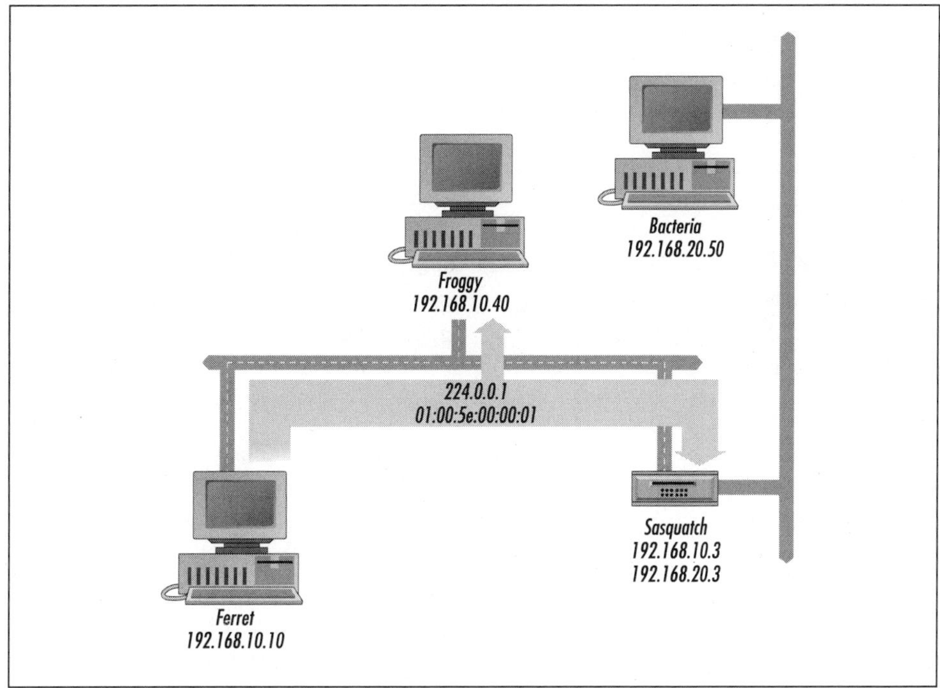

Figure 4-1. Mapping Ethernet addresses to Class D IP addresses

systems must perform some filtering, discarding any IP packets that are destined for a multicast group address (as specified in the IP header) that the device does not want. For example, if the network adapter is monitoring for Ethernet-specific multicast addresses that fall within the duplicate range, then the IP software in use on the listening host must also examine the destination IP address shown in the IP datagram before handing the data to the specified transport protocol for subsequent processing.

Although this presents a challenge for users on Ethernet networks, some topologies have even greater degrees of overlap, and require much greater levels of filtering. For example, Token Ring networks have a limited number of group addresses available to them, so *all* Token Ring multicasts must share the same group address of c0:00:00:04:00:00.

Some networks don't provide any form of group address at all, and are strictly limited to unicast and broadcast frames. On those networks, the topology-specific broadcast address must be used for all multicast data, requiring that hosts filter through all broadcast packets. Note that some point-to-point networks don't even have broadcast addresses. Instead, they have only "send" and "receive" wires. On those networks, multicast routers must use topology-specific unicast frames to deliver data to the destination systems.

Some switches offer an intelligent multicast filtering mechanism, whereby they can interpret an IP multicast request and apply a filter on the switch port for that device, effectively limiting the multicast traffic sent to the device according to the multicast IP addresses that the device has sent out.

Regardless of these issues, the important thing to remember is that IP multicasts use the addressing and delivery mechanisms offered by the underlying network topology, just as every other type of IP packet does. Some network topologies provide better mapping services than others, but almost all of the widely used LAN topologies allow for multicasts using some form of explicit group addressing.

When an application on a host wishes to begin receiving multicast packets, it must inform the local network adapter that it should begin accepting network packets for the specific multicast group (if that service is available, as it is on Ethernet). If a host is directly attached to multiple networks, it may register with any of the network interfaces explicitly, or it may register with all supported interfaces simultaneously. Applications have to explicitly state which networks they want to monitor. Typically, hosts with multiple interfaces will have a "default" multicast interface that they use for reading and writing multicast traffic.

Sometimes this registration occurs at the same time as the network-wide IGMP registration process, and sometimes it occurs just before the IGMP registration process, as a precondition of the IGMP registration request. This is an implementation-specific issue. The important thing to remember is that registering with the network adapter(s) on the local system and registering with the local multicast routers (via IGMP messages) are two separate and distinct acts.

Distributed Multicasting

One of the big differences between IP multicasts and IP broadcasts is that multicast datagrams can be sent to remote networks, while broadcasts are normally restricted to the local network. By being able to forward multicast feeds across network boundaries, multicast routers can get multicast datagrams to hosts around the world, allowing the hosts to participate in global multicasting groups, with multicast datagrams going to every network that has a host that is participating in that particular multicast group.

This process is achieved by using multicasting routers that are particularly aware of multicast traffic and the routing issues associated with that type of traffic. This model involves a couple of theories that are somewhat different from traditional routing.

For one thing, the local multicast router must be listening for multicast packets. The router has to actively monitor the network for IP traffic that has a destination address of 224.0.0.1 through 239.255.255.255, and then forward that data on to any other multicast-enabled network segments that are attached to the router (or any tunnels to remote multicast networks that may be configured). Traditional routers do not monitor the network looking for packets that need to be forwarded, but instead wait for data that needs to be sent to the router (for forwarding) explicitly.

Also, since the destination address is a multicast address and not a unicast address, the multicast router has to forward any multicast data that it sees to every other network segment attached to the multicast router. In addition, since not every network is multicast-enabled (i.e., does not have a multicast router on it), many networks are bridged together using multicast "tunnels," whereby multicast traffic is sent as unicast datagrams to another multicast router at the far end of the tunnel. Regardless of how the networks are connected, the model is the same: multicast routers send multicast data to the other multicast-enabled networks that they know of, and any multicast routers on those networks will pick up the frames and forward the data to any other multicast-enabled networks that they are attached to.

This allows hosts on remote networks to receive locally generated multicast data, and vice versa. And since any additional multicast routers on those networks will see and forward any multicast data that comes onto their network, they will also forward the data on to any other multicast-enabled network segments that they are attached to. This allows the data to be propagated across the entire Internet.

For example, Figure 4-2 shows an IP packet being sent from Ferret to the multicast address of 224.1.2.3. If any remote hosts (such as Fungi) want to monitor that group address, then Sasquatch has to monitor the network on its behalf, pick up any matching data, and then explicitly forward the packets out to the other segments (where they would eventually be received by Fungi).

There are some special considerations with this model that must be followed in order for everything to work smoothly. Otherwise, simply propagating multicasts across the different networks could result in them becoming saturated with unwanted data.

Limited forwarding

The primary rule that multicast routers follow is that they will only forward multicast traffic to the networks that have expressed an interest in that specific type of data. For example, Figure 4-2 shows two subnets. When Ferret sends a multicast datagram to the 224.1.2.3 group address, Sasquatch has to forward the datagram to the 192.168.20.0 network in order for Fungi to receive it. However, Sasquatch will only do this if Fungi has explicitly stated that it was interested in data for the 224. 1.2.3 multicast group.

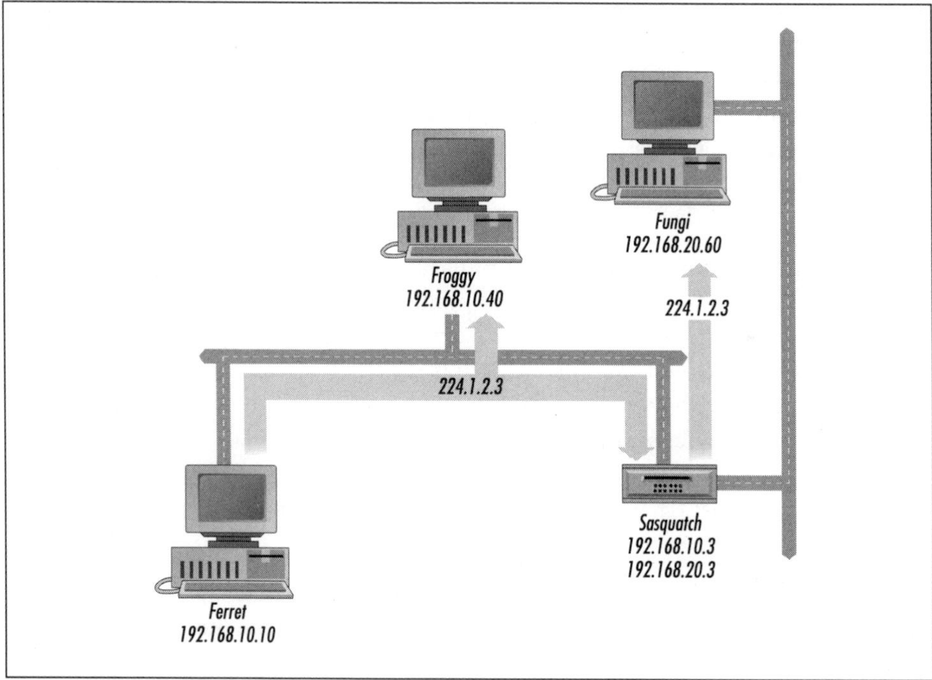

Figure 4-2. Routing in a multicast environment

This "statement of interest" is achieved by using IGMP messages, which are sent by the hosts when they first come onto the network, and which are also sent in response to IGMP queries issued by local multicast routers. There are lots of rules and conditions that are involved with this scenario which are discussed in more detail in "Managing Group Memberships" later in this chapter. However, the basis of the protocol is that hosts announce which multicast groups they want to listen to, and routers use this information to determine which networks they will forward data to. In essence, a multicast router will only forward multicast data to a network if there is an active listener for that group address on that network.

In addition, multicast routers must also forward any group registration information they have to all other multicast routers that they know about. This procedure ensures that other routers know to send multicast data to their networks. Otherwise, upstream routers would not send any data for that multicast group address down to the local network. Note that this process is handled by different multicast routing protocols in different ways, but that they all do the same basic thing: informing other networks of the groups that this particular network wants to receive traffic for.

Time-to-Live considerations

Blindly forwarding multicast data around the Internet could cause significant utilization problems. For this reason, another important aspect of wide-area multicasting is the Time-to-Live value of the multicast IP datagram. As was discussed in Chapter 2, *The Internet Protocol*, the IP datagram's Time-to-Live header field dictates the maximum number of hops that a datagram can take before it must be discarded. Since all multicast datagrams are sent using IP, this field is also used with multicast datagrams, and is also used by multicast routers to keep traffic from propagating across too many multicast routers.

Multicast group addresses in the range of 224.0.0.0 through 224.0.0.255 are reserved for administrative use only, and as such are restricted to the local network. Any data sent to those addresses must have a Time-to-Live setting of 1 in order to keep those messages from being forwarded across multicast routers. RFC 2236 goes so far as to state that even if the Time-to-Live is not set to 1 on those datagrams, they still should not be forwarded.

For example, the all-hosts group address of 224.0.0.1 refers to all of the multicast-aware devices on the local network. Whenever a multicast router wants to locate the active multicast groups in use on the local network, it will send an IGMP query to the 224.0.0.1 group address. In addition, the multicast router must set the Time-to-Live value of that query to 1, preventing any other multicast routers on the local network from forwarding the query to any other networks they may be attached to.

In addition to these considerations, it is also important to note that ICMP errors must not be generated in response to IGMP or multicast datagrams, as that could result in many ICMP messages getting sent for every multicast or IGMP packet. Therefore, if a multicast router sees an IGMP message with the Time-to-Live value set to 1 (normally meaning that the datagram is about to expire and cannot be forwarded), then the ICMP software on that router must not return an ICMP Time Exceeded error message. Instead, the datagram should just be discarded silently. For more information on ICMP, refer to Chapter 5, *The Internet Control Message Protocol*.

Managing Group Memberships

Although any host can send traffic to a multicast group, applications that want to participate in a distributed multicast group as listeners must inform the local multicast routers of the groups that they want to listen for. This is done using IGMP messages that state the multicast group address that the host wants to participate in.

In addition, multicast routers also use IGMP messages to query the local network for hosts that have active memberships in multicast groups that are being routed to the local network. This is basically the entire function of IGMP: routers asking for hosts that are listening for multicast traffic, and hosts telling routers which groups they are listening for.

All IGMP messages have certain requirements. First of all, they must all have the Time-to-Live value of the IP datagram set to "1 hop", thereby preventing them from being forwarded by any routers. In addition, RFC 2236 states that all IGMP messages should set the IP datagram to use the IP Router Alert Option, as discussed in "Router Alert" in Chapter 2.

Membership reports

The process of registering with a router is very straightforward. Whenever an application that needs to participate in a specific multicast group is started, an IGMP "Membership Report" is sent by the host to the multicast address in use by the application. RFC 2236 states that multicast hosts should resend the first Membership Report within a few moments, in case the first one was lost or damaged.

For example, servers running the multicast-enabled Simple Network Time Protocol (SNTP) can use the multicast group address of 224.0.1.1 to automatically pass time-synchronization data across the network to SNTP-enabled clients. Whenever an SNTP system is started, it will immediately send a couple of IGMP Membership Reports to the 224.0.1.1 multicast address, as illustrated in Figure 4-3. Any multicast routers on the local network will see this report, and use this information when building their multicast-forwarding maps.

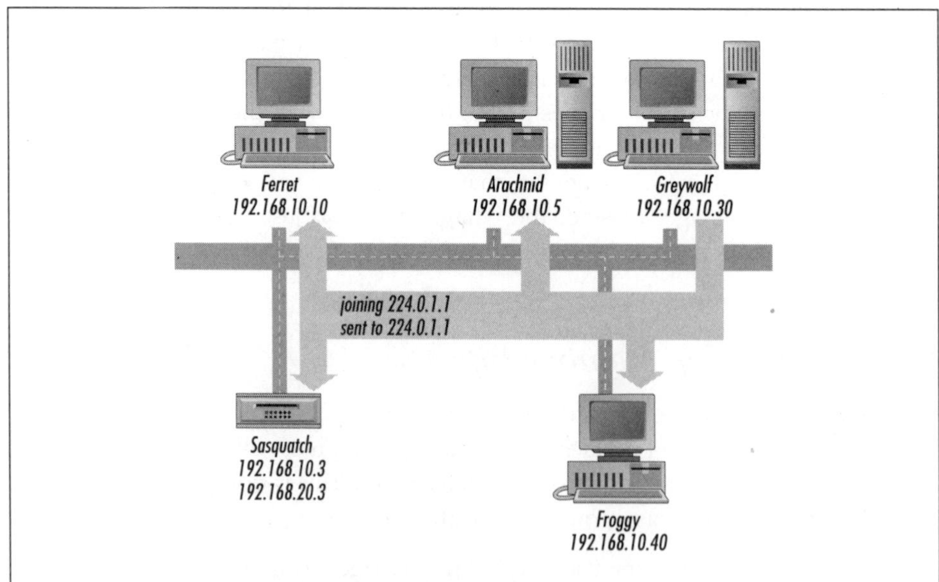

Figure 4-3. An SNTP-enabled system announcing its presence to the network

Membership Reports are also sent in response to IGMP Membership Queries, which are periodically sent by multicast routers on the local network in order to determine which multicast groups still have active memberships. Whenever a query is received, at least one host from each multicast group on the local network must respond with a Membership Report. This procedure is described in more detail in "Membership queries" later in this chapter.

Note that Membership Reports are never generated for the "all-hosts" group address of 224.0.0.1. Although every multicast-enabled host should listen for traffic on that multicast address, no host should ever report its membership in that group.

Leave reports

Another announcement mechanism that is commonly seen with many multicast applications is the "Leave Report," used to announce that a particular host is no longer interested in receiving multicast traffic for a particular group. The idea behind this report is that it can be used to inform a local multicast router that the host is going away, and that the router can stop forwarding multicast data for the specified group address to this network.

There are some special considerations with this type of report. For one thing, the router has to verify that the host that is leaving the multicast group is indeed the last user of the specified group address, otherwise any other hosts on the local network that still wanted to receive traffic for that group wouldn't get it any more. This is achieved through the use of a group-specific query message (as we'll discuss in the next section, "Membership queries"). If no hosts respond to the group-specific query, the router can stop forwarding traffic for that group's multicast address immediately, thereby reducing the local bandwidth consumption.

Furthermore, Leave Reports were introduced in the IGMPv2 specification, and were not a part of the IGMPv1 specification. As such, they will only be used on systems that use IGMPv2, and will be ignored by systems that are using IGMPv1.

It is important to note that Leave Reports are not sent to the multicast address of the group being left as are Membership Reports, but instead are sent to the "all-routers" group address of 224.0.0.2, which is similar to the "all-hosts" address, except that it is only monitored by multicast routers.

Figure 4-4 shows the NTP client from Figure 4-3 announcing that it is leaving the network. In the example network shown, only Sasquatch should receive the Leave Report, since it is the only multicast router on the network.

Devices that do not understand Leave Report messages should silently discard them, as they should all other unknown message types.

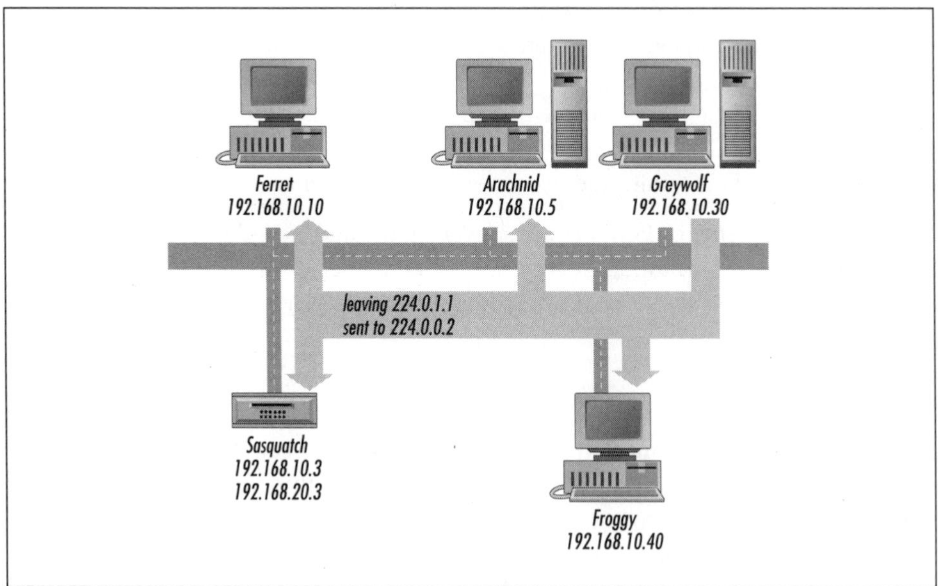

Figure 4-4. An SNTP-enabled system announcing its departure from the network

Membership queries

Another commonly seen IGMP message is the "Membership Query." Queries are sent by multicast routers in order to verify that each of the multicast groups that are currently being forwarded still have listening members on the local network (by default, the interval between queries is 125 seconds). If no hosts respond to a Membership Query, then the router can stop forwarding multicast datagrams for any of the multicast groups that no longer have any active listeners on that network.

Typically, only one multicast router issues these queries. Any other multicast routers on the network then takes a passive role, watching for Membership Reports, but not sending any queries. The "query router" is elected by having the lowest-numbered IP address. If that router stops issuing queries, then the multicast router with the next-higher IP address will become the query router.

Hosts respond to Membership Queries with standard Membership Reports, and the multicast routers use this information to determine which multicast addresses should be forwarded to the local network. If no hosts respond for a multicast address that is already being forwarded, then the multicast router can assume that nobody wants that traffic anymore and can stop forwarding remote datagrams for that multicast address to this network.

Membership Queries are sent to the "all-hosts" address of 224.0.0.1. With IGMPv2, routers are also allowed to send group-specific queries to test for membership in a particular group, if this is needed for some reason. Regardless of the query type, the hosts on the network will respond to the Multicast Query by sending their Membership Reports to the multicast addresses in use by their local applications, just like always. Multicast routers are required to listen for data on every multicast address, so they will see all of the responses.

Figure 4-5 shows an IGMP Membership Query being sent to the "all-hosts" group address of 224.0.0.1. The IGMP messages that are generated in response to the query would be simple Membership Reports—sent to the multicast addresses in use by the applications on those hosts—as shown back in Figure 4-3.

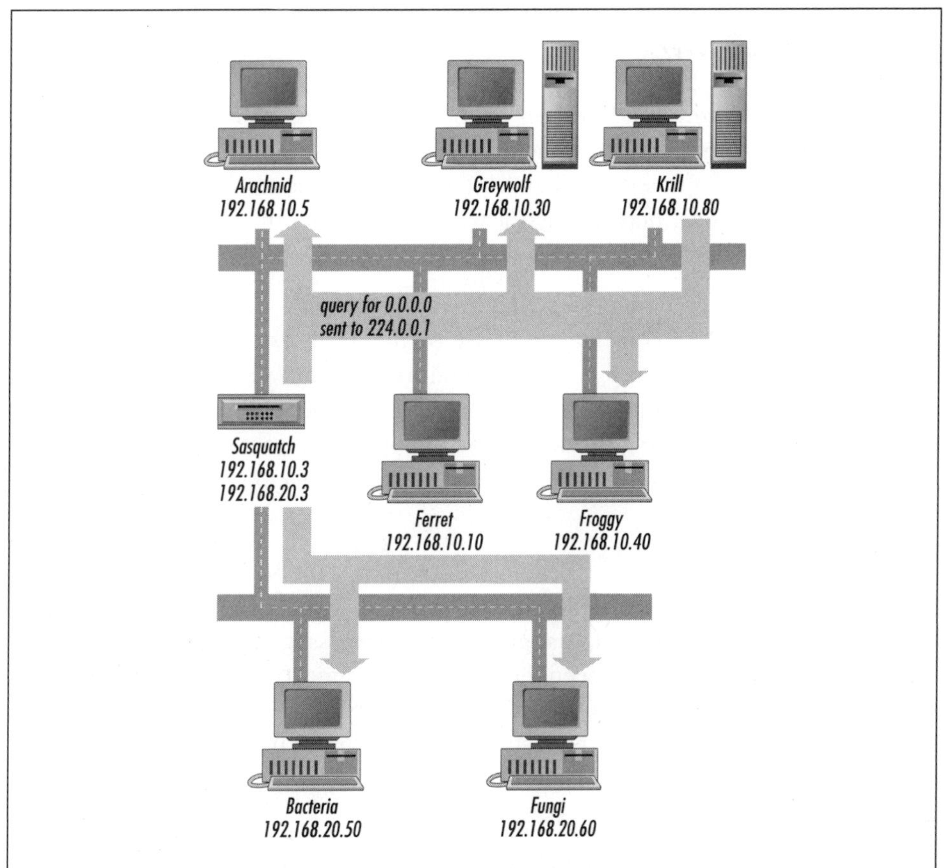

Figure 4-5. An overview of the membership-sampling process

Keep in mind that the purpose of the Membership Query is to locate *any* hosts that are actively listening for a specific group, and is not intended to locate *every* host that may be listening. Since multicast routers only need to know that at least one host is listening for specific multicast addresses, they do not benefit from multiple hosts responding for a single multicast address.

For this reason, hosts incorporate a random length timer that they use before responding to a Membership Query. If no other hosts have responded on behalf of the multicast groups in use on this host before the timer expires, then the host will issue a response. Any other hosts that have not yet responded for that group will then abort their own responses. However, it should be noted that this procedure is conducted on a per-group basis: if a host aborts a response for a group because some other host has already responded to the Membership Query, then it does not abort all of the pending responses; instead it will only abort responses for the groups that have already been responded to by the other hosts.

IGMP Messages

Before a host can receive and process multicast datagrams, it has to do two things: it must inform the local network interface card that it wishes to accept and process network frames for specific multicast groups, and it must inform any multicast routers on the local network that it wishes to receive the IP packets for those multicast groups as well.

How the application communicates with the local network interface card is a function of the specific IP implementation in use on the local system (the process is discussed earlier in this chapter in "Local Multicasting"). However, the mechanisms used by IP to inform the multicast routers on the local network of its desire to participate in certain multicast groups is a function of the Internet Group Management Protocol (this process is discussed earlier in "Managing Group Memberships").

IGM Message Headers

IGMP messages consist of a predefined set of fields that indicate the type of message being passed and the multicast group that the message applies to. Each "message type" is used in specific scenarios and is indicated by a field in the header. Depending on the version of IGMP in use and the type of message being sent, an IGMP message will have four or five fields, with different fields being used for the different versions of IGMP.

Table 4-2 lists all of the fields in IGMPv1 messages, along with their size (in bits) and some usage notes. For more information on these fields, refer to the individual discussions throughout this section.

Table 4-2. The Fields in an IGMPv1 Message

Field	Bits	Description
Version	4	Indicates the version of IGMP in use (always 1).
Message Type	4	Indicates the message type (such as "query" or "report").

Table 4-2. The Fields in an IGMPv1 Message (continued)

Field	Bits	Description
Unused	8	This field is unused with IGMPv1 query messages, and must be filled with zeroes.
Checksum	16	Used to store a checksum of the IGMP message.
Multicast Group	32	The 32-bit IP address of the multicast group that this message is associated with.

Table 4-3 lists all of the fields in IGMPv2 messages, along with their size (in bits) and some usage notes. For more information on these fields, refer to the individual discussions throughout this section.

Table 4-3. The Fields in an IGMPv2 Message

Field	Bits	Description
Message Type	8	Indicates the message type (such as "query" or "report"), and also uses some bits to indicate the version of the message.
Max Response Time	8	Indicates the longest period of time that a host should wait before responding to a query. This field is only used with IGMPv2 query messages, and is unused with IGMPv1 messages.
Checksum	16	Used to store a checksum of the IGMP message.
Multicast Group	32	The 32-bit IP address of the multicast group that this message is associated with.

Note that the size and use of the fields are such that IGMPv2 messages are almost identical to IGMPv1 messages. The only real differences between the two versions is that IGMPv2 messages have subsumed the Version field into the Message Type field, and that the IGMPv1 "Unused" field is now the IGMPv2 Maximum Response Time field.

The total length of a "normal" IGMP message is eight bytes. However, other IGMP messages may be longer, particularly with messages that are specifically used with multicast routing protocols and the like. If the Message Type is recognized as being one of the core messages, IGMPv2 implementation must ignore any additional data after the first eight bytes (although the checksum will be for the entire message, and not just the first eight bytes).

All IGMP messages are sent within IP datagrams directly. Each of these datagrams must have a protocol identifier of 2 and an IP Time-to-Live value of "1 hop". In addition, all IGMPv2 messages should use the Router Alert Option in the header of the IP datagram according to RFC 2236, although many implementations do not follow this suggestion.

Figure 4-6 shows an IGMPv2 Membership Query message, which will be used to dissect the headers of the IGMP Message. Note that this IP packet does not have

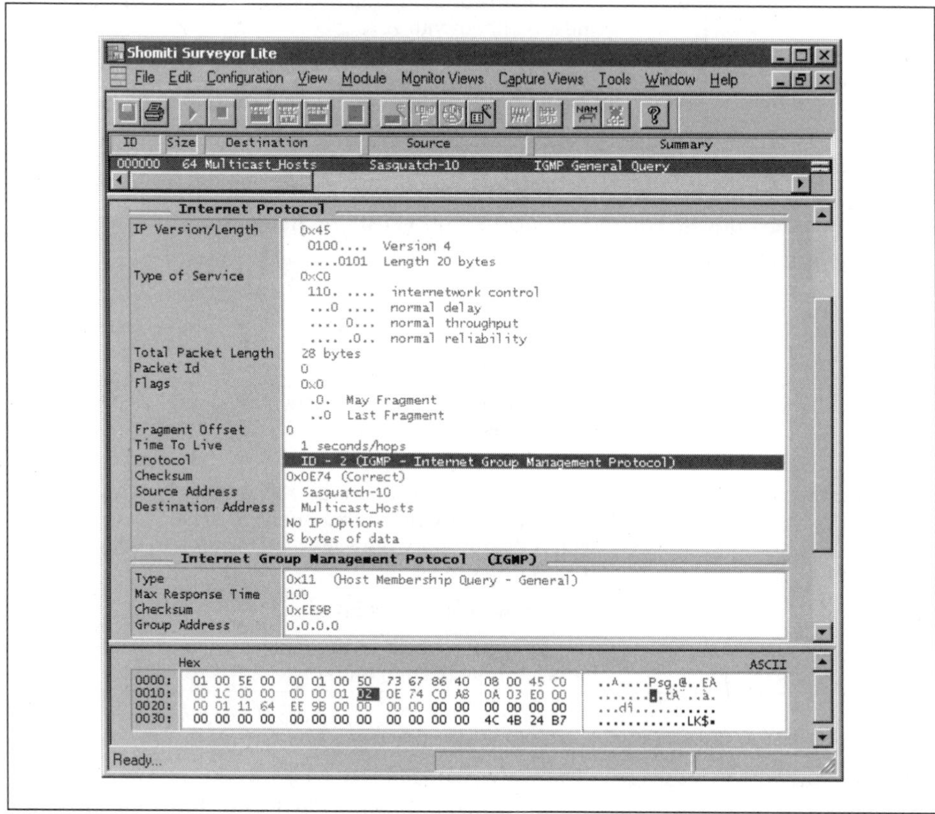

Figure 4-6. A simple IGMP Message

the Router Alert Option, as suggested by RFC 2236 for IGMPv2 messages.

The following sections discuss the header fields in detail.

Version

With IGMPv1 messages, indicates the version of IGMP in use. However, IGMPv2 subsumed this field into the Message Type field, although IGMPv2 messages still set these four bits to 1.

Size

Four bits.

Default Value

1

Defined In

RFCs 1112 and 2236.

Notes

With IGMPv2, this field has been subsumed into the Message Type field, although it is still used to report version information in some cases. In all cases, this field should report a version number of 1, allowing older multicast routers to process the data. If this field reported 2, then IGMPv1 multicast routers would ignore the messages.

Capture Sample

In the capture shown in Figure 4-7, the Version field (i.e., the most significant four bits of the Type field) is set to 1, although the Message Type field shows that this is an IGMPv2 message. All of the messages currently defined for IGMPv2 use 1 in the four-bit version field.

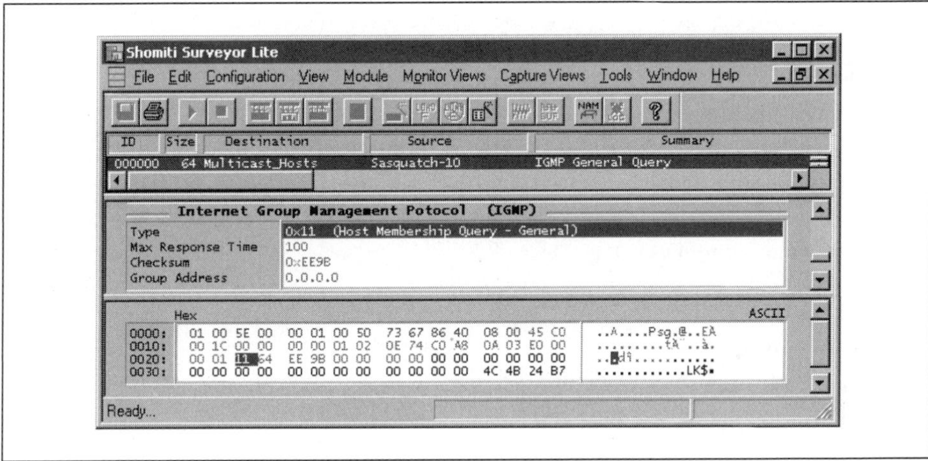

Figure 4-7. The Version field

See Also

"Message Type"

Message Type

Specifies the specific type of message being sent (such as "query" or "report").

Size

Four bits.

Default Value

N/A

Defined In

RFCs 1112 and 2236.

Notes

Each IGMP message is identified by a four-bit numeric code that maps against a specific type of service. There are a variety of message types provided in IGMPv1 and IGMPv2. Table 4-4 lists the different message types, their codes, and descriptions for their use.

Table 4-4. IGMP Message Types and Their Meanings

Code	Message Type	Description
1	Membership Query	Used by IGMPv1 and IGMPv2 multicast routers to locate the multicast groups in use by hosts on the local network.
2	v1 Membership Report	Identifies this message as an IGMPv1 Membership Report.
6	v2 Membership Report	Identifies this message as an IGMPv2 Membership Report.
7	v2 Leave Report	Used by IGMPv2 hosts to announce that they are leaving a multicast group.

Although all of the IGMP messages that are described in RFC 1112 and RFC 2236 use 1 in the version field, each of them use different codes for the message types that are generated by the Membership Reports. For example, Figure 4-8 shows an IGMP Membership Query (identifiable by the Message Type being set to 1).

Unrecognized message types should be silently ignored.

Capture Sample

In the capture shown in Figure 4-8, the Message Type field is set to 1, indicating that this message is an IGMPv2 Membership Query.

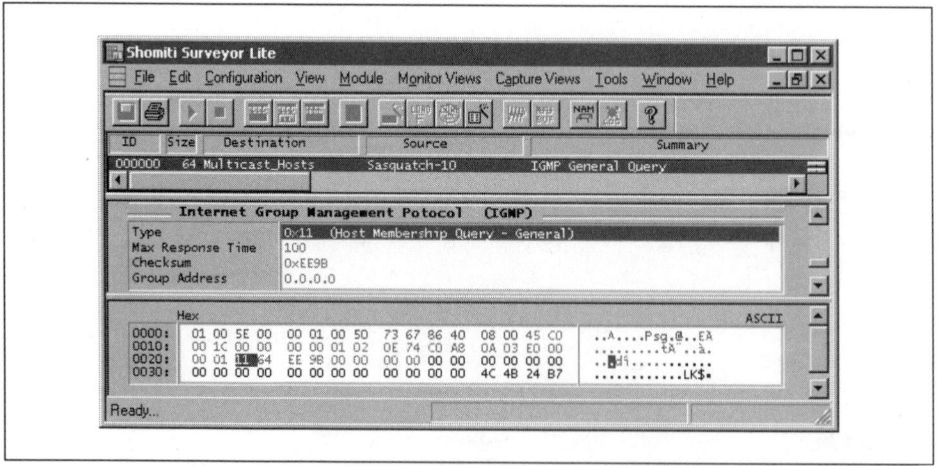

Figure 4-8. The Message Type field

See Also

"Managing Group Memberships"

"IGMP Message Types"

"Version"

"Maximum Response Time"

"Multicast Group"

Maximum Response Time

Identifies the maximum amount of time that a host may wait before responding to an IGMPv2 Membership Query, in tenths of a second. This field is not used with IGMPv1 messages or IGMPv2 Membership Reports.

Size

Eight bits.

Default Value

0

Defined In

RFC 2236.

Notes

This field is almost always set to 0, either because it is unused with IGMPv2 Membership Reports and Leave Reports, or because it originated from an IGMPv1 system.

If the message is an IGMPv2 Membership Query, the value specified in this field is used to inform hosts on a network how much time (in tenths of a second) they have before they must respond. This is useful in situations where hosts are waiting for each other to respond (a process described earlier in "Membership queries"). By providing a maximum response time value, hosts will be forced to choose a random value within the given amount of time.

If the message is an IGMPv1 Membership Query, this value should be set to 0. In that case, IGMPv2 hosts should interpret the 0 to be 100 (or "10 seconds"), and respond within that time frame. Membership Report messages should set this field to 0, since it has no meaning for those messages.

IGMPv1 hosts will ignore this value, if it's defined in a Membership Query.

Capture Sample

In the capture shown in Figure 4-9, the Maximum Response Time field is 100, which is equal to ten seconds.

See Also

"Managing Group Memberships"

"Message Type"

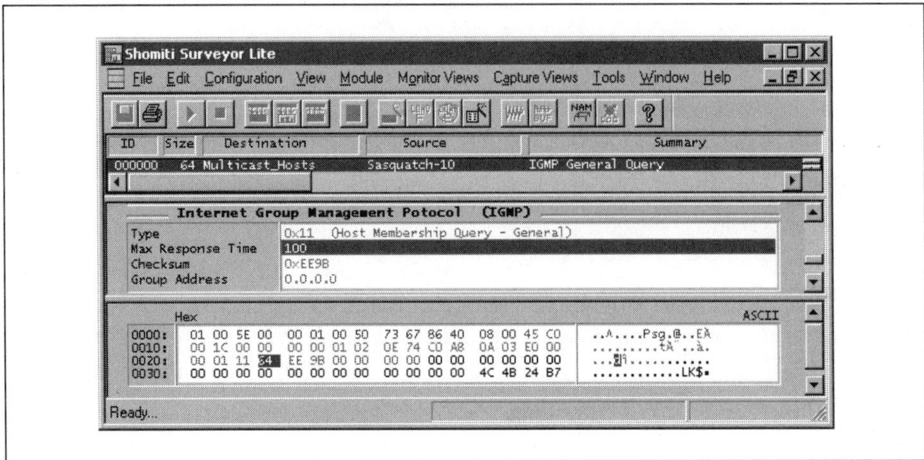

Figure 4-9. The Maximum Response Time field

Checksum

Used to store a checksum of the IGMP message, allowing destination systems to validate the contents of the message and test for possible corruption.

Size

Sixteen bits.

Default Value

N/A

Defined In

RFCs 1112 and 2236.

Notes

The checksum field provides a simple validation scheme for IGMP messages. When calculating the checksum, the sending system looks at the entire message (with the Checksum field set to 0) and performs a simple checksum operation. This procedure is reversed by all recipients before the contents of the message are processed.

Note that the checksum applies to the entire message, even if the message is more than eight bytes long (longer messages may be a result of future versions or external protocols). As long as the Message Type is recognized as an IGMP "core" message, then the segment should be accepted and only the first eight bytes should be processed. However, the checksum value will apply to the entire message, and it is not limited to the first eight bytes of the message.

Also note that the Multicast Group field provides some additional sanity checking, allowing the recipient to verify that the IP datagram's destination multicast address is the same as that used in the Multicast Group field.

- 7-layer decode.

Capture Sample

In the capture shown in Figure 4-10, the Checksum is shown as "ee 9b".

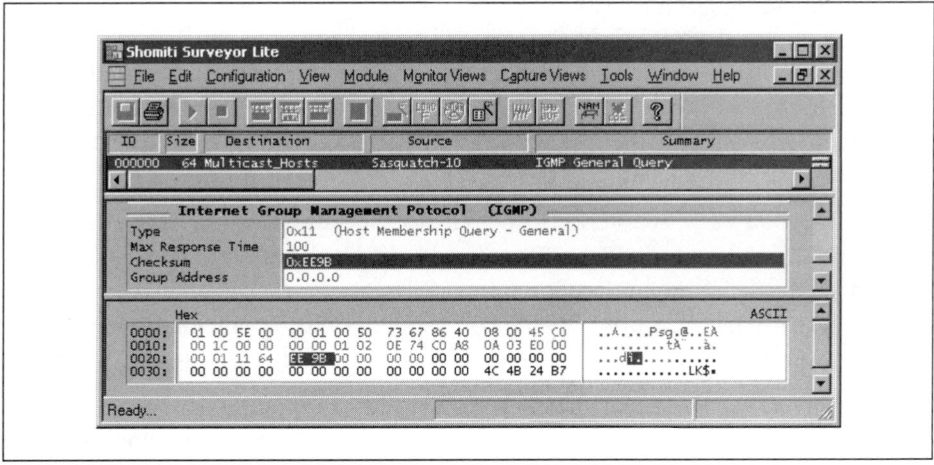

Figure 4-10. The Checksum field

See Also

"Message Type"

"Multicast Group"

Multicast Group

Specifies the multicast group address that this message applies to.

Size

Thirty-two bits.

Default Value

The destination multicast address specified in the IP header, or "0.0.0.0".

Defined In

RFCs 1112 and 2236.

Notes

Membership Queries and reports are not always sent to the multicast group address to which they pertain. Sometimes they are sent to a different address. Therefore, the contents of this field will vary, depending upon the type of message being sent.

IGMPv1 and IGMPv2 "general" queries are sent to the "all-hosts" group address of 224.0.0.1, and the Multicast Group field is set to 0.0.0.0, indicating that the query is for all groups. Group-specific queries (which are normally sent in response to a Leave Report) are also sent to the "all-hosts" address, although the Multicast Group field will be set to the IP address of the specific multicast group being queried.

Membership Reports sent by hosts on the network are sent to the IP address of the multicast group they are joining or reporting, and the Multicast Group field is set to the same multicast group address. This provides an additional validation service to the multicast routers and hosts on the network; if the destination address and the Multicast Group fields do not match, the datagram can be discarded as simply being erroneous.

Finally, IGMPv2 Leave Reports are sent to the "all-routers" group address of 224.0.0.2, while the Multicast Group field shows the IP address of the multicast group that is being left. This provides a mechanism for the Leave Report to specify which group is being abandoned (which will likely result in a group-specific query being generated).

Capture Sample

In the capture shown in Figure 4-11, the Multicast Group field being is shown as "0.0.0.0", which is the all-groups multicast address used with IGMP Membership Queries.

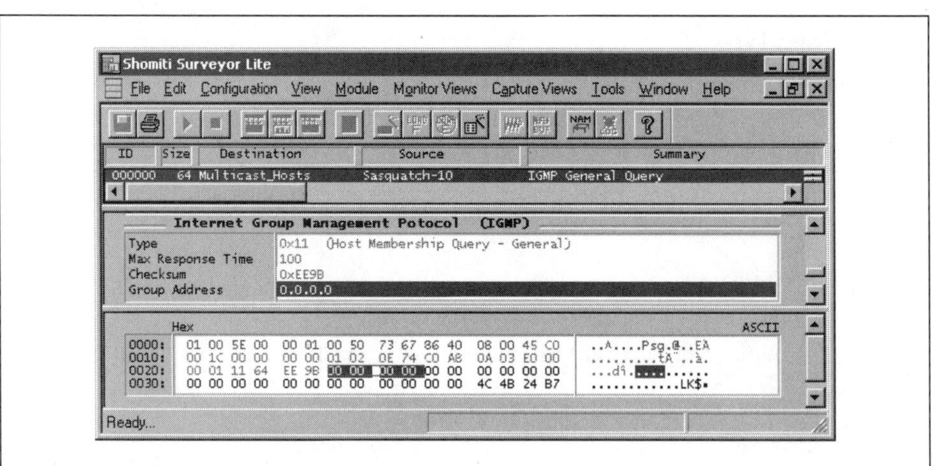

Figure 4-11. The Multicast Group field

See Also

"Membership reports"

"Message Type"

"Checksum"

IGMP Message Types

There are only four IGMP messages defined in RFC 2236, two of which were previously defined for IGMPv1. The message types are listed in Table 4-5.

Table 4-5. IGMP Message Types and Their Meanings

Message Type	Description
Membership Query	Used by IGMPv1 and IGMPv2 multicast routers to locate the multicast groups in use by hosts on the local network.
v1 Membership Report	Identifies this message as an IGMPv1 Membership Report.
v2 Membership Report	Identifies this message as an IGMPv2 Membership Report.
v2 Leave Report	Used by IGMPv2 hosts to announce that they are leaving a multicast group.

For detailed information about each of these message types, refer to the sections that follow.

Membership Query

Membership Query messages are sent by multicast routers whenever they want to verify that hosts are listening for remotely generated multicast traffic that is being forwarded to this network.

IGMP Message Type

The Message Type for Membership Query messages is 1.

Defined In

RFCs 1112 and 2236.

Status

Standard, Recommended.

Generated By

IGMPv1 or IGMPv2 multicast routers.

Notes

Both IGMPv1 and IGMPv2 multicast routers will issue Membership Query messages. The two messages are generally indistinguishable from each other, except that IGMPv2 queries will have data in the Maximum Response Time field.

Membership Queries can be for all groups or for specific groups. If the query is for all groups, then the Multicast Group field will contain 0.0.0.0. If the query is for a specific group, then the Multicast Group field will contain the IP address of the multicast group in question.

Whenever hosts see a Membership Query message, they must respond with a list of the multicast groups that they are actively monitoring, and they must do so within the time-frame provided in the Maximum Response Time field. However, not all hosts will respond to these queries; if another host responds for a multicast group that this host is also participating in, then this host can abort the response for that group. Multicast routers only need one response in order to continue forwarding multicast traffic for any given group.

Capture Sample

The packet capture shown in Figure 4-12 shows a message type of 1, which indicates that this is a Membership Query. By looking at the Maximum Response Time field, we can tell that this is an IGMPv2 query, since IGMPv1 messages did not use this field.

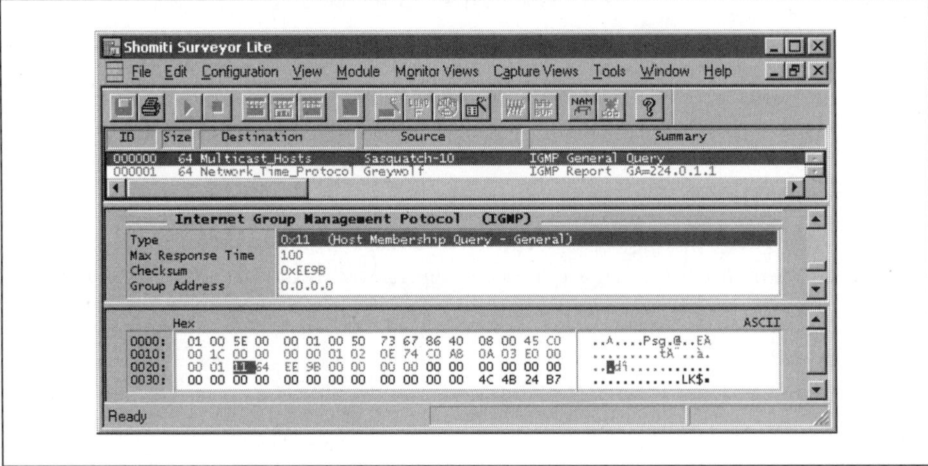

Figure 4-12. An IGMP Membership Query message

See Also

"Managing Group Memberships"

"IGM Message Headers"

"IGMPv1 Membership Report"

"IGMPv2 Membership Report"

"Leave Report"

IGMPv1 Membership Report

IGMPv1 Membership Reports are generated by hosts whenever they start monitoring a multicast address, or whenever they see a Membership Query. IGMPv1 Membership Reports can be generated by IGMPv1 and IGMPv2 hosts.

IGMP Message Type

The IGMP Message Type for IGMPv1 Membership Reports is 2.

Defined In

RFCs 1112 and 2236.

Status

Standard, Recommended.

Generated By

IGMPv1 or IGMPv2 hosts, and multicast routers who are also participating in multicast groups.

Notes

IGMPv1 Membership Reports are generated by IGMPv1 hosts when they first join a multicast group, and are sent in response to IGMPv1 Membership Queries by IGMPv1 and IGMPv2 hosts.

When an IGMPv1 host first joins a multicast group (such as when a multicast application is started on the host), it issues a couple of IGMPv1 Membership Reports, allowing for the possibility that the first one was lost or corrupted. After that, IGMPv1 Membership Reports are not sent unless a multicast router has issued an IGMPv1 Membership Query.

Typically, an IGMPv2 host will respond only to a Membership Query with an IGMPv2 Membership Report when it can tell for certain that an IGMPv2 multicast router is on the network. This is determined by examining the Maximum Response Time field in a Membership Query. If the field is not blank, then the sender is probably an IGMPv2 multicast router.

Not all hosts will respond to Membership Queries. If another host responds for a multicast group that this host is also participating in, then this host can abort the response for that group. Multicast routers only need one response in order to continue forwarding multicast traffic for any given group, so multiple responses only waste network bandwidth.

In some situations, the multicast router will also be a listening host. In those cases, the router will respond as a host to queries that it sees from other multicast routers. Multicast routers never respond to their own queries.

See Also

"Managing Group Memberships"

"IGM Message Headers"

"Membership Query"

"IGMPv2 Membership Report"

IGMPv2 Membership Report

IGMPv2 Membership Reports are generated by hosts whenever they start monitoring a multicast address, or whenever they see a Membership Query. IGMPv2 Membership Reports are generated only by IGMPv2 hosts.

IGMP Message Type

The IGMP Message Type for IGMPv2 Membership Reports is 6.

Defined In

RFC 2236.

Status

Proposed Standard, Elective.

Generated By

IGMPv2 hosts, and multicast routers who are also participating in multicast groups.

Notes

IGMPv2 Membership Reports are generated by IGMPv2 hosts when they first join a multicast group, and are sent in response to IGMPv2 Membership Queries.

When an IGMPv2 host first joins a multicast group (such as when a multicast application is started on the host), it issues a couple of IGMPv2 Membership Reports, allowing for the possibility that the first one was lost or corrupted. After that, IGMPv2 Membership Reports are not sent unless a multicast router has issued an IGMPv2 Membership Query.

Typically, an IGMPv2 host will only respond to a Membership Query with an IGMPv2 Membership Report when it can tell for certain that an IGMPv2 multicast router is on the network. This is determined by examining the Maximum Response Time field in a Membership Query. If the field is not blank, then the sender is probably an IGMPv2 multicast router.

Not all hosts will respond to Membership Queries. If another host responds for a multicast group that this host is also participating in, then this host can abort the response for that group. Multicast routers only need one response in order to continue forwarding multicast traffic for any given group, so multiple responses only waste network bandwidth.

In some situations, the multicast router will also be a listening host. In those cases, the router will respond as a host to queries that it sees from other multicast routers. Multicast routers never respond to their own queries.

Capture Sample

The packet capture shown in Figure 4-13 shows a message type of 6, which indicates that this is an IGMPv2 Membership Report. The Destination Address field of the IP header shows that this message is for 224.0.1.1, which is the well-known multicast address associated with the Network Time Protocol.

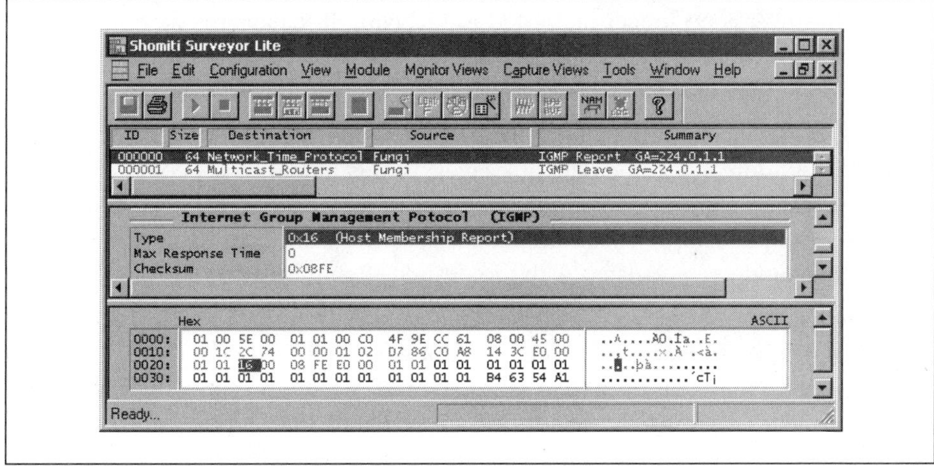

Figure 4-13. An IGMPv2-specific Membership Report message

See Also

"Managing Group Memberships"

"IGM Message Headers"

"Membership Query"

"IGMPv1 Membership Report"

Leave Report

Leave Report messages are generated by IGMPv2 hosts when they stop monitoring a multicast group address for data, and need to inform other devices on the network that they are no longer interested in receiving IP datagrams destined for that multicast group.

IGMP Message Type

The IGMP Message Type for Leave Reports is 7.

Defined In

RFC 2236.

Status

Proposed Standard, Elective.

Generated By

IGMPv2 hosts, and sometimes multicast routers.

Notes

Leave Reports are generated by IGMPv2 hosts when they stop monitoring a multicast group address for data, and need to inform other devices of the fact that this host is no longer interested in receiving IP datagrams destined for the specified multicast group address.

RFC 1112 (which defined IGMPv1) was written primarily for the use and benefit of hosts attached to Ethernet networks, which offered explicit support for multicast addresses at the data-link layer. In this model, hosts could choose to monitor IP multicast addresses—and also could choose to stop monitoring those groups—simply by informing the local network adapter of the Ethernet multicast address associated with the desired IP multicast group.

However, not all networks support this model. In particular, a PPP network that connects a remote user to a network over a dial-up connection offers no support for this type of model whatsoever. If a remote user wanted to monitor a multicast group, they had to send an IGMP Join Report message to the local network, which the dial-up server would have to intercept. At that point, the dial-up server could choose to redirect any multicast traffic for that group address to the remote user. This system has proven to be workable.

Unfortunately, prior to RFC 2236, there has been no way for the downstream device to inform the dial-up server that it wanted to *stop* getting traffic for that group address. Once a remote host subscribed to a group, there was no way for that host to *un*subscribe. IGMPv2 fixed this problem by providing the Leave Report message, which provides just that functionality.

There are other situations where the Leave Report is desirable. For example, it helps to eliminate unnecessary traffic on networks that only have a few multicast listeners, by allowing those hosts to explicitly inform a local IGMP router whenever they are done monitoring a specific group. Although the IGMP router probably would have discovered this information during the next Membership Query cycle, the use of the Leave Report allows for immediate termination (although the router still has to verify the fact that no other hosts are listening for traffic to the specified group address).

Furthermore, in some situations, a multicast router will in fact be the listening host (such a device may be listening for group messages that are specific to a certain routing protocol that is in use by the router). In those cases, the router should also issue Leave Reports when it unsubscribes from those multicast groups.

Capture Sample

The packet capture shown in Figure 4-14 shows a message type of 7, which indicates that this is an IGMPv2 Leave Report. Although the Destination Address in the IP header does not tell us which group this message is for (since it is going to the "all-routers" group address), we can tell from the Group Address field of the IGMP Message that this message is for the Network Time Protocol (224.0.1.1).

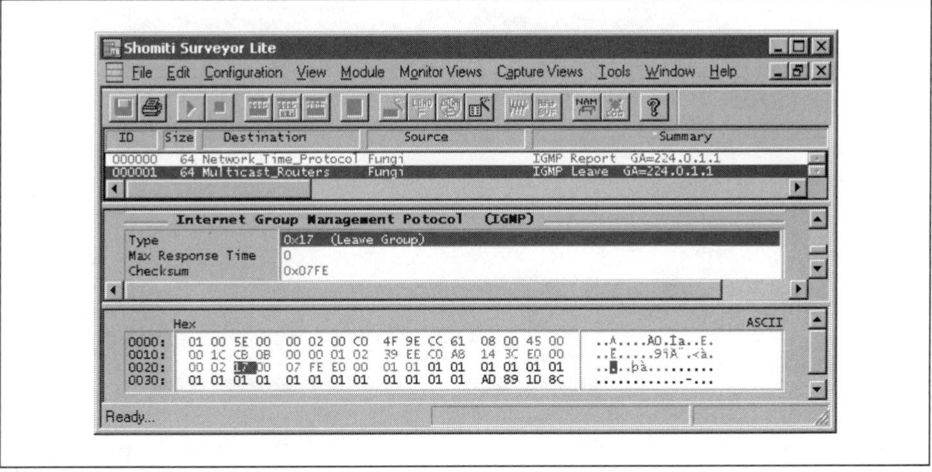

Figure 4-14. An IGMPv2 Leave Report message

See Also

"Managing Group Memberships"

"IGM Message Headers"

"IGMPv2 Membership Report"

Multicasting and IGMP in Action

As far as IP is concerned, multicast datagrams are virtually indistinguishable from other forms of IP traffic. The only way to tell a multicast IP datagram apart from a unicast or broadcast IP datagram is the fact that the destination IP address of the IP datagram that is carrying the multicast data has a Class D address in the range of 224.0.0.0 through 239.255.255.255.

Simple Multicast Traffic

Figure 4-15 shows a simple UDP datagram sent to the multicast address 233.1.1.1. There isn't anything else about this datagram that would indicate that it contains multicast data.

The application used to generate the packet shown in Figure 4-15 is a sample application called *party.exe*, available from Microsoft's public FTP server. Many such applications exist for a wide variety of platforms.

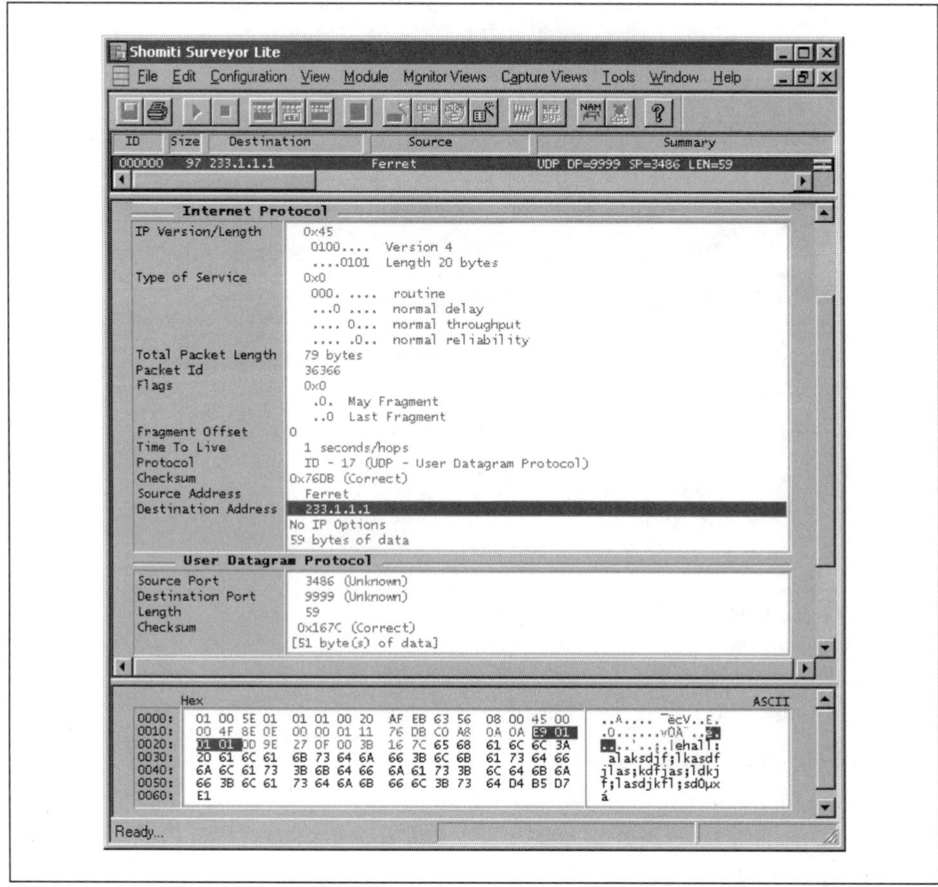

Figure 4-15. A simple UDP datagram sent to a multicast address

Membership and Leave Reports

As was described in "IGMP Message Types" earlier in this chapter, the acts of joining and leaving multicast groups are pretty straightforward: hosts issue multiple join requests when they first start, and later issue a single leave request when they end. A good example of this process can be seen with Microsoft's Windows Internet Name Service (WINS) server, shipped with Windows NT Server 4.0. WINS is a NetBIOS-to-TCP/IP resolution service, capable of automatically locating other WINS servers using IP multicasts. Once these other servers are located, they can replicate name resolution information with each other. Figure 4-16 shows a WINS server being started and then being shut down.

Notice that the WINS server issues two Membership Reports back-to-back. This behavior is specified in RFC 2236, which states that hosts should issue at least two announcements whenever they are started, allowing for the possibility that the first

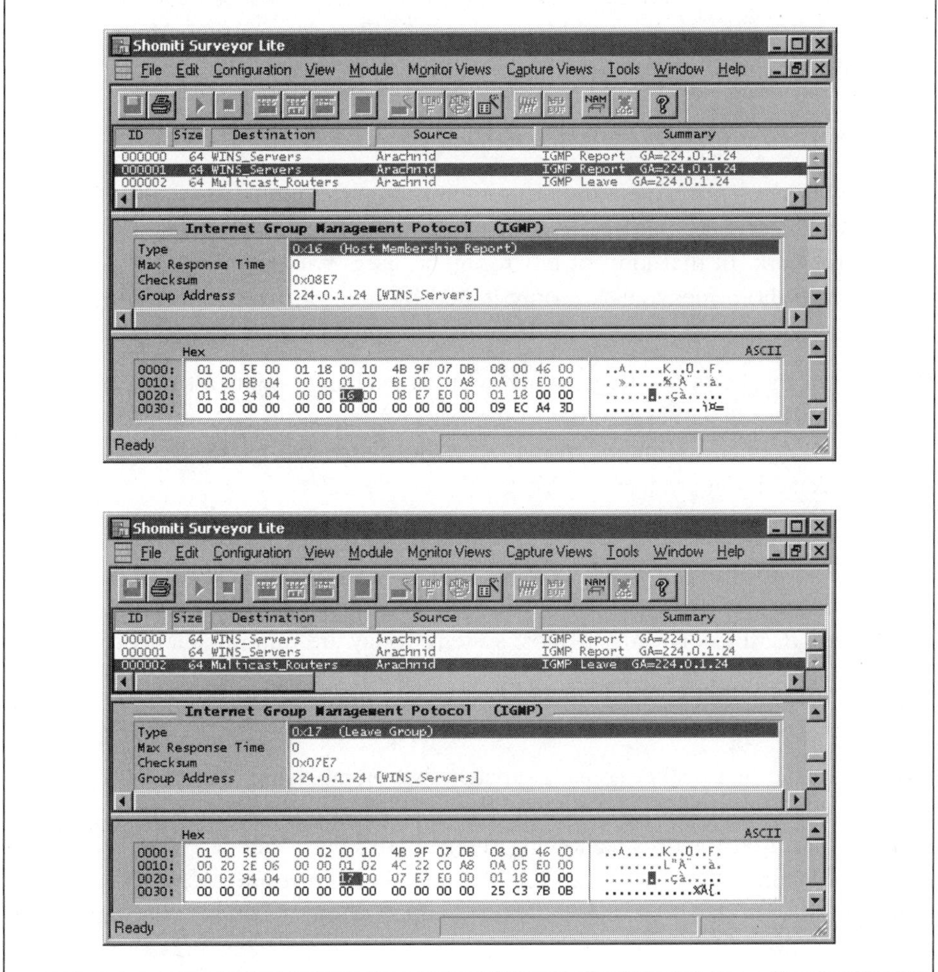

Figure 4-16. A Microsoft WINS server registering and then leaving a multicast group

announcement was lost or corrupted somehow. In the example shown in Figure 4-16, the Windows NT server sends the multicast Membership Report to a WINS-specific multicast address of 224.0.1.24, which is also the proper behavior according to RFC 2236.

After a while, the WINS server is terminated, so the Windows NT host issues an IGMPv2 Leave Report, stating that the host is no longer interested in that particular multicast traffic. Note that the Leave Report is sent to the "all-routers" multicast address of 224.0.0.2, and is not sent to the WINS-specific multicast address of 224. 0.1.24 (only routers are interested in Leave Reports, so that's where they are sent). However, the Group ID of the Leave Report is still set to the 224.0.1.24 multicast group, identifying the group that the application is no longer interested in.

Unfortunately, not all multicast-aware applications follow all of these rules. For a detailed discussion of this problem, refer to "Troubleshooting Multicasts and IGMP" later in this chapter.

Membership Queries and Reports

If a network does not have a multicast router, then the multicast-enabled hosts on that network can only participate with other multicast-enabled hosts that are also on that network. In that kind of environment, users will never see a Membership Query, since those messages are only issued by multicast routers when they need to find out which hosts are actively listening for specific multicast group addresses.

However, if the hosts on the network wish to exchange multicast data with hosts on other networks (either internal to the organization or in far-away places), then multicast routers are required. In that scenario, there will be several Membership Queries issued by the router.

As described in "Managing Group Memberships" earlier in this chapter, at least one host will respond to each of these queries with a Membership Report. The type of report that is issued will depend on whether or not the hosts and routers are running IGMPv1 or IGMPv2. Most systems today are running IGMPv2.

The process of sending Membership Queries and Membership Reports is shown in Figure 4-17.

Notice that the first packet contains an IGMPv2 Membership Query, which is sent to the "all-hosts" address of 224.0.0.1. Every multicast-enabled host is required to monitor that group address, allowing them to see these queries. The last packet shown in Figure 4-17 contains an IGMPv2 membership response for the multicast group address of 224.0.1.1, which is the address associated with the Simple Network Time Protocol (SNTP).

Troubleshooting Multicasts and IGMP

Since IGMP is a very small and lightweight protocol, there aren't many things that can go wrong with it. The only real errors that are likely to occur are problems with programs that implement the specification poorly. For example, the *party.exe* application that is provided by Microsoft does not use the appropriate system calls for generating multicast traffic. As such, it does not cause a Membership Report to be sent when the program is started, and does not cause a Leave Report to be issued when it is stopped.

Another implementation problem can be seen with the SNTP client provided with RedHat Linux 5.2. Although this same client code executes properly on Solaris and Digital Unix systems, RedHat Linux 5.2 had some bugs in the multicasting code

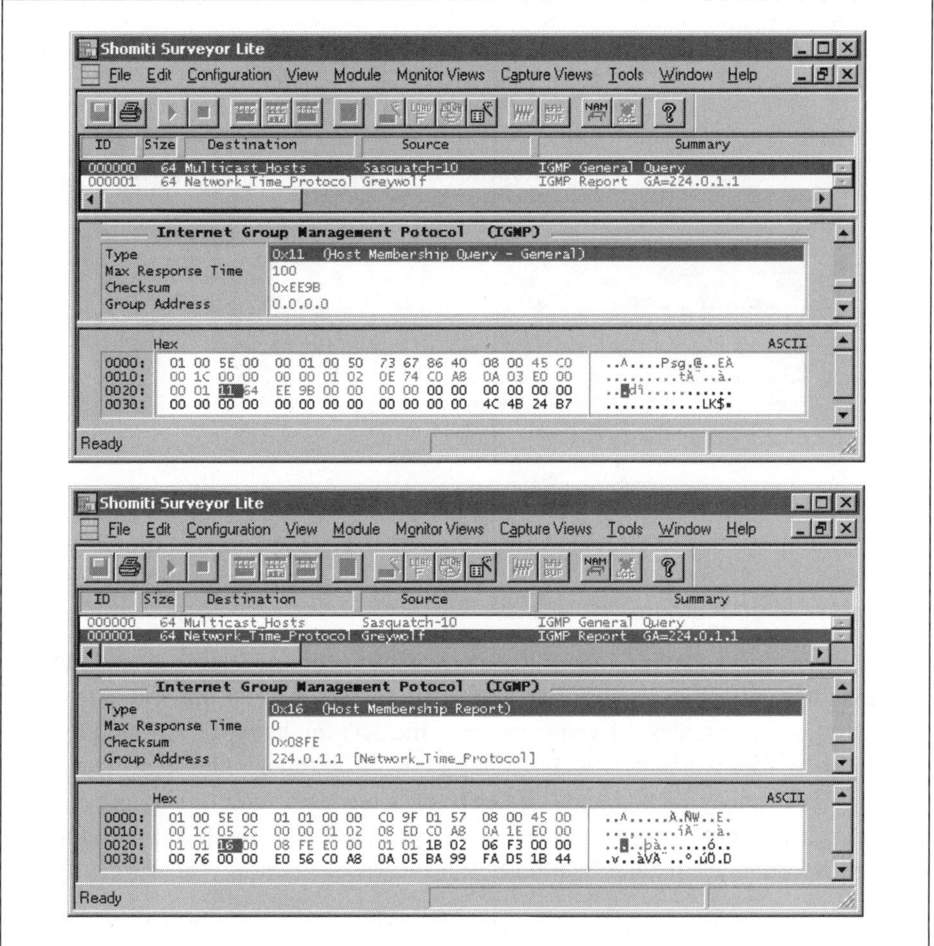

Figure 4-17. A simple exchange of Membership Query and Membership Report messages

that caused some malformed IGMP messages to be sent. Figure 4-18 shows this in detail.

The first mistake that is made is that the SNTP client does not issue multiple Membership Reports when it is started. Instead, only one Membership Report is issued, although RFC 2236 specifically states that applications should issue at least two separate Membership Reports whenever they join a multicast group.

The second mistake—and one that is much more problematic—is that the Leave Report issued by this implementation is completely malformed. Although the client does send the Leave Report to the all-routers multicast group (224.0.0.2), it also specifies that the group it wants to leave is 224.0.0.2, which is not correct. It should be advertising that it wants to leave the 224.0.1.1 group (the well-known

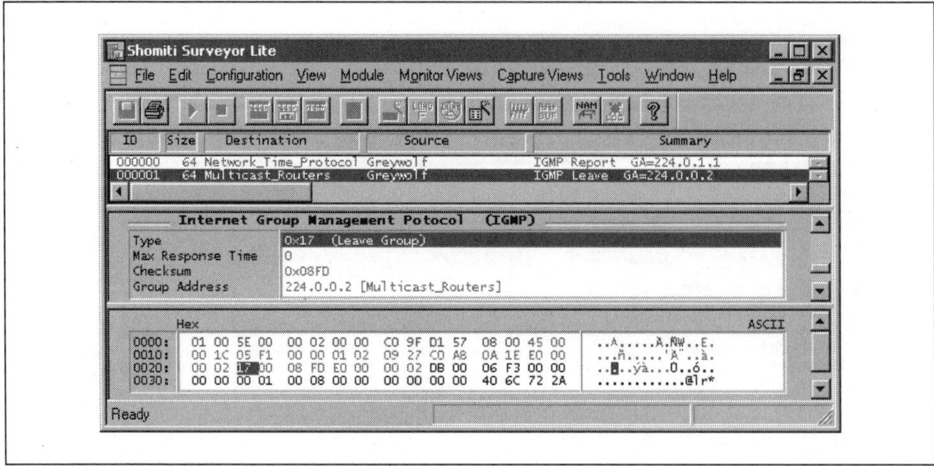

Figure 4-18. A malformed IGMP Leave Report

multicast address for SNTP, the same group that it joined in the previous message). As it stands, this client is offering to leave the all-routers group of 224.0.0.2, rather than the NTP group.

This is the wrong behavior and will likely result in some problems eventually. For example, any multicast routers that are on the network (such as Sasquatch) will never find out that Greywolf wants to leave the NTP multicast group, and as such will continue forwarding NTP data to this network segment. Although that's okay here (we have many NTP clients), if Greywolf were on a remote network accessible via a dial-on-demand connection, we would likely see the link being brought up every so often just for the NTP traffic.

In addition, multicast datagrams are basically indistinguishable from IP datagrams, so one way to test for basic multicasting functionality is to use a program like *ping* to determine which hosts are currently listening for a specific group address.

For example, Figure 4-19 shows a single ICMP Echo Request Query Message being sent from Krill to the all-hosts multicast group address of 224.0.0.1. In response, Krill receives three different ICMP Echo Response Query Messages back, with the IP addresses of the responding systems shown in the *ping* output. Also notice that Krill's implementation of *ping* thinks that two of the responses are duplicates (which they are), although they were returned from different hosts.

Note that many TCP/IP stacks will not respond to ICMP Echo Request messages that are sent to multicast addresses, and that this method is not a sure-fire indicator of the active listeners on a network. For example, there are more than three multicast-aware hosts active on the local network, although Krill only got answers back from three hosts (one of which was itself) in the test shown in Figure 4-19.

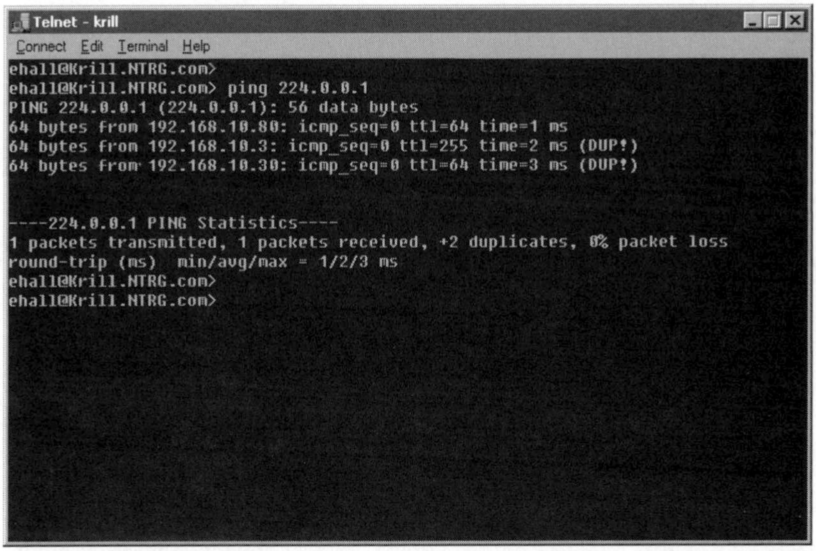

```
Telnet - krill
Connect Edit Terminal Help
ehall@Krill.NTRG.com>
ehall@Krill.NTRG.com> ping 224.0.0.1
PING 224.0.0.1 (224.0.0.1): 56 data bytes
64 bytes from 192.168.10.80: icmp_seq=0 ttl=64 time=1 ms
64 bytes from 192.168.10.3: icmp_seq=0 ttl=255 time=2 ms (DUP!)
64 bytes from 192.168.10.30: icmp_seq=0 ttl=64 time=3 ms (DUP!)


----224.0.0.1 PING Statistics----
1 packets transmitted, 1 packets received, +2 duplicates, 0% packet loss
round-trip (ms)  min/avg/max = 1/2/3 ms
ehall@Krill.NTRG.com>
ehall@Krill.NTRG.com>
```

Figure 4-19. The output from a ping test to the multicast all-hosts address of 224.0.0.1

For a detailed discussion on ways to use *ping*, refer to "Notes on ping" in Chapter 5.

General problems with multicasting will also result from configuration problems with your multicast-enabled routers. Multicasting and IGMP both rely on the presence of a multicast router in order for the multicast datagrams to be forwarded across network boundaries. Although many IP routers offer multicast support, most of them do not have these protocols enabled by default. You may need to enable a multicast-specific routing protocol such as DVMRP (the Distance-Vector Multicast Routing Protocol), or you may need to acquire a new router if the one you currently have does not support either multicast routing or the version of IGMP in use by your hosts.

Also, if you are trying to interact with multicasting traffic from the Internet, then you will need to configure your firewalls to allow that type of traffic through. This is not a widely-supported option at the present time, and the only viable solution may involve the creation of multicast tunnels (using a multicast routing protocol), or the creation of a secure, encrypted virtual private network link. In both cases, you will need to find an external organization that can provide you with those services (although the chances are good that the external organizations are also suffering under security issues with multicast traffic). For more information on this subject, refer to RFC 2588, which covers the issues around IP multicasting and firewalls in great detail.

5

The Internet Control Message Protocol

Summary	The Internet Control Message Protocol provides a mechanism for IP devices to use when they need to exchange information about network problems that are preventing delivery. Although IP is an unreliable protocol that does not guarantee delivery, it is important to be able to inform a sender when delivery is not possible due to a semi-permanent, nontransient error.
Protocol ID	1
Relevant STDs	2 (*http://www.iana.org/*); 3 (includes RFCs 1122 and 1123); 4 (RFC 1812, republished); 5 (includes RFCs 791, 792, 919, 922, 950, and 1112)
Relevant RFCs	792 (Internet Control Message Protocol); 896 (Source Quench); 950 (Address Mask Extension); 1122 (Host Network Requirements); 1191 (Path MTU Discovery); 1256 (Router Discovery); 1812 (Router Requirements)
Related RFCs	1393 (Traceroute Extension)

IP is an unreliable protocol, and as such, delivery is not guaranteed. In this model, if important datagrams are lost, then a higher-layer protocol (such as a transport-layer protocol like TCP or an application-layer protocol like TFTP) will eventually recognize that a problem has occurred and will deal with it. As the theory goes, important data will eventually get through.

However, sometimes a problem crops up that prevents *all* datagrams from getting through to their destination. When these kinds of nontransient errors occur, IP fails for a specific and avoidable reason, and the sender should be notified about the problem so that it can either stop sending data to that destination or modify its behavior so that the specific problem is avoided. IP uses the Internet Control Message Protocol (ICMP) for reporting these kinds of problems.

The ICMP Specification

ICMP is documented in RFC 792, which is included in STD 5 (the IP standard). As such, ICMP is a part of STD 5 and is therefore considered to be an Internet Standard protocol. However, RFC 792 contained some vagaries that were clarified in RFC 1122 (Host Network Requirements) and RFC 1812 (Router Requirements). In addition, much of ICMP's core functionality has been redefined and clarified in STD 2. As such, ICMP implementations need to incorporate RFC 792, RFC 1122, RFC 1812, and STD 2 in order to work reliably and consistently with other implementations.

RFC 792 states that the Protocol ID for ICMP is 1. When a system receives an IP datagram that is marked as containing Protocol 1, it should pass the contents of the datagram to ICMP for further processing. However, ICMP is not a transport protocol and is not used to deliver application data. Rather, ICMP is a control protocol like IGMP, useful for informing devices of network events and changes.

RFC 792 states that ICMP must be used whenever IP itself needs to report a problem. Thus, although ICMP works at a layer above IP, IP also depends on ICMP in order to function properly. ICMP and IP are tightly interwoven, and for all practical purposes are inseparable. For this reason, every IP implementation is also required to include ICMP.

The Need for ICMP

Remember that IP is only responsible for getting datagrams from one host to another, one network at a time. Each IP datagram gets sent as an individual entity capable of following whatever path is available to it. Datagrams are moved across whatever hosts, routers, and networks are capable of getting that specific chunk of data closer to its destination.

In this model, any IP datagram can fail to get delivered for any number of reasons. Some datagrams will get discarded simply because the next-hop router is unavailable, and the current router is unable to forward them. Sometimes a datagram will be destroyed due to the user on the sending system providing a nonexistent destination IP address or port number to their local application. In all of these cases, the system that detects an error will simply destroy the IP datagram that's failing, and move on to the next datagram waiting to be processed.

Depending upon the exact cause of the failure, the system that destroyed the datagram may or may not choose to return an ICMP error message back to the original sender, notifying it of the failure and its cause. Typically this decision is made based on whether the failure is transient or semi-permanent.

Transient failures such as invalid checksums are generally ignored, since it is assumed that the sender will eventually notice the failure and retransmit any important data (which may be handled by TCP or by an application-specific reliability mechanism). The assumption is that if the data wasn't important enough for the sender to use a reliable protocol, then the sender probably doesn't care that delivery failed, and the problem can go unreported. In this model, transient errors can be safely ignored, since it is somewhat unlikely that the next packet will have the exact same problem. Eventually, the transport or application protocol in use will detect the error, and the failure itself does not indicate that there is a problem with the network at large.

Conversely, semipermanent failures (such as invalid destination IP addresses) need to be reported to the sender immediately, since these kinds of failures represent fundamental problems with the network itself, or at least indicate that there is a problem in the way that the sender is trying to use the network. In either case, semi-permanent failures should always be reported back to the sender, thus either causing it to stop sending data to that destination, or forcing it to modify its behavior so that the specific problem is avoided.

ICMP is the protocol used to send failure messages back to a system when a semi-permanent delivery problem has been detected. This includes events such as a destination being unreachable, the IP Time-to-Live value reaching zero, and so forth. In addition, ICMP can be used for exchanging general information about the network, or for probing the network for certain characteristics. For example, the popular *ping* program uses ICMP messages to test basic connectivity between two devices.

In fact, ICMP is essentially just a collection of predefined messages, each of which provide very specific functionality. When a system needs to send an ICMP message, it chooses a message from the dictionary, places the code for the message into an ICMP-specific datagram, and then transmits the ICMP message via IP back to the system that sent the original (failing) datagram.

The recipient will see that the IP datagram contains an ICMP message (as indicated in the IP header's Protocol Type field), examine the message and its data, and then hand the message off to the appropriate protocol for additional processing. If the message is intended for ICMP itself (such a message might be an "echo request" message, generated by *ping*), then ICMP will deal with the message directly and not involve any other protocols.

If the message is intended for IP (such a message might be a "redirect" message, suggesting that the sender should use a different router), then the message will be delivered to the system's IP software for processing. In this example, the IP software should update the local routing table to reflect the path suggested by the message and use that router for any subsequent traffic for the affected destination.

If the message is intended for a transport protocol (such a message might be "destination port is unreachable"), then the message will be delivered to the appropriate transport protocol for processing. The transport protocol should process the message directly and then inform the application protocol of the error, suggesting that it stop sending data to that particular destination socket. Most of the ICMP error messages are meant to be processed by the transport protocols.

When Not to Send ICMP Messages

Just as it is important to know when to send an error message, it is also important to know when an error message should not be sent. For example, any transient error that causes delivery to fail (such as an invalid checksum or a data-link delivery failure) should not be reported. However, the ICMP specifications also state that ICMP error messages should not be generated when their usage will generate an excessive amount of network traffic. For example, RFC 1122 states that ICMP error messages should not be sent as the result of receiving:

- Another ICMP error message (although ICMP error messages *can* be sent in response to ICMP query messages)
- An IGMP message of any kind
- An IP datagram with a destination IP address for a broadcast or multicast address
- An IP datagram with a nonspecific source address (all zeroes, a loopback address, or a broadcast or multicast address)
- A data-link frame with a broadcast or multicast address
- Any fragment—other than the first fragment—from a fragmented IP datagram

The first rule is obvious. You would not want to generate ICMP error messages in response to other ICMP error messages, as a message loop could cause a network storm that would prevent any other packets from getting sent. However, RFC 1122 states that devices can send ICMP error messages in response to ICMP query messages. For example, a router can issue an ICMP Redirect error message in response to an ICMP Echo Request query message that was sent to the wrong router.

The reason that systems shouldn't generate ICMP error messages in response to broadcast or multicast datagrams is to keep network traffic to a minimum. For example, assume that a user on one host broadcasts a UDP message to all of the hosts on the local network, but only a few of the hosts were running the application associated with that UDP traffic. If all of the other hosts on the network sent a Destination Port Unreachable error message back to the sender, then the number of ICMP messages could be quite high. Every time a broadcast was sent, several ICMP error messages would also get generated, which could theoretically overwhelm the network if there were enough of these errors.

With multicast traffic (such as is used for streaming audio or video), this problem would be exacerbated since there could be many thousands of multicast datagrams, which would be followed by many tens- or hundreds-of-thousands of ICMP error messages. On a large shared-access network (such as nonswitched Ethernet), the resulting collisions could theoretically render the network useless. In addition, ICMP error messages should not be generated in response to IGMP messages, for much the same reason.

Note however that ICMP query messages can be sent to a broadcast address, and those messages should be responded to with additional query messages (but should not be responded to with ICMP error messages). For example, a user can use *ping* to send an ICMP Echo Request query message to all of the hosts on the local network, and any of the hosts on that network may respond with ICMP Echo Reply query messages (although this behavior is entirely optional according to RFC 1122). Therefore, the "no errors for broadcast or multicast traffic" rule only applies to ICMP error messages.

Similarly, systems should not return error messages in response to every fragment of a fragmented packet, since this process would also result in multiple messages being sent in response to a single IP datagram. Although the resulting congestion would probably not be as much of a problem as it would be with broadcast or multicast traffic, it would still be an unnecessary utilization of the available network bandwidth.

Reporting on Delivery Problems

As mentioned earlier, ICMP error messages are used when it is necessary to report a problem that is preventing delivery from occurring. Although IP is an unreliable protocol that may fail without warning, it is important for the network to know when problems occur that will prevent delivery from *ever* occurring.

This is a fundamentally different concept from packets simply becoming lost or corrupted. If a system is trying to send data to a destination network that is totally unavailable, then the sending system ought to know that no datagrams are ever going to make it through to the destination system. The problem should be reported to the sending application so it can stop sending data to that destination.

Although ICMP can be used to report on IP failures, it is important to note that ICMP does not make IP a reliable protocol. IP is still capable of losing packets, sending duplicate or out-of-sequence packets, or doing anything else that it wants to. Nor does the lack of ICMP messages mean that the network is functioning perfectly; a host may be ignoring messages for any number of reasons without an ICMP message ever getting returned to the sender.

By the same token, TCP is a reliable transport that uses negotiated connections for data exchange, and as such many of ICMP's error messages are not needed or used by TCP. For example, if an application specified an invalid port number on a destination system, the remote system's TCP software would simply reject the connection request, using the TCP Reset flag. The sender's TCP stack would be informed of the error immediately, and it would be redundant to send an ICMP message stating that the destination port was unreachable. This is true of almost every ICMP error message (but not all of them): TCP just doesn't need to know that a segment was not processed, because it's already keeping track of every segment that it sends.

Conversely, UDP does not have any circuit-management mechanisms, so it has no way to monitor individual segments. As such, UDP benefits greatly from ICMP error messages, and is the principle user of these messages.

Destination Unreachable error messages

A Destination Unreachable error message can signify any number of problems. It can mean that a router was unable to find a path to a remote system, or it can mean that a port number on the destination system is currently unavailable, or it can signal a variety of other problems.

In order to provide more-detailed reporting, the Destination Unreachable message provides a variety of submessages (using the ICMP Message Code field as described later in "Error message headers"). The major Destination Unreachable submessages documented in the various ICMP RFCs include:

Network Unreachable

This error message means that no route for the destination network could be found in the routing table on the reporting router, and is commonly seen when a user tries to connect to a private address that is non-routable across the Internet. This message can also result when datagrams are sent to a router that has corrupt or out-of-date routing tables.

For example, Figure 5-1 shows Ferret (192.168.10.10) trying to send an IP datagram to 192.168.30.10. Since the default route on Ferret points to Sasquatch, Ferret sends the datagram to that router for forwarding. However, Sasquatch does not have a routing table entry for the 192.168.30.0 network, so it returns an ICMP Destination Unreachable: Network Unreachable error message back to the sender.

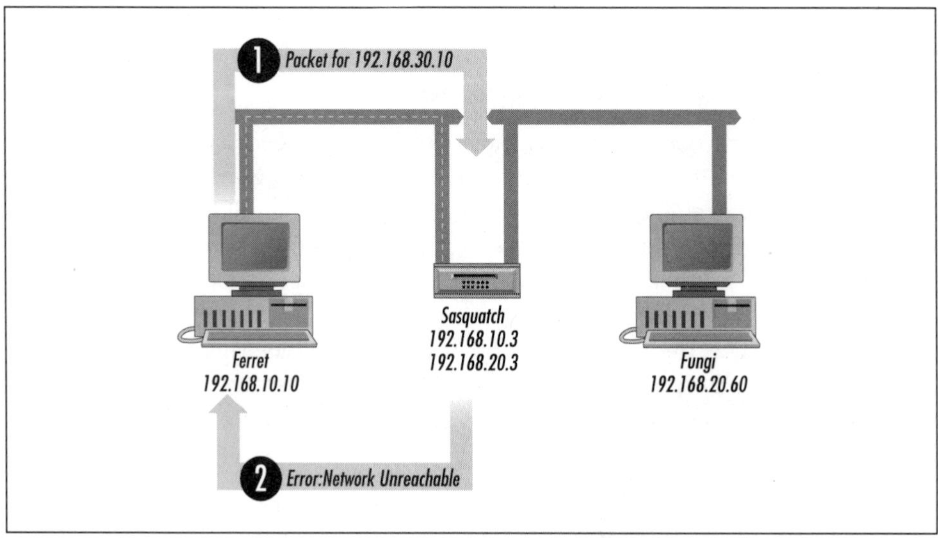

Figure 5-1. A typical scenario for Network Unreachable error messages

It's important to note that this error can be generated by any router between the source and destination systems. Since the problem may be short-term (and thus, may get fixed), Network Unreachable error messages are not meant to be the interpreted as a final word on routing issues, but should only be used to indicate that a temporary routing problem has occurred.

Host Unreachable

This error message means that the IP datagram could not be delivered to the final destination system. This error message is generated by the last-hop router if that router does not know how to reach the destination system in particular. Like the Network Unreachable error, this is only an advisory message and should not be interpreted to mean that the host does not exist.

Protocol Unreachable

This error message indicates that the specified transport protocol is unavailable on the destination system. This message is normally seen when a user tries to use a nonstandard transport protocol (like XTP) to communicate with another host that isn't running that protocol.

Port Unreachable

This error message means that the specified destination port number is not in use on the destination host. Typically, this error indicates that a client application has attempted to connect to a server application that is not loaded or that isn't using the port number expected by the client.

For example, Figure 5-2 shows Ferret trying to send an UDP datagram to port 69 (the well-known port for TFTP) on Froggy. However, Froggy is not running a TFTP server, so it returns an ICMP Destination Unreachable: Port Unreachable error message back to the sender.

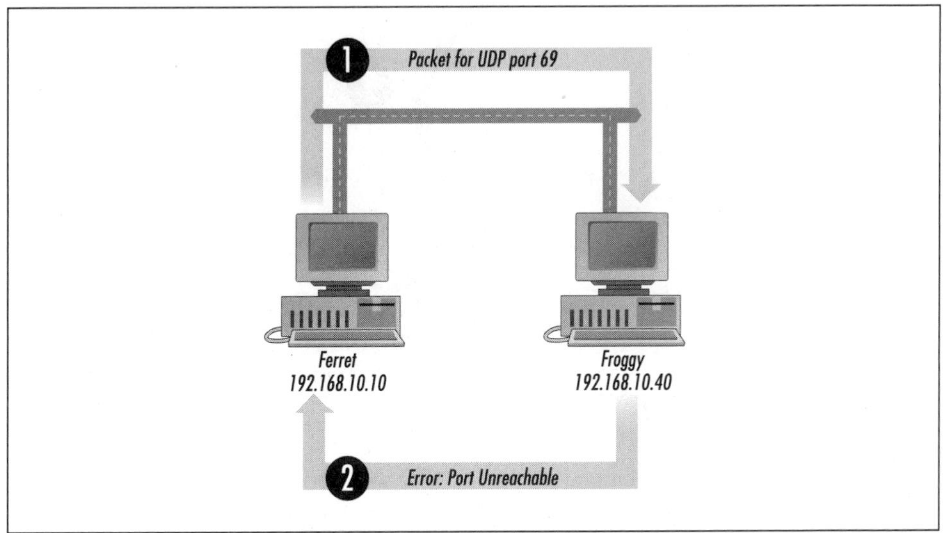

Figure 5-2. A typical scenario for Port Unreachable error messages

Port Unreachable errors are almost always generated by UDP. Since TCP uses a handshake to establish a connection with a remote system, the destination system's TCP stack would use the TCP Reset flag to reject the connection request if the destination port number were not in use by any applications.

Fragmentation Required but DF Bit Is Set

This error message indicates that the IP datagram had to travel across a network whose MTU was smaller than the IP datagram, but the datagram's Don't Fragment flag in the IP header was enabled. Since the router is unable to forward *or* fragment the datagram, it must be rejected.

For example, Figure 5-3 shows the host at 192.168.30.10 trying to send a 16 kilobyte datagram (with the "Don't Fragment" flag set in the IP header) to 192.168.10.10, which is on a segment that offers an MTU of only 1500 bytes. Since the router is unable to forward the datagram without fragmenting it, and the Don't Fragment flag is enabled, the router returns an ICMP Destination Unreachable: Fragmentation Required but DF Bit Is Set error message back to the sender.

Nowadays, the Fragmentation Required but DF Bit Is Set error message is most often seen with Path MTU Discovery, an algorithm defined in RFC 1191 that allows a sending system to discover the largest MTU size for an end-to-end

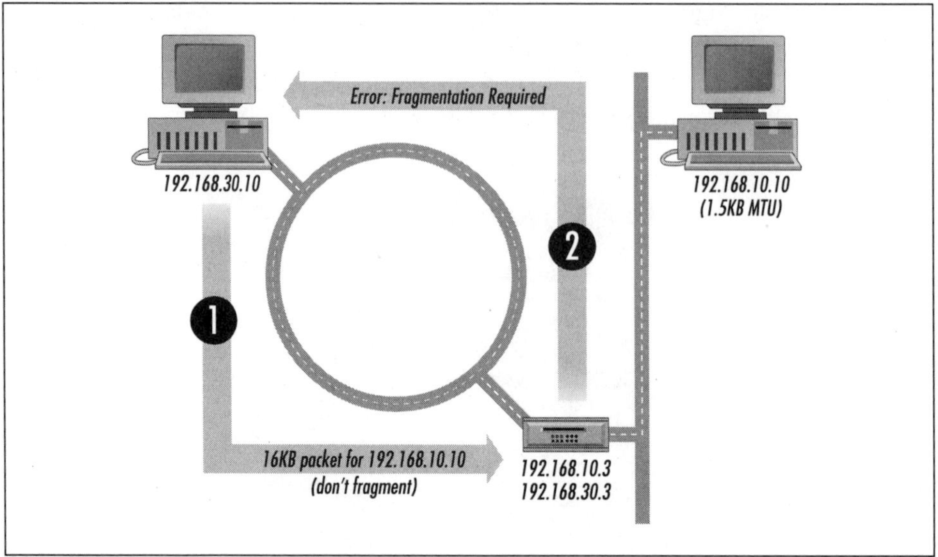

Figure 5-3. A typical scenario for Fragmentation Required error messages

connection. Once the largest-possible MTU has been discovered, the sender can use that MTU on all subsequent datagrams, thereby preventing fragmentation from occurring on that connection. For more information on this procedure, refer to "Notes on Path MTU Discovery" later in this chapter.

Source Route Failed

This error message means that the router was unable to deliver the packet to the next-hop router as specified in the datagram's Source Route IP Option fields. Source routing may fail because an invalid next-hop router was specified, or because the router was unable to send the datagram to the specified next-hop router.

Destination Network Unknown

This error message means that the destination network absolutely does not exist. It should be sent only when the data-link network has unequivocable proof that the destination network really does not exist. This is the opposite of the Network Unreachable error, which only suggests that a path to the destination network could not be found in the current routing tables (although the network may actually exist). Whereas the Network Unreachable error message suggests that a network may not exist, the Destination Network Unknown error message states it as fact.

Destination Host Unknown

This error message means that the destination host absolutely does not exist. It should be sent only when the data-link network has unequivocable proof that the destination system simply does not exist. This is the opposite of the Host

Unreachable error, which only suggests that the destination system cannot be found (although the host may actually exist). Whereas the Host Unreachable error message suggests that a host may not exist, the Destination Host Unknown error message states it as fact.

Network Unreachable for Type-of-Service

This error message is generated by intermediary routers if any of the next-hop networks in between the sender and destination systems either do not support the Type-of-Service value requested in the IP datagram, or do not support the default Type-of-Service. If a device sends an IP packet with a particular Type-of-Service defined, but no path is available that matches that particular Type-of-Service, then the router should reject the packet and inform the sender of the problem.

Host Unreachable for Type-of-Service

This error message is generated by the last-hop router if the last-hop network for the destination system either does not support the Type-of-Service value requested in the IP datagram, or does not support the default Type-of-Service. If a device sends an IP packet with a particular Type-of-Service defined, but the last-hop network does not support that particular Type-of-Service, then the last-hop router should reject the packet and inform the sender of the problem.

Communication Administratively Prohibited

This error message means that the destination system is configured to reject datagrams from the sending system. This error is generally used when firewall restrictions or other security measures are filtering datagrams based on some sort of criteria. This message effectively says, "The destination may be up and running, but it will not get the datagrams that you're sending. Stop sending them."

For example, Figure 5-4 shows Ferret (192.168.10.10) trying to send a datagram to Fungi (192.168.20.60). However, the router Sasquatch is configured to reject all datagrams from the 192.168.10.0 network, so it returns an ICMP Destination Unreachable: Communications Administratively Prohibited error message back to the sender.

Some firewalls are configured not to issue the Communication Administratively Prohibited messages, since such messages may be considered a security risk in their own right. Telling an attacker which hosts are being protected is not necessarily a good idea; sometimes saying nothing is the most secure option.

RFC 1122 also defines "Communication With Destination Network Administratively Prohibited" (code 9) and "Communication With Destination Host Administratively Prohibited" (code 10). However, these messages are reserved for use by U.S. military agencies, and aren't supposed to be used by the general public.

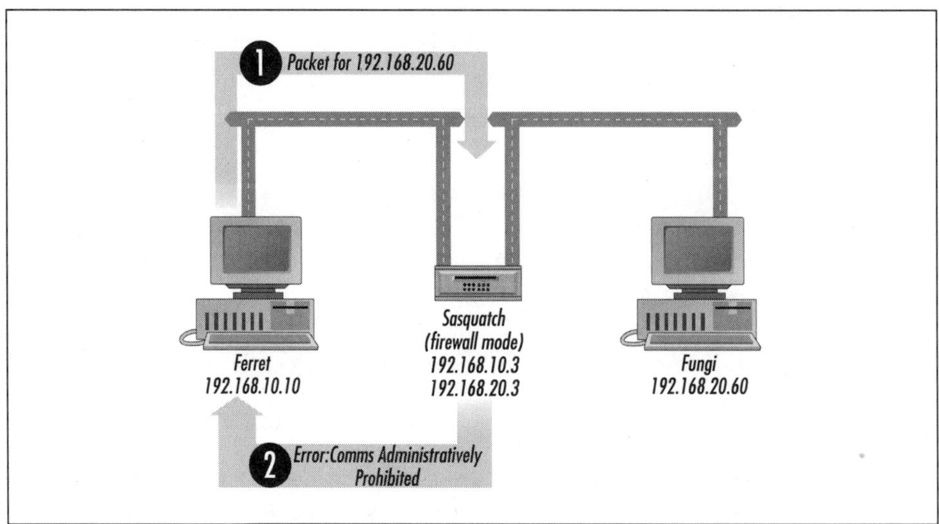

Figure 5-4. Typical scenario for Communications Administratively Prohibited error messages

Host Precedence Violation

This error message means that the sender has specified a Precedence value for the IP datagram that is not supported by the intermediary network, destination network, destination host, or destination application. In order for the source to communicate with the destination, it must change the Precedence value of the IP datagram to a supported value.

Precedence Cutoff in Effect

This error will occur if a sending system defines a specific Precedence value that is lower than the minimum Precedence required on an intermediary or destination network. Such filters are typically found only on very expensive networks. In order for the source to communicate with the destination, it must increase the Precedence value of the IP datagram, or else use a different route for that specific destination.

According to RFC 1122, all Destination Unreachable error messages must be reported to the transport layer that triggered the failure. If the error indicates a "soft failure" (such as Network Unreachable), the transport layer should not abort the connection, but instead should note that the problem occurred. If the connection fails due to this problem, the error may be passed to the application protocol so that it can inform the user of the failure. If the error indicates a "hard failure" (such as Network Unknown), then the connection should be terminated immediately.

For more information on the Destination Unreachable error message, refer to "Destination Unreachable" later in this chapter.

Time Exceeded error messages

Time Exceeded error messages are used to indicate that a forwarding or reassembly operation took too long to complete and that the reporting device is discarding the data. In order to provide more-detailed reporting, the Time Exceeded message provides two different submessages (using the ICMP Message Code field as described later in "Error message headers"). The submessages offered by Time Exceeded include:

Time-to-Live Exceeded in Transit

This error message is used when an IP datagram's Time-to-Live value has reached zero but the datagram has not yet been delivered to its final destination. Since the Time-to-Live field indicates the maximum number of hops that a datagram can take, the router cannot forward a datagram with a Time-to-Live value of zero, and must destroy it instead. Since most systems use Time-to-Live values of 30 or more, the presence of this message generally indicates that a routing loop is preventing the datagram from being delivered.

However, this message is also used with the *traceroute* program to identify the routers in between a source and destination system. For more information on how *traceroute* uses this message, refer to "Notes on traceroute" later in this chapter.

Fragment Reassembly Time Exceeded

This error message is used when a datagram has been fragmented but the destination system has not received all of the fragments within the allotted time (60 seconds on most Unix systems). This message generally indicates that a fragment has been lost in transit somewhere and that the destination system is discarding the other fragments that it has received.

According to RFC 1122, all Time Exceeded error messages must be reported to the transport layer that triggered the failure, although the transport layer should not abort the connection. Instead, the transport layer should note that the problem occurred, and if the connection fails due to this problem, the message may be passed to the application protocol so that it can inform the user of the failure.

For more information on the Time Exceeded error message, refer to "Time Exceeded" later in this chapter.

Redirect error messages

The Redirect error message is used whenever a router needs to inform a sender of a shorter path to the specified destination. This message is typically seen when users only have a single (default) route defined on a network with multiple routers, and they should be sending datagrams for a specific network to a router other than the default. If the users don't send the datagrams to the "better" router, then the default router may use Redirect error messages to inform the sender of the correct router to use.

There are some rules that have to be taken into consideration with this design. First and foremost among them is the fact that Redirect error messages can only be sent when the "better" router is on the same subnet as the host that is sending the packets. This is pretty obvious; if the specified router were on a remote subnet, then the host would not be able to forward packets through it to the destination system. Furthermore, Redirect error messages should be sent only from a router on the same subnet as the original sender, since other routers on other subnets are not likely to know the routing paths available to the sender.

RFC 1122 even goes so far as to state that systems should discard any redirect messages that do not originate from first-hop routers, or messages with a suggested route that does not point to another first-hop router. In addition, RFC 1122 also states that whenever a system receives a Redirect error message, it *must* update its routing tables to use the suggested router if it is on the same network as the device itself. This rule is important, since a failure to update the routing table results in the sender continuously transmitting packets through the wrong gateway.

Figure 5-5 shows Ferret (192.168.10.10) trying to send a datagram for 192.168.30.10 to Sasquatch (which is the default router for Ferret). The router examines its local routing table and sees that the best router for the 192.168.30.0 network is via Canary (192.168.10.1), which is also on the same network as the original sender. Since Canary is "closer" to the final destination network than Sasquatch, Sasquatch issues an ICMP Redirect error message back to Ferret, telling it to use Canary for that traffic.

Note that Sasquatch will go ahead and forward the pending datagram to Canary on Ferret's behalf (as shown in step 3), but after that initial transfer, Ferret should hand all datagrams for the 192.168.30.0 network to Canary directly (as shown in step 4).

Redirect error messages are most commonly seen on networks that rely on the Router Discovery protocol (as described in RFC 1256) for dynamic routing services. Router Discovery makes extensive use of the Redirect error message, and in that environment, these messages do not signify "problems" with the network.

In order to provide more-detailed reporting, the Redirect message provides four different submessages (using the ICMP Message Code field as described later in "Error message headers"). The submessages offered by Redirect include:

Redirect for Destination Network
: This message is used when all traffic for the destination network should go through another router. This is the most common form of the Redirect error

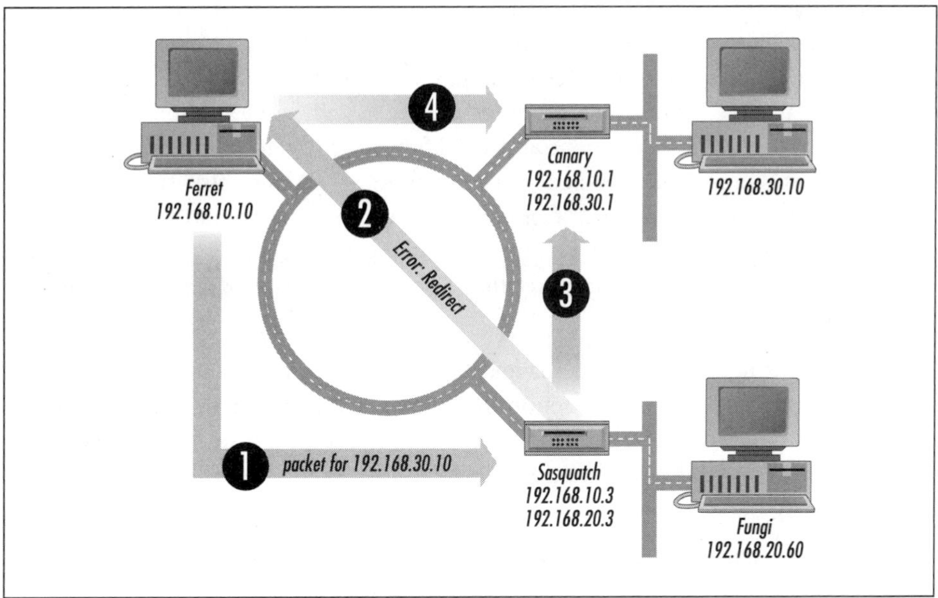

Figure 5-5. A typical scenario for Redirect error messages

message on local networks that rely on Router Discover for dynamic routing services.

Redirect for Destination Host
: This message is used when all traffic for the final destination system should go through another router. Since routing tables can contain host-specific entries (just as they can have network-specific entries), this error is useful if a host-specific redirect is required.

Redirect for Destination Network Based on Type-of-Service
: This error message is used when the sending system has requested a particular Type-of-Service for a specific destination, and all traffic with that Type-of-Service for the destination network should go through another router.

Redirect for Destination Host Based on Type-of-Service
: This error message is used when the sending system has requested a particular Type-of-Service for a specific system, and all traffic with that Type-of-Service for that destination should be sent through another router.

The Redirect message can be a very useful tool for network administrators, since administrators only have to configure their network devices to use a single router, and that router will provide redirection services to the rest of the devices based on its own routing tables. In fact, this is how the Router Discovery protocol works. As the network topology changes, the routers can inform the other devices about the changes dynamically.

However, even though RFC 1122 states that all IP implementations must support Redirect messages, many products do not do so, either failing to update their routing tables or ignoring the Redirect messages entirely. In addition, different implementations support Redirect to different degrees, with some systems taking the redirection message as permanent and modifying their routing tables accordingly, while other systems will only accept the change as a temporary suggestion and will modify their routing tables for only a few minutes. You should verify that your systems fully support the Redirect message to the extent that you require before attempting to implement dynamic routing services across your network using this mechanism.

Note that ICMP Redirect error messages are not sent when a route has been specified using the Source Route IP Option. In that case, the source route takes priority over the optimal path, and the first-hop router specified by the Source Route IP Option must forward the datagram to the next-hop router, regardless of any better paths that may be available.

For more information on the Redirect error message, refer ahead to "Redirect".

Source Quench error messages

The Source Quench error message is perhaps the simplest of all the ICMP error messages. Whenever a device is sending too much data for the destination host to process, the recipient can send an ICMP Source Quench error message back to the sender, suggesting that the sender throttle back on the rate at which it is sending data. If the sender does not slow down, then some packets are likely to be discarded by the congested device.

Source Quench is most often seen when a dial-up server connects a high-bandwidth network (such as a LAN) to a low-bandwidth device (such as a dial-up client). In this kind of scenario, it is easy for a high-powered system on the LAN to transmit more data than the dial-up server can feed to the end-point system. Eventually, the dial-up server will fill its transfer buffers and will have to start dropping packets if the sender doesn't slow down. Source Quench allows the dial-up server to inform the sender of the congestion, effectively requesting it to please stop sending so much data.

According to RFC 1122, all Source Quench error messages must be reported to the transport layer that triggered the failure. In addition, RFC 1122 states that if the Source Quench error message is handed to TCP, then TCP should shrink the congestion window for that virtual circuit to "one segment" and implement the slow start recovery algorithm (as described in "Congestion window sizing" in Chapter 7, *The Transmission Control Protocol*).

It is also important to note that RFC 792 states that either the destination system or any router in between the source and destination systems could issue an ICMP Source Quench error message. However, RFC 1812 states that routers should not send Source Quench error messages, claiming they are of questionable benefit. In fact, RFC 1812 even says that routers can choose not to forward Source Quench error messages if they do not want to.

It is my opinion that this is probably a priori call, however, and that Source Quench is an extremely effective tool for controlling intensive traffic flows (particularly those that use UDP, which does not provide for any flow-control services whatsoever). As such, it is my opinion that Source Quench should be used whenever and wherever possible.

For more information on the Source Quench error message, refer to "Source Quench" later in this chapter.

Parameter Problem error messages

The Parameter Problem error message generally means that something is wrong with the IP datagram itself, and that the datagram is being discarded.

Parameter Problem errors almost always result from an incorrect usage of an IP option. For example, a device may have sent an IP datagram with a malformed Source Route option in the IP header. This datagram would fail to be delivered due to this error, and would get discarded by the recipient (or an intermediary gateway) once the error was detected. Although it might seem that a Destination Unreachable: Source Route Failed error message would be sent in this case, that would not be true since the problem was a malformed option, rather than an undeliverable address.

In order to provide more-detailed reporting, the Parameter Problem message provides three different submessages (using the ICMP Message Code field as described later in "Error message headers"). The submessages offered by Parameter Problem include:

Pointer Indicates the Error
: This error means that there is a specific problem with the datagram's structure (such as a malformed header field). The location of the bad data is provided in the ICMP Message Data field of the Parameter Problem error message, allowing the sender to determine the cause of the failure.

Required Option Is Missing
: This error means that a required IP option has not been defined. This message is used only with the Security options, which are used only by the U.S. military, and are therefore not discussed in this book.

Bad Length

This error indicates that the Header Length and/or Total Packet Length values of the IP datagram do not appear to be accurate.

Note that there is no "checksum failure" submessage. If a checksum does not calculate correctly, then the entire packet is deemed to be corrupt and is discarded without warning. Any portion of the packet may have been corrupted, including the Destination Address field of the datagram's header. In this case, the recipient may not even be the desired destination system, so it should not do anything other than destroy the packet.

For more information on the Parameter Problem error message, refer to "Parameter Problem" later in this chapter.

Probing the Network

Since ICMP is a generic messaging protocol, it is also useful for determining general characteristics about the network. ICMP query messages provide this service, allowing systems to request information about the network in general.

ICMP queries are conversational by nature, with one system seeking information from another, and with the remote system returning the requested information. This process can be seen with the *ping* program's use of Echo Request query messages, which are responded to with Echo Reply query messages. This model is in contrast to the one-way nature of ICMP error messages, which are sent but not responded to.

Echo Request and Echo Reply query messages

One of the simplest tests that a user may wish to perform is verifying that a remote system is up and running on the network. Such a test may be required when basic connectivity appears to be failing.

ICMP provides two query messages that work together to provide just this service. The ICMP Echo Request query message is a probe sent by a user to a destination system, which responds with an ICMP Echo Reply query message.

RFC 1122 states that "every host must implement an ICMP Echo server." Since this service is mandatory, any user should be able to send an ICMP Echo Request to any host on the Internet and receive an ICMP Echo Reply message in return. However, this is not always the case, as firewalls may be blocking the packets (for security reasons), or the packets may simply fail to be delivered.

Furthermore, RFC 1122 also states that every host should implement an end-user–accessible application interface for sending Echo Request query messages to other hosts. Typically this application interface is implemented as a program called *ping*.

Almost every computing environment—even the most basic network print servers and fax gateways—offers some kind of *ping* program for testing basic connectivity. This is expected, since RFC 1122 mandates that any device with a TCP/IP stack must have one.

ping works by sending one or more ICMP Echo Request messages to a destination system, and then measuring the amount of time it took for the ICMP Echo Reply messages to be received from the system being probed. Some implementations do less than this, only printing a message that the destination system "is alive," while others do more than this, allowing the user to specify oversized messages or specific Precedence and Type-of-Service values for the IP datagrams that hold the ICMP Echo Request messages.

Figure 5-6 shows a simple *ping* between two hosts on a local network. In that example, Ferret sends an ICMP Echo Request query message to Froggy, which responds with an ICMP Echo Reply query message. This is a typical example of how *ping* is used on any local network.

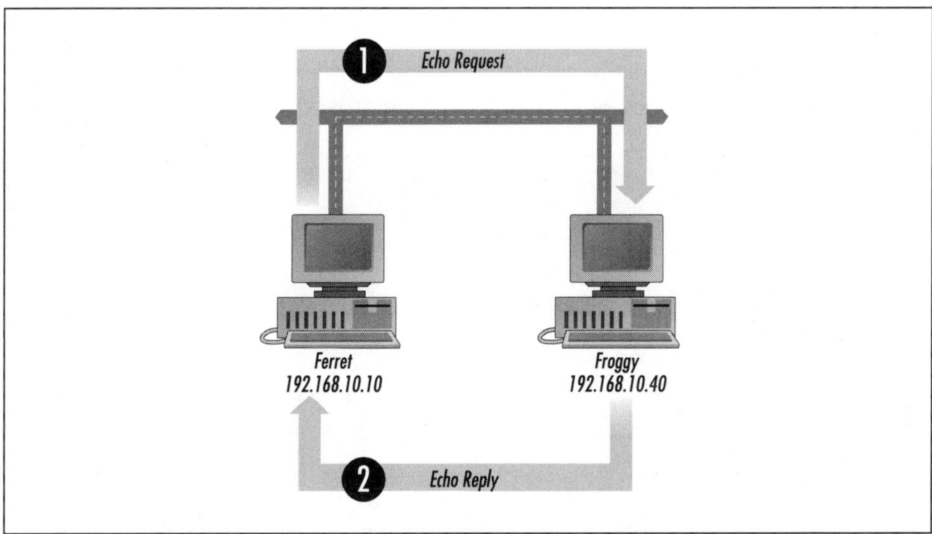

Figure 5-6. A typical exchange of Echo Request and Echo Reply query messages

Although the structure of the Echo Request and Echo Reply messages are described later in detail in "Echo Request and Echo Reply," some aspects of the formatting of these messages are important to understanding how the messages can be used for more-detailed testing. For example, Echo Request messages have an ancillary field for storing test data (called the Optional Data field), allowing the sender to provide customized test data inside the ICMP message. Most *ping* applications use some sort of default data in the test block (such as 64 bytes of 7-bit

US-ASCII text), although many of them will also let you provide your own data in this field, or will at least let you change the quantity of data being sent.

For example, you could choose to have *ping* send 2,000 bytes of data in the Optional Data field. This Echo Request message could then be used to test the effects of fragmentation when the datagram had to be sent across a network with an MTU that was smaller than that (such as an Ethernet segment).

RFC 1122 states that any data that is received in an ICMP Echo Request must be returned in the resulting Echo Reply message, so if your test data made it to the recipient, you should get all of the data back. However, if the recipient does not support fragmentation (and not every IP device does), then an Echo Reply message would still need to be returned. It would only have to contain as much data as would fit within a single message (according to the MTU restrictions of the target system).

This concept is illustrated in Figure 5-7, which shows a Token-Ring–attached device with an MTU of four kilobytes (192.168.30.10) sending a two-kilobyte Echo Request message to an Ethernet-attached device with an MTU of 1500 bytes (192.168.10.10). In order for the router to forward the message to the Ethernet segment, it must split the IP datagram into two fragments, which will be reassembled by the destination host once both fragments have arrived.

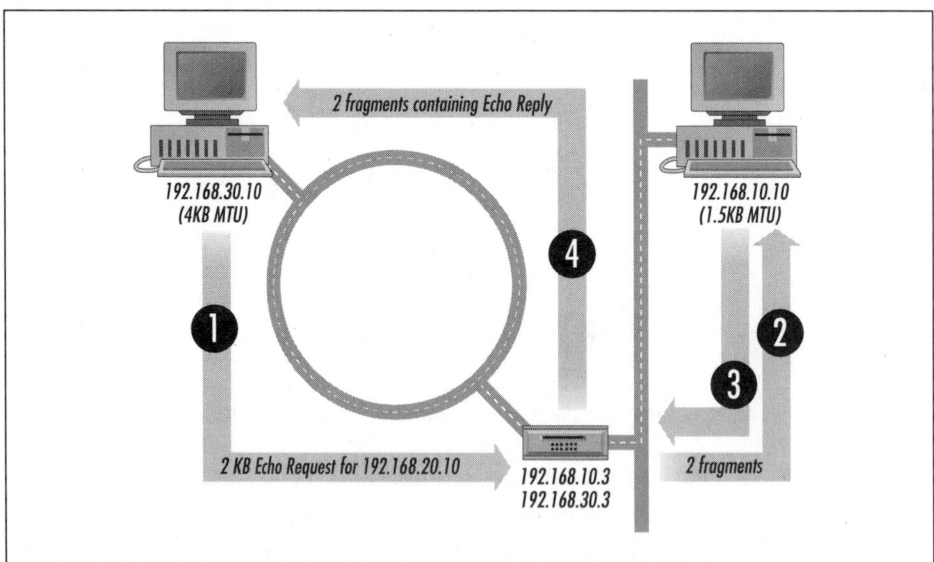

Figure 5-7. Fragmenting Echo Request and Echo Reply query messages

Once the message was received, 192.168.10.10 would respond with an ICMP Echo Reply message that was also two kilobytes long (this datagram would have to be fragmented by the sender before it could be sent, since it exceeds the local network's MTU size). The router would then forward both fragments back to 192.168. 30.10, who would reassemble them into a single datagram before the data is processed. This illustrates how it is possible to use oversized datagrams with *ping* to test fragmentation across a complex network.

Another interesting (but limited) test for *ping* is for a device to send an ICMP Echo Request query message to all of the devices on the local network, by specifying the broadcast address or the all-hosts multicast address for the local network in the Destination Address field of the IP datagram. However, RFC 1122 explicitly states that devices do not have to respond to these queries, and many implementations will not do so. In addition, not all versions of *ping* are capable of dealing with multiple responses to a single request, and will report erroneous information when this situation occurs.

In addition, some *ping* implementations also allow the user to specify the Precedence or Type-of-Service values for the underlying IP datagrams. According to RFC 1122, the remote system is supposed to use those same value in the Echo Reply messages that they return. By specifying non-default values, you can use *ping* to test how well your network handles classified data as opposed to regular (i.e., nonclassified) data, or how traffic is routed according to nondefault Type-of-Service or Precedence values.

Other IP options and services explicitly supported by ICMP Echo Request and Echo Reply query messages are the Source Route, Record Route, and Timestamp IP Options. For example, RFC 1122 states that if an ICMP Echo Request query message is received within an IP datagram that has the Source Route IP Option defined, then the ICMP Echo Reply query message must follow the same route back to the sender, in reverse order.

For more information on the Echo Request and Echo Reply query messages, refer ahead to "Echo Request and Echo Reply."

Timestamp Request and Timestamp Reply query messages

Another pair of ICMP query messages that can be useful for testing the network is the Timestamp Request and Timestamp Reply query messages, which allow a sender to determine the amount of latency that a particular network is experiencing. This gives good insight into the performance characteristics of the network.

As can be imagined, this information also provides more insight than most people want to provide, at least to users outside the local network. For this reason, RFC 1122 states that the Timestamp Request and Timestamp Reply query messages are entirely optional. Indeed, there are only a few TCP/IP implementations that support them.

Timestamp works by having one system send a Timestamp Request query message to another host, with the current time in the Timestamp Request message's Originate Timestamp field. The recipient then creates a Timestamp Reply query message that contains the Originate Timestamp field from the original message, along with new Receive Timestamp and Transmit Timestamp fields.

Once the Timestamp Reply query message is received by the querying device, the different timestamps can be examined, allowing the system to determine the amount of time that it took for the remote system to process the Timestamp Request query message. This data can then be subtracted from the round-trip delivery time, allowing the system to calculate the length of time that it took for the datagrams to travel across the network. This provides a better indication of actual network latency than the Echo Request and Echo Reply query messages, which do not provide any information about the amount of time that the remote system spent processing the ICMP messages.

Note that the timestamps used in the Timestamp Request and Timestamp Reply query messages are based on the number of milliseconds since midnight, using Universal Time (UTC). By using UTC, network devices do not have to worry about timezone issues, since all devices are on the same timezone (UTC).

The ICMP Timestamp Request and Timestamp Reply messages can also be set to use specific Type-of-Service and Precedence values, allowing latency to be measured across specific networks. In addition, RFC 1122 states that if an ICMP Timestamp Request query message is received within an IP datagram that has the Source Route IP Option defined, then the ICMP Timestamp Reply query message must follow the same route back to the sender, in reverse order. This sequence allows a user to measure latency across a specific network path.

Also note that accurate measurements of network latency depend upon each system having accurate (or consistent) time values for their local clocks. Before relying on the Timestamp query messages for latency measurements, synchronize the clocks on the systems being tested using a protocol such as NTP.

For more information on the Timestamp Request and Timestamp Reply query messages, refer ahead to "Timestamp Request and Timestamp Reply."

Address Mask Request and Address Mask Reply query messages

RFC 792 defined a variety of host-configuration messages, allowing diskless systems to obtain IP addresses and other data during the boot process by using ICMP messages. However, the primary ICMP query messages used for this—the Information Request and Information Reply query messages—have since been deprecated and are now obsolete. The Address Mask Request and Address Mask Reply query messages are also somewhat obsolete, although their usage has not been deprecated as of yet.

Essentially, the Address Mask Request and Address Mask Reply query messages allow a host to determine the subnet mask in use on the local network. Once a host has obtained an IP address (which could be obtained via Reverse ARP, BOOTP, or DHCP), they could then send an Address Mask Request message to the local broadcast address of 255.255.255.255. An Address Mask server on the network would then respond with an Address Mask Reply query message that is unicast back to the requesting device directly, providing the host with a subnet mask for the IP address being used.

RFC 1122 states that the Address Mask Request and Address Mask Reply query messages are entirely optional. Indeed, only a handful of systems use these messages today.

For more information on the Address Request and Address Reply query messages, refer to "Address Mask Request and Address Mask Reply" later in this chapter.

Router Solicitation and Router Advertisement query messages

RFC 1256 introduced the concept of a Router Discovery protocol that allows the devices on a network to locate routers using ICMP query messages, rather than having to be configured to use static routing entries or run a full-fledged routing protocol like RIP or OSPF.

The Router Discovery protocol consists of a Router Solicitation query message, which is issued by hosts when they first become active on the network (sent to the all-routers multicast address of 224.0.0.2). Each router on the network should then respond to the Router Solicitation query messages with a unicast Router Advertisement query message, informing the querying device directly of the IP addresses that can be used for packet forwarding. In addition, routers will also issue unsolicited Router Advertisement messages on a periodic basis (sent to the all-hosts multicast address of 224.0.0.1), allowing hosts both to change their routing tables as higher-priority routers become available, and to expire old routers if they are no longer being advertised after a certain length of time.

According to RFC 1256, unsolicited Router Advertisement query messages should be sent to the all-hosts multicast address of 224.0.0.1 through every network interface in use by the router, although directed Router Advertisements that result from Router Solicitations are only unicast back to the requesting device, through the most appropriate interface. Each of these advertisement messages must contain the IP address in use on the local interface, as well as a Preference value for the IP address being published. Network devices then use the IP address with the highest Preference (the lowest number) as their default router.

This process is illustrated in Figure 5-8. In that example, Ferret issues an ICMP Router Solicitation query message to the all-routers multicast group address of 224.0.0.2, which both Sasquatch and Canary respond to (using the ICMP Router Advertisement query message, also sent to the all-routers multicast address of 224.0.0.2). Each response also contains a Preference value for that specific router, with Sasquatch having the highest preference (this router will become the default router for Ferret).

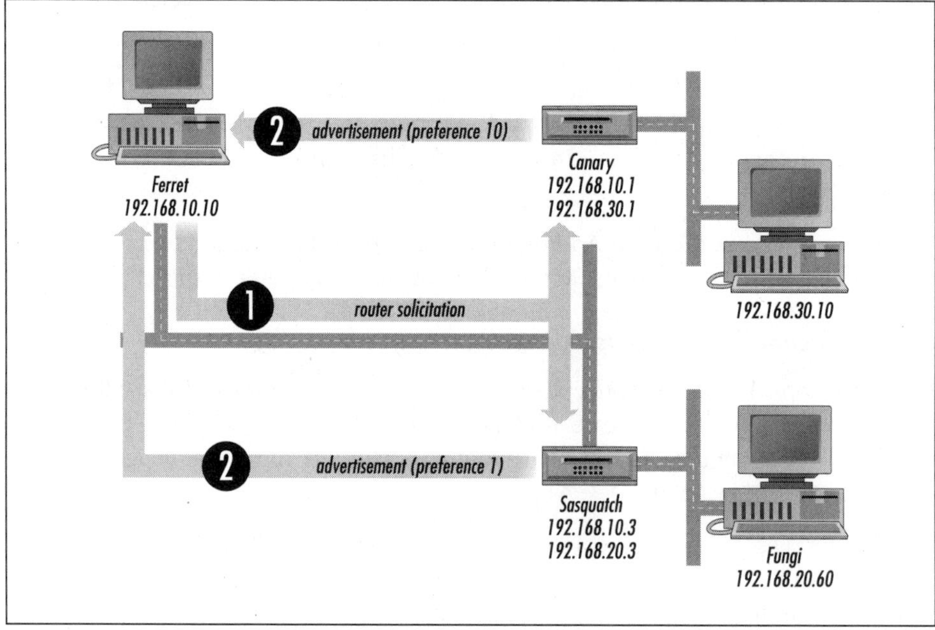

Figure 5-8. Router Discovery using Router Solicitation and Advertisement query messages

Note that routers do not advertise the networks or paths that they can route for. Devices must discover (and build) their own routing tables dynamically, by way of the ICMP Redirect error message discussed earlier in "Redirect error messages." In that model, the Router Discovery client uses the Router Solicitation query message to choose a default route, and then relies on the Redirect error messages whenever the host tries to send a datagram to the default router for delivery, but the router knows of a better path for the specified destination system.

This concept is illustrated in Figure 5-9. As we saw in Figure 5-8, Sasquatch had the strongest preference, and was chosen as the default router by Ferret. If the host wants to send a datagram to 192.168.30.10 (a non-local device), it would send the packets to Sasquatch for delivery. However, Sasquatch would know that Canary was the better router for that destination, so it would return an ICMP Redirect error message back to Ferret, informing it that all traffic for the 192.168.30.0

network should go to Canary. Sasquatch would then forward on the packets it had already received, while Ferret would make note of the new path, and (hopefully) start to use that router for any future datagrams for that destination network.

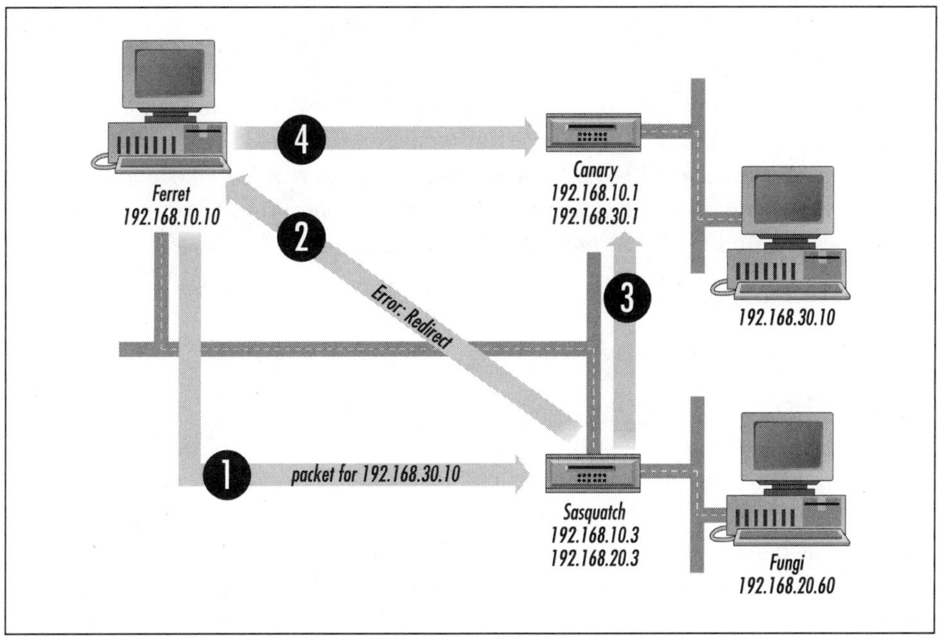

Figure 5-9. Router Discovery using Redirect error messages

On small or isolated networks that have only one or two routers on any given segment, the process of learning about the entire network will only take a few moments and is not nearly as complicated as it sounds here. Conversely, on large and complex networks with many different routers, this process can be significantly more complicated than it sounds here.

For more information on the Router Solicitation and Router Advertisement query messages, refer to "Router Solicitation" and "Router Advertisement," both later in this chapter.

ICMP Messages

ICMP is used for two different types of operations: reporting on problems that prevent delivery (such as "Destination Unreachable" errors), and probing the network through the use of request and reply messages (such as those found in the *ping* program's "Echo Request" and "Echo Reply" ICMP messages).

Every ICMP message is assigned a unique "message type," which is simply a numeric code that represents each of the predefined messages. There are a variety of predefined message types that devices can choose from when they need to send a message to another device. Many of these messages were defined in RFC 792, while others were added in RFC 950, RFC 1122, RFC 1812, and RFC 1256. In addition, some messages have been rendered obsolete (such as the Information Request and Information Reply query messages), and are no longer considered part of the standard dictionary of message types.

For a detailed listing of all of the ICMP Message Types that are currently registered, refer to the Internet Assigned Numbers Authority's (IANA) online registry (accessible at *http://www.isi.edu/in-notes/iana/assignments/icmp-parameters*). Note that RFC 1122 states that if a system receives an ICMP message with a type or code that it does not understand, it must ignore the message.

Table 5-1 lists the Message Types most often used with IPv4.

Table 5-1. Message Types and Their Usage

Type	Message Description	Message Family	Defined In
0	Echo Reply	Query (Reply)	RFC 792
3	Destination Unreachable	Error	RFC 1122
4	Source Quench	Error	RFC 792
5	Redirect	Error	RFC 792
8	Echo Request	Query (Request)	RFC 792
9	Router Advertisement	Query (Reply)	RFC 1256
10	Router Solicitation	Query (Request)	RFC 1256
11	Time Exceeded	Error	RFC 1122
12	Parameter Problem	Error	RFC 792
13	Timestamp Request	Query (Request)	RFC 792
14	Timestamp Reply	Query (Reply)	RFC 792
17	Address Mask Request	Query (Request)	RFC 950
18	Address Mask Reply	Query (Reply)	RFC 950

Since these messages are used for specific types of functionality, they vary widely in their structure and formatting, with some messages having more fields than others. Refer to "Error message headers" for information on the structure of ICMP error messages, and "Query message headers," both later in this chapter, for information on the structure of ICMP query messages.

ICMP Error Messages

ICMP error messages are used whenever a nontransient delivery problem occurs that the sender should be made aware of. A variety of ICMP error messages exist (as described later in "Error message types and codes"), although each of these messages have their own special requirements and treatments. However, all ICMP error messages have the same basic structure, and these fields are described in the next section.

Error message headers

ICMP error messages consist of a predefined set of fields that indicate the type of message being passed, and that also provide message-specific services (such as IP addresses or pointers to corrupt data). These predefined fields are followed by the IP header and the first eight bytes of data from the datagram that caused the error to be generated.

Since delivery problems can occur at any layer, ICMP error messages must include the full header and the first eight bytes of data from the failing IP datagram in order for the sender to see which packet failed, and in order for the sender to notify the transport and application protocols that generated the failure. This process allows the sender to pass the error message to the appropriate layer for subsequent processing.

Table 5-2 lists all of the fields in an ICMP error message's header, along with their size (in bytes), and some usage notes. For more information on these fields, refer to the individual discussions throughout this section.

Table 5-2. Format of the ICMP Error Message

Field	Size	Usage Notes
Message Type	1 byte	Indicates the specific ICMP error message.
Message Code	1 byte	Indicates the specific subclass of the specific ICMP error message.
Checksum	2 bytes	Used to validate the ICMP message's contents.
Message Data	4 bytes	Used for message-specific needs.
Original Headers	20–60 bytes	The full header of the IP datagram that failed.
Original Data	8 bytes	The first 64 bits of the IP datagram's data. This data will contain the Source and Destination Port fields for the transport protocol used by the sender, allowing the transport protocols to determine which specific application generated the failing datagram.

The total length of an ICMP error message is eight bytes. However, this measurement does not include the original datagram's IP headers, which can add anywhere from 20 to 60 bytes of additional data to the message, nor does it include the first eight bytes of data from the failing packet. All told, an ICMP error message can be anywhere from 36 to 72 bytes, including all of these fields.

All ICMP messages are sent within IP datagrams directly. Each of these datagrams must have a protocol identifier of 1. Also, RFC 1122 (Host Network Requirements) states that ICMP error messages sent from hosts should use the default Type-of-Service and Precedence values (0), although RFC 1812 (Router Requirements) states that error messages sent from routers should have a precedence value of 6 or 7.

The remainder of this section discusses the ICMP error messages in detail, using the capture shown in Figure 5-10 for reference purposes.

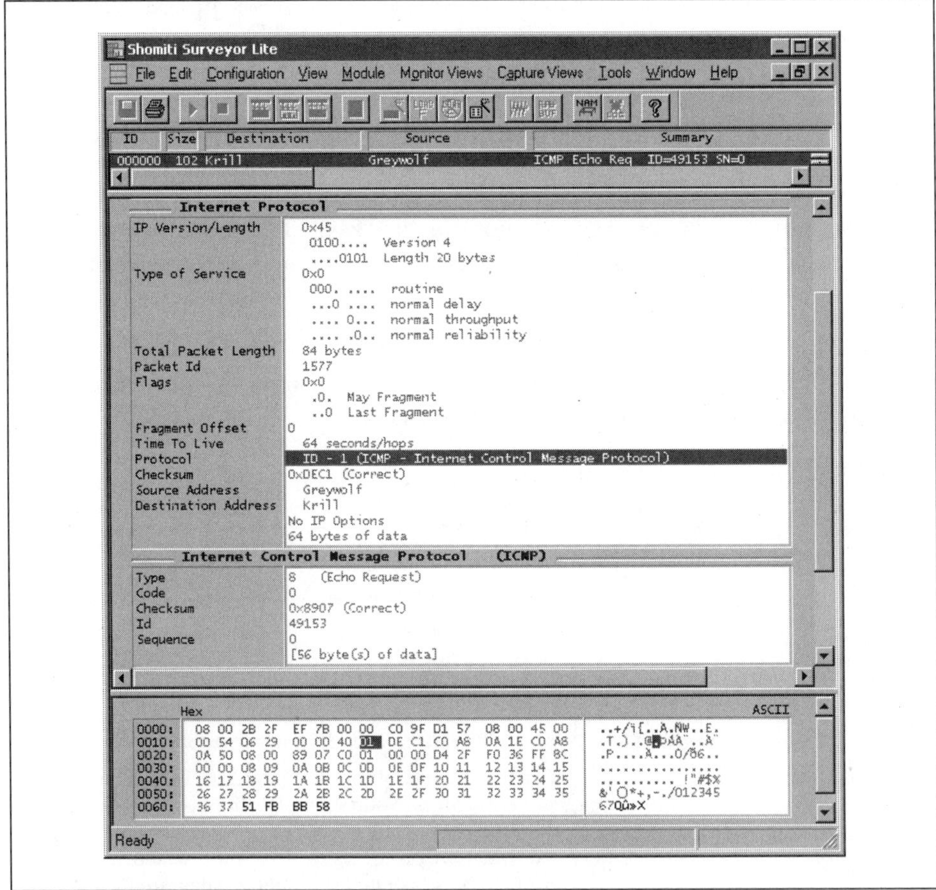

Figure 5-10. A simple ICMP error message

Message Type

The Type field is used to specify the exact ICMP error message being sent.

Size

Eight bits.

Notes

ICMP essentially consists of a predefined dictionary of messages, allowing messages to be exchanged using numeric identifiers. The Type field is used to specify the major class of the message, while the Code field is used to specify the minor class, though some message Types do not have any subtype Codes.

Table 5-3 lists all of the ICMP error message Types used with IPv4, and their meanings.

Table 5-3. ICMP Error Message Types

Type	Message Description	Usage Notes
3	Destination Unreachable	The network, host, or port number specified by the original datagram is unreachable. This could be related to a variety of problems.
4	Source Quench	Either the destination system or an intermediary device is receiving more data than it can process, and is asking the sender to reduce the rate of transfer.
5	Redirect	This message will occur if a device tries to send a datagram to a destination through a router, but the router knows of a shorter path to the destination.
11	Time Exceeded	Either the datagram's Time-to-Live timer expired, or some fragments were not received in time to be reassembled by the destination system.
12	Parameter Problem	Another problem occurred. This error is almost always related to problems with IP or TCP Options.

Capture Sample

In the capture shown in Figure 5-11, the Type field is set to 3, which is used for all Destination Unreachable errors.

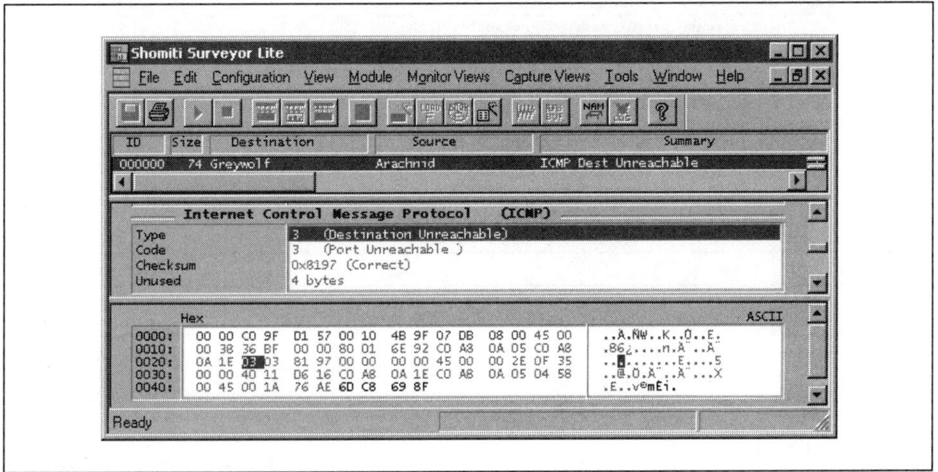

Figure 5-11. The Message Type field

See Also

"Message Code"

Message Code

The Code field is used to specify a specific subtype of the ICMP error message, which was specified in the Type field.

Size

Eight bits.

Notes

ICMP essentially consists of a predefined dictionary of messages, allowing messages to be exchanged using numeric identifiers. The Type field is used to specify the major class of the message, while the Code field is used to specify the minor class, although some message Types do not have any subtype Codes.

The values used in this field vary according to the Message Type for the current error message.

Capture Sample

In the capture shown in Figure 5-12, the Code field is set to 3, which is the value associated with the subtype of "Port Unreachable" when used with Type 3 (Destination Unreachable) error messages.

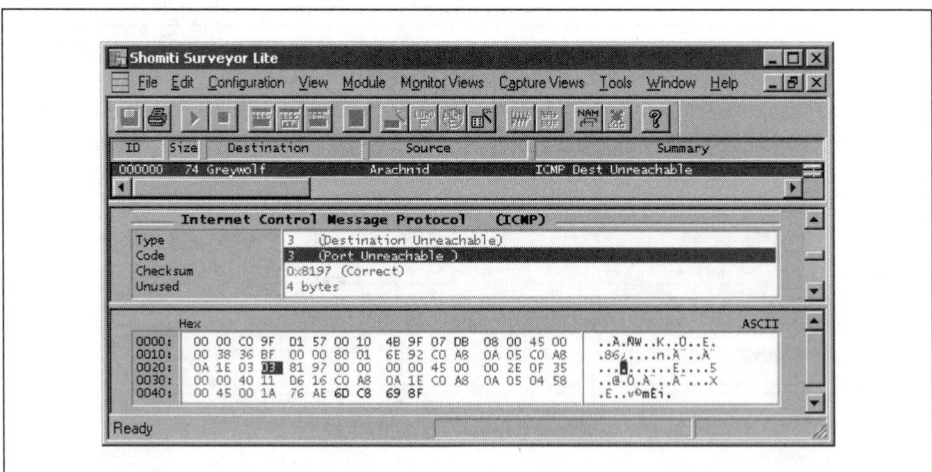

Figure 5-12. The Message Code field

See Also

"Message Type"

Checksum

Used to store a checksum of the ICMP message, allowing destination systems to validate the contents of the message and test for possible corruption.

Size

Sixteen bits.

Notes

The checksum field provides a simple validation scheme for ICMP messages. When calculating the checksum, the sending system looks at the entire message (with the checksum field set to 0) and performs a simple checksum operation. This procedure is reversed by all recipients before the contents of the message are processed.

Capture Sample

In the capture shown in Figure 5-13, the Checksum has been calculated to be hexadecimal "81 97", which is correct.

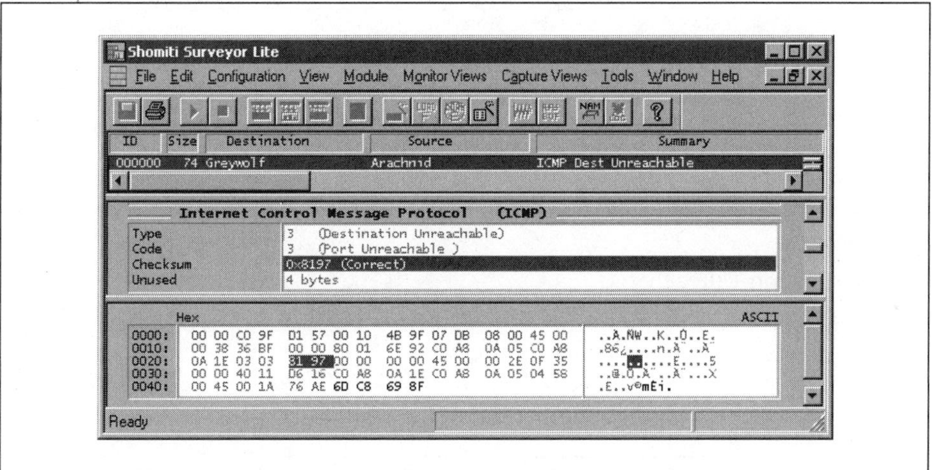

Figure 5-13. The Checksum field

Message Data

Used to provide additional information about the cause of certain ICMP error messages.

Size

Thirty-two bits.

Notes

This field is used differently by each of the ICMP error messages (and is even used differently by some message types). For example, the ICMP Redirect error message uses this field to provide the IP address of a preferred router, while the Destination Unreachable: Fragmentation Required but DF Bit Is Set error message will use this field to provide the Next-Hop MTU (if Path MTU Discovery is supported by the router reporting the error). Most of the ICMP error messages do not use this field.

Capture Sample

In the capture shown in Figure 5-14, the Message Data field is filled with zeroes, indicating that the field is unused.

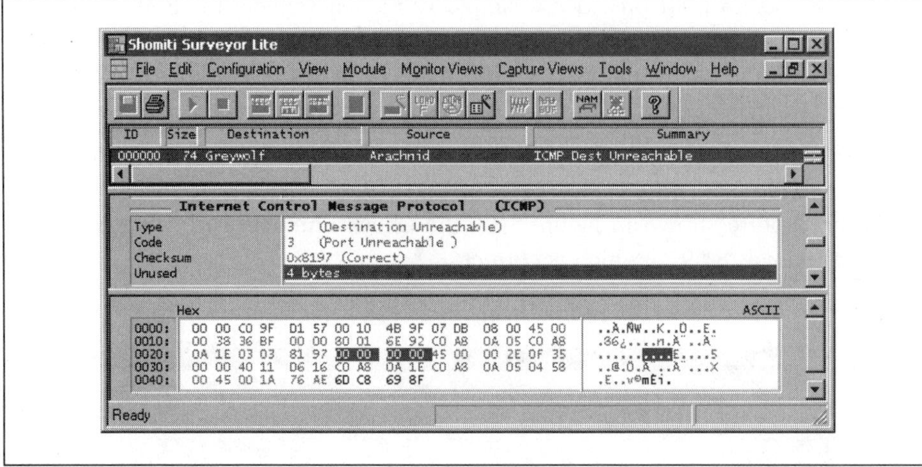

Figure 5-14. The Message Data field

See Also

"Destination Unreachable"

"Redirect"

"Parameter Problem"

Original Headers

In order for ICMP to determine which datagram failed, it must be given information about that datagram. For this reason, the original headers from the failing IP datagram are always included with the ICMP error message.

Size

20 to 60 bytes, depending on the length of the original datagram's IP header.

Notes

IP is a datagram-centric protocol, and not a circuit-centric protocol. As such, it cannot keep track of failed datagrams by referencing a sequence number or some other counter like TCP can. Instead, in order for IP to know when a datagram failed, the headers from the failing datagram must be returned to the sender, allowing it to parse through the information and locate the transport protocol that caused the problem.

This feature is especially important when a host sends many different datagrams to another specific destination. If the host sends hundreds of datagrams and then gets an ICMP error message, which datagram does the failure apply to? The only way to authoritatively answer this question is to examine the failing datagram explicitly.

Typically, this information is used in conjunction with the Original Data field, which allows a transport protocol to determine the application that generated the failing datagram.

Capture Sample

In the capture shown in Figure 5-15, the original headers indicate that the failing datagram was a UDP message sent from Greywolf to Arachnid. The Message Type and Code fields (shown previously) indicate that the datagram was undeliverable because the destination port number for the UDP message was unreachable.

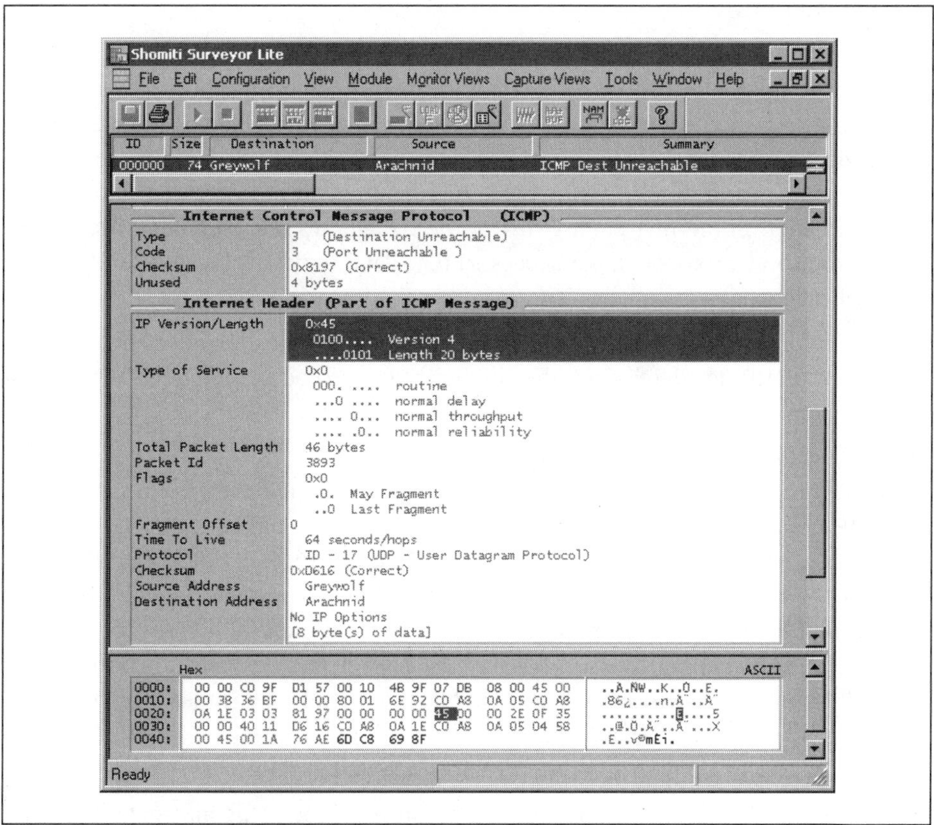

Figure 5-15. The IP headers from the failing IP datagram

See Also

"Message Type"

"Message Code"

"Original Data"

Original Data

Just as ICMP needs to know which IP datagram failed in order to inform the appropriate transport protocol of the problem, the transport protocols also need to know which application sent the failing datagram before they can notify the application of the failure. For this reason, the first eight bytes of data from the failing IP datagram are always included with the ICMP error message, since these bytes contain the source and destination port number fields used by UDP and TCP (or the Message Type and Code fields from ICMP query messages).

Size

Sixty-four bits.

Notes

In order for the transport protocols to know which application generated the failing datagram, they have to be able to examine data that is outside of the original IP headers. All of the upper-layer protocols in use with IP—including TCP, UDP, and ICMP itself—place the source and destination application information in the first eight bytes of the datagram's data segment. As long as the transport protocols have access to that data, they can locate the offending application.

This information is used in conjunction with the Original Headers field, which allows ICMP to determine the higher-layer protocol that sent the failing datagram.

Capture Sample

In Figure 5-15, we saw that the failing datagram originated from UDP. Since UDP uses the first two bytes of the UDP header to indicate the source port, we can tell from the capture shown in Figure 5-16 that the application that sent the failing datagram was using port 1112 on Greywolf (shown as hexadecimal "04 58"). Furthermore, since UDP uses the next two bytes for the destination port number, we can tell that the packet was destined for port 69 (the well-known port number associated with the Trivial File Transfer Protocol) on Arachnid (shown as hexadecimal "00 45").

Therefore, we can tell that this packet failed to be delivered due to there not being a TFTP server running on port 69 on Arachnid. This information should be reported to the application that is using UDP port 1112.

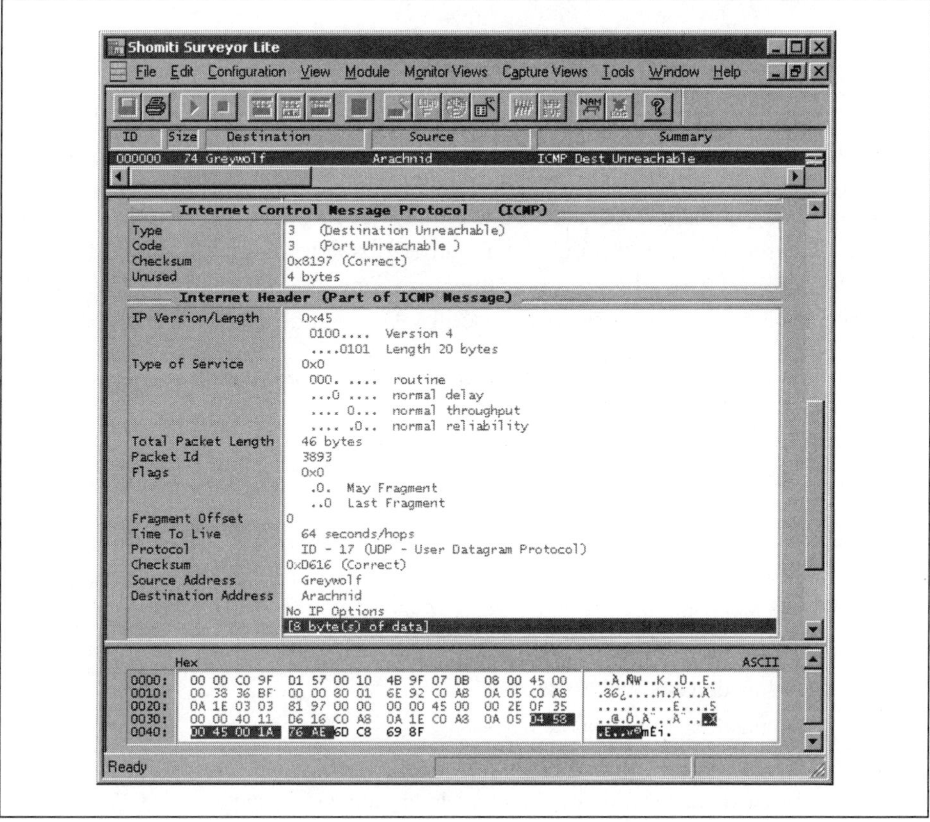

Figure 5-16. The first eight bytes of data from the failing datagram

See Also

"Message Type"

"Message Code"

"Original Headers"

Error message types and codes

The remainder of this section discusses the different ICMP error messages, as listed earlier in Table 5-3.

Destination Unreachable

Destination Unreachable means that the destination network, host, or port number specified in the IP datagram was unreachable. This could be a result of a variety of factors, ranging from a router being unable to find a path to the remote system, to the network refusing to accept connections from this particular sender, among many other factors.

ICMP Message Type

The Message Type for Destination Unreachable is 3.

ICMP Message Codes

Destination Unreachable makes extensive use of the Code field. RFC 792 defined six different possible failure codes, numbered 0 through 5. This list was supplemented by RFC 1122, which added seven additional codes (6 through 12). Finally, RFC 1812 added three more codes (13 through 15), but also declared codes 8 through 10 as either obsolete or inappropriate for non-military usage (for this reason, they are not documented in this book). Table 5-4 lists the Codes currently used by Destination Unreachable

Table 5-4. Codes for Destination Unreachable and Their Meaning

Code	Meaning
0	Network Unreachable
1	Host Unreachable
2	Protocol Unreachable
3	Port Unreachable
4	Fragmentation Required but DF Bit Is Set
5	Source Route Failed
6	Destination Network Unknown
7	Destination Host Unknown
8	Source Host Isolated (obsolete)
9	Destination Network Administratively Prohibited (obsolete)
10	Destination Host Administratively Prohibited (obsolete)
11	Destination Network Unreachable for Type-of-Service
12	Destination Host Unreachable for Type-of-Service
13	Communication Administratively Prohibited
14	Host Precedence Violation
15	Precedence Cutoff in Effect

ICMP Message Data

The ICMP Message Data field is unused with Destination Unreachable error messages (except when Path MTU Discovery is being used), and must be empty. When Path MTU Discovery is being used, the Message Data field is split into two subfields of two bytes each, as shown in Table 5-5.

Table 5-5. The Subfields in an ICMP Message Data Field, as Defined by RFC 1191

Subfield	Bytes	Description
Unused	2	Unused and must be zero
Next-Hop MTU	2	The MTU of the next-hop network

If a router supports Path MTU Discovery and was unable to forward a datagram due to size issues, then it would reject the datagram using the Destination Unreachable: Fragmentation Required but DF Bit Is Set error message, and also inform the original sender of the next-hop network's MTU size using the "Next-Hop MTU" subfield.

Defined In

RFC 792, RFC 1122, RFC 1191, and RFC 1812.

Notes

A Destination Unreachable error message can signify any number of problems, and as such is fairly complex. Refer to "Destination Unreachable error messages" earlier in this chapter for a comprehensive discussion of this error message.

Capture Sample

The packet capture shown in Figure 5-17 shows a Destination Unreachable: Port Unreachable error message being sent to Greywolf from Arachnid. By looking at the failing packet's headers and first eight bytes of data, we can tell that Greywolf had tried to send a UDP message to port 69 on Arachnid, which does not appear to have a listener on that port.

See Also

"Destination Unreachable error messages"

"Notes on Path MTU Discovery"

Source Quench

Source Quench error messages are used when data is arriving too fast to be processed by an intermediate router or by the final destination system, informing the sender that a bottleneck has occurred and that it should slow down the rate of transfer.

ICMP Message Type

The Message Type for Source Quench is 4.

ICMP Message Codes

Source Quench does not use any Codes, and this field must be zero.

ICMP Message Data

The ICMP Message Data field is unused with Source Quench, and must be zero.

Defined In

RFC 792.

Notes

Source Quench is most often used when a router connects a high-bandwidth network (such as a LAN) to a low-bandwidth network or device (such as a

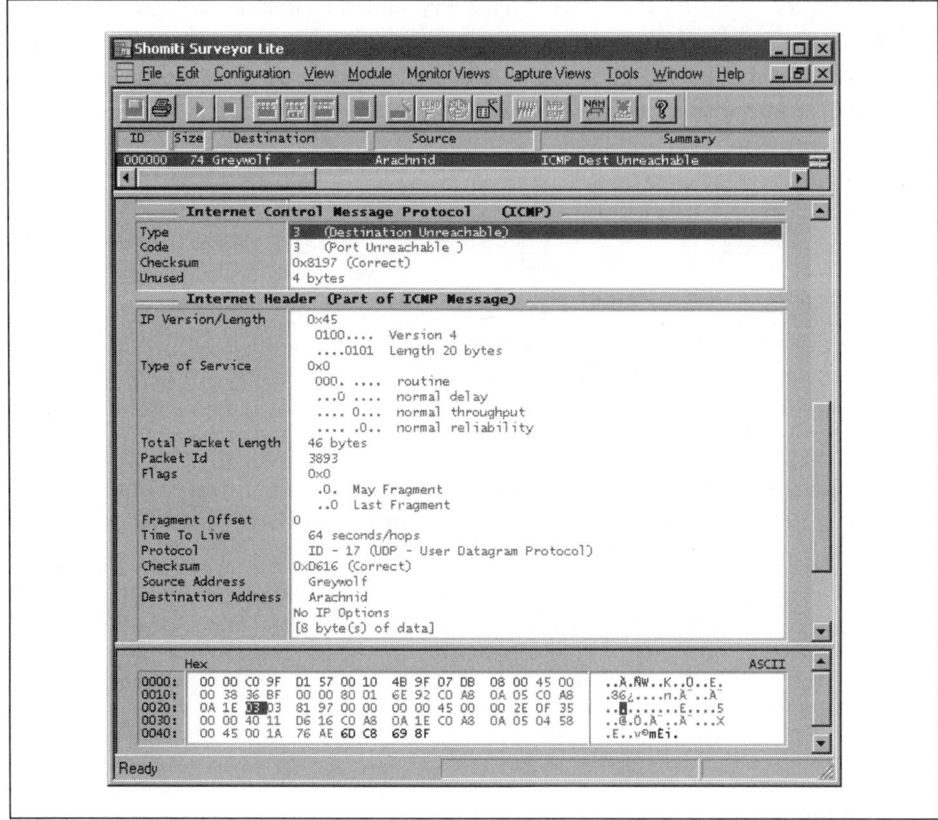

Figure 5-17. An ICMP Destination Unreachable: Port Unreachable error message

dial-up server). In such a scenario, it is easy for a sender to transmit more data than the dial-up server can feed to the end-point system. Eventually, the dial-up server will fill its transfer buffers and will have to start dropping packets if the sender doesn't slow down the rate at which it sends data. Source Quench allows the router (or the destination system) to inform the sending device that the network is congested, and to please stop sending so much data.

RFC 1812 stated that the Source Quench error message had not proven to be of much use in preventing congestion from occurring and that routers were therefore not required to send (or relay) these messages in case congestion did occur. While this is particularly true with TCP-based applications that can rely on TCP's sliding window for flow control services, it is not true for UDP-based applications that could otherwise flood a network. Furthermore, no other protocol or service has yet been standardized that offers similar services, and as such the Source Quench error message still serves an important service in some instances.

Capture Sample

The packet capture shown in Figure 5-18 shows a Source Quench error message being sent from Sasquatch to Ferret. By studying the headers from the original IP packet (as provided in the ICMP message), we can see that the failing packet was a UDP datagram sent from Ferret to Dial-Client, a remote dial-up user. This would indicate that Sasquatch (the dial-up router) was unable to send all of the data it had queued for Dial-Client, and that Ferret needs to slow down the rate of transfer. Ferret should react to this message by momentarily pausing the data transmission.

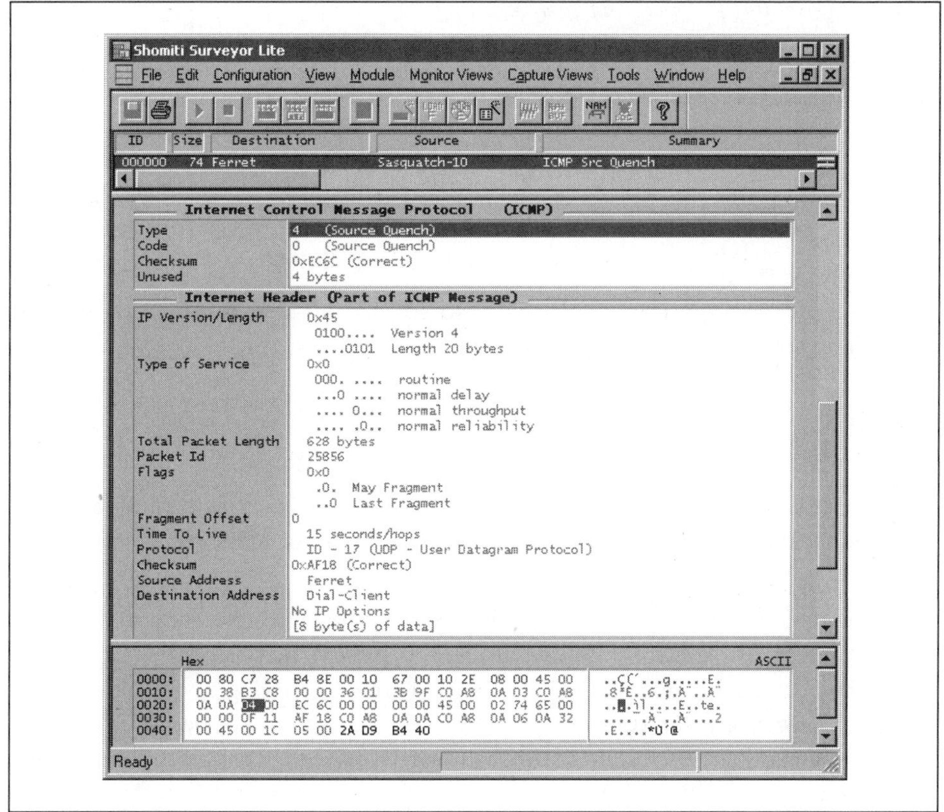

Figure 5-18. An ICMP Source Quench error message

See Also

"Source Quench error messages"

Redirect

The Redirect error message is used when a router needs to tell a host that a different router should be used for a particular destination.

ICMP Message Type

The Message Type for Redirect is 5.

ICMP Message Codes

Redirect uses four different Codes, each of which indicate different types of redirection. Table 5-6 lists the codes used and their meanings.

Table 5-6. Codes for "Redirect" and Their Meanings

Code	Meaning
0	Redirect for Destination Network
1	Redirect for Destination Host
2	Redirect for Destination Network Based on Type-of-Service
3	Redirect for Destination Host Based on Type-of-Service

ICMP Message Data

The ICMP Message Data field is used to specify the alternate router and must contain the 32-bit IP address of that router.

Defined In

RFC 792.

Notes

The Redirect error message is fairly complicated. Refer back to "Redirect error messages" for a comprehensive discussion of this error message.

Capture Sample

In the capture sample shown in Figure 5-19, Sasquatch has sent a Redirect for Destination Host error message to Ferret. Notice that according to the IP header embedded in the ICMP datagram, Ferret was trying to open a connection to *www.ora.com* (O'Reilly & Associates' web site), and that it sent the initial segment to Sasquatch for forwarding. However, Sasquatch knows that Canary (192.168.10.1) offers a better route for that destination, so it returns the Network Redirect message back to Ferret, informing Ferret to use Canary for that destination network. From this point on, Ferret should use Canary as the default route for that destination.

See Also

"Redirect error messages"

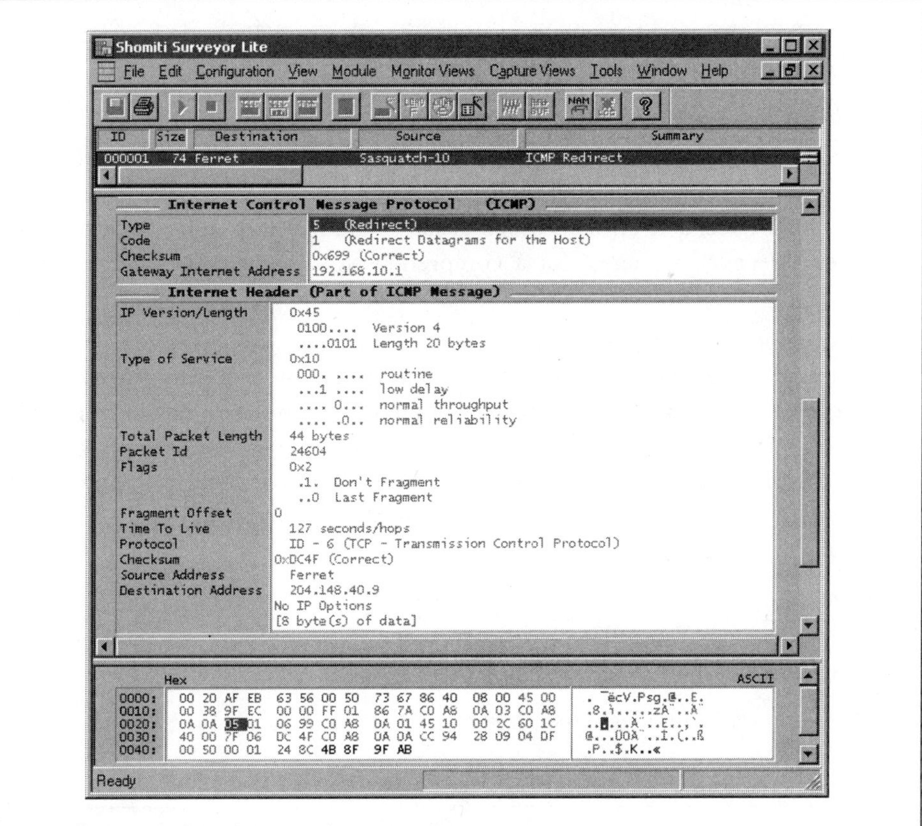

Figure 5-19. An ICMP Redirect for Destination Host error message

Time Exceeded

Time Exceeded messages can be sent when the IP datagram's Time-to-Live value has reached zero but the datagram has not yet been delivered to the final destination. They can also be sent when all of the fragments from an IP datagram have not been received within the allotted time.

ICMP Message Type

The Message Type for Time Exceeded is 11.

ICMP Message Codes

Time Exceeded error messages have two possible Codes, shown in Table 5-7.

Table 5-7. Codes for Time Exceeded and Their Meanings

Code	Meaning
0	Time-to-Live Exceeded in Transit
1	Fragment Reassembly Time Exceeded

ICMP Message Data

The ICMP Message Data field is unused with Time Exceeded and must be zero.

Defined In

RFC 792.

Notes

The Time Exceeded error message is fairly complicated. Refer back to "Time Exceeded error messages" for a comprehensive discussion of this error message.

Capture Sample

In the capture shown in Figure 5-20, a datagram sent from Greywolf to Sasquatch (as seen in the original datagram's IP header) had a very small Time-To-Live value (1 hop). Sasquatch was unable to forward the packet without the Time-To-Live reaching zero, so the packet was destroyed, and a Time Exceeded: Time-to-Live Exceeded In Transit error message was returned to Greywolf.

See Also

"Time Exceeded error messages"

"Time-to-Live" in Chapter 2, *The Internet Protocol*

"Notes on traceroute"

Parameter Problem

RFC 1122 states that the Parameter Problem error message should be used only if no other ICMP error message is appropriate for the particular problem that arose.

ICMP Message Type

The Message Type for Parameter Problem is 12.

ICMP Message Codes

Parameter Problem has three possible Codes, as shown in Table 5-8.

Table 5-8. The Codes for Parameter Problem and Their Meanings

Code	Meaning
0	Pointer Indicates the Error
1	Required Option Is Missing
2	Bad Length

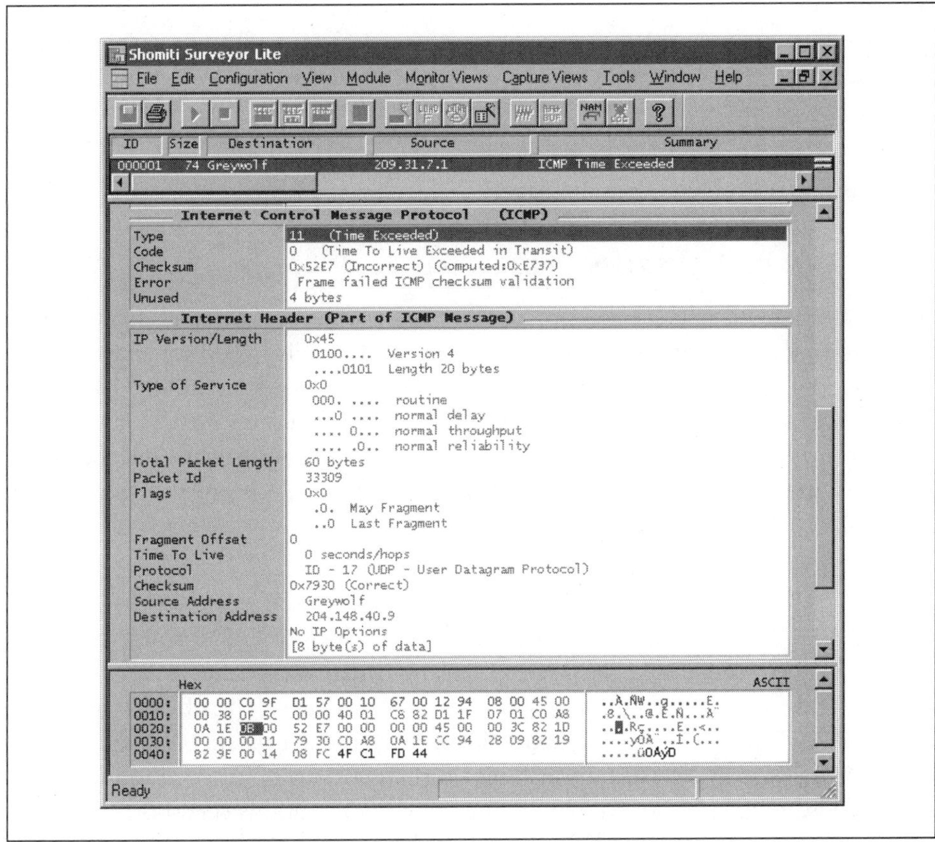

Figure 5-20. An ICMP Time Exceeded: Time-to-Live Exceeded In Transit error message

ICMP Message Data

The ICMP Message Data field is used differently by each of the different Parameter Problem Codes. Table 5-9 shows how the ICMP Message Data field is used for each of the different Codes.

Table 5-9. The Use of the ICMP Message Data Field for Each of the Parameter Problem Codes

Code	Use of ICMP Message Data Field
0	One byte of data, indicating the starting position of the problem
1	One byte of data, set to 130 (indicating a missing security option)
2	Unused and must be zero

Defined In

RFC 792 and RFC 1122.

Notes

The Parameter Problem error message is fairly complicated. Refer back to "Parameter Problem error messages" for a comprehensive discussion of this error message.

See Also

"Parameter Problem error messages"

ICMP Query Messages

ICMP query messages are used to probe the network for specific characteristics (such as host availability and network latency) and are also used for some general purpose lookup services (such as locating routers). A variety of ICMP query messages exist (as described later in "Query message types and codes"), although each of these messages have their own special requirements and treatments. However, all ICMP query messages share some fields, and these fields are described in the next section.

Query message headers

Since ICMP query messages are used for specific types of functionality, they vary widely in their formatting. However, each of them share the same first three header fields, as shown in Table 5-10, along with their size (in bytes) and some usage notes. Beyond these common fields however, each of the ICMP query messages differs widely in their formatting and structure. For more information on these fields, refer to the individual discussions throughout this section.

Table 5-10. Format of the ICMP Query Message

Field	Bytes	Usage Notes
Type	1	Indicates the specific ICMP query message
Code	1	Indicates the subclass of the ICMP query message
Checksum	2	Used to validate the contents of the ICMP query message
Additional Fields	var	Varies by message

The total length of a "normal" ICMP query message is eight bytes. However, this does not include any additional data that may be provided by an ICMP query message's additional fields, which can add a substantial amount of data to a datagram (Echo Request messages can be as large as 64 kilobytes).

All ICMP messages are sent within IP datagrams directly. Each of these datagrams must have a protocol identifier of 1. In addition, RFC 1122 states that ICMP error messages should use the default Type-of-Service and Precedence values when they are sent over IP. However, if a user wishes to set these values to higher levels, then the responses must use the same values they received in the queries.

The following sections discuss ICMP query messages in detail, using the capture shown in Figure 5-21 for reference purposes.

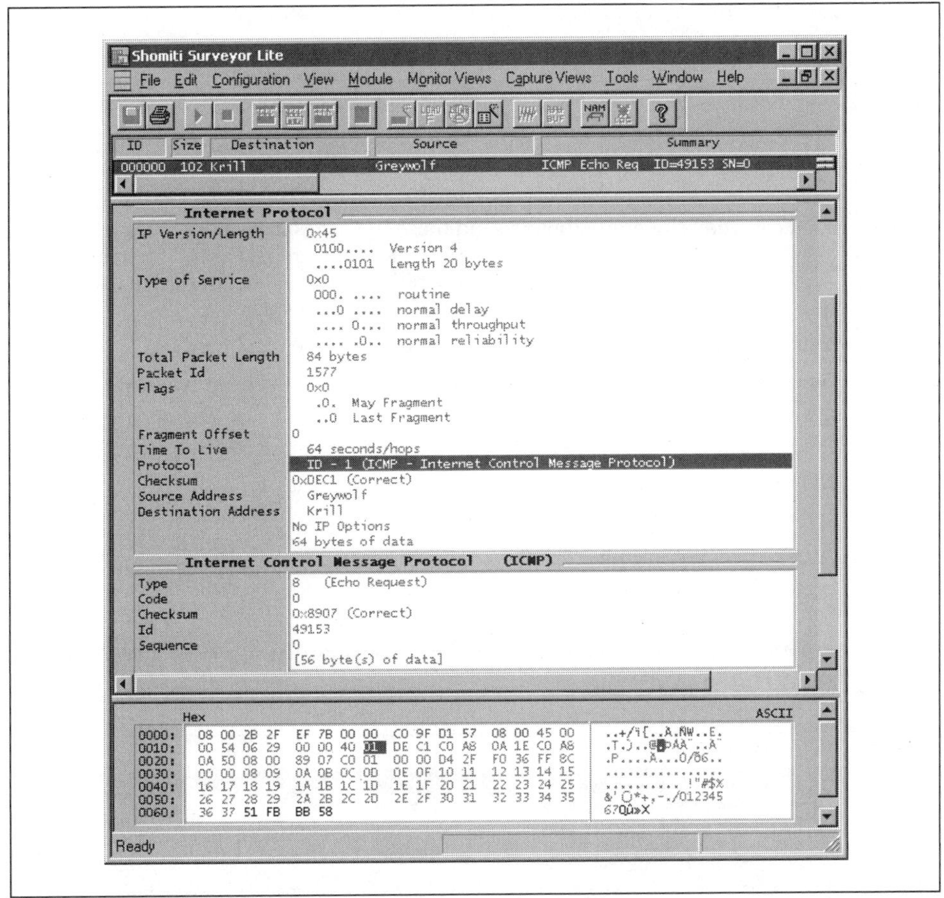

Figure 5-21. A simple ICMP query message

Message Type

The Type field is used to specify the exact ICMP query message being sent.

Size

Eight bits.

Notes

ICMP essentially consists of a predefined dictionary of messages, allowing messages to be exchanged using numeric identifiers. The Type field is used to specify the major class of the message, while the Code field is used to specify the minor class, although some message Types do not have any subtype Codes.

Table 5-11 lists all of the ICMP query message Types used with IPv4 and their meanings.

Table 5-11. ICMP Error Message Types

Type	Message Description	Usage Notes
0	Echo Reply	Used to respond to Echo Request query messages. Typically used by *ping*.
8	Echo Request	Used to test basic connectivity between two or more devices on a network. Typically used by *ping*.
9	Router Advertisement	Routers send these messages in response to a Router Solicitation query message and also send them as periodic updates. Used to inform network devices of available routers on the local network.
10	Router Solicitation	Used to locate routers on the local network.
13	Timestamp Request	Used to test network latency between two or more devices.
14	Timestamp Reply	Used to respond to Timestamp Request query messages.
17	Address Mask Request	Used to request a subnet mask for a device.
18	Address Mask Reply	Used to respond to Address Mask Request query messages.

Capture Sample

In the capture shown in Figure 5-22, the Type field is set to 8, which is used for Echo Request query messages.

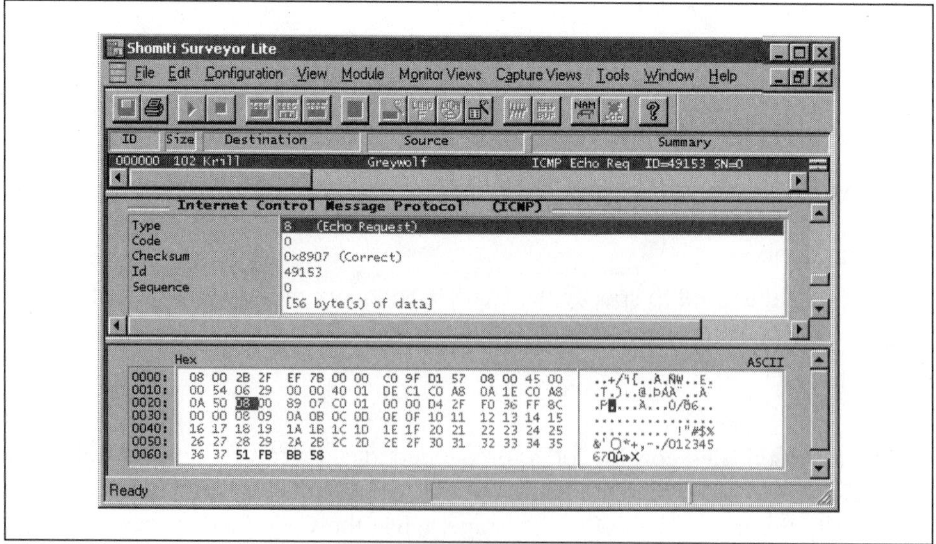

Figure 5-22. The Message Type field

See Also

"Message Code"

Message Code

The Code field is used to specify a specific subtype of the ICMP query message, which was specified in the Type field.

Size

Eight bits.

Notes

ICMP essentially consists of a predefined dictionary of messages, allowing messages to be exchanged using numeric identifiers. The Type field is used to specify the major class of the message, while the Code field is used to specify the minor class, although some message types do not have any subtype Codes.

The values used in this field vary according to the Message Type for the current error message.

Capture Sample

In the capture shown in Figure 5-23, the Code field is set to 0, which is the default for Echo Reply query messages, since those messages do not use the Code field.

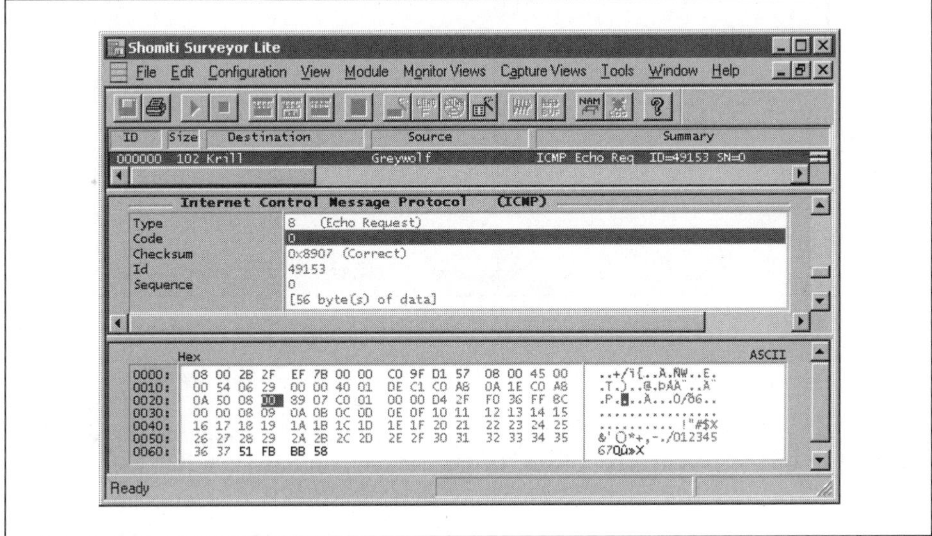

Figure 5-23. The Message Code field

See Also

"Message Type"

Checksum

Used to store a checksum of the ICMP message, allowing destination systems to validate the contents of the message and test for possible corruption.

Size

Sixteen bits.

Notes

The checksum field provides a simple validation scheme for ICMP messages. When calculating the checksum, the sending system looks at the entire message (with the checksum field set to 0) and performs a simple checksum operation. This procedure is reversed by all recipients before the contents of the message are processed.

Capture Sample

In the capture shown in Figure 5-24, the Checksum has been calculated to hexadecimal "89 07", which is correct.

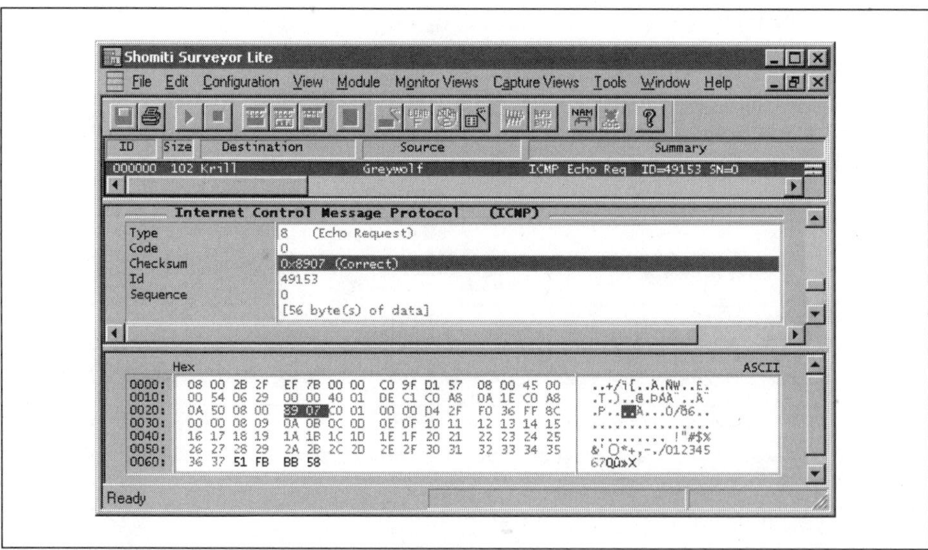

Figure 5-24. The Checksum field

Additional Fields

Each ICMP query message has distinct functionality, and as such has unique fields that are associated with that specific message. The fields that appear from this point on in the message will be unique to the specific Message Type being sent.

Size

Varies according to Message Type.

Notes

Since ICMP query messages are conversational in nature, they provide very specific sets of functionality that are not shared by all other query messages. For example, the functionality provided by Echo Request and Echo Reply messages is nothing at all like the functionality offered by Router Solicitation and Router Advertisement messages. As such, the fields they use for their specific purposes vary considerably.

Capture Sample

The capture shown in Figure 5-25 shows that the Echo Request query message defines several additional fields, including Identifier, Sequence Number, and Optional Data fields. Note that these fields only appear in ICMP Echo Request and Echo Reply query messages. The optional data is the 56 bytes of data following the sequence number.

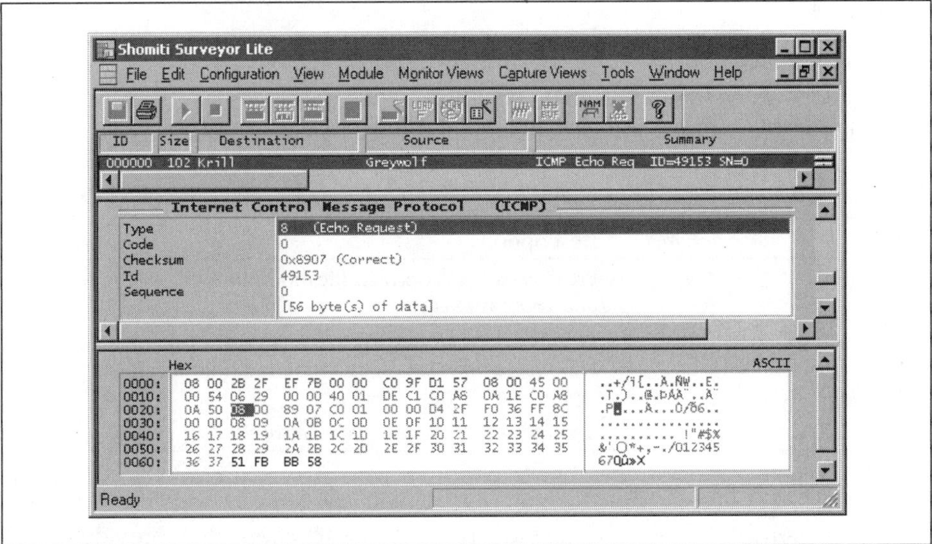

Figure 5-25. The additional fields used with Echo Request query messages

See Also

"Message Type"

"Message Code"

Query message types and codes

The remainder of this section discusses the different ICMP query messages, as listed earlier in Table 5-11.

Echo Request and Echo Reply

Echo Request and Echo Reply query messages provide the ability for one system to see if another system is on the network and functional. Any Echo Request message received by a system must be responded to with an Echo Reply query message.

ICMP Message Type

The Message Type for Echo Request is 8. The Message Type for Echo Reply is 0.

ICMP Message Codes

Neither the Echo Request nor Echo Reply query messages uses any Codes, and this field must be zero. However, some vendors (such as Cisco) use some message codes for specific services. If you see a non-zero value in this field, check the documentation for the sending system to determine what purpose it serves.

Defined In

RFC 792.

Additional Fields

Both the Echo Request and Echo Reply query messages use four additional fields. Table 5-12 lists these fields, their size (in bytes), and their usage.

Table 5-12. The Additional Fields used in Echo Request and Echo Reply Query Messages

Field	Bytes	Description
Identifier	2	Provides a "session identification number" for the request and reply messages
Sequence Number	2	Provides a "counter" for the unique Echo Request and Echo Reply messages, allowing multiple messages to be sent using a single Identifier
Optional Data	varies	Used to store any test data desired

These fields are explained below, but if you are familiar with the *ping* program, then you're probably already aware of the functions they provide.

- The Identifier field provides a kind of "session identification number" to the set of Echo Request and Echo Reply messages being passed. For example, if Ferret were to send multiple Echo Request query messages to Greywolf as part of a single test, then each of the Echo Request (and each of the Echo Reply) messages would all share the same Identifier. This allows Ferret to also send Echo Request messages to another host simultaneously, while keeping all of the ICMP messages separate.
- The Sequence Number field allows the hosts to keep track of the unique Echo Request and Echo Reply messages that are associated with a single Identifier. For example, if Ferret were to send multiple Echo Request queries to Greywolf as part of a single test, then each message would have a

unique Sequence Number (although the Identifier would remain consistent). The Echo Reply messages sent back to Ferret from Greywolf would show the Sequence Number that they applied to.

- The Optional Data field is used to store test data. The Echo Request query message does not need to place any data in the Optional Data field (which is why it is "optional"), but it may place any data here that the user wishes. Any Optional Data received by the final destination must be returned in the Echo Reply query message.

Notes

Echo Request messages are generally issued by a user running the *ping* program (although some network management applications use the Echo Request query message to automate testing). Echo Reply messages are sent only in response to an Echo Request query message. For more information on the *ping* program, refer ahead in this chapter to "Notes on ping."

Capture Sample

In the capture shown in Figure 5-26, Greywolf has sent an Echo Request query message to Krill, to which Krill responds with an Echo Reply query message. Note that both messages contain the same Identifier, Sequence Number, and Optional Data fields.

See Also

"Echo Request and Echo Reply query messages"

"Notes on ping"

Timestamp Request and Timestamp Reply

The ICMP Timestamp Request and Timestamp Reply query messages provide the ability to determine the length of time that ICMP query messages spend in transit, which is extremely useful for measuring the latency across a specific network.

ICMP Message Type

The Message Type for Timestamp Request is 13. The Message Type for Timestamp Reply is 14.

ICMP Message Codes

Neither the Timestamp Request nor Timestamp Reply query messages use any Codes, and this field must be zero.

Defined In

RFC 792.

Additional Fields

Both the Timestamp Request and Timestamp Reply query messages use the same message structure. The additional fields used by these messages are shown in Table 5-13.

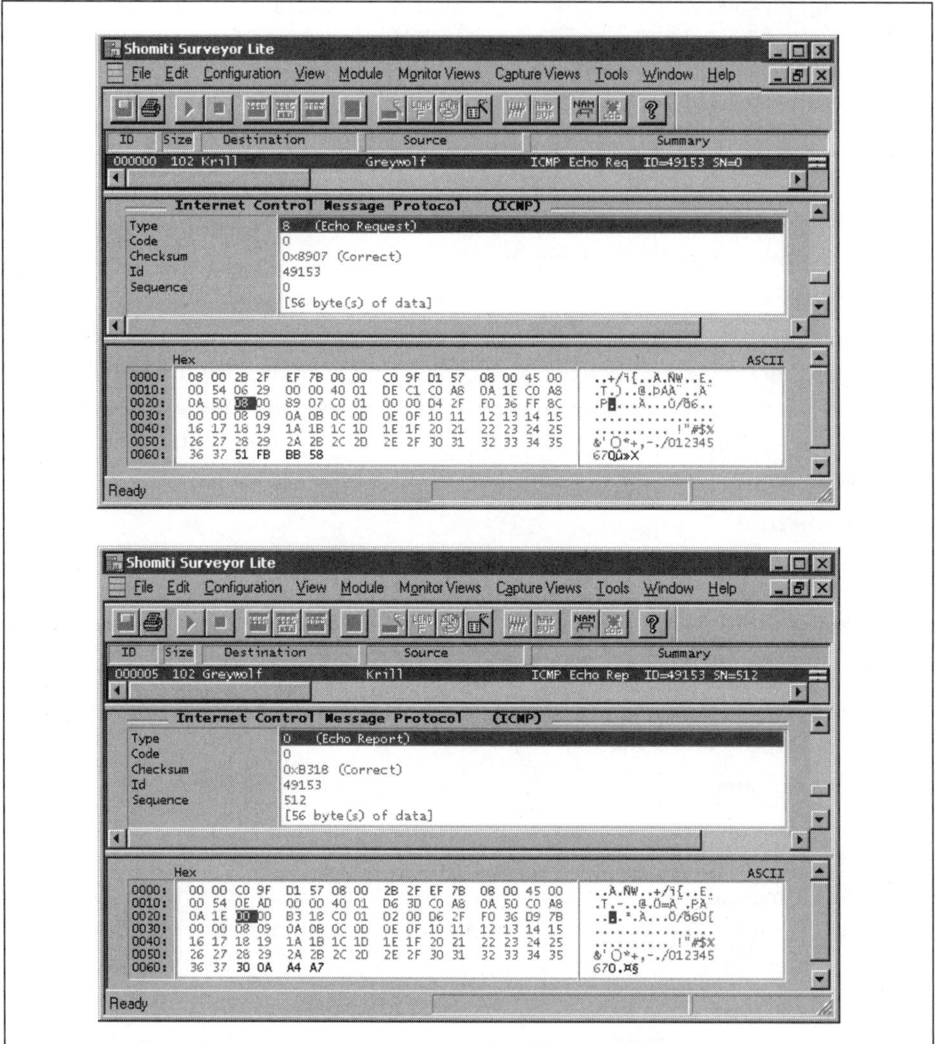

Figure 5-26. A pair of Echo Request and Echo Reply query messages

Table 5-13. Additional Fields in Timestamp Request and Timestamp Reply

Field	Bytes	Description
Identifier	2	Provides a "session identification number" for the request and reply messages.
Sequence Number	2	Provides a "counter" for requests and replies, allowing multiple messages to be used with a single Identifier.
Originate Timestamp	4	The exact time that the Timestamp Request query message was sent.

Table 5-13. Additional Fields in Timestamp Request and Timestamp Reply (continued)

Field	Bytes	Description
Receive Timestamp	4	The exact time that the Timestamp Request was received by the final destination system.
Transmit Timestamp	4	The exact time that the Timestamp Reply was sent back.

These fields are explained below:

- The Identifier field provides a kind of "session identification number" for the Timestamp Request and Timestamp Reply query messages being passed between various hosts. For example, if Ferret sends multiple Timestamp Request queries to Greywolf as part of a single test, then each of the Timestamp Request (and each of the Timestamp Reply) queries would all share the same Identifier. This feature allows Ferret to send Timestamp Request messages to another host simultaneously, while keeping all of the ICMP traffic separate locally.
- The Sequence Number field allows the hosts to keep track of the unique Timestamp Request and Timestamp Reply messages that are sent for a single Identifier. For example, if Ferret sends multiple Timestamp Request queries to Greywolf as part of a single test, then each message would have a unique Sequence Number (although the Identifier would remain consistent). The Timestamp Reply messages sent back to Ferret from Greywolf would show the Sequence Number that they applied to.
- The Originate Timestamp field stores the exact time in milliseconds that the Timestamp Request query message was sent.
- The Receive Timestamp field stores the exact time in milliseconds that the Timestamp Request query message was received by the final destination system. This provides a latency measure.
- The Transmit Timestamp field is used to store the exact time in milliseconds that The Timestamp Reply query message was sent in response to the Timestamp Request query.

Notes

When the system that sent the Timestamp Request query message receives the Timestamp Response query message, it can examine the data stored in the Receive Timestamp and Transmit Timestamp fields, and thereby determine the amount of time used by the remote system to process the ICMP query message. This value can then be subtracted from the round-trip delivery times for the ICMP query messages, providing insight into the latency of the network (as it applies to those messages, anyway).

Timestamp data is based on the number of milliseconds since midnight, using the Universal Time Zone (UTC).

Note that using the Timestamp Request and Timestamp Reply query messages to determine the latency between two devices requires that the devices have identical system times. You must synchronize the clocks on the test systems using a protocol such as NTP before accurate measurements can be obtained.

See Also

"Timestamp Request and Timestamp Reply query messages"

Address Mask Request and Address Mask Reply

The ICMP Address Mask Request and Address Mask Reply query messages provide a host with the ability to determine the subnet mask in use on the local network. This is achieved by sending an Address Mask Request query message to the local broadcast address of 255.255.255.255, which is then responded to with an Address Mask Reply message.

ICMP Message Type

The Message Type for Address Mask Request is 17. The Message Type for Address Mask Reply is 18.

ICMP Message Codes

Neither the Address Mask Request nor Address Mask Reply query messages use any Codes, and this field must be zero.

Defined In

RFC 950.

Additional Fields

Both the Address Mask Request and Address Mask Reply query messages use the same message structure. The additional fields used by these messages are shown in Table 5-14.

Table 5-14. Additional Fields in Address Mask Request and Address Mask Reply Query Messages

Field	Bytes	Description
Identifier	2	Provides a session identification number for the request and reply messages
Sequence Number	2	Provides a counter for requests and replies, allowing multiple messages to be used with a single Identifier
Subnet Mask	4	The subnet mask in use on the local network

These fields are explained below:

- The Identifier field provides a kind of session identification number for the Address Mask Request and Address Mask Reply query messages being passed between various hosts. For example, if Ferret issues multiple Address Mask Request queries as part of a single operation, then each of the Address Mask Request (and each of the Address Mask Reply) queries would share the same Identifier. This feature allows Ferret to send multiple Address Mask Request messages simultaneously, while keeping all of the ICMP traffic separate locally.

- The Sequence Number field allows the hosts to keep track of the unique Address Mask Request and Address Mask Reply messages that are sent for a single Identifier. For example, if Ferret sends multiple Address Mask Request queries as part of a single operation, then each message would have a unique Sequence Number (although the Identifier would remain consistent). The Address Mask Reply messages sent back to Ferret would show the Sequence Number that they were responding to.
- The Subnet Mask field is used to store the subnet mask in use on the local network. This field is unused with Address Mask Requests and must be zero, and is only filled in for Address Mask Reply messages.

Notes

The Address Mask Request and Address Mask Reply query messages were originally provided as ancillary messages for the Information Request and Information Reply query messages, which provided a mechanism for diskless workstations to obtain an IP address during startup. However, the Information Request and Information Reply messages have since been deprecated and are now obsolete. The Address Mask Request and Address Mask Reply query messages are also obsolete, although they have not yet been deprecated. They are quite rare, however.

See Also

"Address Mask Request and Address Mask Reply query messages"

Router Solicitation

When a device that supports the Router Discovery protocol first comes onto the network, it issues a Router Solicitation query message. Routers on the network can then respond with the Router Advertisement query message, informing the device of the available routers.

ICMP Message Type

The Message Type for Router Solicitation is 10.

ICMP Message Codes

Router Solicitation does not use any Codes, and this field must be zero.

Defined In

RFC 1256.

Additional Fields

Router Solicitation query messages have a single four-byte field, which is currently unused, and which must be zero.

Notes

The Router Advertisement and Router Solicitation query messages are both part of the Router Discovery Protocol. However, the Router Advertisement query messages are substantially different from the Router Solicitation query messages. Both messages need to be understood before a complete understanding of the Router Discovery protocol can be reached.

The Router Discovery protocol offers a dynamic-routing service to devices on a network, by way of a handful of ICMP query messages and error messages. When a device first comes onto the network, it will issue an ICMP Router Solicitation query message to the all-routers multicast address of 224.0.0.2 (or to the broadcast address of 255.255.255.255). Any routers that are active on the local network should then respond with unicast Router Advertisement query messages (as described in "Router Advertisement," the next section). In addition, routers will also issue Router Advertisement query messages to the all-hosts multicast address of 224.0.0.1 on a periodic basis, allowing devices to update their list of known routers.

Once a device has chosen a default router, then all traffic will go to that router. If another router exists on the local network that is more appropriate for a specific destination, then the default router should issue an ICMP Redirect error message to the device, informing it of the alternative router. This allows the network devices to build maps of the network dynamically.

Capture Sample

In the capture shown in Figure 5-27, Fungi has sent a Router Discovery query message to the all-routers multicast address of 224.0.0.2. The response to this query is shown later in Figure 5-28.

See Also

"Router Solicitation and Router Advertisement query messages"

"Router Advertisement"

Router Advertisement

When a device that supports the Router Discovery protocol first comes onto the network, it issues a Router Solicitation query message. Routers on the network can then respond with the Router Advertisement query message, informing the device of the available routers.

In addition, routers will send Router Advertisement query messages every seven to ten minutes, allowing the local devices to refresh their lists of available routers.

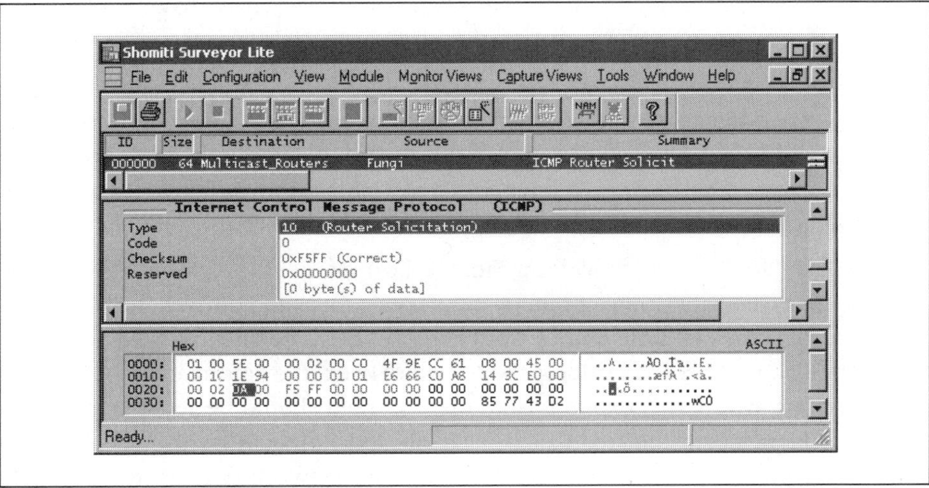

Figure 5-27. An ICMP Router Solicitation query message

ICMP Message Type

The Message Type for Router Advertisement is 9.

ICMP Message Codes

Router Advertisement does not use any Codes, and this field must be zero.

Defined In

RFC 1256.

Additional Fields

The Router Advertisement query message uses several additional fields. Table 5-15 lists these fields, their size (in bytes), and their usage.

Table 5-15. Additional Fields in Router Advertisement Query Messages

Field	Bytes	Description
Number of Addresses	1	The number of addresses in this advertisement
Address Size	1	The number of 32-bit words used to describe each entry
Lifetime	2	The number of seconds that devices should consider this information to be valid
Address Entry *N*	4	The IP address of interface *N* (this field will appear *N* number of times, as defined by the Number of Addresses field above)
Preference for *N*	4	The preference that devices should assign this interface

These fields are used as follows:

- The Number of Addresses field indicates the number of IP address entries in use on this interface. Since the Router Advertisement messages are sent out on each unique interface—some of which may have multiple IP addresses—this field indicates the number of IP addresses in use on this particular interface.

- The Address Size field is used to indicate the size of each IP address, as well as the size of the Preference value being provided for each IP address. The use of Preference values allows the router to dictate how much weight devices should give to each IP address.
- The Lifetime field provides a Time-to-Live metric for this Router Advertisement message. Since routers may come and go, devices will need to expire routing table entries from time to time. The Lifetime field is used to tell the devices how long they should keep the information being provided, before it is expired. Note that this field should be set to a value that is higher than the frequency of unsolicited Router Advertisements, allowing the unsolicited messages to renew the network devices' routing table entries before the Lifetime expires.
- The Address Entry *N* field is used to provide the *N*th IP address. This field will be repeated *N* number of times, as dictated by the Number of Addresses field above.
- The Preference for *N* field is used to provide the Preference value for Address Entry *N*. This field will be repeated *N* number of times, as dictated by the Number of Addresses field above.

Notes

The Router Advertisement and Router Solicitation query messages are both part of the Router Discovery Protocol. However, the Router Advertisement query messages are substantially different from the Router Solicitation query messages. Both messages need to be understood before a complete understanding of the Router Discovery protocol can be reached.

The Router Discovery protocol offers a dynamic-routing service to devices on a network, by way of a handful of ICMP query messages and error messages. When a device first comes onto the network, it will issue an ICMP Router Solicitation query message to the all-routers multicast address of 224.0.0.2 (or to the broadcast address of 255.255.255.255). Any routers that are active on the local network should then respond with unicast Router Advertisement query messages (as described earlier in this section). In addition, routers will also issue Router Advertisement query messages to the all-hosts multicast address of 224.0.0.1 on a periodic basis, allowing devices to update their list of known routers.

Each of the Router Advertisement query messages—regardless of whether they are solicited unicasts or unsolicited multicasts—will contain information about the router that is sending it (as described in the "Additional Fields" reference text above). Devices on the network will then use that information to choose the most appropriate router as their default.

Capture Sample

In the capture shown in Figure 5-28, Sasquatch has sent a Router Advertisement query message directly to Fungi, in response to the query shown in Figure 5-27. Most of the time, Router Advertisement query messages are sent to the all-hosts multicast address of 224.0.0.1, although they can also be unicast directly to a system that has issued a Router Solicitation query message (as shown in Figure 5-27). As can be seen here, this advertisement is only showing a single IP address on the local network and has assigned a preference value of zero to that interface.

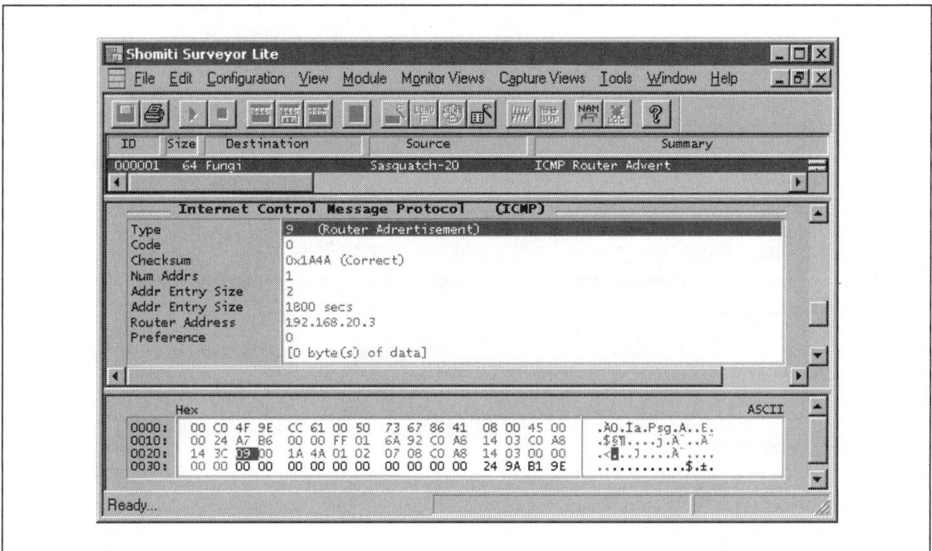

Figure 5-28. An ICMP Router Advertisement query message

See Also

"Router Solicitation and Router Advertisement query messages"

"Router Solicitation"

ICMP in Action

If you were to look at all of the ICMP traffic crossing your network, you would probably be surprised at the amount that gets generated and exchanged during a normal day. This is not necessarily a bad thing, since ICMP is what keeps IP working so well. Most web sites will experience a significant amount of Path MTU

Discovery messages, for example. In addition, sites that move services around on different hosts frequently will see a lot of Destination Unreachable messages, as clients attempt to connect to relocated services.

Notes on Reading ICMP Error Messages

ICMP error messages can be overwhelming, to say the least. They present a lot of information that has be parsed through, deciphered, and generally made sense of.

The easiest way to read an ICMP error message is to break it into manageable chunks. The first portion of the message always identifies the specific ICMP error message being reported, while the remainder of the message consists of the headers and first eight bytes of data from the IP datagram that's being bounced.

For example, Figure 5-29 shows an ICMP Destination Unreachable: Host Unreachable Error message that appears to be very complex on the surface, but actually only consists of a few key pieces of data.

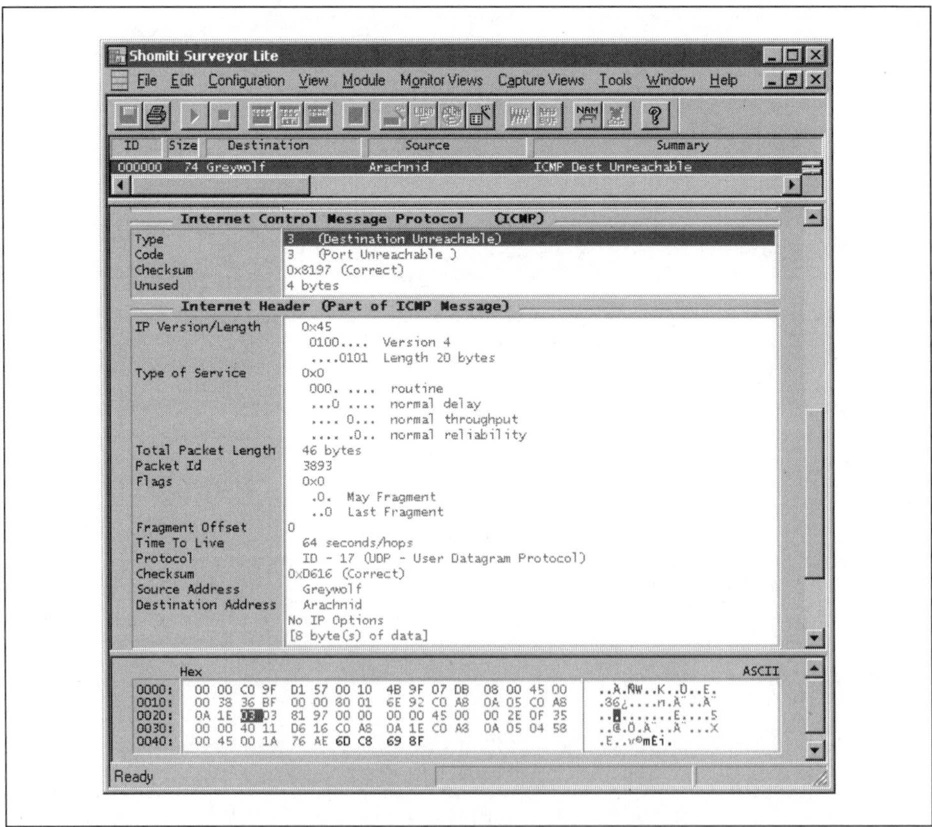

Figure 5-29. An ICMP Destination Unreachable: Port Unreachable error message

By following a few simple steps and answering some simple questions, you can easily decipher the source and cause of the ICMP error message. The questions are:

What is the Message Type?
: The ICMP Message Type for this message is 3, which indicates that it is part of the Destination Unreachable family of error messages.

What is the Message Code?
: The ICMP Message Code for this message is 3, which tells us that this particular Destination Unreachable error message indicates that the destination *port* was unreachable (this is different from the destination host or network being unreachable).

What does it mean?
: We can tell from the discussion of Port Unreachable earlier in "Destination Unreachable error messages" that the Destination Unreachable: Port Unreachable error message means that the destination port number specified by the UDP or TCP message was not in a listening state, which generally indicates that there was no server running on that port number.

What other evidence is there?
: Obviously, the most important piece of evidence for resolving this problem is looking at the destination port number sent in the original message. Since this is an ICMP error message, the original IP datagram has been provided in the message body, so all we have to do is find the Destination Port number field in the original datagram, which points to UDP port 69 (the well-known port for TFTP servers).

What conclusions can we draw?
: We can tell that a host on our internal network tried to send a UDP message to the well-known port for TFTP servers on a remote server. Since the message was rejected, we can assume that this means that there was no TFTP server running on the destination system. Furthermore, we can also assume that this was not a configuration issue at the server, where it was configured to block access to this particular client, since the datagram would have cleared the server's UDP stack (although nothing else may have happened, the packet would have gone through and then been ignored, rather than being blocked at the gate by UDP).

Most ICMP error messages can be read using this same series of procedures. In almost all cases, all the information that you need to diagnose the cause of a failure is presented in the ICMP error message's headers, in the headers from the failing datagram, or in the first eight bytes of data from the failing datagram (which is where the source and destination port numbers are provided for TCP and UDP connections).

Notes on ping

One of the most common uses for ICMP is the *ping* program. According to RFC 1122, every system should implement a user-accessible program for generating ICMP Echo Request and ICMP Echo Reply query messages, and the most common method for this has historically been the *ping* utility. The *ping* program allows a user to test network connectivity between two devices by sending out ICMP Echo Request messages and then measuring the amount of time it took to receive an ICMP Echo Reply message back from the destination system.

Figure 5-30 shows three ICMP Echo Request query messages being sent from Arachnid to Krill, with no special Type-of-Service, Precedence or IP Options defined. In addition, Figure 5-30 shows the response time from Krill back to Arachnid, as well as some summary data for the session. This is pretty typical of Unix-based *ping* programs.

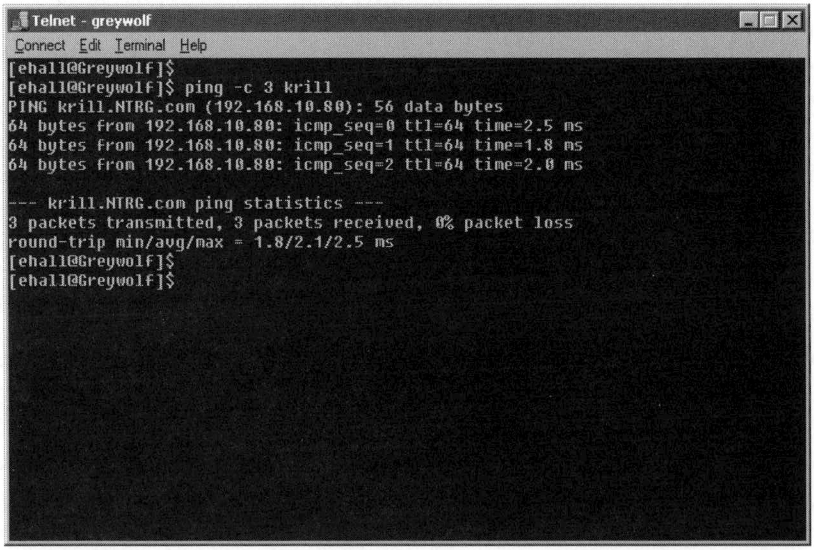

```
Telnet - greywolf
Connect  Edit  Terminal  Help
[ehall@Greywolf]$
[ehall@Greywolf]$ ping -c 3 krill
PING krill.NTRG.com (192.168.10.80): 56 data bytes
64 bytes from 192.168.10.80: icmp_seq=0 ttl=64 time=2.5 ms
64 bytes from 192.168.10.80: icmp_seq=1 ttl=64 time=1.8 ms
64 bytes from 192.168.10.80: icmp_seq=2 ttl=64 time=2.0 ms

--- krill.NTRG.com ping statistics ---
3 packets transmitted, 3 packets received, 0% packet loss
round-trip min/avg/max = 1.8/2.1/2.5 ms
[ehall@Greywolf]$
[ehall@Greywolf]$
```

Figure 5-30. A simple unicast ping test

There are some details that should be paid attention to whenever *ping* is used for network testing and diagnostics. In particular, the Identifier field used for the ICMP Echo Request and Echo Reply query messages is the same across every session, while the Sequence Number fields are unique for every message sent during a session.

For example, Figure 5-31 shows the first Echo Request query message from the *ping* output shown in Figure 5-30, while Figure 5-32 shows the last Echo Reply query message. Notice that each of them share the same Identifier field, although they also have different values in the Sequence Number fields.

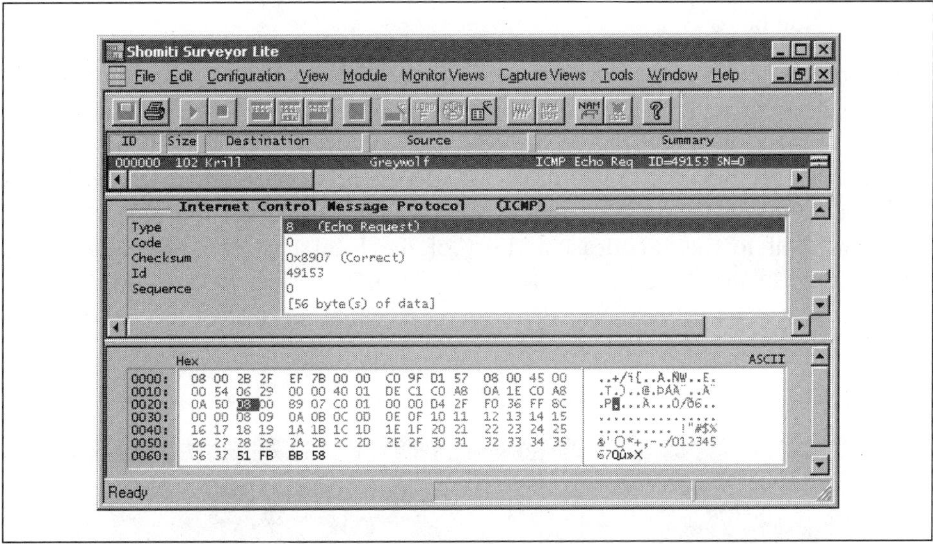

Figure 5-31. The first ICMP Echo Request query message from Figure 5-30

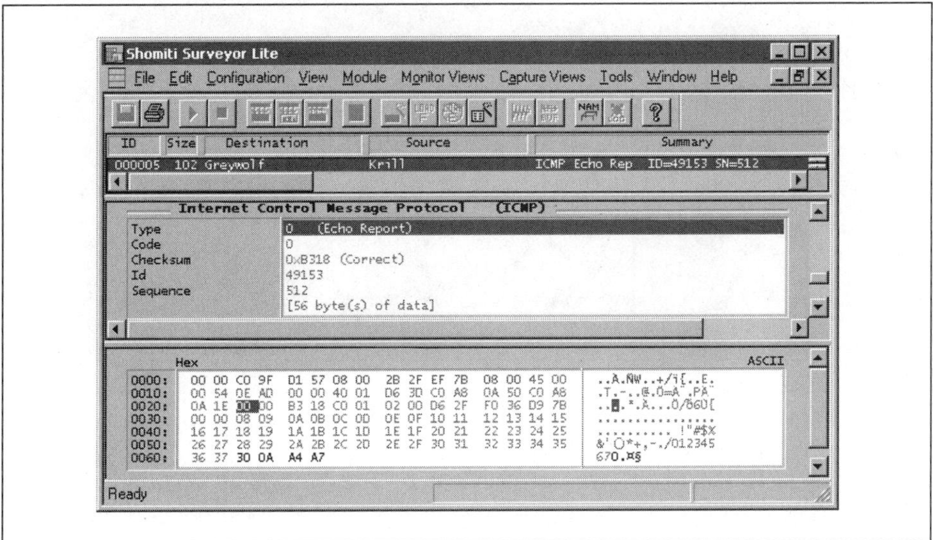

Figure 5-32. The last ICMP Echo Reply query message from Figure 5-30

Another interesting aspect to this particular session is the fact that the Sequence Number fields do not match the sequence numbers shown in Figure 5-30. Whereas *ping* showed sequence numbers of 0 through 2 for the three query messages, we can tell from Figure 5-32 that the Sequence Number fields are actually being incremented by 256 with each Echo Request message getting sent (ranging from 0 through 512). Thus, what *ping* shows as message number 2 actually has the Sequence Number of 512.

Some *ping* programs also allow you to send ICMP Echo Request query messages to a broadcast or multicast address. However, not all of the nodes will necessary respond to the request message, since RFC 1122 states that "an ICMP Echo Request destined to an IP broadcast or IP multicast address may be silently discarded." This behavior occurs in Figure 5-33, where an ICMP Echo Request message was sent from Greywolf to the broadcast address of the local LAN (see the Destination Address field of the IP datagram), but only a handful of the devices on the local network responded to the ICMP Echo Request, while the rest of the systems just ignored it.

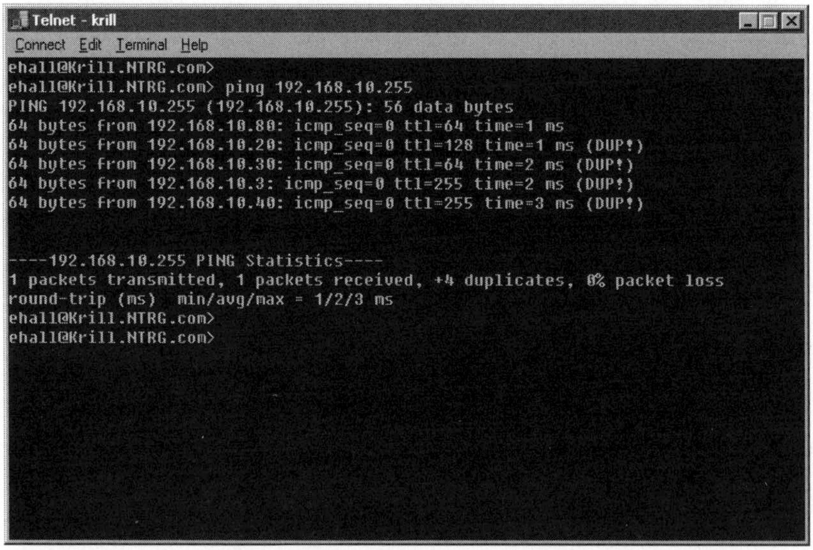

```
Telnet - krill
Connect Edit Terminal Help
ehall@Krill.NTRG.com>
ehall@Krill.NTRG.com> ping 192.168.10.255
PING 192.168.10.255 (192.168.10.255): 56 data bytes
64 bytes from 192.168.10.80: icmp_seq=0 ttl=64 time=1 ms
64 bytes from 192.168.10.20: icmp_seq=0 ttl=128 time=1 ms (DUP!)
64 bytes from 192.168.10.30: icmp_seq=0 ttl=64 time=2 ms (DUP!)
64 bytes from 192.168.10.3: icmp_seq=0 ttl=255 time=2 ms (DUP!)
64 bytes from 192.168.10.40: icmp_seq=0 ttl=255 time=3 ms (DUP!)


----192.168.10.255 PING Statistics----
1 packets transmitted, 1 packets received, +4 duplicates, 0% packet loss
round-trip (ms)  min/avg/max = 1/2/3 ms
ehall@Krill.NTRG.com>
ehall@Krill.NTRG.com>
```

Figure 5-33. A broadcast ping test

Notice that Krill, Greywolf, Weasel, Sasquatch, and Froggy all responded to the Echo Request message sent in Figure 5-33, which had the local network broadcast address of 192.168.10.255 in the IP datagram's Destination Address field. However, neither Ferret, Arachnid, nor Canary responded to the query.

Some implementations of *ping* also let you define specific network characteristics such as the Type-of-Service or Precedence values to be used with the underlying IP datagrams. According to RFC 1122, ICMP Echo Request query messages should use the default Precedence and Type-of-Service values (0), although if you set it higher then the responding system should use the same Precedence and/or Type-of-Service values in their corresponding ICMP Echo Reply Messages.

This concept is illustrated in Figure 5-34. In that example, Ferret sent an ICMP Echo Request query message to Krill, with the Precedence value set to 6 ("flash") and with the "low-latency" Type-of-Service flag defined. On a congested network, this packet would have been sent before any other packets that had a lower priority value, and may have even taken an alternate route (perhaps going across a fiber backbone, rather than across a slower data circuit).

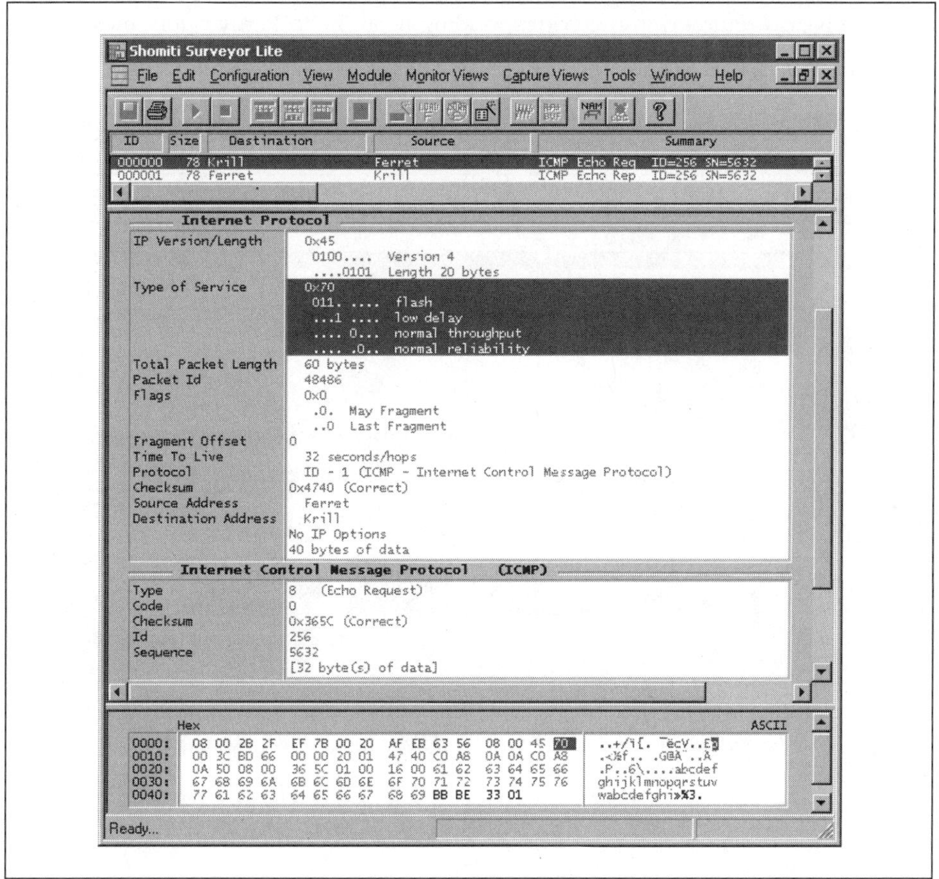

Figure 5-34. A pair of high-priority Echo Request and Echo Reply query messages

Many *ping* applications will also allow you to define your own test data. This can be used to test for fragmentation-related problems, and also to test for problems related to equipment that is interpreting specific bit-patterns as hardware test patterns. For example, "Media-Related Issues" in Chapter 2, *The Internet Protocol*, showed how some WAN equipment will interpret a series of ones or zeroes as a test pattern for the equipment itself, causing it to go into test mode. You can use *ping* to send ICMP Echo Requests with these bit patterns to devices on the other side of the networks, thereby testing for this event. In addition, some implementations will also let you define the amount of data that gets generated by *ping*. This can be useful for determining end-to-end fragmentation and MTU requirements, particularly where a specific size of message seems to have problems.

For example, Figure 5-35 shows a simple *ping* test from Krill to Ferret that uses a predefined pattern of "0011001100110011AAFFAAFFAAFF". This test pattern is incorporated into the Optional Data field of the ICMP Echo Request query message and is also returned in the corresponding ICMP Echo Reply query message.

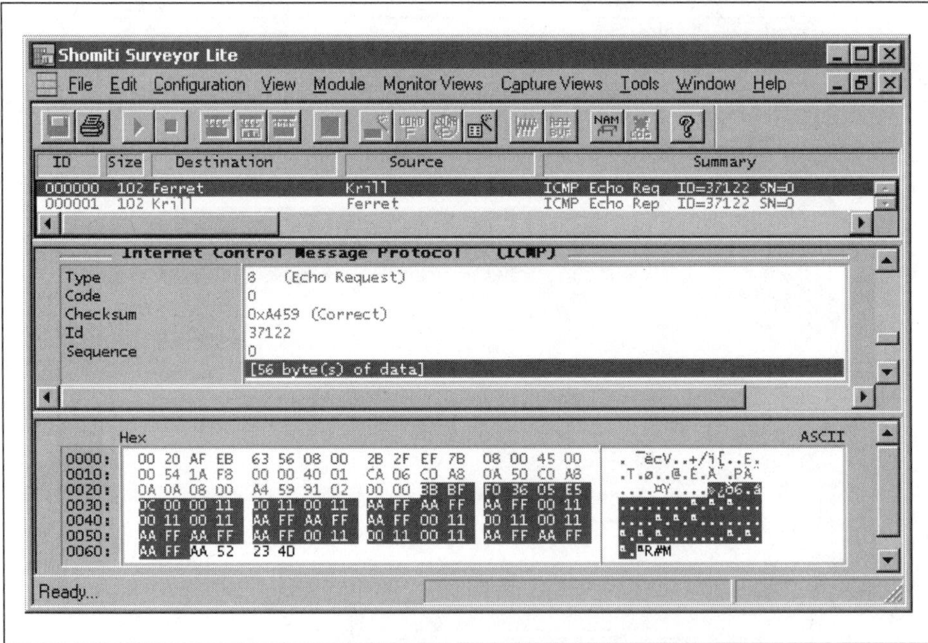

Figure 5-35. A pair of patterned Echo Request and Echo Reply query messages

Ping tests may fail for a variety of reasons, ranging from firewall filters to routing errors on the sender's or receiver's networks. For a comprehensive discussion on these problems, refer to "Troubleshooting ICMP" later in this chapter.

Notes on traceroute

Just as *ping* allows you to verify connectivity between different devices, *traceroute* allows you to identify the route that datagrams are taking on their way to a remote device. This is achieved by sending a series of packets with incrementally larger

Time-to-Live values, and then monitoring for ICMP Time Exceeded error messages as the packets expire on the way to the destination system.

The first packet sent by *traceroute* will have a Time-to-Live value of 1. When the packet is received by the first-hop router on the local network, the router will be unable to forward the datagram without the Time-to-Live value reaching zero, so the router will discard the datagram and send an ICMP Time Exceeded error message back to the sender.

traceroute records the IP address of the router that returned the datagram, and then sends another datagram with the Time-to-Live field set to 2. This time the datagram makes it past the first-hop router to the next router in the path. However, since the Time-to-Live value will have been set to 1 by the first-hop router during the forwarding process, the next-hop router will reject the packet and send an ICMP Time Exceeded error message back to the sending system.

This process is repeated over and over, until the final destination system has been reached. Once that occurs, the local system will have received ICMP Time Exceeded error messages from every router between itself and the final destination system, and will therefore have a complete map of the intermediary network.

It is important to note that different versions of *traceroute* use different types of data for the "seed" datagrams, and the responses you get will probably vary according to the version you use. The original version of *traceroute* was written by Van Jacobsen at the Lawrence Berkeley Labs in Berkeley, California, and is the default version that ships with most Unix systems. Other vendors and TCP/IP implementations ship versions of *traceroute* that work somewhat differently

Van Jacobsen's version of *traceroute* sends three UDP messages for every "send" effort, allowing average latencies to be determined for each hop along the path. In addition, this version of *traceroute* increments the destination UDP port number of each datagram that it sends, allowing the latency times for each datagram to be tracked individually (this is important in case one or more packets gets sidetracked somewhere, and ends up getting returned later than other datagrams sent afterwards).

For example, Figure 5-36 shows a capture of a *traceroute* session between Greywolf and *www.ora.com*. This version of *traceroute* uses the Van Jacobsen model, which sends three UDP datagrams to the destination system in a batch, with each of the datagrams having an incrementally higher destination port number. As the Time-to-Live values of the IP datagrams expire, they are rejected by intermediary routers along the way. This information is then used to display summary data about the latencies of the networks in between the sender and the destination system.

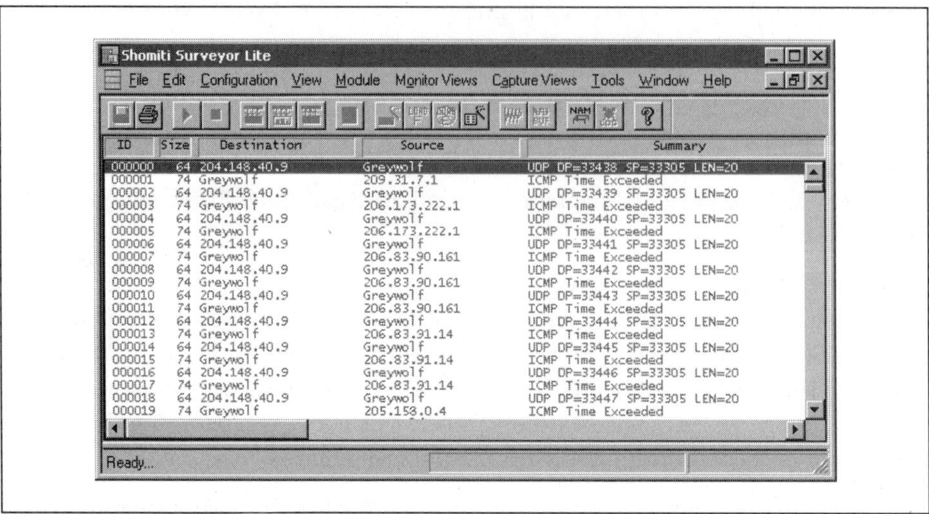

Figure 5-36. traceroute using UDP datagrams

Once the seed UDP datagrams reach the destination system, they may be rejected with ICMP Destination Unreachable: Port Unreachable error messages, although it is also possible that some form of response may come back to the sender via UDP (if one of the target port numbers were active). Regardless, some sort of event should happen that will indicate the complete path has been discovered.

However, that was not the case in this example. Indeed, the last-hop from the *traceroute* shown in this test failed on a continuous basis, due to no response coming back from the remote system, as is shown in Figure 5-37.

This could be a result of a number of factors, although most likely it is due to a firewall on the *ora.com* network blocking the unsolicited UDP messages from entering the network, meaning they will never be seen by the target system. This scenario is quite common, and is discussed in detail in "Firewalls Blocking UDP Messages" in Chapter 6, *The User Datagram Protocol*. It could also be that a firewall is blocking the ICMP response messages, preventing the local system from seeing the resulting messages. This is also quite common and is discussed in detail later in "Troubleshooting ICMP."

The output from the *traceroute* session shown in Figure 5-36 can be seen in Figure 5-38. As can be seen, the last-hop is shown as unknown (the "*" indicates that the request timed out), since *traceroute* is not receiving any responses from either the destination system or any intermediary routers. As such, it continues to increment the Time-To-Live value of the outgoing IP packets, until the process is terminated by the user.

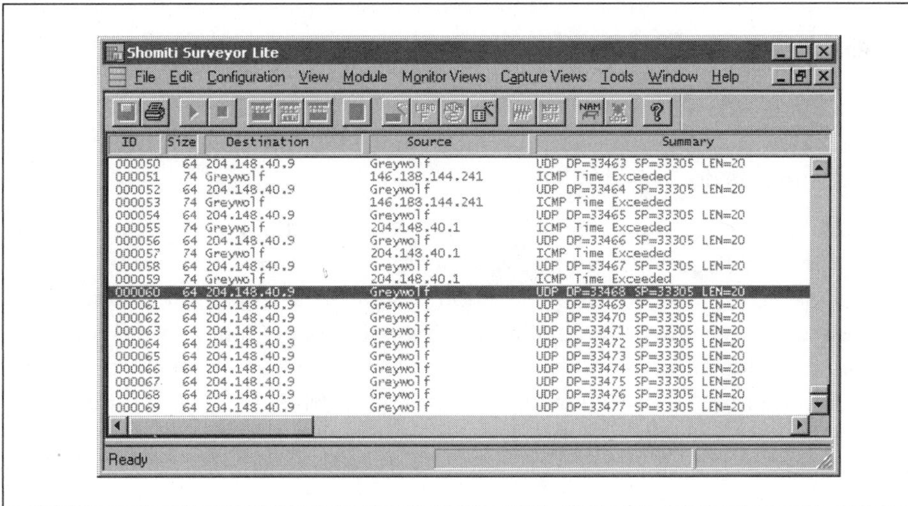

Figure 5-37. UDP traceroute failing, due to firewall blocking

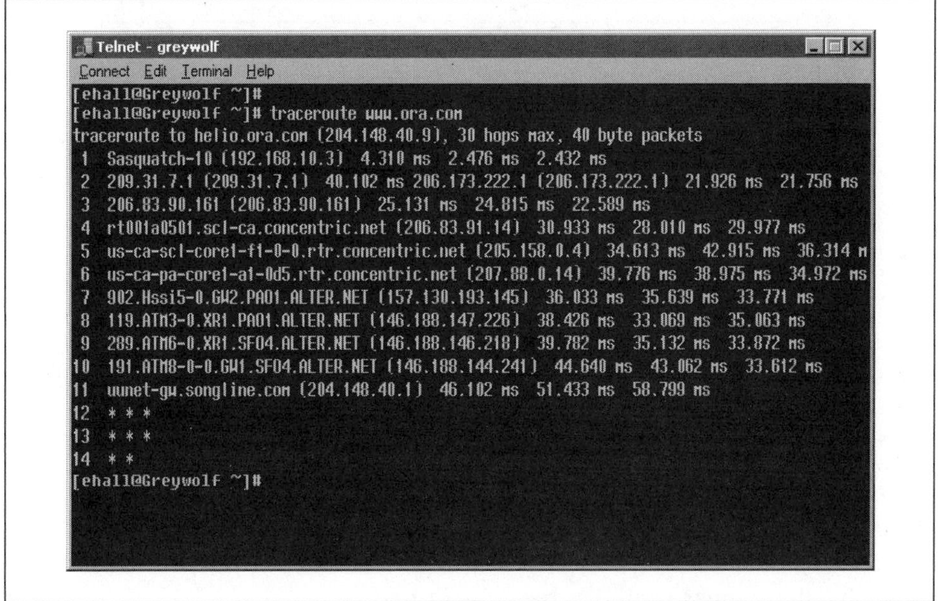

Figure 5-38. Visual output of the traceroute from Figure 5-36

There have been some problems with the Van Jacobsen version of *traceroute*. For one thing, many firewalls block unsolicited UDP datagrams (as discussed above). In addition, the use of incremental UDP port numbers can make these messages appear to be port scans on the destination system, which can trigger false alarms for security-conscious sites.

For these reasons, there are a variety of other *traceroute* programs that use ICMP Echo Request query messages for the seed data, instead of UDP datagrams. Another advantage to using ICMP Echo Request messages is that these messages contain built-in Identifier and Sequence Number fields, which provide better packet-tracking mechanisms for *traceroute* to use in its per-hop calculations than UDP port numbers do.

Figure 5-39 shows a *traceroute* session between Arachnid and *www.ora.com*, using ICMP Echo Request query messages as the seed. Three ICMP Echo Request query messages are sent to the destination system in a batch, with each of the messages having incrementally higher Sequence Numbers (although the Identifier stays the same for all of them). As the Time-to-Live values of the IP datagrams expire, they are rejected by intermediary routers along the way. This information is then used to display summary data about the networks between the sender and the destination system.

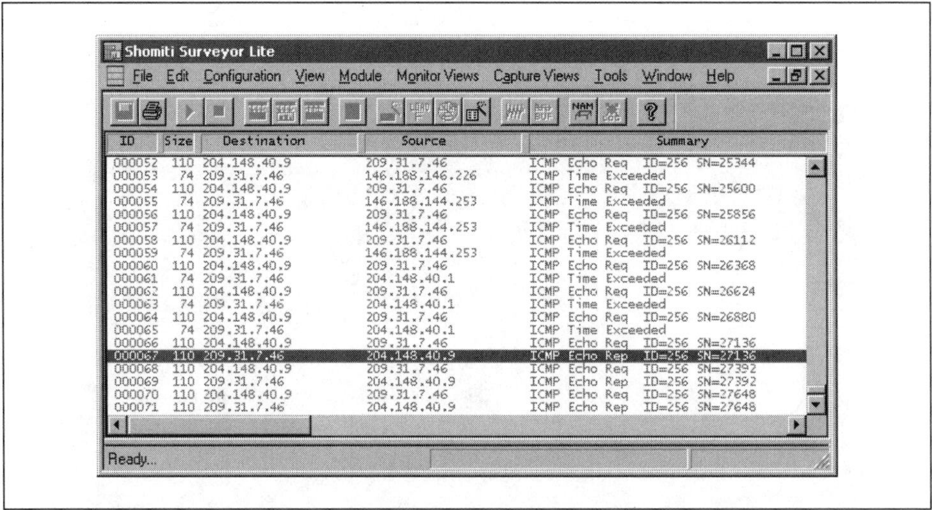

Figure 5-39. traceroute using ICMP Echo Request query messages

Once the seed ICMP Echo Request query messages have reached the destination system, they should be responded to with ICMP Echo Reply query messages, indicating that the complete path has been discovered.

The output from the *traceroute* session shown in Figure 5-39 can be seen in Figure 5-40. This time *traceroute* runs to completion.

There are problems with using ICMP Echo Request messages too, of course. One major problem is that many firewalls also block all forms of ICMP traffic, just as many firewalls will block unsolicited UDP datagrams.

```
Command Prompt

C:\WINNT>
C:\WINNT>tracert www.ora.com

Tracing route to helio.ora.com [204.148.40.9]
over a maximum of 30 hops:

  1    31 ms    47 ms    31 ms  209.31.7.1
  2    15 ms    16 ms    31 ms  206.173.222.1
  3    15 ms    32 ms    15 ms  206.83.90.161
  4    16 ms    31 ms    31 ms  rt001a0501.scl-ca.concentric.net [206.83.91.14]
  5    15 ms    31 ms    32 ms  us-ca-scl-core1-f1-0-0.rtr.concentric.net [205.158.0.4]
  6    63 ms    46 ms    32 ms  us-ca-pa-core1-a1-0d5.rtr.concentric.net [207.88.0.14]
  7    16 ms    47 ms    31 ms  902.Hssi5-0.GW2.PAO1.ALTER.NET [157.130.193.145]
  8    31 ms    31 ms    31 ms  119.ATM2-0.XR2.PAO1.ALTER.NET [146.188.147.238]
  9    32 ms    31 ms    31 ms  188.ATM6-0.XR2.SFO4.ALTER.NET [146.188.146.226]
 10    31 ms    32 ms    46 ms  190.ATM10-0-0.GW1.SFO4.ALTER.NET [146.188.144.253]
 11    47 ms    47 ms    47 ms  uunet-gw.songline.com [204.148.40.1]
 12    47 ms    47 ms    47 ms  helio.ora.com [204.148.40.9]

Trace complete.

C:\WINNT>
C:\WINNT>_
```

Figure 5-40. Visual output of the traceroute from Figure 5-39

The other big problem with this model is that not all TCP/IP implementations return ICMP error messages in response to an ICMP query message. RFC 1122 states that ICMP error messages should not be generated in response to other ICMP error messages. However, devices can (and should) generate ICMP error messages in response to ICMP query messages that fail. Unfortunately, not all vendors have made this distinction, and there are some implementations that do not return ICMP error messages in response to *any* ICMP traffic whatsoever.

RFC 1393 proposed yet another mechanism for *traceroute* programs to use, although this proposal has not been widely accepted. Essentially, RFC 1393 proposed that a device send a single IP datagram that contained an experimental Traceroute IP Option. As the datagram wound its way through the network, routers would issue an experimental ICMP Traceroute message back to the sending system, showing their IP address. By the time the original request datagram gets to the destination system, the sender would have a full map of all the devices on the path.

Although there are benefits to this model (only one seed datagram is required, and the return path could also be discovered independently of the seed path), there are also major problems with it, including the use of the experimental Traceroute IP Option and the experimental ICMP Traceroute message, neither of which have been standardized. For these reasons, this model is not widely supported.

Notes on Path MTU Discovery

Just as *traceroute* allows a system to discover the path taken between two devices, an algorithm called Path MTU Discovery allows the sender to find the most efficient packet size for the connection between two systems. This is particularly important when the two systems are going to exchange a significant amount of data, since sending large datagrams may cause fragmentation (which introduces delay and also increases the risk of errors), while sending small packets generates an excessive amount of traffic. Finding the largest possible MTU on an end-to-end connection allows the systems to send the most amount of data in the least number of packets, thereby keeping fragmentation from occurring.

Path MTU Discovery is described in detail by RFC 1191. Essentially, Path MTU Discovery works by having the sender decrement the size of the IP datagrams until they can be sent to the recipient without being fragmented.

The optimal MTU size is determined by the sender starting with the largest possible size (as determined by their local MTU), and then setting the Don't Fragment flag in the datagram's IP header. If an ICMP Destination Unreachable: Fragmentation Required but DF Bit Is Set error message comes back to the sender, then the datagram is too large to be sent across the network. The sender would then reduce the size of the datagram and try the operation again. This process is repeated until no errors are returned. At this point, the sender can use the last-known MTU of the test datagram as the MTU of the entire network.

In addition, RFC 1191 states that the Message Data field of the ICMP Fragmentation Required but DF Bit Is Set error message should be split into two subfields, one of which is a two-byte field called the "Next-Hop MTU." This field can be used by a rejecting router to specify the exact MTU of the next-hop network. If a router was not aware of this extension, then it would simply return the Fragmentation Required error message, and the sender would have to guess about the next-hop network's MTU size. But if the router were aware of the extension, it could provide the MTU value explicitly, which the sender would use on subsequent probes.

For example, Figure 5-41 shows a capture of a packet containing the Next-Hop MTU data. Since the ICMP Message Data field contains four bytes of hexadecimal data (00 00 02 40), it indicates that the MTU of the next hop is 576 bytes (the first two bytes are ignored, and hexadecimal 0240 is equal to decimal 576). If this were a regular Fragmentation Required error message, the ICMP Message Data field would contain zeroes.

Path MTU Discovery is mostly seen when a remote system is connected on a network with a smaller MTU than the MTU of the sender. This could be a remote Ethernet segment with an MTU that is smaller than the Token Ring network that the sender is on, or a remote dial-up system with an MTU that is smaller than the Ethernet network that the sender is using. Since most end-user networks are Ethernet (which has an MTU of 1500 bytes)—and since most of the Internet backbone

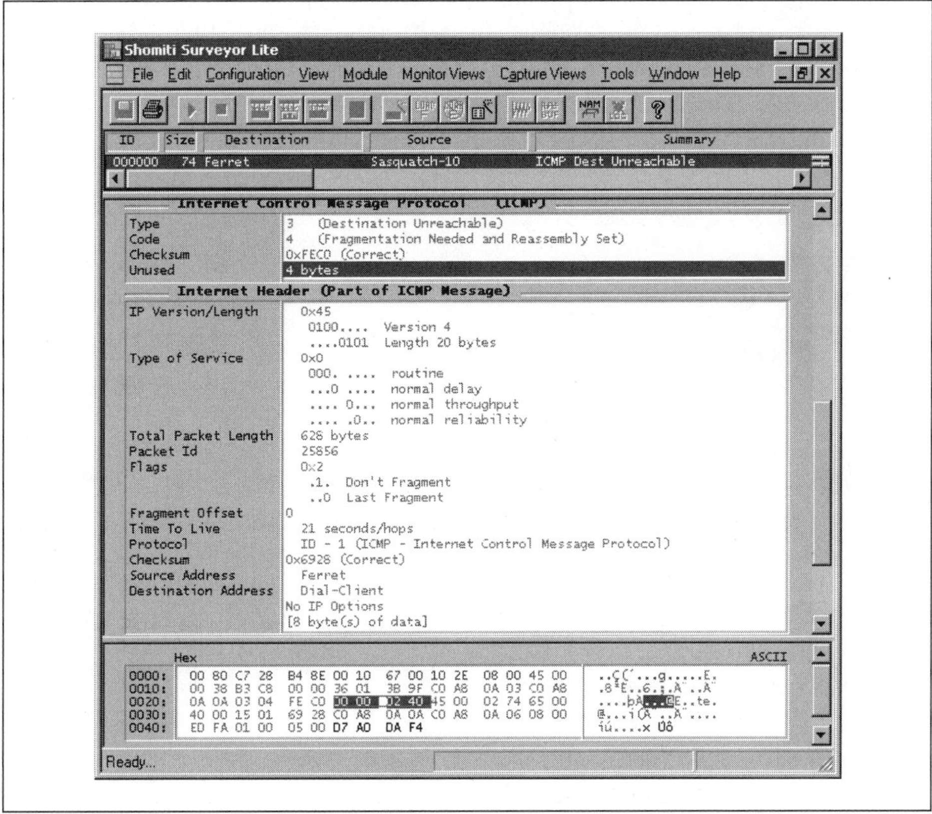

Figure 5-41. A Path MTU-aware Destination Unreachable error message

uses high-speed networks with MTUs that are significantly larger than 1500 bytes—most network-to-network connections that travel across the Internet use the same MTU all of the time.

However, users who try to exchange a lot of data between a host on a Token Ring network and a host on an Ethernet network will likely see a substantial amount of Path MTU Discovery messages. Similarly, users who try to exchange a lot of data between a host on an Ethernet network and a dial-up user who has a small MTU will also see a lot of these kinds of messages.

For example, Figure 5-42 shows a 1500-byte packet being sent from 192.168.10.10 to 192.168.100.10, by way of an Ethernet segment, a data circuit, and a dial-up connection. The Ethernet and leased-line networks both provide MTUs of 1,500 bytes, so the datagram is able to be sent across both of those networks without difficulty. However, once it gets to the router at 192.168.60.70, the datagram is deemed too large to travel across the network and is rejected.

However, the rejecting router supports the Path MTU Discovery extensions defined in RFC 1191, and so it returns an ICMP Destination Unreachable: Fragmentation Required error message with the Next-Hop MTU field showing the next network as being limited to 512-byte MTU sizes. 192.168.10.10 can then use this value for the remainder of the connection, and will resend the data using 512-byte datagrams.

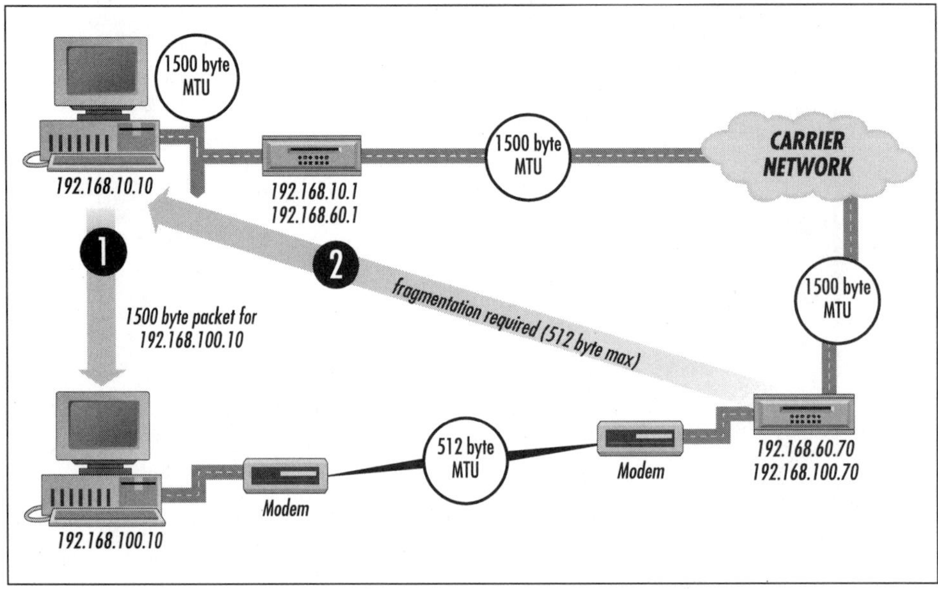

Figure 5-42. An overview of Path MTU Discovery

Unfortunately, there are a lot of problems with Path MTU Discovery, although most of them are related to implementation issues rather than being problems with the protocol itself. The biggest such problem is that many firewalls block the sending and/or receiving of ICMP messages, and in those situations, the ICMP Destination Unreachable error messages will not get returned to the sender of the large datagrams (a phenomenon referred to as "PMTU Black Hole"). Many implementations assume that a lack of error messages means that the datagram went through successfully, so the MTU is fine, which might be wrong in this situation (particularly if the sender's MTU was indeed too large to reach the destination network intact).

One solution to this problem that works with TCP connections in particular is to watch for lost data. If full-sized datagrams are not being acknowledged by the remote TCP end-point, then the sender should reduce the size of the segments being sent and try again until an acceptable MTU is found.

Another workaround to this problem is for the sender to stop using the "Don't Fragment" flag on subsequent datagrams, which would then allow the data to get through the rest of the network (although it would get fragmented if the end-to-end MTU were not large enough to handle the over-sized datagrams). However, some implementations do this in a schizophrenic way, forgetting when they have cleared the flag. For example, a sender may detect that the MTU is too large and then clear the Don't Fragment bit after detecting lost data, only to reset the flag on subsequent packets. This results in three or four sends that are too large, followed by a send without the Don't Fragment flag, followed by more big sends with the flag enabled. Obviously, this will have a negative impact on overall performance.

Note that the alternative *traceroute* mechanism defined in RFC 1393 also provided services for returning the MTU sizes of the next-hop network, using the ICMP Traceroute messages that routers would return. However, RFC 1393 is not widely supported, due to its heavy reliance on experimental and non-standard IP Options and ICMP Messages.

Troubleshooting ICMP

Although ICMP is effective at informing devices of problems with the network, it is also succeptible to these same problems, since it relies on IP for delivery services. Many times, you will encounter a connectivity problem, and get no clue as to the true source of the problem from ICMP. There are several possible causes for not receiving ICMP error messages back from a problem network.

Firewalls Blocking ICMP Traffic

Let's say that you are trying to *ping* a remote web server. Perhaps you are able to connect to it using HTTP, but you are unable to get a response from it when using *ping*. In this case, it is entirely possible that your ICMP Echo Request messages are getting sent to the remote network, but that a firewall at the remote network is filtering out all incoming ICMP messages. In this case, your messages are simply getting eaten by the firewall, and no ICMP messages (neither ICMP query responses, nor ICMP errors) are being sent back.

Although the polite thing to do would be for the remote firewall to send a Destination Unreachable: Communication Administratively Prohibited error message, many network administrators consider these messages to be security holes, and disable their use on their firewalls. In this scenario, you would not receive any message back whatsoever.

Conversely, the problem may be with *your* firewall. It is entirely possible that your network administrator has also blocked all incoming ICMP messages, although outgoing messages are allowed to pass freely. In that situation, your ICMP Echo Request messages may be getting to the remote system—and it may be responding—but your firewall is blocking the responses from getting back into your network.

For example, Figure 5-43 shows Ferret sending an ICMP Echo Request query message to Fungi. Sasquatch is configured to allow traffic out from the 192.168.10.0 network, so it forwards the message on to the destination system. However, when Fungi tries to send an ICMP Echo Reply query message back to Ferret, the firewall blocks the datagram, since it is configured to block all incoming ICMP messages. In this example, Ferret would not be able to successfully *ping* Fungi, even though other forms of IP traffic may work just fine.

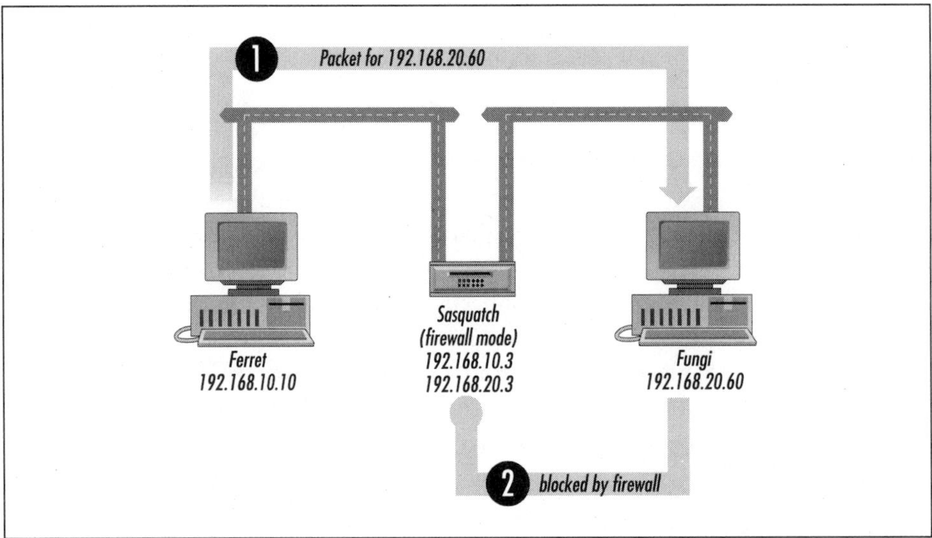

Figure 5-43. An ICMP Echo Reply query message being blocked by a firewall

A variation on this theme is when firewalls filter out *unsolicited* ICMP messages (such as Source Quench and Destination Unreachable) or allow these messages to be sent to predefined internal hosts (such as an internal web server). In this case, you would never receive these warning messages, although you should be able to see ICMP Echo Replies since they were solicited by an earlier ICMP Echo Request message.

This process can result in all kinds of problems, particularly when the firewall interferes with the Path MTU Discovery algorithm. In that scenario, the ICMP Destination Unreachable: Fragmentation Required but DF Bit Is Set error messages being generated on the open Internet are getting blocked by your firewall. Since no errors are making it back to you, the local system is working under the assumption that the destination system is able to handle the larger MTU sizes. In reality, the remote system just cannot handle the larger datagrams.

For all of these reasons, you must monitor the ICMP traffic on both networks simultaneously when you try to use *ping* to diagnose remote connectivity. You would need to monitor the local network to make sure that the Echo Request messages are being sent (and also looking for any Echo Reply messages that may not be getting sent back), and you should also monitor the remote network to ensure that the Echo Request messages are being received and that the Echo Reply messages are also getting sent. If the Echo Replies are getting sent by the remote network but are not getting received by the local network, then either end may be blocking the ICMP traffic at a firewall, or the remote end-point may have routing errors.

Misconfigured Routing Tables

It is also quite possible that your datagrams are going out to the remote destination, and that datagrams are being sent back to your system, but that they are taking a bad route on the way back to your network. This problem occurs when the advertised routes for your network point to an illegal route.

This is a very common problem with new or recently changed networks. It is not at all uncommon for somebody to forget to define the route back to your new network. Remember that just because the datagrams are going out does not mean that return datagrams are coming back on the same route.

Large Quantities of Redirect Error Messages

Some networks are known to generate a large number of ICMP Redirect error messages. Typically this is a result of one of two situations: misconfigured subnet mask on the hosts and routers, or a heavy dependence upon Router Discovery for host configuration.

Router Discovery

If you are seeing a lot of ICMP Redirect error messages in conjunction with Router Discovery, then you are not experiencing a problem (this is almost by definition). It is the prescribed behavior for the Router Discovery Protocol.

Remember that network devices will only choose a single default router, based on the preference values that are advertised by routers when they respond to Router Solicitation query messages. In this model, hosts will use that router for all non-local datagrams until they are informed of a better router for a specific destination system. Therefore, if your network has multiple routers, you will see a multitude of ICMP Redirect error messages on your network, as the devices learn about the various routers and the paths they support.

It may be that you have given the wrong router the highest preference value, and that by assigning a higher preference to another (more frequently used) router, the number of ICMP Redirect error messages on your network could be reduced. Another option would be to concentrate your routers together, allowing only one router to serve the local segment. This would essentially cause all traffic to go through the one remaining router, which would eliminate all ICMP Redirect traffic on the local segment.

For more information on Router Discovery, refer back to "Router Solicitation and Router Advertisement query messages".

Misconfigured subnet masks

Another common cause for high numbers of ICMP Redirect error messages can be seen on networks that have hosts with invalid subnet masks. Whenever these hosts try to connect to another system on the local network, they may think that the destination system is actually on a different network (due to the boundaries of the subnet mask in use), and as such will send the datagrams to the local router for delivery. The router would then inform the sender that the destination system was indeed local to the sender (using a Redirect error message for the job).

The best solution to this problem is to assign the correct subnet mask to the devices on the network, allowing them to communicate with each directly without one of them trying to contact a router first.

First Packet from ping Always Fails

Sometimes, when trying to use *ping* to test connectivity with other devices, the first packet sent will fail to be acknowledged. This could happen for a number of reasons:

ARP cache is empty

If the ARP cache on the sending system does not have an entry for the destination system (assuming that the destination system is local), then the time it takes to locate the hardware address of the destination device may exceed the timeout threshold defined in the *ping* client. In addition, if the size of the ICMP Echo Request Message is larger than the local system's MTU, then another (somewhat rare) condition can also be met, whereby *ping* has flushed the first fragment from its call-back queue, and as such only the second (and subsequent) fragments from the first datagram are getting sent. In that case, the recipient will ignore the IP packet, since it is not complete. These issues are discussed in more detail in "Bursted Duplicate ARP Requests" in Chapter 3, *The Address Resolution Protocol.*

Routing cache is empty
There are millions of networks in use on the Internet today, and most of the routers are simply incapable of keeping track of all the others. In fact, most routers store only a few routing paths in their caches at any given time. In that model, if a packet is getting sent to a network that has not been processed lately, it may take some time for the router to determine the correct network path for the packet to take. This may result in the *ping* client reaching a time-out threshold before the ICMP Echo Request query message is responded to successfully. In that case, *ping* may mark the first few messages as lost.

DNS name cache is empty
If you are using host names with *ping*, then some messages may get delayed during the DNS lookup operation, and may be either bumped out of the queue during processing or erroneously reported as "timed out." In either case, you should always use IP addresses during probe operations (this includes *traceroute* when possible) to keep the name resolution process from interfering with the system tests.

6

The User Datagram Protocol

Summary	The User Datagram Protocol provides a low-overhead transport service for application protocols that do not need (or cannot use) the connection-oriented services offered by TCP. UDP is most often used with applications that make heavy use of broadcasts or multicasts, as well as applications that need fast turnaround times on lookups and queries.
Protocol ID	17
Relevant STDs	2 (*http://www.iana.org/*); 3 (includes RFCs 1122 and 1123); 6 (RFC 768, republished)
Relevant RFCs	768 (User Datagram Protocol); 1122 (Host Network Requirements)

There are two standard transport protocols that applications use to communicate with each other on an IP network. These are the User Datagram Protocol (UDP), which provides a lightweight and unreliable transport service, and the Transmission Control Protocol (TCP), which provides a reliable and controlled transport service.

The majority of Internet applications use TCP, since its built-in reliability and flow control services ensure that data does not get lost or corrupted. However, many applications that do not require the overhead found in TCP—or that cannot use TCP because the application has to use broadcasts or multicasts—will use UDP instead. UDP is more appropriate for any application that has to issue frequent update messages or that does not require every message to get delivered.

The UDP Standard

UDP is defined in RFC 768, which has been republished as STD 6 (UDP is an Internet Standard protocol). However, RFC 768 contained some vagaries that were clarified in RFC 1122 (Host Network Requirements). As such, UDP implementations need to incorporate both RFC 768 and RFC 1122 in order to work reliably and consistently with other implementations.

RFC 768 states that UDP is a stateless, unreliable transport protocol that does not guarantee delivery. Thus, UDP is meant to provide a low-overhead transport for applications to use when they do not need guaranteed delivery.

RFC 768 also states that the Protocol ID for UDP is 17. When a system receives an IP datagram that is marked as containing Protocol 17, it should pass the contents of the datagram to the local UDP service for further processing.

UDP Is an Unreliable, Datagram-Centric Transport Protocol

As we discussed in Chapter 1, *An Introduction to TCP/IP*, sending a message via UDP is somewhat analogous to sending a postcard in that it is totally untrustworthy, providing no guarantees of any kind of delivery. UDP messages are sent and then forgotten about immediately. As such, applications that need a reliable transport protocol should not use UDP.

However, UDP's lightweight model does provide some distinct benefits, particularly in comparison to TCP's highly managed connection model. While TCP provides high levels of reliability through highly managed virtual circuits, UDP offers high performance from having so little overhead. If reliability comes at the expense of performance, then conversely, performance can be gained by eliminating some of the overhead associated with reliability.

In addition, many applications simply cannot use TCP, since TCP's virtual circuit design requires dedicated end-to-end connections between two (and no more than two) endpoints. If an application needs to use broadcasts or multicasts in order to send data to multiple hosts simultaneously, then that application will have to use UDP to do so.

Limited reliability

Although applications that broadcast information on a frequent basis have to use UDP, they do gain some benefits from doing so. Since broadcasts are sent to every device on the local network, it would take far too long for the sender to establish individual TCP connections with every other system on the network, exchange data with them all, and then disconnect. Conversely, UDP's connectionless service allows the sender to simply send the data to all of the devices simultaneously. If any of the systems do not receive one of the messages, then they will likely receive one of the next broadcasts, and as such will not be substantially harmed by missing one or two of them.

Furthermore, streaming applications (such as real-time audio and video) can also benefit from UDP's low-overhead structure. Since these applications are stream-oriented, the individual messages are not nearly as important as the overall stream of data. The user will not notice if a single IP packet gets lost every so often, so it is better to just continually keep sending the next message, rather than stopping everything to resend a single message. These applications actually see error-correction as a liability, so UDP's connectionless approach is a "feature" rather than a "problem."

Similarly, any application that needs only a lightweight query and response service would be unduly burdened by TCP's connection-oriented services and would benefit from UDP's low overhead. Some database and network-lookup services use UDP for just this reason, allowing a client and server to exchange data without having to spend a lot of time establishing a reliable connection when a single query is all that's required.

It should be pointed out that many of the applications that use UDP require some form of error correction, but that this error correction also tends to be specific to the application at hand, and is therefore embedded directly into the application logic. For example, a database client would need to be able to tell when no response came back from a query, and so the database client may choose to just reissue the entire query rather than try to fix a specific part of the datastream (this is how Domain Name System queries work). Applications that use UDP must therefore incorporate any required error-checking and fault-management routines internally, rather than rely on UDP to provide these services.

Another interesting point is that most of the network technologies in use today are fairly reliable to begin with, so unreliable protocols like UDP (and IP) are likely to reach their destinations without much problems. Most LANs and WANs are extremely reliable, losing only tiny amounts of data over the course of their lifetime. On these types of networks, UDP can be used without much concern. Even topologies that are unreliable (such as analog modems) typically provide a modicum of error-correction and retransmission services at the data-link layer.

For these reasons, UDP probably shouldn't be considered *totally* unreliable, although you must always remember that UDP doesn't provide any error-correction or retransmission services within the transport itself. It just inherits any existing reliability that is provided by the underlying medium.

Furthermore, UDP also provides a checksum service that allows an application to verify that whatever data has arrived is probably the same as that which was sent. The use of UDP's checksum service is optional, and not all of the applications that use UDP also use the checksum service (although they are encouraged to do so by RFC 1122). Some applications incorporate their own verification routines within the UDP data segment, augmenting or bypassing UDP's provisional data-verification services with application-specific equivalents.

Datagram-centric transport services

Another unique aspect of UDP is the way in which it deals with only one datagram at a time. Rather than attempting to manage a stream of application data the way that TCP does, UDP deals with only individual blocks of data, as generated by the application protocols in use. For example, if an application gives UDP a four-kilobyte block of data, then UDP will hand that data to IP as a single datagram, without trying to create efficient segment sizes (one of TCP's most significant traits). The data may be fragmented by IP when it builds and sends IP packets for that four-kilobyte block of data, but UDP does not care if this happens and is not involved in that process whatsoever.

Furthermore, since each IP datagram contains a fully formed UDP datagram, the destination system will not receive any portion of the UDP message until the entire IP datagram has been received. For example, if the underlying IP datagram has been fragmented, then UDP will not receive any portion of the message until all of the fragments have arrived and been reassembled by IP. But once that happens, then UDP (and the application in use with UDP) will get and read the entire four-kilobyte message in one shot.

Some UDP stacks require that the application have enough buffers to read the entire datagram. If the application cannot accept all of the data, then it will not get any of the data, since the datagram will be discarded.

Conversely, remember that TCP does not generally cause fragmentation to occur, since it attempts to avoid fragmentation through the use of efficiently sized segments. In that model, TCP would send multiple TCP segments, each of which could arrive independently and be made available to the destination application immediately. Although there are benefits to the TCP design, record-centric applications also have to perform more work when using it instead of UDP, since UDP provides one-shot access to all of the data.

In fact, UDP is particularly useful for applications that have to transfer fixed-length records of data (such as database records or even fixed-length files). For example, if an application needs to send six records from a database to another system, then it can generate six fixed-length UDP datagrams, and UDP will send those datagrams as independent UDP messages (which become independent IP datagrams). The recipient then receives the datagrams as self-contained records and will be able to immediately process them as six unique records.

In contrast, TCP's circuit-centric model would require the same application to write the data to the TCP virtual circuit, which would then break the data into segments for transport across the network. The recipient would then have to read through the segments as they arrived at the destination system, poking through the data and looking for end-of-record markers until all six records were received and found.

For all of these reasons, UDP is a more efficient protocol, although it is still unreliable. As such, application protocols that want to leverage the low-overhead nature of UDP must provide their own reliability services. In addition, these applications typically have to provide their own flow-control and packet-ordering services, ensuring that datagrams are not received out of order. Most applications incorporate a half-duplex data-exchange mechanism in order to provide these services. The application protocol waits for a clear-to-send signal from the remote system, transmits a datagram, and then stops to wait for the clear-to-send signal again.

For example, Trivial File Transfer Protocol (TFTP) clients use acknowledgment messages embedded in UDP datagrams to tell a server that it received the last block of data and that it is ready to receive another block. The TFTP server then sends another block of data as another UDP message and then wait to receive an acknowledgment before sending another block. Although this method is clumsy when compared to TCP's graceful sliding window concept, it has been proven to work over the years.

UDP Ports

UDP does very little. In fact, it does almost nothing, acting only as a very basic facilitator for applications to use when they need to send or receive datagrams on an IP network. In order to perform this task, UDP has to provide two basic services: it must provide a way for applications to send data over the IP software, and it must also provide a way to get data that it has received from IP back to the applications that need it.

These services are provided by a multiplexing component within the UDP software. Applications must register with UDP, allowing it to map incoming and outgoing messages to the appropriate application protocols themselves.

This multiplexing service is provided by 16-bit port numbers that are assigned to specific applications by UDP. When an application wishes to communicate with the network, it must request a port number from UDP (server applications such as TFTP will typically request a pre-defined, specific port number, while most client applications will use whatever port number they are given by UDP). UDP will then use these port numbers for all incoming and outgoing datagrams

This concept is illustrated in Figure 6-1. Each of the applications that are using UDP have allocated a dedicated port number from UDP, which they use for all incoming and outgoing data.

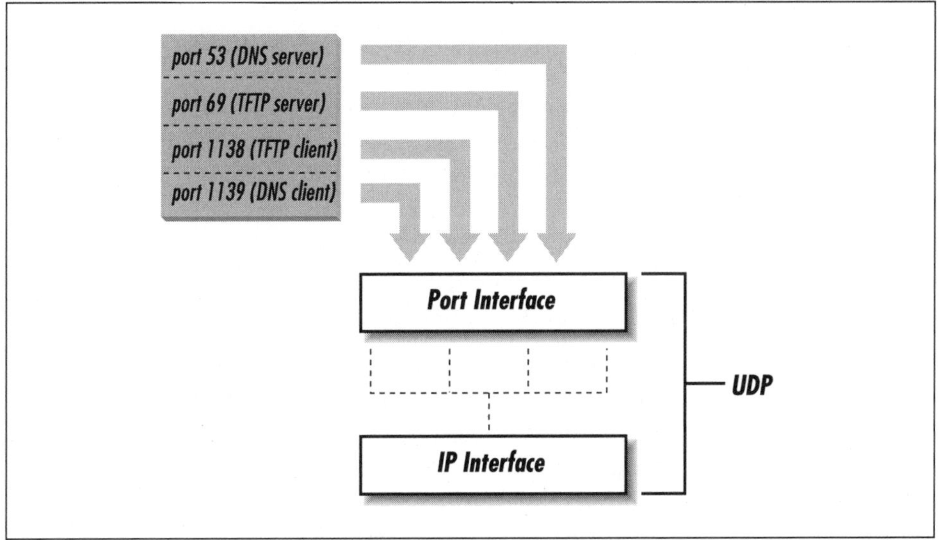

Figure 6-1. Application-level multiplexing with port numbers

When an application wishes to send data over the network, it gives the data to UDP through the assigned port number, also telling UDP which port on the destination system the data should be sent to. UDP then creates a UDP message, marking the source and destination port numbers, which is then passed off to IP for delivery (IP will create the necessary IP datagram).

Once the IP datagram is received by the destination system, the IP software sees that the data portion of the IP datagram contains a UDP message (as specified in the Protocol Identifier field in the IP header), and hands it off to UDP for processing. The UDP software looks at the UDP header, sees the destination port number, and hands the payload portion of the datagram to whatever application is using the specified port number. Figure 6-2 illustrates this concept using the Trivial File Transfer Protocol (TFTP), a small file transfer protocol that uses UDP.

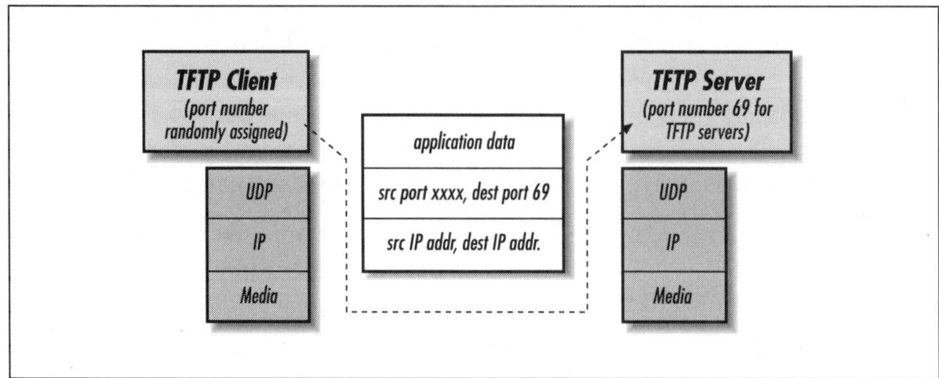

Figure 6-2. Data being sent from a TFTP client to a TFTP server

Technically, a "port" identifies only a single instance of an application on a single system. The term "socket" is used to identify the port number and IP address concantenated together (i.e., port 80 on host 192.168.10.10 would be referred to as the socket 192.168.10.10:80). Finally, a "socket pair" consists of both endpoints, including the IP addresses and port numbers of both applications on both systems. Multiple connections between two systems must have unique socket pairs, with at least one of the two endpoints having a different port number.

Although the concept of socket pairs with UDP is similar to the same concept as it works with TCP, there are some fundamental differences that must be taken into consideration when looking at how connections work with UDP versus how they work with TCP. Most importantly, while TCP can maintain multiple virtual circuits on a single port number through the use of socket pairs, UDP-based applications do not have this capability at all, and simply treat all data sent and received over a port number as data for a single "connection."

For example, if a DNS server is listening for queries on port 53, then any queries that come in to that port are treated as equal, with the DNS server handling the multiplexing services required to distinguish between the different clients that are issuing the distinct queries. This is the opposite of how TCP works, where the transport protocol would create and manage virtual circuits for each of the connections. With UDP, all data is treated as a single "connection," and the application must manage any multiplexing services required on that port.

Well-known ports

Most server-based IP applications use what are referred to as "well-known" port numbers. For example, a TFTP server will listen on UDP port 69 by default, which is the well-known port number for TFTP servers. This way, any TFTP client that needs to connect to any TFTP server can use the default destination of UDP port

69. Otherwise, the client would have to specify the port number of the server that it wanted to connect with (you've seen this in some URLs that use *http://www.somehost.com:8080/* or the like; *8080* is the port number of the HTTP server on *www.somehost.com*).

Most application servers allow you to use any port number you want. However, if you run your servers on non-standard ports, then you would have to tell every user that the server was *not* accessible on the default port. This would be a hard-to-manage implementation at best. By sticking with the defaults, all users can connect to your server using the default port number, which is likely to cause the least amount of trouble.

Some network administrators purposefully run application servers on nonstandard ports, hoping to add an extra layer of security to their network. However, it is my opinion that security through obscurity is no security at all and that this method should not be relied upon by itself.

Historically, only servers have been allowed to run on ports below 1024, as these ports could be used only by privileged accounts. By limiting access to these port numbers, it was more difficult for a hacker to install a rogue application server. However, this restriction is based on Unix-specific architectures, and is not easily enforced on all of the systems that run IP today. Many application servers now run on operating systems that have little or no concept of privileged users, making this historical restriction somewhat irrelevant.

There are a number of predefined port numbers that are registered with the Internet Assigned Numbers Authority (IANA). All of the port numbers below 1024 are reserved for use with well-known applications, although there are also many applications that use port numbers outside of this range. Some of the more common port numbers are shown in Table 6-1. For a detailed listing of all of the port numbers that are currently registered, refer to the IANA's online registry (accessible at *http://www.isi.edu/in-notes/iana/assignments/port-numbers*).

Table 6-1. Some of the Port Numbers Reserved for Well-Known UDP Servers

Port Number	Description
53	Domain Name System (DNS)
69	Trivial File Transfer Protocol (TFTP)
137	NetBIOS Name Service (sometimes referred to as WINS)
161	Simple Network Management Protocol (SNMP)

Besides the reserved addresses that are managed by the IANA, there are also unreserved port numbers that can be used by any application for any purpose, although conflicts may occur with other users who are also using those port numbers. Any port number that is frequently used is encouraged to register with the IANA.

To see the well-known ports used on your system, examine the */etc/services* file on a Unix host, or the *C:\WinNT\System32\Drivers\Etc\SERVICES* file on a Windows NT host.

The UDP Header

UDP messages consist of header and body parts, just like IP datagrams. The body part contains whatever data was provided by the application in use, while the header contains the fields that tell the destination UDP software what to do with the data.

A UDP message is made up of six fields (counting the data portion of the message). The total size of the message will vary according to the size of the data in the body part. The fields in a UDP message are shown in Table 6-2, along with their size (in bytes) and their usage.

Table 6-2. The Fields in a UDP Message

Field	Bytes	Usage Notes
Source Port	2	Identifies the 16-bit port number in use by the application that is sending the data
Destination Port	2	Identifies the 16-bit target port number of the application that is to receive this data
Length	2	Specifies the size of the total UDP message, including both the header and data segments
Checksum	2	Used to store a checksum of the entire UDP message
Data	varies	The data portion of the UDP message

Notice that the UDP header does not provide any fields for source or destination IP addresses, or for any other services that are not specifically related to UDP. This is because those services are provided by the IP header or by the application-specific protocols (and thus contained within the UDP message's data segment).

Every UDP message has an eight-byte header, as can be seen from Table 6-2. Thus, the theoretical minimum size of a UDP message is eight bytes, although this would not leave any room for any data in the message. In reality, no UDP message should ever be generated that does not contain at least some data.

Figure 6-3 shows a UDP message sent from a TFTP client to a TFTP server. In that example, a TFTP session is opened between Greywolf (the client) and Arachnid (the server), with Greywolf sending a file (called *testfile.txt*) to Arachnid. We'll use this message for further discussion of the UDP header fields.

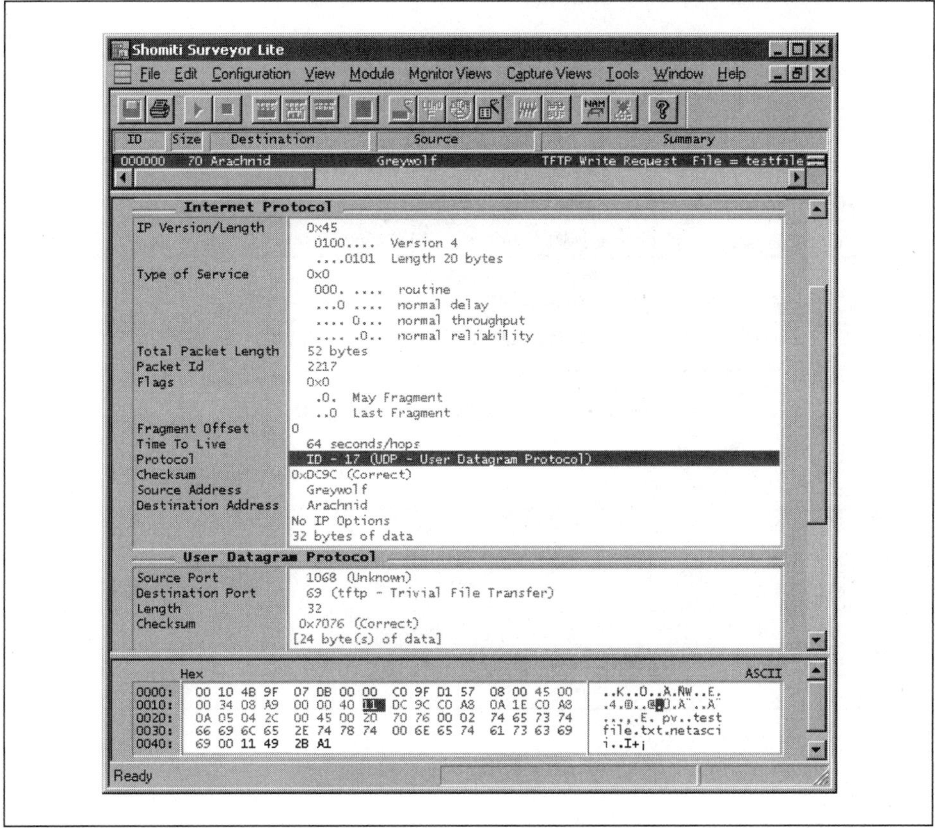

Figure 6-3. A simple UDP message

The following sections describe the header fields of the UDP message in detail.

Source Port

Identifies the message's original sender, as referenced by the 16-bit UDP port number in use by the application.

Size

Sixteen bits.

Notes

This field identifies the port number used by the application that created the data.

Note that RFC 768 states "Source Port is an optional field, when meaningful, it indicates the port of the sending process, and may be assumed to be the port to which a reply should be addressed in the absence of any other information. If not used, a value of zero is inserted."

Although Source Port is optional, it should always be used.

Capture Sample

In the capture shown in Figure 6-4, the Source Port field is set to hexadecimal 04 2c, which equates to decimal 1068.

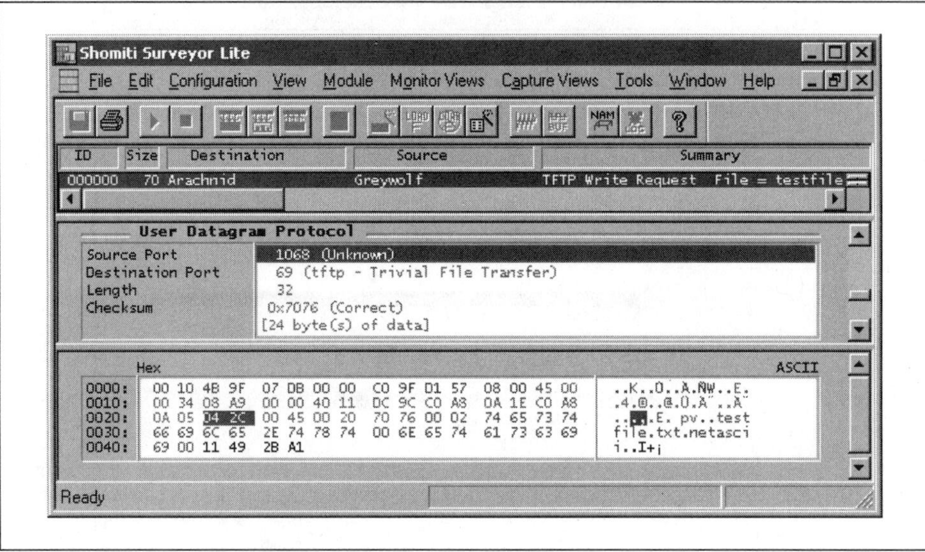

Figure 6-4. The Source Port field

See Also

"Destination Port"

"UDP Ports"

Destination Port

Identifies the message's destination, as referenced by the 16-bit UDP port number in use by the application on the destination system.

Size

Sixteen bits.

Notes

This field identifies the port number used by the destination application.

Capture Sample

In the capture shown in Figure 6-5, the Destination Port field contains the hexadecimal value of 00 45, which equals decimal 69, the well-known port number for TFTP servers.

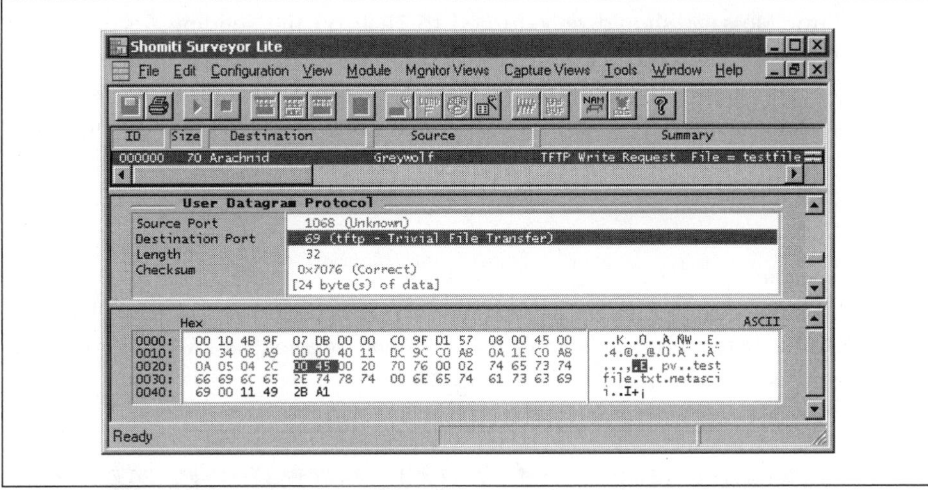

Figure 6-5. The Destination Port field

See Also

"Source Port"

"UDP Ports"

Length

Specifies the length of the entire UDP message in bytes, including both the header and data segments.

Size

Sixteen bits.

Notes

The primary purpose of this field is to inform a system of where the message ends. All UDP headers are eight bytes long, so the minimum size of a UDP message is eight bytes, while the maximum size is 65,535 bytes minus the size of the IP header (which is normally 20 bytes). Determining the size of the data portion of the UDP message can be found by subtracting eight (the size of the UDP header) from the value in this field.

The size of the UDP message is determined by the application. Whatever data gets generated by the application gets sent to IP as one big chunk of data by UDP, which gets turned into one big IP datagram. If the IP datagram is too big for IP to deliver (due to a restricted MTU size), then it is up to IP to fragment the datagram into appropriately sized IP packets, and to get those fragments to the destination system.

If the IP packets require fragmentation but the Don't Fragment bit is set, then the packets will be discarded, and an ICMP Fragmentation Required But DF Set Error Message should be returned to UDP on the sending system. If the UDP layer receives this message, it should relay it back to the calling application, where any necessary error-recovery can be conducted. However, if the application has already gone away, then the error message will never get seen (and therefore never get dealt with). Furthermore, many UDP applications do not care if there are problems after-the-fact, and do not monitor for ICMP error messages at all.

Capture Sample

In the capture shown in Figure 6-6, the Length field shows that this UDP message is 32 bytes long, indicating that the data segment is 24 bytes long (the UDP header is always eight bytes long).

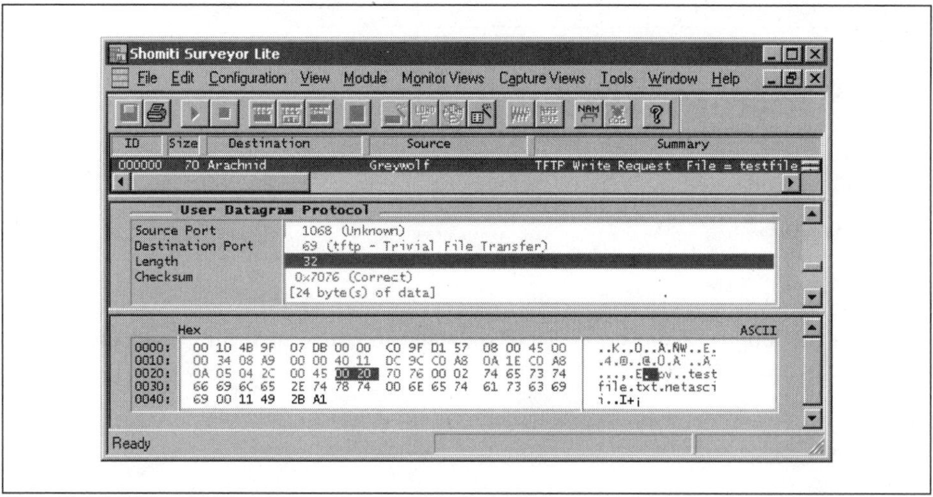

Figure 6-6. The Length field

See Also

"Fragmentation Flags" in Chapter 2, *The Internet Protocol*

"Destination Unreachable error messages" in Chapter 5, *The Internet Control Message Protocol*

Checksum

Used to store a checksum of the UDP message, including both the header and body parts. The checksum allows the destination system to validate the contents of the UDP message and to test for possible data corruption.

Size

Sixteen bits.

Notes

The UDP checksum is entirely optional. Many applications do not use it, particularly those that are performance-sensitive, where the additional processing time required for checksum calculations would induce undesirable delays. However, checksums do provide a certain amount of reliability, and they should be used whenever possible.

Even RFC 1122 states that UDP checksums should be enabled by default (requiring that the user disable them manually). Furthermore, RFC 1122 also states that if a recipient system receives a UDP message with a checksum, then it must use that checksum to verify the integrity of the data. Thus, sending a message without a checksum is optional, but reading and verifying any checksum that does exist is mandatory.

If the checksum is deemed to be invalid, then the message is discarded. Discarding segments is a "silent" error, and no notification of the event is generated or sent. Since UDP does not provide any error-correction mechanisms, this event will go unnoticed, further contributing to UDP's unreliable nature.

When the UDP checksum is calculated, it also includes a "pseudo-header" in the calculations. The pseudo-header includes the source and destination IP addresses, as well as the Protocol Identifier (17 for UDP) and the size of the UDP message (including both the header and the data). The pseudo-header is combined with the UDP header and data segments, and a checksum is calculated. By including the pseudo-header in the calculations, the destination system is able to validate that the sender and receiver are also correct, in case the IP packet that delivered the UDP message got mixed up en route to the final destination.

Capture Sample

In the capture shown in Figure 6-7, the Checksum has been calculated to hexadecimal 76 ed, which is correct.

Troubleshooting UDP

Since UDP provides only simple delivery services, almost all of the problems with UDP are related to delivery problems—perhaps an expected application server is

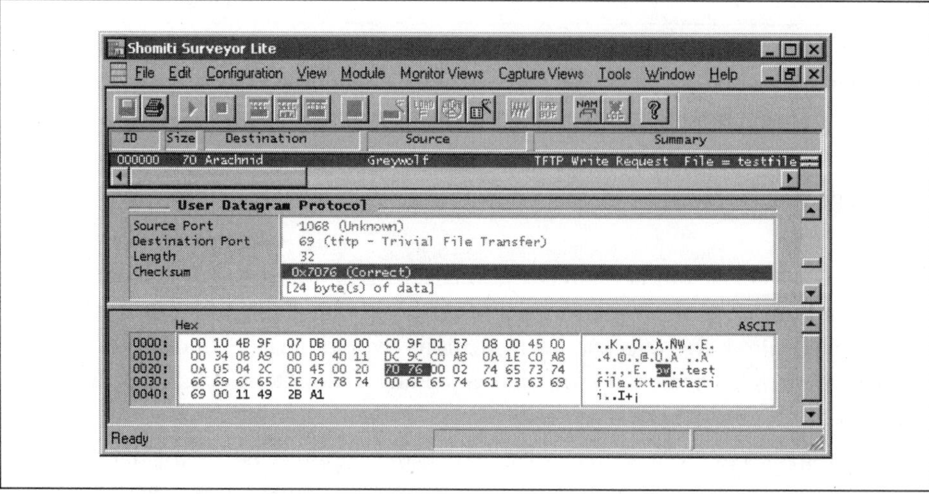

Figure 6-7. The Checksum field

unavailable, or is not running on the expected port number, or is no longer accepting messages for any number of other reasons.

ICMP Destination Unreachable: Port Unreachable Error Messages

In order to effectively debug problems with UDP delivery, you should rely on the ICMP protocol. It is the function of ICMP to report on problems that will keep IP datagrams (or UDP messages) from getting delivered to their destination effectively. For more information on ICMP, refer to Chapter 5, *The Internet Control Message Protocol.*

Figure 6-8 shows a problem with a TFTP client being unable to send data to a TFTP server. In this example, Greywolf has attempted to send data to Arachnid using TFTP. However, Arachnid is not running a TFTP server at this moment, so it returns an ICMP Destination Unreachable: Port Unreachable Error Message back to Greywolf.

If an application receives an ICMP error in response to an action, either it may try to send the data again or it may give up on the operation. Either way, any error-correction services must be implemented by the application, and not by UDP.

Another important point to make here is that many applications will not intercept or display ICMP Error Messages to the users of the application. Therefore, in order to diagnose problems such as this, it may be necessary to capture and decode the traffic on your network, using a tool such as Shomiti's Surveyor Lite.

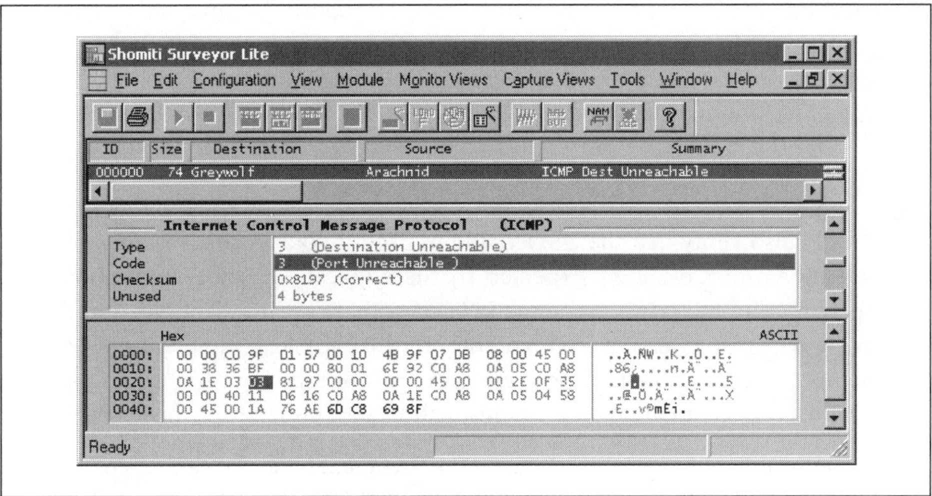

Figure 6-8. An ICMP Destination Unreachable: Port Unreachable Error Message

UDP-Based Application Failures

Since UDP provides a datagram-based transport service that does not offer any of the reliability services found with TCP, UDP-based applications are more prone to failures in a noisy or loss-intensive network. If the network you are using to move IP packets across loses a lot of packets, then this failure will be felt with UDP-based applications before it is noticed by TCP-based protocols.

For example, Sun's Network File Service (NFS) typically uses UDP for remote file-system access, since it benefits from the low-overhead nature of UDP. In addition, NFS typically writes data in large chunks (such as eight-kilobyte blocks), which are then split into multiple IP fragments according to the MTU characteristics of the underlying topology. Once all of the fragments have been received by the destination system, the IP datagram is reassembled and the UDP/NFS message is read and processed. However, if the underlying network loses 20% of the fragments, then the entire IP datagram will not be received (and thus the NFS data will not be processed).

With TCP-based applications, any data that gets lost will be recognized and retransmitted, resulting in slower overall performance, but a functional connection. With UDP however, lost data is gone forever and must be recognized and dealt with by the application. If the network constantly loses data however (such as is seen with sustained congestion levels or 20% packet loss due to line problems), then UDP-based applications that rely on fragmentation will constantly fail.

If you have problems with UDP-based applications such as NFS—but TCP-based applications like FTP work just fine—then you will need to investigate the loss characteristics of the network. You may need to reduce the amount of data that you are sending in a single operation (perhaps setting it equal to the MTU size or smaller), or you may need to use an application protocol that is TCP-based (many NFS implementations also support TCP).

Misconfigured or Missing Services File

You should also verify that the *services* file in use on your system matches up with the well-known port numbers expected by the application. Some applications will ask the system for the port number associated with TFTP, for example, and if your system's *services* file does not have an entry for that application, it will not return a port number to the client. This problem will prevent the client from being able to send any data, since it cannot get the destination port number for the application.

To see the well-known ports used on your system, examine the */etc/services* file on a Unix host, or the *C:\WinNT\System32\Drivers\Etc\SERVICES* file on a Windows NT host.

Firewalls Blocking UDP Messages

Many network managers block all UDP traffic, with the exception of a few critical ports (such as DNS). If you are experiencing problems connecting to remote UDP applications, then you should investigate whether or not a remote firewall is blocking UDP traffic. Note that the problem could also be reversed, with your firewall blocking the return UDP traffic. In this case, your UDP traffic may be leaving the network just fine, but the packets coming back from the remote system may be getting discarded by your own firewall.

Datagrams Are Corrupted or Never Sent

Sometimes, you may notice that a system does not always send the UDP datagrams that you expect it to, or that the first UDP packet from a stream of data does not get sent. Typically, this situation is a result of a lack of entries in the sender's ARP cache for the destination system. Not having an entry, the system is forced to issue an ARP lookup for the destination system, and then wait for a response.

However, many TCP/IP implementations allow only one IP packet to be held in the ARP call-back queue for any given host. If during the act of issuing the ARP lookup the sender receives another out-bound packet for that system, then the first packet is likely to get cleared from the ARP queue in order to make room for the new packet. In this case, the first packet (the one that caused the lookup in the first place) will be destroyed.

This particular problem happens most often when multiple packets are quickly sent to a destination system, or when the size of the UDP or ICMP message exceeds the MTU of the local network, forcing IP to fragment the single message into multiple IP packets. In the latter case, IP will issue two or more ARP requests (depending on the number of fragments generated) for the same destination system, resulting in the ARP agent clearing all but the last fragment from the call-back queue immediately. The last fragment that was sent before an ARP response was received will be the first fragment to get sent on the wire.

When the destination system receives this fragment, it will eventually discard the incomplete IP datagram (possibly returning an ICMP Time Exceeded Error Message), although the amount of time it took for this error to occur (60 seconds is the most common value) may be longer than the client waited for. In that situation, the ICMP error message would not be seen by the client, since it had long since disconnected from UDP.

One way to solve this problem is to create static entries in the ARP cache for the destination system, allowing the sender to immediately send the IP fragments, rather than waiting for the ARP agent to conduct a query first. For more information on issues with the ARP cache, refer to "The ARP Cache" in Chapter 3, *The Address Resolution Protocol*.

This is just another reason why UDP should not be used for important data. If the data is important, you must use TCP to ensure that lost segments are recognized and eventually retransmitted.

7

The Transmission Control Protocol

Summary	The Transmission Control Protocol provides a reliable, connection-oriented transport protocol for transaction-oriented applications to use. TCP is used by almost all of the application protocols found on the Internet today, as most of them require a reliable, error-correcting transport layer in order to ensure that data does not get lost or corrupted.
Protocol ID	6
Relevant STDs	2 (*http://www.iana.org/*); 3 (includes RFCs 1122 and 1123); 7 (RFC 793, republished)
Relevant RFCs	793 (Transmission Control Protocol); 896 (The Nagle Algorithm); 1122 (Host Network Requirements); 1323 (Window Scale and Timestamp); 2018 (Selective Acknowledgments); 2581 (TCP Congestion Control);
Related RFCs	1072 (Extensions for High Delay) 1106 (Negative Acknowledgments); 1146 (Alternate Checksums); 1337 (Observations on RFC 1323); 1644 (Transaction Extensions); 1948 (Defending Against Sequence Number Attacks); 2414 (Increasing the Initial Window); 2525 (Known TCP Implementation Problems); 2582 (Experimental New Reno Modifications to Fast Recovery)

On an IP network, applications use two standard transport protocols to communicate with each other. These are the User Datagram Protocol (UDP), which provides a lightweight and unreliable transport service, and the Transmission Control Protocol (TCP), which provides a reliable and controlled transport service. The majority of Internet applications use TCP, since its built-in reliability and flow control services ensure that data does not get lost or corrupted.

TCP is probably the most important protocol in use on the Internet today. Although IP does the majority of the legwork, moving datagrams and packets around the Internet as needed, TCP makes sure that the *data* inside of the IP datagrams is correct. Without this reliability service, the Internet would not work nearly as well as it does, if it worked at all.

It is also interesting to note that the first versions of TCP were designed *before* IP, with IP being extracted from TCP later. In fact, TCP is now designed to work with any packet-switched network, whether this be raw Ethernet or a distributed IP-based network like the Internet. This flexible design has resulted in TCP being adopted by other network architectures, including OSI's Transport Protocol 4 (TP4) and Apple Computer Corporation's AppleTalk Data Stream Protocol (ADSP).

The TCP Standard

TCP is defined in RFC 793, which has been republished as STD 7 (TCP is an Internet Standard protocol). However, RFC 793 contained some vagaries which were clarified in RFC 1122 (Host Network Requirements). In addition, RFC 2001 introduced a variety of congestion-related elements to TCP, which have been included into the standard specification, although this RFC was superseded by RFC 2581 (a.k.a., RFC 2001*bis*). As such, TCP implementations need to incorporate RFC 793, RFC 1122, and RFC 2581 in order to work reliably and consistently with other implementations.

RFC 793 states that the Protocol ID for TCP is 6. When a system receives an IP datagram that is marked as containing Protocol 6, it should pass the contents of the datagram to TCP for further processing.

TCP Is a Reliable, Connection-Centric Transport Protocol

Remember that all of the transport-layer protocols (including TCP and UDP) use IP for their basic delivery services, and that IP is an unreliable protocol, providing no guarantees that datagrams or packets will reach their destination intact. It is quite possible for IP packets to get lost entirely (due to an untimely link failure on the network somewhere), or for packets to become corrupted (due to an overworked or buggy router), or for packets to get reordered as they cross different networks en route to the destination system, or for a myriad of other problems to crop up while packets are being bounced around the Internet.

For applications that need some sort of guarantee that data will arrive at its destination intact, this uncertainty is simply unacceptable. Electronic mail, TELNET, and other network applications are the basis of many mission-critical efforts, and as such they need some sort of guarantee that the data they transmit will arrive in its original form.

This reliability is achieved through the use of a virtual circuit that TCP builds whenever two applications need to communicate. As we discussed in Chapter 1, *An Introduction to TCP/IP*, a TCP session is somewhat analogous to a telephone conversation in that it provides a managed, full-duplex, point-to-point communications circuit for application protocols to use. Whenever data needs to be sent between two TCP-based applications, a virtual circuit is established between the two TCP providers, and a highly monitored exchange of application data occurs. Once all of the data has been successfully sent and received, the connection gets torn down.

Building and monitoring these virtual circuits incurs a fair amount of overhead, making TCP somewhat slower than UDP. However, UDP does not provide any reliability services whatsoever, which is an unacceptable trade-off for many applications.

Services Provided by TCP

Although it is possible for applications to provide their own reliability and flow control services, it is impractical for them to do so. Rather than developing (and debugging) these kinds of services, it is much more efficient for applications to leverage them as part of a transport-layer protocol, where every application has access to them. This arrangement allows shorter development cycles, better interoperability, and less headaches for everybody.

TCP provides five key services to higher-layer applications:

Virtual circuits

Whenever two applications need to communicate with each other using TCP, a virtual circuit is established between the two TCP endpoints. The virtual circuit is at the heart of TCP's design, providing the reliability, flow control, and I/O management features that distinguish it from UDP.

Application I/O management

Applications communicate with each other by sending data to the local TCP provider, which then transmits the data across a virtual circuit to the other side, where it is eventually delivered to the destination application. TCP provides an I/O buffer for applications to use, allowing them to send and receive data as contiguous streams, with TCP converting the data into individually monitored segments that are sent over IP.

Network I/O management

When TCP needs to send data to another system, it uses IP for the actual delivery service. Thus, TCP also has to provide network I/O management services to IP, building segments that can travel efficiently over the IP network, and turning individual segments back into a data-stream appropriate for the applications.

Flow control

Different hosts on a network will have different characteristics, including processing capabilities, memory, network bandwidth, and other resources. For this reason, not all hosts are able to send and receive data at the same rate, and TCP must be able to deal with these variations. Furthermore, TCP has to do all of this seamlessly, without any action being required from the applications in use.

Reliability

TCP provides a reliable transport service by monitoring the data that it sends. TCP uses sequence numbers to monitor individual bytes of data, acknowledgment flags to tell if some of those bytes have been lost somewhere, and checksums to validate the data itself. Taken together, these mechanisms make TCP extremely reliable.

All told, these services make TCP an extremely robust transport protocol.

Virtual Circuits

In order for TCP to provide a reliable transport service, it has to overcome IP's own inherent weaknesses, possibly the greatest of which is the inability to track data as it gets sent across the network. IP only moves packets around the network, and makes no pretense towards offering any sort of reliability whatsoever. Although this lack of reliability is actually a designed-in feature of IP that allows it to move data across multiple paths quickly, it is also an inherent weakness that must be overcome in order for applications to communicate with each other reliably and efficiently.

TCP does this by building a virtual circuit on top of IP's packet-centric network layer, and then tracking data as it is sent through the virtual circuit. This concept is illustrated in Figure 7-1. Whenever a connection is made between two TCP endpoints, all of the data gets passed through the virtual circuit.

By using this virtual circuit layer, TCP accomplishes several things. It allows IP to do what it does best (which is moving individual packets around the network), while also allowing applications to send and receive data without them having to worry about the condition of the underlying network. And since each byte of data is monitored individually by TCP, it's easy to take corrective actions whenever required, providing reliability and flow control services on top of the chaotic Internet.

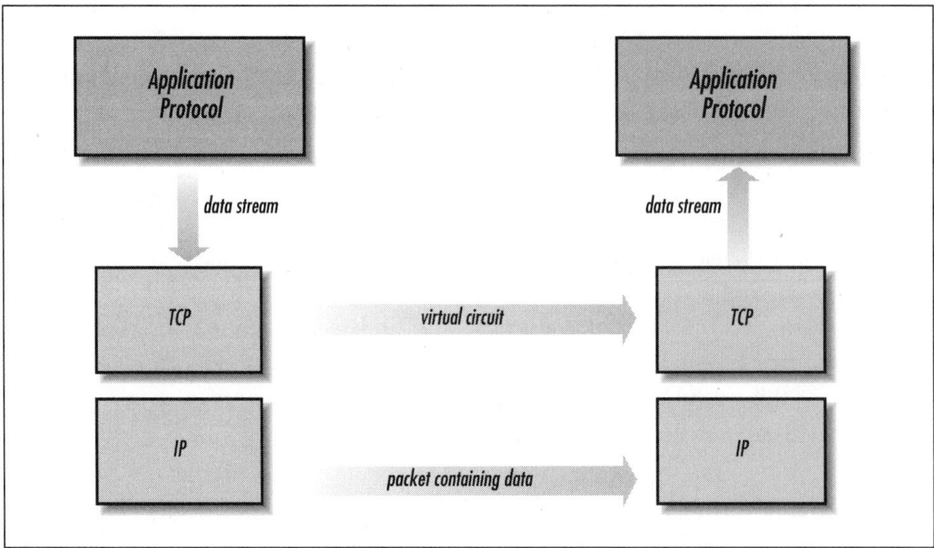

Figure 7-1. An overview of TCP's virtual circuits

These virtual circuits are somewhat analogous to the way that telephone calls work. It is easy to see this corollary if you think of the two TCP endpoints as being the "telephones," and the applications being the users of those telephones.

When an application wants to exchange data with another system, it first requests that TCP establish a workable session between the local and remote applications. This process is similar to you calling another person on the phone. When the other party answers ("Hello?"), they are acknowledging that the call went through. You then acknowledge the other party's acknowledgment ("Hi Joe, this is Eric"), and begin exchanging information ("The reason I'm calling is...").

Likewise, data travelling over a TCP virtual circuit is monitored throughout the session, just as a telephone call is. If at any time parts of the data are lost ("What did you say?"), the sending system will retransmit the lost data ("I said..."). If the connection degrades to a point where communications are no longer possible, then sooner or later both parties will drop the call. Assuming that things don't deteriorate to that point, then the parties will agree to disconnect ("See ya") once all of the data has been exchanged successfully, and the call will be gracefully terminated.

This concept is illustrated in Figure 7-2. When a TCP connection needs to be established, one of the two endpoint systems will try to connect with the other endpoint. If the "call" goes through successfully, then the TCP stack on the remote system will acknowledge the connection request, which will then be followed by an acknowledgment from the sender. This three-way handshake ensures that the connection is sufficiently reliable for data to be exchanged.

Likewise, each clump of data that is sent is explicitly acknowledged, providing constant feedback that everything is going okay. Once all of the data has been sent, either endpoint can close the virtual circuit. However, the disconnect process also uses acknowledgments in order to ensure that both parties are ready to terminate the call. If one of the systems still had data to send, then they might not agree to drop the circuit.

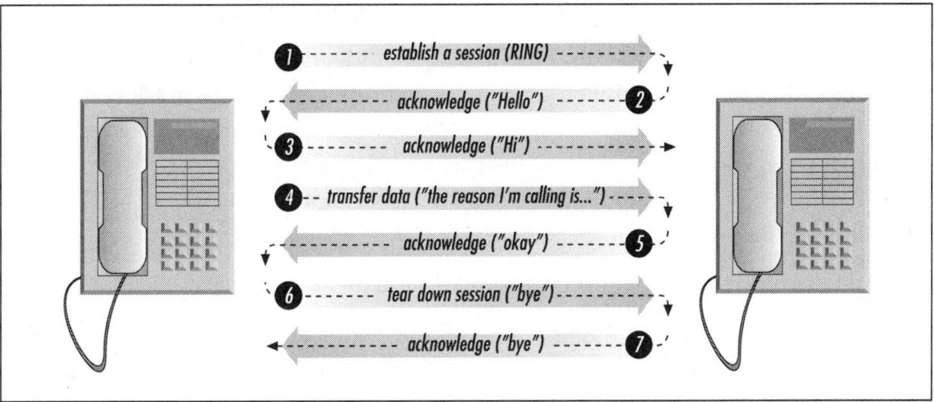

Figure 7-2. TCP virtual circuits versus telephone calls

The virtual circuit metaphor has other similarities with traditional telephone calls. For example, TCP is a full-duplex transport that allows each party to send and receive data over the same virtual circuit simultaneously, just like a telephone call does. This allows for a web browser to request an object and for the web server to send the requested data back to the client using a single virtual circuit, rather than requiring that each end establish its own communication channel.

Every TCP virtual circuit is dedicated to one pair of endpoints, also like a telephone call. If an application needs to communicate with multiple endpoints simultaneously, then it must establish unique circuits for each endpoint pair, just as telephone calls do. This is true even if the same applications are in use at both ends of the connection. For example, if a web browser were to simultaneously request four GIF images from the same server using four simultaneous HTTP "GET" commands, then four separate TCP circuits would be needed in order for the operations to complete, even though the same applications and hosts were being used with all of the requests.

For all of these reasons, it is easy to think of TCP's virtual circuits as being very similar to the familiar concept of telephone calls.

Application I/O Management

The primary benefit of the virtual circuit metaphor is the reliability that it allows. However, another set of key benefits is the I/O management services that this design provides.

One of the main features that comes from this design is that applications can send and receive information as streams of data, rather than having to deal with packet-sizing and management issues directly. This allows a web server to send a very large graphic image as a single stream of data, rather than as a bunch of individual packets, leaving the task of packaging and tracking the data to TCP.

This design helps to keep application code simple and straightforward, resulting in lower complexity, higher reliability, and better interoperability. Application developers don't have to build flow control, circuit-management, and packaging services into their applications, but can instead use the services provided by TCP, without having to do anything special. All an application has to do is read and write data; TCP does everything else.

TCP provides four distinct application I/O management services to applications:

- *Internal Addressing*. TCP assigns unique port numbers to every instance of every application that is using a TCP virtual circuit. Essentially, these port numbers act as extension numbers, allowing TCP to route incoming data directly to the appropriate destination application.
- *Opening Circuits*. Applications inform TCP when they need to open a connection to a remote application, and leave it to TCP to get the job done.
- *Data Transfer*. Whenever an application needs to send data, it just hands it off to TCP, and assumes that TCP will do everything it can to make sure that the data is delivered intact to the destination system.
- *Destroying Circuits*. Once applications have finished exchanging data, they inform TCP that they are finished, and TCP closes the virtual circuit.

Application addressing with TCP ports

Applications communicate with TCP through the use of ports, which are practically identical to the ports found in UDP. Application are assigned 16-bit port numbers when they register with TCP, and TCP uses these port numbers for all incoming and outgoing traffic.

Conceptually, port numbers provide "extensions" for the individual applications in use on a system, with the IP address of the local system acting as the main phone number. Remote applications "call" the host system (using the IP address), and also provide the extension number (port number) of the destination application that they want to communicate with. TCP uses this information to identify the sending and receiving applications, and to deliver data to the correct application.

Technically, this procedure is a bit more complex than it is being described here. When an application wishes to communicate with another application, it will give the data to TCP through its assigned port number, telling TCP the port number and IP address of the destination application. TCP will then create the necessary TCP message (called a "segment"), marking the source and destination port numbers in the message headers, and storing whatever data is being sent in the payload portion of the message. A complete TCP segment will then get passed off to the local IP software for delivery to the remote system (which will create the necessary IP datagram and shoot it off).

Once the IP datagram is received by the destination system, the remote IP software will see that the data portion of the datagram contains a TCP segment (as can be seen by the Protocol Identifier field in the IP header), and will hand the contents of the segment to TCP for further processing. TCP will then look at the TCP header, see the destination port number, and hand the payload portion of the segment off to whatever application is using the specified destination port number.

This concept is illustrated in Figure 7-3. In that example, an HTTP client is sending data to the HTTP server running on port 80 of the destination system. When the data arrives at the destination system, TCP will examine the destination port number for that segment, and then deliver the contents of the segment to the application it finds there (which should be the HTTP server).

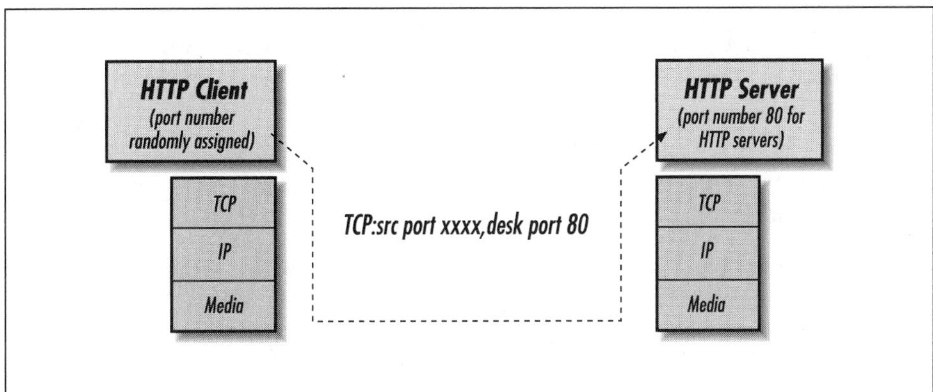

Figure 7-3. Application-level multiplexing with port numbers

Technically, a port identifies only a single instance of an application on a single system. The term "socket" is used to identify the port number and IP address concantenated together (i.e., port 80 on host 192.168.10.10 could also be referred to as socket 192.168.10.10:80). A "socket pair" consists of both endpoints on a virtual circuit, including the IP addresses and port numbers of both applications on both systems.

All TCP virtual circuits work on the concept of socket pairs. Multiple connections between two systems must have unique socket pairs, with at least one of the two endpoints having a different port number.

TCP port numbers are not necessarily linked with applications on a one-to-one basis. It is quite common for some applications to open multiple connections simultaneously, and these connections would all require unique socket pairs, even if there was only one application in use. For example, if an HTTP 1.0 client were to simultaneously download multiple graphic objects from an HTTP server, then each instance of the HTTP client would require a unique and separate port number in order for TCP to route the data correctly. In this case, there would be only one application, but there would be multiple bindings to the network, with each binding having a unique port number.

It is important to realize that circuits and ports are entirely separate entities, although they are tightly interwoven. The virtual circuit provides a managed transport between two endpoint TCP providers, while port numbers provide only an address for the applications to use when talking to their local TCP provider. For this reason, it is entirely possible for a server application to support several different client connections through a single port number (although each unique virtual circuit will have a unique socket pair, with the client-side address and/or socket being the unique element).

For example, Figure 7-4 shows a single HTTP server running on Arachnid, with two active virtual circuits (one for Ferret, and another for Greywolf). Although both connections use the same IP address and port number on Arachnid, the socket pairs themselves are unique, due to the different IP addresses and port numbers in use by the two client systems. In this regard, virtual circuits are different from the port number in use by the HTTP server, although these elements are also tightly related.

Most of the server-based IP applications that are used on the Internet today use what are referred to as "well-known" port numbers, as we discussed in the previous chapter. For example, an HTTP server will listen on TCP port 80 by default, which is the well-known port number associated with HTTP servers. This way, any HTTP client that needs to connect to any HTTP server can use the default destination of TCP port 80. Otherwise, the client would have to specify the port number of the server that it wanted to connect with (you've seen this in some URLs that use *http://www.somehost.com:8080/* or the like; *8080* is the port number of the HTTP server on *www.somehost.com*).

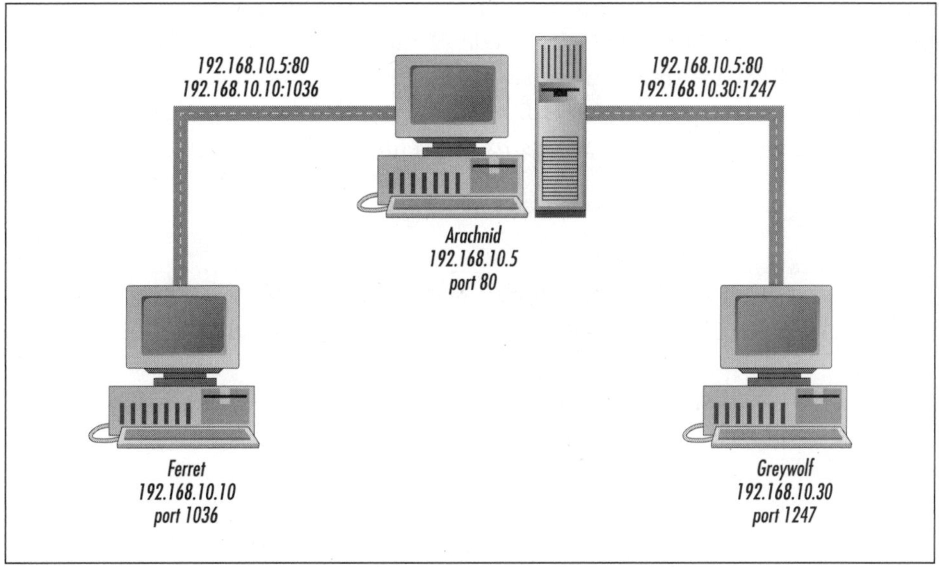

Figure 7-4. An HTTP server with two connections, using two distinct socket pairs

Most servers let you use any port number and are not restricted to the well-known port number. However, if you run your servers on non-standard ports, then you would have to tell every user that the server was *not* accessible on the default port. This would be hard to manage at best. By sticking with the defaults, all users can connect to your server using the default port number, which is likely to cause the least amount of trouble.

Some network administrators purposefully run application servers on nonstandard ports, hoping to add an extra layer of security to their network. However, it is my opinion that security through obscurity is no security at all, and this method should not be relied upon by itself.

Historically, only server-based applications have been allowed to run on ports below 1024, as these ports could be used only by privileged accounts. By limiting access to these port numbers, it was more difficult for a hacker to install a rogue application server. However, this restriction is based on Unix-specific architectures and is not easily enforced on all of the systems that run IP today. Many application servers now run on operating systems that have little or no concept of privileged users, making this historical restriction somewhat irrelevant.

There are a number of predefined port numbers that are registered with the Internet Assigned Numbers Authority (IANA). All of the port numbers below 1024 are reserved for use with well-known applications, although there are also many applications that use port numbers outside of this range. Some of the more common port numbers are shown in Table 7-1. For a detailed listing of all of the port numbers that are currently registered, refer to the IANA's online registry (accessible at *http://www.isi.edu/in-notes/iana/assignments/port-numbers*).

Table 7-1. Some of the Port Numbers Reserved for Well-Known TCP Servers

Port Number	Description
20	File Transfer Protocol, Control Channel (FTP)
21	File Transfer Protocol, Data Channel (FTP-Data)
23	TELNET
25	Simple Mail Transfer Protocol (SMTP)
80	Hypertext Transfer Protocol (HTTP)
110	Post Office Protocol, v3 (POP3)
119	Network News Transfer Protocol (NNTP)

Besides the reserved addresses that are managed by the IANA, there are also "unreserved" port numbers that can be used by any application for any purpose, although conflicts may occur with other users who are also using those port numbers. Any port number that is frequently used should be registered with the IANA.

To see the well-known ports used on your system, examine the */etc/services* file on a Unix host, or the *C:\WinNT\System32\Drivers\Etc\SERVICES* file on a Windows NT host.

Opening a circuit

Applications communicate with each other using the virtual circuits provided by TCP. These circuits are established on an as-needed basis, getting created and destroyed as requested by the applications in use. Whenever an application needs to communicate with another application somewhere on the network, it will ask the local TCP provider to establish a virtual circuit on its behalf.

There are two methods for requesting that a virtual circuit be opened: either a client will request an open so that data can be sent immediately, or a server will open a port in "listen" mode, waiting for a connection request to arrive from a client.

The simplest of the two methods is the "passive open," which is the form used by servers that want to listen for incoming connections. A passive open indicates that the server is willing to accept incoming connection requests from other systems, and that it does not want to initiate an outbound connection. Typically, a passive open is "unqualified," meaning the server can accept an incoming connection from anybody. However, some security-sensitive applications will accept connections only from predefined entities, a condition known as a "qualified passive open." This type is most often seen with corporate web servers, ISP news servers, and other restricted-access systems.

When a publicly accessible server first gets started, it will request that TCP open a well-known port in passive mode, offering connectivity to any node that sends in a connection request. Any TCP connection requests that come into the system destined for that port number will result in a new virtual circuit being established.

Client applications (such as a web browser) use "active opens" when making these connection requests. An active open is the opposite of a passive open, in that it is a specific request to establish a virtual circuit with a specific destination socket (typically this will be the well-known port number of the server that is associated with the specific client).

This process is illustrated in Figure 7-5. When an HTTP client needs to get a document from a remote HTTP server, it issues an "active open" to the local TCP software, providing it with the IP address and TCP port number of the destination HTTP server. The client's TCP provider then allocates a random port number for the application and attempts to establish a virtual circuit with the destination system's TCP software. The server's TCP software verifies that the connection can be opened (Is the port available? Are there security filters in place that would prevent the connection?), and then respond with an acknowledgment.

If the destination port is unavailable (perhaps the web server is down), then the TCP provider on the server system rejects the connection request. This is in contrast to UDP, which has to rely on ICMP Destination Unreachable: Port Unreachable Error Messages for this service. TCP is able to reject connections explicitly and can therefore abort connection requests without having to involve ICMP.

If the connection request is accepted, then the TCP provider on the server system acknowledges the request, and the client would then acknowledge the server's acknowledgment. At this point, the virtual circuit would be established and operational, and the two applications could begin exchanging data, as illustrated in Figure 7-5.

The segments used for the handshake process do not normally contain data, but instead are zero-length "command segments" that have special connection-management flags in their headers, signifying that a new virtual circuit is being established. In this context, the most important of these flags is the Synchronize flag, used by two endpoints to signify that a virtual circuit is being established.

For example, the first command segment sent by the client in Figure 7-5 would have the Synchronize flag enabled. This flag tells the server's TCP software that this is a new connection request. In addition, this command segment will also

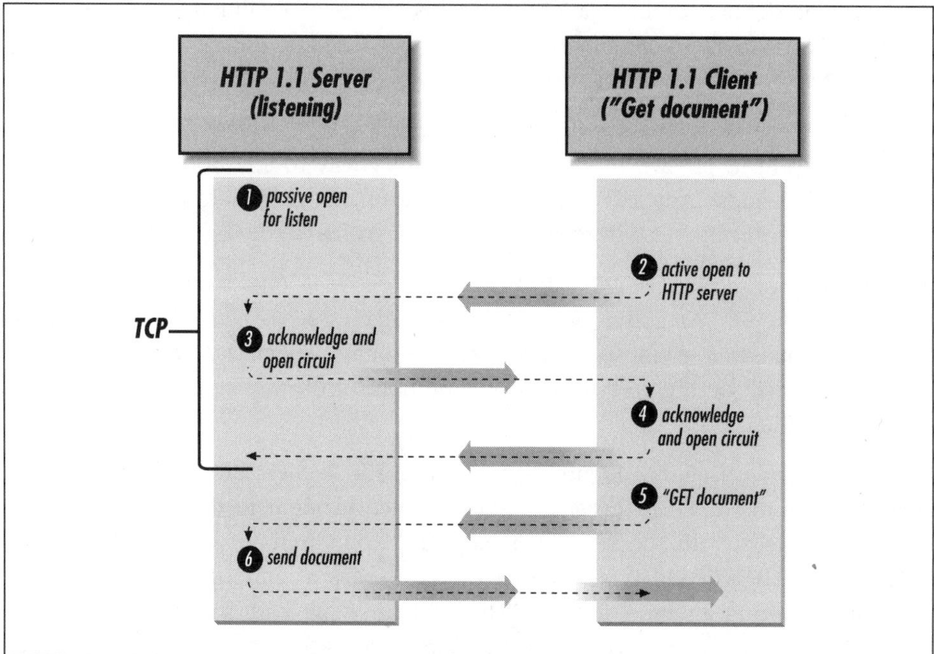

Figure 7-5. A TCP virtual circuit being established

provide the starting byte number (called the "sequence number") that the client will use when sending data to the server, with this data being provided in the Sequence Identifier field of the TCP header.

If the server is willing to establish a virtual circuit with the client, then it will respond with its own command segment that also contains the Synchronize flag and that also gives the starting sequence number that the server will use when sending data back to the client. This command segment will also have the Acknowledgment flag enabled, with the Acknowledgment Identifier field pointing to the client's next-expected sequence number.

The client will then return a command segment with the Acknowledge flag enabled to the server, and with its Acknowledgment Identifier field pointing to the server's next-expected sequence number. Note that this segment does not have the Synchronize flag enabled, since the virtual circuit is now considered up and operational, with both systems now being able to exchange data as needed.

It is entirely possible for two systems to issue active opens to each other simultaneously, although this scenario is extremely rare (I know of no applications that do this purposefully). In theory, such an event is possible, although it probably happens only on very slow networks where the circuit-setup messages pass each other on the wire.

For more information on the Synchronize and Acknowledgment flags, refer to "Control Flags" later in this chapter. For more information on the sequence and acknowledgment numbers, refer to "Reliability" also later in this chapter.

Exchanging data

Once a virtual circuit has been established, the applications in use can begin exchanging data with each other. However, it is important to note that applications do not exchange data directly. Rather, each application hands data to its local TCP provider, identifying the specific destination socket that the data is for, and TCP does the rest.

Applications can pass data to TCP in chunks or as a contiguous byte-stream. Most TCP implementations provide a "write" service that is restricted in size, forcing applications to write data in blocks, just as if they were writing data to a file on the local hard drive. However, TCP's buffering design also supports application writes that are contiguous, and this design is used in a handful of implementations.

TCP stores the data that it receives into a local send buffer. Periodically, a chunk of data will get sent to the destination system. The recipient TCP software will then store this data into a receive buffer, where it will be eventually passed to the destination application.

For example, whenever a web browser issues an HTTP "GET" request, the request is passed to TCP as application data. TCP stores the data into a send buffer, packaging it up with any other data that is bound for the destination socket. The data then gets bundled into an IP datagram and sent to the destination system. The recipient's TCP provider then takes the data and passes it up to the web server, which fetches the requested document and hands it off to TCP. TCP sends chunks of the document data back to the client in multiple IP packets, where it is queued up and then handed to the application.

This concept is outlined in Figure 7-6, which shows an HTTP client asking for a document from a remote HTTP server. Once the TCP virtual circuit is established, the HTTP client writes "GET document" into the local send buffer associated with the virtual circuit in use by the client. TCP then puts this data into a TCP segment (creating the appropriate TCP headers), and sends it on to the specified destination system via IP. The HTTP server at the other end of the connection would then take the same series of steps when returning the requested document back to the client.

The important thing to remember here is that application data is transmitted as independent TCP segments, each of which requires acknowledgments. It is at this layer that TCP's reliability and flow control services are most visible.

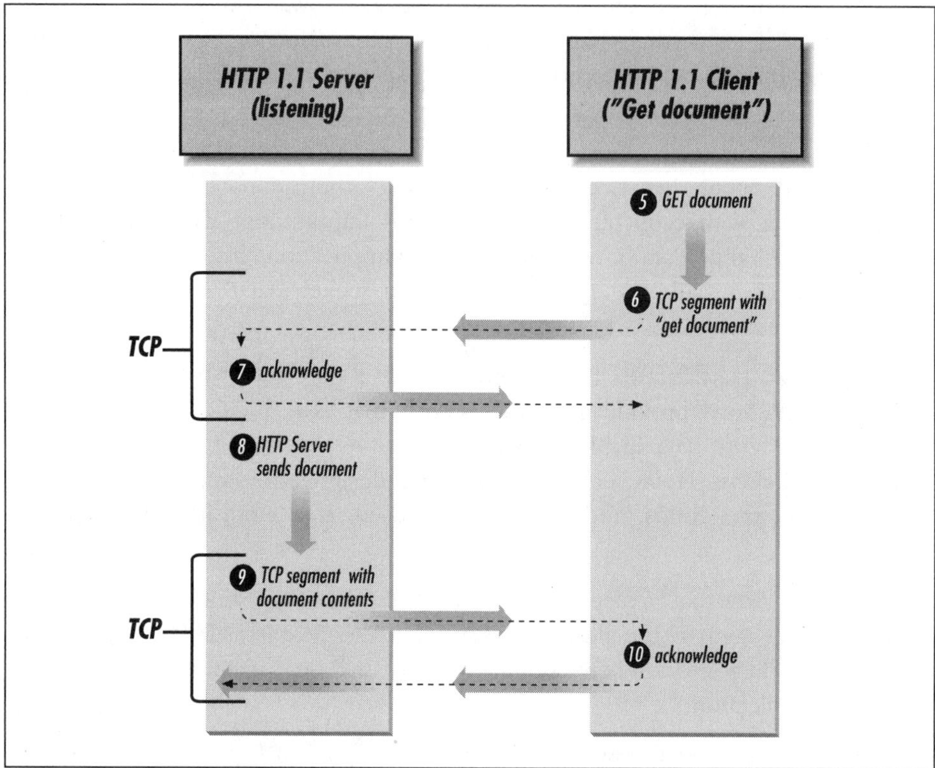

Figure 7-6. Data being exchanged over a TCP virtual circuit

For more information on how TCP converts application data into IP datagrams, refer ahead to "Network I/O Management."

Closing a circuit

Once the applications have exchanged all of their data, the circuit can be closed. Closing a circuit is similar to opening one, in that an application must request the action (except in those cases where the connection has collapsed, and TCP is forced to terminate it).

Either end of the connection may close the circuit at any time, using a variety of different means. The two common ways to close are "active closes" that initiate a shutdown sequence and "passive closes" that respond to an active close request.

Just as building a circuit requires a bidirectional exchange of special command segments, so does closing it. One end of the connection requests that the circuit be closed (the active close at work). The remote system then acknowledges the termination request and responds with its own termination request (the passive close). The terminating system then acknowledges the acknowledgment, and both endpoints drop the circuit. At this point, neither system is able to send any more data over the virtual circuit.

Figure 7-7 shows this process in detail. Once the HTTP client has received all of the data, it requests that the virtual circuit be closed. The HTTP server then returns an acknowledgment for the shutdown request, and also sends its own termination request. When the server's shutdown request is received by the client, the client issues a final acknowledgment, and begins closing its end of the circuit. Once the final acknowledgment is received by the server, the server shuts down whatever is left of the circuit. By this point, the connection is completely closed.

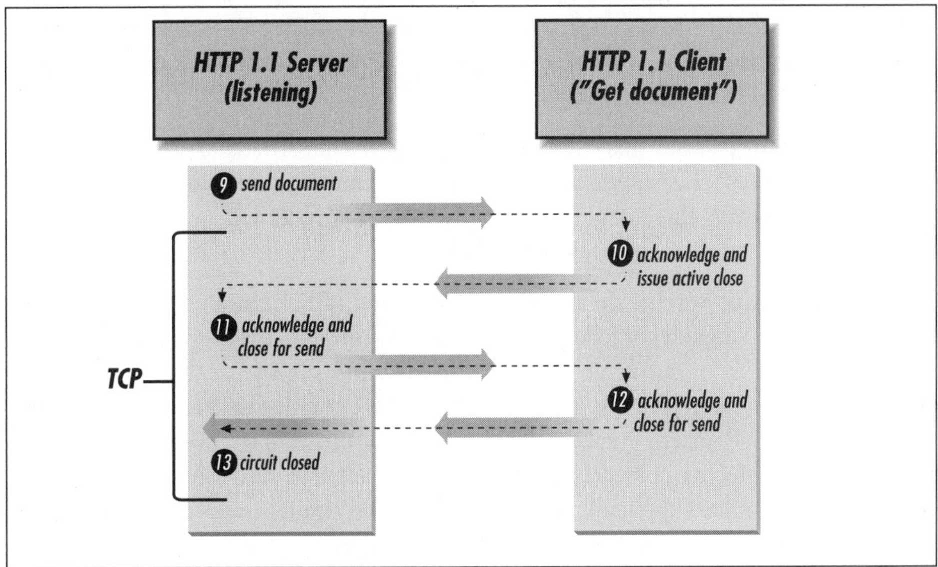

Figure 7-7. A TCP virtual circuit being torn down

Just as TCP uses special Synchronize flags in the circuit-setup command segments, TCP also has special Finish flags that it uses when terminating a virtual circuit. The side issuing the active close sends a command segment with the Finish flag enabled and with a sequence number that is one byte higher than the last sequence number used by that side during the connection. The destination system responds with a command segment that also has the Finish flag enabled and with its sequence number also incremented by one. In addition, the Acknowledgment Identifier field for this response will still point to the next-expected sequence number, even though no other data should be forthcoming. In this regard, the Finish flag is considered to be one byte of data (just like the Synchronize flag), and as such must be acknowledged explicitly.

Once the Finish segments have been exchanged, the terminating system must respond with a final acknowledgment for the last Finish segment, with the

Acknowledgment Identifier also pointing to the next-expected sequence number (even though there should not be another segment coming). However, this last segment will not have the Finish flag enabled, since the circuit is considered to be "down" and out of action by this point.

It's important to note that either endpoint can initiate the circuit-termination process, and there are no hard and fast rules for which end should do it, although typically it is left to the client to perform this service since it may make multiple requests over a single connection. POP3 is a good example of this process, as POP3 allows a client to submit multiple commands during a single session. The client would need to dictate when the circuit should be closed with this type of application. However, sometimes a server issues the active close. For example, Gopher servers close the virtual circuit after sending whatever data has been requested, as do HTTP 1.0 servers.

It's also important to note that "server" applications keeps the *port* open until the application itself is terminated, allowing other clients to continue connecting to that server. However, the individual *circuits* will be torn down on a per-connection basis, according to the process described above.

Sometimes, the two systems do not close their ends of the circuit simultaneously. This results in a staggered close—also known as a "half-close"—with each end issuing passive close requests at different times. One example of this type can be found in the *rsh* utility, which is used to submit shell commands to *rsh* servers. On some systems, once an *rsh* command has been sent the client will close its end of the connection, effectively switching the virtual circuit into half-duplex mode. The server will then process the shell command, send the results back to the client (for display or further processing), and then close its end of the connection. Once both ends have been closed, the circuit is dropped.

Another option for closing a circuit is to simply drop it without going through an orderly shutdown. Although this method will likely cause unnecessary traffic, it is not uncommon. Typically, this method should only happen if an application is abruptly terminated. If an application needs to immediately close a circuit without going through the normal shutdown sequence, then it will request an immediate termination, and TCP will issue a segment with the Reset flag set, informing the other end that the connection is being killed immediately.

For more information on the Finish, Reset, and Acknowledgment flags, refer ahead to "Control Flags." For more information on the sequence and acknowledgment numbers, refer ahead to "Reliability."

Application design issues

Some applications open a connection and keep it open for long periods of time, while others open and close connections rapidly, using many circuits for a single operation.

For example, if you instruct your web browser to open a document from an HTTP 1.0 Web server, the HTTP client issues an active open to the destination HTTP 1.0 server, which then sends the document to the client and close the TCP connection. If there are any graphic objects on that document, the HTTP client has to open multiple unique connections for each of those objects. Thus, opening a single web page could easily result in twenty or more circuits being established and destroyed, depending on the number of objects embedded in the requested web page.

Since this model generates a lot of traffic (and uses a lot of network resources on the server), this process was changed with HTTP 1.1, which now allows a single circuit to be used for multiple operations. With HTTP 1.1, a client may request a page and then reuse the existing circuit to download objects embedded within that page. This model results in significantly fewer virtual circuits being used, although it also makes the download process synchronous rather than asynchronous.

Most applications use a single circuit for everything, keeping that circuit open even when there may not be any noticeable activity. TELNET is one example of this, where the TELNET client will issue an active open during the initial connection, and then use that virtual circuit for everything until the connection is terminated. After logging in, the user may get up and walk away from the client system, and thus no activity may occur for an extended period of time, although the TCP connection between the two systems would remain active.

Whether the circuits are torn down immediately or kept open for extended periods of time is really a function of the application's design goal, rather than anything mandated by TCP. It is entirely possible for clients to open and close connections rapidly (as seen with web browsers that use individual circuits for every element in a downloaded document), or to open a single connection and maintain it in perpetuity (as seen with TELNET).

Keep-alives

Although RFC 793 does not make any provision for a keep-alive mechanism, some TCP implementations provide one anyway. There are good reasons for doing this, and bad ones as well.

By design, TCP keep-alives are supposed to be used to detect when one of the TCP endpoints has disappeared without closing the connection. This feature is particularly useful for applications where the client may be inactive for long periods of time (such as TELNET), and there's no way to tell whether the connection is still valid.

For example, if a PC running a TELNET client were powered off, the client would not close the virtual circuit gracefully. Unfortunately, when that happened the TELNET server would never know that the other end had disappeared. Long periods of inactivity are common with TELNET, so not getting any data from the client for an extended period would not cause any alarms on the TELNET server itself. Furthermore, since the TELNET server wouldn't normally send unsolicited data to the client, it would never detect a failure from a lack of acknowledgments either. Thus, the connection might stay open for infinity, consuming system resources for no good purpose.

TCP keep-alives allow servers to check up on clients periodically. If no response is received from the remote endpoint, then the circuit is considered invalid and will be released.

RFC 1122 states that keep-alives are entirely optional, should be user-configurable, and should be implemented only within server-side applications that will suffer real harm if the client were to disappear. Although implementations vary, RFC 1122 also states that keep-alive segments should not contain any data, but may be configured to send one byte of data if required for compatibility with non-compliant implementations.

Most systems use an unsolicited command segment for this task, with the sequence number of the command segment set to one byte less than the sequence number of the next byte of data to be sent, effectively reusing the last sequence number of the last byte of data sent over the virtual circuit. This design effectively forces the remote endpoint to issue a duplicate acknowledgment for the last byte of data that was sent over that connection. When the acknowledgment arrives, the server knows that the client is still there and operational. If no response comes back after a few such tests, then the server can drop the circuit.

Network I/O Management

When an application needs to send data to another application over TCP, it writes the data to the local TCP provider, which queues the data into a send buffer. Periodically, TCP packages portions of the data into bundles (called "segments"), and passes them off to IP for delivery to the destination system, as illustrated in Figure 7-8.

Although this process sounds simple, it involves a lot of work, primarily due to segment-sizing issues that TCP has to deal with. For every segment that gets created, TCP has to determine the most efficient segment size to use at that particular moment, which is an extremely complex affair involving may different factors.

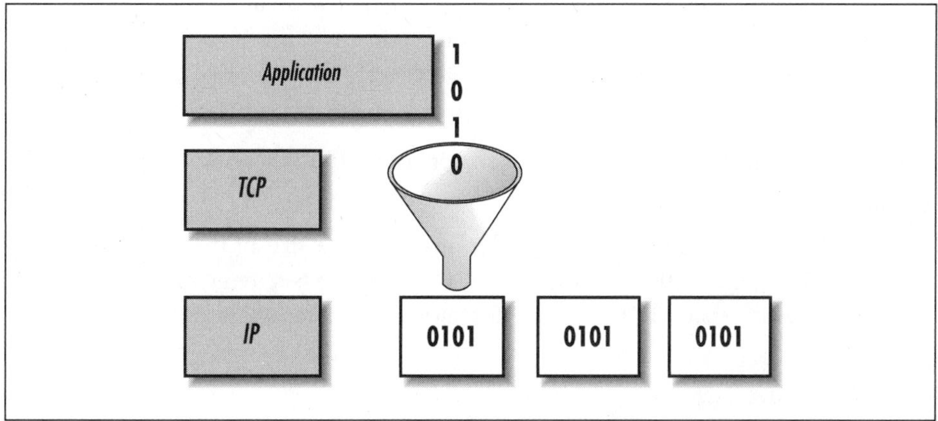

Figure 7-8. An overview of TCP's data-encapsulation process

However, this is also an extremely important service, since accurately determining the size of a segment dictates many of the performance characteristics of a virtual circuit.

For example, making the segment too small wastes network bandwidth. Every TCP segment contains at least 40 bytes of overhead for the IP and TCP headers, so if a segment only contained one byte of data, then the byte ratio of headers-to-data for that segment would be 40:1, a miserable level of throughput by anybody's standard. Conversely, sending 400 bytes of data would change this ratio to 1:10, which is better, although still not very good. Sending four kilobytes of data would change this ratio to 1:100, which would provide excellent utilization of the network's capacity.

On the other hand, sending too much data in a segment can cripple performance as well. If a segment were too big for the IP datagram to travel across the network (due to topology-specific restrictions), then the IP datagram itself would have to be fragmented in order for it to get across that network. This situation would not only require additional processing time on the router that had to fragment the packet, but it would also introduce delays to the destination system, as the receiving IP stack would have to wait for all of the IP fragments to arrive and be reassembled before the TCP segment could be passed to TCP for processing.

In addition, fragmentation also introduces reliability concerns. If a fragment is lost, then the recipient's fragmentation timers have to expire, and an ICMP Time Exceeded error message has to be issued. Then the sender has to resend the entire datagram, which is likely to result in even more fragmentation occurring. Furthermore, on networks that experience known levels of packet loss, fragmentation increases the network's exposure to damage, since a single lost fragment will destroy a large block of data. But if the data were sent as discrete packets to begin with, the same lost packet would result in only that one small segment being lost, which would take less time to recover from. For all of these reasons, avoiding fragmentation is also a critical function of accurately determining the most effective segment size for any given virtual circuit.

Determining the most effective segment size involves the following factors:

Send buffer size
: The most obvious part of this equation involves the size of the send buffer on the local system. If the send buffer fills up, then a segment must be sent in order to make space in the queue for more data, regardless of any other factors.

Receive buffer size
: Similarly, the size of the receive buffer on the destination system is also a concern, as sending more data than the recipient can handle would cause overruns, resulting in the retransmission of lost segments.

MTU and MRU sizes
: TCP also has to take into consideration the maximum amount of data that an IP datagram can handle, as determined by the Maximum Transfer Unit (MTU) size of the physical medium in use on the local network, the Maximum Receive Unit (MRU) size of the destination system's network connection, and the MTU/MRU sizes of all the intermediary networks in between the two end-point systems. If a datagram is generated that is too large for the end-to-end network to handle, then fragmentation would definitely occur, penalizing performance and reliability.

Header size
: IP datagrams have headers, which will steal anywhere from 20 to 60 bytes of data from the segment. Likewise, TCP also has variable-length headers which will steal another 20 to 60 bytes of space. TCP has to leave room for the IP and TCP headers in the segments that get created, otherwise the datagram would be too large for the network to handle, and fragmentation would occur.

Data size and timeliness
: The frequency at which queued data is sent is determined by the rate at which data is being generated. Obviously, if lots of data is being generated by an application, then lots of TCP segments will need to be sent quickly. Conversely, small trickles of data will still need to be sent in a timely manner, although this would result in very small segments. In addition, sometimes an application will request that data be sent immediately, bypassing the queue entirely.

Taking all of these variables into consideration, the formula for determining the most efficient segment size can be stated as follows:

MESS = ((lesser of (send buffer, receive buffer, MTU, or MRU)) – headers)
or (data + headers)

Simply put, the most efficient segment size is determined by finding the lowest available unit of storage (send buffers, receive buffers, or the MTU/MRU values in use) minus the required number of bytes for the IP and TCP headers, except in those situations where there is only a little bit of data to send. In that case, the size of the data (plus the required headers) will determine the size of the segment that is being sent.

By limiting the segment size to the smallest available unit of storage, the segment can be sent from one endpoint to another without having to worry about fragmentation. In turn, this allows TCP to use the largest possible segment for sending data that can be sent end-to-end, which allows the most amount of data to be sent in the least amount of time.

Buffer size considerations

Part of determining the most efficient segment size is derived from the size of the send and receive buffers in use on the two systems. If the send buffer is very small, then the sender cannot build a very large segment. Similarly, if the receive buffer is small, then the sender cannot transmit a large segment (even if it could build one), as that would cause overruns at the destination system, which would eventually require the data to be retransmitted.

Every system has a different default buffer size, depending upon its configuration. Most PC-based client systems have eight kilobyte send and receive buffers, while many server-class systems have buffers of 16 kilobytes or more. It is not uncommon for high-end servers to have 32 or 48 kilobyte send and receive buffers. However, most systems will let you specify the default size for the receive buffers on your system, and they will also let the application developer configure specific settings for their particular application.

Sometimes the size of the local system's send buffer is the bottleneck. If the send buffer is very small, then the sending device just won't be able to generate large segments, regardless of the amount of data being written, the size of the receive buffer, or the MTU/MRU sizes in use on the two networks. Typically, this is not the case, although it can be in some situations, particularly with small hand-held computers that have very limited system resources.

Similarly, sometimes the size of the receive buffers in use at the destination system will be the limiting factor. If the receive buffer on the destination system is very small, then the sender must restrict the amount of data that it pushes to the receiving endpoint. This is also uncommon, but is not unheard of. High-speed Token Ring networks are capable of supporting MTUs of 16 kilobytes and more, while the PCs attached to those networks may only have TCP receive buffers of eight kilobytes. In this situation, the segment size would be restricted to the available buffer space (eight kilobytes), rather than the MTU/MRU capabilities of the network (16 kilobytes).

Obviously, a sender already knows the size of its send buffers, but the sender also has to determine the size of the recipient's receive buffer before it can use that information in its segment-sizing calculations. This is achieved through the use of a 16-bit "Window" field that is stored in the header of every TCP segment that gets sent across a virtual circuit. Whenever a TCP segment is created, the sending endpoint stores the current size of their receive buffers into the Window field, and the recipient then reads this information once the segment arrives. This allows each system to constantly monitor the size of the remote system's receive buffers, thereby allowing them to determine the maximum amount of data that can be sent at any given time.

In addition, the Window field is only 16 bits long, which limits the size of a receive buffer to a maximum of 64 kilobytes. RFC 1323 defines a TCP option called the Window Scale option that allows two endpoints to negotiate 30-bit window sizes, allowing for sizes up to one gigabyte to be advertised.

For more information on the Window field, refer to "Window." For information on how to calculate the optimal default receive window size for your system, refer to "Notes on Determining the Optimal Receive Window Size." For more information on how the window value affects flow control, refer to "Receive window size adjustments." For more information on the TCP Window Scale option, refer to "Window Scale." All of these sections appear later in this chapter.

MTU and MRU size considerations

Although buffer sizing issues can have an impact on the size of any given segment at any given time, most of the time the deciding factor for segment sizes is based on the size of the MTU and MRU in use by the end-to-end network connection.

For example, even the weakest of systems will have a TCP receive buffer of two or more kilobytes, while the MTU/MRU for Ethernet networks is only 1.5 kilobytes. In this case (and almost all others), the MTU/MRU of the Ethernet segment will determine the maximum segment size for that system, since it indicates the largest amount of data that can be sent in a single datagram without causing fragmentation to occur.

Typically, the MTU and MRU sizes for a particular network are the same values. For example, Ethernet networks have an MTU/MRU of 1500 bytes, and both of these values are fixed. However, many dial-up networks allow an endpoint system to define different MTU and MRU sizes. In particular, many dial-up systems set the MTU to be quite small, while also setting the MRU to be quite large. This imbalance can actually help to improve the overall performance of the client, making it snappier than a fixed, medium-sized MTU/MRU pair would allow for.

To understand why this is so, you have to understand that most dial-up systems are clients, using applications such as POP3 and TELNET to retrieve large amounts of data from remote servers. Having a small MTU size forces the client to send segments quickly, since the MTU is the bottleneck in the segment-sizing calculations. Conversely, having a large MRU on a dial-up circuit allows the client to advertise a larger receive value, thereby letting the server send larger blocks of data down to the client. Taken together, the combination of a small MTU and a large MRU allows a dial-up client to send data quickly while also allowing it to download data in large chunks.

For example, one endpoint may be connected via a dial-up modem using a 1500-byte MRU, while the other node may be connected to a Token Ring network with a four-kilobyte MTU, as shown in Figure 7-9. In this example, the 1500-byte MRU would be the limiting factor when data was being sent to the dial-up client, since it represented the bottleneck. Furthermore, if the dial-up client had a 576 byte MTU (regardless of the 1500-byte MRU), then that value would be the limiting factor when data was being sent from the dial-up client up to the Token Ring–attached device.

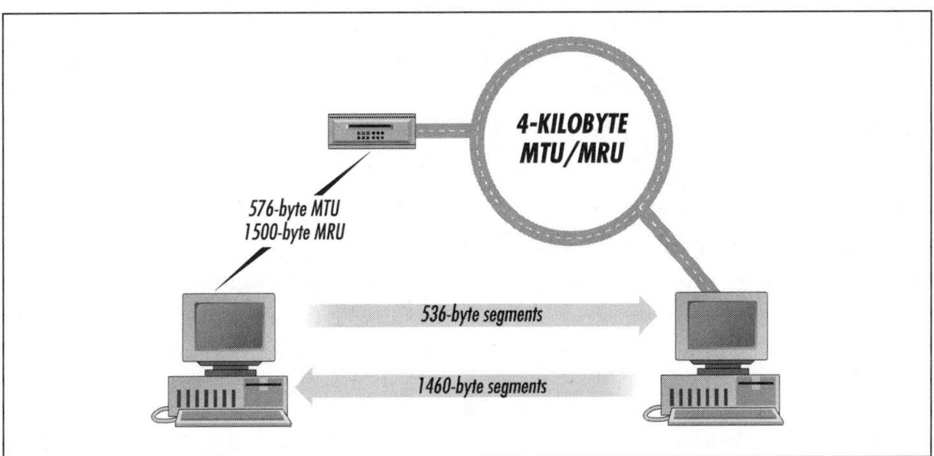

Figure 7-9. An overview of the segment-sizing process, using MTU and MRU values

Regardless of whether or not the client has a large or small MTU, it should be obvious that senders have to take the remote system's MRU into consideration when determining the most efficient segment size for a virtual circuit. At the same time, however, the sender also has to worry about the size of its local MTU. Both of these factors will determine the largest possible segment allowable on any given virtual circuit.

In order for all of this to work, both systems have to be able to determine each other's MRU sizes (they already know their own MTU sizes), and then independently calculate the maximum segment sizes that are allowed for the virtual circuit.

This determination is achieved by each system advertising its local MRU during the circuit-setup sequence. When each system sends its TCP start segments, it also includes its local MRU size (minus forty bytes for the IP and TCP headers) in those segments, using a TCP option called the Maximum Segment Size option. Since each system advertises its MRU in the start segments, it is a simple procedure for each of the systems to read the values and compare it with its own MTU values.

In truth, the MSS value advertised in the MSS option field tends to be based on the sender's MTU, rather than the MRU. Only a handful of systems actually use the MRU for their MSS advertisements. Although RFC 732 states that the MSS should be derived from the MRU, RFC 1122 clarified this position, stating that the MSS should be derived from the largest segment size that could be *reassembled*, which could be just about any value (although most implementations set this to the MTU size). Also, since most networks have fixed MTU/MRU pairs, most vendors set this value to the MTU size, knowing that it is the largest segment they can send. While this probably isn't the most technically accurate approach, it is what most implementations have chosen.

Note that RFC 793 states that the use of the MSS option is entirely optional, and therefore not required. If a system did not include an MSS option in its start segments, then a default value of 536 bytes (which is 576 bytes minus 40 bytes for the TCP and IP headers) should be used as the default. However, RFC 1122 reversed this position, stating that the MSS option is mandatory and must be implemented by all TCP providers.

Also note that some BSD-based systems can send only segments with lengths that are multiples of 512 bytes. So, even if an MTU of 576 bytes were available, the segments generated by these systems would be only 512 bytes long. Similarly, circuits capable of supporting MTU sizes of 1.5 kilobytes would use segments of only 1,024 bytes in length.

For a list of the default MTU sizes used with the most-common network topologies, refer to Table 2-5 in Chapter 2, *The Internet Protocol*. For more information on the MSS option, refer to "Maximum Segment Size."

Path MTU discovery

Even though TCP systems are able to determine the MTU values in use by the endpoints on a virtual circuit, they are not be able to determine the MTU sizes of the networks in between the two endpoints, which may be smaller than the MTU/MRU values in use at either of the endpoint networks. In this scenario, fragmentation would still occur, since the MTU of the intermediary system would require that the IP datagrams be fragmented.

For example, if two systems are both on Token Ring networks using four-kilobyte MTUs, but there is an Ethernet network between them with a 1.5 kilobyte MTU, then fragmentation will occur when the four-kilobyte IP datagrams are sent over the 1.5 kilobyte Ethernet network. This process will lower the overall performance of the virtual circuit and may introduce some reliability problems.

By itself, TCP does not provide any means for determining the MTU of an intermediate network, and must rely on external means to discover the problem. One solution to this problem is to use a technique called Path MTU Discovery, which incorporates the IP Don't Fragment bit and the ICMP Destination Unreachable: Fragmentation Required error message to determine the MTU of the end-to-end IP network.

Essentially, Path MTU Discovery works by having one system create an IP packet of the largest possible size (as determined by the MTU/MRU pair for the virtual circuit), and then setting the Don't Fragment flag on the first IP packet. If the packet is rejected by an intermediary device (due to the packet being too large to forward without being fragmented), then the sender will try to resend the packet using a smaller segment size.

This procedure is repeated until ICMP errors stop coming back. At this point, the sender could use the size of the last-tested packet as the MTU for the entire network. Unfortunately, some systems assume that "no error messages" means that the packet was delivered successfully, without conducting any further testing to verify the theory. However, some routers and firewalls do not return ICMP errors (due to security concerns or configuration errors), which may result in the ICMP errors not being returned to the sender.

This unreliability can cause a situation known as "Path MTU Black Hole," where the sender has chosen to use an MTU that is too large for the end-to-end network, but the network is unable or unwilling to inform the sender of the problem. In this scenario, the sender continues sending data with an MTU that is too large for the intermediary network to forward without being fragmented (which is prohibited by the sender). Some implementations are aware of this problem, and if it appears that packets are not getting through then they reduce the size of the segments that they generate until acknowledgments are returned, or they clear the Don't Fragment flag, allowing fragmentation to occur.

For a complete discussion on this subject, refer to "Notes on Path MTU Discovery" in Chapter 5, *The Internet Control Message Protocol*.

Header size considerations

As we discussed in Chapter 2, *The Internet Protocol*, most IP packets have a 20-byte header, with a maximum of 60 bytes being used for this data. TCP segments also have their own header information, with a minimum value of 20 bytes (the most common), and a maximum size of 60 bytes. Taken together, most TCP/IP datagram have 40 bytes of header data (20 from IP and 20 from TCP), with the maximum amount of header data being limited to 120 bytes (60 bytes from IP and TCP each).

Whenever TCP creates a segment, it must leave room for these headers. Otherwise, the IP packet that was generated would exceed the MTU/MRU pair in use on that virtual circuit, resulting in fragmentation.

Although RFC 1122 states that TCP implementations must set aside 40 bytes of data when a segment is created, this isn't always enough. For example, some of the new advanced TCP options utilize an additional 10 or more bytes. If this information isn't taken into consideration, then fragmentation will likely occur.

TCP is able to determine much of this information, but not always. If the underlying IP stack also utilizes IP options that TCP is not aware of, then TCP will not make room for them when segments are created. This will also likely result in fragmentation.

For more information on IP header sizes, refer to "The IP Header" in Chapter 2, *The Internet Protocol*. For more information on TCP header sizes, refer to "The TCP Header" later in this chapter.

Data considerations

Remember that applications write data to TCP, which then stores the data into a local send buffer, generating a new segment whenever it is convenient or prudent to do so. Although segment sizes are typically calculated based on the available buffer space and MTU/MRU values associated with a given virtual circuit, sometimes the nature of the data itself mandates that a segment be generated, even if that segment won't be the most efficient size.

For example, if an application sends only a little bit of data, then TCP will not be able to create a large segment since there just isn't much data to send to the remote endpoint. This is regardless of the inefficiencies of sending small amounts of data; if there isn't a lot of data to send, TCP can't send large segments.

The decision process that TCP goes through to figure out when to send small amounts of data incorporates many different factors. If an application is able to tell TCP how much data is being written—and if TCP isn't busy doing other stuff—then TCP could choose to send the data immediately. Conversely, TCP could choose to just sit on the data, waiting for more data to arrive.

Sometimes, an application knows that it will be sending only a little bit of data, and can explicitly tell TCP to immediately send whatever data is being written. This service is provided through the use of a "push" service within TCP, allowing an application to tell TCP to go ahead and immediately send whatever data it gets.

The push service is required whenever an application needs to tell TCP that only a small amount of data is being written to the send buffer. This is most often seen with client applications such as POP3 or HTTP that send only a few bytes of data to a server, but it can also be seen from servers that write a lot of data. For example, if an HTTP server needed to send *more* data than would fit within a segment; the balance of the data would have to be sent in a separate (small) segment. Once the HTTP server got to the end of the data, it would tell TCP that it was finished and to go ahead and send the data without waiting for more. This step would be achieved by the application setting the Push flag during the final write.

Some applications cause the Push flag to be set quite frequently. For example, some TELNET clients will set the Push flag on every keystroke, causing the client to send the keystroke quickly, thereby causing the server to echo the text back to user's display quickly.

Once TCP gets data that has been pushed, it stores the data in a regular TCP segment, but it also sets a Push flag within that segment's TCP header. This allows the remote endpoint to also see that the data is being pushed. This is an important service, since the Push flag also affects the receiving system's segment-handling process. Just as a sending TCP will wait for more data to arrive from an application before generating a segment, a receiving TCP will sometimes wait for more segments to arrive before passing the data to the destination application. But if a receiver gets a segment with the Push flag set, then it is supposed to go ahead and send the data to the application without waiting for any more segments to arrive.

An interesting (but somewhat irrelevant) detail about the Push flag is that the practical usage is quite a bit different from the behavior defined in the standards. Although RFC 793 states that "A sending TCP is allowed to collect data … until the push function is signaled, then it must send all unsent data," most TCP implementations do not allow applications to set the Push flag directly. Instead, most TCP implementations simply send data as they receive it (most of the time, applications write data to TCP in chunks rather than in continuous streams), and TCP will set the Push flag in the last segment that it sends. Some implementations will even set the Push flag on every segment that they send.

Similarly, many implementations ignore the Push flag on data they receive, immediately notifying the listening application of all new data, regardless of whether the Push flag is set on those segments.

Another interesting flag within the TCP header is the Urgent flag. The Urgent flag can be used by an application whenever it needs to send data that must be dealt with immediately. If an application requests that a segment be sent using the Urgent flag, then TCP is supposed to place that segment at the front of the send queue, sending it out as soon as possible. In addition, the recipient is supposed to read that segment ahead of any other segments that may be waiting to be processed in the receive buffer.

Urgent data is often seen with TELNET, which has some standardized elements that rely on the use of the TCP Urgent flag. Some of the standardized control characters used with TELNET (such as interrupt process and abort output) have specific behavioral requirements that benefit greatly from the "out-of-stream" processing that the Urgent flag defines. For example, if a user were to send an interrupt process signal to the remote host and flag this data for Urgent handling, then the control character would be passed to the front of the queue and acted upon immediately, allowing the output to be flushed faster than would otherwise happen.

However, the use of the Urgent flag has been plagued by incompatibility problems ever since RFC 793 was first published. The original wording of that document did not clarify where the urgent data should be placed *in the segment*, so some systems put it in one place while other systems put it in another. The wording was clarified in RFC 1122, which stated that the urgent pointer points to the last byte of data in the stream. Also of interest is the fact that the urgent pointer can refer to a byte location somewhere up ahead in the stream, in a future segment. All of the data up to and including the byte position specified by the urgent pointer are to be treated as a part of the urgent block. Unfortunately, some systems (such as BSD and its derivatives) still do not follow this model, resulting in an ongoing set of interoperability problems with this flag in particular.

For more information on the Push and Urgent flags, refer to "Control Flags" later in this chapter.

Flow Control

When an application needs to send data to another application over TCP, it writes the data to the local TCP provider, which queues the data into a send buffer. Periodically, TCP will package portions of the data into segments and pass them off to IP for delivery to the destination system.

One of the key elements to this process is flow control, where a sending system will adjust the rate at which it tries to send data to the destination system. A change in rate may be required due to a variety of reasons, including the available buffer space on the destination system and the packet-handling characteristics of the network. For this reason, TCP incorporates a variety of flow control mechanisms, allowing the sending system to react to these changes easily.

Originally, RFC 793 proposed only a handful of flow control mechanisms, most of which were focused on the receiving end of the connection. Of these services, the two most important were:

Receive window sizing
: TCP can send only as much data as a receiver will allow, based on the amount of space available in the remote system's receive buffer, the frequency at which the buffers are drained, and other related factors. Therefore, one way for a receiver to adjust the transfer rate is to increase or decrease the size of the buffer being advertised. This in turn controls how much data a sender can transmit at once.

Sliding receive windows
: In addition to the Window size being advertised by a receiver, the concept of a "sliding window" allows the sender to transmit segments "on credit," before acknowledgments have arrived for segments that were already sent. This lets an endpoint send data even though the preceding data has not yet been acknowledged, trusting that an acknowledgment will arrive for that data shortly.

These mechanisms put the destination system in charge of controlling the rate at which the sender transmits data. As the original theory went, the receiver was likely to be the point of congestion in any transfer operation, and as such needed to have the last word on the rate at which data was being sent.

Over time however, the need for sender-based flow control mechanisms has been proven, particularly since network outages may occur, which will require the sender to reduce its rate of transmission, even though the receiving system may be running smoothly. For this reason, RFC 1122 mandated that a variety of network-related flow control services also be implemented. Among these services are:

Congestion window sizing
: In order to deal with congestion-related issues, the use of a "congestion window" is required at the sending system. The congestion window is similar in concept to the receive window in that it is expanded and contracted, although these actions are taken according to the underlying IP network's ability to handle the quantity of data being sent, rather than the recipient's ability to process the data.

Slow start
: In an effort to keep congestion from occurring in the first place, a sender must first determine the capabilities of the IP network before it starts sending mass quantities of data over a newly established virtual circuit. This is the purpose of slow start, which works by setting the congestion window to a small size and gradually increasing its size, until the network's saturation point is found.

Congestion avoidance

Whenever network congestion is detected, the congestion window is reduced, and a technique called congestion avoidance is used to gradually rebuild the size of the congestion window, eventually returning it to its maximum size. When used in conjunction with slow start, this helps the sender to determine the optimal transfer rate of a virtual circuit.

Taken together, the use of the receive and congestion windows gives a sending system a fairly complete view of the state of the network, including the state of both the recipient and the congestion on the network.

A note on local blocking

Although there are a variety of flow control mechanisms found with TCP, the simplest form of flow control is "local blocking," whereby a sending system refuses to accept data from a local application. This feature is needed whenever TCP knows that it cannot deliver any data to a specific destination system—perhaps due to problems with the receiver or the network—and the local send buffer is already full. Having nowhere to send the data, TCP must refuse to accept any new data from the sending application.

Note that TCP cannot block incoming network traffic (coming from IP). Since TCP is unable to tell which application a segment is destined for until its contents have been examined, TCP must accept every segment that it gets from IP. However, TCP may be unable to deliver the data to the destination application, due to a full queue or some other temporary condition. If this happens, TCP could choose to discard the segment, thereby causing the sender to retry the operation later (an effort which may or may not succeed).

Receive window size adjustments

In the section entitled "Network I/O Management," I first mentioned the TCP header's Window field, suggesting that it provided an insight into the size of the receive buffer in use on a destination system. Although this is an accurate assessment when looking at TCP's segment sizing process, the primary purpose of the Window field is to provide the receiving system with flow control management services. The Window field is used to tell a sender how much data a recipient can handle. In this model, the recipient dictates flow control.

According to RFC 793, the window field "specifies the number of octets ... that the receiving TCP is currently prepared to receive." In this scenario, a sending system can transmit only as much data as will fit within the recipient's receive buffer (as specified by the Window field) before an acknowledgment is required. Once the sender has transmitted enough data to fill the receive buffer, it must stop sending data and wait for an acknowledgment from the recipient before sending any more data.

Therefore, one way to speed up and slow down the data transfer rate between the two endpoint systems is for the receiving system to change the buffer size being advertised in the Window field. If a system that had been advertising an eight-kilo398byte window suddenly started advertising a 16-kilobyte window, the sender could pump twice as much data through the circuit before having to wait for an acknowledgment.

Conversely, if the recipient started advertising a four-kilobyte window, then the sender could transmit only half as much data before requiring an acknowledgment (this would be enforced by the sender's TCP stack, which would start blocking writes from the sending application when this occurred).

An important consideration here is that recipients are not allowed to arbitrarily reduce their window size, but instead are only supposed to shrink the advertised window when they have received data which has not yet been processed by the destination application. Arbitrarily reducing the size of the receive window can result in a situation where the sender has already sent a bunch of data in accordance with the window size that was last advertised. If the recipient were to suddenly reduce the window size, then some of the segments would probably get rejected, requiring the sender to retransmit the lost data.

What happens when the receive buffer goes to zero, effectively preventing the sender from sending any data whatsoever? The answer varies by implementation, but generally speaking the sender will simply stop sending data until the receiver is ready to take data again. Any segments that were already sent may be rejected (or may get accepted), and as such the sender will have to deal with this issue when the window opens again.

Also, many systems implement an incremental fall-back timer, where they will probe the receiver for a window update periodically whenever this situation occurs. In this scenario, the sender will probe the receiver, and if the size of the window is still zero, then the sender will double the size of its probe timer. Once the timer expires, the sender will probe the receiver again, and if the receive window is still zero, the timer will get doubled again. This process will continue as long as the probe results in an acknowledgment—even if the window remains at zero—up to an implementation-specific maximum (such as 64 or 128 seconds).

As soon as the stalled system is able to begin accepting more data, it is supposed to send an unsolicited acknowledgment to the remote system, advising it that the window is "open" again.

Since the Window field is included in the header of every TCP segment, advertising a different buffer size is a very straightforward affair. If the recipient is willing to speed up or if it needs to slow down, it simply changes the value being advertised in the Window field of any acknowledgment segment that is being returned, and the sender will notice the change as soon as the segment containing the new value is received. Note that there may be some delay in this process, as it may take a while for that segment to arrive.

The size of the buffer also affects the number of segments that can be received, in that the maximum number of available segments is the Window size divided by the maximum segment size. Typically, systems will set their window size to four times the segment size (or larger), so if a system is using one kilobyte segments, then the smallest window size you would want to use on that system would be four kilobytes.

Unfortunately, since the Window field is only 16 bits long, the maximum size that can be advertised is 65,535 bytes. Although this is plenty of buffer space for most applications, there are times when it just isn't enough (such as when the MTU of the local network is also 64 kilobytes, resulting in a Window that is equal to only a single segment). One way around this limitation is the Window Scale option, as defined in RFC 1323. The Window Scale option allows two endpoints to negotiate 30-bit window sizes, allowing up to one gigabyte of buffer space to be advertised.

While it may seem best to use very large window sizes, it is not always feasible or economical to do so. Each segment that is sent must be kept in memory until it has been acknowledged. A hand-held system may not have sufficient resources to cache many segments, and thus would have to use small window sizes in order to limit the amount of data being sent.

In addition, there is a point at which the size of the receive window no longer has any effect on throughput, but instead the bandwidth and delay characteristics of the virtual circuit become the limiting factors. Setting a value larger than necessary is simply a waste of resources and can also result in slower recovery. For example, if a sender sees a large receive window being advertised then it might try to fill that window, even though a router in between the two endpoints may not be able to forward the data very quickly. This delay can result in a substantial queue building up in the router, and if a segment ever does get lost, then it will take a long time for the recipient to notice the problem and the sender to correct it. This would result in extremely long gaps between retransmissions, and may also result in some of the queued data getting discarded (requiring even more retransmissions).

For more information on the Window field, refer to "Window." For more information on the TCP Window Scale option, refer to "Window Scale." For detailed instructions on how to calculate the most optimal window size for a particular connection, refer to "Notes on Determining the Optimal Receive Window Size." All of these sections appear later in this chapter.

Sliding receive windows

Even though large window sizes can help to increase overall throughput, they do not provide for *sustained levels* of throughput. In particular, if a situation required the use of a synchronous "send-and-wait" design that required a system to send data and then stop to wait for an acknowledgment, the network would be quite jerky, with bursts of writes followed by long pauses. This problem is most noticeable on networks with high levels of latency that cause extended periods of delay between the two endpoints.

In an effort to avoid this type of scenario, RFC 1122 states that a recipient should issue an acknowledgment for every two segments that it receives, if not more often. This design causes the receiver to issue acknowledgments quickly. In turn, these acknowledgments arrive back to the sender quickly.

Once an acknowledgment has arrived back at the sending system, the outstanding data is cleared from the send queue, thereby letting the sender transmit more data. In effect, the sending system can "slide" the window over by the number of segments that have been successfully acknowledged, allowing it to transmit more data, even though not all of the segments have been acknowledged yet.

As long as a sender continues receiving acknowledgments, it is able to continue sending data, with the maximum amount of outstanding segments being determined by the size of the recipient's receive buffer. This concept is illustrated in Figure 7-10, which shows how a sender can increment the sliding window whenever it receives an acknowledgment for previously sent data. For example, as the sender is transmitting segment number three, it receives an acknowledgment for segment number one, allowing the sender to move the send buffer forward by one segment.

The key element here is that the sender can transfer only as many bytes of data as the receiver can handle, as advertised in the Window field of the TCP headers sent by the recipient. If the recipient's receive window is set to eight kilobytes and the sender transmits eight one-kilobyte segments without having received an acknowledgment, then it must stop and wait for an acknowledgment before sending any more data.

However, if the sender receives an acknowledgment for the first two segments after having sent eight of them, then it can go ahead and send two more, since the window allows up to eight kilobytes to be in transit at any time. On networks with low levels of latency (such as Ethernet), this feature can have a dramatic impact on

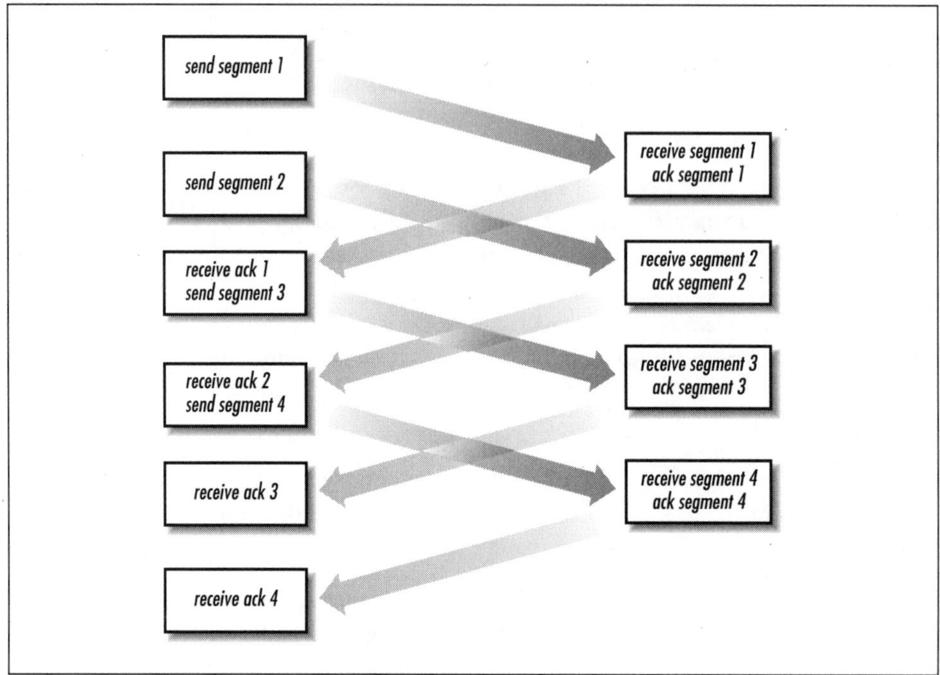

Figure 7-10. An overview of TCP's sliding window mechanism

overall performance, providing for sustained levels of high utilization. On networks with very high levels of latency (such as those that use satellite links), the effect is less pronounced, although it is still better than the send-and-wait effect that would otherwise be felt.

In situations where the window size is smaller than the MTU, a sliding window is harder to implement. Some systems will write only a single segment (up to the maximum allowed by the advertised receive buffer), and then stop to wait for an acknowledgment. Other systems will reduce the size of the local send buffers to half (or less) of the advertised receive window, thereby forcing multiple small segments to be written in an effort to increase the number of acknowledgments that are generated.

Another problem can occur with some TCP implementations that do not issue acknowledgments for every two segments that are received, but instead issue acknowledgments when they have received enough data to fill two *maximum-sized* segments. For example, if the system has a local MTU of 1500 bytes, but is receiving data in 500-byte chunks, then such a system would only issue acknowledgments for every six segments that arrive (6 × 500 = 3000, which is MTU times two). This process would result in a substantially slower acknowledgment cycle that could cause problems if the sender had a small send window. Although this problem is somewhat rare, it does happen.

For systems that implement this procedure correctly (sending acknowledgments for every two segments that are received, regardless of the maximum segment size), this design can substantially improve overall performance. By using the sliding window technique—and by using large windows—it is quite possible for two fast systems on a fast network to practically saturate the connection with data.

For more information on how frequent acknowledgments can impact performance, refer ahead to "Delayed acknowledgments."

The Silly Window Syndrome

The amount of buffer space that a system advertises depends on how much buffer space it has available at that given moment, which is dependent upon how quickly applications can pull data out of the receive buffer. This in turn is driven by many factors, such as the complexity of the application in use, the amount of CPU time available, the design of the TCP stack in use, and other elements.

Unfortunately, many of the first-generation TCP-based applications did a very poor job of cleaning out the receive buffers, taking only a few bytes at a time. The system only advertised a receive buffer of a few bytes. In turn, a sender would transmit only a very small segment, since that was all that was being advertised by the recipient. This process would repeat incessantly, with the recipient taking another few bytes out of the receive queue, advertising a small window, and then receiving yet another very small segment.

To prevent this scenario (known affectionately as the "Silly Window Syndrome"), RFC 1122 clarified the amount of buffer space that could be advertised, stating that systems could only advertise a non-zero window if the amount of buffer space available could hold a complete segment (as defined by the value shown in the MSS option), or if the buffer space was at least half of the "normal" window size. If neither of these conditions are met, then the receiver should advertise a zero-length window, effectively forcing the sender to stop transmitting.

The Nagle algorithm

The Silly Window Syndrome is indicative of a problem at the receiver's end of the virtual circuit. Data is not being read from the receive buffers quickly, resulting in small window sizes being advertised, which in turn causes the sender to transmit small segments. The result is that lots of network traffic gets generated for very small amounts of data.

However, a sending system can also cause these kinds of problems, although for totally different reasons. Some applications (such as TELNET) are designed to send many small segments in a constant barrage, which causes high levels of network utilization for small amounts of data. Other situations in which this is a problem are applications that write data only in small chunks, such as writing 10 megabytes of data in 512-byte blocks. The number of packets that will get generated in that model are extremely wasteful of bandwidth, particularly when this same transfer could be done using larger writes.

One solution proposed to this kind of problem is the Nagle algorithm, which was originally described in RFC 896. Simply put, the Nagle algorithm suggests that segments that are smaller than the maximum size allowed (as defined by the MSS option of the recipient or the discovered MTU of the end-to-end path) should be delayed until all prior segments have been acknowledged or until a full-sized segment can be sent. This rule forces TCP stacks to merge multiple small writes into a single write, which is then sent as a single segment.

On a low-latency LAN, the Nagle algorithm rarely comes into play, since a small segment will be sent and acknowledged very quickly, allowing another small segment to be sent immediately (effectively eliminating the use of the Nagle algorithm). On slow WAN links though, the Nagle algorithm comes into play quite often, since acknowledgments take a long time to be returned to the sender. This results in the next batch of small segments getting bundled together, providing a substantial increase in overall network efficiency.

For these reasons, use of the Nagle algorithm is encouraged by RFC 1122, although its usage is not mandatory. Some applications (such as X Windows) react poorly when small segments are clumped together. In those cases, users must have the option of disabling the Nagle algorithm on a per-circuit basis. However, most TCP implementations do not provide this capability, instead allowing users to enable or disable its use only on a global scale, or leaving it up to the application developer to decide when it is needed.

This limitation can be somewhat of a problem, since some developers have written programs that generate inefficient segment sizes frequently, and have then gone and disabled the use of the Nagle algorithm on those connections in an effort to improve performance, even though doing so results in much higher levels of network utilization (and doesn't do much to improve performance in the end). If those developers had just written their applications to use large writes instead of multiple small writes, then the Nagle algorithm would never come into effect, and the applications would perform better anyway.

Another interesting side effect that appears when the Nagle algorithm is disabled is that the delayed acknowledgment mechanism (as described later in "Delayed acknowledgments") does not tend to work well when small segments are being generated, since it waits for two full-sized segments to arrive before returning an acknowledgment for those segments. If it does not receive full-sized segments due to a developer having turned off the Nagle algorithm, then the delayed acknowledgment mechanism will not kick in until a timer expires or until data is being returned to the sender (which the acknowledgments can piggyback onto).

This can be a particular problem when just a little bit of data needs to be sent. The sender will transmit the data, but the recipient will not acknowledge it until the timer expires, resulting in a very jerky session.

This situation can also happen when a small amount of data is being generated at the tail-end of a bulk transfer. However, the chances are good that in this situation the remote endpoint is going to generate some sort of data (such as a confirmation status code or a circuit-shutdown request). In that case, the delayed acknowledgment will piggyback onto whatever data is being returned, and the user will not notice any excess delays.

For all of these reasons, application developers are encouraged to write data in large, even multiples of the most-efficient segment size for any given connection, whenever that information is available. For example, if a virtual circuit has a maximum segment size of 1460 bytes (the norm for Ethernet), the application should write data in even multiples of 1460 (such as 2,920 byte blocks, or 5,840 byte blocks, and so forth). This way, TCP will generate an even number of efficiently sized segments, resulting in the Nagle algorithm never causing any delay whatsoever, and also preventing the delayed acknowledgment mechanism from holding up any acknowledgments.

Congestion window sizing

TCP's use of variable-length, sliding windows provides good flow control services to the receiving end of a virtual circuit. If the receiver starts having problems, it can slow down the rate at which data is being sent simply by scaling back the amount of buffer space being advertised. But if things are going well, the window can be scaled up, and traffic can flow as fast as the network will allow.

Sometimes, however, the network itself is the bottleneck. Remember that TCP segments are transmitted within IP packets, and that these packets can have their own problems outside of the virtual circuit. In particular, a forwarding device in between the two endpoints could be suffering from congestion problems, whereby it was receiving more data than it could forward, as is common with dial-up servers and application gateways.

When this occurs, the TCP segments will not arrive at their destination in a timely manner (if they make it there at all). In this scenario, the receiving system (and the virtual circuit) may be operating just fine, but problems with the underlying IP network are preventing segments from reaching their destination.

This problem is illustrated in Figure 7-11, which shows a device trying to send data to the remote endpoint, although another device on the network path is suffering from congestion problems, and has sent an ICMP Source Quench error message back to the sender, asking it to slow down the rate of data transfer.

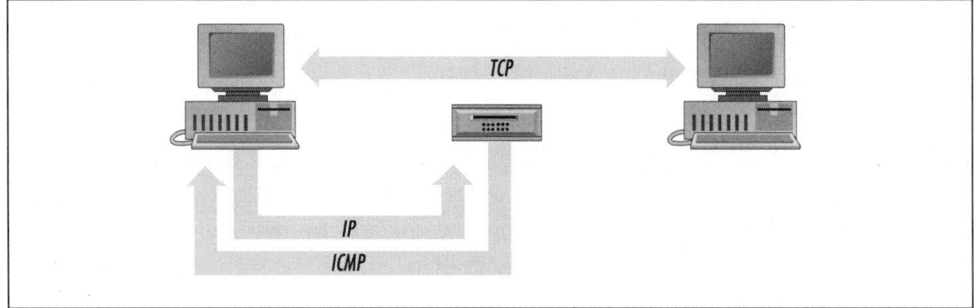

Figure 7-11. Detecting congestion with ICMP Source Quench error messages

Congestion problems can be recognized by the presence of an ICMP Source Quench error message, or by the recipient sending a series of duplicate acknowledgments (suggesting that a segment has been lost), or by the sender's acknowledgment timer reaching zero. When any of these problems occur, the sender must recognize them as being congestion-related, and take counter-measures that deal with them appropriately. Otherwise, if a sender were to simply retransmit segments that were lost due to congestion, the result would be even more congestion. Orderly congestion recovery is therefore required in order for TCP to maintain high performance levels, but without causing more congestion to occur.

At the heart of the congestion management process is a secondary variable called the "congestion window" that resides on the sender's system. Like the receive window, the congestion window dictates how much data a sender can transmit without stopping to wait for an acknowledgment, although rather than being set by the receiver, the congestion window is set by the sender, according to the congestion characteristics of the IP network.

During normal operation, the congestion window is the same size as the receive window. Thus, the maximum transfer rate of a smooth-flowing network is still restricted by the amount of data that a receiver can handle. If congestion-related problems occur, however, then the size of the congestion window is reduced, thereby making the limiting factor the sender's capability to transmit, rather than the receiver's capability to read.

How aggressively the congestion window is reduced depends upon the event that triggered the resizing action:

- If congestion is detected by the presence of a series of duplicate acknowledgments, then the size of the congestion window is cut in half, severely restricting the sender's ability to transmit segments. TCP then utilizes a technique known as "congestion avoidance" to slowly increment the size of the congestion window, cautiously ramping up the rate at which it can send data, until it returns to the full throttle state.
- If congestion is detected by the TCP acknowledgment timer reaching zero or by the presence of an ICMP Source Quench error message, then the congestion window is shrunk so small that only one segment can be sent. TCP uses a technique known as "slow start" to begin incrementing the size of the congestion window until it is half of its original size, at which point the congestion avoidance technique is called into action to complete the ramp-up process.

Slow start and congestion avoidance are similar in their recovery techniques. However, they are also somewhat different and are used at different times. Slow start is used on every new connection—even those that haven't yet experienced any congestion—and whenever the congestion window has been dropped to just one segment. Conversely, congestion avoidance is used both to recover from non-fatal congestion-related events and to slow down the rate at which the congestion window is being expanded, allowing for smoother, more sensitive recovery procedures.

Slow start

One of the most common problems related to congestion is that senders attempt to transmit data as fast as they can, as soon as they can. When a user asks for a big file, the server gleefully tries to send it at full speed immediately.

While this might seem like it would help to complete the transfer quickly, in reality it tends to cause problems. If there are any bottlenecks between the sender and receiver, then this burst-mode form of delivery will find them very quickly, causing congestion problems immediately (most likely resulting in a dropped segment). The user may experience a sudden burst of data, followed by a sudden stop as their system attempts to recover one or more lost segments, followed by another sudden burst. Slow start is the technique used to avoid this particular scenario.

In addition, slow start is used to recover from near-fatal congestion errors, where the congestion window has been reset to one segment, due to an acknowledgment timer reaching zero, or from an ICMP Source Quench error message being received.

Slow start works by exponentially increasing the size of the congestion window. Every time a segment is sent *and acknowledged*, the size of the congestion window is increased by one segment's worth of data (as determined by the discovered MTU/MRU sizes of the virtual circuit), allowing for more and more data to be sent.

For example, if the congestion window is set to one segment (with the segment size being set to whatever value was determined during the setup process), a single segment will be transmitted. If this segment is acknowledged, then the congestion window is incremented by one, now allowing two segments to be transmitted simultaneously. The next two segments in the send buffer then get sent. If they are both acknowledged, they will each cause the congestion window to be incremented by one again, thus adding room for two more segments (with the congestion window being set to four segments total). All of the segments do not have to be acknowledged before the congestion window is incremented, as shown in Figure 7-12.

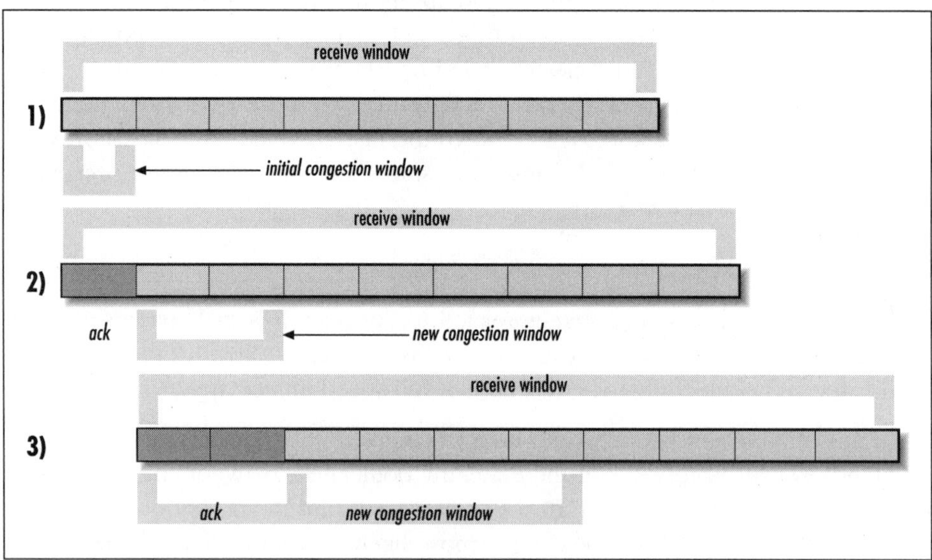

Figure 7-12. An overview of the slow start algorithm

If a connection is new, then the process is repeated until congestion is detected or the size of the congestion window is equal to the size of the receive window, as advertised by the receiver's Window field. If the ramping process is successful, then the virtual circuit will eventually be running at full speed, with the flow control being dictated by the size of the recipient's receive buffer. But if congestion is detected during the incrementing process, the congestion window will be locked to the last successful size. Any further congestion problems will result in the congestion window being reduced (as per the process described earlier in "Congestion window sizing").

However, if the slow start routines are being used to recover from a congestion event, then the slow start procedure is used only until the congestion window reaches half of its original size. At this point, the congestion avoidance technique is called upon to continue increasing the size of the congestion window (as described soon in "Congestion avoidance"). Since congestion is likely to occur again very quickly, TCP takes the more cautious, linear-growth approach outlined with congestion avoidance, as opposed to the ambitious, exponential growth provided with slow start.

Note that although RFC 1122 mandates the use of slow start with TCP, the procedure was not fully documented until RFC 2001 was published. Therefore, many of the earlier systems do not incorporate the slow start routines described here.

In addition, RFC 2414 advocates the use of four segments as the seed value for slow start, rather than the one segment proposed in RFC 2581 (TCP Congestion Control), which is arguably an improvement with applications that send more than one segment. For example, if an application needed to send two segments of data but the initial congestion window was locked at "one segment," then the application could send only one of those segments. As such, the remote endpoint would not receive all of the application data, and the delayed acknowledgment mechanisms would force a long pause before an acknowledgment was returned. But by setting the initial congestion window to "two segments," the sender can issue two full-sized segments, which will result in the recipient issuing an acknowledgment immediately. Although this allows connections to ramp-up faster, note that RFC 2414 is only experimental and is not required to be implemented in any shipping TCP implementations.

Congestion avoidance

The congestion avoidance routines are called whenever a system needs to use a slower, more sensitive form of congestion avoidance than the exponential mechanisms offered by the slow start procedure. A slow congestion avoidance mechanism may be required when a system detects congestion from the presence of multiple duplicate acknowledgments, or as part of the recovery mechanisms that are utilized when an acknowledgment timer reaches zero.

Although duplicate acknowledgments are not uncommon (and are allowed for by TCP's error-recovery mechanisms), the presence of many such acknowledgments tends to indicate that an IP datagram has been lost somewhere, most likely due to congestion occurring on the network. As such, RFC 1112 states that if three or more duplicate acknowledgments are received, then the size of the congestion window should be cut in half, and the congestion avoidance technique is to be used in an effort to return the network to full throttle.

Another scenario where congestion avoidance is used is if the sender's acknowledgment timer has expired, which means that *no* acknowledgments are coming back from the other end. This signifies that there are serious congestion problems, or that the other system has left the network. In an effort to recover from this event, the congestion window is shrunk so small that only one segment can be sent. Then the slow start mechanism is called upon and used until the congestion window is half of its original size. Congestion avoidance is then used to return the network to full speed, albeit at a slower, more cautious rate.

Congestion avoidance is very similar to slow start in that the size of the congestion window is expanded whenever acknowledgments arrive for segments that have been sent. However, rather than incrementing the congestion window on a one-for-one basis (as is done with slow start), the congestion window is incremented by only one segment when *all of the segments sent within a single window* are acknowledged.

For example, assume that a system's congestion window is set to allow four segments, although the recipient's receive window is advertising a maximum capacity of eight segments. Using congestion avoidance, a system would send four segments and then wait for all of them to be acknowledged before incrementing the size of the congestion window by one (now being set to "five segments").

If this effort was a success, then the next five segments would be sent, and if all of them were acknowledged, then the congestion window would be increased to six. This process would continue until either congestion occurred again or the congestion window equals the size of the receive window being advertised by the recipient ("eight segments" here).

Note that it doesn't matter if the remote system sends back a single acknowledgment for all of the segments previously sent, or if individual acknowledgments are returned for each of the segments. With congestion avoidance, *all* of the segments must be acknowledged before the size of the congestion window will be incremented.

Also note that although RFC 1122 mandates the use of congestion avoidance with TCP, the procedure was not fully documented until RFC 2001 was published. Therefore, many of the earlier systems do not incorporate the congestion avoidance routines described here.

Reliability

The most often touted TCP service is reliability, with TCP's virtual circuit design practically guaranteeing that data will get delivered intact. Using this design, TCP will do everything it can to get data to the proper destination, if at all possible. If this is not possible—perhaps due to a failure in the network or some other catastrophic event—then naturally TCP won't be able to deliver the data. However, as long as the network and hosts are operational, TCP will make sure that the data is delivered intact.

TCP's reliability service takes many forms, employing many different technologies and techniques. Indeed, RFC 793 states that TCP must be able to "recover from data that is damaged, lost, duplicated, or delivered out of order." This is a broad range of service, and as such TCP's reliability mechanisms tend to be somewhat complex.

The most basic form of reliability comes from the use of checksums. TCP checksums are used to validate segments (including the TCP headers and any associated data). Furthermore, checksums are mandatory with TCP (as opposed to being optional as they are with UDP), requiring that the sender compute them, and that the recipient compare them to segments received. This provides a simple validation mechanism that lets a receiver test for corrupt data before handing the data off to the destination application.

Although checksums are useful for validating data, they aren't of any use if they never arrive. Therefore, TCP also has to provide delivery services that will ensure that data arrives in the first place. This service is provided by TCP's use of sequence numbers and acknowledgments, both of which work together to make TCP a reliable transport. Once a segment has been sent, the sender must wait for an acknowledgment to be returned stating that all of the data has been successfully received. If a segment is not acknowledged within a certain amount of time, the sender will eventually try to send it again. This design allows TCP to recover from segments that get lost in transit.

Furthermore, the use of unique sequence numbers allows a receiver to reorder any segments that may have come in out of sequence. Since IP is unpredictable, it is entirely possible that some datagram will be routed over a slower link than the rest of the datagrams, causing some of them to arrive in a different order than they were sent. The receiving TCP system can use the sequence numbers to reorder segments into their correct sequence—as well as eliminate any duplicates—before passing the data off to the destination application.

Taken together, these services make TCP an extremely reliable transport protocol, which is why it is the transport of choice for most Internet applications.

In summary, the key elements of TCP's reliability service are:

Checksums
: TCP uses checksums for every segment that is sent, allowing the destination system to verify that the data within the segment is valid.

Sequence numbers

Every byte of data that gets sent across a virtual circuit is assigned a sequence number. These sequence numbers allow the sender and receiver to refer to a range of data explicitly, and also allows the recipient to reorder segments that come in out of order, as well as eliminate any duplicates.

Acknowledgments

Every byte of data sent across a virtual circuit must be acknowledged. This task is achieved through the use of an acknowledgment number, which is used to state that a receiver has received all of the data within a segment (as opposed to receiving the segment itself), and is ready for more data.

Timers

Since TCP uses IP for delivery, some segments can get lost or corrupted on their way to the destination. When this happens, no acknowledgment will be received by the sender, which would require a retransmission of the questionable data. In order to detect this error, TCP also incorporates an acknowledgment timer, allowing the sender to retransmit lost data that does not get acknowledged.

In practice, these mechanisms are tightly interwoven, with each of them relying on the others in order to provide a totally reliable implementation. They are discussed in detail in the following sections.

TCP checksums

TCP checksums are identical to UDP checksums, with the exception that checksums are mandatory with TCP (instead of being optional, as they are with UDP). Furthermore, their usage is mandatory for both the sending and receiving systems. RFC 1122 clearly states that the receiver must validate every segment received, using the checksum to verify that the contents of the segment are correct before delivering it to the destination application.

Checksums provide a valuable service in that they verify that data has not been corrupted in transit. All of the other reliability services provided by TCP—the sequence numbers, acknowledgments, and timers—serve only to ensure that segments arrive at their destination; checksums make sure the data inside the segments arrives intact.

Checksums are calculated by performing ones-complement math against the header and data of the TCP segment. Also included in this calculation is a "pseudo-header" that contains the source and destination IP addresses, the Protocol Identifier (6 for TCP), and the size of the TCP segment (including the TCP headers and data). By including the pseudo-header in the calculations, the destination system is able to validate that the sender and receiver information is also correct, in case the IP datagram that delivered the TCP segment got mixed up on the way to its final destination.

TCP must validate the checksum before issuing an acknowledgment for the segment. If a segment is received with an invalid checksum, then the segment must be discarded. Discarding the segment is a "silent" event, with no notification of the failure being generated or sent.

This is required behavior, since the recipient has no way of determining which circuit the segment belongs to if the checksum is deemed invalid (the header could be the corrupt part of the segment). In such a situation, an error message could be sent to the wrong source, thereby causing additional (and unrelated) problems to ensue. Instead, the segment is thrown away, and the original sending system would eventually notice that the data was not successfully received (due to the acknowledgment timer expiring), and the segment would eventually be reissued.

Since each virtual circuit consists of a pair of sockets, the receiver has to know the IP address of the sender in order to deliver the data to the correct destination application. If there are multiple connections to port 80 on the local server (as would be found with an HTTP server), TCP has to know which system sent the data in order to deliver it to the right instance of the local server. Although this information is available from IP, TCP verifies the information using the checksum's pseudo-header.

Note that RFC 1146 introduced a TCP option for alternative checksum mechanisms. However, the Alternative Checksum option was classified as experimental, and RFC 1146 has since expired. Therefore, the Alternative Checksum option should not be used with any production TCP implementations.

Sequence numbers

A key part of TCP's reliability service is the use of sequence numbers and acknowledgments, allowing the sender and receiver to constantly inform each other of the data that has been sent and received. These two mechanisms work hand-in-glove to ensure that data arrives at the destination system.

RFC 793 states that "each [byte] of data is assigned a sequence number." The sequence number for the first byte of data within a particular segment is then published in the Sequence Identifier field of the TCP header. Thus, when a segment is sent, the Sequence Identifier field shows the starting byte number for the data within that particular segment. Note that sequence numbers do not refer to segments, but instead refer to the starting byte of a segment's data block.

Once a segment is received, the data is verified by the recipient (using the checksum), and if it's okay, then the recipient will send an acknowledgment back to the sender. The acknowledgment is also contained within a TCP segment, with the

Acknowledgment Identifier field in the TCP header pointing to the next sequence number that the recipient is willing to accept. The acknowledgment effectively says "I received all of the data up to this point and am ready for the next byte of data, starting at sequence number *n*."

When the acknowledgment arrives, the sender knows that the receiver has successfully received all of the data contained within the segment, and the sender is then able to transmit more data (up to the maximum amount of data that will fit within either the receiver's current receive window or the sender's current congestion window). This process is illustrated in Figure 7-13. In that example, the sender has identified the first byte of data being sent as 1, while the acknowledgment for that segment points to the first byte of data from the *next* segment that the receiver expects to get (101).

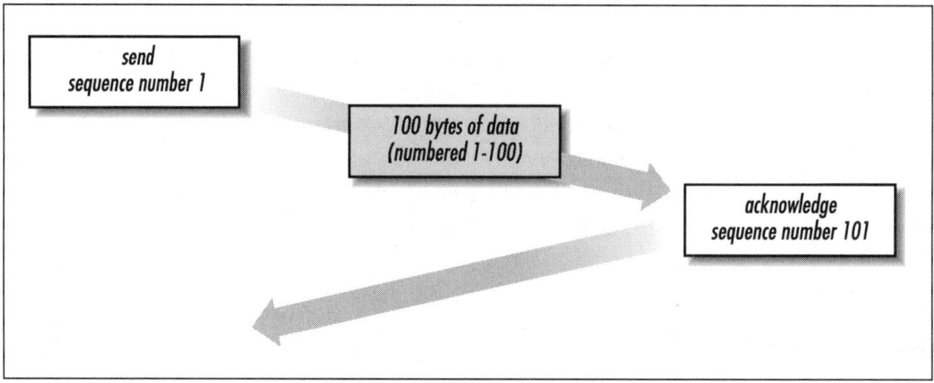

Figure 7-13. Using sequence numbers to track data

In practice, sequence numbers should rarely be numbered 1. Sequence numbers are 32-bit integers, with a possible range in values from zero through 4,294,967,295. RFC 1122 states that systems must seed the sequence number value on all new circuits using a value derived from the local system's clock. Therefore, the first byte of data being sent across a virtual circuit should not be numbered 1, but instead should be numbered according to a value derived from the current time. Some systems violate this principle, starting at 1 even though they're not supposed to.

The main reason for seeding the sequence number with the system clock is for safety. If sequence numbers always start at a fixed integer (like 1), there is an increased opportunity for overlapping to occur, particularly on circuits that are opened and closed rapidly. For example, if two systems used the same port numbers for multiple connections, and a segment from the first connection got lost in transit, that segment may arrive at the destination during the next connection, thereby appearing to be a valid sequence number. For this reason, all TCP implementations should always seed the sequence number for all new connections using a value derived from the local system's clock.

In addition, RFC 1948 discussed how this information could be used to launch a variety of attacks against a system, and that using predictable sequence numbers was not only a technical problem but a security risk as well. Essentially, predictable sequence numbers also mean that acknowledgment numbers can be predicted. Given that information, it is easy for a remote hacker to send fake packets to your servers, providing valid IP addresses and acknowledgment numbers. This loophole lets the bad guy compromise your systems without ever seeing a single packet. Unfortunately, some systems still use highly predictable sequence numbers today, and this problem has not gone away entirely.

Another concern with sequence numbers is that they can wrap around during long data transfers. Although there are more than four billion possible sequence numbers, this is not an infinite amount, so reusing sequence numbers will certainly happen on some circuits, particularly those that are kept open for extended periods of time. For example, if a 10-gigabyte file was transferred between two hosts, then the sequence numbers used on that virtual circuit would have to wrap around twice, with some (if not many) of the sequence numbers getting reused at some point. When this occurs, a segment that got lost or redirected in transit could show up late and appear to be a valid segment.

In order to keep reused sequence numbers from causing these kinds of problems, the recipient must limit the active sequence numbers to a size that will fit within the local receive buffer. Since the receive buffer limits the amount of data (in bytes) that can be outstanding and unacknowledged at any given time, a recipient system can simply ignore any segments with sequence numbers that are outside the boundaries of the current window range.

For example, if a recipient has an eight-kilobyte receive buffer, it can set an eight-kilobyte limit on the data that it receives. If it is currently processing segments with sequence numbers around 100,000, then it can safely ignore any segments that arrive with sequence numbers less than 92,000 or greater than 108,000.

In addition, IP's built-in Time-To-Live mechanism also helps to keep older segments from showing up unexpectedly and wreaking havoc. If an IP datagram has a medium-sized Time-To-Live value, then the datagram may be destroyed before it ever reaches the destination. However, most TCP implementations set the Time-To-Live value at 60 seconds (a value recommended in RFC 1122). Since this value tends to be greater than the acknowledgment timer, it is quite possible that a sender will reissue a segment that has not been acknowledged, and that the old datagram will show up unexpectedly. Since the two segments would have the same sequence number, the recipient should be able to detect that they are duplicates, and simply discard the duplicate segment.

Another way to deal with this problem is to use the TCP Timestamp option to identify when a particular segment was sent. On extremely fast networks (such as those using Gigabit Ethernet), it takes only 17 seconds to completely cycle through all four billion sequence numbers. Since the Time-To-Live value on most IP datagrams is substantially larger than this, there is a high probability of an old datagram showing up with a recently used sequence number. RFC 1323 provides a solution to this problem, using the TCP Timestamp option as a secondary reference for each unique segment. When used together, these two mechanisms keep old segments from wreaking havoc when sequence numbers are being reused.

Since the Sequence Identifier field is a standard part of the TCP header, every segment that is sent must have a Sequence Identifier field, even if it is a segment that doesn't contain any data (such as acknowledgments). There's an obvious problem here: it does not contain any data, so what should it use for the Sequence Identifier? After all, the sequence number is supposed to refer to the first byte of data.

If a segment does not contain any data, then the next byte of data *expected to be sent* is used in the Sequence Identifier field of the TCP header. This sequence number would continue to be used until some data was actually sent, forcing the sequence number to be incremented.

Figure 7-14 illustrates how zero-length segments reuse sequence numbers. As the sender pumps data down to the recipient, the latter has to periodically acknowledge the data that it has received. These acknowledgments are sent as individual segments, with each segment having a Sequence Identifier in the TCP header. Since the client isn't sending any data, it is using the next byte it expects to send as the sequence number. This sequence number will be reused until data actually does get sent, at which point the client's sequence number will be incremented.

One drawback of this approach is that these acknowledgment segments are non-recoverable if they get lost or become corrupted. Since each of these segments contain duplicate sequence numbers, there's no way for the other end of the connection to uniquely identify them. The remote endpoint cannot ask that sequence number *n* be resent, because there are lots of segments with that sequence number. In addition, sequence number *n* has *not yet been sent anyway*, since the Sequence Identifier field is referring to the next byte of data *expected* to be sent.

However, this does not mean that the connection will collapse if a zero-length segment is lost. Since zero-length segments typically contain acknowledgments, if one of them is lost then the acknowledgment will be lost as well. But if the sender has sent more data beyond that segment, then the recipient will likely return an acknowledgment for a higher-numbered sequence anyway, obviating the need for that particular acknowledgment to be resent. If the sender is not sending any more data, then it will eventually notice the missing acknowledgment, and resend the

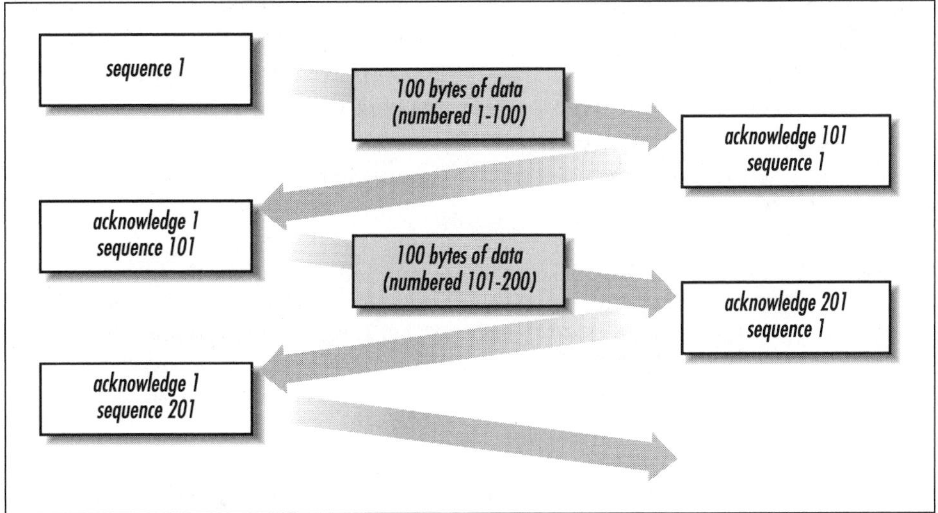

Figure 7-14. Reusing sequence numbers with command segments

questionable data. This action should result in the recipient re-issuing the lost acknowledgment, providing full recovery.

Some of the other zero-length command segments that get used—such as the command segments used to open and close virtual circuits—have their own special sequence number considerations. For example, "start" segments that use the Synchronize bit use a sequence number that is one lower than the sequence numbers used for data, while "close" segments that use the Finish or Reset bits use sequence numbers that are one greater than the sequence numbers used for data. By using sequence numbers outside the range of the sequence numbers used for data, these particular segments will not interfere with actual data delivery, and can be tracked individually if necessary.

For more information on the Synchronize, Finish, and Reset flags, refer to "Control Flags" later in this chapter.

Acknowledgment numbers

Acknowledgment numbers and sequence numbers are closely tied, working together to make sure that segments arrive at their destination.

Just as sequence numbers are used to identify the individual bytes of data being sent in a segment, acknowledgment numbers are used to verify that all of the data in that segment was successfully received. However, rather than pointing to the first byte of data in a segment that has just arrived, the acknowledgment number points to the next byte of data that a recipient expects to receive in the next segment.

This process is illustrated earlier in Figure 7-13. In that example, the sender transmits 100 bytes of data, using a sequence number of 1 to identify the first byte of data in the segment. The receiver returns an acknowledgment for the segment, indicating that it's ready to accept the next segment (starting at sequence number 101). Notice that the acknowledgment does not point to bytes 1 or 100, but instead points to 101, the next byte that the receiver expects to get.

In truth, acknowledgment numbers are closer in concept to a flow control throttle rather than being explicit acknowledgments. Rather than saying "I got the data," they say "I'm ready for more data, starting at byte number *n*."

This design is commonly referred to as being "cumulatively implicit," indicating that all of the data up to (but not including) the acknowledgment number has been received successfully, rather than explicitly acknowledging that a particular byte has been received. Implicit acknowledgments work well when data is flowing smoothly, as a receiver can continually request more data. However, when things go bad, implicit acknowledgments are not very robust. If a segment gets lost or corrupted, then the recipient has no way of informing the sender of the specific problem. Instead, it must re-request the next expected byte of data, since that's all the cumulatively implicit acknowledgment scheme allows for.

Remember that the sliding window mechanism allows a sending system to transmit as many segments as can fit within the recipient's advertised receive buffer. If a system is advertising an eight-kilobyte window, and the sender is using one-kilobyte segments, then as many as eight segments may be issued and in transit at any given moment. If the first segment is lost or damaged, the recipient may still get the remaining seven segments. Furthermore, it should hold those other segments in memory until the missing data arrives, preventing the need for all of the other segments to get resent.

However, the recipient must put the segments back into their original order before passing the data up to the destination application. Therefore, it has to notify the sender of the missing segment before it can process the remaining seven segments.

Most network protocols use either *negative* acknowledgments or *selective* acknowledgments for this service. Using a negative acknowledgment, the recipient can send a message back to the sender stating "segment *n* is missing, please resend." A selective acknowledgment can be used to notify the sender that "bytes *a* through *g* and bytes *s* through *z* were received, please resend bytes *h* through *r*."

However, TCP does not use negative or selective acknowledgments by default. Instead, a recipient system has to implement recovery using the implicit acknowledgment mechanism, simply stating "all bytes up to *n* have been received." When a segment is lost, the recipient has to resend the acknowledgment, thereby informing the sender that it is still waiting for a particular sequence number. The original sender then has to recognize the duplicate acknowledgment as a cry for help, stop transmitting new data, and resend the missing data.

Note that RFC 1106 introduced an experimental TCP option that allowed for the use of negative acknowledgments. However, the Negative Acknowledgment option was never widely used, and RFC 1106 has since expired. Therefore, the Negative Acknowledgment option should not be used with any production TCP implementations.

In addition, RFC 1072 introduced selective acknowledgments to TCP, by way of a set of TCP options. However this work has been clarified in RFC 2018. Using the selective acknowledgment options described therein, a TCP segment can precisely state the data it has received—and thus the data that's missing—even if those blocks of data are non-contiguous. In this model, a receiver uses the normal acknowledgment scheme to state that it is looking for sequence number *n*, and then supplements this information with the Selective Acknowledgment Data option, stating that it also has bytes *y* through *z* in the receive queue. The sender would then resend bytes *n* through *x*, filling the hole in the receiver's queue. For a more detailed discussion on Selective Acknowledgments, refer to "Selective Acknowledgments Permitted" and "Selective Acknowledgment Data" both later in this chapter.

The cumulatively implicit acknowledgment scheme used by TCP is illustrated in Figure 7-15. In that example, each segment contains 100 bytes. The first segment is received successfully, so the recipient sends an implicit acknowledgment for bytes zero through 100 back to the sender. The second segment, however, is lost in transit, so the recipient doesn't see (or acknowledge) it.

When the third segment arrives, the recipient recognizes that it is missing bytes 101 through 200, yet having no way to issue a negative acknowledgment, it repeats the previous implicit acknowledgment, indicating that it is still waiting for byte 101.

What happens next depends on a variety of implementation issues. In the original specification, the sender could wait until an acknowledgment timer for sequence number 101 had expired before resending the segment. However, RFC 1122 states that if three *duplicate* acknowledgments are received for a segment—and if no other acknowledgments have been received for any subsequent segments—then the sender should assume that the segment was probably lost in transit. In this

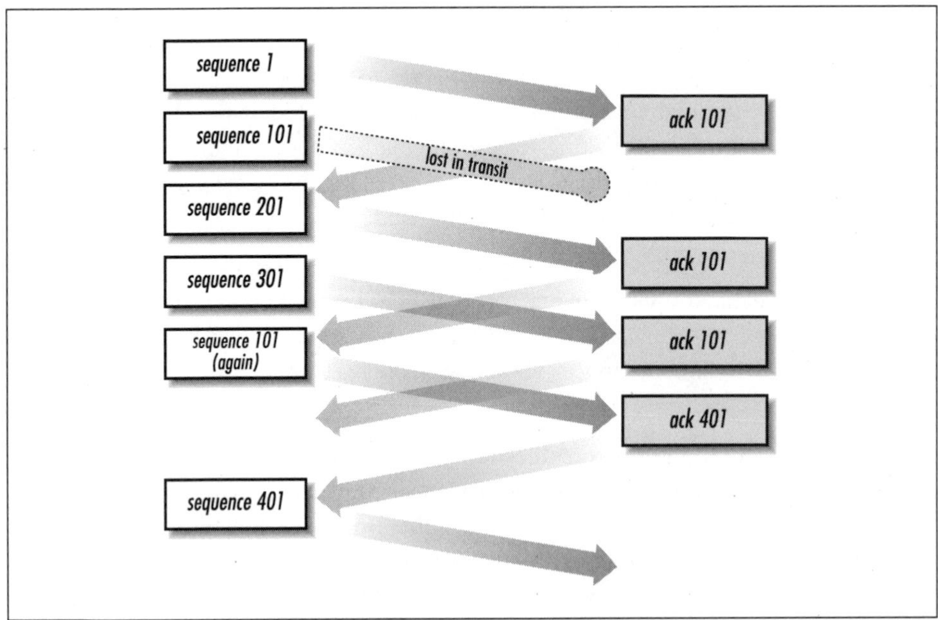

Figure 7-15. Detecting data loss from multiple duplicate acknowledgments

case, the sender should just retransmit the questionable segment rather than waiting for the acknowledgment timer for that segment to expire. This process is known as *fast retransmit*, which is documented in RFC 2581.

It is important to note that fast retransmit does not work when the data has been lost from the tail-end of the stream. Since no other segments would have been sent after the lost segment, there would not be any duplicate acknowledgments, and as such fast retransmit would never come into play. In those situations, the missing data will be discovered only when the acknowledgment timer for that segment expires.

Regardless of the retransmission strategy used, once the sender had resent the lost segment, it would have to decide whether or not it needed to resend all of the segments following the lost segment, or simply resume sending from the point it left off when the missing segment was discovered. The most common mechanism that is used for this is called *fast recovery*, which is also described in RFC 2581. The fast recovery algorithm states that if data was retransmitted due to the presence of multiple duplicate acknowledgments, then the sender should just resume transmitting segments on the assumption that none of the subsequent segments were lost. If in fact there were other lost segments, then that information would be discovered in the acknowledgments for the retransmitted segment. This position assumes that multiple segments are not likely to have been lost, and is accurate most of the time.

Of course, this also depends on whether or not the recipient actually kept any other segments that may have been sent. Although RFC 1122 states that the recipient should keep the other segments in memory (thereby allowing for reassembly to occur locally rather than requiring a total retransmission), not all systems conform to this recommendation.

Another related issue is "partial acknowledgment," whereby a recipient has lost multiple segments. When that happens, the sender may discover and resend the first lost segment through the use of the fast retransmission algorithm. However, rather than getting an acknowledgment back for all of the segments sent afterwards, an acknowledgment is returned that only points to some of the data sent afterwards. Although there aren't any standards-track RFCs that dictate how this situation should be handled, the prevailing logic is to have the sender retransmit the next-specified missing segment and then continue resending from where it left off.

This process illustrates the importance of the recipient's receive buffer, particularly as it pertains to the sender. Every time the recipient received another segment that was out of order, it would have to store this data into the receive buffer until the missing segment arrived. This in turn would take up space in the receive buffer, and so the recipient would have to advertise a smaller receive buffer every time it sent a duplicate acknowledgment for the missing segment. This would in turn cause the sender to slow down (as described earlier in "Receive window size adjustments"), with the sender eventually being unable to send any additional segments. Once the recipient got the missing segment, it would reorder the segments and then pass the data off to the destination application. Then it could advertise a large receive buffer again, and the sender could resume sending data.

Depending on the size and condition of the receive buffer, the sender may be able to resume sending data from where it left off (in our example, sequence number 401), without waiting for an acknowledgment for the next segment. This really depends on the number of unacknowledged segments currently outstanding and the maximum amount of unacknowledged data allowed by the recipient.

For example, if the size of the receive buffer was 800 bytes (using 100–byte segments)—and if only two segments were currently unacknowledged—then once the sender had resent the missing data, it could go ahead and resume transmitting additional segments without waiting for an acknowledgment for those other segments. But if the receive buffer had been cut down to just two hundred bytes, then the sender could not send any more data until the two outstanding segments had been acknowledged.

For more details on how the receive buffer controls flow control in general, refer back to "Flow Control." For more information on the selective acknowledgment option, refer ahead to "Selective Acknowledgment Data."

Acknowledgment timers

Most of the time, spurious packet loss is dealt with by using the fast retransmit and fast recovery algorithms, as defined in RFC 2581. However, those algorithms are not always usable. For example, if the link has failed completely, then multiple duplicate acknowledgments will not be received. Also, if the last segment from a transmission were the one that got lost, then there would not be any additional segments that would cause multiple duplicate acknowledgments to get generated. In these situations, TCP has to rely on an acknowledgment timer (also known as a retransmission timer) in order to detect when a segment has been lost in transit.

Whenever a sender transmits a segment, it has to wait for an acknowledgment to arrive before it can clear the segment from the outbound queue. On well-heeled networks, these acknowledgments come in quickly, allowing the sender to clear the data immediately, increment the sliding window, and move on to the next waiting segment. But if a segment is lost or corrupted and no acknowledgment ever arrives, then the sender has to rely on the timer to tell it when it should resend unacknowledged data.

Determining the most efficient size for the acknowledgment timer is a complex process that must be handled carefully. Setting the timer too short would result in frequent and unnecessary retransmissions, while setting the timer too long would result in unproductive delays whenever loss actually occurred.

For example, the acknowledgment timer for two systems connected together on a high-speed LAN should be substantially shorter than the timer used for a slow connection over the open Internet. Using a short timer allows failure to be recognized quickly, which is desirable on a high-speed LAN where latency is not much of an issue. However, setting a long timer would be more practical when many slow networks were involved, as it would not be efficient to continually generate duplicate segments when the problem is slow delivery (rather than packet loss).

Most systems start with a default acknowledgment timer, and then adjust this timer on a per-circuit basis according to the round-trip delivery times encountered on that specific connection. However, even this approach can get complicated, because the default timer is likely to be inappropriate for many of the virtual circuits, since some of them will be used for slow, long-haul circuits while others will be used for local and fast connections.

For example, most modern systems use a default timer of 3000 milliseconds, which is really too large for local area networks that have a round-trip time less than 10 milliseconds (even though this is the recommended default in RFC 1122). Conversely, many earlier implementations had a default timer of 200 milliseconds, which is far too short for many dial-up and satellite links, resulting in frequent and totally unnecessary retransmissions.

Also, the round-trip delivery times of most networks change throughout the day, due to changes in network utilization, congestion, and routing updates that affect the path that segments take on the way to their destination. For these reasons, the default setting is only accurate some of the time, and must be modified to reflect the specific latency characteristics of each virtual circuit throughout the connection's lifetime.

The two formulas used for determining round-trip delivery times are *Van Jacobsen's algorithm* and *Karn's algorithm*. Van Jacobsen's algorithm is useful for determining a "smoothed round-trip time" across a network, while Karn's algorithm offers techniques for adjusting the smoothed round-trip time whenever network congestion is detected. Although these two algorithms are outside the scope of this book, understanding their principles is required in order to fully understand how they can impact TCP acknowledgment timers.

The basis of Van Jacobsen's algorithm is for a sender to watch the delay encountered by acknowledgment segments as they cross the network, constantly tweaking the variables in use according to the specific amount of time it takes to send a segment and then receive an acknowledgment for that segment.

Although Van Jacobsen's original algorithm used acknowledgments to determine round-trip times for specific segments, this model did not provide for guaranteed accuracy, as multiple acknowledgments could arrive for a single segment (due to loss or due to the use of acknowledgments to command segments, each of which would share the same sequence number). In order to provide for a more accurate monitoring tool, RFC 1072 introduced a pair of TCP options that could be used for measuring the round-trip time of any given circuit, called the Echo and Echo Reply options. However, this work was abandoned in favor of a generic Timestamp option, as defined in RFC 1323.

RFC 1323 uses two fields in a single Timestamp option, allowing both systems to monitor the precise round-trip delivery time of every segment that they send. Whenever a system needs to send a segment, it should place the current time into the Timestamp Value field of the Timestamp option in the TCP header of the outgoing segment. When the remote system receives the segment, it will copy that data into the Timestamp Reply field of the response segment, and place its own timestamp into the Timestamp Value field. Upon receipt of the response, the original sender will see the original timestamp for the original segment, and can compare that data to the current time allowing it to determine the exact amount of latency for the network. In addition, the field-swapping operation will also be repeated, allowing the remote end to determine the same information. For more information on the Timestamp option, refer to "Timestamp" later in this chapter.

Karn's algorithm amplifies the basic round-trip time formula, although it focuses on how to deal with packet loss or congestion. For example, Karn's algorithm suggests that it is best to ignore the round-trip times on packets that get lost (i.e., where no acknowledgment has been received) in order to prevent one failure from unnecessarily tilting the smoothed round-trip time determined from using Van Jacobsen's algorithm. Karn's algorithm also suggests that the value of the acknowledgment timer should be doubled whenever questionable data has been retransmitted due to the acknowledgment timer expiring, in case the problem is with temporary link failure or congestion.

In this model, if the retransmitted segments also go unacknowledged, then the acknowledgment timer will be doubled yet again, with the process repeating until a system-specific maximum has been reached. This could be a maximum number of retransmissions, or a maximum timer value, or a combination of the two.

Systems based on BSD typically limit the length of the retransmission timer to either five minutes or a maximum of twelve attempts, whichever comes first. Windows-based systems limit retransmissions to five attempts, with each retransmission doubling the acknowledgment timer. Other implementations do not double the retransmission timer, but instead use a percentage-based formula or a fixed table, hoping to recover faster than blind-doubling would allow. Regardless, remember that the value that is being incremented or doubled is based on the smoothed round-trip time for that connection, so the maximum acknowledgment timer value could be either quite large or quite small.

Some systems have shown problems in this area, failing to double the size of their retransmission timers whenever the timer expired. As such, these systems would send a retransmission, and then continue resending the data in short fixed intervals. Since these systems had low timers anyway (200 milliseconds was the default), a dial-up user connecting to this system would tend to get at least two or three retransmissions of the very first segment, until the round-trip smoothing started to kick in.

Also, some systems will cache the learned round-trip time for future use, allowing any subsequent connections to the same remote system (or network) to use the previously learned round-trip latency values. This feature allows the new connection to start with a default that should be appropriate for the specific endpoint system, instead of starting at the system default value (which is almost always wrong).

RFC 1122 mandates that both Van Jacobsen's algorithm and Karn's algorithm be used in all TCP implementations so that acknowledgment timers will get synchronized quickly. Subsequent experimentation has shown that these algorithms do in fact help to improve overall throughput and performance, regardless of the networks in use.

However, there are also times when these algorithms can actually cause problems to occur, such as when Karn's algorithm results in an overly slow reaction to a sudden change in the network's characteristics. For example, if the round-trip time suddenly goes through the roof due to a change in the end-to-end network path, the acknowledgment timer on the sender will most likely get triggered before the data ever reaches the destination. When that happens, the sender will resend the unacknowledged data, the size of the retransmission timer will get doubled, and the acknowledgments for the questionable data may also be ignored (since retransmissions aren't supposed to interfere with the smoothed round-trip time). It will take several attempts before the smoothed round-trip time will get updated to reflect the true round-trip latency of the new network path.

Delayed acknowledgments

Figure 7-15 earlier in this chapter shows the receiver sending an acknowledgment every time it receives a segment from the sender. However, this is not necessarily an effective use of resources. For one thing, the receiver has to spend CPU cycles on calculating the acknowledgment, as does the sender when it gets the acknowledgment. Furthermore, the use of frequent acknowledgments also generates excessive amounts of network traffic, thereby consuming bandwidth that could otherwise be used by the sender to transmit data.

Rather than acknowledging every segment, it is better for the receiver to only send acknowledgments on a periodic basis. A mechanism called Delayed Acknowledgment is used for this purpose, allowing multiple segments to be acknowledged simultaneously. Remember that acknowledgments are implicit, stating that "all data up to *n* has been received." It is therefore possible for a recipient to acknowledge multiple segments simultaneously by simply setting the Acknowledgment Identifier to a higher inclusive value, rather than sending multiple distinct acknowledgments. Not only does this consume less network resources, but it also requires less computational resources on the part of the two endpoints.

This concept is illustrated in Figure 7-16. In that example, the recipient only sends an acknowledgment after receiving two segments. This approach not only generates less traffic, but it also allows the sender to increment their sliding window by two segment sizes, thereby helping to keep traffic flowing smoothly.

RFC 1122 states that all TCP implementations should utilize the delayed acknowledgment algorithm. However, RFC 1122 also states that TCP implementations who do so must not delay an acknowledgment for more than 500 milliseconds (to prevent the sender's acknowledgment timers from reaching zero).

RFC 1122 also states that an acknowledgment should be sent for every two full-sized segments received. However, this depends upon the ability of the recipient to clear the buffer quickly, and also depends upon the latency of the network in

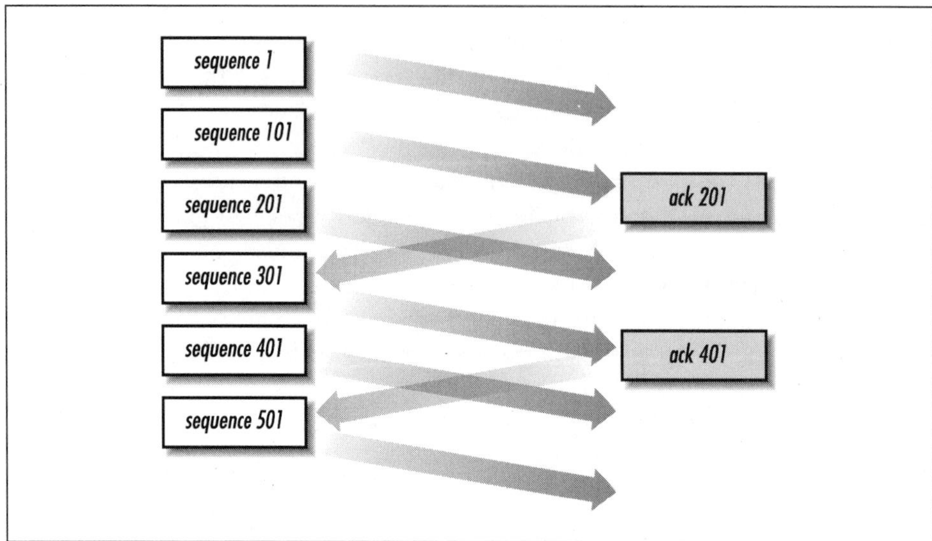

Figure 7-16. An overview of the delayed acknowledgment algorithm

use. If it takes a long time for cumulative acknowledgments to reach the sender, this design could negatively impact the sender's ability to transmit more data. Instead of helping, this behavior would cause traffic to become bursty, with the sender transmitting lots of segments and then stopping to wait for an acknowledgment. Once the acknowledgment arrived, then the sender would send several more segments, and then stop again.

Furthermore, some applications (such as TELNET) are "chatty" by design, with the client and server both sending data to each other on a regular basis. With these applications, both systems would want to combine their acknowledgments with whatever data had to be sent, reducing the number of segments actively crossing the network at any given moment. Delayed acknowledgments are also helpful here, as the two systems can simply combine their acknowledgments with whatever data is being returned.

For example, assume that a TELNET client is sending keystrokes to the server, which must be echoed back to the client. This would generate lots of small segments by both systems, not only for the keystroke data, but also for the acknowledgments that would be generated for each segment containing the keystroke data, as well as for the segments containing the data being echoed back to the client.

By delaying the acknowledgment until the segment containing the echoed data is generated, the amount of network traffic can be reduced dramatically. Effectively, rather than sending an acknowledgment as soon as the client's keystroke data segment had been verified, the server would delay the acknowledgment for a little while. Then, if any data was being returned to the client (such as the echoed keystroke), the server would just set the Acknowledgment Identifier in that segment's TCP header, eliminating the need for a separate acknowledgment segment. When combined with the Nagle algorithm, delayed acknowledgments can really help to cut down the amount of network bandwidth being consumed by small segments.

Unfortunately, there are also some potential problems with this design, although they are typically only seen when used in conjunction with Path MTU Discovery. These problems occur whenever a system chooses to delay an acknowledgment until two full-sized segments have been received, but the system is receiving segments that are not "fully sized." This can happen when two devices announce large MTUs using the MSS option, but then the sender determines that a smaller MTU is required (as detected with Path MTU Discovery). When this happens, the recipient will receive many segments, but will not return an acknowledgment until it has received enough data to fill two full-sized segments (as determined by the MSS option).

In this case, the sender will send as much data as it can (according to the current limitations defined by the congestion window and the local sliding window), and then stop transmitting until an acknowledgment for that data is received. However, the recipient will not return an acknowledgment until the 500-millisecond maximum for delayed acknowledgments has been reached, and then will send one acknowledgment for all of the segments that have been received. The sender will increment its sliding window and resume sending data, only to stop again a moment later, resulting in bursty traffic.

This scenario happens only when Path MTU Discovery detects a smaller MTU than the size announced by the MSS option, which should be a fairly rare occurrence, although it does happen often enough to be a problem. This is particularly problematic with sites that use Token Ring, FDDI, or some other technology that allows for large MTU sizes, with an intermediary network that allows for only 1500-byte MTU sizes. For a more detailed discussion of this problem, refer to "Partially Filled Segments or Long Gaps Between Sends" later in this chapter.

The TCP Header

TCP segments consist of header and body parts, just like IP datagrams. The body part contains whatever data was provided by the application that generated it, while the header contains the fields that tell the destination TCP software what to do with the data.

A TCP segment is made up of at least ten fields. Unlike the other core protocols, some TCP segments do not contain data. In addition, there are a variety of supplementary header fields that may show up as "options" in the header. The total size of the segment will vary according to the size of the data and any options that may be in use.

Table 7-2 lists all of the mandatory fields in a TCP header, along with their size (in bits) and some usage notes. For more detailed descriptions of these fields, refer to the individual sections throughout this chapter.

Table 7-2. The Fields in a TCP Segment

Field	Bits	Usage Notes
Source Port	16	Identifies the 16-bit port number in use by the application that is sending the data.
Destination Port	16	Identifies the 16-bit target port number of the application that is to receive this data.
Sequence Identifier	32	Each byte of data sent across a virtual circuit is assigned a somewhat unique number. The Sequence Identifier field is used to identify the number associated with the first byte of data in this segment.
Acknowledgment Identifier	32	Each byte of data sent across a virtual circuit is assigned a somewhat unique number. The Acknowledgment Identifier field is used to identify the next byte of data that a recipient is expecting to receive.
Header Length	4	Specifies the size of the TCP header, including any options.
Reserved	6	Reserved. Must be "zero."
Flags	6	Used to relay control information about the virtual circuit between the two endpoint systems.
Window	16	Identifies the size of the receive buffer in use on the system that generated this segment.
Checksum	16	Used to store a checksum of the entire TCP segment.
Urgent Pointer	16	Identifies the last byte of any urgent data that must be dealt with immediately.
Options (optional)	varies	Additional special-handling options can also be defined using the options field. These options are the only thing that can cause a TCP header to exceed 20 bytes in length.
Padding (if required)	varies	A TCP segment's header length must be a multiple of 32 bits. If any options have been introduced to the header, the header must be padded so that it is divisible by 32 bits.
Data (optional)	varies	The data portion of the TCP segment. Not all TCP segments have data, since some of them are used only to relay control information about the virtual circuit.

Notice that the TCP header does not provide any fields for source or destination IP address, or any other services that are not specifically related to TCP. This is because those services are provided by the IP header or by the application-specific protocols (and thus contained within the data portion of the segment).

As can be seen, the minimum size of a TCP header is 20 bytes. If any options are defined, then the header's size will increase (up to a maximum of 60 bytes). RFC 793 states that a header must be divisible by 32 bits, so if an option has been defined, but it only uses 16 bits, then another 16 bits must be added using the Padding field.

Figure 7-17 shows a TCP segment being sent from Arachnid (an HTTP 1.1 server) to Bacteria (an HTTP 1.1 client). This segment will be used for further discussion of the TCP header fields throughout the remainder of this chapter.

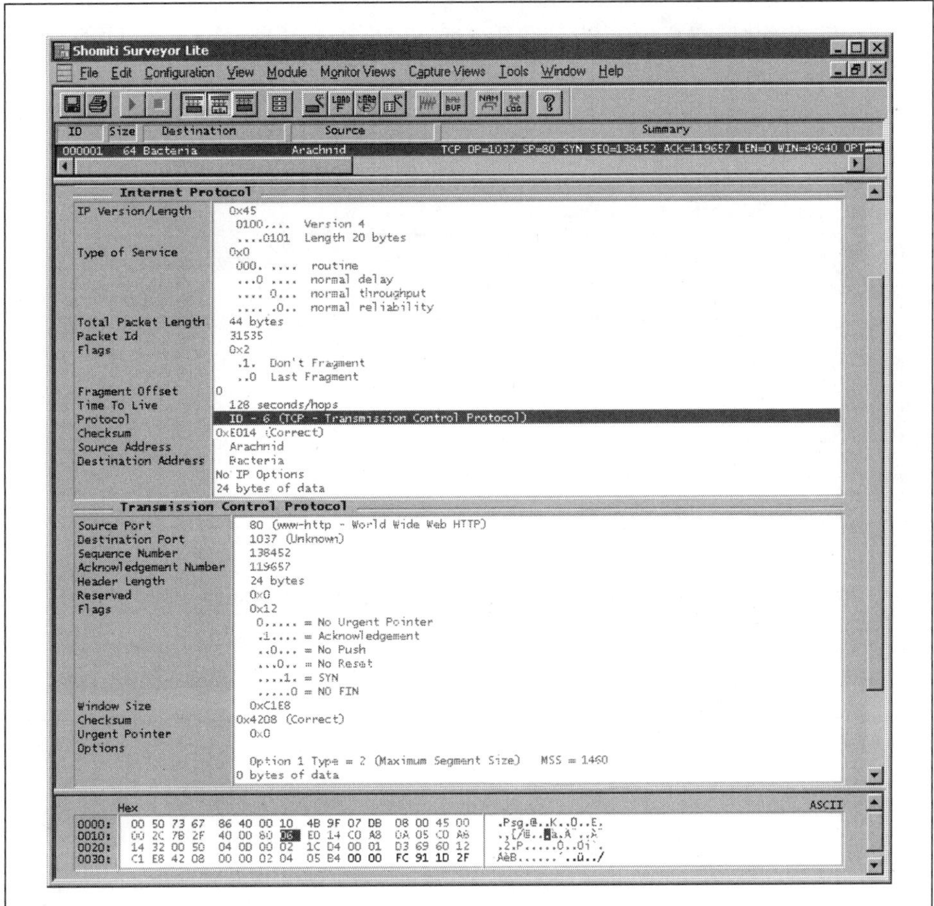

Figure 7-17. A typical TCP segment

Source Port

Identifies the application that generated the segment, as referenced by the 16-bit TCP port number in use by the application.

Size

Sixteen bits.

Notes

This field identifies the port number used by the application that created the data.

Capture Sample

In the capture shown in Figure 7-18, the Source Port field is set to hexadecimal 00 50, which is decimal 80 (the well-known port number for HTTP). From this information, we can tell that this segment is a reply, since HTTP servers only send data in response to a request.

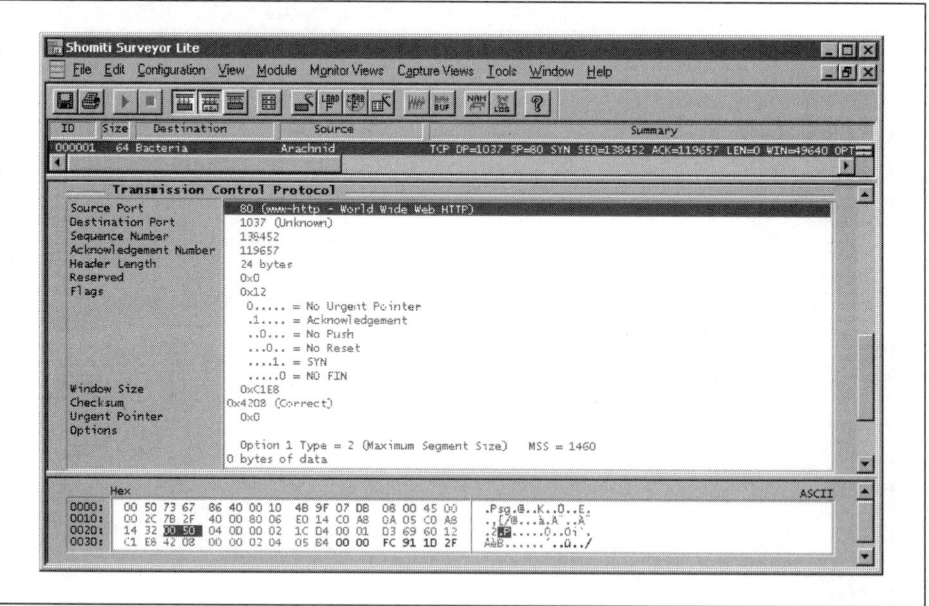

Figure 7-18. The Source Port field

See Also

"Destination Port"

"Application addressing with TCP ports"

Destination Port

Identifies the application that this segment is for, as referenced by the 16-bit TCP port number in use by the application on the destination system.

Size

Sixteen bits.

Notes

This field identifies the port number used by the destination application.

Capture Sample

In the capture shown in Figure 7-19, the Destination Port field is set to hexadecimal 04 0d, which is decimal 1037. This is the port number that the HTTP client is using.

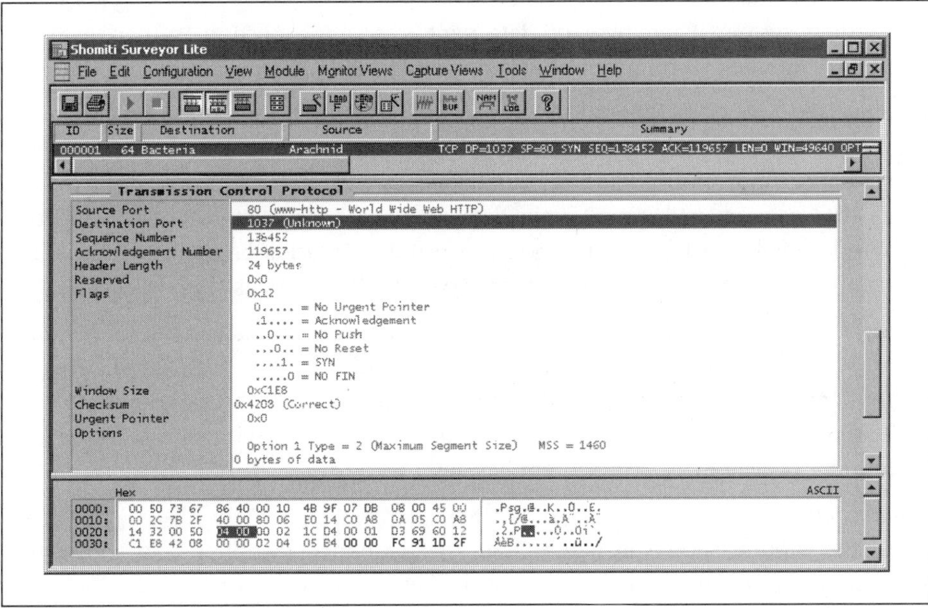

Figure 7-19. The Destination Port Number field

See Also

"Source Port"

"Application addressing with TCP ports"

Sequence Identifier

Identifies the first byte of data that is stored in the data portion of the segment.

Size

Thirty-two bits.

Notes

Every byte of data sent across a virtual circuit is given a somewhat unique sequence number. As the data is stored into segments for delivery, the sequence number of the first byte of data in the segment is placed into the Sequence Identifier field.

The primary purpose of the Sequence Identifier field is to allow the recipient to sort data into its proper order. This step is required since the underlying IP network is unreliable and may destroy, delay, or duplicate some IP packets, causing the TCP segments within them to arrive out of order (if they arrive at all). By numbering the bytes inside of the segment, the recipient is able to put the data back into its proper order, eliminate duplicates, and recognize missing blocks of data.

Sequence numbers are supposed to be seeded by the system clock of the sending system. Each byte of data sent over a connection is then given a unique number, starting from the seed value.

Since the Sequence Identifier field is only 32 bits long, there are only enough values for four gigabytes of data. With very large data transfers, some sequence numbers may get reused. Typically this is not a problem, however, as the recipient will accept only data that has been sent recently, using the Window field's value as a boundary constraint. In addition, some systems utilize the Timestamp option to further separate old segments from new ones.

Since TCP virtual circuits are full-duplex, each endpoint is capable of sending and receiving data simultaneously. As commands and data are passed between the applications in use on the two systems, the sequence numbers and acknowledgment numbers for each endpoint will increment according to the amount of data that each of them has sent.

Capture Sample

In the capture shown in Figure 7-20, the Sequence Identifier field shows the sequence number of the first byte of data in this segment as 138452.

See Also

"Acknowledgment Identifier"

"Sequence numbers"

Acknowledgment Identifier

Identifies the next byte of data that a system is expecting to receive from the remote endpoint.

Size

Thirty-two bits.

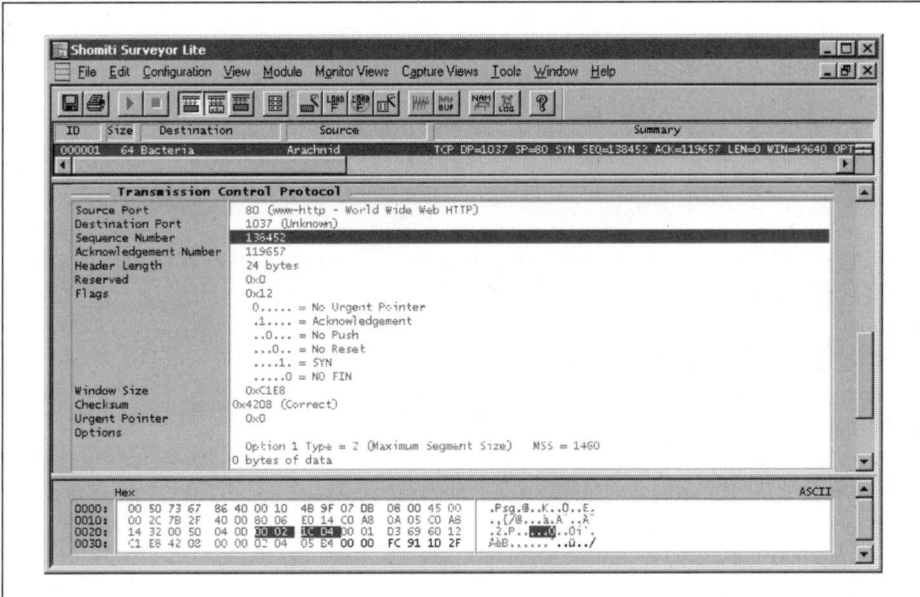

Figure 7-20. The Sequence Identifier field

Notes

Every byte of data sent across a virtual circuit is given a somewhat unique sequence number. As data is received, the recipient states that it is ready to receive the next segment, starting at the sequence number provided in the Acknowledgment Identifier field.

The Acknowledgment Identifier acts as an implicit, cumulative acknowledgment, saying that all data up to (but not including) this sequence number has been received. In truth, the Acknowledgment Identifier acts like a flow-control throttle rather than an acknowledgment, since it identifies the data it is ready to receive, rather than the data it has already received.

If a segment gets lost or corrupted, then the recipient will not receive it and will continue to publish the same acknowledgment number in each segment that it sends. In this way, a sender can recognize that data has been lost and recover from the error by resending the questionable data.

Since TCP virtual circuits are full-duplex, each endpoint is capable of sending and receiving data simultaneously. As commands and data are passed between the applications in use on the two systems, the sequence numbers and acknowledgment numbers for each endpoint will increment according to the amount of data that each of them has sent.

Capture Sample

In the capture shown in Figure 7-21, the Acknowledgment Identifier field is set to 119657, which is the sequence number of the next byte of data that Arachnid expects to receive from Bacteria.

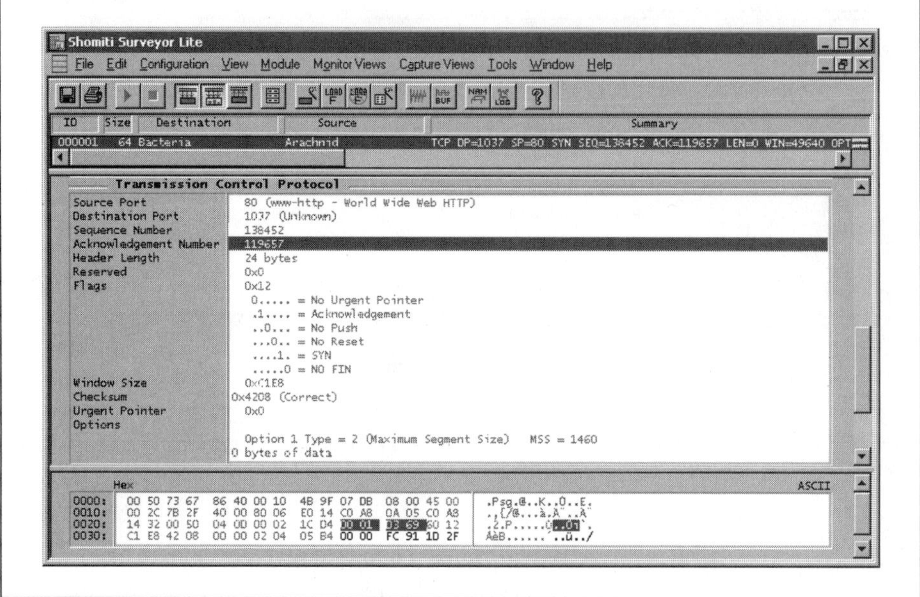

Figure 7-21. The Acknowledgment Identifier field

See Also

"Sequence Identifier"

"Acknowledgment numbers"

Header Length

Identifies the size of the TCP header, in 32-bit multiples.

Size

Four bits.

Notes

The primary purpose of this field is to inform the recipient where the data portion of the TCP segment starts. Due to space constraints, the value of this field uses 32-bit multiples. Thus, 20 bytes is the same as 160 bits, which would be shown here as 5 (5 × 32 bits = 160 bits = 20 bytes). Since each of the header's mandatory fields are fixed in size, the smallest this value can be is 5.

If all of the bits in this field were "on," the maximum value would be 15. Thus, a TCP header can be no larger than 60 bytes (15 × 32 bits = 480 bits = 60 bytes).

Note that TCP does not define "total length" like UDP does, but rather only defines "header length," like IP. In order to determine the amount of data contained in a segment, the destination system must calculate the entire length of the IP datagram (as described in "Total Packet Length" in Chapter 2, *The Internet Protocol*), and then subtract the size of the TCP header from that value. The resulting value provides both the number of bytes of data stored in this segment and the starting position for the data.

Capture Sample

In the capture shown in Figure 7-22, the Header Length field shows the size of the TCP header as hexadecimal 6 which indicates that the TCP header is 24 bytes long. Although the default size is only 20 bytes, this segment contains some TCP options, which are making it a little bit larger than normal.

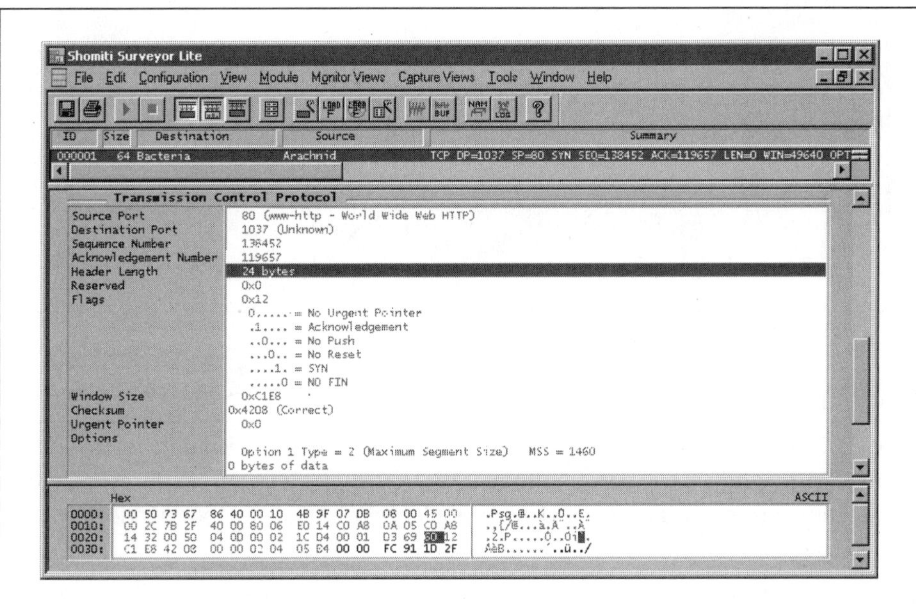

Figure 7-22. The Header Length field

See Also

"TCP Options"

"Padding"

Reserved

These bits are currently unused, and must be set to "zero."

Size

Six bits.

Capture Sample

In the capture shown in Figure 7-23, the Reserved field contains zeroes.

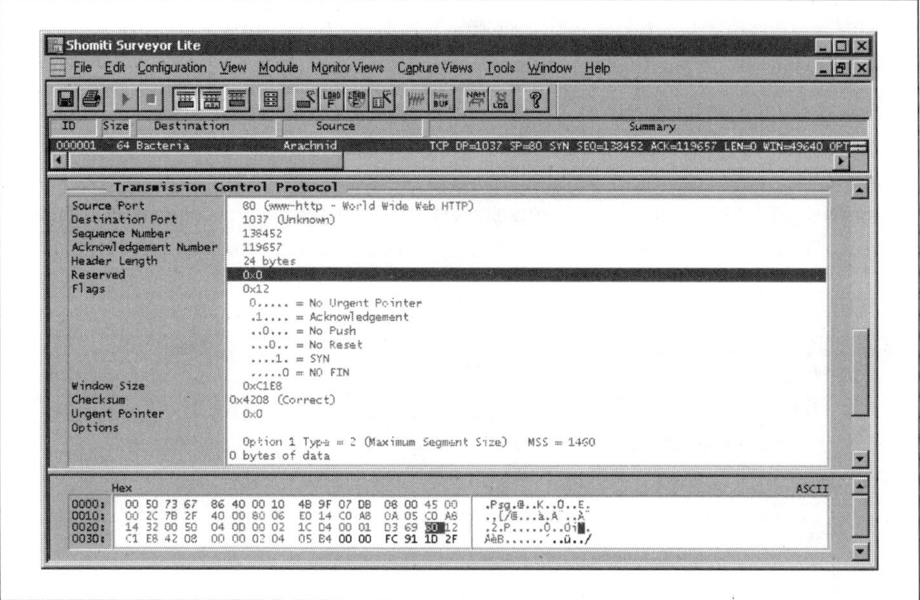

Figure 7-23. The Reserved field

Control Flags

Since TCP uses a point-to-point virtual circuit for all communications, it needs to be able to manage the flow of information across the virtual circuit at different times. The Control Flags are used to provide circuit-management services to the TCP endpoints.

Size

Six bits.

Notes

There are six different flags in the Control Flags field, with each flag being represented by an "on" or "off" condition.

Each of the Control Flags provide a variety of different service to TCP. Some of the flags provide circuit-management services, while others provide data-management services. The flags and their meanings are listed in Table 7-3.

Table 7-3. The Control Flags and Their Meanings

Control Flag	Usage
Urgent	If the Urgent flag is set, then this segment contains urgent data, up through the sequence number referenced by the Urgent Pointer field. If this flag is not set, then the Urgent Pointer field should be ignored.
Acknowledgment	If the Acknowledgment flag is set, then this segment contains an acknowledgment. Every segment (except for the very first segment that was used to initialize the circuit, and the Reset segments that are used to abort connections) should have this flag set.
Push	If the Push flag is set, then this segment contains data that is being "pushed" by the sending application. Typically, the Push flag is used to indicate that all of the data has been transferred, and is conceptually similar to an end-of-record marker.
Reset	The Reset flag should be seen only when a virtual circuit must be aborted because it cannot be torn down in an orderly fashion (due to errors), or when an incoming connection request is for an invalid socket and therefore must be rejected.
Synchronize	When a virtual circuit is first established, the two endpoint TCP providers must synchronize their sequence numbers before they can issue meaningful acknowledgments. During the handshake process, each endpoint sends a segment with the Synchronize flag set, and also provides the sequence numbers that will be used for the virtual circuit. Both systems will then have the necessary information to proceed orderly, and can begin exchanging data as needed.
Finish	When all of the data has been exchanged between the two endpoint systems, the virtual circuit can be closed. This is achieved by one system issuing a segment with the Finish flag set. If the other end is ready to close the virtual circuit, it will return a segment with the Finish flag set as well. The connection is then terminated.

The Urgent and Push flags are both used by applications to identify certain characteristics of the data being exchanged between the two endpoints:

- Urgent is used in conjunction with the Urgent Pointer field to identify that the data contained within the segment (up through the sequence number published in the Urgent Pointer field) needs to be processed immediately. All segments that arrive with the Urgent flag set "on" are to be treated as top-priority. Segments that have sequence numbers in the Urgent Pointer field but that do not have the Urgent flag set "on" should be treated as normal.
- As written in RFC 793, the Push flag is supposed to be used by applications whenever they wish to have the send buffer flushed immediately.

This may be necessary if the application needs to send only a little bit of data, which would normally require the sending TCP software to wait for additional data before generating a segment. However, many TCP providers do not provide applications with access to the Push flag directly, and will instead set the Push flag whenever a write operation is completed. Some systems will even set the Push flag on every segment that they generate, regardless of any other factors.

For more information on how the Urgent and Push flags work with applications, refer back to "Data considerations," earlier in this chapter.

The Acknowledgment, Reset, Synchronize, and Finish flags are used by the TCP endpoints directly, allowing them to control certain characteristics of the virtual circuit:

- The Synchronize flag is used whenever a virtual circuit needs to be established. When an application issues an "open" request to the local TCP provider, TCP will issue a segment with the Synchronize flag "on." The segment will contain all of the normal headers (including a Sequence Identifier field that identifies the starting sequence number that will be used by the local TCP provider for that virtual circuit). The recipient will then respond with a TCP segment of its own, which will also have the Synchronize bit "on," with its local sequence number in the Sequence Identifier field.
- The Acknowledgment flag is used with every segment that is sent across a virtual circuit, except for the very first segment and some Reset segments. Since the very first segment is a connection request, there cannot have been any data received that could be acknowledged. However, the response to the connection request—and every other segment sent thereafter—will be a response of some sort, and therefore must have the Acknowledgment flag set. The other exception to this rule is with Resets, which may be issued without any accompanying acknowledgment data.
- Once all of the data has been exchanged between the two endpoint systems, one system may wish to close the connection. This is achieved through the use of the Finish flag, which is pretty much the opposite of the Synchronize flag. When an application issues a "close" request to the local TCP provider, the latter will issue a segment with the Finish flag set. If the recipient is willing to close the connection, then it will respond with a segment that will also have the Finish flag set. The virtual circuit will then be torn down.
- If the virtual circuit must be terminated abruptly—possibly due to a loss of communication with the other endpoint system—or if an incoming

connection request does not map to an active listener, then the terminating system will issue a segment with the Reset flag set. This acts as an informational notice that the circuit is being terminated, rather than acting as an agreement to terminate like the Finish flag.

For more information on the circuit-management flags, refer in this chapter to the sections entitled "Opening a circuit," "Closing a circuit," and "TCP in Action."

Capture Sample

In the capture shown in Figure 7-24, the Acknowledgment and Synchronize flags are both enabled, indicating that this segment is a part of the circuit-setup exchange.

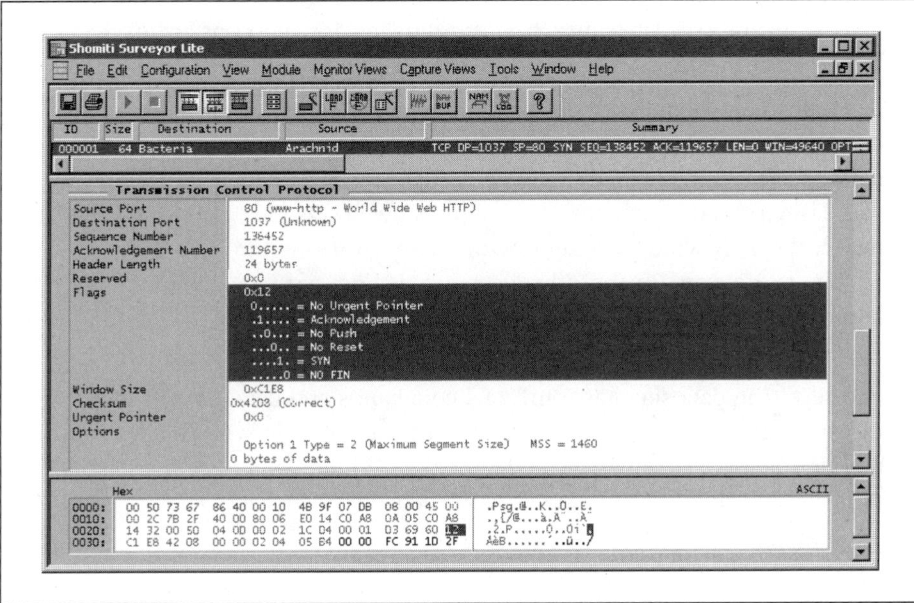

Figure 7-24. The control flags

See Also

"Data considerations"

"Opening a circuit"

"Closing a circuit"

"TCP in Action"

Window

Identifies the amount of receive buffer space available on the sending system, in bytes.

Size

Sixteen bits.

Notes

A key part of TCP's flow control service involves having each system keep track of the other's available receive buffer space. By advertising a small receive buffer, one end of the virtual circuit can effectively force the other end to stop sending data temporarily, while increasing the size of the buffer allows the other end to send larger amounts of data without having to wait for acknowledgments. The size of the receive buffer is advertised in the Window field of every TCP segment's header, allowing for the constant exchange of buffer status messages.

Since this field is limited to 16 bits, the maximum amount of buffer space that can be advertised is 64 kilobytes. This amount has proven to be too small for many networks, particularly satellites and Token Ring networks, both of which can easily send 64 kilobytes of data in a single frame. To get around this limitation, the TCP Window Scale option has been defined in RFC 1323, allowing 30 bits to be used in the advertisement, letting systems advertise buffers as large as one gigabyte.

Since TCP virtual circuits are full-duplex, each endpoint is capable of sending and receiving data simultaneously. As commands and data are passed between the applications in use on the two systems, each system will have to adjust the amount of space being advertised. Since the Window field is a mandatory part of the TCP header, this process is easily achieved.

Capture Sample

In the capture shown in Figure 7-25, the Window field is set to hexadecimal C1 E8, which is decimal 49,640. On an Ethernet network with a Maximum Segment Size of 1460 bytes, that value would allow 34 segments to be in-flight at any given time.

See Also

"Buffer size considerations"

"Notes on Determining the Optimal Receive Window Size"

"Partially Filled Segments or Long Gaps Between Sends"

"Window Scale"

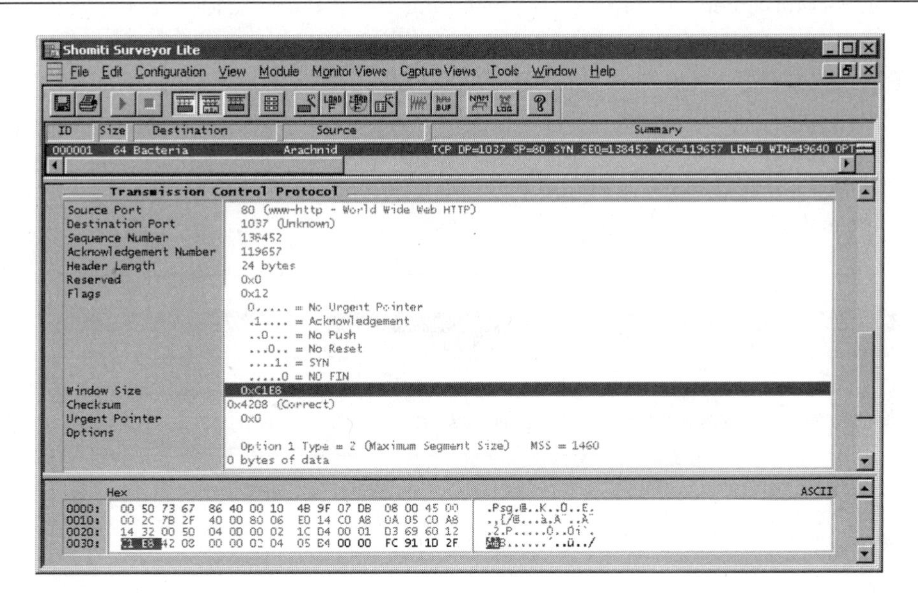

Figure 7-25. The Window field

Checksum

Used to store a checksum of the TCP segment, including both the header and body parts. The checksum allows the destination system to validate the contents of the TCP segment and to test for possible corruption.

Size

Sixteen bits.

Notes

Unlike UDP, the TCP checksum is mandatory. The sending system must calculate a checksum, and the receiving system must validate the contents of the TCP segment using the checksum.

If the checksum is deemed to be invalid, then the segment is discarded before it is processed. Discarding segments is a "silent" error, and no notification of the event is generated or sent. Therefore, the sender will not be made aware of the failure until the next acknowledgment is generated by the recipient, informing the sender that the recipient is still waiting for the next byte.

When the TCP checksum is calculated, a "pseudo-header" is included in the calculations. The pseudo-header includes the source and destination IP addresses, as well as the Protocol Identifier (6 for TCP) and the size of the TCP segment (including both the header and the data). The pseudo-header is combined with the TCP header and data, and a checksum is calculated using ones-complement arithmetic. By including the pseudo-header in the calculations, the destination system is able to validate that the sending and receiving hosts are correct, in case the IP datagram that delivered the TCP segment got mixed up en route to the final destination.

Capture Sample

In the capture shown in Figure 7-26, the Checksum field is calculated as hexadecimal 42 08, which is correct.

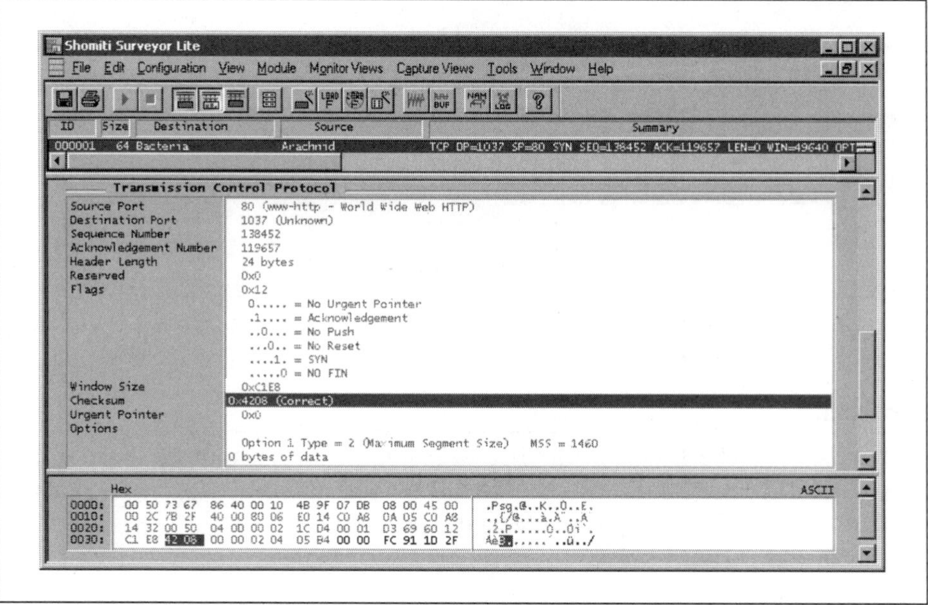

Figure 7-26. The Checksum field

See Also

"Reliability"

Urgent Pointer

Identifies the sequence number of the last byte of any urgent data that may be in this segment.

Size

Sixteen bits.

Notes

TCP offers the ability to flag certain bytes of data as "urgent." This feature allows an application to process and forward any data that must be dealt with immediately, without the data having to sit in the send queue for processing. Instead, the data is packaged into a segment, the Urgent flag is set in the TCP header, and a byte off-set marking the end of urgent data is specified in the Urgent Pointer field.

It is important to note that the Urgent Pointer does not use a Sequence Number to specify the end of urgent data, but instead uses an off-set in the current stream, indicating the location where urgent data ends. A recipient of a TCP segment with the Urgent flag enabled must add the value provided in the Urgent Pointer to the Sequence Number field of the current segment, and use the resulting value to determine the ending sequence number. What this means is that the Urgent Pointer off-set can refer to a byte location in another TCP segment, allowing urgent data to span across multiple segments if needed.

This mechanism reflects a specific design as mandated in RFC 1122. Unfortunately, this design was not always clear, and many TCP implementations take a different interpretation. Most notably, many BSD-based systems use the Urgent Pointer to refer to the byte following the off-set specified in the Urgent Pointer, rather than the specified off-set itself. Other systems have other problems, and many implementations simply do not support urgent data at all.

If urgent data is supported correctly on your system, then any segment that arrives with the Urgent flag enabled should be treated as containing urgent data. Conversely, any segment that arrives with a value in the Urgent Pointer field—but with the Urgent flag off—should be treated as normal data.

Capture Sample

In the capture shown in Figure 7-27, the Urgent Pointer field is set to 0, indicating that the first byte of data in this segment would be urgent, if the Urgent Flag were enabled (which it is not).

See Also

"Control Flags"

"Data considerations"

TCP Options

The TCP header provides everything needed for two endpoint systems to establish a connection, exchange data, and tear down the virtual circuit. However, some additional functionality beyond what is provided for in the TCP header is needed at times. When this is the case, TCP options must be used.

Size

Varies as needed. The default is zero bits, while the maximum is 40 bytes (a restriction imposed by the limited bits available in the Header Length field).

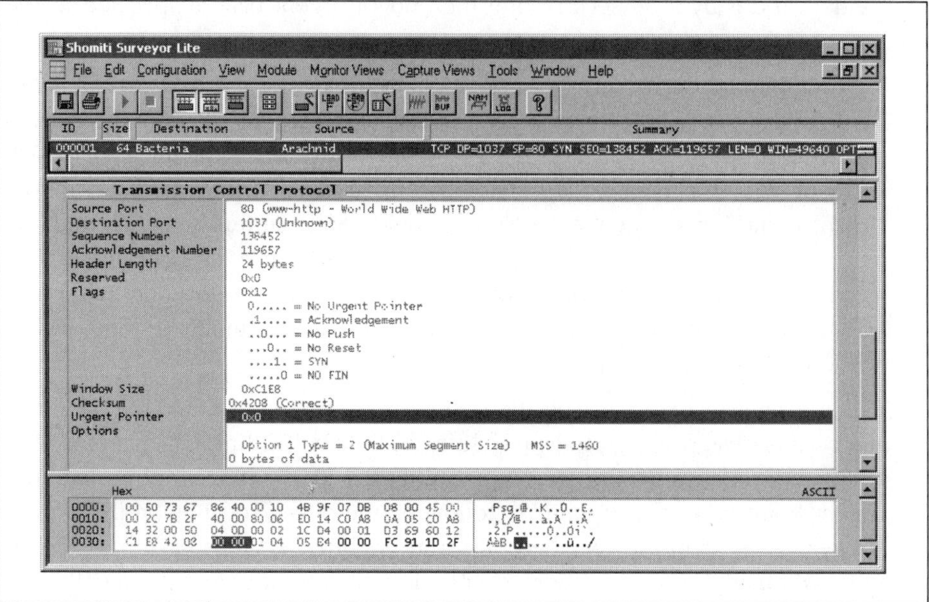

Figure 7-27. The Urgent Pointer field

Notes

By default, no options are defined within a TCP header, meaning that this field does not exist. The TCP header can have as many options as will fit within the space available (up to 40 bytes), if any are required.

Each option has unique characteristics. For more information on the various options and their ramifications, refer to "Notes on TCP Options" later in this chapter.

Capture Sample

In the capture shown in Figure 7-28, the options field contains the Maximum Segment Size option, which is normal for circuit-setup segments (this option is explained in detail in "Maximum Segment Size" later in this chapter).

See Also

"Header Length"

"Padding"

"Notes on TCP Options"

Padding

Used to make a TCP segment end on a 32-bit boundary.

Size

Varies as needed.

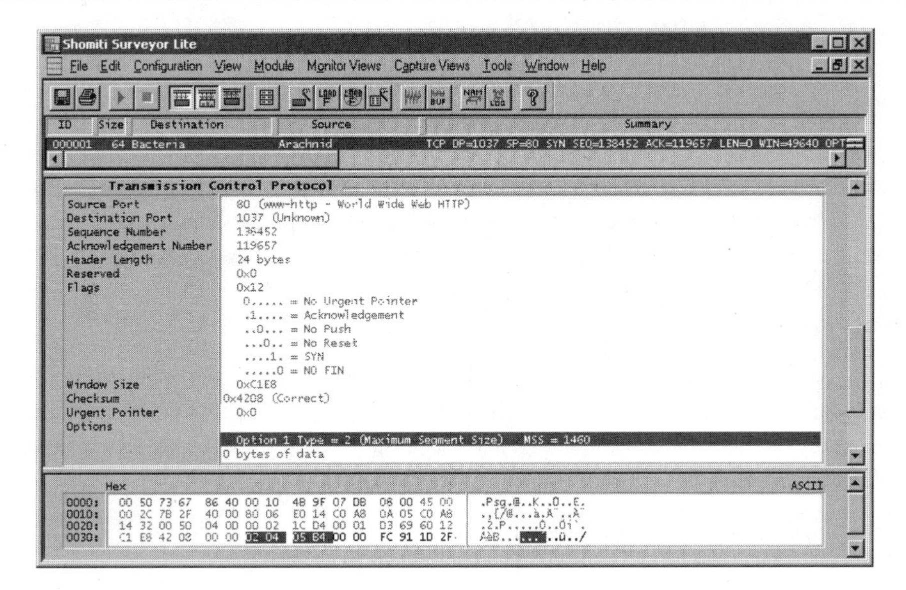

Figure 7-28. The options field

Notes

The length of a TCP header must be divisible by 32 bits in order for its length to fit within the Header Length field. Most TCP headers are 160 bits long, since that's the size of a normal header when all of the mandatory fields are used. However, if any options have been defined, then the TCP header may need to be padded in order to make it divisible by 32 again.

See Also

"Header Length"

"TCP Options"

Notes on TCP Options

TCP options are conceptually similar to IP options, although their usages are quite different. For one thing, IP options are mostly used to define special-handling services for IP datagrams being sent across the Internet, while TCP options are mostly used to extend TCP's native circuit-management services.

RFC 793 originally defined three option types, only one of which is required (the Maximum Segment Size option, used by the two endpoint systems during circuit setup to exchange information about their local MTU/MRU sizes). Over the years however, the list of options has grown dramatically.

RFC 1072 introduced the Window Scale, Selective Acknowledgment and Echo/Echo Reply options. However, the Window Scale option was redefined in RFC 1323, and the Echo/Echo Reply options were replaced with a single Timestamp option in RFC 1323 as well. Selective Acknowledgments were also redefined, although not until RFC 2018.

In addition, RFC 1106 defined an alternative to the Window Scale option called the Big Windows option, and also defined a Negative Acknowledgment option as a possible enhancement to TCP's native cumulatively implicit acknowledgment scheme. However, RFC 1106 was never ratified, nor was it implemented on many systems.

Table 7-4 lists the current options that are commonly used and some notes on their usage. For a detailed listing of all of the TCP options that are currently registered, refer to the IANA's online registry (accessible at *http://www.isi.edu/in-notes/iana/assignments/tcp-parameters*).

Table 7-4. The Current Most-Used Options

Type	Name	Description
0	End of Option List	Used to mark the end of all the options.
1	No operation	Used for internal padding, when multiple options are present, or when an option needs to start on a 32-bit boundary.
2	Maximum Segment Size	Used to exchange MRU sizes during the circuit setup handshake.
3	Window Scale	Allows TCP to use and publish window sizes that are larger than the 64 kilobytes maximum allowed by the Window field of the TCP header.
4	Selective Acknowledgment Permitted	Used to allow the use of selective acknowledgments on a virtual circuit.
5	Selective Acknowledgment Data	The selective acknowledgment, if specified using the Selective Acknowledgment Permitted option (using option-type of 4).
8	Timestamp	Used to determine the round-trip delivery time for a segment, allowing the two endpoints to determine reasonable acknowledgment timers.

Each option is specified using three fields: an eight-bit option field for the option's type, an eight-bit field for the option's length, and a variable-length field for the option's data. The option-type field identifies the specific option in use, while the option-size field indicates the amount of data used for the entire option (including the option-type, option-size, and option-data fields). Since each option contains different types of information, the option-length field is required in order for the

TCP software to determine where the option-data field ends (and where the next option-type field begins).

Figure 7-29 shows a TCP circuit-setup message between Bacteria and Arachnid, with Bacteria providing several different TCP options. This capture will be used to further discuss some of the more common TCP options throughout the remainder of this section.

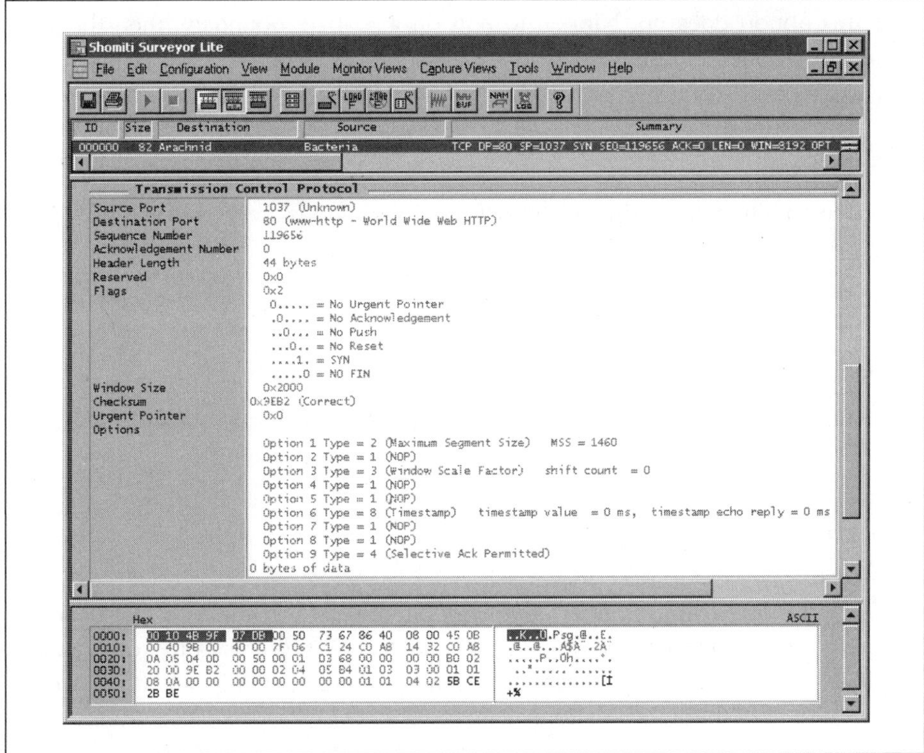

Figure 7-29. A TCP segment with some common TCP options

End of Option List

Used to mark the end of all the options in a TCP header.

Type

0

Size

Eight bits.

Defined In

RFC 793.

Status

Standard.

Notes

This option comes at the end of all the options, and not after every option. The End of Option List option does not have option-length or option-data fields. It is simply a one-byte option used to mark the end of all the options in a TCP header.

If this option does not happen to end on a 32-byte boundary, then the TCP header will need to be padded.

As you may have noticed from Figure 7-29, this option is not required.

No Operation

Used to internally pad the options field if multiple options are provided.

Type

1

Size

Eight bits.

Defined In

RFC 793.

Status

Standard.

Notes

If a TCP header has multiple options defined, then sometimes it makes sense to have them start on an even 32-bit boundary. When this is the case, multiple No Operation options can be chained together, filling out the space in between the other (real) options.

The No Operation option does not have option-length or option-data fields. It is simply a one-byte option used to internally pad the TCP header.

Capture Sample

In the capture shown in Figure 7-30, the No Operation option is used to internally pad the options field.

Maximum Segment Size

Used by both endpoints to publish their local MTU or MRU values during the circuit-setup process.

Type

2

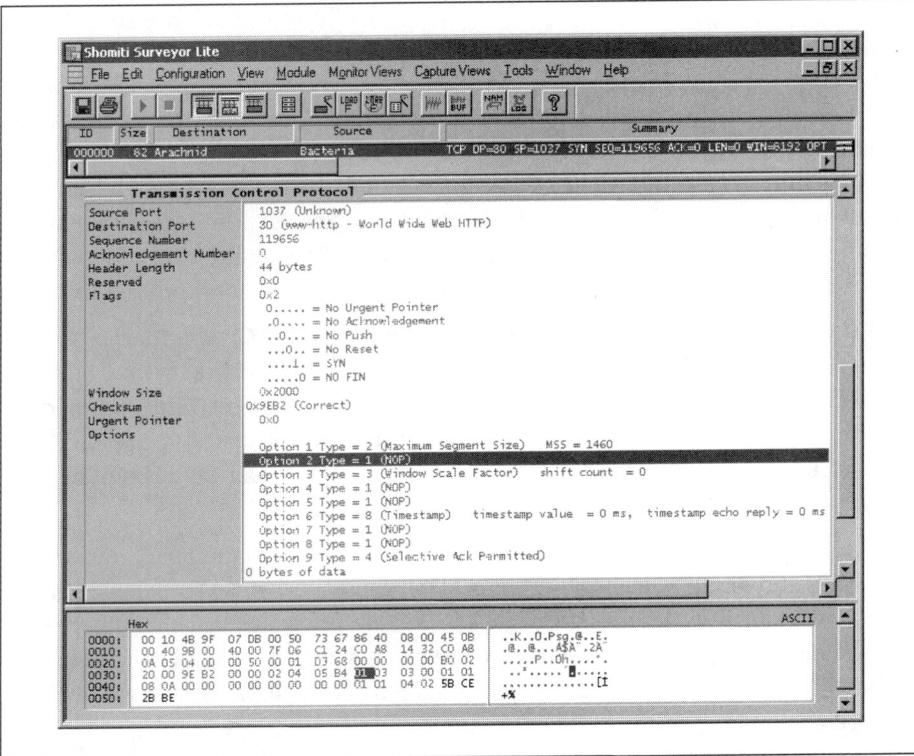

Figure 7-30. The No Operation option

Size

Thirty-two bits total (sixteen bits are used for the option-data field).

Option Fields

Table 7-5 lists the format of the Maximum Segment Size option.

Table 7-5. The Format of the Maximum Segment Size Option

Field	Size (Bytes)	Purpose
Option Type	1	Identifies this option as the Maximum Segment Size option
Option Size	1	Identifies the total length of the option (including all of the fields and data)
MRU	2	Used to publish the MRU (or more often, the MTU) of the local network

Defined In

RFC 793.

Status

Standard.

Notes

Before two endpoints can begin exchanging data, they must first understand the segment sizing restrictions that will be imposed upon them by the other end of the connection. Part of this process involves discovering the remote system's Maximum Transfer Unit or Maximum Receive Unit size. The Maximum Segment Size option provides this service, allowing the two endpoints to publish their local MTU/MRU sizes during the synchronization process.

When an application issues an "open" request to TCP, TCP will issue a startup segment with the Synchronize flag set, and with the local network's MRU or MTU information placed inside of the Maximum Segment Size option data field. The remote system will respond with a segment that also has the Synchronize flag set, and with its MRU or MTU size stored in the Maximum Segment Size option data field of the response segment.

The value advertised in the option-data field for the Maximum Segment Size option is typically the local system's MTU minus 40 bytes (20 bytes each for the TCP and IP headers). Although RFC 793 clearly states that the MSS option "communicates the maximum receive segment size," RFC 1122 changed this to be the largest size that can be reassembled. Most implementations use the MTU with this option.

Also, note that some systems do not take into consideration any extra IP options or TCP options that would reduce the maximum segment size being advertised, and only subtract 40 bytes from the MTU when sending this option. This setup may cause problems down the road, depending on the options that are being used on that circuit. For example, if the first segment has only this option defined, then none of the remaining segments will have any extra TCP options (so TCP does not need to leave room for any additional TCP options). However, if the systems agree to use the TCP Timestamp option and the Selective Acknowledgments option, then it is very likely that some segments will have those options, so the advertised value should leave room for the extra space. Otherwise, later segments may end up being larger than the maximum size advertised, and thus will be fragmented.

The Maximum Segment Size option must not appear in any segment other than the first two (the ones that contain the Synchronization flag), and must be ignored if it shows up anywhere else.

If a system does not specify a value with the Maximum Segment Size option, then RFC 1122 states that a default value of 536 (IP's default of 576 bytes, minus 40 bytes for the IP and TCP headers) should be used.

Capture Sample

In the capture shown in Figure 7-31, the Maximum Segment Size option shows 1460 bytes, which is the MTU of the local Ethernet network minus 40 bytes for the TCP and IP headers. Although the TCP header in this example is more than 20 bytes, the normal TCP header size (for the duration of the session) will only be 20 bytes long, so that is the value set aside by the Maximum Segment Size option.

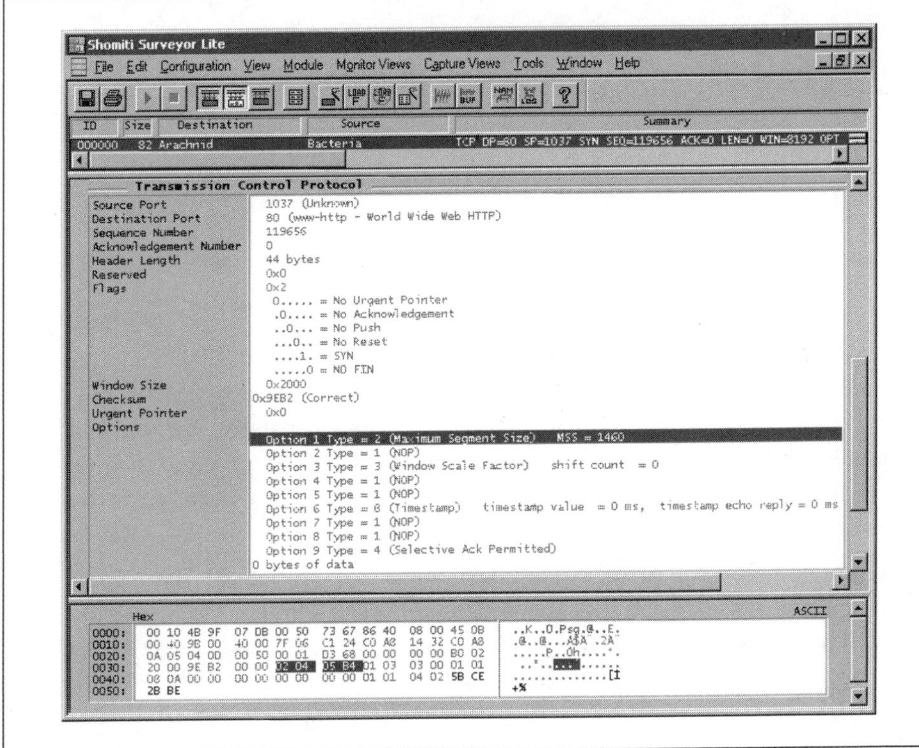

Figure 7-31. The Maximum Segment Size option

See Also

"MTU and MRU size considerations"

Window Scale

Used to publish receive buffer sizes that are larger than the 64 kilobytes allowed by the Window field of the TCP header.

Type

3

Size

Twenty-four bits total (eight bits for the option-data field).

Option Fields

Table 7-6 lists the format of the Window Scale option.

Table 7-6. The Format of the Window Scale Option

Field	Size (Bytes)	Purpose
Option Type	1	Identifies this option as the Window Scale option
Option Size	1	Identifies the total length of the option (including all of the fields and data)
Scale	1	Identifies the scale factor of the Window being advertised

Defined In

RFC 1323.

Status

Proposed standard.

Notes

Before two endpoints can begin exchanging data, they must first understand the buffer size restrictions that will be imposed upon them by the other end of the connection. Systems can only transmit as much data as the recipient can handle, and must wait for data to be acknowledged before attempting to send any more data. This is a key component of TCP's flow control and reliability services.

Although every TCP header contains a Window field that is used to advertise the current status of the sending system's receive buffers, this field is only 16 bits long. Thus, the maximum receive buffer size that can be advertised in the Window field is 64 kilobytes, which isn't large enough for many applications.

The Window Scale option provides a way around this hard limit, allowing the value advertised in the Window field to be scaled up to a maximum of one gigabyte. The Window Scale option does this by publishing the number of bit positions that the binary value advertised in the Window field should be shifted to the left.

If the Window field were advertising 16 bits in the "on" position (which would normally be interpreted as 64 kilobytes of buffer space), and the Window Scale option's option-data field showed a value of 4, then the 16 original bits would be shifted to the left by four places, becoming the 16 most-significant bits of a new 20-bit window value (now equal to one megabyte).

Both endpoints on a virtual circuit must agree to use the Window Scale option in order for it to be valid. If both systems do not agree to use the Window

Scale option, then both systems should assume that the other endpoint does not understand the option, and the Window field must be interpreted literally.

In order for both systems to use the Window Scale option, they must pass the option during the circuit-setup negotiation. The Window Scale option should not appear in any segment other than the first two segments (those containing the Synchronization flag), and should be ignored if it shows up anywhere else.

Note that the Window Scale option was originally defined in RFC 1072, with clarifications being made in RFC 1323. An alternative "Big Windows" option was defined in RFC 1106, although this option was experimental, and RFC 1106 has since expired. All production TCP implementations should use the Window Scale option as defined in RFC 1323, and none of them should use the Big Windows option defined in RFC 1106.

Capture Sample

In the capture shown in Figure 7-32, the Window Scale option shows 0, which indicates that this system understands the Window Scale option, but that this system is not using it for any data.

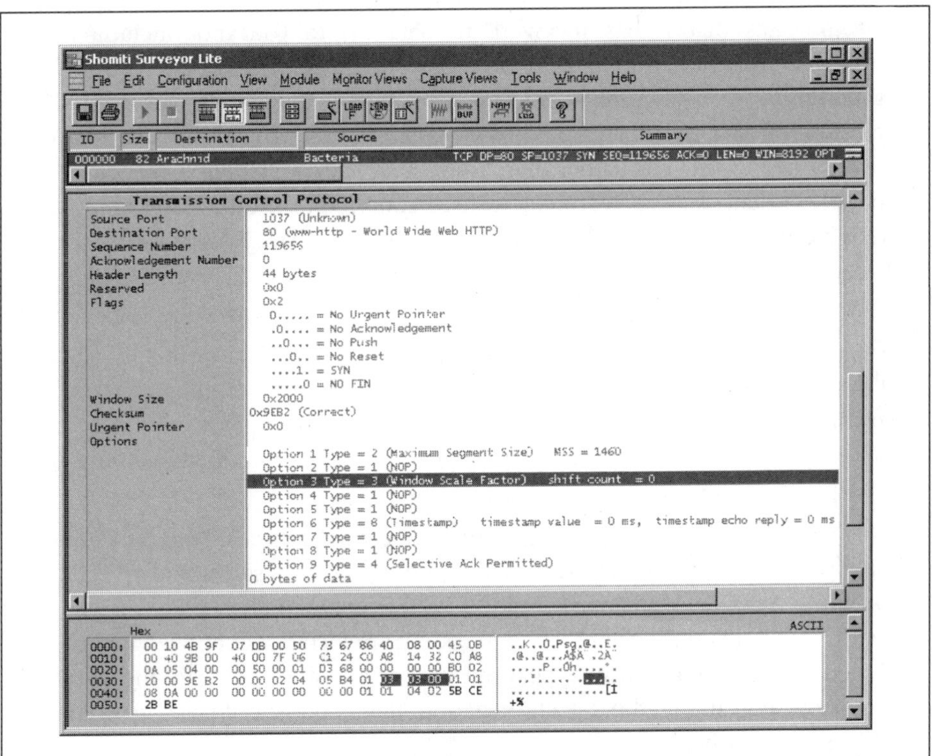

Figure 7-32. The Window Scale option

See Also

"Buffer size considerations"

"Receive window size adjustments"

Selective Acknowledgments Permitted

Indicates that selective acknowledgments are allowed on this virtual circuit.

Type

4

Size

Sixteen bits (the Selective Acknowledgment option does not use an option-data field).

Defined In

RFC 2018.

Status

Proposed standard.

Notes

TCP uses cumulative, implicit acknowledgments by default, whereby a recipient indicates that it has received all data up to (but not including) the sequence number represented in the Acknowledgment Identifier field. Although the use of cumulative, implicit acknowledgments works well when the flow of data is uninterrupted, it is a clumsy mechanism to use when data has not been received. Rather than being able to request that a particular segment be resent, the receiver must instead continue to use the last byte of consecutive data received in its acknowledgments. This may force the sender to retransmit all of the data from that point on, even though some of the data may have arrived safely.

The Selective Acknowledgment Data option (described later in this chapter) allows recipients to issue acknowledgments for specific ranges of data. Any missing segments can then be resent as discrete entities. However, before the Selective Acknowledgment Data option can be used, both systems must agree to support and use it.

This is achieved through the use of the Selective Acknowledgments Permitted option. During the initial handshake period, both systems must place the Selective Acknowledgments Permitted option in the TCP headers of the segments that contain the Synchronize flags. The Selective Acknowledgments Permitted option should not appear in any segment other than the first two segments containing the Synchronization flag, and should be ignored if it shows up anywhere else.

The Selective Acknowledgments Permitted option does not contain an option-data field. It only contains the option-type field (storing the option-type of 8), and a length field ("two bytes").

Capture Sample

In the capture shown in Figure 7-33, the Selective Acknowledgments Permitted option is being passed, indicating that this system understands how to deal with Selective Acknowledgments, should they be required.

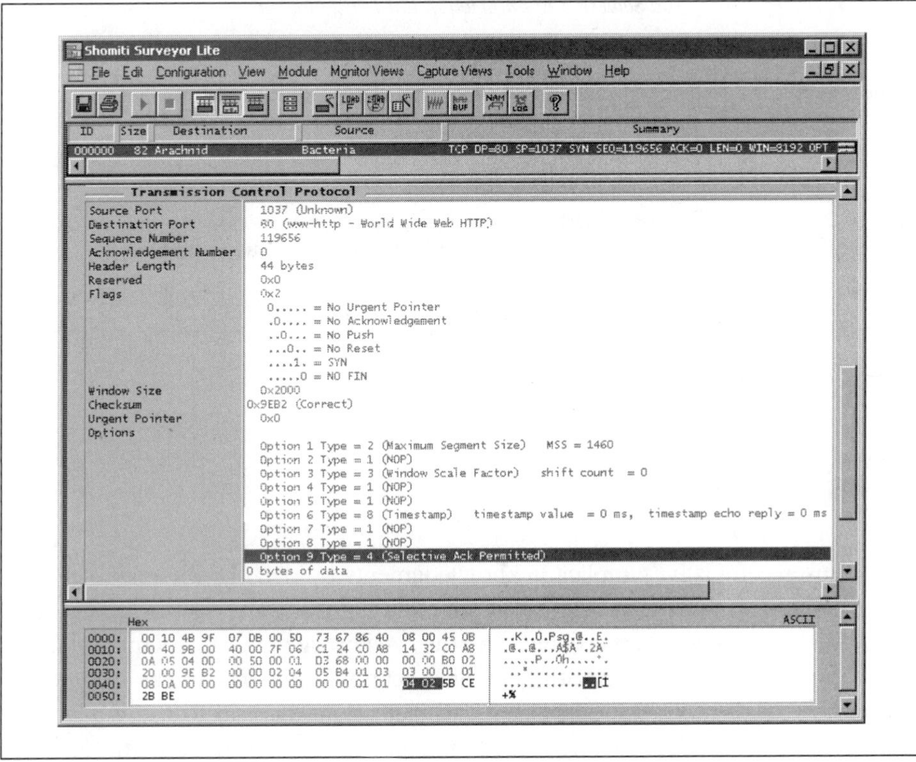

Figure 7-33. The Selective Acknowledgments Permitted option

See Also

"Selective Acknowledgment Data"

"Acknowledgment Identifier"

"Acknowledgment numbers"

Selective Acknowledgment Data

Used to report noncontiguous blocks of data received by a system.

Type

5

Size

Varies according to the number of blocks being acknowledged, but at least 10 bytes (eight bytes for the two sequence number boundaries used to identify a single block of data). The size of this field can expand to fill all available space if multiple blocks of data are reported simultaneously.

Option Fields

Table 7-7 lists the format of the Selective Acknowledgment Data option.

Table 7-7. The Format of the Selective Acknowledgment Data Option

Field	Size (Bytes)	Purpose
Option Type	1	Identifies this option as the Selective Acknowledgment Data option.
Option Size	1	Identifies the total length of the option (including all of the fields and data).
Start of Block	4	Marks the beginning of a higher, noncontiguous block of data that the sender has received successfully.
End of Block	4	Marks the end of a higher, noncontiguous block of data that the sender has received successfully.

Defined In

RFC 2018.

Status

Proposed standard.

Notes

TCP uses cumulative, implicit acknowledgments by default, whereby a recipient indicates that it has received all data up to (but not including) the sequence number represented in the Acknowledgment Identifier field. Although the use of cumulative, implicit acknowledgments works well when the flow of data is uninterrupted, it is a clumsy mechanism to use when data has not been received. Rather than being able to request that a particular segment be resent, the receiver must instead continue to use the last byte of consecutive data received in its acknowledgments. This may force the sender to retransmit all of the data from that point on, even though some of the data may have arrived safely.

The Selective Acknowledgment Data option allows for the use of selective acknowledgments, thereby allowing recipients to issue acknowledgments for specific ranges of data. Any missing data can then be resent. Selective Acknowledgments work by allowing a recipient to specify any blocks of data that have been received which are higher than the sequence number referenced to in the Acknowledgment Identifier field, and which are stored in the recipient's receive buffer. A sending system could then resend the missing blocks of data as discrete segments.

Each block of non-contiguous data that the recipient has received is specified with two fields in the Selective Acknowledgment Data option. The start-of-block field points to the sequence number of the first byte of non-contiguous data received, and the end-of-block field points to the sequence number of the last byte of non-contiguous data received. These fields can be repeated as many times as necessary, up to the maximum amount of free space available in the TCP header.

The Selective Acknowledgment Data option includes normal acknowledgment data that is combined with the Selective Acknowledgment Data option to identify the exact problem. If the recipient has received segments containing the byte ranges of one through 100 and 201 through 300, but is missing bytes 101 through 200, then a normal acknowledgment will be generated with the Acknowledgment Identifier pointing to sequence number 101. However, the TCP header of that acknowledgment segment would also contain a Selective Acknowledgment Data option that pointed to the byte range of 201 through 300, since those segments had been received. The original data sender would then recognize that sequence numbers 101 through 200 were missing, and retransmit just that data.

The Selective Acknowledgment Data option can appear in the header of any TCP segment that is acknowledging data, but may only be used on virtual circuits where both endpoints have agreed to use selective acknowledgments by way of the Selective Acknowledgments Permitted option.

Although the use of selective acknowledgments is still quite rare, it is becoming more common.

See Also

"Selective Acknowledgments Permitted"

"Acknowledgment Identifier"

"Acknowledgment numbers"

Timestamp

The Timestamp option allows both endpoints on a virtual circuit to constantly measure the latency between itself and the other end. Since the two endpoints may experience different levels of delay, both systems have to test the network independently, using a single option.

Type

8

Size

Ten bytes total (including two four-byte fields for timestamp data).

Option Fields

Table 7-8 lists the format of the Timestamp option

Table 7-8. The Format of the Timestamp Option

Field	Size (Bytes)	Purpose
Option Type	1	Identifies this option as the Timestamp option.
Option Size	1	Identifies the total length of the option (including all of the fields and data).
Timestamp Value	4	Used by the sender of this particular segment to place a timestamp into, for comparison upon receipt.
Timestamp Echo Reply	4	Used as a holder for the original value of the Timestamp Value field, prior to the Timestamp Value field being overwritten.

Defined In

RFC 1323.

Status

Proposed standard.

Notes

Before two endpoints can begin exchanging data, they must first understand the characteristics of the underlying network, particularly in terms of how much latency and delay a particular virtual circuit is experiencing. This is required, since understanding the round-trip delivery time is necessary in order to establish an appropriate threshold for the acknowledgment timers. Setting a low acknowledgment timer threshold on a slow network would result in an excessive amount of retransmissions, while setting a high acknowledgment timer threshold on a fast network would result in errors going unnoticed.

The Timestamp option provides a mechanism by which the round-trip delivery times for a specific virtual circuit can be detected. Whenever data is being sent, one of the two TCP endpoints places a timestamp into the Timestamp Value field. The receiver then responds by placing its own timestamp into the Timestamp Value field, and moving the original data into the Timestamp Echo Reply field. This process is repeated continually, with each system "acknowledging" the timestamp they have most-recently received. By continually repeating the process, both endpoints can constantly monitor the network for changing latency, thereby constantly updating their acknowledgment timer thresholds appropriately.

Since this model allows both systems to monitor the network—and because it relies on multiple exchanges—the Timestamp option can (and should) appear in most of the segments sent by any system that supports it. However, both systems also have to agree to use the Timestamp option, and as such it is required to be in the circuit-startup segments (those that contain the Synchronize flag). Note that many systems do not support this option, and its usage is still quite rare.

Capture Sample

In the capture shown in Figure 7-34, the Timestamp option shows a Timestamp Value of 0 (which is wrong; the specifications clearly state that the seed value should be derived from the system clock, using the current time), and a Timestamp Reply of 0 (which is correct, since this system has not yet received a Timestamp Value from the remote endpoint).

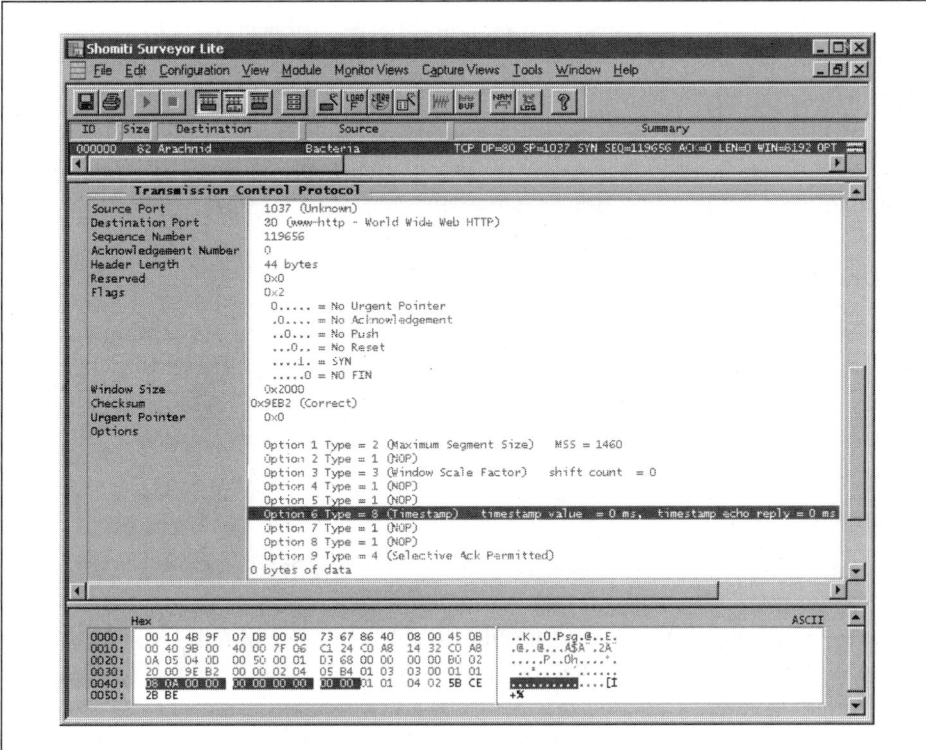

Figure 7-34. The Timestamp option

See Also

"Acknowledgment timers"

TCP in Action

Since TCP offers such a wide variety of services, it is easy to understand why so many applications choose to use it as a transport. Among the core services that TCP provides are application and network management, flow-control and reliability, all of which are implemented using TCP's virtual circuit architecture.

The thing to remember is that TCP's virtual circuit design is what makes all of the services offered by TCP possible. Without virtual circuits, TCP's buffering, flow control and reliability services would be much more difficult to implement. But by using this design, these services come for free, at least to the applications that use them.

In order to illustrate how these services work, a variety of diagrams and captures are shown throughout the remainder of this section. Figure 7-35 shows what happens during a TCP session, from the moment that an application is loaded until a circuit is terminated, while Figure 7-38 shows what happens on the wire when TCP opens and closes virtual circuits. Figure 7-39 shows what happens when many small segments are sent using an interactive application such as Echo, while "Bulk Data Transfer and Error Recovery" shows what happens when large blocks of data are sent using applications such as Chargen.

A Complete Session

Figure 7-35 shows a complete TCP session between an HTTP 1.0 client and server, taken from the examples given in "Opening a circuit," "Exchanging data," and "Closing a circuit." Although this example shows an overview of the steps, it does not provide detailed insight into each of the segments being sent between the two endpoints. This information will be shown later in this section.

The order of events are as follows:

1. Before anything else can happen, applications have to register with their local TCP provider, allocating a port number for use. In this example, the HTTP server has requested that port 80 (the well-known port number for HTTP) be opened in passive mode, allowing incoming requests from HTTP clients to get satisfied. For more information on TCP port numbering mechanism, refer to "Application addressing with TCP ports."
2. In this example, a user wishes to retrieve a document from the HTTP server, so he enters the URL of the document into the HTTP client. The HTTP client issues an active open request to the local TCP provider, which then begins the

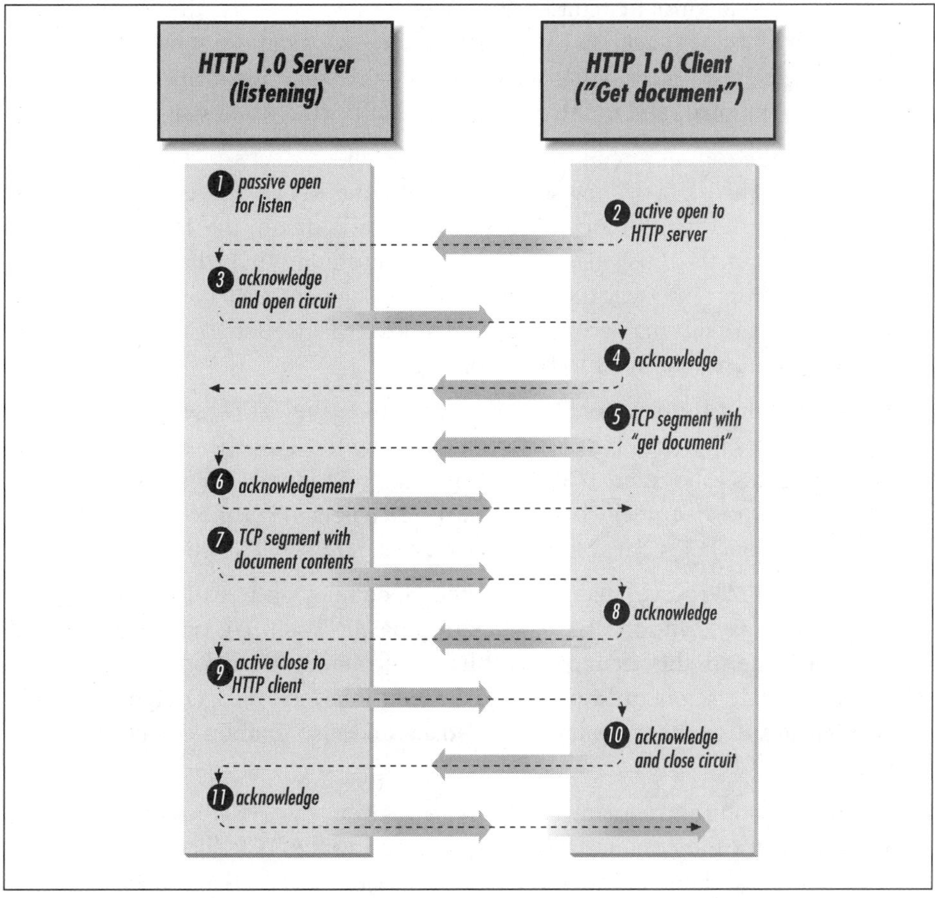

Figure 7-35. A complete TCP session

process of establishing a virtual circuit between the local and remote TCP systems. For more information on active and passive opens, refer to "Opening a circuit."

3. During the circuit-setup process, the TCP stack in use at the HTTP client sends a command segment to the TCP stack in use at the destination system. Since the HTTP server is operational and willing to accept the connection, the remote TCP provider responds with a similar command segment, allowing the virtual circuit to be established. Since this is a new virtual circuit, both segments must have the Synchronize flag enabled. In addition, the segment shown in step three must have the Acknowledge flag enabled, since it is a response to the original segment that was sent by the HTTP client's TCP software. For more information on the Synchronize and Acknowledgment flags, refer to "Control Flags."

4. In order for the virtual circuit to get established completely, the HTTP client's TCP stack must also acknowledge the Synchronize segment sent by the HTTP server. Once the server's TCP stack receives this acknowledgment, the circuit will be operational, and the two endpoints can begin exchanging data.
5. Now that the virtual circuit is up, the HTTP client issues a "GET document" command. This data is not sent directly to the HTTP server however, but instead is passed to the local TCP software. In addition, the HTTP client will likely have set the Push flag for this data, informing TCP that no additional data is coming. TCP will then create a TCP segment that contains this data, with the Push flag enabled in that segment's TCP header. For more information on the Push flag, refer to "Control Flags."
6. Upon receiving the segment issued in step five, the HTTP server's TCP provider validates the contents of the segment using the TCP checksum routines. If the segment is valid, then TCP passes the data off to the HTTP server, and then issue an acknowledgment back to the HTTP client's TCP provider. For more information on TCP's checksum characteristics, refer to "TCP checksums."
7. Once the HTTP server has located the document and read its contents, it writes the data to the local TCP stack, setting the Push flag once it is finished with the write. In this example, TCP has determined that all of the data will fit within a single segment (a process described in "Network I/O Management"), so it creates a segment containing the data, and also enables the Push flag on that segment.
8. Upon receiving the segment issued in step seven, the HTTP client's TCP provider validates the contents of the segment using the TCP checksum routines, and then issues an acknowledgment after passing the validated data off to the HTTP client application.
9. Once the HTTP server receives the acknowledgment issued in step eight, it requests TCP tear down the virtual circuit. TCP then issues a command segment with the Finish flag set to the remote HTTP client's TCP provider. Note that if this connection were using HTTP 1.1 instead of HTTP 1.0, the client would request the virtual circuit be closed, rather than the server. For more information on the Finish flag, refer to "Control Flags."
10. The HTTP client's TCP stack recognizes the request to tear-down the circuit, and if the HTTP client didn't object, TCP responds with a command segment that also had the Finish flag set. For more information on how virtual circuits are terminated, refer to "Closing a circuit."
11. Upon receiving the confirmation issued in step 10, the HTTP server's TCP provider issues an acknowledgment, and the virtual circuit would be terminated.

All told, ten unique segments are required in order to satisfy two simple operations (the "get document" request, and the sending of the document back to the client). Although this seems like a lot of overhead, this all happens fairly quickly. Furthermore, it only seems like a lot of wasted effort because everything went smoothly. If there had been any problems—such as a segment getting lost or corrupted—then it would be easier to appreciate the value that this overhead provides.

Also note that the session as shown in Figure 7-35 is just an example, and will not necessarily mirror the exact behavior that you will see in all cases. For example, some HTTP 1.0 servers do not gracefully close their virtual circuits, but instead simply force the connection closed immediately after sending the requested document, even though this causes huge problems whenever loss occurs, since the clients are unable to request lost data (the server isn't listening, and therefore won't process the retransmission request).

In addition, some servers will return an HTTP header before the document itself, using a separate application write. This would result in a single small segment being written before the document contents were returned to the client, which may or may not result in another acknowledgment. The point is that implementations vary widely, and the example shown here is just an example of how one implementation may do it, which is not to say that all implementations will do it in the same way.

Notes on Virtual Circuit State Changes

Whenever a TCP-based application is loaded, the application has to register with TCP. Server applications do this whenever they issue a passive open, while clients do this whenever they issue an active open to a server.

Once registered, applications are linked with virtual circuits, with the virtual circuits going through a variety of different changes throughout the circuit's lifetime. For example, when a server is first loaded it enters the "LISTEN" state, where it sits and waits for a connection request. When a connection request arrives, the virtual circuit goes into the "SYN-RECEIVED" state (signifying that a connection request has arrived). Once the handshake is finished—but before any data is exchanged across the virtual circuit—the virtual circuit changes to the "ESTABLISHED" state, and when the applications are finished, the virtual circuit enters one of many different "ENDING" states, depending upon who terminated the circuit and how.

Most operating systems provide tools for monitoring the connectivity state of the virtual circuits that are currently in use on that particular system. This information is useful for debugging TCP, and for also monitoring the network activity on the system. On most Unix and derivative systems, this information can be gleaned by issuing the *netstat* command. The output of this command will be similar to what is shown in Figure 7-36.

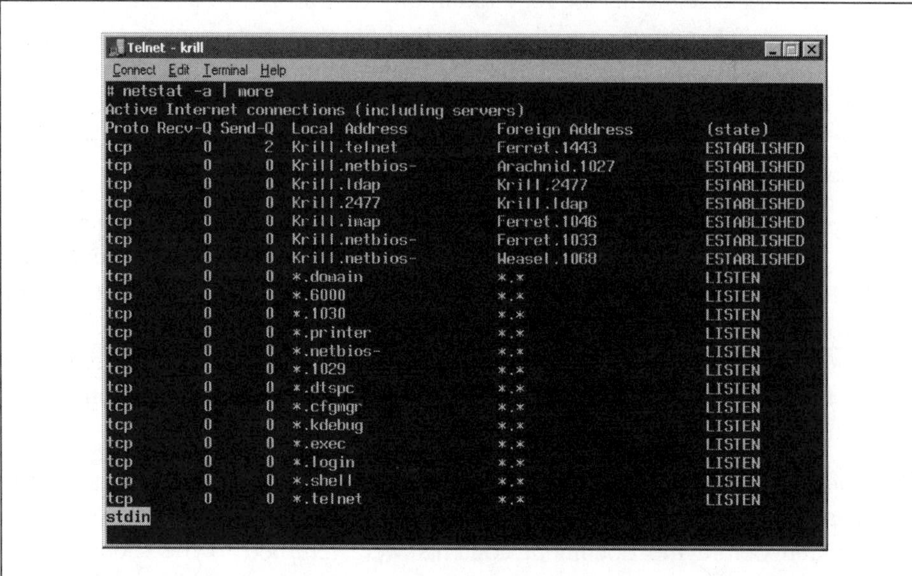

Figure 7-36. Using netstat to view the state of active virtual circuits

Each virtual circuit will be in different states at different times, depending upon their current situation. Table 7-9 lists the common states that TCP virtual circuits go through, and their meaning.

Table 7-9. The Various Circuit States and Their Meanings

Circuit State	Description
LISTEN	A server application has been loaded, and has opened a port in passive mode. TCP is now waiting for incoming connection requests.
SYN-SENT	A client application on the local system has issued an active open to a remote host. TCP has sent a startup segment with the Synchronize flag enabled, and is waiting for the remote system to respond with a startup segment that also has the Synchronize flag enabled.
SYN-RECEIVED	TCP on the server has received a startup segment with the Synchronize flag enabled from a remote client, has responded with its own startup segment, and is now waiting on an acknowledgment for that segment.
ESTABLISHED	The virtual circuit is operational. This state occurs on both endpoints once the three-way handshake has completed.
FIN-WAIT-1	The local application has issued an active close for the virtual circuit, and TCP has sent a shutdown segment with the Finish flag enabled. However, TCP is still waiting for the remote system to acknowledge the segment and respond with a shutdown segment of its own. No additional data will be sent from this system, although data will be accepted from the remote system until the circuit is completely terminated.

Table 7-9. The Various Circuit States and Their Meanings (continued)

Circuit State	Description
CLOSE-WAIT	A shutdown segment with the Finish flag enabled has been received (as discussed in FIN-WAIT-1), and the local TCP has returned an acknowledgment for that segment back to the sender. However, the local TCP cannot respond with its own shutdown segment until the local application issues its own close operation, which has not yet occurred.
FIN-WAIT-2	The local TCP has sent a shutdown segment with the Finish flag enabled (as described in FIN-WAIT-1), and an acknowledgment has arrived from the remote endpoint for that segment (as described in CLOSE-WAIT above). However, the remote application has not yet performed a close operation, preventing the remote TCP from issuing its own shutdown segment.
LAST-ACK	A shutdown segment with the Finish flag enabled has been received (as discussed in FIN-WAIT-1), and the local application has approved the shutdown request by issuing its own close operation. This results in the local TCP sending its own shutdown segment with the Finish flag enabled, although the circuit will not be destroyed until an acknowledgment for this shutdown segment is received.
CLOSING	This state is somewhat rare, and typically indicates that a segment has been lost on the network. In this case, the local TCP has sent a shutdown segment with the Finish flag enabled (as described in FIN-WAIT-1 above), and a shutdown segment has been received from the remote endpoint (as described in LAST-ACK), although the remote system has not yet sent an acknowledgment for the shutdown segment that was sent by the local system in FIN-WAIT-1. This normally indicates that the acknowledgment was lost in transit.
TIME-WAIT	The circuit-shutdown operation has completed, but TCP is keeping the socket open for a while to allow for any laggard segments that might have gotten lost en route. This is to prevent any new connections to that port number from accidentally reusing any sequence numbers that may have been used in the previous connection. Note that this state occurs only on the host that issued the active close, since the remote system is not likely to receive any more data from the terminating host.
CLOSED	Nothing is happening; the circuit is closed and TCP has released all of the resources it had been using with the virtual circuit. This state should never appear since there would not be a virtual circuit to show.

Notice that there is a pretty straightforward series of events that are followed when the virtual circuit is established, although there can be several different states that an endpoint can go through when a virtual circuit is terminated. That is because the model for establishing connections is almost always the same (as described in "Opening a circuit"), while the shutdown sequence can take a variety of different paths, with either the client or server initiating the action, and doing so in a number of different ways at different junctures in the data-exchange process.

Figure 7-37 shows a simple operation, with the circuit being terminated in a clean, orderly sequence by an HTTP server.

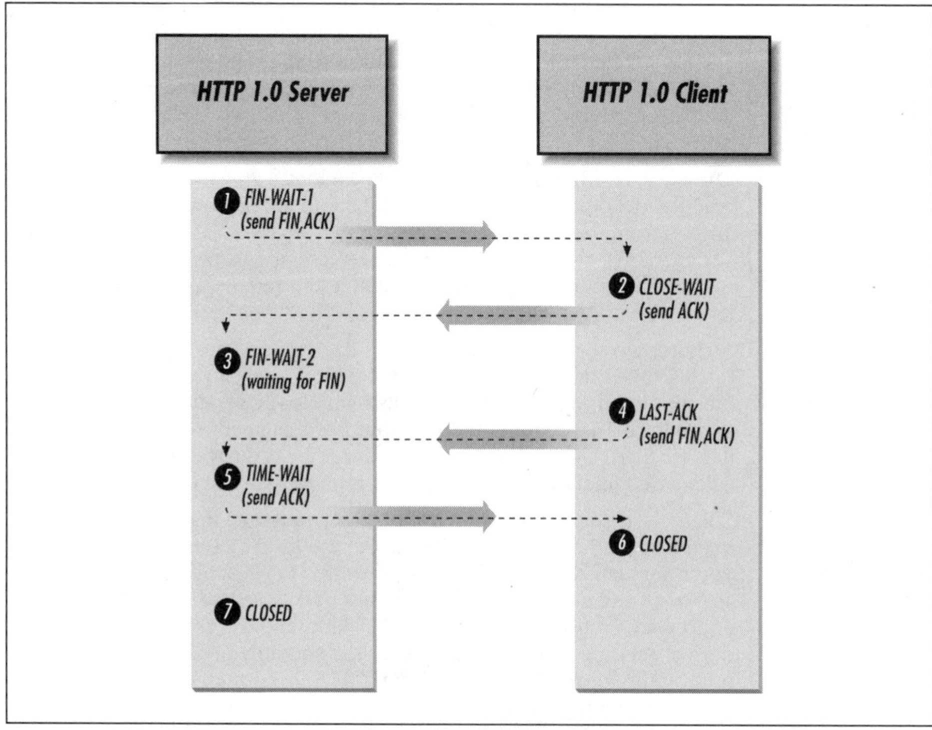

Figure 7-37. A simple circuit-shutdown sequence of state-changes

In the example shown in Figure 7-37, the following state-changes have occurred:

1. The HTTP server issued a close-for-send, resulting in the TCP stack sending a shutdown request to the remote endpoint (a segment with the Finish and Acknowledgment flags enabled, although the acknowledgment is for the last-accepted byte of data). This is the FIN-WAIT-1 state.
2. The client's TCP stack receives the request, and issues an acknowledgment for the segment. However, it has to inform the client of the shutdown request—and wait for the client' s approval—before responding with its own Finish flag. At this point, the client's TCP stack is in the CLOSE-WAIT state.
3. The server's TCP stack goes into the FIN-WAIT-2 state, while it waits for the client to respond with a Finish flag.
4. The HTTP client approves the shutdown request, so the TCP stack on that system sends a shutdown segment with the Finish flag enabled (and repeats the acknowledgment returned in step 2). The client has entered the LAST-ACK

state, and as soon as the server's TCP returns an acknowledgment it will close the circuit completely and then enter the TIME-WAIT state.

5. Once the server's TCP stack receives the Finish flag sent in step 4, it will return an acknowledgment and completely close the circuit. The server's TCP stack will then go into the TIME-WAIT state, where it monitors the local socket for any spurious segments that may arrive late. After waiting for two times the maximum segment lifetime, the socket will enter the CLOSED state. (The server is the only one to enter TIME-WAIT since it issued the active close.)
6. Upon receiving the acknowledgment sent in step 5, the client's TCP stack will close the connection completely and enters the CLOSED state or disappears entirely.
7. After the server's TIME-WAIT timer expires, the virtual circuit will enter the CLOSED state or disappear entirely. However, there will still likely be at least one occurrence of the HTTP server still sitting in the LISTEN state, waiting for new connection requests.

This is a simple example of how things are supposed to work. However, that does not mean that things always go this way. Many times segments get lost at the end of the connection, and when that occurs the two endpoints can choose to close the circuit down anyway. This may result in a lot of Reset segments, since the other endpoint may not be fully aware of the circuit shutdown. For more information on how to tell when this has happened, refer to "Lots of Reset Command Segments."

Opening and Closing Virtual Circuits

Figure 7-38 shows a dataless TCP session between a Discard client and server. The Discard client on Arachnid connects to the Discard server on Greywolf, and then disconnects. No data is sent between the two systems whatsoever.

Discard is a simple application that takes characters from a client and then throws them away. Since Discard does so little, it is really only useful for testing basic TCP connectivity between two systems.

The order of events are as follows:

1. The first segment sent in the exchange is the circuit-setup request, being sent from port 4854 on Arachnid to port 9 (the well-known port number for Discard servers) on Greywolf. This segment is being used to initialize the virtual circuit, and as such has the Synchronize flag set. Furthermore, this segment is advertising a beginning sequence number of 138,806. In addition, notice that the Acknowledgment flag is not set and that the Acknowledgment Identifier field is set to zero. Since this is the first segment to be sent, there is nothing to

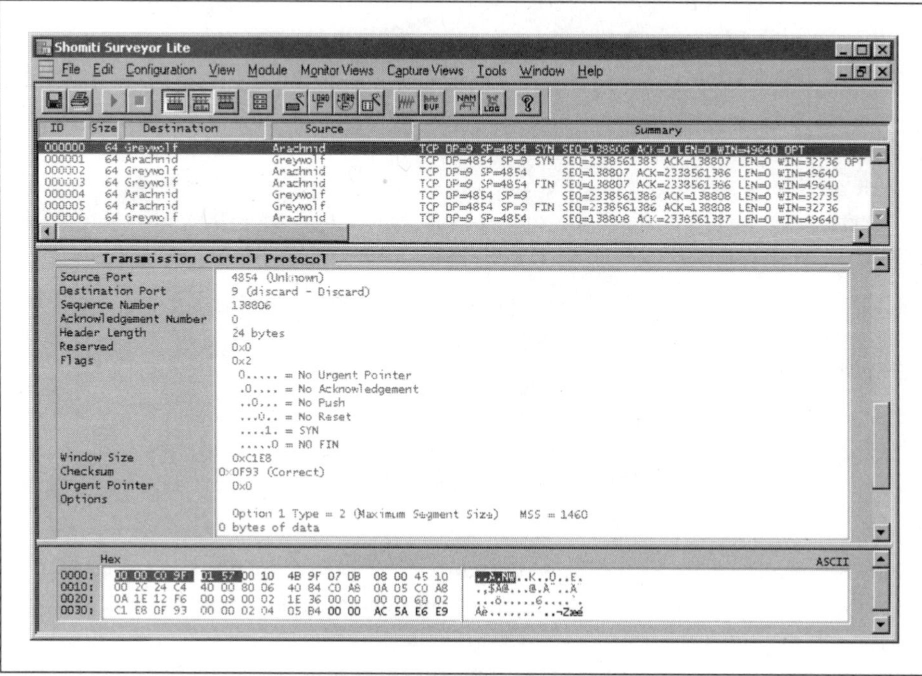

Figure 7-38. A Discard client exchanging data with a Discard server

acknowledge, so these fields are cleared. For more information on these flags, refer to "Control Flags."

Also, since this is the first segment, the Maximum Segment Size option is being used to advertise Arachnid's MRU (minus 40 bytes for the IP and TCP headers). For more information on the MSS option, refer to "Maximum Segment Size."

At this point, Arachnid is in the SYN-SENT state.

2. Segment two is a response from Greywolf back to Arachnid, agreeing to open the virtual circuit. This is identifiable by the Synchronize flag also being set. Also, notice that Greywolf is advertising its own sequence number (2,338,561,385), and is also using the Maximum Segment Size option to advertise the local MRU.

   Furthermore, since this is a response to segment one, this segment has the Acknowledgment flag enabled, with the Acknowledgment Identifier pointing to the next byte of data that Greywolf expects to receive from Arachnid (138,807).

   At this point, Greywolf is in the SYN-RECEIVED state.

3. In order to complete the handshake process, Arachnid's TCP stack returns an acknowledgment for segment two in segment three. Since the circuit-setup is now completed, the Synchronize flag is not set in this segment. However, the Acknowledgment flag is enabled, with the Acknowledgment Identifier pointing to the next byte of data that Arachnid expects to receive from Greywolf (2,338,561,386).

   In addition, notice that the Sequence Identifier of this segment has been incremented (now being set at 138,807). In order for TCP to track circuit-startup and shutdown messages as distinct entities, it uses special sequence numbers for these segments that are outside the range of sequence numbers that may be used by any data sent across the virtual circuit. Although no data is being sent over this connection, TCP is still incrementing the local sequence number in case any data does get sent, thereby keeping the startup sequence number unique. For more information on sequence numbers and their usage with command segments, refer to "Sequence numbers."

   Once this acknowledgment is received by Greywolf, both systems will be in the ESTABLISHED state.

4. The Discard client on Arachnid requests that the virtual circuit be terminated, resulting in the local TCP stack issuing a segment with the Finish bit set. Notice that the Sequence Identifier of this segment is still set at 138,807. Since no data was sent, the sequence number remains unchanged. If any data had been sent however, then the sequence number would have been incremented.

   At this point, Arachnid is in the FIN-WAIT-1 state.

5. Greywolf issues an acknowledgment for the segment it just received. However, notice that this response does not have the Finish flag enabled. Remember that in order for a close to complete, the applications in use on the virtual circuit have to agree to the request. While Greywolf is off getting permission from the Discard server to terminate the connection, it goes ahead and returns an acknowledgment for the request, so that Arachnid will know that the request was received. Once the request has been approved by the Discard server, then Greywolf will respond to the circuit-termination request with a segment that also has the Finish flag set.

   At this point, Greywolf is in the CLOSE-WAIT state. Once Arachnid receives this acknowledgment, it will be in the FIN-WAIT-2 state.

6. Greywolf issues another segment almost immediately, this time setting the Finish flag, and repeating the acknowledgment number issued in segment five.

   At this point, Greywolf is in the LAST-ACK state.

7. In order to terminate the circuit, Arachnid must issue an acknowledgment to Greywolf, indicating that it received the circuit-termination confirmation sent

in segment six. In addition, notice that the Sequence Identifier of this segment has been incremented (now being set at 2,351,319,118). This allows the acknowledgment to the shutdown request to be tracked independently of the request itself.

Arachnid is the only host in the TIME-WAIT state. Greywolf goes into the CLOSED state, or the circuit disappears from the state table.

What's most interesting about this example is that no end-user data was sent at all. Rather, the Discard client on Arachnid connected to the Discard server on Greywolf, and then disconnected almost immediately. Remember that TCP does not care about data whatsoever, and instead focuses strictly on managing virtual circuits. Whether or not an application chooses to send data has no effect on TCP's circuit-management duties.

Interactive Data Exchange

Figure 7-39 shows a simple TCP session between an Echo client and server. The Echo client on Arachnid connects to the Echo server on Greywolf, sends the characters "t," "e," "s," and "t," and then disconnects.

Echo is a simple application that takes characters from a client and then echoes the characters back. As such, Echo is a good example of how TCP handles interactive applications that send and receive many small segments.

The order of events are as follows:

1. [Segments 0–2] The Echo client on Arachnid allocates a TCP client port (4868), and establishes a TCP connection with the Discard server's well-known port (TCP port 7) on Greywolf.
2. [3] The Echo client sends the letter "t" (hex 74). In addition, notice that the Sequence Identifier of this segment has been incremented by one (now being set at 138,921) allowing data that is sent after the circuit has been established to be tracked separately from the segments used to establish the connection. Also, notice that the Push flag is set on this segment, indicating that the application requested that TCP clear the send buffer immediately, an act that also forces the recipient to clear its receive buffer immediately as well. For more information on the Push function, refer to "Data considerations."
3. [4] Greywolf's Echo server responds to the segment by returning a segment that contains the same data that it received. Notice that this segment also has the Acknowledgment flag enabled, with the Acknowledgment Identifier field pointing to sequence number 138,922. Because one byte of data was received, Greywolf has added one byte to the Sequence Identifier of the segment that it received from Arachnid, and is using the resulting value to identify the next

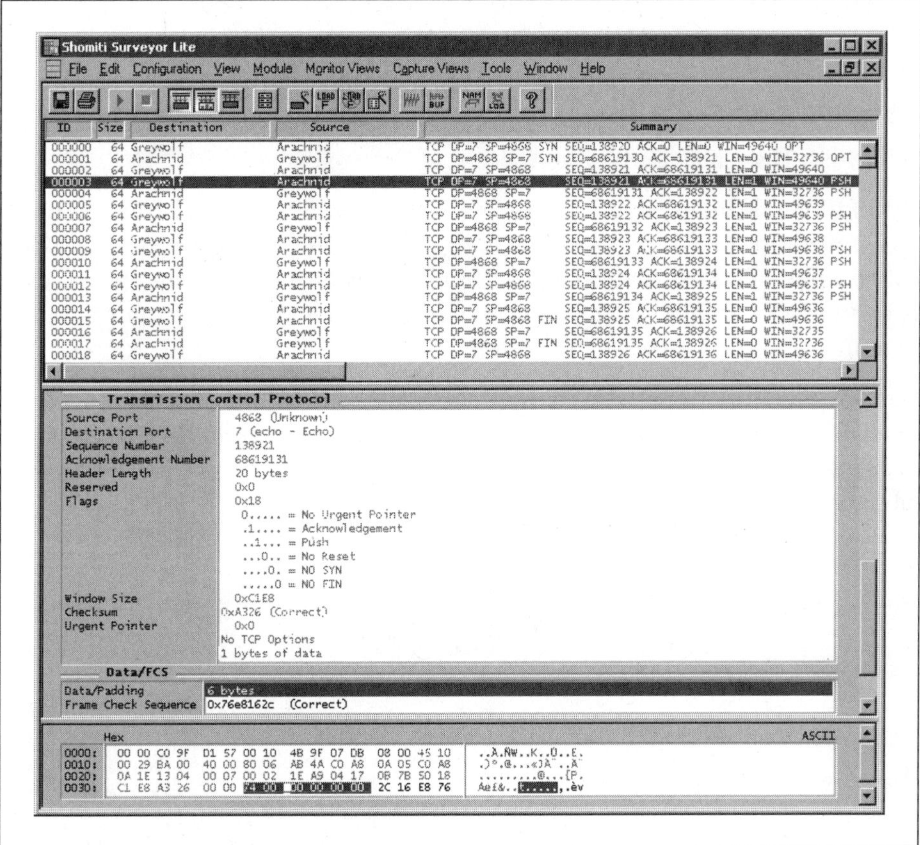

Figure 7-39. An Echo client exchanging data with an Echo server

byte of data it is expecting to receive from Arachnid. For more information on how acknowledgment numbers are chosen, refer to "Acknowledgment numbers."

The important detail here is that Greywolf has consolidated the acknowledgment to segment number three with the outbound data (the echo reply), thereby eliminating the need to send two distinct segments. For more information on this subject, refer to "Delayed acknowledgments."

4. [5] When Arachnid receives the echoed data back from Greywolf, it must acknowledge it. However, unlike segment four, there is no additional data being returned to Greywolf right now, so the acknowledgment is sent on its own. Also, notice that the acknowledgment number used in this segment points to the next byte of data that Arachnid expects to receive from Greywolf, which is one byte plus the sequence number used by Greywolf when

the echoed data was sent to Arachnid. This process really illustrates the full-duplex nature of TCP virtual circuits.

5. [6–14] The process described in steps 2 through 4 are repeated for the letters "e," "s" and "t."
6. [15–18] The virtual circuit is torn down.

The most important aspect of this session is the way in which the sequence numbers and acknowledgments work hand-in-glove on a fully bidirectional basis. Since TCP is a true full-duplex transport, each endpoint is allowed to send as much data as required by the applications in use. As such, each endpoint must provide their own unique sequence numbers, which must be acknowledged by the recipient.

Another interesting aspect of this capture is the way in which the Echo server combines its acknowledgments with the echoed data being sent back to the Echo client. By delaying the acknowledgment until there is data to be sent, Greywolf substantially reduces the number of segments required.

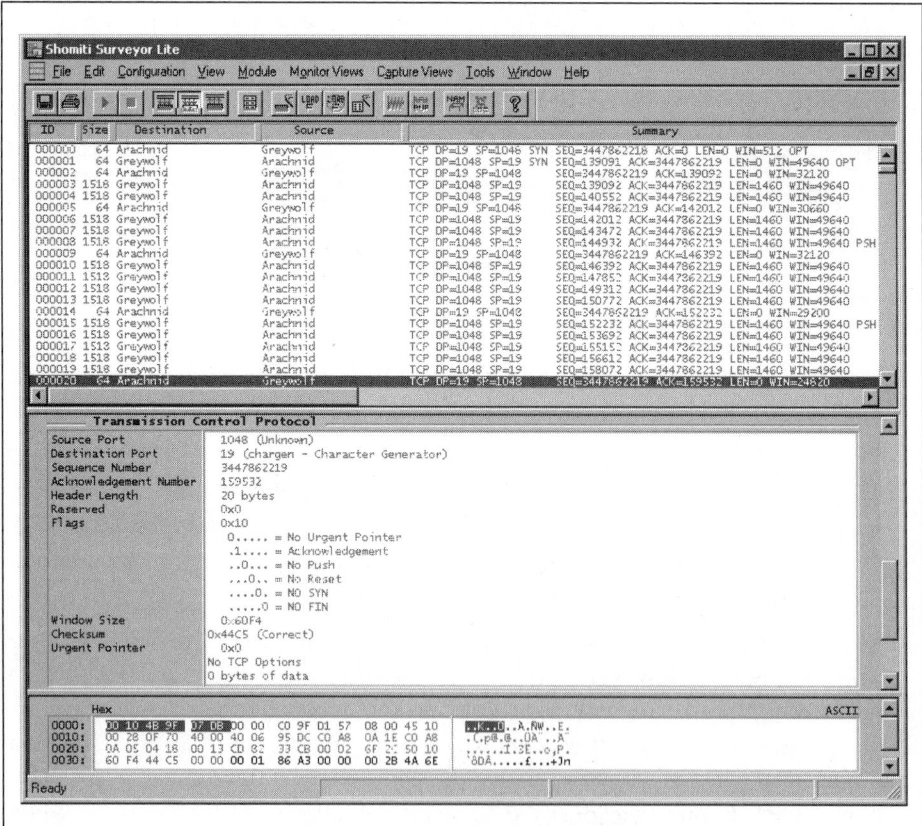

Figure 7-40. A Chargen client exchanging data with a Chargen server

Bulk Data Transfer and Error Recovery

Figure 7-40 shows a more-complex TCP session between Greywolf (the Chargen client) and Arachnid (a Chargen server). Greywolf connects to Arachnid and receives several segments of data. Due to a variety of events, this session gets fairly complicated. As such, the discussion is continued in Figure 7-41, Figure 7-42, and Figure 7-43.

Chargen is a simple application that generates streams of character data as soon as a connection is established. Chargen sends the data as a continuous stream, with the stream being broken into segments according to the segment-sizing calculations performed during circuit setup (as described in "Network I/O Management"). As such, Chargen is a good example of how TCP handles applications that send large quantities of data.

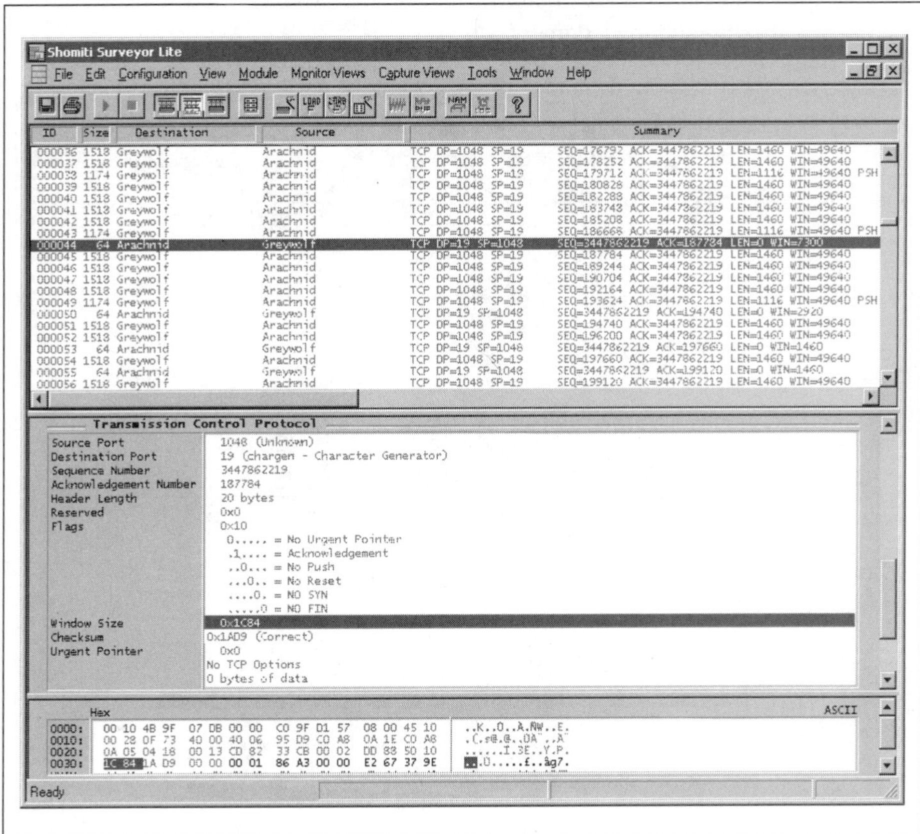

Figure 7-41. Chargen data exchange, continued

The order of events are as follows:

1. [Segments 0–2] The Chargen client on Greywolf allocates a TCP client port (1048), and establishes a TCP connection with the Chargen server's well-known port (TCP port 19) on Arachnid.
2. [3–4] Once the circuit is established, the Chargen server on Greywolf immediately starts sending data to the Chargen client on Arachnid. Notice that Arachnid sends two segments, and then waits for Greywolf to return an acknowledgment for that data. This will be shown to be an important detail in a moment.
3. [5] Greywolf acknowledges the data sent in segments three and four, and increments the byte number used in the Sequence Number field to show that these segments are different from the ones used in the circuit-setup procedure.
4. [6–8] Arachnid sends three more segments back-to-back, and then pauses to wait for another acknowledgment.

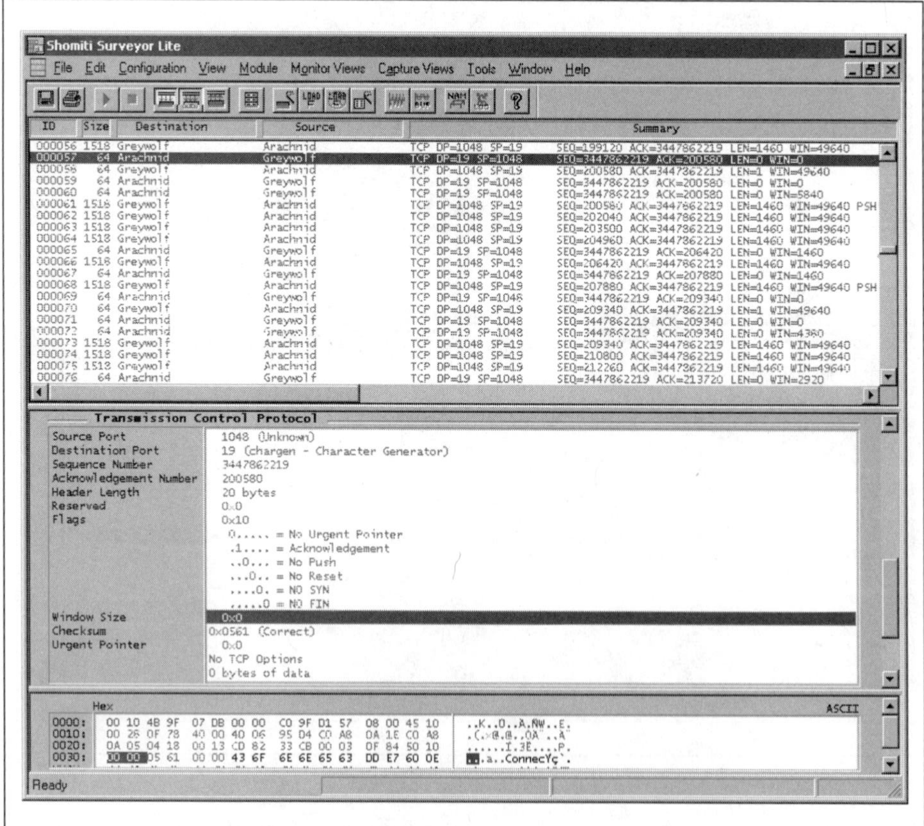

Figure 7-42. Chargen data exchange, continued

5. [7–9] Greywolf acknowledges the data.
6. [10–13] Arachnid sends four more segments and then stops. This linear growth pattern would seem to indicate that Arachnid is using the congestion avoidance algorithm to enlarge the size of its congestion window, rather than using slow start. Congestion avoidance increments the size of the sender's congestion window by one segment whenever an acknowledgment is received for all of the segments already issued (linear growth), while slow start increments the sender's congestion whenever *any* segment is acknowledged (exponential growth). Since Arachnid is only sending one additional segment before stopping to wait for an acknowledgment, it appears that congestion avoidance is being used instead of slow start. For more information on these mechanisms, refer to "Slow start" and "Congestion avoidance."

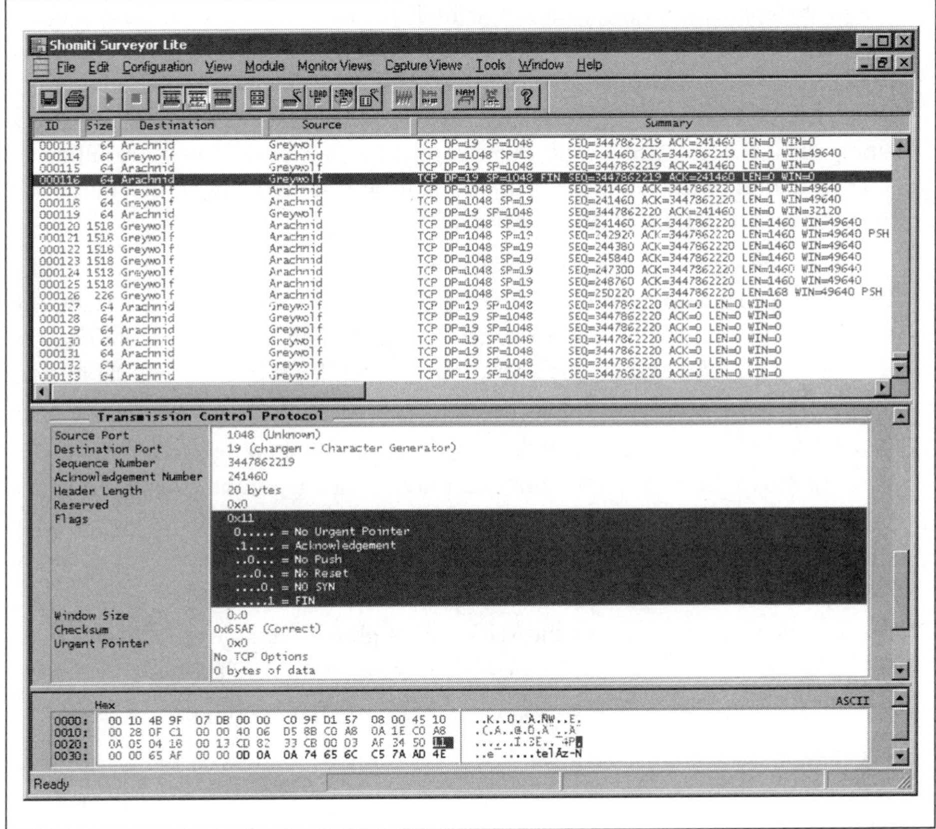

Figure 7-43. Chargen data exchange, continued

7. [14] Greywolf acknowledges all of the data sent. However, notice that the size of Greywolf's receive window (as advertised by the Window field of the TCP

header) is starting to shrink a little bit, suggesting that it is not able to process the data as fast as it is coming in.

8. [15–19] Arachnid sends five more segments.
9. [20] Greywolf acknowledges all of the segments, but its Window is still shrinking.

   This process continues through segment 44, with Arachnid sending one extra segment before stopping to wait for an acknowledgment, while Greywolf continues to acknowledge all of the data that it has received (although its Window continues to shrink).

   One other pattern that is beginning to emerge is that Arachnid is setting the Push flag on every fifth segment. This pattern indicates that the Chargen server on Arachnid is handing data to TCP in chunks of 7,300 bytes each. Whenever this write occurs, then the data is "pushed" to TCP, who sets the Push flag on the outgoing segment. This does not affect the delivery of the data, since the application writes are a multiple of the maximum segment size. Otherwise, the segments containing the Push flag would probably be less than full-sized, since all of the data up to the Push would be sent immediately, resulting in smaller-than-normal segments. For more information on how the Push flag affects delivery, refer to "Data considerations."

10. [Segment 44] Greywolf has been given eight segments, and it is acknowledging them all. However, by this point the size of its receive window has shrunk to the point where it will start to affect Arachnid's ability to send more data. In this case, the Window advertisement only shows 7,300 bytes of available storage in Greywolf's receive queue.
11. [45–49] Arachnid sees the small Window. Instead of sending nine segments as would be expected from the congestion avoidance algorithm, Arachnid sends only five segments, since that is all that would fit within the smaller receive queue (5 segments of 1460 bytes = 7300 bytes, the size of Greywolf's receive queue).
12. [50] Greywolf acknowledges the data, although it is unable to process all of the data right away, and the Window field only shows 2,920 bytes.
13. [51–52] Arachnid sends two segments, which is all that would fit.
14. [53] Greywolf acknowledges the data, but only advertises a 1460-byte Window.
15. [54] Arachnid sends one segment.
16. [55–56] The process described in steps 14 through 15 are repeated.

17. [Segment 57] This time, Greywolf returns a zero-length Window advertisement along with the acknowledgment, suggesting that it cannot accept any more data at this time.
18. [58] Arachnid sends a window probe to Greywolf, checking to see if the receive queue has opened up any. Looking at the length of this segment, we can tell that this is a one-byte probe, and based on the Sequence number that is being provided, we can tell that Arachnid is trying to send the next byte of data (but just the next byte) as its probing mechanism. For more information on window probing, refer to "Receive window size adjustments."
19. [59] Greywolf responds to the probe with another zero-length window. Notice that the acknowledgment number still points to 200580, which is the same as it was in the zero-length window advertisement sent in step 17.
20. [60] A few moments later, Greywolf sends an unsolicited acknowledgment to Arachnid with a Window size of 5,840 bytes. This would indicate that Greywolf has processed some of the data in its receive queue, and is ready to receive more data. This use of an solicited acknowledgment is called a "window update," and is documented in "Receive window size adjustments."
21. [61–64] Arachnid sends four segments, to fill the window.
22. [65–68] Greywolf responds with a 1460-byte Window advertisement, which Arachnid fills with another segment, and these steps are repeated.
23. [69] Greywolf sends another zero-length Window advertisement.
24. [70–75] Arachnid sends another window probe, which Greywolf responds to with another zero-length Window advertisement. After a while, Greywolf advises that it can handle 4380 bytes of data, which Arachnid sends as three segments.
25. [76–115] Greywolf advises a 2920-byte window, which Arachnid fills. Things never really get off the ground again, and Greywolf continues to alternate between small and zero-length Window advertisements, while Arachnid continues trying to send whatever data it can.
26. [Segment 116] The Chargen client on Greywolf informs its local TCP stack that it is going to close down. This results in Greywolf sending a circuit-shutdown request segment to Arachnid. Notice however that Greywolf is still advertising a zero-length window. Although Greywolf cannot currently accept any data, it will be able to send a shutdown message, which Greywolf must be able to accept. At this point, Greywolf is in the FIN-WAIT-1 state.
27. [117] Arachnid returns an acknowledgment for the shutdown request. However, it does not return its own shutdown-request segment (the Chargen server must approve the request first). At this point, Arachnid is in the CLOSE-WAIT

state, although it may also try to send any data that is waiting in the outbound queue.

28. [118] Arachnid sends another window probe to Greywolf. Apparently, there is still a substantial amount of data in Arachnid's send queue, which must be dealt with before the virtual circuit can be terminated.

29. [119] Greywolf returns a fairly large Window size advertisement in response to the window probe sent in step 28. Greywolf has also received the acknowledgment for the shutdown request it sent in step 27, so it is now in the FIN-WAIT-2 state.

30. [120–126] Arachnid sees the large window, and sends five full-sized segments plus one small segment to Greywolf in a burst (this is probably data that Arachnid had in the send queue). Once this data was acknowledged, Arachnid would likely send a circuit-shutdown segment of its own, in response to the one sent by Greywolf in step 26.

31. [127–133] However, Greywolf is not waiting around for Arachnid to issue a shutdown segment, and instead has closed the connection permanently. Since the TCP stack on Greywolf has nowhere to send the data that it just received, it rejects each of the segments (although this information is not visible from this capture, each of the segments sent during this step all have the Reset flag enabled). As a result of this action, Arachnid closes its end of the connection immediately as well. Greywolf enters the TIME-WAIT state. Greywolf had issued the active close in Step 26.

A variety of TCP's concepts are illustrated in this example. For one thing, notice that bulk data transfers act quite a bit differently from the interactive applications shown earlier in "Interactive Data Exchange." Rather than each endpoint sending small data segments, only one end is transferring data in this example. As such, issues such as flow control and congestion management are much more important.

The congestion management is most easily seen in this example, whereby the amount of data that Arachnid could send was severely constrained by the size of its local congestion window, as well as the size of Greywolf's receive window. Another interesting aspect to this exchange is the fact that Arachnid did not use the slow start mechanisms at any time, although it should have done so at the very beginning. Instead, Arachnid used the congestion avoidance algorithm to ramp up the size of its congestion window.

Note that Arachnid was not sending acknowledgments every other segment, as recommended by RFC 1122. Instead, it was acknowledging data whenever it noticed a problem, or whenever it was convenient to do so. Would sending acknowledgments for every other segment made much of a difference? Probably not, although it would have made the transfer go smoother, instead of being jerky like it was at the very beginning (during the congestion avoidance ramp-up).

Finally, note that the size of the receive window in use by Greywolf is too large for this particular network session. By advertising a large Window size, Arachnid was able to queue up more data, than the network could handle. This resulted in problems when Greywolf tried to end the connection, since Arachnid had to clear its buffers before it could do anything else. If Greywolf had been advertising a small buffer consistently, then data still would have flowed across the network, but Arachnid would not have queued up a lot of data for sending, resulting in faster recovery times. For more information on sizing the receive window, refer to "Notes on Determining the Optimal Receive Window Size."

Notes on Determining the Optimal Receive Window Size

Almost all of TCP's flow control services depend upon the size of the Window field that is advertised by a recipient, since this value dictates the maximum amount of data that can be sent during steady-state operations (i.e., after slow start has fully opened the initial congestion window) without the sender having to stop and wait for an acknowledgment. As such, this value determines the smooth flow of data more than just about any other element, so correctly determining the appropriate size of a system's receive window is central to achieving efficient throughput on a virtual circuit.

Although an application can set the size of the receive window in use with that application, most applications just use the system-wide default, which is only sometimes appropriate for the typical usage of that system. Therefore, one way to improve performance for any given system is to optimize the system-wide default for the receive window in use on that system, so that it more accurately reflects the typical usage.

In fact, setting this value accurately is crucial to achieving optimal performance. Setting the receive window too small results in an artificial bottleneck, where the receiver's window is smaller than the amount of data that the network can handle. In this model, the sender has to wait for the recipient to acknowledge data before it can send any more data, even though the network may be idle and have plenty of excess capacity. This results in connections running slower than they could, which is something that nobody wants.

Conversely, setting the window too large results in a waste of system resources (some systems allocate memory according to the size of the receive buffers), and can also introduce problems where the sender and receiver attempt to put more data into the network than the network can handle. In that situation, unnecessary delays are added to the exchange, network throughput becomes a noticeable bottleneck, and recovery times get very high.

For example, if a remote system is advertising a large receive window, then the sender may actually try to fill that window, even though the network path is unable to forward that much data in a timely fashion. If any of that data gets lost, then the sender will not discover this until the next segment has made it through the network to the recipient (which could take a long time) and an acknowledgment has been returned (more time). Then when the sender resent the lost data, that segment would have to sit in the queue on a router somewhere until all of the other segments that had already been processed were delivered (even more time). If the receive window were better sized, then none of these delays would have occurred, and recovery could have occurred much more quickly. Therefore, setting the window to be too large is not just ineffective, but it actually causes recovery problems whenever the network suffers from congestion.

Determining the most-efficient receive window size is a function of the specific virtual circuit in use with the particular applications on that system. For example, the optimal settings will be quite a bit different for a system that is acting as a Web server for a site that gets many dial-up users over a relatively slow leased line, versus a system that is acting as a mail server for a highly distributed enterprise.

The factors that affect the optimal receive window size are the bandwidth of the typical virtual circuit (represented in bits-per-second), and the amount of round-trip latency (expressed in seconds) found on that circuit. The product of the bandwidth multiplied by the round-trip latency represents the maximum amount of data that can be in-flight on the network at any given time, and therefore represents the optimal window size for that virtual circuit. Setting a value that is larger than this can cause recovery problems, while setting a value that is smaller than this works against effective network utilization.

Determining these basic values can be somewhat complicated. For one thing, you must remember that the maximum throughput is a function of the entire end-to-end link, which may not be nearly as fast as your local connection. Just because you have a 100 MB/s Ethernet card in your web server does not mean that you should perform your calculations based on 100 MB/s throughput. Instead, you must determine the throughput of the entire connection, which is not always easy to do. If you know that all of the connections to that server are originating on your LAN, then you can just use the defaults, but if the system is also serving resources for users on many different remote networks, then you have to determine the end-to-end bandwidth based on the destination network and all of the intermediary networks in between.

You also have to determine the latency times for the typical connections, using the round-trip latency for the typical connections. Although it may seem that latency should only be measured "one-way" (from the sender to the recipient), remember that the acknowledgments also have to come back across the network, and that the sender can continue to transmit data while those acknowledgments are in flight.

Fortunately, measuring latency is somewhat easier since tools such as *ping* or *traceroute* can be used. However, you have to be somewhat cautious with these tools, ensuring that they do not send large messages in their tests, as the time it takes to deliver all of the bits from a large packet will obviously be longer than the time it takes to deliver a small one. Obviously, you will not get a response until the remote end has received all of the message that you sent, and until your system has received all of the response data. When you are testing for latency with these tools, make sure to use a message size that is typical of the segment size for the application data that is predominately in use on that system. For applications like TELNET, this should be small messages, while applications like HTTP and SMTP will typically use a mix of small and large segments.

Remember that kilobits and megabits are based on multiples of 1024 and not 1000. To figure out how many bits-per-second a 19.2 KB/s modem can send, you have to multiply 19.2 by 1024, and to figure out how much throughput a 1.5 MB/s circuit offers you have to multiply 1.5 times 1024 times 1024. Also remember that some topologies will have additional throughput constraints, such as the use of parity bits.

Taken together, bandwidth times latency tells us how much data a particular virtual circuit can handle. For example, multiplying the throughput of a 19.2 KB/s modem (19.2 × 1024) by an average round-trip time of 60 milliseconds (.06) tells us that the maximum amount of data in-flight over that virtual circuit at any given time is 1,180 bits. Actually, the calculations return 1179.648, although circuits cannot send fractions of bits, so we have rounded up.

Some examples of this formula at work are shown in Table 7-10.

Table 7-10. Maximum Bits-in-Flight from Calculating Bandwidth Times Delay

Bits-per-Second	Round-Trip Latency	Maximum Bits-in-Flight
19.2 KB/s (modem)	.060 seconds	1,180
19.2 KB/s (modem)	.120	2,360
53 KB/s (modem)	.060	3,257
53 KB/s (modem)	.120	6,513

Table 7-10. Maximum Bits-in-Flight from Calculating Bandwidth Times Delay (continued)

Bits-per-Second	Round-Trip Latency	Maximum Bits-in-Flight
64 KB/s (satellite)	.200 (fast)	13,108
64 KB/s (satellite)	.400 (normal)	26,215
384 KB/s (DSL)	.060	23,593
384 KB/s (DSL)	.120	47,186
1.5 MB/s (T-1)	.060	94,372
1.5 MB/s (T-1)	.120	188,744
10 MB/s (Ethernet)	.002 (local)	20,972
10 MB/s (Ethernet)	.010 (multi-hop)	104,858
100 MB/s (Ethernet)	.002	209,716
100 MB/s (Ethernet)	.010	1,048,577

As can be seen, the number of bits-in-flight change dramatically according to the bandwidth and latency characteristics of the virtual circuit. Circuits that have high levels of latency (referred to as "long pipes") take more time for data to be propagated to the destination than short pipes do, allowing more bits to get stuffed into the pipe at any given time, regardless of the bandwidth ("size") of that pipe. For example, the first two entries from Table 7-10 show a 19.2 KB/s modem with 60 milliseconds of round-trip latency versus the same modem with a 120 millisecond latency. Since the second connection is twice as long, it can hold twice as much data from end-to-end.

Just as round-trip latency affects the amount of data in-flight, so does the capacity (or the bandwidth) of the connection. In this regard, fat pipes can carry more data than a skinny pipe can, regardless of the length of the pipe. For example, the 100 mb/s Ethernet link shown in Table 7-10 has 10 times the capacity than a 10 MB/s link, and thus can have 10 times as much data in-flight.

In a scenario where a network has lots of bandwidth and high levels of latency (the "long, fat pipe"), the number of bits-in-flight can really add up. For example, the T-1 circuit with latencies of 120 milliseconds has a substantially larger requirement than long, thin pipe offered by the 19.2 KB/s modem with 120 millisecond latencies, or the short, fat pipe offered by the 10 MB/s Ethernet LAN with 2 milliseconds of latency.

Once the number of bits-in-flight have been determined, then that value must be converted to a byte value, since the Window field advertises buffer space in terms of the available number of bytes (not bits). Therefore, you have to divide the value by eight in order to determine the optimal size in bytes. However, a key consideration in this is to make sure that the byte value is an even multiple of the MTU for the virtual circuit. This is to ensure that the sender can always transmit two fully sized segments, thereby preventing the Silly Window Avoidance algorithm from holding up small segments, and also preventing the Delayed Acknowledgment algorithm from holding up acknowledgments (a problem discussed in "Partially Filled Segments or Long Gaps Between Sends").

For example, if the MTU between two endpoints is 1460 bytes, then the Window field must be a multiple of 2920 bytes, but if the end-to-end MTU is only 536 bytes, then the Window field must be a multiple of 1072. Also recall that many BSD-based systems only use multiples of 512 for their MTU size (regardless of the MTU that is offered by the network), and this has to be taken into consideration if you're using those systems.

Typically speaking, the value used for the receive window should be at least a multiple of four, since a receive window that was smaller than that would not allow for a steady exchange of data. If the receive window were only two times the MTU, then the use of delayed acknowledgments on the receiver would result in a very staggered exchange. Upon seeing a window size of "two segments," the sender would transmit two segments and then stop to wait for an acknowledgment, while the two segments worked their way through the network to the recipient. Once received, the recipient's acknowledgment would also have to work its way back to the sender, whereupon the sender could transmit two more segments. This would result in a very jerky exchange of data.

In addition, setting the receive window to just "two segments" will prevent fast retransmit from occurring whenever there is lost data. Remember that the fast retransmit algorithm depends upon the sender getting three or more acknowledgments for the same segment, which suggests that the receiver lost that segment, but has also gotten at least some segments sent later. If the receive window is only set to "two segments" then the sender will only be able to send two segments at a time, and the recipient will only get one of them, meaning that the recipient will only be able to issue one duplicate acknowledgment (and even that one duplicate acknowledgment will likely be delayed according to the Delayed Acknowledgment algorithm). Without the additional duplicate acknowledgments, the sender cannot utilize the fast retransmit algorithm, and will have to wait until the acknowledgment timer gets triggered, which will then cause other things to happen.

In the end, the state of the virtual circuit will become very messy, although all of this could have been avoided by just setting the recipient's receive window to four segments or greater. In fact, many systems set the default receive window size to 4 * MTU in an effort to avoid just these kinds of problems. It may be required that you go higher than this value, but you should not go lower than this without a very good reason.

With that in mind, some example Window sizes are shown in Table 7-11.

Table 7-11. Possible Window Sizes, Based on the Maximum Number of Bits-in-Flight and the Available MTU

Bits per Second	Latency	Bits	Bytes	MTU	Window
19.2 KB/s (modem)	.060 seconds	1,180	148	1460 * 4	5,840
19.2 KB/s (modem)	.120	2,360	295	1460 * 4	5,840
53 KB/s (modem)	.060	3,257	408	1460 * 4	5,840
53 KB/s (modem)	.120	6,513	815	1460 * 4	5,840
64 KB/s (satellite)	.200 (fast)	13,108	1,639	536 * 4	2,144
64 KB/s (satellite)	.400 (normal)	26,215	3,277	536 * 8	4,288
384 KB/s (DSL)	.060	23,593	2,950	1468 * 4	5,840
384 KB/s (DSL)	.120	47,186	5,899	1460 * 6	8,760
1.5 MB/s (T-1)	.060	94,372	11,797	1460 * 10	14,600
1.5 MB/s (T-1)	.120	188,744	23,593	1460 * 18	26,280
10 MB/s (Ethernet)	.002 (local)	20,972	2,622	1024 * 4	4,192
10 MB/s (Ethernet)	.010 (multi-hop)	104,858	13,108	1460 * 10	14,600
100 MB/s (Ethernet)	.002 (local)	209,716	26,215	1460 * 18	26, 280
100 MB/s (Ethernet)	.010 (multi-hop)	1,048,577	131,073	1460 * 90	131,400

This process should illustrate just how complicated the art of determining valid window sizes can be. However, by doing these calculations on a regular basis—particularly for the most-commonly accessed systems on your network—you can optimize the delivery times on your TCP network dramatically. For example, if your users are talking to a mail server that is many hops away on a 100 MB/s Ethernet LAN, it may be that large window sizes will improve throughput dramatically (although you may be better off with mail servers that were closer to the user, and thus had lower latencies).

Troubleshooting TCP

Most of the problems that users will experience will be related to application-specific issues, and should not be related to TCP. However, since TCP offers such a wide breadth of services, there are many things that can go wrong with a virtual circuit throughout a session.

Rejected Connections

The most common failing that TCP has is related to the inability of a client to connect to a remote system. This can be caused by either the client specifying a destination port number that does not have a listening application associated with it (such as trying to connect to a nonexistent web server), or by the listening server refusing to accept a connection due to a configuration issue. Figure 7-44 shows what a session looks like when the specified destination does not have a listening application associated with it, while Figure 7-45 shows what a session looks like when the destination server refuses to accept the connection.

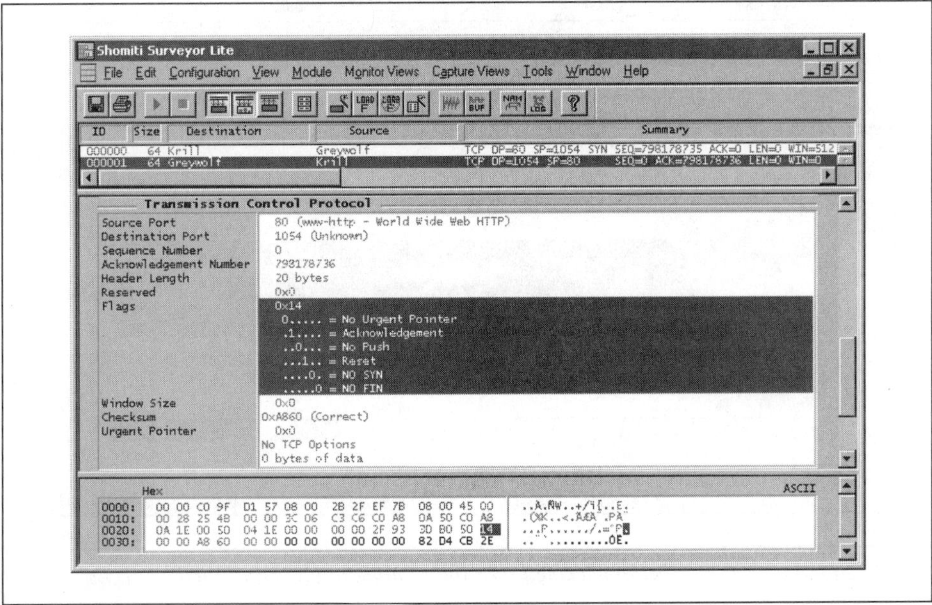

Figure 7-44. A connection being rejected because there's no listener

As stated, the most likely cause for this error is that the destination port number specified in the active open is not active. In the example shown in Figure 7-44, the destination port number of 80 (the well-known port number for HTTP) was inactive, meaning that no web server was available on the destination host.

Notice that the destination system's TCP provider simply rejects the connection request. In the first segment, the client attempts to establish a connection, and the server responds with a Reset segment. This tells the client to just go away. The circuit never even gets established, with no Synchronize segment being returned.

Figure 7-45 shows what happens when a destination application has been misconfigured. In that example, the virtual circuit gets established (as indicated by the completed Synchronize process), but the listening application aborts the connection before any data is transferred (immediately starting the circuit-shutdown process).

The most likely cause for this occurring is that the remote system is unwilling to provide services to this client, although this does not get discovered until after the connection has been established. In the example shown in Figure 7-45, the destination TELNET server's security rules were configured to not allow a connection from the client system. Although the TCP virtual circuit was started successfully,

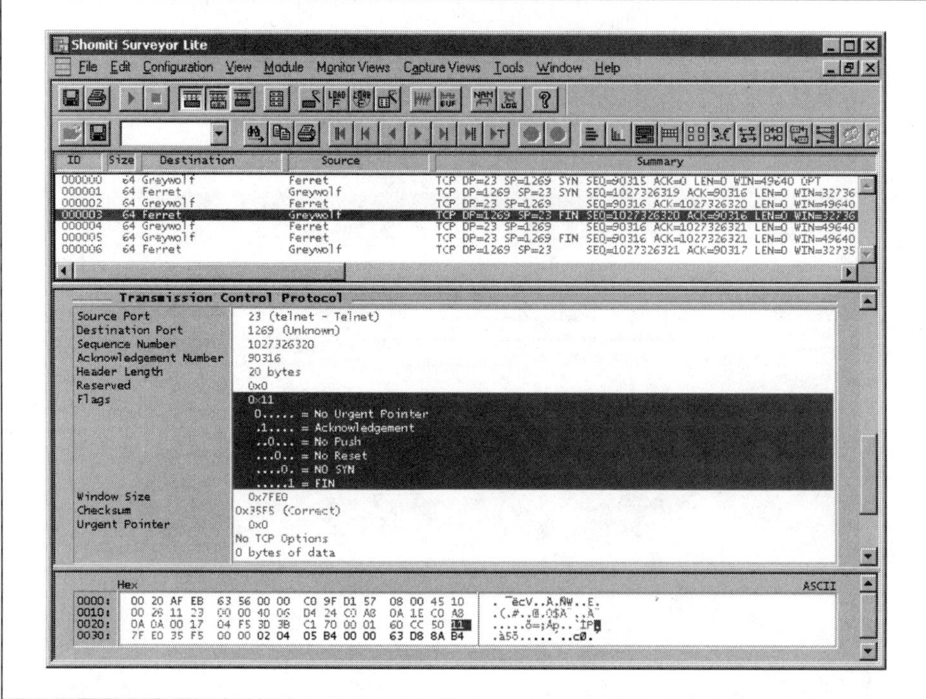

Figure 7-45. A connection being accepted and then immediately terminated

the TELNET server closed the circuit immediately by marking the packed FIN, indicating that the application was loaded and running in LISTEN mode, but that it didn't want to talk to this particular client.

Lost Circuits

Sometimes the connection is established just fine, but then the virtual circuit starts to collapse, with one side appearing to just disappear off the network. Most of the time, that's exactly what has happened: the remote endpoint has lost physical connectivity with the rest of the network for some reason, possibly due to power failure, link failure, or any number of other potential problems.

This scenario is illustrated in Figure 7-46, which shows an HTTP client on Greywolf requesting a document from the HTTP server on *www.ora.com*. After issuing the "GET /" request, Greywolf loses physical connectivity with the network.

Segments four through ten show the HTTP server on *www.ora.com* attempting to send the contents of the requested document back to Greywolf. However, since Greywolf is no longer "live" on the network, it is unable to acknowledge the data, nor is it able to issue a Finish or Reset segment back to the server. Since the server has not been told that the circuit has been torn down (since it hasn't been), it just assumes that the data has been lost, and continually tries to resend the questionable data.

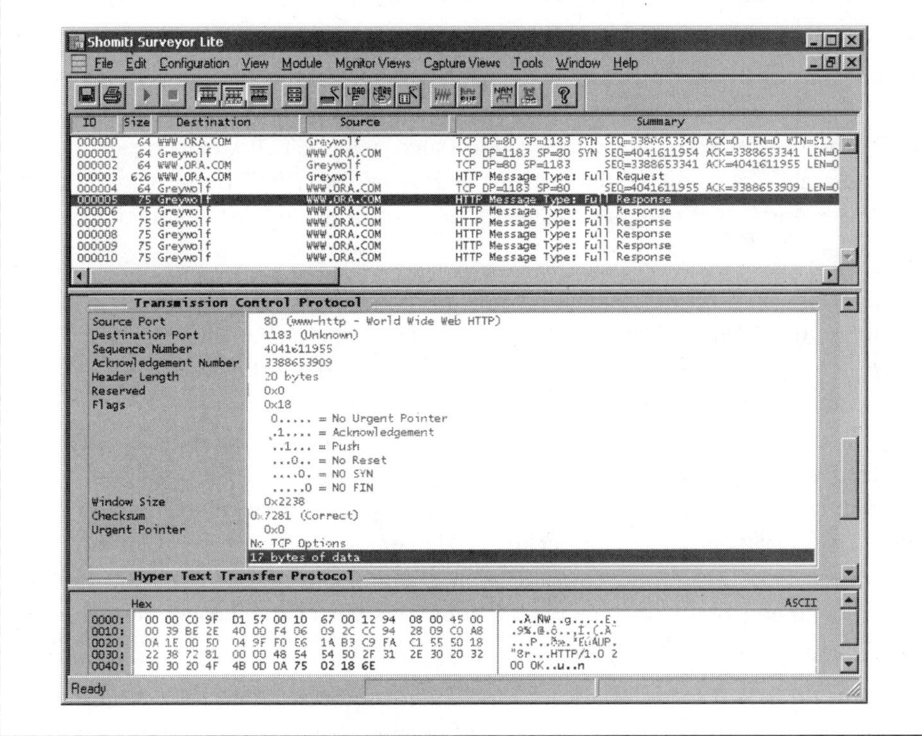

Figure 7-46. A connection getting dropped due to loss of carrier

What isn't shown in Figure 7-46 is that the time between the retry operations is increasing while *www.ora.com* continues trying to resend the data to Greywolf. Since Greywolf is not acknowledging the data, *www.ora.com* keeps trying to send the data, and keeps doubling the size of its acknowledgment timers. This process will continue for a while, until *www.ora.com* gives up and drops the connection. The number of times that *www.ora.com* will retry the operation—and the length of time between retransmissions—will be a function of the stack in use on that system. For more information on this subject, refer to "Acknowledgment timers."

Partially Filled Segments or Long Gaps Between Sends

In order to maximize network utilization, TCP employs several algorithms that work towards filling the network with the most amount of data, using the least amount of segments. Among these mechanisms are the Nagle algorithm (as discussed in "The Nagle algorithm"), the silly window avoidance algorithm (as discussed in "The Silly Window Syndrome"), and delayed acknowledgments (as discussed in "Delayed acknowledgments"). However, sometimes these mechanisms can actually trigger delays on a virtual circuit, rather than preventing them.

Interactions between Nagle and delayed acknowledgments

The Nagle algorithm is used to prevent senders from transmitting unnecessary small segments by mandating that a small segment cannot be transferred until all of the previously sent segments have been acknowledged, or until a full-sized segment can be sent. Thus, if an application (such as an HTTP client) needs to send one-and-a-half segments of data, then the first segment will be sent immediately but the second (small) segment will not be sent until the first segment has been acknowledged.

However, delayed acknowledgments are designed to prevent excessive acknowledgments by holding them until either two full-sized segments have been received, a timer expires, or data is being returned to the sender (which the acknowledgment can then piggyback onto). In this scenario, the first full-sized segment described above would not get acknowledged immediately, since two full-sized segments had not been received, nor would there be any data being returned since not all of the application data had been received by the HTTP server as of yet. Instead, the acknowledgment would not be sent until the acknowledgment timer had expired, which could take as long as 500 milliseconds, depending upon the implementations and the characteristics of the virtual circuit in use on that connection.

Sometimes this will show up as an application protocol taking a long time to get off the ground, particularly when a connection has already been established between the two endpoints (this is most often seen with application protocols such as HTTP that generate small amounts of data which are larger than a single segment, but smaller than two full-sized segments). At other times, this problem may manifest itself as a single trailing segment that appears to get held up for a long time (which can be seen with any TCP-based application).

The HTTP problem is illustrated in Figure 7-47. In that example, the HTTP client is sending 1500 bytes of data to the HTTP server, but because the client is using the Nagle algorithm, the sixty bytes of overflow data are delayed until the first segment has been acknowledged. But since the server is using the delayed acknowledgments mechanism, it is waiting for two full-sized segments before returning an acknowledgment, which is causing the overflow data to be held up on the HTTP client.

When these events occur, the result is long pauses between the first and second data segments. The only real cure for this situation is to disable the use of the Nagle algorithm on the system that is sending the one-and-a-half segments of application data, although in all likelihood you will need to have access to the application source code to make this change.

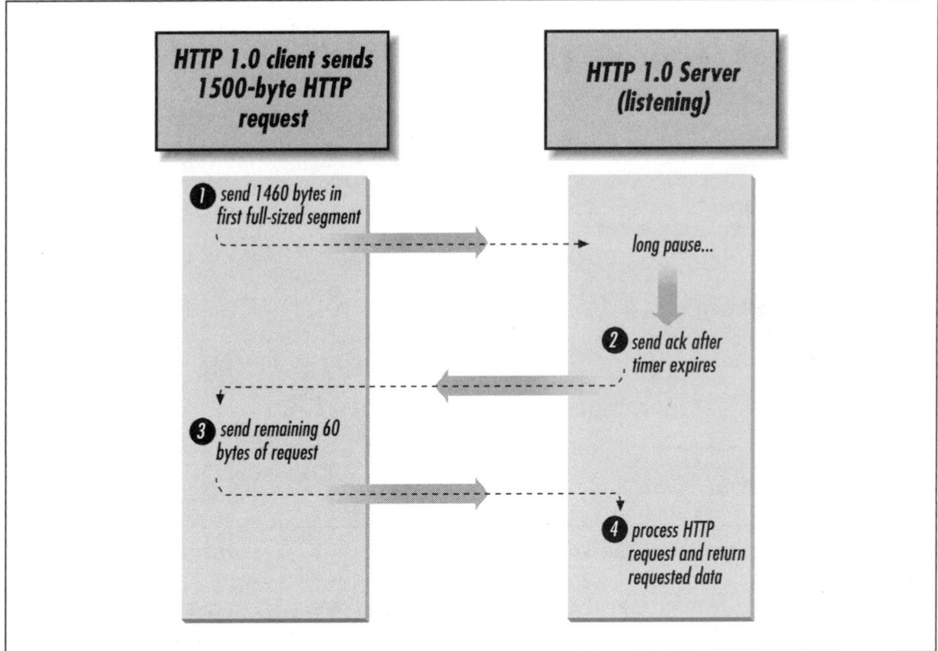

Figure 7-47. A negative interaction between the Nagle algorithm and delayed acknowledgments

Once the Nagle algorithm is disabled on an application, the sender can transmit the small segment immediately, thereby causing all of the data to get to the remote endpoint immediately, where it can be processed. The remote system is likely to return some sort of data as a result of receiving all 1500 bytes of data (such as a requested web page), which the delayed acknowledgment could ride on.

This process is shown in Figure 7-48. In that example, the client has disabled the use of the Nagle algorithm and is now free to send small segments to the server without waiting for acknowledgments. As a result, the HTTP server gets the entire HTTP request quickly and is able to return the data (and the acknowledgment) quickly as well.

If you notice long delays with these kinds of applications, check to see if the client is sending more data than will fit within a single segment (but not so much data as to fill two fully sized segments). If so, then you may be able to disable the use of the Nagle algorithm on the client, which will allow it to send the small segment immediately. The server can then bundle the acknowledgments for those segments with whatever data is going to be returned by the application protocol, using the delayed acknowledgment mechanism to its advantage.

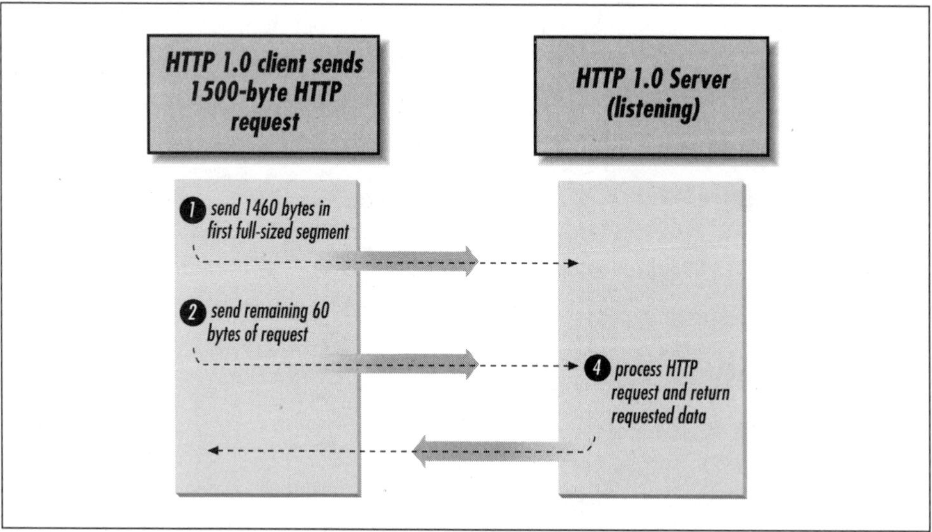

Figure 7-48. Flow control with the Nagle algorithm disabled

These problems can occur in the other direction as well. In some cases, the web server may be sending more data than can fit within a single segment, but that does not fill two full-sized segments. In those cases, the server may also be suffering from the use of the Nagle algorithm. However, you should be much more cautious about disabling the use of the Nagle algorithm on servers, since they also tend to send large amounts of data (such as GIF images) that benefit from clustering small blocks of data into a single transmission. As a result, disabling the use of the Nagle algorithm on a server may cause other problems due to a large amount of small segments.

It is important to realize that this problem occurs only with applications that frequently generate writes that are smaller than two full-sized segments of data. Application developers should not disable the Nagle algorithm if they are writing many small blocks of data that are larger than two full-sized segments, since those writes should be clumped together, thereby preserving network utilization.

Sometimes you can tell the size of the block of data that an application is writing by looking for the Push flag, since this flag is often set on every application write. For example, if an application is writing data to TCP in four-kilobyte chunks, then there may be a Push flag at the end of every four kilobytes of data sent via TCP. Note that this method is not fool-proof, since some TCP stacks will set the Push flag on every segment that they send, but it can be used with many implementations.

Wrong MTU sizes

Another set of performance problems can occur whenever a system chooses to delay an acknowledgment until two full-sized segments have been received, but the system is receiving segments that are smaller than the system's local MTU. In this situation, the sender may send many segments, which the recipient does not acknowledge.

This particular scenario most-often happens when two devices announce large MTUs during the circuit-setup process (using the MSS option), but the sender then determines that a smaller end-to-end MTU is required in order to transfer data to the recipient (this is typically detected using Path MTU Discovery). The sender will therefore only transmit small segments to the recipient, who will not return an acknowledgment until enough data has been received to fill two full-sized segments (according to its understanding of the end-to-end MTU, which is still reflective of the local MTU).

This introduces all kinds of performance problems during slow start and congestion avoidance, since the sender's congestion window will only allow a few segments to be sent before waiting on an acknowledgment to arrive. Eventually the recipient's delayed acknowledgment timer would expire, and it would send one acknowledgment for all of the data that it had received, thereby allowing the sender to increment its congestion window and resume sending data, resulting in a very bursty ramp-up process.

However, it is important to realize that this scenario only happens when the sender's Path MTU Discovery routines detect a smaller end-to-end MTU than the size announced by the MSS option. If both endpoints are using the same MTU for the local and intermediary networks, then this problem will never occur. But if the intermediary path is smaller than the MTU of the two endpoints, then it will likely occur quite frequently.

For example, if the two endpoints both have MTUs of 1500 bytes (common for Ethernet), but an intermediary path is only providing an MTU of 536 bytes (somewhat common on older leased lines and dial-up circuits), then the recipient may continually delay acknowledgments, since it is only receiving what it believes to be small, undersized segments. This problem also occurs frequently with systems who use Token Ring, FDDI and other large MTU sizes over a 1500-byte intermediary network (1500 bytes is the most common MTU found on the Internet).

Uneven MTU multiples

Another interesting opportunity for problems occurs when the receive window size being advertised by a recipient is not an even multiple of the MTU in use on the virtual circuit. This results in problems with Silly Window Avoidance causing transmission delays. As you may recall, the Silly Window Syndrome can occur when the recipient's TCP stack advertises a small window size, resulting in the sender transmitting a few bytes (to fill the advertised space), with the process repeating ad infinitum. In order to prevent this behavior, RFC 1122 stated that a system could only advertise a non-zero window if the receive buffers could store one fully sized segment.

However, this becomes a problem when the receive buffers on a system are not an even multiple of the MTU in use on the network, or when the application attempts to write data in blocks that are not an even multiple of the MTU. For example, if a system has a default receive window of four kilobytes but is receiving 1460-byte segments, then the sender can only transmit three fully sized segments, since the Nagle algorithm delays the fourth segment until an acknowledgment arrives for the third segment, or until a fully sized segment can be sent. However, as noted above, the recipient will not issue an acknowledgment until it has received two fully sized segments, or until a timer expires.

As such, the sender sends only three segments of data, and then stops to wait for an acknowledgment before sending the final small segment (the Nagle algorithm at work). Once the acknowledgment for the first two segments had been received, then the sender would transmit the fourth segment (which may or may not result in an acknowledgment from the remote system, according to whether or not the recipient is issuing acknowledgments for every two segments that it receives, or only for every two full-sized segments it receives). This would result in a fast send of three segments, followed by a long pause for the final (small) segment.

Most TCP implementations attempt to avoid this problem by forcing the receive window to be at least four times the size of the local MTU (as discussed in "Notes on Determining the Optimal Receive Window Size"). However, this is still a problem with applications that write data in blocks that are not an even multiple of the end-to-end MTU (which is more important than the local MTU). In an effort to prevent this from occurring, some operating systems (such as BSD) will not delay sending the final segment from a write. For implementations that do not do this though, it can be problematic.

Small send windows and excessively delayed acknowledgments

A variety of performance problems can also occur when the sending system is using a small send window, while the recipient is using a large receive window and is delaying acknowledgments for too long. Although this requires an odd mixture of conditions to occur, it is not so rare as to not be a problem.

For example, some server-class systems intentionally delay acknowledgments for more than every-other segment, in an attempt to reduce network utilization and overhead, with some systems delaying acknowledgments until 50% or 60% of the receive window has been filled. When this mechanism is used to exchange data with other large-scale systems on a half-duplex network, the long gaps between acknowledgments allow the network to send more data in less time. However, when this model is used on systems with small send windows (such as is common with PC-based implementations), it can then trigger serious performance problems.

Although the vast majority of "send" activity comes from server-class systems with large send windows (such as HTTP servers, or POP3 mail servers), a lot of network traffic also gets generated by PC clients that are sending mail messages with large binary attachments to an SMTP server, or who are uploading large data files to an FTP server, and so forth. Typically, these systems do not have very large send windows (most of them only have send windows that are four times the local MTU).

When these systems try to send data to a system that is delaying acknowledgments until half of the receive window has been filled—and when the receive window on that system is substantially larger than the sender's send window—the sender will have to stop transmitting once the send window has been filled with outstanding, unacknowledged data. If the recipient is not returning acknowledgments for that data (due to an excessively long delay timer), then this will result in very bursty traffic, with the sender transmitting four or so segments, and then stopping until the remote system's acknowledgment timer expires.

Excessive or Slow Retransmissions

One of the most important aspects of TCP's reliability service is the use of acknowledgment timers (also called retransmission timers), which ensure that lost segments get recognized as such in a timely manner, resulting in the quick retransmission of that data. However, as was pointed out earlier in "Acknowledgment timers," accurately determining the correct timer values to use on any given virtual circuit is a complex process. If the value is set too low, then the timer will expire too frequently, resulting in unnecessary retransmissions. Conversely, if the value is set too high, then loss may not be detected quickly, resulting in unnecessary delays.

On some systems, you may notice that there are a high number of excessive retransmissions on new circuits (indicating that the default timer is set too low for those virtual circuits), or you may see very long gaps in between retransmissions (indicating that the default acknowledgment timer is set too high). Although these values are typically changed on a per-circuit basis as the smoothed round-trip time is calculated, the default settings can be problematic on new connections, where the smoothing has yet to begin in earnest.

For example, if the default acknowledgment timer is set to 3000 milliseconds, then the system may not detect a lost segment until three full seconds after the segment was sent. This would obviously cause problems with applications that only send one or two segments at a time (such as mail and web clients, that only send a little bit of data). The result would be a very long pause, followed by a retransmission, which may or may not succeed.

Conversely, if the default acknowledgment timer is set to 200 milliseconds, but you are connecting to a site that is on a very slow link, then you may see the same segments getting sent multiple times. Although this does not penalize applications that only send a couple of segments at once (mail and news clients, for example), it would be quite annoying to those applications that send many segments (such as an FTP upload, or a disk-sharing protocol), since those applications would be constantly resending data, at least until the smoothed round-trip time were sufficiently incremented.

Most operating systems allow you to define the default value for the acknowledgment timers in use on those systems. You should determine the most appropriate default timer according to the typical connection scenarios in use on your network (i.e., use *ping* or *traceroute* to determine typical latency times), and then refer to the system documentation to see how to set the default acknowledgment time to those values.

Slow Throughput on High-Speed Networks

The author has seen poorly written network drivers cause significant throughput problems on TCP/IP networks, particularly with regards to buffer management on the receive queue. In those instances, the sending and receiving systems are never able to get beyond the slow start ramp-up activity, as the recipient is unable to acknowledge more than a couple of segments at a time, due to poor buffer management within the device driver itself.

In this scenario, the sender transmits four segments as part of the slow start algorithm, but the recipient only returns an acknowledgment for the first two segments (or more accurately, fails to acknowledge the third and fourth segments). The sender will interpret this behavior as network congestion and reduce the size of its congestion window to one segment. This process will complete ad infinitum, with the sender never getting beyond a couple of segments. Unfortunately, the only way to resolve this problem is to either replace the recipient's network driver, or to replace the network card entirely.

Another set of problems for this are discussed earlier in "Partially Filled Segments or Long Gaps Between Sends."

Lots of Reset Command Segments

A high number of TCP command segments with the Reset flag enabled can indicate a variety of things, although typically it boils down to the recipient getting a segment that "apparently is not intended for the current connection," according to RFC 793. However, RFC 793 also goes on to state that "A reset must not be sent if it is not clear that this is the case," leaving it up to the recipient to make the decision.

For example, Reset segments will be sent whenever a remote endpoint attempts to establish a connection to a non-existent socket on the local system. If a web browser tries to establish a connection to port 80 (the well-known port number for HTTP), but there is no server listening on that port, then the local system's TCP stack should return a Reset segment in response to the incoming Synchronize requests.

Reset segments can also be sent if the local socket is no longer valid for a previous connection. In that case, the local application has completely closed its end of the connection but the remote system is still sending data. When those segments arrive, the local TCP stack should just reply with an equal number of Reset segments. This can happen due to the remote endpoint refusing to close their end of the connection after the local system has sent the requisite circuit-termination segments (using the Finish flag), and can also occur if the virtual circuit had to be destroyed due to an excessive number of retransmissions. In both of those cases, the connection has fallen apart and was terminated abruptly by the server, so any additional segments received for that virtual circuit must be refused.

Generally speaking, applications are supposed to close their connections gracefully, so that particular scenario should only happen when fatal errors occur. However, some applications use abrupt closes on their ends of the virtual circuit in an attempt to boost performance, rather than closing the connection gracefully. For example, some HTTP servers don't try to close their virtual circuits gracefully, but instead just do a full close once they've sent all of the requested data. The theory behind this practice is that it is faster to terminate the connection than to go through the laborious task of exchanging shutdown segments. However, this also means that the client will not be able to request any data that was lost, since the server has closed the connection without waiting for acknowledgments to arrive for all of the data that was sent. Any subsequent requests for retransmission will just get rejected, resulting in a stalled client. Welcome to the World Wide Wait!

Another situation where resets can occur is if an application has crashed, leaving TCP thinking that the socket is still valid, although nothing is servicing the receive queues associated with that port number. In that situation, TCP may accept data on behalf of the application, until the buffer is full. If the queue never gets serviced, then eventually TCP should start issuing Reset segments for any new data that it receives, while continuing to advertise a zero-length window.

Weird Command Segments

As the Internet has gained in popularity, it has attracted people of every ilk, not all of whom have the best intentions. In particular, over the past few years there has been a large increase in the number of hackers who have taken a strong liking to TCP/IP (many of whom are probably reading this book), and who are using network probing tools to discover the layout of your network and the weak points on your servers. If you see weird looking command segments, then the chances are good that your network is being probed by one of the commonly available programs that are the tools of the trade for these users.

Figure 7-49 shows what one type of probe looks like, with Greywolf sending a lamp-test segment to Weasel, in an effort to discover the operating system in use on that host. This segment has the Urgent, Push, Synchronize, and Finish flags enabled. The way in which Weasel responds to this illegal segment can be used as

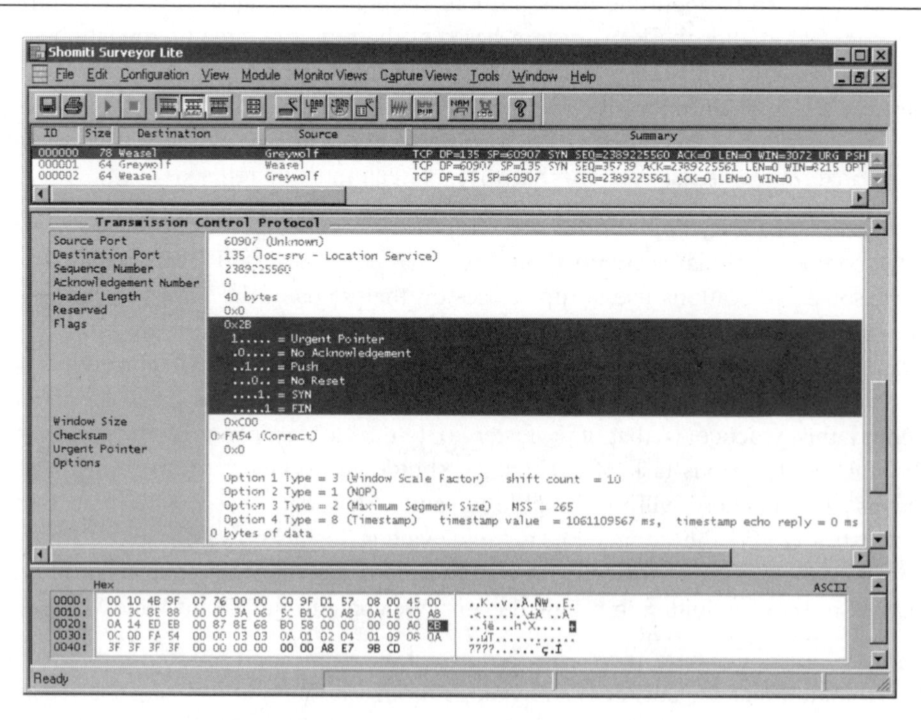

Figure 7-49. A lamp-test segment

a clue towards discovering the operating system in use on that host (although this information has to be combined with many other such probes). As can be seen by the next segment, unfortunately Weasel responded to this command segment with an Acknowledgment and Synchronize segment of its own, allowing the connection to continue. It certainly should not have done this, upon seeing the Finish flag of the original command segment.

Other types of probe segments can consist of simple half-opens, whereby the hacker is testing to see whether or not a server is listening on a known port, or the false-reset segment where a command segment is sent with just the Reset flag enabled, even though no connection has yet been established.

When you see these types of segments, you should examine your security infrastructure for any possible holes that may be being exploited by these segments. A good firewall should block most of these probes.

Path MTU Discovery-Related Problems

Over the years, there have been many implementation-specific problems from the use of Path MTU Discover with TCP.

For a comprehensive discussion on this subject, refer to "Notes on Path MTU Discovery" in Chapter 5, *The Internet Control Message Protocol.*

Misconfigured or Missing Services File

You should verify that the *services* file in use on your system matches up with the well-known port numbers expected by the applications you are using. Some applications will ask the system for the port number associated with "SMTP" for example, and if your system's *services* file does not have an entry for that application, it will not return a port number to the client.

This will prevent the client from being able to send any data, since it cannot get the destination port number for the application.

To see the well-known ports used on your system, examine the */etc/services* file on a Unix host, or the *C:\WinNT\System32\Drivers\Etc\SERVICES* file on a Windows NT host.

Miscellaneous Interoperability Problems

A variety of interoperability problems with different vendors' TCP implementations have been documented. Some of these problems have been seen in the sample captures shown in this chapter (such as Greywolf failing to use slow start, as shown in "Bulk Data Transfer and Error Recovery").

For more information on these problems, refer to RFC 2525, entitled "Known TCP Implementation Problems."

The Internet Standardization Process

Throughout this book, there have been many references to specifications and documents, such as the RFCs and STDs that define the various protocols and data formats in use on the Internet. How these documents get developed is an interesting aspect of the Internet community, and one that needs to be discussed in order to fully understand how the Internet really works.

RFC 2026 gives an overview of the Internet standardization process. It is a must-read for anybody who wants to get a true understanding of the process. This appendix attempts to summarize this document (and others) for those people who are interested only in an overview.

Perhaps the best analogy comes from Ed Krol's book, *The Whole Internet User's Guide and Catalog*, in which Krol says that the Internet is kind of like a church. It has a council of elders, every member has an opinion on how things should work, and you can either choose to participate or you can choose not to participate. This is a pretty accurate assessment.

Although the defining element of "what the Internet is" is the conformance to Internet-based standards and services, it is important to note that the use of these standards is strictly voluntary. There is no "Internet Police force" that goes around and makes you use IP and SMTP, for example. Instead, your usage of these protocols is entirely optional.

However, by *not* using these standards, you would also be making a choice of being isolated from the rest of the Internet community. Therefore, most people find that using these standards makes more sense than not using them, and as such they remain extremely popular. However, their popularity is also directly related to the usability and functionality that these protocols and services provide. After all, if the protocols didn't work, then they wouldn't be very popular.

Developing a protocol to perform a simple task is easy; anybody can write a simple protocol in just a few minutes by giving it some thought. However, making a protocol that is usable on a wide variety on computing platforms (as is the case with TCP/IP) is significantly harder, and takes a lot more work. You have to develop the protocol within very simple host constraints (taking into consideration old platforms, odd-ball platforms, etc.), and the protocol also has to be generic enough so as not to present implementation challenges for a large number of users. If a protocol is hard to implement or use, then it will not be widely adopted. And after all that, the protocol still has to be functional enough to satisfy the design goals. This can be extremely difficult to do when you're having to deal with systems that will only exchange seven-bit ASCII characters, for example.

This is the task of the developers of the protocols and services used on the Internet. They must develop protocols that are both functional and usable on a wide variety of systems. Also, they have to do this so well that vendors and users alike will actually want to use these protocols for their networking services. Remember that the Internet standards are not mandated by anybody, and that acceptance is only realized when people *want* to use them.

The Internet Authorities

There are a variety of interrelated organizations that work to develop, promote, and standardize the protocols and services used on the Internet. The most visible of these organizations is the Internet Engineering Task Force (IETF). In a nutshell, the protocols and services used on the Internet are developed by volunteers, who work within a collaborative development environment sponsored by the IETF.

The IETF has a sister organization called the Internet Engineering Steering Group (IESG), which is the body that ratifies specifications as standards. All of the voting members of the IESG are also participants within the IETF. In addition, a related organization—called the Internet Architecture Board (IAB)—provides think-tank services on behalf of the IETF, examining the broader technology issues that are affecting the usage and adoption of Internet standards (such as support for international character sets).

As part of this service, the IAB also has a dedicated research organization, called the Internet Research Task Force (IRTF), which delves into particularly thorny and complex issues. The IAB also has two administrative organizations that facilitate the usage of the standards that get developed. These groups are the Internet Assigned Numbers Authority (IANA) and the RFC Editor.

You can find more information on each of these organizations in the following sections.

The Internet Engineering Task Force

The IETF consists of a handful of areas, each of which are focused on particular topics of interest (such as routing or security). Each area is chaired by an Area Director, who is responsible for guiding the development of the protocols and services within the group.

The IETF areas are further broken into working groups that conduct research and development on specific protocols within the relevant area. For example, the Applications Area has working groups on HTTP, SMTP, and other application protocols.

The majority of the work performed by each of the working groups is conducted using mailing lists. In addition to the mailing lists, the IETF holds face-to-face meetings three times a year, allowing the working group participants to get together and hash out issues in person. Anyone can subscribe to any of these mailing lists or attend these meetings.

For more information on the IETF, visit their web page at *http://www.ietf.org/*.

The Internet Engineering Steering Group

Although the IETF is where the protocol development effort takes place, the IESG is the organization that actually moves these protocols along the standards track.

Whenever an IETF working group finishes a proposal, it is submitted to the IESG for consideration. If the IESG thinks the protocol is useful and functional, they vote to advance the work along a standards track until it eventually becomes an Internet standard. Note that the IESG is the body responsible for making things "standards" or "informational." This process is discussed in more detail in "The Standards-Track Process" later in this chapter.

The IESG membership is made up entirely of the IETF Area Directors, who themselves are nominated by the IETF. In many regards, the IETF and the IESG are inseparable and sometimes indistinguishable.

For more information on the IESG, visit their web page at *http://www.ietf.org/iesg/*.

The Internet Architecture Board

Perhaps the most critical function that the IAB serves is to provide think-tank services for the Internet in general, dealing with such issues as overall architecture, support for international character sets, and so on. The IAB also acts as a pseudo-appellate court for users to go to when they feel that the IESG has made a critical error in the standardization process. The IAB is also responsible for interacting with other standards bodies (such as IEEE, ITU, and ISO).

The IAB consists of thirteen voting members. Twelve of these board positions are filled by a nomination process sponsored by the IETF. The thirteenth position is an ex officio seat provided to the current chair of the IETF. In addition, the chairs of the IANA and the IRTF are also invited to attend all IAB meetings, although they do not have any votes.

For more information on the IAB, visit their web page at *http://www.iab.org/*.

The Internet Research Task Force

When the IAB encounters a particularly deep or thorny problem that must be researched in depth, it can request the Internet Research Task Force (IRTF) to review the problem and report back with their findings. The work performed by the IRTF does not typically result in any new standards, but instead tends to take the form of suggestions that the IAB follows when a working group is established to create a new protocol or specification.

For more information on the IRTF, visit their web page at *http://www.irtf.org/*.

The Internet Assigned Numbers Authority

Since many different protocols and data types exist, and since many of these documents use numeric or keyword assignments that must not be duplicated, a registry is required to act as a central clearinghouse for these types of assignments. This is the purpose of the Internet Assigned Numbers Authority (IANA).

The IANA keeps track of every type of assignment specified in the different RFCs and STDs, including mundane lists such as the protocol identifiers (like 17 for UDP and 6 for TCP) and esoteric lists such as the different MIME media types.

For more information on the IANA, visit their web page at *http://www.iana.org/*.

The RFC Editor

The RFC Editor is the office that is responsible for publishing RFCs, for assigning them unique identifiers, and for the final editorial review of the documents. This is mostly provided as an administrative service for the benefit of the standards process, and is not a clerical service (the RFC Editor does not fix spelling mistakes, for example).

Although the RFC Editor and IANA are different organizations, they have historically been served by the same person. This precedent has recently changed, however.

For more information on the office of the RFC Editor, visit their web page at *http://www.rfc-editor.org/*.

Internet Documents (Drafts, RFCs, and STDs)

The process for developing standards in the Internet community is simple on the surface, but arduous in practice. Not only does it require the robust participation of various contributors, but it must also be able to stand up to the harsh criticism of its detractors. For these reasons, it can easily take several years for an otherwise simple and straightforward protocol to make it all the way through the various stages, finally emerging as an official standard for the Internet community.

RFC 2026 defines an Internet standard as "a specification that is stable and well-understood, is technically competent, has multiple, independent, and interoperable implementations with substantial operational experience, enjoys significant public support, and is recognizably useful in some or all parts of the Internet." This is a tall order to fill for anybody. Even companies such as Sun and Novell—who have many years of experience in developing network protocols and services—would have a hard time delivering a protocol that stood up to that definition. This is an even taller order when the process is opened to any and all participants, some of whom may have their own agendas.

The process itself can also be somewhat convoluted. Depending on the number of revisions and drafts that a document may go through, the process can either be a straightforward series of clearly delineated steps, or it can turn a simple proposal into a complex schema that becomes something totally different from its original goals.

The Standards-Track Process

When the process works like it's supposed to, the IAB charters the IESG with creating an IETF working group to research and develop a protocol or other specification that addresses a specific problem. The working group hammers out the issues, develops a syntax or structure that addresses the problem, and then publishes a draft proposal.

The draft is then posted to the IETF's servers for peer review, at which time people make whatever comments they have about the proposed solution. If any significant errors are found or if any other major changes need to be made, the draft may be replaced at any time with a new version of the document.

After a waiting period of at least two weeks, a draft can be proposed to the IESG as the final specification. If the IESG accepts the draft, it becomes a Request for Comments (RFC), and is assigned a unique identifier. If the RFC is for an IESG-sanctioned standard, then it becomes a Proposed Standard immediately upon its acceptance.

An RFC remains a Proposed Standard until at least two interoperable implementations have been built and demonstrated, and for at least six months following publication as a Proposed Standard. At this point, the RFC may become a Draft Standard if the IESG approves of the change in status.

RFCs must remain as Draft Standards for at least four months, or until a face-to-face IETF meeting has occurred, whichever is longer. The last step for an RFC is to become an official Internet Standard, once the specification has been proven to work widely and reliably.

Changes to the documents

Over time, the state of the technology may change to such a degree that fundamental alterations must be made to a proposal. Typically, changes that require radical modifications will result in the creation of a new IETF working group, or a re-chartering of the existing working group.

Minor changes that do not have a significant impact on the technology are allowed at any time, although typically these changes are made whenever a document moves to the next step in the standards process. For example, a Proposed Standard may require some minor modifications, and those changes could be incorporated into the document when it becomes a Draft Standard.

However, no changes (except for typographical or spelling errors) are allowed to be made to a document when it moves from the Draft Standard stage to the Internet Standard stage.

If the changes made at any of these transition points are severe, the new document may be required to re-enter the process as a Proposed Standard, effectively requiring that the process be restarted.

Requirement levels

Because there are so many different types of documents published, not all of which are suggested or required, RFC 2026 also defines a set of "requirement levels" that should be applied to each RFC that gets published. These requirement levels are listed in Table A-1.

Table A-1. Requirement Levels Listed in RFC 2026

Level	Description
Required	The specification is required in order for an implementation to be considered as Internet-compliant. For example, RFC 791 and RFC 1122 are required to be followed in order for a vendor's implementation of the IP protocol to be considered compliant.

Table A-1. Requirement Levels Listed in RFC 2026 (continued)

Level	Description
Recommended	The specification is not required in order for the implementation to be considered as Internet-compliant, but experience shows that the system and/or network would benefit from the specification being implemented.
Elective	Neither the system nor the network will be helped or harmed by the specification being implemented.
Limited Use	The specification should be used only in extraordinary situations. This is commonly seen with experimental and historic RFCs that may cause some problems if implemented in production implementations.
Not Recommended	This is the same as "limited use," except its usage is strongly discouraged. RFCs labelled as "not recommended" should only be used when they absolutely have to be.

STD 1 acts as a clearinghouse for the status of each RFC, and also provides the current requirement level status for each of them. Only standards-track documents will have requirement levels.

Off-Track Documents

Not all of the available RFCs out there are standards-track documents. In fact, many of the RFCs currently floating around are not even on their way to becoming sanctioned Internet standards in any shape or form. Such a document may be an informational notice provided by a vendor, a historical note or procedure, or an experiment that is simply being documented for everybody to see.

In all of these cases, the RFCs are simply provided as public knowledge, and nobody is required to implement any of them. In some cases, vendors who implement the mechanisms detailed in these documents may actually cause interoperability problems.

Informational RFCs

Sometimes a vendor or consultant will choose to share information with the Internet community, and this information can be published as an Informational RFC.

Informational RFCs may be anything, ranging from the simple to the extraordinarily complex. For example, there are some Informational RFCs that advocate certain technologies or make observations about specific implementations. Conversely, some complex protocols (such as NFS) are also published as Informational RFCs, in the hopes that doing so will lead to a broader adoption of the proprietary service.

Sometimes a protocol that is published as an Informational RFC will be adopted on a widescale level. For example, Gopher (RFC 1436) and Ph (RFC 2378) have both achieved a large number of implementations over the years, although both of these protocols were published as Informational RFCs.

Historical RFCs

Any RFC that gets replaced by another RFC is automatically labelled as Historic.

In addition, it is possible that a new technology will simply make an existing specification obsolete. When this happens, one or more existing specifications may need to be retired. In this case, the existing RFCs and standards will also be marked as Historical RFCs.

Note that historic specifications are kept in the archives for reference purposes. Users should be careful to verify that the document they are reading is not an historical one that has no bearing on the current state of things.

Experimental RFCs

Experimental RFCs are typically the result of ongoing research projects that are experimenting with new technologies or approaches for doing something. These documents are only published for the benefit of public record.

Under no circumstances should a vendor incorporate any Experimental RFCs into a shipping product. Interoperability problems are likely to occur if this warning is ignored.

Best Common Practice (BCP) RFCs

Besides the standards-track and off-track documents, the IETF also publishes some other documents from time to time that are known as Best Common Practice (BCP) documents. These documents are most likely to be informational in nature, offering advice to the reader about how to do something, rather than prescribing a set methodology for doing it. Although these documents are also published as RFCs, they are most often referred to as BCPs. An example of this is RFC 2026—also published as BCP 9—which describes the Internet standardization process that much of this appendix refers to.

For Your Information (FYI) RFCs

Another variant on the informational theme is the "For Your Information" series of RFCs. FYIs are mostly informational in nature, although their intended target reader is the end user who is trying to make heads or tails about the Internet in general. Although these documents are also published as RFCs, they are most-often referred to as FYIs. An examples of the FYI series includes RFC 1178—also published as FYI 5—which describes why computers have hostnames.

B

IP Addressing Fundamentals

IP Addresses

IP uses an anarchic and highly distributed model, with every device being an equal peer to every other device on the global Internet. This structure was one of IP's original design goals, as it proved to be useful with a variety of different systems, it did not require a centralized management system (which would never have scaled very well), and also it provided for fault-tolerance on the network (no central management means no single point of failure).

In order for systems to locate each other in this distributed environment, nodes are given explicit addresses that uniquely identify the particular network that the system is on, and that also uniquely identify the system to that particular network. When these two identifiers are combined, the result is a globally unique address.

This concept is illustrated in Figure B-1. In that figure, the network is numbered 192.168.10, and the two nodes are numbered 10 and 20. Taken together, the fully qualified IP addresses for those systems would be 192.168.10.10 and 192.168.10.20.

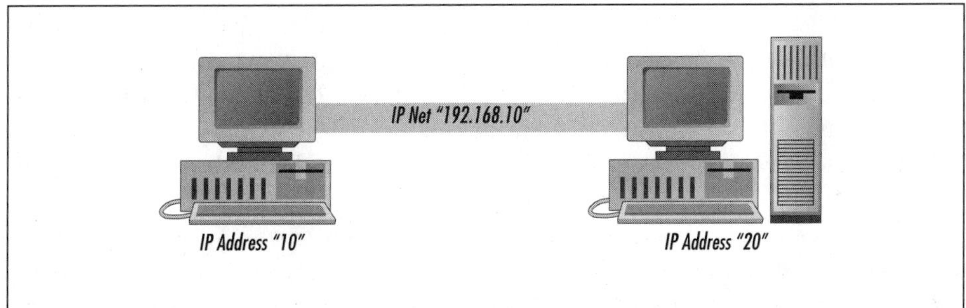

Figure B-1. IP addresses consist of a network address and a node address

An IP address is actually a 32-bit binary number (in binary, 192.168.1.20 corresponds to 11000000101010000000000101000010100). However, the 32-bit IP address actually consists of two sub-addresses, with one part identifying the network and the rest identifying the host to the network, with an imaginary boundary separating the two.

Subnet Masks

The particular location of the boundary marker within the 32-bit address is determined through the use of a *subnet mask*. The subnet mask is another 32-bit binary number that acts like a filter when it is applied to the IP address. By comparing a subnet mask with an IP address, systems can determine which portion of the IP address relates to the network and which portion relates to the host. Anywhere the subnet mask has a bit set to 1, the underlying bit in the IP address is part of the network address, while anywhere the subnet mask is set to 0, the related bit in the IP address is part of the host address.

For example, assume that the IP address of 11000000101010000000000101000010100 has a subnet mask of 11111111111111111111111100000000. In this example, the first 24 bits of the 32-bit IP addresses are used to identify the network, while the last eight bits are used to identify the host on that network.

The size of the network—i.e., the number of devices that can be used on a particular network—is a function of the number of bits that are used to identify the host portion of the address. If a subnet mask shows that 24 bits are used for the network portion of the address, then there are only eight bits available for the host portion of the address block, allowing only 256 possible host addresses for that specific network. Similarly, if the subnet mask showed that 16 bits were used for the network, then the remaining 16 bits can be used for the host portion of the address space, allowing for 65,535 possible host addresses on that particular network.

If a network administrator needs to split a single network into multiple virtual networks, the bit-pattern in use with the subnet mask can be changed to allow as many networks as are required. For example, assume that we want to split the 192.168.10 network into two smaller networks. All we would have to do in this situation is change the subnet mask of the devices on the network so that they used 25 bits for the network instead of 24 bits (the default for that address). This would turn our original network of 192.168.10 into two distinct networks with 128 possible addresses on each network (instead of a single network with 256 host addresses). In this case, the first network would have a range of network addresses between 192.168.10.0 through 192.168.10.127, while the second network would have a range of addresses between 192.168.10.128 through 192.168.10.255.

Whenever you split a network into multiple subnets, you must reserve any host addresses that are made up entirely of ones or zeros, to be used by the network itself. This is so that each subnet will have a network-specific address (the all-zeroes address) and a broadcast address (the all-ones address). This means that you will lose two possible host addresses from each subnet that you create. If you split a 24-bit network into two 25-bit networks with 128 possible addresses, then only 126 of those addresses can be used for host address assignments (the all-zeroes and all-ones addresses from each subnet must be set aside for the subnets themselves).

Table B-1 shows some of the most common subnet masks (in decimal notation), and the number of networks and hosts (after subtracting for the all-zeroes and all-ones addresses) that result from them.

Table B-1. Common Subnet Masks, with Available Number of Networks and Hosts

Subnet Mask	Network Bits	Nets per Mask	Host Bits	Hosts per Net	Network Class
255.255.0.0	16	1	16	65,534	Class B masks (default)
255.255.128.0	17	2	15	32,766	Class B masks
255.255.192.0	18	4	14	16,382	Class B masks
255.255.224.0	19	8	13	8,190	Class B masks
255.255.240.0	20	16	12	4,094	Class B masks
255.255.248.0	21	32	11	2,046	Class B masks
255.255.252.0	22	64	10	1,022	Class B masks
255.255.254.0	23	128	9	510	Class B masks
255.255.255.0	24	1	8	254	Class C masks (default)
255.255.255.128	25	2	7	126	Class C masks
255.255.255.192	26	4	6	62	Class C masks
255.255.255.224	27	8	5	30	Class C masks
255.255.255.240	28	16	4	14	Class C masks
255.255.255.248	29	32	3	6	Class C masks
255.255.255.252	30	64	2	2	Class C masks
255.255.255.254	31	128	1	0	Class C masks

When you split a network into multiple subnets, all of the systems on those subnets must use the same subnet mask in order to communicate with each other directly. If they use different subnet masks, then they will think they are on different networks, and will not be able to communicate with each other without going through a router first.

You must also remember that the subnet masks are only used by the *internal* systems; external systems will not be aware of the subnet masks in use on your internal networks. As such, external systems will still route data to your network according to the subnet mask associated with the address block assigned to you by your ISP. They will continue to send packets to the routers published for the unsegmented network, and your internal routers will have to determine the appropriate subnet mask for the specific destination system in order to successfully deliver the data.

Subnet Classes

Until recently, network addresses were clumped into three distinct classes, each of which provided different-sized blocks of network addresses for organizations to use on their internal networks. The only real difference between these network classes was the number of bits used in the subnet mask to identify the network portion of the addresses, which in turn dictated the number of hosts that could be used on that network. These address classes are shown in Table B-2.

Table B-2. Common Subnet Mask Classes

Class	Network Portion	Host Portion
A	11111111	00000000 00000000 00000000
B	11111111 11111111	00000000 00000000
C	11111111 11111111 11111111	00000000

The number of networks available with each of the subnet classes—and the number of hosts possible on each of those networks—varies widely between the different classes. This concept is illustrated in Table B-3, which shows that there are only a few Class A networks available, although each of them can have millions of possible hosts. Conversely, there are a couple of million possible Class C networks, although they can only serve 254 devices each (after subtracting the all-ones and all-zeroes addresses).

Table B-3. Available Number of Networks and Hosts for the Default Subnet Classes

Class	Network Bits	Nets per Class	Host Bits	Hosts per Net
A	7	125	24	16,777,213
B	14	16,383	16	65,533
C	21	2,097,151	8	254

Networks that are very large would want to use the Class A subnet mask, since Class A networks can have millions of nodes on a single large network. The most common users of Class A addresses have historically been the global service providers with extremely large, world-wide networks. In practice, Class A networks are too large to be usable as single entities (I do not know of any data-link topologies that are capable of handling 16 million devices on a single network). For this reason, Class A networks have typically been split into several virtual networks, as described in "Subnet Masks" earlier in this chapter.

Organizations with networks that have thousands (but not millions) of nodes have been the typical users of Class B networks. This group includes universities, large commercial enterprises, and mid-level network service providers. Class B networks were also commonly split into multiple networks, since a single network of 65,535 devices would not work efficiently (if it worked at all).

Almost all networks used the Class C subnet mask, since most companies have fewer than 100 employees (the average network only has around forty nodes). In fact, most of the Class A and Class B networks were simply broken into multiple Class C networks, since they represent the most common network size. For these reasons, Class C networks have historically been the most popular with the general public.

There is a fourth class of addresses—known as Class D addresses—which is used exclusively for multicast applications. Class D addresses use all 32 bits to identify a *group* of hosts, each of which can accept data sent to that specific IP address. For more information on multicasting and Class D addresses, refer to Chapter 4, *Multicasting and the Internet Group Management Protocol.* There's also a Class E, which is reserved for experimentation.

Class-Based Routing

Since the network portion of a packet's destination IP address determines the destination network, routing a packet requires examining the IP address, determining the network portion of that address, and then sending the traffic to that specific network. However, IP packets do not carry subnet mask data around with them, and only contain the 32-bit IP address of the destination system. Without this information, devices are unable to determine what portion of the IP address belongs to the network, and which portion belongs to the host, meaning they cannot determine the destination network number and thus cannot route the packets.

In order to resolve this problem, IP systems had to use some other form of logic to determine which portion of the IP address applied to the destination network, and which portion applied to the destination system. This was achieved through the use of the address classes defined above, and the way in which network addresses were assigned.

Class A network addresses always have the first bit of their IP address set to 0. Since Class A networks only use the first eight bits for the network number, this leaves seven bits for the network portion of the address, allowing for 128 possible network numbers. However, the "all-on" and "all-off" networks (numbered 0 and 127) were also reserved, so there were really only 126 possible network numbers (1 through 126). Therefore, any IP packet with a destination network of 1.x.x.x through 126.x.x.x is for a Class A network, and therefore has a subnet mask of 11111111000000000000000000000000.

Class B addresses have their first bit set to 1 and the second bit set to 0. Since Class B addresses use the first 16 bits to identify the network portion of the address, this leaves 14 bits to identify each network segment, for a maximum of 16,383 networks. However, the all-on and all-off network numbers are also reserved and therefore unavailable, reducing the maximum number of available addresses to 16,381, ranging from 128.1 through 191.254. Any packet that has one of these addresses is a Class B address, and has a subnet mask of 11111111111111110000000000000000.

Class C addresses have their first two bits set to 1 and the third bit set to 0. Class C addresses use the first 24 bits to identify the network portion of the address, so there are 21 bits available, allowing for 2,097,151 possible Class C network addresses. However, both of the extreme networks are also reserved here as well, reducing this quantity to 2,097,149, with a possible range of network numbers from 192.0.1 through 223.255.254. Any packet that has one of these addresses is a Class C address, and thus has a subnet mask of 11111111111111111111111100000000.

This concept is illustrated in Table B-4. As you can see, a device can determine the class of the IP address in use by examining the first four bits of the first octet of the destination IP address.

Table B-4. The First Four Bits from the Major Network Classes

Class	Leading Bits	Possible Values
A	0*xxxxxxx*	0.0.0.0 through 127.255.255.255
B	10*xxxxxx*	128.0.0.0 through 191.255.255.255
C	110*xxxxx*	192.0.0.0 through 223.255.255.255
D	1110*xxxx*	224.0.0.0 through 239.255.255.255 (multicasting)
E	1111*xxxx*	240.0.0.0 through 255.255.255.255 (experimental)

By examining the first four bits of the destination IP address, devices could determine what type of IP address was in use, and could then use that information to determine the subnet mask for that IP address as well. Once this information was gleaned, the device could apply the appropriate subnet mask to the IP address in question, determine which portion of the address belonged to the network (versus belonging to the host), and then determine the router for that network.

Classless Inter-Domain Routing (CIDR)

All told, there are around 4.3 billion possible host addresses (there are fewer if you don't consider Class D and E addresses, which cannot be used as host addresses). Unfortunately, the class-based structure of the addressing scheme used by IP placed heavy restrictions on the distribution of these addresses.

Every time a Class A address was assigned to an organization, almost 17 million host addresses went with it. If all 126 of the Class A networks were assigned, then two billion of the possible addresses were gone. If all of the available Class B networks were assigned, then another billion host addresses were gone as well.

Class C addresses represented the biggest problem, however, for two reasons. First, there are fewer IP addresses available in all of the Class C networks than there are with the other classes (only about 600 million possible node addresses are available from all of the Class C networks combined). Second, Class C networks were the most popular, since they reflected the size of the majority of the LANs in use.

However, every time a Class C address was assigned, 256 possible host addresses went with it. Organizations who had three segments but who only had 60 devices were wasting over 700 possible addresses (3 segments × 254 addresses = 762 addresses – 60 active nodes = 702 inactive addresses). Whether or not all of the addresses were actually put to use or not is irrelevant because they were assigned to a specific network and could not be used by anybody else. This problem is even worse with Class B addresses, since an organization with a few hundred nodes might have been given a Class B address, in which case they would be wasting several thousand IP addresses.

To some readers, the logic for having different "classes" of addresses may seem vague at best. With the current design, there are only 2,113,662 possible networks. If all of the networks used Class C addressing, then there would be 16,777,124 networks, with 254 nodes on each of them. Surely this would be a better design!

Remember, however, that TCP/IP networks are inherently router-based, and that it takes much less overhead to remember a few networks than to remember millions of them. Having to process 16 million networks would quickly overwhelm even the fastest of routers, and network traffic would either slow to a crawl or would fail completely. Having network classes allowed routers to deal with large networks, which allowed the routers to run faster (in some cases, it allowed them to work at all).

Remember also that the original architecture of the Internet consisted mostly of large networks connecting to each other directly, and didn't look much like the hierarchical design that is used today. It was easy to give one huge address block to the military and another big block to Stanford University. In that model, routers only had to remember one IP address for each of those networks, and could reach millions of hosts through each of those routes.

Today however, things are considerably different, and organizations of all sizes are connecting to the Internet. Some networks are still quite large, requiring many thousands of network numbers in order to satisfy their requirements, while some organizations are quite small, consisting of only a handful of PCs that need direct connectivity to the Internet. In this evolving environment, class-based routing does not scale very well, although there still exists the need for bundled networks so that routers do not have to remember millions of separate routers and network paths.

This problem has been resolved through the use of variable-length subnet masks; instead of assigning network numbers in 24-, 16-, or 8-bit subnet masks, addresses are assigned to organizations using the most-appropriate subnet mask for the number of devices on that network. If a network only has eight PCs, then they would only be assigned a 28-bit subnet mask for that network, which would provide them with 16 addresses (14 of which would be usable by the hosts).

This system results in a substantially less amount of wasted address space, although it also results in more routing entries that must be managed somewhere. However, another key part of the classless address assignment architecture is that network numbers are assigned hierarchically, with top-level service providers getting big network numbers (possibly as large as 13 bits, which offers 524,288 host addresses). Those organizations then assign subnets from within their allocated address space.

This process allows a single routing entry for the top-level ISP to be used for all of the networks underneath it. Rather than the top-level routers having to store routing information for the 32,000+ networks that could result from segmenting the large block into 28-bit networks, they only have to remember one route for the entire 13-bit network.

Internet-Legal Versus Private Addressing

Although the pool of IP addresses is somewhat limited, most companies have no problems obtaining them. However, many organizations have already installed TCP/IP products on their internal networks without obtaining "legal" addresses from the proper sources. Sometimes these addresses come from example books or are simply picked at random (several firms use networks numbered 1.2.3, for example).

These addresses are not legal, and will not be usable when these organizations attempt to connect to the Internet. These firms will eventually have to reassign Internet-legal IP addresses to all of the devices on their networks, or they will have to invest in address translation gateways that re-write outbound IP packets so that they appear to be coming from an Internet-accessible host.

Even if an address translation gateway is installed on the network, these firms will never be able to communicate with the sites that are the registered owners of the IP addresses in use on the local network. For example, if you choose to use the Class A address block of 36 on your corporate network, then your users will never be able to access the computers at Stanford University, which is the registered owner of that particular address block. Any attempt to connect to a host at 36.x.x.x would be interpreted by the local routers as a request for a local system, so packets would never leave your local network.

Not all firms have the luxury of using Internet-legal addresses on their hosts, for any number of reasons. There may be legacy applications that use hard-coded addresses, or there may be too many systems across an organization for a clean upgrade to be successful.

If you do not wish to obtain Internet-legal addresses, then you should at least be aware that there are groups of *private* Internet addresses that can be used on internal networks by anyone. These address pools have been set aside in RFC 1918, and therefore cannot be assigned to any organization. As such, these addresses can be used by anyone, although only on an internal-use basis. The Internet's backbone routers are explicitly configured not to route packets with these addresses, so they are completely useless outside of an organization's internal network. The address blocks available are listed in Table B-5.

Table B-5. "Private Addresses" Provided in RFC 1918

Class	Range of Addresses
A	Any addresses in 10.*x*.*x*.*x*
B	Addresses in the range of 172.16.*x*.*x* through 172.31.*x*.*x*
C	Addresses in the range of 192.168.0.*x* through 192.168.255.*x*

Since these addresses can not be routed across the Internet, you must have an address translation gateway or firewall, or else you will not be able to communicate with any hosts on the Internet. These gateways are available from a number of vendors.

An important note here is that since nobody can use these addresses on the Internet, it is safe to assume that anybody who is using these addresses is also utilizing an IP gateway. Therefore, you will never see these addresses used as a destination on the Internet. However, if your organization establishes a private connection to a partner company who is also using these addresses, then you will encounter the same difficulties described above, and your firms will not be able to interconnect completely.

It is always best to use formally assigned, Internet-legal addresses whenever possible. If this is not possible for some reason, then you should use one of the private address pools described in Table B-5. Never use random, self-assigned addresses if you can possibly avoid it, as this will only cause connectivity problems for you and your users.

C

Using the CD-ROM

This book includes a CD-ROM that contains various pieces of software, documentation, and other tools designed to help you get the most out of the content of this book. These tools are contained in various folders on the CD-ROM.

Contents of the CD-ROM

The CD-ROM contains several different software programs and support files. The main programs found on the CD-ROM are:

Shomiti Systems' demonstration software
: The demonstration software provides an overview of the Shomiti Systems' product line, allows you to install the Surveyor Lite network monitoring and packet capture tool, and also provides product tutorials. For information on running the demonstration software, refer to "Installing and Using the Demonstration Software" later in this chapter.

Shomiti Systems' Surveyor Lite
: Surveyor Lite can be used to view packets on a live network and examine the details of the various protocols described in this book. Surveyor Lite is limited to specific protocols and will only capture 100 packets at a time, but it can be used indefinitely. For information on running Surveyor Lite, refer to "Installing and Using Surveyor Lite".

Shomiti Systems' Surveyor (15-day evaluation version)
: Surveyor "Time Lock" is a full version of the Surveyor software, which expires after a trial period of fifteen days. It can do everything that Surveyor Lite can do and much more (it is not limited in protocol support or the number of captured packets). Additional add-on components provided with the fifteen-day evaluation version of Surveyor include expert analysis, packet generation, and remote monitoring tools. For information on running the evaluation version of

Surveyor, refer to "Installing and Using the 15-Day Evaluation Version of Surveyor" later in this chapter.

The root directory of the CD-ROM contains two executable programs:

SETUP.EXE
: This program will install the Shomiti System's multimedia demonstration software and various support programs. Once this software has been installed, you can view information about Shomiti Systems' various product offerings, install the Surveyor Lite limited-use network monitoring and capture software, and access product tutorials.

SHOMITI.EXE
: This is the main executable program for the multimedia demonstration software. This software can be installed using the *SETUP.EXE* program described above, or it can be run from the CD-ROM directly. Note that the *SHOMITI.EXE* program will perform properly only if all of the necessary support programs are already installed on the computer, and it may not function for all users in all cases; full installation of the demonstration software via the *SETUP.EXE* program is highly recommended.

The rest of the CD-ROM contains support files for the demonstration software, and reference material for the book itself. Some of these files will be installed automatically by the *SETUP.EXE* program described above, while some of them will not:

CAPTURES
: Capture files for the various samples shown in this book, for use with Surveyor Lite and/or the fifteen-day evaluation copy of Surveyor. These capture samples can be loaded into Surveyor or Surveyor Lite directly from the CD-ROM.

DOCS
: Product literature for Shomiti Systems' line of network–analysis products, in Adobe Acrobat format.

MOVIES
: Animation files used by the demonstration software. These are support files and are not meant to be accessed directly.

READER
: Apple's QuickTime player, for use by the demonstration software. This software can be installed directly or by using the main setup program (described later in "Installing and Using the Demonstration Software").

RFCS
: All of the Requests for Comments (RFCs) that were available from the IETF at the time this book was published. These documents are viewable with most text editors.

SCMS

Lotus' ScreenCam player and various animation files, for use by the demonstration software. This software can be installed directly or by using the main setup program (described later in "Installing and Using the Demonstration Software").

SOFTWARE

This folder contains a subfolder called *SURVEYOR*, which contains the demonstration version of Shomiti Systems' Surveyor Lite software. The demonstration version is limited to 100 captures, but can be used as often as needed. This software can be installed directly (described in "Installing and Using Surveyor Lite") or by way of the demonstration software (described later in "Installing and Using the Demonstration Software").

TIMELOCKED_SURVEYOR

This folder contains various subfolders that comprise Shomiti Systems' regular Surveyor software. This software is limited to a fifteen-day evaluation period, although it does not have the usage limitations found with Surveyor Lite. Other components found in the subfolders under this directory are Shomiti Systems' Expert Analyzer add-on, Packet Blaster packet-generation add-on, and Remote Monitor add-on. This software can be installed only directly, and is not installed by the main setup program. For instructions on installing this software, refer to "Installing and Using the 15-Day Evaluation Version of Surveyor" later in this chapter.

XTRAS

Various files used by the demonstration software. These are support files and are not meant to be accessed directly.

Installing and Using the Software

Each of the different components available on the CD-ROM have different installation procedures, although the system requirements and support procedures are the same for all of them. Please refer to the appropriate section of this appendix for information on installing the desired software.

System Requirements

The following system specifications are a minimum set of requirements for using the bundled software:

- Microsoft Windows 95, Microsoft Windows 98, or Microsoft Windows NT 4.0/ SP 3 with Administrative privileges
- Pentium 100 Mhz processor or higher

- 4x or higher CD-ROM drive
- 16MB RAM Windows 95
- 32MB RAM Windows NT 4.0
- 800 x 600 Video SVGA display (or higher)
- 16-bit color (or higher)
- MPC-compatible sound card and speakers (only required for demonstration software)
- 16-bit or 32-bit NDIS driver for any 10/100 Ethernet or 4/16 Token Ring adapter card (only required for use with Surveyor or Surveyor Lite); ODI and/or Packet Driver drivers are not supported

Installing and Using the Demonstration Software

1. Insert the CD-ROM into your CD-ROM drive.
2. If autorun is enabled on this system and the CD-ROM drive, the installation program for the demonstration software will start automatically. If autorun is not enabled on this system or the CD-ROM drive, you can access the installation program by loading the *SETUP.EXE* program in the root directory of the CD-ROM.
3. The installation software will ask if you want to install version 3 of the Adobe Acrobat viewer. It is highly recommended that you accept this option, unless you know for certain that you have a later version of the Acrobat viewer already installed.
4. The installation software will install the files necessary for the demonstration program, and a shortcut will be placed in your Start menu for running the program.
5. After installation is completed, the multimedia demonstration software will be launched. At the end of the demonstration, you will have the option of installing other software components (such as Surveyor Lite). Click the button labelled "Main" to view the additional installation options.

Installing and Using Surveyor Lite

You can install Surveyor Lite in one of two ways:

- After installing and viewing the demonstration software.
- Run the *SETUP.EXE* program from the *\SOFTWARE\SURVEYOR* directory on the CD-ROM.

If you wish to install Surveyor Lite from within the demonstration software:

1. Locate the "Launch Shomiti CD-ROM" icon in the Start menu, and click it. Click the button labelled "Main" to skip to the main menu, and then click the text labelled "Software and Documentation," which will give you the option of installing Surveyor Lite.
2. Insert the CD-ROM into your CD-ROM drive when prompted, if it isn't already.
3. If autorun is enabled on this system and the CD-ROM drive, the installation program for the demonstration software will start automatically. If you want to install only Surveyor Lite, cancel the installation of the demonstration software. If you want to install the demonstration software, refer back to "Installing and Using the Demonstration Software". Otherwise, jump to step 4 in the list below.

If you wish to install Surveyor Lite without installing the demonstration software:

1. Insert the CD-ROM into your CD-ROM drive when prompted, if it isn't already.
2. If autorun is enabled on this system and the CD-ROM drive, the installation program for the demonstration software will start automatically. If you want to install only Surveyor Lite, cancel the installation of the demonstration software. If you want to install the demonstration software, refer back to "Installing and Using the Demonstration Software." Otherwise, continue with the next step.
3. Locate the *SETUP.EXE* program within the *\SOFTWARE\SHOMITI* directory of the CD-ROM and double-click it to start the installation of Surveyor Lite.
4. Once the installation program has been launched, you will be prompted for registration details. Enter your name and company into the dialog box, and use the string "12345" for the product serial number.
5. Surveyor Lite will be installed into the directory of your choice, and a shortcut will be created in the "Shomiti Systems" folder within your Start menu. After installation is completed, Surveyor Lite can be started immediately.
6. The first time that Surveyor Lite is started, you will be given the option of specifying any hardware capture devices from Shomiti Systems that you may have on this computer. These devices provide better capturing and monitoring services than generic network adapters tend to allow (although most adapter cards work fine for casual monitoring and analysis). If you do not have any Shomiti capture cards installed on this system, click the OK button without selecting any additional devices or options.

For information on using Surveyor Lite to monitor or capture packets, refer to the online help provided with the program.

Installing and Using the 15-Day Evaluation Version of Surveyor

1. Insert the CD-ROM into your CD-ROM drive, if it isn't already.
2. If autorun is enabled on this system and the CD-ROM drive, the installation program for the demonstration software will start automatically. If you want to install only Surveyor, cancel the installation of the demonstration software. If you want to install the demonstration software, refer back to "Installing and Using the Demonstration Software." Otherwise, continue with the next step.
3. Launch the *SETUP.EXE* program in the *\TIMELOCKED_SURVEYOR\SURVEYOR* directory of the CD-ROM and double-click it to start the installation of the fifteen-day evaluation version of Surveyor.
4. Once the installation program has been launched, you will be prompted for registration details. Enter your name and company into the dialog box, and use the string "12345" for the product serial number.
5. Surveyor will be installed into the directory of your choice, and a shortcut will be created in the "Shomiti Systems" folder within your Start menu. After installation is completed, Surveyor can be started immediately.
6. The first time that Surveyor is started, you will be given the option of specifying any hardware capture devices from Shomiti Systems that you may have on this computer. These devices provide better capturing and monitoring services than generic network adapters (although most adapter cards work fine for casual monitoring and analysis). If you do not have any Shomiti capture cards installed on this system, click the OK button without selecting any additional devices or options.

For information on using Surveyor Lite to monitor or capture packets, refer to the online help provided with the program.

In addition to the full-decodes and capture support offered by the evaluation version of Surveyor, you can also install any of the following components:

Expert
: Provides detailed analysis of network events and conditions

Packet Blaster
: Allows you to edit and generate custom packets, or to replay protocol events

Remote
: Allows you to monitor capture devices on remote network segments (requires additional components from Shomiti Systems)

Each of these components can be installed by selecting the *SETUP.EXE* program found in the appropriate subdirectories under the *\TIMELOCKED_SURVEYOR*

SURVEYOR folder on the CD-ROM. You must install the evaluation version of Surveyor prior to installing the add-on modules.

Getting Help with Shomiti Systems' Products

For assistance with Shomiti Systems' products, please contact Shomiti Systems directly:

Shomiti Systems
1800 Bering Drive
San Jose, CA 95121
Support: 1-408-437-4059
Support email: *support@shomiti.com*
Sales: 1-408-437-3940
U.S. Toll-Free Sales: 1-888-SHOMITI
Sales email: *info@shomiti.com*

Please note the following known issues:

Sound problems
: Some multimedia and game programs install Intel's RSX 3-D Sound System on your computer. RSX is known to cause sound distortion and breakups with other multimedia packages. Microsoft and Intel recommend that you remove the RSX software by using the Uninstall utility in your Control Panel.

Color problems
: First, try setting your display settings for the 800×600 resolution at 65,535 colors. This is required for proper viewing of the CD and running the Surveyor software. Setting the display for other color depths (such as 256 colors) may result in mismatched colors, while using a lower screen resolution will result in cropped images. If you cannot run your display at the 800×600 resolution, you will still be able to view most of the CD, although some screens will not be completely visible.

Problems accessing the tutorials
: You may or may not be able to run the tutorials directly from the CD-ROM drive. It is highly recommended that you install the demonstration software (as described earlier in "Installing and Using the Demonstration Software"). The tutorials were recorded using Lotus ScreenCam, and if you try to run more than one simultaneously, you may experience difficulties. On some very fast systems, the sound track may end slightly before the screen action, which will cause an error message. Just click OK to dismiss the error message. It will not effect anything.

Problems viewing the Acrobat PDF documents

If you have an older version of Adobe Acrobat on your system and you experience errors when launching any of the PDF documents, please install the version of Acrobat found in the *DOCS* folder of the CD-ROM.

Bibliography

Books

This book would not be possible without the prior work of others. I made extensive use of following works:

Black, Uyless. *TCP/IP and Related Protocols.* New York, NY: McGraw-Hill, Inc., 1992.

Comer, Douglas. *Internetworking with TCP/IP, Volume I, 3rd Edition.* Englewood Cliffs, NJ: Prentice-Hall, Inc., 1995.

Comer, Douglas, and David Stevens. *Internetworking with TCP/IP, Volume III.* Englewood Cliffs, NJ: Prentice-Hall, Inc., 1993.

Feit, Sidnie. *TCP/IP: Architecture, Protocols, and Implementation.* New York, NY: McGraw-Hill, Inc., 1993.

Hunt, Craig. *TCP/IP Network Administration.* Sebastopol, CA: O'Reilly & Associates, Inc., 1992.

Jamsa, Kris, and Ken Cope. *Internet Programming.* Las Vegas, NV: Jamsa Press, 1995.

Lynch, Daniel, and Marshall T. Rose. *Internet System Handbook.* Reading, MA: Addison Wesley Longman, Inc., 1993.

Malamud, Carl. *Stacks: Interoperability in Today's Computer Networks.* Englewood Cliffs, NJ: Prentice-Hall, Inc., 1992.

McConnell, John. *Internetworking Computer Systems.* Englewood Cliffs, NJ: Prentice-Hall, Inc., 1988.

Roberts, Dave. *Internet Protocols Handbook.* Scottsdale, AZ: The Coriolis Group, Inc., 1996.

Stallings, William. *Networking Standards.* Reading, MA: Addison Wesley Longman, Inc., 1993.

Stevens, W. Richard. *TCP/IP Illustrated, Volume I.* Reading, MA: Addison Wesley Longman, Inc., 1994.

Request for Comments

Request for Comments (RFCs) define the Internet protocols and services that we all use on a daily basis. RFCs are available from the RFC Editor's web site (*http://www.rfc-editor.org/rfc.html*), as well as from several mirror sites around the world.

The following RFCs were used extensively in the development of this book:

RFC 768 *User Datagram Protocol*
J. Postel. August, 1980.

RFC 781 *A Specification of the Internet Protocol (IP) Timestamp Option*
Z. Su. May, 1981.

RFC 791 *Internet Protocol*
J. Postel. September, 1981.

RFC 792 *Internet Control Message Protocol*
J. Postel. September, 1981.

RFC 793 *Transmission Control Protocol*
J. Postel. September, 1981.

RFC 813 *Window and Acknowledgment Strategy in TCP*
D. Clark. July, 1982.

RFC 815 *IP Datagram Reassembly Algorithms*
D. Clark. July, 1982.

RFC 826 *Ethernet Address Resolution Protocol*
D.C. Plummer. November, 1982.

RFC 896 *Congestion Control in IP/TCP Internetworks*
J. Nagle. January, 1984.

RFC 903 *Reverse Address Resolution Protocol*
R. Finlayson, T. Mann, J.C. Mogul, M. Theimer. June, 1984.

RFC 919 *Broadcasting Internet Datagrams*
J.C. Mogul. October, 1984.

RFC 922 *Broadcasting Internet Datagrams in the Presence of Subnets*
J.C. Mogul. October, 1984.

RFC 950 *Internet Standard Subnetting Procedure*
J.C. Mogul, J. Postel. August, 1985.

RFC 1072 *Extensions for High Delay*
V. Jacobsen, B. Braden. October, 1988.

RFC 1075 *Distance Vector Multicast Routing Protocol*
D. Waitzman, C. Partridge, S.E. Deering. November, 1988.

RFC 1108 *U.S. Department of Defense Security Options for the Internet Protocol*
S. Kent. November, 1991.

RFC 1112 *Host Extensions for IP Multicasting*
S.E. Deering. August, 1989.

RFC 1122 *Requirements for Internet Hosts, Communication Layers*
R.T. Braden. October, 1989.

RFC 1123 *Requirements for Internet Hosts, Application and Support*
R.T. Braden. October, 1989.

RFC 1191 *Path MTU Discovery*
J.C. Mogul, S.E. Deering. November, 1990.

RFC 1256 *ICMP Router Discovery Messages*
S. Deering. September, 1991.

RFC 1323 *TCP Extensions for High Performance*
V. Jacobson, R. Braden, D. Borman. May, 1992.

RFC 1337 *TIME-WAIT Assassination Hazards in TCP*
R. Braden. May, 1992.

RFC 1349 *Type of Service in the Internet Protocol Suite*
P. Almquist. July, 1992.

RFC 1393 *Traceroute Using an IP Option*
G. Malkin. January, 1993.

RFC 1433 *Directed ARP*
J. Garrett, J. Hagan and J. Wong. March, 1993.

RFC 1455 *Physical Link Security Type of Service*
D. Eastlake, III. May, 1993.

RFC 1469 *IP Multicast over Token-Ring Local Area Networks*
T. Pusateri. June, 1993.

RFC 1584 *Multicast Extensions to OSPF*
J. Moy. March, 1994.

RFC 1644 *T/TCP: TCP Extensions for Transactions, Functional Specification*
R. Braden. July, 1994.

RFC 1700 *Assigned Numbers*
J. Reynolds, J. Postel. October, 1994.

RFC 1812 *Requirements for IP Version 4 Routers*
F. Baker. June, 1995.

RFC 1868 *ARP Extension: UNARP*
G. Malkin. November, 1995.

RFC 1918 *Address Allocation for Private Internets*
Y. Rekhter, B. Moskowitz, D. Karrenberg, G. J. de Groot, and E. Lear. February, 1996.

RFC 1948 *Defending Against Sequence Number Attacks*
S. Bellovin. May, 1996.

RFC 2001 *TCP Slow Start, Congestion Avoidance, Fast Retransmit, and Fast Recovery Algorithms*
W. Stevens. January, 1997.

RFC 2018 *TCP Selective Acknowledgment Options*
M. Mathis, J. Mahdavi, S. Floyd, A. Romanow. October, 1996.

RFC 2026 *The Internet Standards Process, Revision 3*
S. Bradner. October, 1996.

RFC 2113 *IP Router Alert Option*
D. Katz. February, 1997.

RFC 2131 *Dynamic Host Configuration Protocol*
R. Droms. March, 1997.

RFC 2236 *Internet Group Management Protocol, Version 2*
W. Fenner. November, 1997.

RFC 2365 *Administratively Scoped IP Multicast*
D. Meyer. July, 1998.

RFC 2390 *Inverse Address Resolution Protocol*
T. Bradley, C. Brown, A. Malis. August, 1998.

RFC 2400 *Internet Official Protocol Standards*
J. Postel, J. Reynolds. September, 1998.

RFC 2525 *Known TCP Implementation Problems*
V. Paxson, M Allman, S. Dawson, W. Fenner, J. Griner, I. Heavens, K. Lahey, J. Semke, B. Volz. March, 1999.

RFC 2581 *TCP Congestion Control*
M. Alman, V. Paxson, W. Stevens. March, 1999.

RFC 2582 *New Reno Modifications to Fast Recovery*
S. Floyd, T. Henderson. March, 1999.

RFC 2588 *IP Multicasting and Firewalls*
R. Finlayson. May, 1999.

Index

A

B

D

G

H

O

P

S

T

U

K

L

M

N

About the Author

Eric A. Hall has been involved with computers and networking for over twenty years, both personally and professionally. He got his start in computers as a child by writing games in Basic on an IBM S/360 at his father's office, and got his first real taste of distributed networking by running a FidoNet BBS node out of his home town in Nashville, TN.

More recently, Eric has served as the Labs Director for *Network Computing* magazine (designing and managing two of their test centers), has worked for two Internet startups, and has designed and managed Fortune 500 networks. Eric continues to serve as an independent consultant for a variety of network-related companies, and continues to write for the trade press on occasion.

Eric also tries to travel frequently, and has lived for extended periods on three of the seven continents.

Colophon

Our look is the result of reader comments, our own experimentation, and feedback from distribution channels. Distinctive covers complement our distinctive approach to technical topics, breathing personality and life into potentially dry subjects.

The animals on the cover of *Internet Core Protocols* are trout. Trout belong to the family *Salmonidae*, one of the 435 families of *Osteichthyes*, the class of bony fish. Some species of trout, like their cousins the salmon, are anadromous. This means they systematically leave their freshwater, natal streams to feed in the ocean before expending most of their life's energy swimming hundreds of miles back to spawn in the exact streams in which they hatched.

The trout in the upper left is a blueback char (*Salvelinus alpinus*). Most often referred to as arctic char, the sea-going variety is typically 2–8 pounds, with a deep blue-green back, brilliant silver sides, and occasional violet-pink spots. It is found farther north than any other freshwater fish. Circumpolar in distribution, arctic char roam marine environments off the coasts of Alaska, Canada, Greenland, Iceland, the U.K., and Scandinavia, eating zooplankton and small fish.

The fish on the lower right is the North American brook trout (*Salvelinus fontinalis*, meaning spring char), a stream-dwelling, small (1-3 pound) trout indigenous to the streams around the Great Lakes. Its olive-green back is marked with dark wavy lines and its sides have pale yellow and red spots, creating camouflage as seen from above when the sun shines through the water. During warm months, they eat insects and their larvae; in the cold months, they feed on larvae only, which they find on the lake bottom.

There are many dangers threatening trout and other salmonid. Dams and irrigation projects impede their upstream journeys, preventing reproduction; over-harvesting affects the ocean populations and over-fishing threatens stream-dwellers. A reduction in ocean productivity, due to weather phenomena such as El Nino, depletes their food sources. Even environmental protection laws can have an unintended impact—they can boost the populations of predators such as sea lions and seals, who hunt in the estuaries where the fish must stay for days while adjusting to saline changes between environments.

Nicole Arigo was the production editor and copyeditor for *Internet Core Protocols*. Colleen Gorman was the proofreader; Maureen Dempsey, Mary Anne Weeks Mayo, and Jane Ellin provided quality control. The illustrations that appear in this book were produced by Robert Romano and Rhon Porter using Macromedia Free-Hand 8 and Adobe Photoshop 5. Ellen Troutman wrote the index.

Edie Freedman designed the cover of this book, using a 19th-century engraving from the Dover Pictorial Archive. Kathleen Wilson designed the cover layout and CD label with QuarkXPress 4.04 using the ITC Garamond font. The inside layout was designed by Nancy Priest and Alicia Cech and implemented in FrameMaker 5.5 by Mike Sierra. The text and heading fonts are ITC Garamond Light and Garamond Book. This colophon was written by Sarah Jane Shangraw.

Whenever possible, our books use RepKover™, a durable and flexible lay-flat binding. If the page count exceeds RepKover's limit, perfect binding is used.

INTRODUCING MEDIA PRACTICE

Sara Miller McCune founded SAGE Publishing in 1965 to support the dissemination of usable knowledge and educate a global community. SAGE publishes more than 1000 journals and over 800 new books each year, spanning a wide range of subject areas. Our growing selection of library products includes archives, data, case studies and video. SAGE remains majority owned by our founder and after her lifetime will become owned by a charitable trust that secures the company's continued independence.

Los Angeles | London | New Delhi | Singapore | Washington DC | Melbourne